MW01119894

SIGN LANGUAGES

What are the unique characteristics of sign languages that make them so fascinating? What have recent researchers discovered about them, and what do these findings tell us about human language more generally? This thematic and geographic overview examines more than forty sign languages from around the world. It begins by investigating how sign languages have survived and been transmitted for generations, and then goes on to analyze the common characteristics shared by most sign languages: for example, how the use of the visual (rather than the auditory) system affects grammatical structures. The final section describes the phenomena of language variation and change. Drawing on a wide range of examples, the book explores sign languages both old and young, from British, Italian, Asian and American to Israeli, Al-Sayyid Bedouin, African and Nicaraguan. Written in a clear, readable style, it is the essential reference for students and scholars working in sign language studies and Deaf studies, as well as an indispensable guide for researchers in general linguistics.

DIANE BRENTARI is Professor of Linguistics and Director of the ASL Program at Purdue University. She is the author of *A Prosodic Model of Sign Language Phonology* (1998) and has published widely in the area of sign language phonology and morphology. Her current research involves the crosslinguistic analyses of sign languages.

CAMBRIDGE LANGUAGE SURVEYS

This series offers general accounts of the major language families of the world, with volumes organized either on a purely genetic basis or on a geographical basis, whichever yields the most convenient and intelligible grouping in each case. Each volume compares and contrasts the typological features of the languages it deals with. It also treats the relevant genetic relationships, historical development and sociolinguistic issues arising from their role and use in the world today. The books are intended for linguists from undergraduate level upwards, but no special knowledge of the languages under consideration is assumed. Volumes such as those on Australia and the Amazon Basin are also of wider relevance, as the future of the languages and their speakers raises important social and political issues.

Volumes already published include
Chinese *Jerry Norman*
The languages of Japan *Masayoshi Shibatani*
Pidgins and Creoles (Volume I: Theory and structure; Volume II: Reference survey) *John A. Holm*
The Indo-Aryan languages *Colin Masica*
The Celtic languages *edited by Donald MacAulay*
The Romance languages *Rebecca Posner*
The Amazonian languages *edited by R. M. W. Dixon and Alexandra Y. Aikhenvald*
The languages of Native North America *Marianne Mithun*
The Korean language *Ho-Him Sohn*
Australian languages *R. M. W. Dixon*
The Dravidian languages *Bhadriraju Krishnamurti*
The languages of the Andes *Willem Adelaar with Pieter Muysken*
The Slavic languages *Roland Sussex and Paul Cubberley*
The Germanic languages *Wayne Harbert*
Sign languages *Diane Brentari*

SIGN LANGUAGES

edited by
DIANE BRENTARI

CAMBRIDGE
UNIVERSITY PRESS

CAMBRIDGE UNIVERSITY PRESS
Cambridge, New York, Melbourne, Madrid, Cape Town, Singapore,
São Paulo, Delhi, Dubai, Tokyo

Cambridge University Press
The Edinburgh Building, Cambridge CB2 8RU, UK

Published in the United States of America by Cambridge University Press, New York

www.cambridge.org
Information on this title: www.cambridge.org/9780521883702

First published 2010

Printed in the United Kingdom at the University Press, Cambridge

A catalogue record for this publication is available from the British Library

ISBN 978-0-521-88370-2 Hardback

CONTENTS

FIGURES

TABLES

CONTRIBUTORS

Kinda Al-Fityani
University of California, San Diego

Mark Aronoff
State University of New York, Stony Brook

Robert Bayley
University of California, Davis

Brita Bergman
Stockholm University

Penny Boyes Braem
Center for Sign Language Studies, Basel

Diane Brentari
Purdue University, West Lafayette, IN

Carlo Cecchetto
Università degli Studi di Milano-Bicocca

Rachel Channon
University of Connecticut, Storrs

Marie Coppola
University of Chicago

Kearsy Cormier
DCAL Research Centre, London

Quinn Duffy
Boston University

Petra Eccarius
Indiana University – Purdue University, Indianapolis

Elisabeth Engberg-Pedersen
University of Copenhagen

Susan Fischer
University of California, San Diego

Carlo Geraci
Università degli Studi di Milano-Bicocca

Qunhu Gong
Fudan University, Shanghai

Carolina González
Purdue University, West Lafayette, IN

Tommi Jantunen
University of Jyväskylä

Trevor Johnston
Macquarie University, Sydney

Diane Lillo-Martin
University of Connecticut, Storrs

Ceil Lucas
Gallaudet University

Dorothy Lule
Kyambogo University, Kampala

David McKee
Victoria University of Wellington

Rachel McKee
Victoria University of Wellington

Gaurav Mathur
Gallaudet University

Laura Mazzoni
Università degli Studi di Pisa

Irit Meir
The University of Haifa

Ronice Müller de Quadros
Universidade Federal de Santa Catarina

Carol Neidle
Boston University

Victoria Nyst
Leiden University

Carol Padden
University of California, San Diego

Roland Pfau
University of Amsterdam

Elena Antinoro Pizzuto
National Research Council (CNR), Rome

Josep Quer
ICREA and Universitat Pompeu Fabra, Barcelona

David Quinto-Pozos
University of Illinois at Urbana-Champaign

Claire Ramsey
University of California, San Diego

Christian Rathmann
Universität Hamburg

Paolo Rossini
National Research Council (CNR), Rome

Wendy Sandler
The University of Haifa

Galini Sapountzaki
University of Thessaly

Adam Schembri
DCAL Research Centre, London

Ann Senghas
Barnard College of Columbia University, NY

Felix Sze
The Chinese University of Hong Kong

Ritva Takkinen
University of Jyväskylä

Gladys Tang
The Chinese University of Hong Kong

Harry van der Hulst
University of Connecticut, Storrs

Lars Wallin
Stockholm University

Ronnie B. Wilbur
Purdue University, West Lafayette, IN

Sherman Wilcox
University of New Mexico, Albuquerque

Piotr Wojda
Pope John Paul II
Catholic University of Lubin

Bencie Woll
DCAL Research Centre, London

Sandro Zucchi
Università degli Studi di Milano-Bicocca

SIGN LANGUAGE ABBREVIATIONS

ABSL	Al-Sayyid Bedouin Sign Language
AdaSL	Adamorobe Sign Language
ArSL	pan-Arab Sign Language
ASL	American Sign Language
Auslan	Australian Sign Language
BANZSL	British, Australian and New Zealand Sign Language
BSL	British Sign Language
CSL	Chinese Sign Language
DGS	German Sign Language
DSGS	Swiss German Sign Language
DSL	Danish Sign Language
FinSL	Finnish Sign Language
GhSL	Ghanaian Sign Language
GSL	Greek Sign Language
HKSL	Hong Kong Sign Language
HSL	Hausa Sign Language
HZJ	Croatian Sign Language
IPSL	Indo-Pakistani Sign Language
ISL	Israeli Sign Language
JSL	Japanese Sign Langauge
KSL	Korean Sign Language
KuSL	Kuwaiti Sign Language
LaSiMa	Mali Sign Language
LGP	Portuguese Sign Language
LIS	Italian Sign Language
LIS-SI	Swiss Italian Sign Language
LIU	Jordanian Sign Language
LSA	Argentinian Sign Language

LSB	Brazilian Sign Language
LSC	Catalan Sign Language
LSE	Spanish Sign Language
LSF	French Sign Language
LSF-SR	Swiss French Sign Language
LSL	Libyan Sign Language
LSM	Mexican Sign Language
NicaSL	Nicaraguan Sign Language
NSL	Norwegian Sign Language
NZSL	New Zealand Sign Language
ÖGS	Austrian Sign Language
PJM	Polish Sign Language
PSL	Palestinian Sign Language
SLN, NGT	Dutch Sign Language; Sign Language of the Netherlands
SSL	Swedish Sign Language
TSL	Taiwan Sign Language
UGL	Ugandan Sign Language
VSL	Venezuelan Sign Language

NOTATIONAL CONVENTIONS

Upper case letters: e.g., 'FATHER.' Glosses of lexical signs

Lower case letters with underline between words: e.g., 'rocket_lands_on$_i$.' Glosses of material in a classifier construction articulated by a single form.

Subscripted letters: e.g., 'rocket_lands_on$_i$.' The subscript indicates spatial loci.

Subscripted numbers: e.g., $_0$GIVE$_3$. The subscript indicates verb agreement.

Carat symbol '^': e.g., BLACK^NAME 'bad reputation.' This indicates a compound.

Annotated line above a signed gloss: e.g., $\cdot\overline{\text{MOTHER.}}^{\,t}$ This indicates a simultaneously articulated nonmanual property.

Underlined letter(s): e.g., CAFETERIA; VIDEOTAPE. The underlining indicates elements of a sign that are derived from the manual alphabet.

1

Introduction

Diane Brentari

What are the unique characteristics of sign languages that make them so interesting? How is linguistic theory enriched by research on sign languages? *Sign Languages: A Cambridge Language Survey* tries to answer these questions. It is a collective work for which the whole is much greater than the sum of its parts. Differences among sign languages and Deaf communities will be described in its chapters as well as the common themes that point to convergence in the field. This volume addresses three areas of crosslinguistic study involving the family of sign languages: "transmission" of sign languages from one generation to the next, "shared crosslinguistic characteristics" and "variation and change." The study of sign languages is still relatively young, and while the majority of scholarship on these languages has come from just a few of them, a great effort has been made to represent as full a range as possible in this book. More than forty sign languages are treated in this volume. Among the sign languages represented in this volume are older sign languages, including British, Italian and American Sign Language as well as younger sign languages such as Israeli, Al-Sayyid Bedouin and Nicaraguan Sign Languages. Sign languages from developing countries as well as economically more advanced countries are included. A wide range of geographic locations is also represented: Latin America, Asia, the Mid-East, Africa, as well as Northern, Southern and Eastern European countries. Naturally the set represented here is not all-inclusive, due in part to concerns for space, but also due to the fact that the sign languages of many parts of the world have not yet been studied.

Sign Languages highlights three related areas of linguistics to which sign languages have contributed, and each is represented by its own part in this book. The first addresses how sign languages are transmitted from one generation to the next in different parts of the world, and how transmission is influenced by socio-political-cultural factors. The languages in this section were chosen because there is little known about them in the existing literature. Probably the most common assumptions about sign transmission comes from American Sign Language, British Sign Language and French Sign Language (LSF), which were not included in this section precisely because there is an existing literature.[1] These languages have been transmitted primarily through the schools for the Deaf – not necessarily because a sign language was a language of instruction, but because the school environment provided a community within which grammaticalization could take place. We will see in the sign languages represented in this section of the book that the school environment is not the only way that sign languages are transmitted. Factors internal to the Deaf community, such as identity, cohesiveness and stability, and those external to it will be considered.

The matter of language transmission is relevant to cultural studies and anthropological linguistics. It also has a profound effect on linguists doing fieldwork, insofar as the users of a language in decline may begin to lose the sense of what and what is not grammatical. The second part of the book highlights those crosslinguistic characteristics of sign languages that are stable and unique to this language family.[2] Here we will see such issues as iconicity and modality addressed crosslinguistically in, for example, systems of aspect and verb agreement. These examples were chosen because similar results across several sign languages have been found. The third area of scholarship to which sign languages have made a great contribution is language variation and change. Here we address synchronic variation but also how sign languages change in historical time, examining not only the effects of time on a stable sign language, but also how such languages emerge from gesture systems to become sign languages.

In the next sections of this introduction, I will describe a small selection of the chapters and orient the reader concerning some of the ways in which such work has contributed to the study of culture and language more generally. In trying to encapsulate why all linguists might want to become familiar with work on sign languages, allow me to summarize three reasons why sign languages present a unique perspective on the study of language. The first is *communication modality*; that is, what properties of structure are motivated by the visual/gesture nature of the phonetic systems that are used to produce and perceive them? Since sign languages are minority languages and visual (as opposed to auditory), linguists who study them help to shift focus of discussion from one where the facts of the spoken language "channel" are taken for granted to one where both the auditory and the visual channels can be considered. This matter is crucially important in phonology because recognition of modality differences exhibited in sign languages leads back to a reconsideration of the impact of these channel differences on spoken languages. No doubt the effect of the visual/gestural modality on sign languages is no less than the effect of the auditory/vocal modality in spoken languages, yet relatively little spoken language work addresses the question of how much of the auditory/vocal communication modality of spoken languages is present in their phonological architecture; for example, in the organization of syllables. Work on sign language phonology opens up a space for linguists working on spoken languages to address such questions.

The second element of scholarship to which sign languages contribute is *iconicity* in language, which is one particular type of modality effect. Signed and spoken languages both contain iconicity, but because sign languages are visual/gestural and the visual properties of entities and actions are so readily accessible, they are utilized in abundance in sign languages. How iconicity is used in the emergence of language in creating novel forms and in historical change are questions that can be taken up seriously in sign languages because there is a large amount of data with which to work. The use of iconicity in no way implies that sign language lack "duality of patterning," one of the fundamental design features of language (Hockett 1966), because as many of the chapters in this book show, it is not the source of structure that makes a system linguistic, but the distribution and use of elements within that system that constitute its grammar. Several chapters in this volume take up topics that involve iconicity in various forms.[3]

The third body of work on sign languages that helps us better understand our capacity for language is the work on the *emergence* of language; that is, the possibility of tracing the route from gesture to language. Speakers gesture when they talk, have always done so, and while these gestures are important in many ways (McNeill 1992, Goldin-Meadow 2003a), co-speech gesture systems do not possess self-standing grammars. Yet sign languages often begin when a single individual creates a system to use in his/her local environment. Sign language linguistics can study how non-linguistic gestural systems become linguistic over time in a way that cannot be traced in spoken languages. Two intermediate populations that function in between these two ends of the continuum of gesture and language are home sign systems, which are invented by isolated deaf individuals without a language model, and young sign systems that are less than a hundred years old. The opportunity that we have to study the stages of language change from gesture to sign language is extremely useful in understanding how a language can take shape in historical time. Two chapters of the volume address aspects of the system that change over time as language emerges.

In reading all of the chapters included here, I hope that it will become clear that a single theory of language cannot explain everything about this structurally related group of sign languages. Theories that address a wide range of cultural, societal and demographic factors, those addressing general cognitive systems, and those specific to abstract linguistic structure are needed. And perhaps because the set of sign languages studied here comes from all over the world (yet is still relatively small, compared to the number of families of spoken languages), we can see these theoretical perspectives played out on a smaller stage. Factors "external" to a linguistic system, such as cultural traditions, attitudes about language, the size of the community, the system (or systems) of deaf education, language environment and the cohesiveness of the community, to name a few, play a large role in understanding language transmission; this will be brought out in the first section of the book. Mufwene (2008) calls the contribution of such external factors "ecological" in nature, and he applies an approach of population dynamics to the phenomena of pidgins, creoles, language dominance and language extinction, as well as language transmission. He writes (2008: 182):

> No group of speakers passes on a ready-made grammar to a new group of speakers, no individual speaker does to any other speaker (Meillet 1929, Hagège 1993, DeGraff 1999) ... As with the development of any social competence, this (re)construction process ... depends on both the learners' individual skills and on the particular network that he/she has participated in.

With respect to factors that shape languages from within, both cognitive and generative linguistic approaches are represented in this volume. Cognitive linguistics has been interested in general factors that could be responsible for language structure and variation within it; namely, those not specific to language but which are part of our general perceptual, articulatory, cognitive or physiological systems (Givón 1984, Langacker 1987, Hopper & Traugott 1993, Bybee, Perkins & Pagliuca 1994). Engberg-Pedersen's and Wilcox, Rossini and Pizzuto's chapters are positioned in this framework. On the other hand, constituent structure at all levels of grammar – phonology, morphology, syntax, semantics – have been prevalent themes in generative linguistics and its predecessors since the early 1900s (Sapir 1925, Trubetzkoy 1939, Jackobson 1941, Hockett 1954, Chomsky 1957, to name a few), and no less in signed than in spoken languages. Sign languages exhibit a set of common characteristics, while still allowing for variation in constraint rankings and parameter settings. The chapters by Neidle and colleagues and Müller de Quadros and Lillo-Martin are representative works in this framework.

1   Language transmission

Looking closely at the transmission of sign languages from one generation to the next in a given country is like checking in on the basic health of the Deaf community, similar to taking its pulse. In the case of spoken languages, researchers who have worked on endangered and dying languages have long observed that if a language is no longer transmitted in the home from parents to children and if the cultural environment that is central to its use no longer exists, the language has little chance of surviving (Fishman 1991). Sign languages are not typically transmitted in the home, except for the small percentage of Deaf children born to Deaf parents. Approximately 1 in 1,000 live births results in a *deaf* child, but less than 10 percent of these (i.e., less than 1 in 10,000) is likely to be born into a culturally *Deaf* home, one where sign language is a daily presence.[4] And it is "sign language that plays the major role in developing Deaf identity … [t]herefore further research into sign transmission, dissemination, and preservation are critical activities that need to be undertaken if [these] minority sign languages are to survive" (Lule & Wallin, this volume: p. 118, p. 130).[5] The chapters contained in this volume describe how practices of sign language transmission differ in diverse areas of the world, and in so doing tap into how much power the Deaf community has over its own destiny in these locations. This is because control over language transmission is a way of ensuring that the most important manifestation of "Deaf culture" has a future. By "Deaf community" and "Deaf culture" I want to include all of the potential ways that this might manifest itself – historically as well as today.[6] The pressures and tensions surrounding the practices of language transmission are the expression of different power relations, and the work of Michel Foucault captures their interplay in a general way, aptly applied here to language transmission (2001: 1006):

> We cannot then speak of *power* if we want to undertake an analysis of power, but we have to speak of *powers* and try to localize them in their historical and geographical specificity … A society is not a unitary body in which one and only one power would exert itself, but it is in reality a juxtaposition, a connection, a coordination, a hierarchy, also, of different powers, which nevertheless remain in their specificity … Society is an archipelago of powers.[7]

Reading the chapters of this volume, we see a set of sources of power emerge that is relevant to the issue of language transmission. Crucially, none of the factors mentioned below is considered positive or negative on its own; every factor must be studied with respect to its own local network.[8] Some specific factors *internal* to Deaf communities that influence language transmission are:

size: How large is the Deaf community relative to the surrounding spoken language community?

proximity: Is it relatively easy for Deaf community members to stay in contact with one another?

cohesion: Is there an infrastructure for the Deaf, such as associations of the deaf, sports clubs, artistic traditions, or religious organizations? Is there consensus among Deaf community members concerning important issues, such as what variety of sign language should be taught to deaf and hearing people?

self-awareness: How much do deaf people consider themselves a group separate from the surrounding spoken language community?

longevity: How long has the community been aware of itself as a group?

Some specific factors *external* to Deaf communities that might influence language transmission are:

economic situation: What is the general state of the economy in the country?

mono- vs. multicultural environments: Is the surrounding spoken and signed language community homogeneous or heterogeneous with regard to culture and ethnicity?

educational intervention: What are the mechanisms for educating deaf children and what are the related educational policies?

governmental intervention: Is there official or unofficial recognition of sign language as a minority language? Are there explicit or implicit policies of eugenics concerning "human perfection"?

availability of technology: Is technology, such as the Internet and video technology, readily and inexpensively available so that it can provide a surrogate community in cyberspace?

medical intervention: What degree of influence does the medical community have in matters related to deafness?

availability of interpreters: Is interpreting a viable profession? Who pays for their services? How are interpreters trained?

There is a complex interplay between internal and external factors regarding practices of language transmission in each community represented in this volume. Let us look at just a couple of cases in some depth here. Schools, especially residential schools, have long been considered important in sign language transmission because, regardless of their communication policy, they provide a community for the language to grow and be passed to the next generation of signers. Some well-studied Deaf communities have had schools for the deaf since the period between 1750 and 1850. We will look at two of these countries – Sweden and Poland. Each is situated differently with respect to language transmission today.[9] Three more examples discussed here are communities where schools currently play relatively little role in the transmission of the language – Mexico, Uganda and the Arab World – again with different ambient situations based on the interplay of internal and external factors regarding language transmission.

The chapter by Bergman and Engberg-Pedersen describes the case of the Swedish Deaf community, which may appear small (8–10,000), unless it is considered as a proportion of the population as a whole, which is also quite small (approximately 9,000,000). The Swedish Deaf community is relatively old: there is evidence of Swedish Sign Language in 1759, even before the direct and indirect influence of the French across Europe after the founding of the first Deaf school in Paris in 1761.[10] There are six special schools for deaf and hard-of-hearing children, and the first of these appeared in 1809. More recently, in the 1960s, a member of the Swedish Parliament became the president of the Swedish Deaf Association, and in the 1970s there was an alliance established between parents of deaf children and the Swedish Deaf Association. This alliance has created a larger group that has been able to influence government policies. At first these policies introduced a general notion of "sign language," and the type of sign language taught to parents was more like Signed Swedish, with the signs following Swedish word order rather than that of Swedish Sign Language.[11] But Swedish Sign Language was officially recognized by the Riksdag (Swedish Parliament) in 1981 in a declaration stating deaf people's right to be bilingual, and a bilingual curriculum was adopted as well. Qualified interpreters and interpreter training are available, as is technology, and the economic situation is relatively strong. Currently Swedish Sign Language is largely taught by Deaf instructors; it is one of the languages offered in the regular school system for hearing pupils, and it is the third most popular choice among language options after French and Spanish, English being obligatory for all children. Approximately 100,000 hearing people are considered to have some signing skill. The universities in Malmö and Stockholm have two to three semester programs in Swedish Sign Language as a "foreign" language. We can conclude from this sketch that the internal and external factors that contribute to language transmission are working together in Sweden to provide a favorable environment for the future of Swedish Sign Language.

The second example is the case of Polish Sign Language transmission. Wojda (this volume: p. 146) writes in his conclusion:

> The [Polish] deaf community tends to lack group cohesiveness. The slogans about "Deaf culture" are not often reflected in everyday experiences. They are understood by only a few individuals who mainly acquire their understanding and meaning of culture from the surrounding Polish spoken language community ... For a deaf person in Poland, learning a spoken language is often a primary concern. Thus, dividing the Deaf community into those who are culturally Deaf vs. all others remains problematic.

As in Sweden, the first school for the deaf in Poland was established in the early 1800s – 1817 to be exact – but as recently as the 1990s, artificial hybrid communication systems, similar to Signed Polish, have been used in deaf classrooms, taught to hearing sign language students and even used to promote bilingual education. The confusion stems, in part, from the policy set by the Polish Deaf Association, which controls sign language teaching. It had been decided that it would be extremely difficult to describe the grammar of Polish Sign Language sufficiently to teach this language, so instead an artificial system thought to be more comprehensible to hearing people was taught, which uses the word order of Polish and can include the mouth movements of Polish words. This state of affairs has existed for decades, and it has affected deaf people as well, because teachers of the deaf learn this type of signing and then use it and ascribe high status to it in the classroom. Since the hybrids are often considered "cultured" signing, some native signers have adopted this style of signing. This creates an environment in which it is difficult to determine what Polish Sign Language really is, because it has altered signers' judgments about what constructions are grammatically acceptable. Sports clubs have fostered social cohesion, but the community has not mobilized itself to establish the unique status of Polish Sign Language. The external factors of the Polish Deaf community are quite encouraging – a good economy, a well-established national Deaf association, the existence of schools for the deaf – but the lack of self-awareness (an internal factor) contributes to a language transmission situation that puts Polish Sign Language in a precarious position.

Ramsey and Quinto-Pozos (this volume) describe a situation in Mexico where a residential school did exist but was closed in the 1960s. Many members of the community are somewhat distant from one another, so there is lack of cohesion among community members, and few have access to computers or the Internet. Language transmission of Mexican Sign Language has therefore migrated to other spaces – to church groups, for example – and sometimes to a type of mentorship situation that takes place when a skilled signer (*padrino*) works with a young signer to improve his/her skills. Alejandro López, one of the Deaf lay teachers at a church with a strong Deaf presence, commented that, to his dismay, there are now "eight or nine kinds of signing" in Mexico. He elaborated on this, saying that "in the past we only had one way to sign but since then things have gotten bad. It's all mixed up now" (p. 59). There is little support from external sources (government or international Deaf groups), and the lack of internal cohesion creates a difficult language transmission situation in this country. A healthy situation of dialectal variation may result from such a situation, but the worry is that without access to a large number of strong language models of any one variety, the language may be in a state of decline.

Our next example is Uganda. Like Mexico, there is little support from the government, but fortunately the government has not interfered with efforts by the Deaf community to create a cohesive community. Progress has been made in the last twelve years. The preamble to the Ugandan constitution now states that, "The state shall promote the development of a sign language for the deaf."[12] Ugandan Sign Language is also mentioned in some government policies, such as the Persons with Disabilities Act 2006. There is wide linguistic diversity in Uganda with approximately forty-three spoken languages, primarily from the Bantu and the Nilo-Saharan families; however, English is the language that deaf children learn to read and write, and Ugandan Sign Language is what deaf students learn to sign. There is also some interference from Signed English, perceived by some Deaf people as useful for upward mobility in the world of work. Deaf people are very proud of developing a Ugandan Sign Language theatre group as well as an Ugandan Sign Language dictionary, which grew out of collaboration with the Deaf Association of Denmark and the linguists Lars Wallin and Dorothy Lule. The Ugandan Deaf community has an optimistic future and a favorable language transmission situation, thanks to a growing community awareness that has not been diminished by external factors.

Our last case of sign language transmission is the sign languages of the Arab world (Al-Fityani and Padden, this volume). Three factors make the Deaf communities in this area of the world unique: (1) the high level of isolation and large family groups, (2) the high level of consanguinity among these families creating a higher than normal incidence of recessive genetic traits, and (3) large family groups with a higher than normal incidence of deafness means that the schools play a less important role in transmission, and there is a relatively high degree of sign language use within family and community settings. Thus, unlike the situation in the many other parts of the world represented in this volume, in this area of the world where there are large, extended families, there is more opportunity to learn a sign language from birth, and therefore a great chance that sign languages will be transmitted within families across generations. As Al-Fityani and Padden report, there is a wide range of language variation in this region, yet the Council of Arab Ministers of Social Affairs, a committee within the League of Arab States, has encouraged a standard pan-Arab Sign Language. This has been met with wide resistance, in large part due to the fact that when this artificial variety of sign language is presented during interpreted television news broadcasts, Deaf viewers say they cannot understand it. The authors write, "the underlying assumption that sign languages of the region are similar enough to be standardized may in fact be erroneous. It may be risky to engineer a 'standardized' sign language in the Arab world, given the difficulty of standardizing languages that are historically unrelated" (p. 452). While it is unlikely that such a move could jeopardize the transmission of sign languages in families and the local cohesion of these groups, this type of action by a governmental body may have consequences in school settings, and the energy and resources of the various affected Deaf communities may need to mobilize in a cooperative fashion in order to combat it.

In sum, d/Deaf people have many different identities that emerge from their own personal interactions, and these identities may or may not include that of being an active citizen in a Deaf-World. The factors in their external language environments have many different characteristics as well. Each situation can be described in terms of relationships of power, and these relations result in a set of practices used to transmit a sign language. For these reasons sign language transmission is a fascinating field of study, as the chapters of this volume amply demonstrate.

2   Shared crosslinguistic characteristics

In this section the shared properties of sign languages are described. These chapters describe issues that are common to a wide range of sign languages – e.g., word order, the expression of aspect, productivity and changes due to pressures of ease of perception and ease of production. Since this volume is designed to highlight the features of sign languages that make them unique, more attention in this introductory chapter will be paid to those properties not commonly seen nor commonly studied in spoken languages, and which contribute to our understanding of language more generally.

2.1   The lexicon

One common characteristic across sign languages is the organization of the lexicon, but languages of the world – signed and spoken – have lexicons composed of words with different origins. For example, Itô and Mester (1995a, 1995b) propose a core-periphery model for Japanese that involves several components (Yamoto, Mimetic, Sino-Japanese and Foreign). Brentari and Padden (2001) proposed a three-part lexicon for ASL (see Figure 1.1), which has been extended to many sign languages. In such models, the lexical components are established based on phonological and morphological properties as well as historical origins. Many sign languages share this type of lexical structure in part because of shared historical paths involving the interaction with the written and spoken means of communication surrounding them, and because of the use of iconicity in grammar in classifier constructions (described in more detail later on). The three lexical components of signed language lexicons are core, foreign and spatial, and these three components will be described briefly.

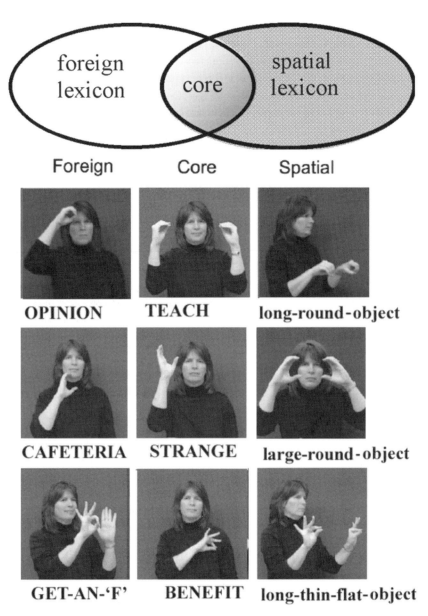

Figure 1.1 *The three components of the ASL lexicon with representative vocabulary items of each: foreign (left); core (middle); spatial (right).*

Figure 1.1 shows ASL examples from each component using the same three handshapes (i.e., ⟨symbol⟩, ⟨symbol⟩ and ⟨symbol⟩; from Brentari & Eccarius, this volume).[13] In the core component, the three manual parameters of handshape, place of articulation and movement are *phonological* and combine with other elements to form stems – i.e., the parameters *have no meaning*. Examples are TEACH, STRANGE and BENEFIT. The foreign component of the lexicon has forms that have a relationship with the surrounding spoken language or another sign language. Foreign forms include the set of initialized forms, which have a handshape of the manual alphabet as an affix and are built from stems in the core. The handshape as a whole is *morphological* because it *has meaning;* it expresses the meaning of the letter of the manual alphabet. In these signs the other manual parameters are phonological. Examples are OPINION, CAFETERIA, and GET-AN-'F'. Signs borrowed from the gesture systems of the surrounding spoken language or from another sign language would also be members of the foreign component, and all such signs may move towards the core as they obey more and more of the phonological constraints of the language or allow more types of morphological processes. The spatial component includes spatial signs (UP, DOWN, etc.) and classifier constructions. In classifiers, all of the parameters (and potentially smaller features internal to the parameters) *have meaning*, and this part of the lexicon contains a great deal of visual iconicity.[14] Classifier constructions are polymorphemic complexes with a verbal root – the movement – and affixes that involve place of articulation and handshape. In Figure 1.1, the forms are given for 'long_thin_round_object' (such as a round pipe), '[person]_look through_binoculars', and 'long_ thin_ flat_object' (such as a piece of paper or fabric).

2.2   Productivity

Iconicity is productive in sign languages, yet it is not equally productive across all components within a given sign language. Brentari and Eccarius (this volume) describe the differential use of iconicity in classifier handshapes, appealing to the systematic morphological possibilities available to different types of classifier handshapes crosslinguistically. Classifier handshapes representing the whole object show more complexity in finger selection, while handling and size/shape specifiers, which show the physical dimensions of the object, show more complexity in the joint configuration of the handshape. And even though iconicity never disappears from sign languages, it is generally weakened over time, both at the word level (Frishberg 1975) and at the level of the grammar as a whole. Forms become more conventionalized, and these grammaticized forms are distributed in a systematic way phonologically.

Engberg-Pedersen (this volume) argues that the degree of iconicity is correlated with the degree of productivity in the analysis of two falling events. She compares a more "typical" falling event with a more "atypical" one. In the more "typical" falling event, a boy falls from a tree. In this case one participant in the event (the tree) is a "ground" (as opposed to figure), stable (not moving) and inanimate, and the other participant (the boy) is the "figure" (as opposed to ground), active and animate. This configuration of participants is a typical one in a two-handed classifier construction (McIntire 1980, Padden 1988, Perniss 2007). Across seven of the nine sign languages analyzed by Engberg-Pedersen, the same handshape – the V-handshape (✌) – is used to indicate the "boy," demonstrating that these sign languages have taken the same route towards grammaticization of this form. Also, despite the apparent iconicity of V-handshape indicating a bipedal figure, with the fronts of the fingers indicating the front of the body (and therefore the knuckles would indicate the knees), when the figure expressed by this classifier handshape loses control and falls, the iconicity of the front of the legs and the front of the hand is suppressed. This loss of iconicity is not uniform across the spatial component of sign language grammars, as Engberg-Pedersen shows. She also analyzes an "atypical" falling event with two animate participants (a deer and a boy), where both move and neither is the obvious figure or ground (see Perniss 2007). In this case, there is a greater degree of iconicity overall and a great deal more variation, which is attributed to, among other factors, the various possible points of view taken by the signer.

Another area where iconicity is evident in sign languages is in movement. Wilbur (this volume) has analyzed the relationship between movement, iconicity, and meaning in many sign languages. She recently developed the Event Visibility Hypothesis, which is a formal account of how iconicity is mapped between the phonology and the semantics in the event structure of sign language predicates, both in the core and in the spatial lexical components. These distinctions are part of the semantic *Aktionsart* of the event, which include achievements and accomplishments, as well as states and processes (Vendler 1967). Wilbur has argued that these structural components of predicates are one reason why sign languages look so similar to one another.

2.3   Verb agreement

The topic of verb agreement is much discussed in the sign language literature and in this volume, both in the section on shared crosslinguistic characteristics and in the language variation and change section (Mathur and Rathmann, this volume, Padden *et al.*, this volume). The complexity of an analysis of verb agreement in sign languages is also associated with iconicity, since the spatial, referential loci (called "R"-loci) may participate in a visual iconic relationship with the transfer of objects in space. While there is variation in the number of mechanisms chosen, most – if not all – sign languages indicate the transfer of grammatical themes, as well as agreement with object and subject arguments using paths in signing space. However, the distribution of these mechanisms, while iconic at their origin, is highly grammaticized. Because R-loci indicate the location of the object and changes from discourse to discourse, the phonological realization of agreement for a given lexical item also changes, even if the agreement system of a given sign language is internally consistent and systematic. This is often referred to as the "listability" problem, which must determine how the infinite number of spatial loci using various types of iconicity is resolved into a set of discrete agreement morphemes. Solutions to the listability problem are outlined in Mathur and Rathmann's chapter, and they conclude that while, "The phenomenon [of agreement] has several properties in signed languages that make it look different than verb agreement in spoken languages," agreement is the appropriate mechanism to describe this phenomenon in sign languages. Because of the listability problem, the terms for these verbs vary: "agreement" (Lillo-Martin 1991), "directional" (Baker-Shenk & Cokely 1980, Meier 1982) and "indicating" (Liddell 2000) have all been applied to this phenomenon.

2.4   Simultaneity

Another important issue that must be taken up in the analyses of all sign languages is the matter of increased simultaneity of structure in signed as compared with spoken languages. This is not to say that there is little simultaneity in spoken languages. On the contrary, intonation systems and tonality are highly productive simultaneous elements of spoken languages; however, monosyllabic spoken languages with a large inventory of simultaneous elements are rare. This general difference between signed and spoken languages is due, in part, to the difference in using the visual vs. the auditory modality to construct a language. In general, the visual system is better at processing simultaneous information, while the auditory system is better at processing sequential information.[15] This is a crucial issue from the point of view of research tools, analysis and, ultimately, for investigating just how much this difference in degree affects the phonological representation of signed vs. spoken forms. This issue of simultaneity in sign languages is taken up in several chapters of the volume (Pfau and Quer on nonmanual properties, Jantunen and Takkinen on syllable structure, and van der Hulst and Channon on notation systems).

3   **Language variation**

Languages exhibit variation over historical time and across communities. Some of the mechanisms described in this section show that despite similar general grammatical mechanisms shared by sign languages, the particular expression of these mechanisms is different across sign varieties.

3.1   Diachronic variation

Diachronic change can mean a change from one stage to another of a given language (e.g., Frishberg 1975) or a change from a non-linguistic system to a linguistic one. In this section there are two contributions of the latter type, one from work being done in Nicaragua (Coppola & Senghas), which follows the role of deictic points from their *locative* use by signers who were the first students at the school in Managua and who communicated primarily in a pidgin form of Nicaraguan Sign Language ("Cohort 1") to their *nominal* use by signers who use the creolized form of the language ("Cohort 3"). The distribution of locative and nominal uses changes across cohorts, revealing a way that a form can be extended, grammaticized and made more abstract over time. In the second contribution, Padden and colleagues describe factors that affect the rate of change in two sign languages that are approximately the same age – Al-Sayyid Bedouin Sign Language (a village sign language with a relatively small number of signers) and Israeli Sign Language (a national sign language with a relatively large number of signers). They argue that the degree of different types of iconicity operating in agreement verbs in the two languages is different, and this difference is attributed, in part, to the size of the signing communities involved. Al-Sayyid Bedouin Sign Language makes reference to the body of the signer as the grammatical subject and as one of the R-loci; therefore, agreement verbs are situated along the "Z" axis (from the signer's body outward). In contrast, Israeli Sign Language, like many older sign languages such as those of Europe, uses the "X" axis (in front of the signer from one side to the other) for representing the R-loci of agreement verbs. These two chapters are important because they demonstrate facts about historical change and rate of change in different types of signing communities, and because they illuminate internal structural principles at work in the grammars of these languages.

3.2   Synchronic variation

The chapter by Lucas and Bayley (this volume) focuses on variation in American Sign Language that are correlated with ethnicity and region (often regions associated with residential schools for the Deaf), with particular attention to phono-logical variation – e.g., in one- vs. two-handed forms, and in forms that undergo the phonological process of phonological "lowering." Lowered signs show a shift in place of articulation from the forehead to a place closer to the cheek/chin. Schembri, *et al.* (2007), discuss variation in lexical choice, conversational style and use of fingerspell-ing in the sign language that includes the major portions of Great Britain, Australia and New Zealand, referred to by the acronym BANZSL. Such variation is correlated with such variables as age, gender and region. Besides variation within a single language, there are chapters in this section that deal with variation across sign languages. A lexicostatistical methodology is used to analyze variation in the chapter by Al-Fityani and Padden (this volume) on the sign languages of the Arab world. The degree of phonological variation among lexical items in the sign languages of this region is measured and then used to argue that these are indeed different sign languages. Tang and colleagues (this volume) analyze variation among four sign languages with different historical roots – Japanese, Swiss German, Hong Kong and American Sign – to demonstrate that while the inventory of prosodic cues across sign languages may be the same, the distribution and co-occurrence of these cues differ across sign languages. Fischer and Gong (this volume) focus on the sign languages of East Asia to demonstrate variation in handshape among these sign languages and also to compare and contrast them with sign languages from Europe and the United States. Finally, variation is sometimes exhibited by the lack of a set of structures. Nyst (this volume) observes that in some of the local sign languages of West Africa there are few classifier constructions than can be seen in the older sign languages of Europe, Asia and the Americas.

In sum, this volume is both a thematic and a geographic survey of sign languages, grouped around the themes of transmission, shared characteristics and variation and change. In concluding, let me also briefly explain the impetus for this project. The vision for *Sign Languages* had its origins in 2001, while I was traveling to ten different countries to collect data for a crosslinguistic project. I had the opportunity not only to address the specific questions of the project, but also to discuss these issues at length with my collaborators (both Deaf and hearing) from each country. From that experience, the idea for this book took shape. It grew by more frequent contact with new communities and the increased opportunity to ask broader questions in subsequent projects. My deepest thanks are extended to all of the contributors to this volume who worked tirelessly to write chapters that distill an enormous amount of material into a few drops of dense, yet accessible essence. It is difficult enough to turn a ton of rose petals into a gallon of rose water, but to get that gallon of rose water down to one drop of perfume takes patience, discipline and focus, and I am extremely grateful for the effort.

PART I
History and transmission

2

Transmission of sign languages in Northern Europe

Penny Boyes Braem and Christian Rathmann

1 Introduction

This chapter presents case studies of sign language transmission in European countries in which the majority of inhabitants all speak a Germanic-based language. Owing to space constraints, we are focusing in this chapter on Switzerland, Germany and the Netherlands as examples of the past and current practices of language transmission in this part of Europe, but by no means should this overview be interpreted as being inclusive of other countries of the region.

2 Transmission of the three sign languages of Switzerland

2.1 The spoken language situation in Switzerland

Switzerland recognizes four "*National* Languages," which are those used by the majority of people in different geographical regions of the country: Eighteen cantons are primarily German-speaking, five French, one Italian, one bilingual French/ German and one trilingual canton where German, Italian and Rhaeto-Romansh are spoken. "National Languages," however, have historically not been the same as the "*Official* Languages," which are those that can be used legally at the federal level. Romansh, for example, became an official language only in 1996. The "mother tongues" actually spoken by Swiss people in their families and local communities are not necessarily either "national" or "official" languages. "Mother tongue" languages used by a large number of persons on a daily basis include the several regional dialects of "Swiss German" and, as approximately 20 percent of the population living in Switzerland have foreign roots, such languages as Spanish, Portuguese, Serb, Croatian, Albanian and English.

There is no standardized form of the Swiss-German and Rhaeto-Romansch dialects learned by many persons as a mother tongue. Spoken Swiss German is lexically and grammatically different from the "Standard German" spoken in neighboring Germany and has no conventional written form. As a consequence,

Swiss German hearing children learn to read and write "Standard German" and not their mother tongue, Swiss German.

This somewhat complex spoken language situation has consequences for Swiss deaf persons. Deaf children from the Swiss German cantons usually do not learn the spoken but unwritten Swiss German dialects of their communities but are taught to read and write "Standard German." Their hearing families also usually speak with them in Standard German, although this is not a mother tongue of any of them. Deaf children from Rhaeto-Romansh areas have traditionally attended schools for the Deaf in the German-speaking cantons, where they are taught to speak, read and write in Standard German (Boyes Braem *et al.* 2000). Needless to say, the children from other cultural and linguistic backgrounds also have home languages, such as Portuguese or Albanian, which are different from whatever official Swiss language is their school language.

2.2   The sign language situation in Switzerland

The three sign languages used in Switzerland are

> Swiss German Sign Language (Deutschschweizerische Gebärdensprache, DSGS),
> Swiss French Sign Language (Langue des Signes Suisse romande, LSF-SR) and
> Swiss Italian Sign Language (Lingua dei Segni Italiana, LIS-SI).

There are no official statistics on deaf persons in Switzerland, but estimates based on the internationally used formula of 0.01 signing deaf persons per thousand of a population, as well as on membership in various clubs and organizations and on clients of interpreter services, would indicate that of the *c.*7.5 million inhabitants of Switzerland, there are *c.*7,500 Deaf signers, with *c.*5,500 in the eighteen primarily German-speaking cantons, 1,700 in the seven primarily French cantons and 300 in the Italian canton. Whether the traditional formula is still valid for the younger generations of deaf children who now routinely receive cochlear implants is an important open question for future research. There are, in addition, *c.*13,000 hearing signers in the country, an estimate based on the number of participants in sign language classes. There are no figures for children of deaf adults (CODAs).

In the past, signers learned their languages either from Deaf family members or, if they came from hearing families, from Deaf peers at a regional school for the deaf. This has changed radically in the past two decades, due primarily to the fact that, beginning in the 1980s, an increasingly large number of deaf children have received cochlear implantations at an early age and have been educated only in the spoken language of their region, with no contact with signers. Many signers in these more recent deaf generations have learned sign language as adolescents from the adult Deaf community.

2.2.1   *Official recognition of sign language*

The sign languages of Switzerland are not recognized as either "National" or "Official Languages" in the Swiss Constitution. Part of the state's reasoning for refusing the Swiss Deaf Association's 1993 petition that sign languages be officially recognized was that the users of these languages were not all located in one geographical "territory."

In 1994, the Swiss Parliament did pass a postulate that "recommends sign language for the integration of the deaf and urges, together with the oral language, its support in the fields of education, training, research and communication."[1] This postulate represented a first step but falls short of an official recognition that sign languages are the natural languages of Deaf people. Any implementation of most of the recommendations in the postulate, especially those concerning educational practices, is left up to the decisions of the numerous different cantonal institutions and governmental offices. In 2002, in a federal law on nondiscrimination of disabled people, a special Article was added to specify that the government could financially help institutions and cantons that encourage sign languages, and that sign language can also be used for official administration proceedings (for example in courts, with social agencies, etc.). It also stipulates that official political speeches on television by members of the Swiss Federal Council (Bundesrat) be translated by sign language interpreters. As a result of the 1994 Postulate and the 2002 and earlier regulations, the federal government now subsidizes sign language classes, the inter-cantonal training of sign language teachers and of sign language interpreters.

2.3   Descriptions of the three Swiss sign languages

None of the Swiss sign languages are standardized and all are composed of regional dialects that differ primarily at the lexical level. The five variants of DSGS and five variants of LSF-SR are related to the traditional residential schools for the Deaf in these regions. The regional dialects of DSGS are Basel, Bern, Lucerne, St. Gallen and Zurich. Although living in a different country, the deaf persons in Liechtenstein use a sign language which seems to be closely related to that used in the Swiss German cantons. The main regional varieties of LSF-SR are those of Geneva, Lausanne, Neuchatel, Fribourg and Sion. No research has been done on regional variation of LIS-SI, but deaf persons have informally reported that there are two main varieties of this language, centered on the cities of Lugano and Bellinzona.

The sign language used in German Switzerland, DSGS, is similar to the sign language used in the southern parts of Germany, LSF-SR to the sign language used in France (LSF) and LIS-SI to Italian Sign Language (LIS). An interesting study that remains to be done is of the extent to which these Swiss sign languages could be considered regional dialects of the sign languages of these neighboring countries, a question that is reflected in the use of abbreviations for these languages. Signers in French and Italian Switzerland usually refer to their languages with the abbreviations that are used for the related sign languages in neighboring countries. DSGS has been used in research publications, but Swiss German signers do not usually refer to their language with any abbreviation.

It is not unusual for a Swiss Deaf person to know more than one of the Swiss sign languages through personal contacts as well as national associations (such as the Swiss Deaf Sports Association), as well as one or more foreign sign languages (especially German, French, Italian and American sign languages). Owing to frequent encounters with persons using other sign languages, including Deaf refugees and immigrants from other countries, many Swiss Deaf signers are also fluent in some form of international signing.

Loan items from other sign languages do find their way into the lexicons of Swiss sign languages, but the direction of borrowing seems to be asymmetrical. Signers of DSGS report a high regard for the aesthetic qualities of LSF-SR and are relatively open to borrowing signs from that language. Signers of LSF-SR, in contrast, report resistance to borrowing from DSGS, which is viewed as the language of the majority group of Swiss Deaf. Signers of DSGS, on their part, report a resistance to borrowings from German Sign Language (DGS), due, again, to feelings of a minority needing to protect itself against a neighboring majority language. In general, deaf persons in Ticino have more contact with deaf in Italy than with the deaf in the German and French areas of Switzerland, which represent "dominating majorities" and with whom they do not share a common spoken language. The LIS-SI variety used around Bellinzona is more strongly influenced by sign languages of immigrants from the former Yugoslavia, Lithuania and Poland.

Signers of DSGS tend to use voiceless mouthings of German-like words or word beginnings with their signing for lexical, prosodic and stylistic purposes (Boyes Braem 2001b). Signers of LSF-SR use more fingerspelling with their signing compared to signers of DSGS, who until very recently have used this very little. As few DSGS signers are as yet as fluent in producing or reading fingerspelling, the use of "initialized" signs is not common for the creation of new DSGS signs. Both fingerspelling and mouthings are used with the signing of LIS-SI.

Deaf signers of both LSF-SR and DSGS have reported that they feel their languages have changed over the past couple of decades, primarily in an expansion of the vocabulary with new lexical items replacing the older signing generation's paraphrases or simply mouthings alone for describing concepts for which there are no signs. DSGS signers also report that more "signed German" lexical items have crept into their language from the younger generations of Deaf that have attended the Zurich school for the deaf, where a ten-year program of "signed German" was introduced in the 1980s (Maye, Ringli & Boyes Braem 1987).

2.4   Swiss sign languages in deaf education

2.4.1   *Education and attitudes toward deaf persons in the past*

2.4.1.1   *First schools for the deaf in Switzerland*   The first classes for the deaf in German Switzerland were begun in 1777 in the canton of Zurich and involved the use of local signs as well as spoken German. It was in Zurich in 1783 that the historical debate took place between the German proponent of the oral methodology, Samuel Heinicke, and proponents of Abbé Charles-Michel de l'Epée's "methodological signs." Schools for the deaf were established in Switzerland between 1811 and 1838, including Johan Heinrich Pestalozzi's school in Yverdon.[2] All of these schools used sign language together with the spoken language in a "combined method" and employed deaf teachers (Caramore 1988, 1990). As all teachers of the deaf were, until 1924, trained directly in the schools, they became increasingly influenced by the hiring of many fellow-teachers from Germany. By the middle of the nineteenth century already, before the 1880 Congress of Milan, the Swiss schools had become so strongly influenced by German oral methods that they had turned away from their earlier support of deaf teachers and signing.

2.4.1.2   *Eugenics movement and deaf people in Switzerland*   Eugenics, a theory of improving the human race through breeding, had an influential following in Switzerland in the first part of the twentieth century and was implemented through several measures affecting the so-called "degenerate" elements of the population, in which deaf persons were included. After World War I, the proponents of eugenics saw the increase in the deaf school population in contrast to the stagnating general population as a danger that the congenitally impaired sections of the population were increasing at the cost of the non-impaired citizens.

According to the then director of the Zurich "Deaf and Dumb Institute,"

> The aim of the caretaking of the deaf and dumb is, and must remain, to
> make itself superfluous. We should not let ourselves be satisfied with

> raising our children to be people who strive to be good, capable and
> able to take care of themselves. We have the duty to help shape the
> research and to stem the tide of deafness. (Hepp & Nager 1926:11)

The Swiss medical and educational authorities did not chose, however, to adopt the
extreme measures of the National Socialists in neighboring Germany, but rather
relied on other means, such as the clergy forbidding marriages of deaf persons,
placement of deaf women in institutions where their becoming pregnant was less
likely, abortions, as well as voluntary – and as a last resort, obligatory – sterilization. These attempts to eradiate deafness continued in Switzerland until the 1950s.
The Deaf community began only in the 1990s to re-examine this historical period
(Winteler 1995, Boyes Braem *et al.* 2000).

2.4.2   *Current educational situation*

2.4.2.1   *Cochlear implantation, parents' associations and counseling services*   The
practice of cochlear implantation is widespread throughout Switzerland, with the
entire cost of the procedure covered by the federal Disability Insurance. In 2006,
approximately 80 percent of deaf infants were implanted, many of them at as early
as thirteen months of age and the medical staff usually does not encourage parents
to use sign language with their deaf child. The Swiss Association of Parents of Deaf
Children as well as most counseling services for parents do officially mention sign
language as a possible form of communication, but their activities in practice,
especially in German Switzerland, concentrate primarily on information about
cochlear implantation and oral education.

In the late 1990s and early 2000, several playgroups using sign language were
started up all over the country; however, most of these playgroups no longer exist,
due to the lack of interest of new parents of young deaf children.

2.4.2.2   *Primary and secondary school education*   The number of pupils in the
day and residential schools for the Deaf has been steadily decreasing over the
past decade, as the large majority of Swiss deaf children who have received a
cochlear implant are integrated into classes with hearing children, usually without
signing support. The small number of deaf children still attending the traditional
residential schools tends to have additional disabilities or come from immigrant
families.

In French Switzerland, the schools for the deaf in Geneva, Fribourg and
Lausanne do have bilingual (LSF-SR/French) programs. In German Switzerland,
the Basel school has one experimental bilingual classroom and the Zurich school
offers a few classes per week taught in sign language by Deaf teachers.[3] In Italian

Switzerland, although in the past there was a school for the deaf, currently there is no regional school for the small population of deaf children.

After primary school, many Swiss deaf students now attend public high schools with hearing children but some chose to attend a residential secondary school for the deaf in Zurich or in Fribourg,[4] or a vocational training school for the deaf in Zurich.[5] At these schools, almost all of the main teachers are hearing, and few have fluent sign language skills. As approximately two-thirds of the students at the vocational training school are hard of hearing (often due to early cochlear implants), communication between the students themselves can also take place in the spoken language rather than in sign language. At the secondary school for the deaf, signing takes place mainly in the dormitory.

2.4.2.3 *College and university-level education*   In order to enter any Swiss university or technical college (*Fachhochschule*), one must have a special diploma (*Matura/Baccalauréat/Maturità*) from a secondary school. Secondary schools for the deaf have in the past not offered this kind of diploma and consequently there have been very few deaf Swiss who have been qualified to enter universities in this country. For those who do make it into a university or college, sufficient interpreting services are often not available for those who wish them.

In the absence of other Swiss university programs that are easily accessible for Deaf persons, the part-time program for training Deaf teachers of sign language[6] has functioned since 1990 as a center for higher education for signing deaf students, a kind of Swiss German "mini-Gallaudet." This program has been taught in sign language and includes several courses on sign language linguistics and Deaf culture. Deaf persons have also participated as team members as well as informants in all research and development studies of DSGS, from which they receive a kind of "on-the-job" training in research principles and techniques.

2.5   Swiss sign language in Deaf communities

Deaf clubs and associations began springing up in many regions of the country in the later nineteenth century providing places where the Deaf could communicate with signs. This was done, however, in face of strong disapproval by the teachers and professionals, who considered themselves to be the public representatives of the deaf. Until the 1920s, deaf who could not demonstrate good oral skills were regarded as peculiar or rebellious, which, until the 1940s, put them in danger of becoming "mentally retarded" wards of the state (Gebhard 2007). In this environment, it is not surprising that many deaf persons chose not to sign when in public, or even to regard signing as a "real" language. In the first church services for the deaf, one of the first ministers, Eugen Sutermeister (1929), himself deafened as a child, was also a proponent of a ban on signing.

The local associations and clubs were united into a national "Swiss Deaf and Dumb Association" (Schweizerische Taubstummenverein) in 1873. It was, however, not until 1987 that the French and German areas began publications of their own and the dominance of the hearing professionals began to break down (Gebhard 2007). In the early 1980s, the three regional Deaf Associations in the German, French and Italian parts of the country also began to fight for the public recognition of the Deaf person to sign, although at the beginning this was referred to as "signing" and only later as "sign language." In 2006, the three regional associations joined together into one national organization, the Swiss Federation of the Deaf (SGB-FSS),[7] which, among other things, was responsible for almost all sign language courses in the country as well as the development of sign language learning materials. There are currently more materials available for DSGS than for the other Swiss languages, although the newly nationalized Swiss Deaf Association is currently making plans for producing such products for LSF-SR and LIS-SI as well.[8]

In recent years, a growing number of regional "Communication Forums" ("Kofos") in the French and German cantons have become important places for conveying information in sign language on political and social topics. In both French and German Switzerland, there is a tradition of sign language theatre and "Deaf slams," competitions with signed poetry and stories, have become increasingly popular. Deaf Websites and Blogs have also become forums in which Swiss Deaf routinely discuss, among other things, matters relating to their sign languages.

As a counterpart to the many Swiss deaf groups that use and advocate sign languages, there are also organizations, in both the German and French areas, of oral-only communicating deaf persons, who advocate not using sign language.[9]

As Switzerland is such a small, and linguistically diverse, country, networking with Deaf signers from other countries is an important influence on the form and transmission of its sign languages. Swiss French Deaf have contact with signers over the border in France, a connection that was particularly important in setting up the first LIS-SR sign language courses and interpreter training programs in the 1980s. Congresses and cultural events in Germany in the early 1990s had a great influence on the linguistic self-awareness of all Swiss Deaf and a renewed look at some form of signing in the classroom for educators. Several Swiss Deaf from the French and German areas have, since the 1980s, attended Gallaudet University in the United States for shorter or longer periods of time.

2.6   Swiss sign languages in society

2.6.1   *Sign language courses and sign language interpreting in Switzerland*
All teachers of sign language courses in Switzerland are themselves deaf. In German Switzerland, there is a permanent training program for these teachers; in the French area, there have been intermittent programs; there have been no equivalent programs in the Italian canton.

Part-time programs for interpreter training began in 1984 in Lausanne/Geneva for LIS-SR and in Zurich in 1986 for DSGS.[10] In Italian Switzerland, there has been only one interpreter training program (1996–1999). Despite these programs, there are clearly not enough trained interpreters for the ever-growing demand in all areas of the country, and the deaf client is often upset by not receiving requested interpreting services.

2.6.2   *Sign language in the Swiss Media/Internet*
In 1998, the bimonthly television program in German Switzerland, which communicated in DSGS, was dropped entirely from the public television. In order to fill the information gap left for a Deaf audience, an Internet TV program (www.focus-5.tv) was begun by Deaf persons in 2003 with reports in DSGS, ASL and International Signing. In French Switzerland, the TV program in LSF-SR for the Deaf ("signes") was never cancelled. In Italian Switzerland, there is no television program for the Deaf on the Italian Swiss television. Since 2007, all Swiss national television stations are legally required to provide sign language interpretation of at least one program per day and, in 2008, the national Swiss television stations in all three areas of the country began, in addition, the interpretation of one daily news program into the local sign languages.

The Swiss government is now required by law to provide official information in sign language on some of its official websites, and some private companies are also beginning to provide information in sign languages. Also available on the Web are DSGS lexicons for technical terms, explanations of health topics in SLF-SR, as well as SignWriting Notation for both of these languages.[11]

2.7   Sign language research and development

Research on sign languages in Switzerland has been greatly hampered by the fact that, in contrast to most of its neighboring countries, there are no departments or faculty positions in any university that specialize in sign language or have permanent faculty positions for sign language research. There has been more research published on DSGS than on the other two Swiss sign languages, with the Swiss National Science Foundation funding most of the major projects.[12]

There being no permanent presence of sign language research at the university level, it is not surprising that few Swiss PhD dissertations involving sign language have been done in Switzerland.[13] In German Switzerland, seminar and master papers involving sign language have been done primarily at the Universities of Basel and Bern, a few of which have been published by a small association founded in 1982 to further sign language research (www.vugs.ch). In French Switzerland, Professor François Grosjean at the University of Neuchatel has been one of the most prominent proponents of sign language in this country. His short but influential text "The right of the deaf child to grow up bilingual" has been reprinted in at least thirty different language[14] and several of his students have also produced unpublished masters papers on topics related to sign language.

2.8   Opinions on the future of sign language in Switzerland

The Swiss Constitution guarantees the individual the freedom to use privately any language. In this sense, there is no official oppression of sign languages and, as noted above, some laws allow the use of sign languages in some contexts. On the other hand, there is no official recognition of sign languages as natural languages of Deaf persons. Deaf persons are still regarded, especially by Swiss medical personnel, primarily as disabled persons.

For these societal and cultural reasons, as well as the current practice of not encouraging sign languages in the education of cochlear-implanted deaf children, all three Swiss sign languages are considered by many persons to be endangered languages. However, from the point of view of other (often Deaf) persons, the languages are not ultimately endangered and will always, in some form, be used by Deaf persons.

3   Transmission of sign language in Germany

3.1   The sign language situation in Germany

The sign language used in the German Deaf Community is referred to as Deutsche Gebärdensprache (DGS), German Sign Language, a term widely used in the German Deaf community. As with spoken languages, DGS has a number of regional dialects.[15] One of the regional dialects that has been systematically documented is the Munich dialect (Mally 1993b).

3.1.1   *Number of sign language users*

There are no official figures on the number of sign language users in Germany, nor for hearing children of Deaf signing parents who have acquired DGS as a first language. The German Deaf Association (DGB; www.gehoerlosenbund.de) registered 33,383 deaf and hard-of-hearing members in 1991 and 29,833 in 2005. The reasons for the decline in membership include the improvement of technology (e.g. access to telecommunication) and individual lifestyle choices (e.g. decline of Deaf volunteers in Deaf organizations and clubs) within the Deaf population (Worseck & von Meyenn 2007). At the same time, the website of the German Deaf Association states that there are 100,000 Deaf and deaf individuals living in Germany. According to a census conducted in West Germany in 1950, the prevalence rate for "prelingual deafness" was estimated to yield about 43,000 deaf individuals (van Cleve 1987:252). It is difficult to judge how many of these deaf people are actually signers, as there has been no formal census of sign language users.

3.2   History of sign language and the Deaf community in Germany

3.2.1   *First institutes for the deaf and deaf organizations in the eighteenth and nineteenth centuries*

In spite of the lack of empirical documentation on how DGS has emerged and stabilized, it is assumed that the precursors of DGS appeared in the second half of the eighteenth century and the first half of the nineteenth century. Its appearance was likely fostered by the establishment of residential schools for the Deaf, beginning with the very first "Institute for the Deaf and Dumb" founded in Leipzig by Samuel Heinicke in 1778. Some of the first deaf students at these first institutes became teachers there, and consequently, the combined method (i.e., the use of both signed and spoken languages in the classroom) became popular. Thus, while the oralist so-called "German Method" had a significant impact on German deaf education in the following centuries, it was not apparent that it had an immediate effect due to the many Deaf teachers at schools for the deaf.[16]

A second factor that played a significant role in the transmission and dissemination of sign language in Germany in the nineteenth century was the establishment of numerous Deaf clubs, associations and organizations, and newspapers, and the organization of national and European conferences.[17]

The establishment of Institutes for the Deaf as well as Deaf clubs and associations as Deaf "places" (in the sense of Padden & Humphries 2005) resulted in a critical mass of Deaf individuals. This fact implies that it has led to an increase in the number of Deaf marriages and Deaf children born to Deaf families.

3.2.2   *Oralist movement backlashes in late nineteenth and early twentieth centuries*

A wave of "oralism" using "the German method" occurred after the Second International Congress on the Education of the Deaf and Dumb, held in Milan, Italy, in September, 1880.[18] Although only one (hearing) representative from Germany attended the congress, the resolutions had a huge impact on deaf education in Germany: Deaf teachers were forced to leave their jobs, no new Deaf teachers were hired and ultimately the use of sign language was banned from the classroom.

Although the thriving German Deaf community saw these events as a disaster, it tirelessly organized various protests against the implementation of the Milan resolutions. Their two main demands (reintroduction of the "combined method" and reemployment of Deaf teachers) remained mainly unheard until the 1980s (Beecken *et al.* 1999).

3.2.3   *National Socialism (1933–1945)*

A second major backlash against the dissemination and transmission of DGS took place during the era of National Socialism from 1933 to 1945. The National Deaf Association (Reichsverband der Gehoerlosen Deutschlands, also known as ReGeDe) was founded in Weimar in 1927 and was necessary at that time, as a large number of Deaf people were unemployed and there was the beginning of sterilization for people with hereditary deafness ("Lex Zwickau," Boeters 1926).

3.2.3.1   *Laws of 1933 (Gleichschaltung)*   When Adolf Hitler came to power in 1933, the laws to consolidate institutional powers (*Gleichschaltung*) were passed, which had a negative effect on the transmission and dissemination of DGS. ReGeDe lost its ability to operate as an independent national association with its own political agenda of preserving sign language and became – either directly or indirectly – involved in the compulsory sterilization of Deaf persons as well as responsible for the exclusion of Deaf Jews from Deaf associations and clubs. ReGeDe was ultimately dismantled in 1945, leaving the Deaf community with no formal organization to advocate its human rights, including the right to use sign language.

3.2.3.2   *Jewish Deaf people and the Holocaust*   During the Holocaust, approximately 6,000 Deaf Jewish people were murdered in concentration camps. The ultimate effect was that a significant portion of the transmission and dissemination of DGS was practically "shut down." After World War II, only about twenty-two Deaf Jews remained in Germany. Many other Deaf Jewish people emigrated outside of Germany. The language of the Jewish German Deaf who emigrated to Israel seems, along with contact with other signed languages, to have influenced the lexicon of Israeli Sign Language as can be seen by the relatively high degree of similarity between the lexical items of DGS and Israeli Sign Language.

3.2.3.3 *Deaf people and eugenics* In 1933, Germany passed a law called "The Law for the Prevention of Offspring with Hereditary Diseases" (*Gesetz zur Verhütung erbkranken Nachwuchs*). Approximately 17,000 people who had a history of hereditary deafness were sterilized against their will during this time. Church organizations, ReGeDe and the teachers of the deaf actively cooperated with law enforcement agencies and hospitals in enforcing the law by giving them contact information for candidates eligible for sterilization and even explained to deaf children and their parents that there were benefits to this program (Biesold 1999). About 5 to 10 percent of the Deaf community comes from deaf families, and their main contribution to the Deaf community is to maintain the transmission of their language and culture. All of these Deaf from Deaf families were likely included in the 17,000 who were sterilized, thus making it impossible for them to pass on their language and culture to future generations of Deaf and hearing children.

When the government realized that the sterilization of deaf people through the above-mentioned law was not sufficient for eliminating disabled people "unworthy of life," it initiated a pilot project called the "T4 program" in 1939 to test practical means of gassing people to their death. Under this program, 75,000 to 250,000 people with intellectual or physical disabilities were murdered, including some Deaf persons (Klee 1985). The method developed under the T4 program was subsequently used at concentration camps to kill Jewish people, including Deaf Jewish people.

The rise of National Socialism had a huge impact on the transmission and dissemination of DGS. The *Gleichschaltung* weakened ReGeDe's ability to advocate for the Deaf community and eliminated Jewish members who happened to be strong leaders; the Holocaust wiped out the Deaf Jewish community; and compulsory sterilization for deaf individuals went unchecked, damaging their self-esteem. The effects of National Socialism continued to reverberate through the postwar decades.

3.2.4 *Germany after the war*

When Germany was divided into zones controlled by American, French, British and Soviet administrations after the war, Deaf people started to reestablish local Deaf clubs and associations. In West Germany, a coalition of these groups was formed in 1948, with one of its aims being the fight for compensation for the many deaf people who were sterilized. A law mandating compensation for these individuals was not passed until three decades later, in 1965 (Federal Law of Rehabilitation, *Bundesentschädigungsgesetz BEG*). Deaf people in the eastern Zone administered by USSR were not allowed to form a Deaf association until 1957.

During this postwar period, two independent worlds grew up: The world of teachers and administrators in deaf education who took a deficit-oriented view toward deaf people, and the world of Deaf people, which thrived with mostly sports-oriented Deaf clubs and associations in which the use of DGS again thrived. A diglossic situation emerged in which it was considered appropriate to use DGS in private at Deaf clubs or at home but not in public, whereas those who were oral and/or could use the contact language, Sign Supported German (LBG, Lautsprachbegleitende Gebaerden) were considered to be "smart" and "intelligent" people. A number of Deaf people were ashamed to use DGS in public.

3.2.5   *Resurgence of German Sign Language (and German Deaf community) after the 1970s*

The resurgence of DGS (and German Deaf community) had four catalysts: Deaf activism in the late 1970s onward, linguistic research on DGS, the emergence of the bilingual approach in deaf education and the Deaf community's rediscovery of its identity as a linguistic-cultural minority.

3.2.5.1   *Deaf activism in the 1970s*   The first catalyst came about in the late 1970s when Getrud Mally and Volkmar Jaeger, Deaf activists from Munich and Leipzig respectively, responded to the apathy of the Deaf associations that came about after the rise of National Socialism (Mally 1993a). These activists and their friends sought to reevaluate their Deaf identity and language, and founded a "Communication Forum" and publications that were, and still are, used to raise awareness issues of the education, culture, identity and sign language of the Deaf. These discussions were like an earthquake within the Deaf community.

3.2.5.2   *New research on DGS*   A second catalyst occurred in the 1970s when Professor Siegmund Prillwitz at the University of Hamburg was asked by Jochen Kohnert, a professor of deaf education, to investigate ways of enhancing the literacy skills of deaf children in written German. After visiting the school for the deaf in Hamburg, Prillwitz became fascinated with how deaf children conversed with each other using their hands. Around the same time, a deaf man, Wolfgang Schmidt, after a visit to Gallaudet University, began discussing with fellow deaf people, Heiko Zienert and Alexander Meyenn, whether the concept of ASL as a language on its own could be applied to

Germany. It was then that the term "*Deutsche Gebärdensprache*" came into common use, replacing the previously used term "*Gebärden*." Eventually these three deaf men met Prillwitz and, in 1982, started a research project together on the structure of DGS at the University of Hamburg. They presented their research findings at a congress for Deaf education in 1985 (Prillwitz *et al.* 1985), where they claimed that the communication form that deaf people were accustomed to using was German Sign Language, a full-fledged language with its own lexicon and grammar and not to be confused with Signed German. That discovery was a mind-blowing event for the Deaf community and for educators of the deaf, not only in Germany but also in neighboring German-speaking countries.

The Center (now Institute) of German Sign Language and Communication of the Deaf was founded at the University of Hamburg in 1986 by Professor Siegmund Prillwitz. Its research agenda is quite extensive, ranging from lexicographic projects to the description of DGS, the development of educational materials, notational systems (HamNoSys, *Hamburger Notationsystem*), the development of sign corpora databank and language acquisition studies.[19] The institute has had two full-time degree programs (Sign Languages and Interpreting) since 1992 and has hosted a number of international congresses on sign languages and Deaf history. Convinced that the dissemination of research findings played an important role in the awareness of sign languages as full-fledged languages and the existence of Deaf culture, Prillwitz founded a publishing company, Signum Press (www. signum-verlag.de), in the late 1980s.

At the University of Frankfurt, the focus of research on DGS, under the direction of Professor Helene Leuninger, mainly lies in language production (within the field of psycholinguistics). The research team has also been actively engaged in various projects including the formal description of DGS and bilingualism, the documentation of a religion-related lexicon and the development of courses specially designed for sign language teachers and interpreters.[20]

In 1995, an interdisciplinary research group at RWTH University of Aachen was established by Professor Ludwig Jaeger, a linguist in the German Department; Professor Walter Huber from the Medical School and Professor Klaus Willmes-von Hinckeldey, both neuroscientists at the Medical School. Their agenda is fourfold: (a) development of assessment tools, (b) development of instructional materials, (c) research on psycholinguistic and neurolinguistic processes of DGS and German and on DGS as a medium of communication and (d) information technology.[21]

In the late 1980s and early 1990s, Jens Hessmann and Horst Ebbinghaus led a research project at the Free University of Berlin, investigating the role of mouthing in DGS, and raising the issue of multimodality of sign languages, which is still

34   *Sign Languages*

under debate today. Hessmann is currently professor and directs the sign interpret-
ing training program at the University of Applied Sciences in Magdeburg-Stendal.
Professor Ebbinghaus established the interpreter training program at the West-
Saxonian University of Applied Sciences Zwickau in 2000 (now directed by
Professor Vaupel) and has been responsible for the Deaf Studies program at
Humboldt University in Berlin since 2003.[22]

One important research question, which has not yet been researched, is
whether there has been any change in the community and their use of DGS
since the first gatherings of Deaf individuals in the nineteenth century. Such
analyses await an analysis of historical materials, such as early documentary
films with DGS, which were banned during the National Socialist era and were
only rediscovered in the late 1980s. As another starting point for an analysis of
change in DGS, the second author has conducted ethnographic interviews with
German Deaf sign language users, who have noted that older sign language
users tend to use more mouthing and less signing space, while younger sign
language users tend to use condensed signs, signing space and neologisms more
often than the older signers.

The discovery that DGS was a full-fledged language led to highly controversial
debates on the methods of deaf education. First, Signed German (LBG) was
introduced in the classrooms. In the early 1990s, the school for the deaf in
Hamburg started the first bilingual project to use DGS, which met with success
(Günther 2004). As a result, a number of other schools adopted the bilingual
approach and DGS has become one of the requirements for a degree in deaf
education. The success of the bilingual project also led to the formation of a
professional association of teachers of the Deaf supporting the bilingual approach
(Deutscher Fachverband fuer Gehoerlosen- und Schwerhoerigen paedagogik,
DFGS) and the association of Parents of Deaf Children (www.gehoerlose kinder.
de) becoming involved in awareness activities, ensuring that DGS be included in
the education of Deaf children. Other organizations involving the use of sign
language are the National Association of Sign Language Interpreters (BGSD)
and an association for specialists working with hearing children and their Deaf
parents (Leben auf dem Trapez/Life on the Trapeze).

3.2.5.3 *The modern Deaf community* Another important catalyst took place
within the Deaf community in the form of a paradigm shift from a focus
on disability to putting more weight on the celebration, preservation and
dissemination of DGS. The German Deaf Association (DGB) under Ulrich
Hase started a political campaign to get the government to recognize sign
language, resulting in a number of bills that came into law (discussed in

the next section). The DGB launched its first German Deaf Culture Festival in Hamburg in 1993, which has continued to be held in various cities until the present.[23] More deaf events celebrating sign language and Deaf culture began being held and became an integral part of the German Deaf community.[24]

Communication forums (*Kommunikationforen*), following the early model in Munich, were founded in several German cities with the purpose of furthering socio-political discussion among Deaf sign language users. Several advocacy and interest groups centering on DGS and/or the German Deaf community have also emerged.[25]

The discovery of DGS as a language had an effect on the media. The weekly TV program for the Deaf (*Sehen Statt Hoeren*) changed its paradigm from Signed German to using DGS, with Deaf presenters and producers in the late 1980s. Efforts have been made to deliver television news in DGS, most notably in Phoenix (a private German channel), and recently a small number of programs in German WebTV became accessible for DGS users.[26] DGS has also become more visible on the Internet in the form of translations of German texts.[27]

3.2.5.4 *Official recognition of German Sign Language*   In more recent years, a number of federal and state laws have been passed or revised which acknowledge the linguistic right of Deaf people to use DGS in the public domain, connected with laws for the disabled.[28] There is still no law mentioning that Deaf children have the linguistic right to use DGS in educational settings.

The Constitution of the Federal Republic of Germany (*Grundgesetz fuer Bundesrepublik Deutschland*) does not include any information about the official language status of DGS. Because the constitution and all laws are written in German, it is widely assumed that German is considered the official language in Germany. At the same time, there is a number of federal laws that are relevant for administrative agencies and courts stating that German is the official language.

The German government has adopted and ratified the European Charter for Regional or Minority Languages of 1992,[29] which became German law in January 1999. The charter defines the linguistic and cultural rights and protection of regional and minority languages in a wide range of public and private domains. To date, the German federal government and/or state governments have officially listed Danish, Friesian, Sorbian and Romani as minority languages and Lower German as a regional and minority language. There is no mention of the linguistic and cultural rights and protection of DGS.

The German federal and state governments have partially followed the European Parliament Resolution on Sign Languages of June 17, 1988,[30] concerning the official recognition of sign languages.

One issue that remains is how the official recognition of sign language at the governmental level can be conducted – under either a linguistic and cultural minority model or an accessibility model? The latter model seems to be the case for Germany, as the laws mentioned above seem to be of the kind that allows the Deaf community access to the larger society; they are not necessarily of the kind that protects the interests of the community.

3.3   Current issues

This section raises three issues that currently face the transmission of DGS: (a) endangerment by cochlear-implant technology and other biotechnology, (b) multilingualism and multiculturalism within the German Deaf community and (c) confronting the events that occurred during the period of National Socialism.

3.3.1   *Cochlear implants and biotechnology*

As in many industrialized countries, more and more deaf children in Germany are receiving cochlear implants (CI). Currently, about 80 percent of children with hearing loss of 100 db and above, and 50 percent of children with hearing loss of 80–100 db receive CIs. The majority of deaf children appear to have no opportunity for exposure to DGS during their language development. Doctors and professionals at CI clinics strongly recommend that parents not use DGS with their children (unless a serious delay in speech development is diagnosed) and do not actively seek cooperation with the German Deaf Association or with sign linguists and professionals working at bilingual schools. Consequently, fewer deaf children are enrolled at schools for the deaf. This trend could be interpreted as the next backlash against the transmission of a full-fledged sign language and might turn out to be irreversible. For this reason, huge efforts have gone into raising awareness of the importance of sign language in deaf children's bilingual development (see, e.g., Szagun 2003 and Hintermair 2007). The efforts have come from various levels, e.g. academia through their research, the German Deaf Association through distributing materials, and a number of individuals through scheduled activities.[31]

At the time of this publication, a bill on Human Fertilization and Embryology is under discussion in the House of Lords in the United Kingdom.[32] Clause 14, Section 4, Number 9 of this bill states that "persons or embryos that are known to have a gene, chromosome or mitochondrion abnormality involving a significant risk that a person with the abnormality will have or develop – (a) a serious physical or mental disability; (b) a serious illness or (c) any other serious mental condition, must not be preferred to those that are not known to have such an abnormality." As it prevents the birth of certain kinds of people, including deaf people, and deafness is considered as a "serious disease," it raises two questions for the transmission of DGS that remain to be addressed. First, how can the current draft be compared with the earlier described German "Law for the Prevention of Offspring with Hereditary Diseases"? Second, if the bill is passed in the United Kingdom, will it in turn cause another serious backlash against sign language transmission in the European Union, including Germany, in the twenty-first century?

3.3.2   *Multilingualism and multiculturalism within the German Deaf community*

The sociolinguistic situation in the German Deaf community has taken on a new dimension as a result of new patterns of migration in Germany during the past few decades. There are ethic minority groups (e.g., Turkish, Polish, Bosnian or Russian) within the German Deaf community as well as multiethnic Deaf marriages and children growing up with two sign languages. There is an increase in the enrollment of linguistically and culturally diverse Deaf children at schools of the deaf. The new sociolinguistic dimension raises several interesting questions: How is sign language transmission conducted within this context? What is the nature of language contact between DGS and other sign language(s) brought by immigrants? How do Deaf immigrants acquire DGS as a second sign language, and how are they integrated into the German Deaf community?

3.3.3   *Coming to terms with the past*

Finally, there is the question of how the history of sign language transmission in the era of National Socialism has been dealt with inside the German Deaf community. This issue has received attention recently, but the process of reconciliation has apparently been difficult. For example, to date the current German Deaf Association has acknowledged its role during the era of National Socialism with respect to Deaf Holocaust and sterilization. Most recently, they have officially offered a public apology for its role.[33] At the same time, thanks largely to the efforts of the Deaf educator, Horst Biesold, and other Deaf individuals,[34] research and education have begun in Germany on the backlash against sign language transmission during the time of National Socialism (Biesold 1999, Zaurov 2003). In the summer of 2006, the sixth International Deaf History conference was hosted in Berlin by the Interest Group of Deaf of Jewish Descent (Interessengemeinschaft

Gehörloser Jüdischer Abstammung in Deutschland IGJAD) with its main focus on the Deaf Holocaust and it was the first of its kind on German soil.

The German Association of Teachers for the Deaf (Bundes deutscher Hörgeschädigtenlehrer) has distributed a public apology for its involvement in the compulsory sterilization of Deaf individuals. However, to date, there has been no open dialogue between the German Deaf community and the association on several questions such as the following: How was it possible that teachers and directors who were actively involved in the compulsory sterilization were able to continue their job at schools for the Deaf until their retirement and acted as if compulsory sterilization never happened? Why was the association not involved in ensuring that Deaf people suffering from sterilization received appropriate compensation from the government? In sum, the German Deaf community has been tremendously creative and resilient in transmitting DGS against great obstacles. Second, it is evident that with backing from research findings on German Sign Language, the German Deaf community is able to ensure the continuation of sign language transmission. In addition, the influence of DGS on the ISL lexicon is also a type of language transmission and survival when the language was in danger at home.

4   Transmission of sign language in the Netherlands

4.1   The sign language situation in the Netherlands

In English, the language is referred to as Sign Language of the Netherlands (SLN), and in Dutch as Nederlandse Gebarentaal (NGT).

There are no official statistics on the number of persons who use NGT; estimates are *c*.10,000 Deaf signers. Crasborn (personal communication) thinks these numbers are probably too high and argues that using a formula of .033 percent of the national population would provide a more accurate estimate of 5,500 signers. The number of fluent signers who show fairly little influence of spoken Dutch (sign-supported Dutch) may well be much lower than this. There are no estimates for the number of hearing (including CODA) signers.

As of 2007, NGT was not yet legally recognized in any Dutch law, although efforts are being made to get legal recognition within an education and a health law (Baker 2000). The Dutch Ministry of Education funds the Dutch Sign Center[35] and there are official national programs for teachers, for interpreter training, and for note-takers for deaf students needing to focus on signed communication in the classroom.[36] There is also an official right to have sign language interpreters through the national Health Care Insurance (AWBZ), although the number of hours and settings are limited.

There has been a distinction in the Netherlands between deaf and hard-of-hearing persons, influenced by their separate schools since the middle of the twentieth century.

Both younger and older Dutch Deaf have a positive attitude toward Dutch, although they might not always like to use their voice.

In the Netherlands, although there are individual deaf persons who do not advocate sign language, there has never been an "oral" deaf group that opposes sign language. The Deaf community usually accepts hearing teachers and researchers, as long as they have sufficient signing skills and a "Deaf" attitude. Within Dutch society, NGT is culturally accepted as a language.

4.2   Description of the Sign Language of the Netherlands

The Sign Language of the Netherlands seems to have evolved from signs used in the Deaf communities, which grew up around the regional schools for the Deaf (see Schermer 1990). The language is related generally to those used in Western Europe and North America (DGS, LSF, BSL and ASL). Slobin and Hoiting (1994) have argued that NGT typologically is, like most sign languages, a verb-framed language, in contrast to spoken Dutch or English, which are satellite-framed languages.[37]

4.3   Signing in deaf education in the Netherlands

4.3.1   *Deaf education in the past*

The first school for the deaf was established in Groningen in 1790 by H. D. Guyot, who followed de l'Epée's methodological use of local signs to teach a spoken language and also used fingerspelling. The "oral method" became more influential already in the middle of the nineteenth century, although there is some evidence that some teachers continued to use sign-supported Dutch through this period (Hoiting & Slobin 2001).

The inclusion of sign language in deaf education which took place in the period 1950–1990 was helped to a great extent by several individuals: Bernard Tervoort at the University of Amsterdam; Truus van der Lem from the Dutch Foundation for the Deaf and Hard-of-hearing Child (NSDSK), Anne Bouwmeester who taught at the Groningen School, as well as NGT sign language teachers such as Martie Koolhof, Bea Visser and Wim Emmerik (Tervoort 1987, Knoors 1999).

4.3.2   *Current educational situation*

4.3.2.1   *Cochlear implantation*   Today, cochlear implantation is widely used on young deaf children. The baby's deafness is diagnosed in his/her first week of life and implantations are carried out at the age of two years or even younger. Sign language is mentioned, but not encouraged, in the CI counseling programs. After implantation, the child is classified as "deaf" for only one year, after which there are no official indications of deafness or needs for special schools or guidance, although the child might still be eligible for government-funded use of interpreters. Children with a CI are usually educated in mainstreaming programs (with or without special assistance from sign language interpreters) or in combinations of hearing and deaf schools.[38]

4.3.2.2 *Parents' association and preschool*   Deaf children of deaf parents usually acquire sign language at home. A national parent guidance program at different centers linked to the schools for the deaf is open to all parents of preschool (0–5 years) deaf children. The Dutch parents' association FODOK (www.fodok. nl) is active and supports the use of sign language and bilingualism for all deaf children.

Throughout the Netherlands, there are playgroups and kindergartens using signing for deaf and hard-of-hearing children.[39]

4.3.2.3 *Primary and secondary school education*   The Netherlands has five regional schools for the deaf,[40] some of which are for both deaf and hard-of-hearing children (the Bosschool in Arnhem and the Polanoschool in Rotterdam). There is one residential school for the deaf.

Since 1995, the five schools for the deaf have followed a bilingual (sign language, spoken/written language) program. The schools' official policy is usually to offer signed Dutch to deaf children with a CI and NGT to children without a CI. All the schools for the deaf, supported by the Dutch Ministry of Education, put together and published a national sign language curriculum (Werkgroep Sprong Vooruit 2005). In actual practice, however, there is a great deal of variation in how much sign language is actually used. There are several signing teachers and interpreters working at these schools and in the parent guidance programs.

Although one can become a teacher of the deaf without any prior knowledge about the deaf or signing skills, most schools offer an in-service training program, which includes sign language courses. Currently two main deaf institutes[41] are developing a description of communication and sign language skills for their employees.

There is one residential secondary vocational school for the deaf in Haren for pupils who do not want to be in a hearing secondary school as well as two secondary schools for the hard-of-hearing. Mainstreaming into schools with

hearing children (with or without special assistance from sign language interpreters) has increased, especially for deaf children with a cochlear implant.

Hard-of-hearing children have, in the past decades, gone to schools with hearing
children who have language disorders. In these schools, there has been a gradual
acceptance of communication in sign-supported Dutch (Fortgens & Knoors 1994).
Even within the schools for the deaf, there has been a recent revival of sign-
supported Dutch, due to the growing number of deaf children with cochlear
implants. Terpstra and Schermer (2006) have done a study of the contact situation
of NGT and Dutch in classroom situations. Signed Dutch courses have also
become popular for persons who have suddenly become deaf.[42]

4.3.2.4 *College and university education* Some deaf and hard-of-hearing students attend regular colleges or universities, often supported by interpreters in
sign language or by speech-to-text interpreters. The only universities that offer
courses in sign language are the University of Amsterdam and the Hogeschool
Utrecht. At Radboud University Nijmegen, students can have a minor in sign
linguistics as part of their major course of studies in linguistics.

Deaf students are usually supported in their studies by an interpreter. At the
Hogeschool Utrecht, a deaf student can obtain a bachelor degree as an NGT
teacher, or a Master's degree in Deaf Studies.

4.4 Sign language in Deaf life in the Netherlands

4.4.1 *National Deaf Association*

The National Deaf Association (Dovenschap; www.dovenschap.nl) was established in 1977, as an umbrella organization of local, regional and national organizations for and of Deaf people. One of Dovenschap's primary goals is the legal
recognition of the Sign Language of the Netherlands, which includes investigations
into recognition of the language in laws other than the constitution.

4.4.2 *Regional and local groups*

Several Dutch cities have Deaf clubs, which function as meeting places for the local
signing Deaf and are also where sign language courses take place.

More and more theatre productions, both for children and adults, are made
accessible by using interpreters. A national theater for the Deaf (Handtheater)
produces plays in NGT.[43] Once every couple of years there is an international Deaf
Film Festival,[44] which offers films produced by and for Deaf people. Signed poetry
began to be actively developed in the 1980s and 1990s by Dutch Deaf poets, such

as the well-known Wim Emmerik (Emmerik *et al.* 1993, Emmerik *et al.* 2005, Crasborn 2006).

4.5   Sign language in Dutch society

4.5.1   *Sign language courses in the Netherlands*
Deaf persons who have been trained at the Dutch Sign Center or at the teacher training college, Hogeschool Utrecht, teach the sign language courses.

The courses use printed and DVD sign language materials developed by the Dutch Sign Center for both NGT and Signed Dutch for different groups of learners (parents of deaf children; teachers of deaf children and the general public), as well as DVD-Videos with signed material on different themes aimed at young children.[45] Since 2002, these courses, as well as the schools for the deaf, have had available a standardized basic lexicon of NGT in the form of DVD-ROMs and online.

4.5.2   *Sign language interpreting in the Netherlands*
As of 2009, there are 238 officially registered sign language interpreters in the Netherlands and an unknown number of unregistered interpreters. A NGT teacher and interpreter training program was established in 1997 at the Instituut Gebaren, Taal of Dovenstudies in the Hogeschool Utrecht (www.hu.nl). Specialized training is available for the deaf blind, as well as to become a "transliterator" in written Dutch.

Interpreting situations occur in educational, counseling, church, courtroom, theatre and cinema settings. The interpreters have their own professional organization and a registry of interpreters.[46]

4.5.3   *Sign language in the Dutch media and internet*
A daily morning news program is translated into sign language. Many but not all television programs are subtitled. A website (www.doof.nl) provides information on deaf- and sign language-related issues. There is one journal by/for the deaf, *Woord en Gebaar* (www.woordengebaar.nl), and articles about sign language appear in the Dutch newspapers on a regular basis.

4.6   Sign language research and development

Research on NGT has been well established since the early 1980s. The primary centers for research on sign language currently include the University of Amsterdam (www.uva.nl) and the Department of Linguistics at the Radboud

University Nijmegen,[47] both of which have several active projects, as well as offering BA, MA and PhD degrees, for which several students have written theses on sign language topics. The Dutch Sign Center (www.gebarencentrum.nl) does research and also develops NGT dictionaries and course materials.

Research activities on NGT have been, or are being, done in a wide range of areas. There has been a great deal of research on the lexicon of the language, beginning with the "Communicative Competence" (KOMVA) project (1982–1990), which resulted in the first lexicon of NGT with dialect variants.[48] Since 2002, all national lexicons on CD and DVD-ROMs have been produced by the Dutch Sign Center, which has been supported since 2004 by the federal government and is recognized as the National Lexicography Institute on Dutch Sign Language. A web-based lexicon database containing 12,000 signs has been developed and is maintained by the Dutch Sign Center.[49] A standardized lexicon for education, including many newly developed signs was also produced for second language (L2) learners and schools for the deaf (Schermer 2003).

Deaf persons in Groningen and younger signers in general seem to use more fingerspelling than signers in other parts of Holland. Employing "initialized" signs derived from fingerspelling is a strategy used by some in the deaf community. While there is extensive use of mouthing (Schermer 1990, 2001) by signers, some researchers report that this strategy used in the signing context for disambiguating concepts does not often lead to stable new lexical items (Crasborn, personal communication). Hoiting and Slobin (2001) also report some interesting, though not widespread, borrowing of lexical items from spoken Dutch into NGT. Lexical studies have also been done on name signs, variation and lexical databases.[50]

There has been considerable development of transcription, notation and technological tools in the Netherlands. The KOMVA notation system has been used since 1982 (Schermer & Harder 1985). The media tagging system ELAN, developed and distributed for free by the Max Planck Institute in Nijmegen, is being increasingly used for transcriptions, especially since it has been further developed to serve the specific needs of users of all languages.[51] Crasborn and his group have developed a notation and database tool for phonology research, "SignPhon."[52]

A first study of adult sign discourse was based on the first KOMVA corpus of NTG (Schermer 1985 and 1990). Using more recent digital and Internet technology, Crasborn's group at Radboud University Nijmegen has begun developing a large online annotated corpus of video data from NGT.[53]

Numerous studies of NTG have also been done in the following areas: phonology,[54] morphology and syntax,[55] prosody,[56] acquisition,[57] sign language assessment[58] and interpreting.[59]

4.6.1   *Deaf people and research*

There are still few deaf signers involved as linguistic researchers. As of 2007, there are deaf researchers working at Radboud University Nijmegen, the Dutch Sign Center, the Sign Linguistics Program at the University of Amsterdam and the Hogeschool Utrecht.

Written reports on sign language research appear regularly in magazines such as *Woord en Gebaar* and *Van Horen Zeggen*. The Dutch Sign Center regularly organizes workshops for signers about "new" signs and its lexicon standardization project, as well as an annual workshop on selected grammatical topics. The interpreters' association, NBTG, also organizes workshops on different topics in interpreting.

4.7   Opinions on the future of sign language in the Netherlands

Some researchers have expressed the opinion that NGT is not an endangered language in the Netherlands (Trude Schermer, personal communication). Among the projects that will help to preserve NGT and Deaf culture are the national lexicography database at the Dutch Sign Center and the Handtheater in Amsterdam, as well as the Corpus NGT project.

However, other persons in the field report they are worried about the emphasis by the medical profession on spoken language for deaf children with a cochlear implant and feel this may well become a threat to the social wellbeing and development of these children, as well as to the Deaf community (Beppie van den Bogaerde, personal communication). Crasborn summarizes the complexity of the future prospects and nature of signing in the Netherlands as follows (personal communication):

> Our Corpus NGT project is aimed at recording the present state of the language, including regional and age variation. Since already most deaf people show influence of Dutch in their everyday signing, I expect sign supported Dutch to have taken over in the deaf community in, say, 2050. This decrease of NGT usage is not a big change to deaf communication, but on the other hand, already many more people (including the hearing L2 users) use sign supported Dutch of some type rather than "pure" NGT – even though we still have to find out what exactly that is.

5   **Concluding remarks**

Although the sign languages used in these countries are varied and not necessarily related to each other, in all of these countries over the past thirty years, these languages have received a growing recognition and appreciation by both deaf and hearing groups.[60] This development has been due to the increased self-awareness and empowerment of the Deaf signers in these countries and, in no small part, to a growing body of linguistic research on these sign languages. However, being prosperous middle European countries with strong medical communities, all of these countries also have experienced a strong trend during this same period to provide deaf children with cochlear implants at a very young age. The result is that while the present adult generation of Deaf, as well as the larger hearing community, know more about and take more pride in the local sign languages than thirty years ago, the majority of the younger generations of Deaf with cochlear implants are either learning no sign language at an early age, or using a sign language heavily influenced by the spoken language of their region.

3

Transmission of sign languages in Latin America

Claire Ramsey and David Quinto-Pozos

1 Introduction

Language transmission is a natural and hence nearly invisible phenomenon for many of the world's language communities. Typically, and without noticeable difficulty, infants acquire the spoken languages of their families and caregivers. Transmission attracts notice when family languages are not national languages, when children must learn national languages in other contexts, for example through social institutions like schools. This is a common occurrence all over the world, and can have serious impacts on teaching and learning, as well as on relations among families and schools. Often the addition of a national language to the home language in a child's language repertoire does not affect the home language. For example, although a Dutch immigrant child in Vancouver, Canada, may use Dutch for very limited functions and fail to pass it on to her own Canadian-born children, the continuity of the Dutch language itself is not threatened. In other cases, notably those of some sign languages, minority language status threatens the survival of the language itself.

Transmission of sign languages in almost all geographic contexts is difficult to take for granted. The processes it depends on are not obvious, although the problems it confronts reflect the social, political and economic pressures that other minority languages overcome to survive. When a deaf child is born into a hearing family, parents who do not know a natural sign language cannot pass it along to their child. Additionally, hearing loss is usually interpreted as a deviation from normality. In these cases, transmission of a language across generations is no longer invisible. In fact, it draws extraordinary attention from a range of professionals including physicians, speech language pathologists, audiologists and educators. The most common response is not to seek the culturally rooted response of Deaf people, that is, a sign language, but the medically rooted response of hearing people, tactics to return the child to normalcy, hearing and speaking (Ramsey & Noriega 2000). Nonetheless, sign languages come into being, and are transmitted and maintained over generations despite conditions that work against them, especially obstacles to transmission in the family.

With these observations about language transmission, and the special circumstances of sign language transmission as our foundation, in this chapter we take up transmission and related issues in the sign languages of Latin America, highlighting the case of Lengua de Señas Mexicana, (LSM); the sign language used in much of Mexico.[1] The sign languages we discuss here trace their origins to posited processes of creolization which began at a school. Ideological shifts emanating from Milan at the end of the nineteenth century made their way to New World deaf education, with well-known consequences. Inclusion, the powerful twentieth century ideological and economic shift in schooling, has also had an effect on sign language transmission in Latin America. Here we offer a picture of life for Deaf Mexicans during the twentieth century and describe the consequences of ideological shifts on LSM. We want to show the extent to which life for Deaf people in a developing country like Mexico contrasts with Deaf life in other nations, as well as portray the attitudes, concerns and anxieties about language transmission, continuity and stability that arise when ideology drastically reorganizes education and, from Deaf people's point of view, brings potentially negative consequences.

2   Method

Because information about Latin American sign languages, their transmission and their communities is scarce and difficult to access, this chapter is not evenly weighted and does not treat the many Latin American sign languages evenly. Note that descriptions of LSM and the sociolinguistic context of signing in Mexico City make up the majority of the chapter, primarily because the authors have each conducted long-term research in Mexico about LSM and so have recent and detailed data available. For example, data about contact between LSM and American Sign Language (ASL) are based on Quinto-Pozos (2002, 2008). The remainder of of the LSM section of the chapter is based on data generated during an ongoing project designed to describe the transmission and continuity of LSM in the twentieth and early twenty-first centuries (Ramsey & Ruiz Bedolla, in progress). The first stage of this project consisted of an investigation of the Mexican national school for the deaf, La Escuela Nacional para Sordomudos (ENS). The key informants, the "ENS signers" referred to here, either attended ENS or married a husband who attended ENS. We report data generated by life history interviews of twenty-three elderly Deaf signers, nineteen of whom attended ENS, and four of their wives. Although we offered anonymity to the ENS signers, none of them saw a reason for protecting their privacy. On the contrary, they wanted to be identified with their real names in all publications. We have complied with their wishes with the permission of the University of California, San Diego Institutional Review Board.

In contrast, descriptions of the sign languages in other countries in Latin America are based on reviews of literature and information supplied by generous contacts with experience with Deaf signers and education in several countries. There is much less information available about Deaf people across Latin America, and as noted, published information is limited. Additionally, it is critical to note that Latin America is not a monolith. On the contrary, it is a huge, highly diversified geographic area that includes twenty-nine nations,[2] two spoken national languages (Spanish and Portuguese) which vary across national boundaries, and hundreds of indigenous languages and peoples. The literature on sign languages used in Latin American countries is both scarce and uneven. Some countries have very active sign language research communities, e.g. Brazil and Nicaragua; others produce less literature, e.g. Honduras. Journals that publish this literature are not always easy to access.

We found minimal ethnographic and sociolinguistic work published about Deaf people in Central and South America. This gap in knowledge naturally determined the content we could include in this chapter, for example information about deaf education and its role in language transmission. (See the Appendix for a summary of features of deaf education in Latin America.) It also indicates a pressing research need. Deaf education across most of Latin America is influenced by the Salamanca Statement (UNESCO 1994), which was introduced at the World Conference on Special Needs Education in 1994 and ratified by the ninety-two nations and twenty nongovernmental organizations (NGOs) in attendance. Its guidelines prompted rapid and profound ideological changes in education for students with disabilities by declaring that integration of students with disabilities into typical schools was the best way to promote education for all. Although most Latin American nations promote integrated education for Deaf students, at least in name, implementation of this change in ideology was hampered by limited economic and human resources, embedded attitudes about the learning potential of students with disabilities and, in the case of Deaf students, long-term national preferences for clinical oral education without supports for integrated students.

3   Transmission of Mexican Sign Language (LSM)

3.1   LSM and education for Deaf students in Mexico

From the nineteenth century to the present (early twenty-first century), three public institutions have been positioned to support or limit the transmission of LSM, La

Escuela Nacional para Sordomudos (ENS), La Secretaria de la Educación Pública (SEP), and El Instituto Nacional para la Comunicación Humana (INCH). Through the Decree of April 15 (1861), President Benito Juárez laid the foundations of a national school for the deaf in Mexico, ENS. The school opened as a municipal school in Mexico City in November 1867, with three students, under the direction of Eduardo Huet, a Deaf Frenchman, who came from Brazil, where he had started a school for the deaf in 1857. The original plan was that the school would have six students, three girls and three boys, and six teacher candidates, three women and three men. The teacher preparation objective of the school was never implemented (Jullian Montañez 2003). In 1967, the school was closed.

Although a Deaf man was involved with the creation of the Mexican school, neither sign-medium instruction nor Deaf teachers played a major role in the school. In the twentieth and twenty-first centuries, secondary and higher education has been virtually closed to Deaf people in Mexico, especially those who sign. Accordingly, very few Deaf people earn normal school or university degrees, and formally trained Deaf teachers are almost nonexistent. We know of three small private schools[3] currently operating in Mexico City that have decided to use LSM as the medium of instruction. These schools welcome Deaf signers as teachers, despite the lack of teacher preparation available to Deaf people, and provide in-service type professional development for all of their teachers, Deaf and hearing. It is worth noting that special preparation in deaf education is not widely available for hearing preservice teachers either. Special education training, and preparation in speech and hearing sciences are widely available, especially training in oral methods of instruction. But preparation for supporting the specific learning needs of deaf children who sign is currently available only through a diploma program at the Tijuana Baja California campus of the Universidad Pedagógica Nacional. Training for interpreters is equally difficult to find in Mexico. The first, and to date the only, diploma program in sign language interpreting in Mexico opened in 2006 at the Universidad Autónoma de Baja California, also in Tijuana Baja California.

Although it is undeniable that oralism still dominates deaf education in Mexico, a shift toward signing as the medium of instruction has begun in some states, and Deaf Mexicans' advocacy of sign-medium schooling occurs in both Mexico City and the provinces. One indicator of potential change is the SEP's publication of a Spanish–LSM dictionary (Dirección de Educación Especial en el Distrito Federal 2004), which was developed by a team of Deaf and hearing signers. The introduction to the dictionary recognizes that teachers are using LSM with Deaf children. The dictionary is unevenly distributed across teachers in the republic, however, and is not widely available to parents, families and friends of Deaf children. Accordingly, SEP's dictionary is a recognition that some Deaf children are signers but does not constitute either a policy statement in favor of signing or a widespread effort to transmit LSM across the Deaf or hearing populations. As a result, there are few education personnel in Mexico who have the signing skills needed to use LSM as a medium of instruction or to teach it to Deaf children and their families.

For about a century, 1867 to 1967, ENS played a major role in the transmission of LSM to a proportion of Deaf young people. During the years the ENS signers attended the school, from the 1930s into the 1950s, enrollment was approximately 200 students, in ten cohorts of about 20 students each. ENS signers estimate that there were fifteen teachers for the morning session, and an additional eight teachers who came in the afternoons to teach vocational workshops. Boys and girls attended the school together. Students who did not have families with whom they could live in Mexico City stayed in *internados*, privately run boarding houses near the school. It is unclear what proportion of Mexico's deaf children were able to attend ENS. However, analysis of the ENS signers' narratives suggests that many parents, especially those in the provinces, did not know that the school existed. In these cases, they learned about the school through somewhat random avenues (e.g. seeing a person signing on the street, conversations with strangers, or assistance from an itinerant priest). Additionally, several ENS signers had older deaf siblings or relatives who were unschooled, in all cases because the school was not known to their families. This suggests that a small proportion of the school-aged Deaf population attended ENS while it was open.

The historical relationship of LSM with Mexico's ENS is a typical example of the relationships with schools that many of the world's sign languages present. That is, the school created a site for Deaf people to come together, and as a result a variety of signing evolved there. In the case of ENS, we can speculate that Huet used French signs, and that during his years in Brazil, they mixed with the varieties of signing that Brazilian Deaf students brought to the school. Huet possibly also used this creole variety, the probable foundation of LSB (the sign language of Brazil). Although we know nothing about the signing of the earliest students, Jullian (2003) indicates that there were signing Deaf people in Mexico City in the nineteenth century prior to the opening of ENS. At least two European signers, one French, the other Spanish, had advertised their services as teachers for the deaf between 1820 and 1830. Although neither specified his teaching method, one specifically advertised that he was deaf from birth. Additionally, Rivas-Palacio, who is known to have based his characters on real people, included a pair of Deaf siblings (Anselmo and Maria) in his 1868 novel *Monja y Casada, Virgen y Mártir* (Nun and Wife, Virgin and Martyr). Last, there is little doubt that varieties of home sign made their way into the signing at the school as time passed. Taken together these data suggest that processes of creolization as a result of language mixing when the school came into existence created the foundation of LSM as we know it today. Deaf people in Mexico revere Benito Juárez for his role in LSM's origin.

3.2   Role of families

Families with two or more generations of Deaf people provide continuity for sign languages. Deaf parents use the language with their Deaf and hearing children, and their childen are native signers who can potentially transmit the language to others. Members of Deaf families, in turn, routinely serve as language models and provide socialization to new signers. Through them the language finds an avenue beyond the intimate boundaries of Deaf families to other Deaf people who do not have signing family members. This pathway is key to continuity of sign languages.

Among the above-mentioned ENS signers, although several Deaf families are represented, having Deaf parents, siblings or other kin did not provide dependable access to LSM. For example, one signer's Deaf mother was unschooled, did not know LSM and used idiosyncratic home sign with him. In addition, eight ENS signers had a total of fourteen Deaf siblings, half of whom were unschooled. Four eventually learned LSM, but three did not. In one family with two Deaf children, one attended ENS and became an LSM signer, and the other did not. The remaining unschooled Deaf siblings eventually learned LSM from their siblings or in-laws who attended ENS, or from other Deaf people, often at church.

3.3   Role of ENS

Although many ENS signers communicated with their hearing families using home sign or what they describe as *signos naturales* (natural signs, which we take to mean broadly iconic gestures and pointing), most counted their first visit to the school (at a mean age of 10.25 years) as their first exposure to signing. Most were surprised to see so many other children signing, were intrigued and confused, and feared they would not learn to sign. Still the ENS signers report learning their first signs from students they met at the school. However, most also claimed that they did not learn to sign well until they left the school. Many reported their search in young adulthood for a signing mentor or *padrino* who would help them become better signers (Ramsey & Ruiz Bedolla 2006).

All nineteen former ENS students told us how they came to be enrolled at the school. In thirteen of the cases, a family member or priest knew about the school. However in six cases, neither parents nor any local person had heard of a school for a deaf child. These included both urban and rural families. These six students ended up at the school through coincidences and luck. In one family, parents persisted in asking around and finally heard about someone whose cousin worked as a secretary to someone who knew about the school, the "friend of a friend" phenomenon. Another father was at a park on a Sunday, noticed some people signing, approached them to ask where they had learned, and was told about the school. The old priest left a rural parish and the new one had been in Mexico City and visited the school. Someone passing through a village had heard there was a school in the capital but did not know where it was. In short, during these years information about education for deaf children was not widely distributed. This is a peculiar situation among human languages, most of which do not confront such constraints being passed from one generation to the next. ENS's potential role as a site of LSM transmission rested on fragmented information about its existence and location.

During the time our informants attended ENS there were no Deaf teachers, although the first school director, Huet, is reported to have been Deaf. The limited information available about the school suggests that it was an oral school which tolerated signing (Consejo Nacional para la Cultura y las Artes 2006). ENS signers repeatedly mentioned two hearing teachers who were regarded as good signers (Luis Gomez and Simon, whose surname is not known) and one hard-of-hearing teacher (Fidel Lopez) had reportedly attended Gallaudet. Dispositions toward signing varied. While some teachers punished children who signed, most were simply non-signers who had no interest in learning LSM but tolerated it among the students. As a result, among our informants, teachers at ENS were not considered LSM models or agents of language socialization. Instead ENS signers describe leaving school and seeking older Deaf people at clubs or at church, Deaf parents of school friends, or Deaf co-workers who could provide models of fluent LSM as well as contact with Deaf people.

3.4   Role of Church, mentors and *padrinos*

Of the nineteen signers who attended ENS, five reported attending San Hipólito Church (a Catholic church in Mexico City on the opposite side of the Alameda from the school, which has served Deaf people since the early twentieth century). The church continues to offer not only mass in LSM but instruction in LSM for Deaf people, including religious teaching and basic academic and vocational skills. Others named Deaf people who served as LSM mentors (*padrinos*). For example, Gela Bedolla did not attend ENS, nor did her two older Deaf sisters. However, each older sister had a boyfriend and eventual husband who had attended ENS. These young men were around the house under Gela's mother's properly maternal eye and provided access to LSM for all three Deaf sisters, their mother and some of their hearing siblings. (Most of our male informants recalled Gela's mother, who was a signer, and who accompanied her three Deaf daughters and her hearing daughters, all LSM signers, to parties at the Deaf clubs.) Gela received access to LSM earlier than most students at ENS since she was under ten years of age when her sisters' signing Deaf husbands joined her family. Young men who had recently left ENS sought *padrinos* in clubs. Daniel López provided a lengthy history of his efforts to improve his signing and told about his LSM mentors, including the son of Deaf signing parents and an older Deaf club member. Although these young men first gained access to LSM at the school, most date their beginnings as signers to the time the *padrinos* began to help them.

In sum, the ENS signers' reports of their early lives, their first access to LSM and their schooling, paint a picture of LSM transmission as uneven and, while associated with a school, not completely dependent on a school. Institutions of the larger society (e.g., the Church) and Deaf social institutions (e.g., clubs) played an important role, for schooled as well as unschooled Deaf people. Importantly, even during the years when ENS was functioning, transmission of LSM across generations was not straightforward. We cannot assume that structural features of a sign language's sociolinguistic context in today's developed world hold true for LSM. For example, Deaf family members may transmit the sign language to other members, but we cannot assume that they do. Schools and classes for Deaf students may not support transmission. Access to schooling may be far from universal for Deaf students. Indeed, it is more likely that patterns of sign language transmission in developing countries will be different from those that linguists are accustomed to observing in developed nations.

3.5   Shifts in policy and ideology in Mexico

In 1967, ENS was closed (Adams 2003, B. Fridman [personal communication, May 2006], Consejo Nacional para la Cultura y las Artes 2006). In Fridman's view, closing ENS was the outcome of the forces set in motion in Milan in 1880. The long period of the Mexican Revolution, 1909 to 1920, delayed the effects of Milan on deaf education in Mexico, but as civil life again consolidated in the 1920s and 1930s, the prominence of oralism slowly grew. ENS's *internados* closed in the early 1930s, and reportedly the level of tolerance for LSM in the school went down (although LSM was not eliminated, as the ENS signers attest). Teachers who did not sign replaced signing teachers, and as some ENS signers reported, signing in classrooms was punished. ENS lost its own building and moved to share a building with the school for the blind (Adams 2003). By the 1950s educational policy for Deaf students was heavily influenced by medicine. In 1967 when the school was closed, an institute devoted to human communication, INCH (Instituto Nacional para la Comunicación Humana) took on its function. Putting Deaf education under the umbrella of medicine increased the distance between deaf education policy, which was now officially medicalized, and educators. As Fridman commented, schooling at ENS devolved into "recess and workshops." Teaching at INCH, in contrast, was clinical, focusing on audition, speech and speech reading. Many ENS signers, as well as others involved in current Mexican deaf education, report that INCH personnel believed that deaf children needed clinics and rehabilitation before they could benefit from education.[4] For some time ENS and INCH schooling existed in parallel. (One ENS signer, Alejandro López, reports that he left ENS for INCH because his mother wanted him to get hearing aids.) When the decision was made in the mid-1960s to physically move ENS to the INCH campus, ENS closed but did not reopen at INCH. Teachers did not make the move, and Adams (2003) reports that few students transferred. ENS now exists on paper only.

Additionally, although INCH deals with the public health aspects of speech and language for deaf children, the SEP (Mexico's centralized education department) administers special education throughout the republic. Deaf children, like all Mexican children, may attend government-supported SEP schools. Mexico is a signatory to the UNESCO Salamanca Declaration (1994), and as a result implemented a series of structural reforms aimed at integrating students with disabilities into SEP schools, with access to a common core curriculum (Ramos & Fletcher 1998). Rhodes (2000) describes the range of services that hypothetically are available to support integration in SEP schools. Fletcher *et al.* (2003) describe the consequences and resulting difficulties of the rapid implementation of integration for elementary teachers, special education teachers and students.

As in the United States (e.g., Ramsey 1997), the ideology that motivated integration in Mexico focuses on all children's right to education and on creating avenues to access. It does not take into consideration deaf students' complex language and learning needs, or the special skills that their teachers must develop. Although signing with deaf children is a reality in Mexico and is encouraged in many SEP and private schools, it is not widespread and not yet a matter of special education or public health policy.[5] As in other countries where oral education dominates, preparation to work with deaf children is highly clinical, sign language has a limited public presence, and parents often hesitate to consider signing with their Deaf children. Even in schools where signing is permitted or encouraged, the staff who work with Deaf children have few resources for learning LSM, especially if they are located outside major cities like Mexico City or Guadalajara. Notably, provision of sign language interpreters is not regarded as the kind of support deaf students need in order to be integrated in SEP schools. The few interpreters one may see in schools are typically funded by parents, research projects or other charitable parties.

Additionally, one surprising integration strategy has been the creation of *Centros de Atención Multiple* (CAMs), where all students with disabilities are consolidated into one school. Rhodes (2000) explains that CAMs are opened in areas where the population of students with disabilities is too small to support separate programs, however, CAMs exist all over the republic, including Mexico City and Guadalajara. In practice a Deaf student integrated in a CAM may be as isolated as a solitary Deaf student integrated with hearing students, and equally poorly served, since matching teachers' knowledge and skills with student needs is usually not possible in CAMs, and so-called "categorical" services (that is, separate services for each disability) are viewed as contrary to integration efforts. In Mexico, Deaf students are easily isolated from other Deaf students as well as from signers. Mexico's move away from strict oralism has barely begun, and the fundamental expectations of oral education, that deaf students will speak and speech-read, use residual hearing (assuming they can afford hearing aids and batteries) and assimilate with hearing people, remain powerful. Current policies favoring integration mesh very well with ideologies that assume that Deaf children will learn to assimilate with hearing people if signing is withheld from them.

3.6 Continuity of LSM

Social and political policies unintentionally disperse Deaf people and increase threats to the already fragile continuity of sign languages. Signers in countries with intact systems of deaf education, especially where signing is not prohibited in public schools and has a large public presence; where there are millions of hearing signers (as there are in the United States); and where Deaf people have access to higher education and may enter the teaching force, become researchers and contribute knowledge to the field, rarely consider the continuity of sign languages. Even in the United States, where the Deaf community worries about shrinking residential school enrollments and the high proportion of Deaf preschoolers with cochlear implants, there are still many Deaf signers available to transmit ASL and provide continuity across generations.

We have recent evidence about what happens when a school opens (e.g., Nicaragua [Senghas, Román & Mavillapalli 2006]). Mexico offers evidence about what happens when a national school closes. Our efforts to understand continuity in LSM began with a study of the transmission of LSM to the ENS signers and of the ways LSM signers transmitted their language to future generations (Ramsey & Ruiz Bedolla 2004, Ramsey 2007). Accordingly, we discuss here the ENS signers' children and the ENS signers' grandchildren. First, ENS served as a site of LSM transmission during much of the twentieth century until the school closed. Not surprisingly, in our study all of the ENS signers with children (a total of fifty children, seven Deaf and forty-three hearing, who are all adults now) reported using LSM at home. In addition there are three Deaf grandchildren in the ENS signing group we studied. In one three-generation family of Deaf people, the father (and his Deaf wife, who was not interviewed) transmitted LSM to their three Deaf children. One of their sons married a Deaf woman and has two sons, one Deaf and one hard-of-hearing. Accordingly, this family represents transmission of LSM across three generations. One member of the child generation, and one grandchild work as LSM native consultants with Christian missionaries in ongoing linguistic research and Bible translation. They, along with several other Deaf people with no familial connection to ENS, are contributing to the continuity and maintenance of LSM primarily through providing videotaped samples of signing, although these video documents are not intended for use with deaf children so do not provide direct LSM transmission to younger generations.

Clear breaks in continuity are also evident among the ENS signers. In several cases their adult children live in the United States or Canada, or have been out of touch with their Deaf parents for many years. Presumably while some of these children would sign LSM with their parents if they had maintained contact, it is unlikely that their hearing children, the ENS signers' grandchildren, would know it.

The remaining hearing children of ENS signers (between thirty-five and forty) all of whom were reported to have been signers in childhood,[6] have a varied record of transmitting the language to the grandchild generation. Twelve ENS signers report that their children sign well. In these cases, LSM has been maintained into adulthood because the parents and children continue to have close relationships. Others report that their hearing children, although signers in childhood, have not all maintained LSM into adulthood. From these reports we know that all of the hearing children of the ENS signers were signers in childhood, and most of them are signers in adulthood, too. However, unless they have a Deaf child themselves, or unless they participate in projects like those mentioned immediately above, their lives do not include transmitting LSM to others, and the continuity of the language breaks with their generation.

There are two exceptions to this pattern. One, Fabiola Ruiz Bedolla, is a hearing native signer and a psychologist at one of the private schools where LSM is the medium of instruction. Children enter this school as young as eighteen months, and approximately five Mexico City Deaf couples have selected it for their Deaf child. In addition to providing support groups for hearing parents of Deaf children, she teaches LSM to them. She also teaches LSM classes that include both hearing people and Deaf young people who were raised orally and who now want to learn LSM. Her sister is a middle-school teacher, who periodically interacts with Deaf students who visit her school's computer lab. They both use LSM with younger generation Deaf people and so are transmitting the language across generational and family lines.

In general, though, for the ENS signers, opportunities for contact with younger generations of Deaf people are scarce. As noted, Deaf people have limited opportunities to enter the teaching profession. Nor are clubs as numerous as they once were. For example, one traditional Deaf club in Mexico City maintains its own space but is now open only on Sunday afternoons; members are elderly; very few young people visit, so this club is not a dependable site of language transmission across generational lines. Members are very concerned about the future of their club since it is difficult to recruit new members. In Mexico City informal gatherings may be supplanting clubs. For example, on Thursday nights a mixed-age group of Deaf men meets at a restaurant. This informal and somewhat closed group began in 2004 when three ENS signers started getting together casually. On some Thursdays, groups as large as twenty-five men gather. This group, as well as another casual gathering on Friday nights at another restaurant, attracts younger generations of Deaf people. The latter gathering includes women, hearing signers and students of LSM, and some hearing families with Deaf children, who learn about the gathering from teachers or other parents. Each of these gatherings offers potential as a site of informal language transmission.

Churches offer the best opportunities for Deaf people to take roles where they can teach LSM, use LSM as a medium of instruction, and transmit it to Deaf and hearing people. Use of LSM by hearing missionaries is a key outreach strategy of several Protestant denominations active in Mexico (e.g., Testigos de Jehova). In addition, at San Hipólito Catholic Church two of the ENS signers have served as lay pastors and teachers to priests and younger Deaf people. The first of these Deaf lay pastors is Alejandro López, who has taught LSM to priests and also works with Deaf adults who have not learned conventional LSM prior to adulthood. The second is Rodolfo Verduzco, who, after he retired, went to San Hipólito to help out by "teaching the story of Jesus." These two are the only ones of the twenty-three ENS signers who have managed to occupy roles that permit them to transmit LSM actively, beyond their own families.

Because there will always be deaf people without real facility and access to spoken Spanish, LSM is not likely to become extinct, but its continuity in a broad sense is difficult to anticipate. As shown above, few of the ENS signers and their hearing and Deaf children and grandchildren are in positions to transmit LSM beyond their own families. With few exceptions, the ENS signers, their children or their grandchildren will likely be the last LSM signers in their families unless more Deaf people are born to the same signing families. This fact is not lost on the ENS signers, most of whom expressed anxiety and a sense of betrayal over the closure of the school, the dispersal of Deaf children across many integrated schools and the loss of interest in the clubs that sustained them in their youth. They do not view themselves as part of a national-level Deaf community and claim that Mexico has not one community but many (and willingly list the ones that they dislike or disapprove of). Among the ENS signers, many yearn for a community like the US Deaf community that they have heard about from Deaf North Americans who visit Mexico or that they have participated in while living in the United States.

3.6   Stability and LSM

In addition to concerns about the continuity of LSM and future Deaf generations' timely access to it, ENS signers express concern about the stability of the language. Instability comes about, according to this view, from dispersal and isolation of Deaf children from other Deaf people, from weakened ties to the past and from contamination of LSM from various sources.

Just as the ENS signers reported their own shared origin legend about the school, there are several shared elements in accounts about its closure. One common theme is that doctors wanted to be in charge of deaf education, so they maneuvered to take over the school. A less frequent but widespread belief is that the principal (and in some tellings the teachers) of ENS sold the school and kept the proceeds, thereby enriching themselves while betraying Benito Juárez's promise to take care of Deaf people forever. (The former ENS building was destroyed in the 1985 earthquake, and several ENS signers believe that its destruction was Divine Retribution.) Deaf narrators lay out the following case. When the school closed, Deaf children no longer had a place where they could be educated together. Dispersing them all over the city and the Republic kept them from learning LSM, which weakened the language and disrupted shared Deaf life. Benigno Ruiz expressed the vulnerability of the language when he explained that without a national school "there is no gathering of deaf students to place a structure on the language of signs." He continued, "Since schools are dispersed there are variants in signs now, some make one kind, others make other signs, or they move the schools because of money or they quit using signs and become oral schools, and, well, it's all bad."

A second recurring concern focuses on the consequences for LSM of Deaf children losing their connection to "the old ways," that is, LSM as it was used at ENS. Not surprisingly for Deaf people who recount their histories as signers in detail and name *padrinos* of LSM, the signs they use symbolize their identities as signers and as Deaf people (e.g., Alejandro López's sense of himself as a signer rests on "the signs I learned from elderly Deaf people like Andrés [Sierra] and Gaspar [Sanabria]"). For them, links to past signers are links to ancestors. Especially important are the elderly Deaf people they met as children, who in turn had met ENS students from the 1860s and 1870s. For most of the ENS signers, the "old ways" include fingerspelling of Spanish words, which they believe is an indicator of intelligence that young Deaf people are unable to demonstrate because their education is inadequate. Several ENS signers claimed that it is limiting to use only signs, and that being able to fingerspell is key to being able to ask questions about word meanings, about objects and about knowledge of the world. Again, not fingerspelling is seen as indicating a break with the way LSM was signed in the past. This state of affairs is identified as evidence of instability in the language that could undermine the potential of Deaf people to learn and advance, and that threatens the language as well as Deaf Mexicans.

Finally, strong disapproving attitudes circulate about variation in LSM, including contamination from non-LSM signing.[7] Alejandro López, one of the Deaf lay teachers at San Hipólito Church, commented that, to his dismay, there are now "eight or nine kinds of signing" in Mexico. We suspect that he and the other ENS signers who expressed their disapproval of LSM variation were reporting observations of lexical variation. Their comments are not linguistic but social, an argument that disturbing and excessive variation is the expectable result of ENS closing, the continuing dominance of oral education, the fragmentation of schooling for deaf students, and dispersal and the isolation of Deaf children. Alejandro elaborated, "in the past we only had one way to sign but since then things have gotten bad. It's all mixed up now." We can view the emotions of Lopez alongside data provided by linguists' descriptions of LSM. Bickford (1991) describes phonological variation that he primarily attributes to age differences between signers, and Guerra Currie (1999) provides an in-depth analysis of phonological parameters of sign formation to support her claim that variation is evident in handshape and movement, whereas place of articulation is relatively stable and less prone to dialectal influence. Faurot *et al.* (1999) suggest that social characteristics like religious differences between signers (e.g., Catholic versus Protestant), levels of education and geographical distribution of signers also account for variation in the language. Purported regional variation is also viewed as a problem by members of the Deaf community. Several informants reported that in Guadalajara and Monterrey new ways of signing have emerged, but that they are not "natural," hence not really LSM. "Natural" as our informants used it indicates "what is familiar to us," "what we define as LSM." It would be surprising if people who have had minimal opportunities for schooling used the definitions of "natural" common among linguists or held technical knowledge about common patterns of change in languages. Instead, here we interpret their observations and accompanying sentiments as expressions of loyalty to familiar ways of communicating and anxiety over societal changes that appear to eliminate Deaf people's role in maintaining LSM. Irma Valverde expressed the crux of the matter for the ENS signers, commenting that "They push us aside because they have new signs. Now the teachers are hearing."

3.7   LSM contact with ASL

Contact with ASL is a fact, as the work of Quinto-Pozos (2002) indicates. Movement across the border in both directions is common. Not surprisingly, entire families of Deaf individuals move north of the border. Often such families use LSM in the household, although Spanish may also play a role in communication, while their interactions with American Deaf people or service providers (e.g., interpreters, educators, social workers, etc.) show elements of ASL and/or English. As a result, Mexican Deaf who immigrate to the United States often learn at least some ASL in order to communicate. Over time, ASL may influence LSM production resulting in various types of interference between LSM and ASL, which LSM users in Mexico easily detect.

A substantial number of Deaf Mexicans have lived in the United States. Many settle in border towns, but there is a Mexican diaspora, and immigrants live in all parts, rural and urban, of the United States. They move for better employment opportunities, better support services such as sign language interpreters or accessible telecommunications, and even better educational opportunities for their children. Social services for Deaf people in Mexico are limited, and currently there is little accommodation for communication between deaf and hearing individuals. As a result, opportunities for training and advancement of Deaf people in the workplace are few. Deaf education in Mexico is also limited.

While there are Mexican Deaf individuals who cross the border regularly (some on a daily basis) but who live in Mexico, there are also Deaf Mexican families who live in US border towns and interact with other Deaf from Mexico. For example, in one city of the Texas Valley, several Mexican families, composed mostly of Deaf parents with their Deaf children and hearing children, live in one mobile home park, a permanent neighborhood made up of mobile homes. Additionally, Mexican Deaf interact with American Deaf in border towns at community gatherings, such as events planned by social service providers, religious settings and gatherings at people's homes.

Deaf and hearing signers of ASL from the United States travel to Mexico for various reasons and interact with Deaf Mexicans. ASL signers conduct missionary work, engage in linguistic and other research, and travel for business or personal reasons. This contact takes linguistic form, but social and cultural impacts are also likely, although we currently know little about them. ASL signers in the United States may learn some LSM signs in order to communicate with Deaf individuals from Mexico, but it appears more generally to be the case that the Mexican Deaf in the United States, whether they stay in border areas or move further into the country, learn ASL in order to communicate with ASL signers. LSM may be the language that Mexican Deaf families used in Mexico, but ASL is often learned quickly from members of the US Deaf community in order to communicate, albeit minimally in some cases, with them. Deaf children also learn elements of ASL from their Deaf friends at school or English-based signed from their teachers and/or interpreters at school. In sum, Mexican Deaf signers of LSM travel to or live in US border towns and elsewhere throughout the country, and they learn ASL and interact with US Deaf. This has set the stage for contact between two signed languages.

Linguistic interference is one result of contact between LSM and ASL. Quinto-Pozos (2002, 2008) describes the effects of interference on phonology, syntax, the use of nonmanual signals and mouthing as an accompaniment to lexical signs. For example, phonological interference is seen in the use of the LSM F-handshape in signs that require the ASL F-handshape (e.g., the ASL signs FAMILY, FRIDAY). The two handshapes differ minimally, but the differences can be recognized, at least from a phonetic point of view, in language production. A more obvious example of interference from ASL on the LSM of Mexican Deaf individuals is the code-switching of signs within a phrase. In particular, Quinto-Pozos points out the occurrence of single signs from ASL within strings of LSM signs, often semantic equivalents of the LSM signs.

Quinto-Pozos's border study does not show a border-dweller's LSM production if she were in the interior of Mexico, far from settings where ASL is the dominant sign language. If the LSM signers who have spent time in the United States signed LSM with elements of ASL, it seems obvious that LSM monolingual signers might feel that the stability of LSM is being compromised by influence from the signing neighbors to the north. Indeed, from the perspective of ENS signers in Mexico City, potential influence of ASL, and borrowing or copying from ASL add to LSM's instability and endangerment. The consensus among the ENS signers is that even though US Deaf people are admirable for many reasons, ASL is simply not beautiful, while LSM is. ENS signers were in agreement that ASL contamination is a destabilizing force for LSM, although again, their responses to ASL signs are based on their concerns about their community rather than on linguistic evidence. In addition, Mexicans in general are uneasy about the relationship between their country and the United States. Our informants' language attitudes express a particularly Deaf version of many Mexicans' perspective about the United States. A well-known comment is credited to Porfirio Diaz (Mexico's president between the 1870s and 1911), "¡Pobre México! ¡Tan lejos de Dios y tan cerca de los Estados Unidos!" (Poor Mexico, so far from God and so close to the United States!).

3.8   Summary of LSM transmission

The ENS generation's history suggests that even when ENS was active, gaining access to LSM was not without difficulties. The signers in our sample who attended ENS were late learners whose first access to LSM occurred after they were ten years of age on average. First access for those who were unschooled or did not attend ENS was extremely late – fifteen years on average. Ramsey (2007) has analyzed the first data in a study of the post-ENS generation (18- to 40-year-olds), and found the mean age of first contact with LSM to be 13.75 for informants with hearing parents (n = 4), suggesting that conditions of transmission after ENS closed did not improve. (Having Deaf parents in the post-ENS generation was a dependable source of access to LSM in infancy, however.) The language continues to face difficulties recruiting new signers with potential consequences for both the language and for signers. Although it has not been addressed in research yet, we assume that a high proportion of very late learners is not optimal for a language, although it is not necessarily an endangerment factor. Nonetheless, there is evidence that being a late learner has consequences for the linguistic development of the signer (e.g., Mayberry & Eichen 1991).

4   Transmission of Latin American sign languages

We traced the key themes identified in Mexico, the role of schools in sign language origin, transmission and risk, routes of transmission across generations, continuity and stability, in the Latin American sign language literature and among personal contacts with linguists and educators from several Latin American nations. Knowledge on these topics is difficult to come by and unevenly reported. Even demographic information about the numbers and distribution of Deaf people is difficult to find. It is clear that there are profound gaps in our knowledge, which should be filled to complete a picture of sign language transmission in Latin America.

4.1   The role of education

We presume that Deaf education in Latin America, as in Mexico, influenced the evolution and transmission of signed language. In most cases where there is reported information, early signing communities were influenced greatly by European educators of the deaf who traveled to Latin American countries and helped to establish some of the first schools in those countries. In particular, educators of the deaf from France and Spain seemed to have used their sign languages, at least in part, for instruction. Those languages, as noted earlier with the case of LSM, likely mixed with home signs and other elements of sign languages that deaf people may have already developed or adopted from previous contact with other signers. These elements then creolized into early forms of the languages that became, over time, the national sign languages of each of the countries.

A Latin American case that has received widespread attention in the research and other literatures is that of Nicaragua. Even though deaf children were brought together as early as 1946 within educational settings, it appears that no sign language emerged until after the establishment of a center for special education in Managua in 1977. It was the opening of the Centro Nacional de Educación Especial, with thirty-two deaf students in its first class, that is cited as being the beginning of the Nicaraguan Deaf community and Nicaraguan Sign Language. Apparently, before the 1970s, deaf Nicaraguan children and adults had little contact with each other: deaf individuals were generally kept apart by societal attitudes that discouraged their interaction, the few children in school did not interact with each other outside of school, and of course, methodologies rooted in oralism did not permit the use of signed language (even in the form of home signs and gestures) in the classroom (Senghas 2003). However, in some accounts the children did use manual means to communicate with their teachers and peers, mostly outside of the classroom, but even that does not seem to have been enough to support the development of a signed language and a Deaf community (Polich 2000). This is truly an instructive case because it shows that bringing deaf children together for education is not, in and of itself, sufficient for a sign language to develop, despite the common assumption based on various sign languages that are believed to have developed among children in school settings.

4.2   Transmission across generations

Transmission of Latin American sign languages across generations seems to occur, in many cases, at social clubs for the Deaf and social events in the community. While it may be the case that, like Mexico, religious organizations serve to regularly bring together members of the Deaf community, information about such activities is not common in the literature on Latin American Deaf communities and their sign languages. Certainly, Deaf social clubs in Latin America form an integral part of Deaf communities, and their members engage in activities of the clubs (e.g., competing in sports, organizing to fight for linguistic and other human rights, and coming together with the goal of socialization) on a regular basis. Information about the length of existence of some of those clubs is often available, which suggests that the members take pride in recording and remembering when the clubs were formed. For example, in 1966, sports clubs began to be formed in the Deaf community in Ecuador, and in the mid-1970s male members of the clubs traveled to Venezuela and Colombia to compete with Deaf athletes from those countries (Santillán 1994). Officially recognized associations of Deaf people in Ecuador, such as the Fray Luis Ponce de León Society, were formed the 1970s and 1980s. The first Deaf clubs in Brazil were established in 1913 after some Deaf from São Paulo visited Argentina and observed activities of the associations there (Campos de Abreu 1994, Campello 1994). And, the first national organization of Deaf persons in Peru was formed in 1960 (Paliza Farfan 1994).

4.3   Continuity of sign languages in Latin America

Transmission and continuity in sign languages is a recent interest. Prior to Ramsey and Ruiz Bedolla's work, the limited literature about LSM did not address issues of continuity, not because these concerns did not exist but because researchers' interests centered on morphology (Fridman-Mintz 2005) or acquisition and syntax (Hawayek & Cappelli 2004). Likewise, concerns about the continued use and acquisition of Latin American sign languages for future generations is a topic that has not been explicitly addressed in the literature. Even in Argentina, a stronghold of oralism into the twenty-first century, the Deaf community seems to be vibrant and LSA appears not to be threatened by educational philosophies. There are Deaf associations in nine cities throughout the country (Massone & Curril 2004) and Argentine deaf people are in contact with each other because of social activities and sports events (Massone & Menéndez 1992). Peru's education for deaf children also follows oralism, despite its early signed language influence from nuns who came from Spain (Paliza Farfan 1994), but there is little indication that Peruvian Sign Language is particularly vulnerable at the current time.

   Yet, concerns about continuity take an indirect form in the Latin American literature. One perceived threat to sign languages and their communities is the general lack of Deaf instructors in the schools and the poor signing skills of hearing teachers. Oviedo (1996) provides an analysis of the signed language of deaf children in a Venezuelan school, and compares it to their hearing teachers' signing. By comparing the children's language to that of adult users of Venezuelan Sign Language (VSL), he comes to the conclusion that the children are using VSL at school, whereas the teachers only manage to use a "contact code" that contains elements of both Spanish and VSL grammatical features. This is true in spite of the bilingual model of Deaf education followed in Mérida where he conducted his study.

It is also true that hearing educators rarely consult Deaf people about educational programming and planning. This has generally been true in most countries of Latin America, but it has been specifically mentioned by writers from Ecuador (Benalcázar 1994) and Uruguay (Behares & Massone 1996). For example, in Uruguay, in spite of the fact that bilingual education has been in place since 1987, hearing teachers tend to control deaf teachers and the power differential leads to various problems within the deaf education system. It is possible that rich ethnographic research in Latin American Deaf communities, which is currently scarce, would reveal similar issues across the continent's Deaf people, even those whose communities are currently vibrant.

4.4   Stability of Latin American sign languages

Whether or not language contact is a factor in the stability of other Latin American sign languages is unclear. Part of the problem is that the degree to which other such sign languages come into contact with neighboring sign languages is unknown. To our knowledge, there are no other studies of contact between two or more Latin American sign languages. From the brief writings of Santillán (1994) and Velásquez García (1994), we know that Ecuadorian Sign Language may have been influenced by VSL and Colombian Sign Language because of sports competitions that have been held over the years. Additionally, the adoption of the US dollar as official currency in Ecuador in 2000 has reportedly led to Deaf immigrants from Colombia and Peru entering Ecuador in an attempt to earn more for their labor than they would if working in their home countries. This may have resulted in frequent contact between Ecuadorian Sign Language users and those of the other two sign languages – a language contact situation that may be altering each of those languages over time. Further, the SIL Ethnologue (Gordon 2005) lists a number of Latin American sign languages that have been influenced by ASL – either through missionary work or collaborations between US educators of the Deaf and those of Central and South American countries. In spite of the reported contact between and among Latin American sign languages, the suggestion that such contact is being perceived as affecting the stability of any sign language has, to our knowledge, not been made. This may be an artifact of the lack of descriptive ethnographic research in those settings. However, based on knowledge that is available, contact among Latin American sign languages does not generate explicit concerns about stability. This contrasts with the beliefs of Mexican Deaf people who report concern about consequences of LSM–ASL contact for the vitality of LSM. We acknowledge that historic relations between Mexico and the United States have led to heightened awareness of and resistance to North American influences in Mexico, and this coupled with the long shared border may motivate Mexican Deaf people's concerns about ASL. US influence in other Latin American countries may be interpreted differently and have different meanings from those that arise in Mexico.

Language variation, not surprisingly, is another characteristic common to LSM and other Latin American sign languages. Latin American sign languages exhibit significant variation. For example, Peru's sign language is said to vary widely based on whether or not a Deaf person is from a city or from a rural area (Paliza Farfan 1994). This is even true of countries such as Brazil where much recognition of the natural sign language and research has taken place over the years. Vianna Martins (2006) describes a project in Rio Grande do Sul to expose the rural deaf of that area to Brazilian Sign Language.

5   LSM and Latin American sign languages: summarizing current knowledge

One of our initial assumptions is that sign languages face obstacles to transmission that other human languages need not concern themselves with. This is true even if communities of signers are stable and do not feel a sense of language endangerment. Continuity is a long-term phenomenon that is difficult to perceive during an individual lifetime. Transmission generally occurs in intimate circles, families and friends, which need not take a broader or longer-term perspective. The fact remains, however, that sign languages are rarely passed from parents to infants. In ideological climates that stigmatize deafness and promote assimilation enacted through oral teaching methods and integrated education settings, hearing parents of newly diagnosed deaf infants are hesitant to seek sign language for their deaf children. The fragility of sign language transmission is the consequence of social institutions.

The case of Mexico suggests that while ideological preference for oral education does not eliminate sign languages, it places barriers around them. In particular, obstacles to access in infancy and early childhood, when sign languages can provide the strongest and longest lasting developmental contribution to individual Deaf signers, are worrisome for all sign languages and for all signers. A second obstacle, equally worrisome for individual signers and for sign languages, is generated by fervor for inclusive education. This obstacle to access is created primarily by the intentional dispersal of Deaf students over many school sites. The resulting isolation creates conditions where development and transmission of a conventional language is almost impossible, especially when hearing itinerant special education consultants are permitted to use a sign language but do not have access to instruction themselves so do not manage the language well. Zeal for assimilationist ideologies like oral schooling and integration is based on misunderstanding of the basic developmental and learning needs of humans, and failure to correctly interpret what language is and the role it fulfills in our humanity. Thankfully, signing with deaf children, from preschool, is slowly gaining ground in Mexico, and the rapid structural reforms of the 1990s are viewed by many educators as a very imperfect work in progress that must be adjusted to Deaf students' needs. Other Latin American nations have made commitments to bilingual Deaf education, although we note the reported scarcity of Deaf people as teachers. Change is slow but it is not impossible.

In Mexico, private and public education currently provide a small amount of support for the transmission of LSM. As in other nations, few Deaf signers fill teaching roles. Churches provide much more support and include limited numbers of Deaf signers in teaching roles. Little is known about participation of Deaf teachers in churches in Latin America. Reportedly clubs are numerous and robust in much of the region. In contrast, in Mexico, informal gatherings, such as the weekly Deaf events at restaurants in Mexico City, are the largest public opportunities for signers to transmit LSM across family and generational boundaries. Some Deaf children and their hearing families attend these events, and although formal teaching does not take place, these events are potential sites of LSM access for those who might need it most.

Educational institutions are powerful, practically as well as ideologically. In Mexico, despite the strong beliefs of Deaf signers, the closing of ENS cannot wholly be blamed for the transmission and continuity difficulties that LSM currently faces, since the same difficulties existed while the school was active. However, over time the separation of Deaf children from other signers, the limited role of fluent signing adults in the education of Deaf children and the lack of sign-medium schooling will contribute to a high proportion of very late learners of LSM among Deaf Mexicans, as it will in other nations. In addition, it is likely that economic disparities between urban and rural regions will continue to influence sign language transmission across Latin America. The rapid spread of inclusive schooling across Latin America, often with limited attention to deaf students' learning needs, is a risk factor the consequences of which we cannot yet describe. Hallahan (1998) expresses concern that the focus on full inclusion distracts attention from the learning needs of students with disabilities, and notes that the costs (for personnel and resources) of integrated education have been underestimated and the needed investments have not been made. Kweller (2005) makes a similar point specifically about deaf education in Latin America. Recent regional UNESCO meetings on education for all in Latin America have reported that inclusive education of quality has been difficult to implement, primarily because resources and funding are not available (World Enable.net 2003, Regional Bureau of Education for Latin America and the Caribbean 2007a, 2007b, Intergovernmental Regional Committee of the Regional Education Project for Latin America and the Caribbean 2007).

Finally, we return to an early theme, the relationship between sign language origins and schooling. Ironically, the origins of sign languages are tightly bound, in historical fact and in legend, with the beginnings of deaf education across Latin America. From the Mexican Deaf perspective, the two ideologies that dominate Deaf education across Latin America, oralism and integrated schooling (the Appendix indicates that these two ideologies are indeed spread across the entire region), threaten sign languages. The fact that we do not have direct knowledge of similar concerns across Latin America does not mean Deaf people are not concerned, only that there are gaps in our knowledge. While the influence of oralism may be waning in parts of the region, integrated schooling holds ideological, economic and political power that is very difficult to challenge, despite the fact that a range of problems with inclusive schooling have been identified. Padden and Rayman (2004) highlight the role of both schools and Deaf clubs in the vitality of sign languages. In fact, they take the position that "the human dimensions of language capacity and grammatical structure depend deeply on cultural institutions such as the school and the deaf associations whose role is to make possible durability and complexity" (p. 263). Assuming that their conclusions are accurate, and there is little reason to think that they are not, sign languages need both schools and Deaf clubs to foster their transmission, continuity and stability. Indeed, signers need them also, since Padden and Rayman suggest that future signers will not enjoy the full benefits of their human heritage as language users without them. Elderly LSM signers acknowledge the risk. Even if other sign language communities do not anticipate endangerment of their languages, many of them are at risk of losing the sustenance of schools by virtue of oralism and integration, and clubs, by virtue of aging memberships and difficulties recruiting younger members who have been educated in isolation from their Deaf peers. Eventually the fragile lines of sign language transmission may fray and lead to difficulties with continuity. Transmission and continuity in sign languages in developed and developing nations merit attention and research, first to describe the extent of the problem, its relationship to educational policies and the mechanisms by which it works, and second, to raise awareness and press for alternative outcomes for both sign languages and individual signers.

Appendix *Deaf education philosophies and practices in Latin America*

Country	Population estimate	Philosophy	Inclusion and supports	Deaf instructors
Argentina	No reports found.	Oralism from beginnings through present times (Alisedo & Skliar 1993), although Signed Spanish in a few schools in 1983, but not widespread (Massone & Curiel 2004). Socialization of young deaf children to signed language by their peers at school (Behares & Massone 1996, Massone & Menéndez 1992). Despite lack of support for signed communication in educational settings, deaf people become skilled signers – through Deaf associations and sports activities (Massone & Menéndez 1992).	No reports found.	No reports found.
Brazil	No reports found.	Education may have begun in a residential school setting with the French "manual" method (i.e., the use of signed language), but it changed to oralism after the 1880 Milan Congress and continued until the 1980s or 1990s (Berenz 2003). São Paulo schools continue to follow oralism (Gordon 2005). Acquisition and growth of the signed language occurred for many years at the residential school in Rio de Janeiro despite oralism (Berenz 1998). Over the years, a mix of oralism and education via signed language, including Total Communication, occurred (Ribeiro Hutzler 1994, Campus de Abreu 1994). Currently, bilingualism is being encouraged, in some areas, as an educational philosophy (Skliar & de Quadros 2004).	"many deaf children very often enter regular school without knowing either Portuguese (the national language of Brazil) or Brazilian Sign language (BSL)" ... "teachers tend to communicate with them using Signed Portuguese, a modality of Simultaneous Communication" (Kelman & Branco 2004: 274–275).	Deaf people are becoming involved in courses to become language professionals (Skliar & de Quadros 2004). Deaf teachers co-teach with hearing (Kelman & Branco 2004).

Appendix (*cont.*)

Country	Population estimate	Philosophy	Inclusion and supports	Deaf instructors
Bolivia	350–400 signers in 1988 based on Powlison 1988.	Oralism appears to be the primary philosophy (Gordon 2005). Some use signed language in a new program in La Paz (www.manosquehablan.com.ar/noticias/2007/02/16337.php).	No reports found.	No reports found.
Chile	150,000–200,000 signers (Nippon Foundation 2007).	No reports found.	Both special schools and "differential groups" in traditional schools are offered for special education students (www.StateUniversity.com 2007).	No reports found.
Colombia	50,000 in Bogotá in 1992 (Gordon 2005).	First schools, established in the 1920s, followed oralism (Paulina Ramirez, personal communication, September 10, 2007). Beginning of bilingual education in the mid-1990s (Ramirez). Some bilingual programming occurring by 1998 for deaf children under five years old (Tovar 1998, Ramirez). Total Communication in some schools in 1980s (Ramirez).	Currently, interpreter preparation at the Universidad del Valle (Ramirez).	Apparently, no Deaf instructors by 1998 (Tovar 1998). Deaf instructors proposed (Ramirez).
Costa Rica	44, 000 (Buhler 2007).	Oral, Total Communication, bilingual.	No reports found.	No reports found.

Country	Deaf population	Educational methods	Educational inclusion/interpreters	Instructors
Cuba	670,000 (Gordon 2005).	Oralism, bilingual proposed (Vanguardia 2005).	Integration is the goal. First group of trained interpreters will graduate in 2008 (Vanguardia 2005).	No specific information although efforts are being made to train more sign language instructors (Vanguardia 2005).
Dominican Republic	No reports found.	Voice for the Deaf (no date) reports that most deaf children receive at most three years of schooling.		No reports found.
Ecuador	64,692 to 150,000 (Gordon 2005).	Oral, Total Communication. Bilingual methods proposed by Federación Nacional de Sordos rejected by government (Voces en Silencio 2006).	Special schools and inclusion, no interpreters (Voces en Silencio 2006).	No reports found.
El Salvador	150,000–349,000 (Gordon 2005).	No reports found.	No reports found.	No reports found.
Guatemala	100,00 to 650,000 (Gordon 2005).	Oralism in first school (Fray Pedro Ponce de León) in 1954 (Julio Roberto Bámaca, personal communication, April 15, 2008). Total Communication, oralism, sign language and manual alphabet, varies by school (Comité Prociegos y Sordos de Guatemala 2006, Gerner de García, personal communication, April 2, 2007).	Educational inclusion is supported (Comité Prociegos y Sordos de Guatemala 2006). Some interpreters in private schools and at the Universidad Galileo (Bámaca).	Fewer than ten Deaf instructors in 2008 (Bámaca).
Honduras	70,000 (Logos International Ministry Association, no date), 322,000 (Gordon 2005).	Public education for deaf students is not available (Logos International Ministry Association, no date).	None in public education (Logos International Ministry Association, no date).	One in 2003, two in 2006 (Hudspeth 2006).

Appendix (*cont.*)

Country	Population estimate	Philosophy	Inclusion and supports	Deaf instructors
Mexico	1,300,000 to 5,590,207 (Gordon 2005).	Primarily oral with LSM-medium instruction in some schools.	Inclusion is widespread. Itinerant auxiliary teachers provide support. Interpreters are not used to support integrated deaf students.	Very few, primarily in private schools.
Nicaragua	1,000 deaf signers (Senghas, personal communication).	Oralism in the first school established in 1946 in Managua (Polich 2000). Bilingual education, or the use of signed language for instruction, followed in more than one school, although that is not necessarily the official philosophy (Senghas, personal communication).	Within an afternoon high school program for Deaf students, an interpreter facilitates communication for the hearing teacher who provides lessons to the students, but no widespread provision of interpretation for deaf children to attend hearing public schools (Senghas, personal communication).	Deaf signers of Nicaraguan Sign Language are being trained to be teachers for Deaf children (Shepard-Kegl 2006) and some Deaf adults serve as teaching assistants in classrooms with deaf students (Senghas, personal communication).
Panama	159,256 (Gordon 2005).	No reports found.	No reports found.	No reports found.
Paraguay	316,214 (Gordon 2005).	No reports found.	No reports found.	No reports found.
Peru	No reports found.	Oralism appears to be the dominant philosophy (Paliza Farfan 1994, Gordon 2005). Although Total Communication may also be used in some schools (Paliza Farfan 1994).	No reports found.	No reports found.

	Population estimate	Education	Interpreting/relay services	Teachers
Puerto Rico	8,000–40,000 (Gordon 2005).	No reports found.	No reports found.	No reports found.
Uruguay	Population estimate: 15,000 profoundly deaf persons (Lockwood 2002).	No instruction in signed language prior to 1985 (Behares & Massone 1996). Implementation of bilingual education in 1987 (Behares & Massone 1996).	Interpreters in some secondary schools since 1996 (Lockwood 2002). National relay service (ANTEL) since 1999; 24-hour services since 2002 (Lockwood 2002).	Deaf adults as instructors (Behares & Massone 1996) or teacher aids (Lockwood 2002).
Venezuela	15,000–40,000 signers (Pérez 2008).	Oral education from 1935 to 1985 (Pérez 2008). Total communication practiced since 1985, although some programs aim to be bilingual, but fall short because of teachers who do not sign LSV (Oviedo 1996; Pérez 2008).	Some interpreters in schools for deaf students (Liceos de Sordos) (Pérez, personal communication).	Mostly Deaf teacher aids currently, but some Deaf are attending universities with the goal of becoming teachers for the Deaf. (Pérez, personal communication).

Note: Population estimates include children and adults, and unless indicated, the figures may also include non-signing deaf individuals.

4

Transmission of sign languages in the Nordic countries

Brita Bergman and Elisabeth Engberg-Pedersen

1 Introduction

Scandinavia is the name of the three independent countries Denmark, Norway and Sweden; the term "the Nordic countries" includes also Finland and Iceland. The histories of these five countries are interwoven politically, linguistically and culturally with relations also to Greenland and the Faeroe Islands. As the present volume includes chapters with analyses of Danish Sign Language, Finnish Sign Language and Swedish Sign Language, the focus in this chapter will be on these three languages. But Danish Sign Language has influenced the sign languages used in Norway, Iceland, Greenland and the Faeroe Islands, so we will briefly sketch the role of Danish Sign Language in these other countries and regions at the end of the section on Danish Sign Language.

The Nordic Council for the Deaf was founded in 1907. One of its original aims was to create a common Nordic sign language, an aim that led to the compilation of the first sign dictionary in Finland (Hoyer 2005) and the second sign dictionary in Denmark. Discussions about common Nordic signs continued at the Nordic congresses for the deaf[1] up through the century (Hoyer 2005), and as late as 1979 a sign dictionary was published in Denmark with some of the signs marked with an "N," indicating that these signs were new and agreed upon by the Nordic deaf associations (Plum *et al.* 1979). However, these normative endeavors were not continued and were criticized not the least by deaf people themselves (Hoyer 2005).

Today the Nordic Council for the Deaf has representatives from the deaf associations in Denmark, the Faeroe Islands, Finland, Iceland, Norway and Sweden. Among its goals is official recognition of sign language as "the first language of deaf persons."[2]

In the following sections, the languages are presented in alphabetical order. In the final section, we will draw forth some parallels and differences in the transmission and status of the three sign languages.[3]

2   Danish Sign Language

2.1   The name of the language, the number of users and official recognition

The traditional Danish name for Danish Sign Language (in some international publications, abbreviated DSL) is *tegnsprog* or *tegnsproget* ("sign language"/"the sign language") and, more recently, *dansk tegnsprog* ("Danish Sign Language"). The Ministry for Education used the name *tegnsprog* in publications from 1982 and 1991 (Undervisningsministeriet 1982, 1991), but the term *dansk tegnsprog* in a publication from 2007 (Undervisningsministeriet 2007). In Danish no acronym or abbreviation of the name is used.

There are no official statistics of the number of deaf users of Danish Sign Language in Denmark, but the Danish Deaf Association (Danske Døves Landsforbund, abbreviated DDL) estimates that the number is about 5,000 out of a population of approximately 5,500,000.

The Danish Deaf Association has fought hard to have Danish Sign Language officially recognized, especially after the official recognition of Swedish Sign Language in 1981 and Finnish Sign Language in 1995. Nevertheless, Danish Sign Language is still not officially recognized as a (minority) language in Denmark. Generally languages are recognized in the Danish legislation only in the special contexts where they are or should be used. Danish, for instance, is officially recognized as the language used in courtrooms, but nowhere is it stated that the legislation should be written in Danish or that Danish is the official language of Denmark; it is taken for granted. Partly because of this tradition of not recognizing languages per se, it is difficult to have Danish Sign Language officially recognized as a minority language in Denmark.

2.2   Danish Sign Language in deaf education

In the beginning of the nineteenth century, the medical doctor Peter Atke Castberg (1779–1823) conducted experiments in Copenhagen with electric stimulation of deaf persons' hearing. The results were very discouraging, however, and extremely painful for the patients, and Castberg ultimately gave up the experiments. But during two visits to discuss similar experiments at the Institute for Deaf-Mutes in Kiel in 1802 and 1803, he saw children signing. A further inspiration was the French playwright Jean-Nicolas Bouilly's piece *L'Abbé de l'Epée*, which was performed in theatres all over Europe at the beginning of the nineteenth century. The play, which is based on real events, is about the founder of deaf education in Paris,

Abbé Charles-Michel de l'Epée, and his encounter with a deaf young man found on the road and believed by some to be the son of a nobleman.

After his unsuccessful experiments, Castberg was provided with a grant from the King of Denmark to study deaf education in Europe for two years (1803–1805), including de l'Epée's school in Paris. At his return in 1805, Castberg began teaching eight deaf children, and on April 17, 1807, the King signed the charter for Døvstumme-Institutet i Kiøbenhavn (The Institute of the Deaf-Mute in Copenhagen).

Castberg was very positive about the use of sign language in the teaching of deaf children and was critical of de l'Epée's so-called "methodical signs" invented to represent grammatical categories of spoken French. We know little about the kind of signing that the children brought into the institute at the time. Among Castberg's first pupils were two pairs of deaf siblings. Castberg also wrote that two of his first pupils "always conversed, like deaf-mutes in general," supposedly in sign language (Castberg 1809:7). So there is reason to believe that the children used one or more home sign systems, if not a sign language, from the start. In his writings, Castberg complained that the signs used by deaf people for the same concept varied a lot but found that the best way to create signs that were consistent with the nature of sign language was to ask deaf persons of some intelligence to make a sign, once the concept had been explained to them. According to one of his students, Castberg was himself a very skilled signer.

Already in 1808, the first manual alphabet was printed. The manual alphabets used in Denmark are one-handed and stem from the Spanish alphabets (Padden & Gunsauls 2003) with some variations, which were probably due to inevitable changes through their use over time. In 1977, the Danish Deaf Association decided to adopt what they described as the "international manual alphabet." It is identical to the American manual alphabet with minor differences and supplemented by three signs for the final three letters of the written Danish alphabet (æ, ø and å).

The teaching at the institute in Copenhagen was also dominated by signing after Castberg's death in 1823. In 1845, however, one of the teachers, H. V. Dahlerup, received a grant to study the German oral method. After his return, he got permission to use the German method with a few children, an experiment that ended with an exam in 1849. The board of the institute was not impressed and allowed a continuation of the speech method only for children who were described awkwardly as *uegentligt døvstumme*, i.e., 'not genuinely deaf-mute' children (Holm *et al.* 1983:23). Dahlerup left the institute and founded a private school based on the speech method, a school that grew in importance especially after it was taken over by J. Keller in 1855. Following a heated debate between Keller and the headmaster of the institute, H. R. Malling Hansen, the authorities decided in 1867 that all deaf children should be admitted to the institute. After one month, the children were tested and it was decided who was "genuinely deaf-mute" and should remain at the institute, and who was "not genuinely deaf-mute" and should be transferred to Keller's school. The system of separating the children according to these somewhat obscure criteria continued for years.

Malling Hansen thought that some of the "genuinely deaf-mute" children at the institute might also benefit from the speech method, and he introduced speech training and training in lip-reading alongside instruction in signing. After further inspiration from Germany, Malling Hansen suggested in 1879 that the children be separated into even smaller groups. In 1880, the king signed a law on the teaching of deaf children with a fourfold separation of the pupils: (1) the most intelligent "genuinely deaf-mute" children to be taught by the speech method at the Deaf-Mute Institute in Fredericia in western Denmark; (2) the less intelligent "genuinely deaf-mute" children to be taught by the sign method at the Deaf-Mute Institute in Copenhagen; (3) the "not genuinely deaf-mute" children to be taught by the speech method at Keller's school in Copenhagen; and (4) the mentally retarded deaf children to be taught by the speech method with some use of signs in a special section of Keller's school. This series of events beginning in 1845 indicate that oralism was underway in Denmark long before the Milan Congress in 1880.

In 1890, a new school based on the speech method was founded in the middle of the country, in the town of Nyborg. It was decided that the children should live in families in the town, partly because that would prevent them from signing in the dormitories.

The first headmaster in Nyborg, Georg Forchhammer, invented the "mouth–hand system," a set of handforms that show the articulation of the consonants as you speak (Birch-Rasmussen 1989). This system is still used by some signers when there is no sign for a concept, and, like the manual alphabets, it has given rise to derived signs.

The debate about the use of signing or a purely oralist method in the teaching of deaf children continued up through the twentieth century and took place especially in *Nordisk tidskrift för dövundervisningen* (Nordic Journal of Deaf Education).

By the end of the 1950s, the school in Nyborg was changed to a boarding school for young people from about sixteen years of age, the only one in the country for deaf students of this age. Since almost all deaf signers attend the school for one or two years, it has had a standardizing influence on Danish Sign Language.

In the 1980s the former Deaf-Mute Institute in Copenhagen, now called Skolen på Kastelsvej, started experimenting with bilingual education. Alongside the international wave promoting the use of sign languages in deaf education, the main advocates of Danish Sign Language were the Danish Deaf Association, the parents' association Bonaventura, founded in 1914, and the Center for Total Communication of the Deaf, founded in 1973 (1997–2009 now the Center for Sign Language and Sign Supported Communication (KC)).

In 1982, the Ministry for Education sent out regulations stating that children with hearing problems should be instructed in the same curriculum as all other children. The regulations focus on the practical organization of the teaching, but sign language is mentioned among other means of communication that teachers for the deaf should include when they give counsel to parents and the teachers of mainstreamed deaf children (Undervisningsministeriet 1982). In 1991, Danish Sign Language was introduced as part of the curriculum for the children in the special schools for deaf children (Undervisningsministeriet 1991).

Teachers for the deaf who are not already signers take courses in Danish Sign Language organized by the schools for the deaf or at a regional center for teaching the language.

Since the beginning of the new millennium, almost all deaf children have been provided with cochlear implants (CIs). In 2006 Percy-Smith published a report on the linguistic and social abilities of about 85 percent of all deaf children with a cochlear implant in Denmark in 2004. The tests included auditive, communicative, impressive and expressive tests of Danish spoken language and parents' reports on their child's social life. It was concluded that there is a strongly significant statistical correlation between the type of linguistic code used in the children's home (whether it includes manual signs or not) and the children's Danish language scores and their social wellbeing. The parents' choice of linguistic code is interpreted as the main causal factor in furthering the child's acquisition of Danish and their social development. Left unquestioned is another possibility – of whether the parents' choice of linguistic code and the child's scores on the spoken-language tests might both depend on the child's ability to benefit from their CI. The government's attitude to the education of deaf children is that it is the parents' choice whether they want their child to go to a school for the deaf or be mainstreamed. Based on Percy-Smith's report and international – especially British – literature on the importance of training CI-children's hearing, the staff at the clinics counseling parents of deaf children with cochlear implants discourages the use of signs and sign language to their child. The number of children in the schools for the deaf and the number of parents attending courses in Danish Sign Language have consequently decreased drastically in recent years. It is too early to know whether some of the children with cochlear implants will learn Danish Sign Language later in life.

2.3   Danish Sign Language outside deaf education

The first deaf club, Døvstummeforeningen af 1866 (The Deaf-Mute Association of 1866), was founded in Copenhagen in 1866 by three deaf artisans who had all attended the Institute in Copenhagen. The opening of the club marked the beginning of what the sociologist Jonna Widell (1994) describes as "the Opening phase of Deaf culture in Denmark," lasting until 1893. The club supported its members in such emergencies as unemployment, disease and death. After its foundation deaf clubs were established in most major cities.

In 1893, some teachers at the schools in Nyborg and Fredericia founded an association, Effata, for their former students with the aim of integrating them in society without the use of sign language. The same year, the Deaf-Mute Association of 1866 in Copenhagen made the preservation of Danish Sign Language its main goal. For the next approximately eighty years, Danish Sign Language was primarily transmitted from one generation of deaf children to the next within the schools and within the deaf community in deaf clubs and marriages between deaf individuals, with some support from society, however, especially in religious life. Signing had had a strong foothold in religious services for deaf people in the Copenhagen Institute right from 1807. The first minister for the deaf was appointed in 1900, and in 1904, the first church for the deaf was consecrated in Copenhagen. Today religious services for the deaf take place all over the country. In the years 2000–2003, a number of biblical and liturgical texts were translated into Danish Sign Language. They are now available as a DVD (Det Danske Bibelselskab 2004).

The Danish Deaf Association was founded in 1935. The fight for Danish Sign Language has always been high on its agenda, and over the years, it has successfully lobbied for, among other issues, deaf persons' right to interpreting and TV-broadcast news in Danish Sign Language. In 2003, the association managed to get a grant from the Ministry for Social Affairs for a digital dictionary of Danish Sign Language. The first version of the dictionary was published on the web in 2008 (*Ordbog over Dansk Tegnsprog 2008*).

At the request of the Danish Deaf Association, the Center for Total Communication of the Deaf offered the first course in Danish Sign Language in 1973; it was a course for people who already worked as interpreters. Around 1980, the demand for qualified interpreters became very strong, and in order to obtain some standard of interpretation, the Center for Total Communication of the Deaf, again at the request of the Danish Deaf Association, ran a number of courses for people who already knew Danish Sign Language, in particular hearing children of deaf parents. At the same time the Danish Deaf Association urged the Ministry for

Education to establish a program for interpreters, and in 1986, the first group of students with no knowledge of Danish Sign Language was admitted to a two-year full-time program for interpreters run by the center. In 1996, the program was extended to 3.5 years with the first year focused on teaching the students Danish Sign Language. The steady flow of qualified interpreters made it possible for deaf people to become better integrated in Danish society; interpreters make it possible for a greater number of deaf students to join further education and for deaf people in general to take part in social life in their local communities and their hearing children's schools and to access news broadcast on TV in Danish Sign Language.

In 1977, the World Congress for the Deaf was held in Copenhagen, and the Center for Total Communication of the Deaf organized at the city hall an exhibit, "Deaf in Denmark," which was open to the general public. The center is still one of the main resources for information on Danish Sign Language and the teaching of Danish Sign Language, especially in the program for interpreters.

In 1973, an association offering evening classes to deaf people bought a building, Castberggård, in a village in the west of Denmark, and in 1986 it became a folk high school[4] for the deaf, offering courses of up to thirty weeks in subjects of general interest, courses in Danish Sign Language to parents and others, and the international course Frontrunners, a course in leadership and empowerment for deaf persons. The means of communication at the school is Danish Sign Language.

There is no possibility of studying Danish Sign Language in a university context. Linguistic research on the language takes place in the linguistics department of the University of Copenhagen and at the Center for Sign Language and Sign Supported Communication. Elisabeth Engberg-Pedersen wrote a doctoral dissertation on the language in 1993, and one deaf signer, Janne Boye Niemelä, has a Master's degree in linguistics with specialization in Danish Sign Language.

DeafFilm Video was established by the Ministry for Social Affairs in 1963. In the early days, it produced and distributed films to the deaf clubs. Today it produces programs in Danish Sign Language, broadcast by public television, and signed interpretations of news programs, broadcast on a special digital canal.

2.4   Transmission of Danish Sign Language: conclusions

The history of the transmission of sign language in Denmark mirrors to some extent the history of European sign languages in general, beginning with the establishment of the first school for the deaf based on instruction in signing in the early nineteenth century. In the course of the century more and more hearing educators focused on the problems of acquiring a spoken language with no hearing and abandoned signing. But having acquired a functional sign language and being able to sustain themselves economically, deaf adults founded deaf clubs and associations, thereby securing a signing community.

In the 1960s and 1970s, it became increasingly clear that an oralist education could not provide many deaf children with the basic skills of reading and writing. A combination of a general focus in Danish society on providing all children with sufficient basic education, the work of individual deaf and hearing enthusiasts, international trends toward the use of Total Communication, and the fact that there was still a strong deaf community, fertilized the soil for the increased use of Danish Sign Language in all aspects of deaf people's lives. Many deaf adolescents joined advanced educational programs and were employed as teachers of the deaf, teachers of Danish Sign Language, social workers for the deaf and administrators in organizations for the deaf. Somewhat paradoxically, the empowerment of the deaf had the consequence that the deaf clubs lost importance, and fewer deaf people wanted to participate in voluntary work.

At the turn of the millennium, Danish Sign Language had a very strong position among deaf people, their families and professionals working with them and had become visible in the Danish society at large especially through TV broadcasts and the interpreter training program advertised broadly to young people. But since the year 2000, the decline in the number of parents attending courses in Danish Sign Language and the number of deaf children in the schools for the deaf has made the future status of Danish Sign Language somewhat unpredictable.

2.5   Norway, Iceland, Greenland and the Faeroe Islands

In 1807, at the official start of deaf education in Denmark, both Iceland and Norway were parts of the Kingdom of Denmark. One of the first students at the school for the deaf founded by Castberg, himself Norwegian by birth, was the Norwegian Andreas Christian Møller. Møller became a teacher at the school in Denmark for a few years, but then returned to Norway, which had become a relatively independent region in a union with Sweden, and founded the first Norwegian school for the deaf in Trondheim in1825. The signing used in the school may have been based on the form of manual communication in use among deaf Norwegians before this school was founded and may have been influenced by Danish Sign language through Møller, as well as Swedish Sign Language from a Swedish deaf teacher (Schröder 1993). Today Norwegian Sign Language and Danish Sign Language are seen by the users as two distinct languages, but there has not been any study of their degree of similarity.

Iceland, with a population of about 300,000 inhabitants, remained part of the Kingdom of Denmark up to 1944, and about twenty-four deaf Icelandic children attended the Institute in Copenhagen at least until the first Icelandic teacher was employed in Iceland in 1867. Today the Deaf Association of Iceland (Félag heyrnarlausra) estimates that there are about 150 active users of Icelandic Sign Language. The language has a high percentage of signs that are similar to their equivalents in Danish Sign Language (Aldersson & McEntee-Atalianis 2007).

Greenland and the Faeroe Islands are still members of what is called Det danske rigsfællesskab (The Danish Community of the Realm) alongside Denmark, but have extensive self-government. Greenland, which has a population of about 56,000, is a huge impassable island, of which about 80 percent is covered by ice. This explains why it took so long before the first deaf Greenlandic children received proper education for deaf children. In 1957, two deaf Greenlandic children were sent to a school for the deaf in Denmark, beginning a practice that continued until the mid 1970s. In 1978, the first school for the deaf was founded in Sisimiut, which, however, has very few children today. The government seems to expect it to be possible for the children to stay in their villages after cochlear implantation and attend schools for hearing children with no sign language support. The sign language used among deaf Greenlanders is very close to Danish Sign Language but possibly considered a separate language by the signers.

The Faeroe Islands consist of eighteen islands in the Atlantic north of the British Isles and have a population of about 50,000 inhabitants. Until 1962 deaf children were sent to Denmark to go to school, but from 1962 the children have been instructed in the capital Tórshavn. The Faeroe Islands have a deaf association, Deyvafelag Føroya, with about forty-five active members.

3   Finnish Sign Language

3.1   The name of the language, the number of users and official recognition

Finland was part of a union with Sweden for almost 700 years up to 1809 when the country was conquered by the Russian tsar and then became a grand duchy in a union with Russia. After the Russian Revolution in 1917, Finland became an independent nation. Even today, the country, with approximately 5,200,000 inhabitants, has two official spoken languages, Finnish, which is the primary language of more than 92 percent of the population, and Swedish – or Finland-Swedish – which is the primary language of about 5.5 percent.

The Finnish name of Finnish Sign Language (sometimes abbreviated FinSL) is *suomalainen viittomakieli* ('Finnish sign language') or simply *viittomakieli* ('sign language'). Besides Finnish Sign Language, there is *finlandssvenskt teckenspråk*

(Finland-Swedish Sign Language, abbreviated FinSSL), which is the sign language of deaf people with a background in Finland-Swedish families (Hoyer 2004; see the papers in 2005, and Hoyer, Londen & Östman 2006). The number of signers of this language is estimated to be about 150–200 signers or about 3 percent of all deaf signers in Finland, which the Finnish Association of the Deaf (Kuurojen Liitto ry) estimates to be about 5,000.

In 1995, Finnish Sign Language was included in the Finnish Constitution, where it is said that "[t]he rights of persons using Sign Language and of persons in need of interpretation or translation aid owing to disability shall be guaranteed by an Act" (quoted from the webpage in English of the Finnish Association for the Deaf, www. kl-deaf.fi). Sign language is further mentioned as the language of instruction and as a part of the curriculum in educational laws and in a law on the Research Institute for the Languages of Finland from 1996, where research on the language and the preservation of the purity of the sign language are mentioned as some of the institute's duties. Moreover, deaf persons are guaranteed interpretation services free of charge to manage their everyday affairs, in study programs, in pre-trial investigations and administrative affairs. Among the general requirements for naturalization is satisfactory oral and written skills in Finnish or Swedish or, alternatively, skills in Finnish Sign Language.

3.2   Finnish Sign Language and deaf education

In 1834, the eight-year-old Carl Oscar Malm (1826–1863) was sent from Finland to the Manilla School for deaf children in Stockholm, which had seven students from Finland in the period 1810–1860 (Mesch 2006). Malm, who was particularly gifted, was a student there until 1845 when he became an assistant teacher. Soon after, however, he returned to Finland to teach deaf people there, and in 1846, he founded a private school in Borgå on the south coast. Malm applied in 1853 for economic support for his private school or for funding for a new school in Helsinki or in the Finland-Swedish city of Åbo, but his application was turned down. In 1858, the senate and the tsar finally accepted a proposal for a school in Åbo, and Malm became a teacher there in 1859 (Wallvik 2006).

In the 1870s and 1880s, the German oralist method was discussed at the Nordic congresses for teachers of the deaf, and by the end of the century, it had become the main method in the schools for the deaf in Finland. In consequence, the deaf teachers were dismissed and signing was forbidden (Hoyer 2005). Moreover, the schools became either Finnish or Swedish (the schools in Borgå and Jakobstad). The children were divided into three groups according to intelligence, but in reality the division depended on whether the children were expected to learn to speak or not. Until 1932, when the school was closed, the children who went to the (Swedish) school in Jakobstad were taught by a method based on writing and the use of some signs. In the years 1998–2002, twenty-eight deaf individuals who were born between 1918 and 1952 and had attended the school in Borgå were interviewed about their experiences and described how they had come to the school with almost no signs and had learned sign language from older children. Some of the teachers punished the children for signing, while others used pointing and some gestures in their instructions (Hoyer 2005).

In the 1960s, there was a growing demand for sign language courses, a demand that the Finnish Association of the Deaf tried to meet. The demand became even stronger when Finnish Sign Language was increasingly recognized in legislation. Today, there is still a lack of teachers with signing skills in Finland, and many deaf children in Finland do not receive instruction in Finnish Sign Language in spite of the educational act mentioning the possibility that the language of instruction be sign language (Hoyer 2005, see also the webpage of the Finnish National Association of the Deaf).

The Service Foundation for the Deaf, which is a private organization funded by money from the public Slot Machine Association, started the project "Good Future for Deaf Children" in 1995. The project's aim is to familiarize hearing families with deaf children, with deaf persons and deaf culture, to teach Finnish Sign Language to them as well as to create a natural signing environment for the deaf children during the course weeks and weekends (Takkinen, Jokinen & Sandholm 2000). Most of the children who attend the program have a cochlear implant, but the parents of these children have decided to make both languages – Finnish and Finnish Sign Language – available to their child.

As more children began receiving cochlear implants, the hearing centers became less positive toward signing, and the number of parents choosing to use signed communication with their children has diminished since the 1980s and 1990s (Takkinen 1995).

3.3   Finnish Sign Language outside deaf education

One of Malm's first students, David Fredrik (Fritz) Hirn, who succeeded Malm as a teacher in Åbo, was one of the founders of the first Finnish deaf club in Åbo in 1886 and, in 1905, of the Finnish Association of the Deaf in Helsinki. Today the Finnish Association of the Deaf has forty-one local clubs as members. Encouraged by the discussions of a common Nordic sign language at the beginning of the century, Fritz Hirn and his wife Maria Hirn, who was a photographer like her husband, compiled the first dictionary with drawings and photos of 344 signs and published it in three parts (1910, 1911 and 1916). Later dictionaries published in 1965 and 1973 included many signs that were newly coined and not used by deaf people (Salmi & Laakso 2005). The 1998 dictionary (Malm 1998) was compiled according to linguistic principles with translation equivalents and examples of the signs' use.

The first ministers for the deaf were appointed in 1908, and all through the twentieth century Finnish Sign Language or spoken Finnish with signs was used in religious services. One of the ministers, Lauri Paunu, was active in research on Finnish Sign Language and took part in compiling dictionaries in the 1960s and 1970s. Another minister, Eino Savisaari, who had deaf parents, argued in the 1970s against sign-supported Finnish and in favor of "the genuine sign language" and research on this language (Hoyer 2005). In 1998, the Evangelical Lutheran Church of Finland established a group for translation of prayers and liturgical texts. It has also translated the Gospel according to Saint Luke into Finnish Sign Language.

In a 1998 legislative act on public broadcasting, the TV and radio broadcasting company became obliged to produce programs in "Sign Language." The programs are limited to five minutes of daily news in Finnish Sign Language. In addition, before elections, the major political debates are interpreted into Finnish Sign Language.

Since the early 1900s, there has been a strong and lively theatre and poetry recital tradition among the deaf. In 1988, the Kuurojen teatteri (*Dövas teater*, "Deaf Theater") under the Finnish Association of the Deaf was established (Wallvik 2006). The theatre, now called Teatteri Totti, has been subsidized since 2006 by the government.

Research on Finnish Sign Language was begun at the University of Helsinki in 1982. In the first linguistic description of Finnish Sign Language from 1985, Terhi Rissanen characterized Finland-Swedish Sign Language as a distinct language, and not just the dialect of the school in Borgå (Hoyer 2005). Since 1984, research on Finnish Sign Language has been the responsibility of the Research Institute for the Languages of Finland, at which a permanent research post was established in 1988.

The University of Jyväskylä began offering instruction in Finnish Sign Language in 1992 with two programs on Finnish Sign Language, one for signers and one for non-signers. Since 1998, the Department of Education at this university has offered a teacher-training program for deaf and hearing signers, i.e., a program with the same curriculum as other teacher-training programs, but taught in Finnish Sign Language. And since 2004, its Department of Languages has offered a Master's program in the language. Courses on Finnish Sign Language can serve as partial fulfillment of the requirement of two foreign languages for Master's degrees.

The University of Turku offers a basic-level course on Finnish Sign Language as part of the linguistics program in collaboration with the Diaconia University of

Applied Sciences, which has an interpreter training program. At the universities of Turku and of Helsinki, postgraduate studies of topics in Finnish Sign Language are possible within the linguistics programs.

The first Finnish deaf person to get a PhD in sign linguistics was Johanna Mesch with a thesis on tactile sign language for the deaf–blind at Stockholm University (Mesch 1998). Three PhD theses on Finnish Sign Language have been completed: Takkinen (2002) on acquisition, Fuchs (2004) on the phonetics of movement and Rainò (2004) on personal name signs.

In 1978, the Finnish Association of the Deaf started the first courses for interpreters for persons who already knew Finnish Sign Language. These were followed by a one-year course in Turku in 1983, a course that was extended to two years in 1986 and later to three years. Since 1998, two polytechnic institutes, the Diaconia University of Applied Sciences in Turku and Humak University of Applied Sciences in Kuopio and Helsinki (from 2001), have been in charge of all interpreter training, with now four-year programs.

4   Swedish Sign Language

4.1   The name of the language and the number of users

The traditional Swedish name of Swedish Sign Language (in international publications often abbreviated SSL) is *teckenspråk* or *teckenspråket* ("sign language"/"the sign language") and in older texts also *åtbördsspråket* ("the gesture language"), though since the 1990s the language is often referred to as *svenska teckenspråket* ('Swedish Sign Language'), which is the name used in the recent reports from the Swedish Government survey on the status of Swedish Sign Language (Swedish Government survey 2006a, 2006b). In Swedish no acronym for the language is used.

There are no official statistics of the number, or hearing status, of the users of Swedish Sign Language, but the officially accepted estimation is 8,000–10,000 deaf users (who were born deaf or became deaf during childhood or adolescence) (Swedish Government survey 2006b). An increasing number of hard-of-hearing and deafened adults also learn Swedish Sign Language, and the estimated number of hearing people with some sign language skills is 100,000 out of a population of approximately 9,150,000.

4.2   Swedish Sign Language and early deaf education

A popular myth about the origin of Swedish Sign Language is that it comes from France. The assumption seems to be that as the teaching method used by de l'Epée (the initiator of deaf education in Paris in the 1770s) spread, not only the method, but also the language was adopted. It has not been possible to find evidence supporting this view, either in terms of persons who could have been the mediators, or in terms of linguistic characteristics.

An early reference to signed communication in Sweden is made in a 1759 description of the Ålhem parish written by a teacher at Kalmar Grammar School, who mentions a deaf man "who conveys his thoughts well by signs, as dumb people often do" (quoted from Bergman 1979:7).

At the beginning of the nineteenth century several initiatives were taken to teach deaf children. One of the pioneers, G. A. Silverstolpe, communicated with his pupils through signs (Prawitz 1913), as did Per Aron Borg (1776–1839), who is justifiably regarded as the founder of deaf education in Sweden. Borg began to teach deaf and blind pupils in 1808, and in 1809 he established the General Institute for the Blind and the Deaf-Mute – now known as the Manilla School – in Stockholm. In one of his unpublished manuscripts, Borg provides further support for the assumption that sign language communication existed in Sweden before deaf education was initiated: "the language or, more correctly, the foundation for a language which has existed as long as there have been deaf and dumb people in the world, which is their natural language and which they would never abandon even if they were in full possession of the written and spoken language; I mean the *Natural Sign Language*" (quoted from Bergman 1979:7; Borg's emphasis).

In his writings, Borg describes how the students practice together to gain uniformity of sign language and facial expression. It is interesting to note how sign language at that time was not only regarded as the mode of communication, but also treated as a subject of its own.

Borg's interest in teaching the deaf is indirectly attributable to abbé de l'Epée. In the periodical *Döfstumvännen* (The Deaf-Mute's Friend) in 1876, Ossian Edmund Borg mentions that his father had seen Bouilly's theatre piece *L'Abbé de l'Epée* (see section 2.2). Later, Borg read de l'Epée's book on teaching the deaf, which is evident from the fact that his translations of a number of passages from de l'Epée appear in his own writings.

In a different manuscript, Borg writes that in the fourth lesson he intends to introduce the pupils to a manual alphabet, but he appears doubtful about the possibility of carrying out the idea. If that assumption is correct, Borg did not know of the alphabet that de l'Epée and others had already been using for decades. With a few minor differences Borg's alphabet is still used in Sweden. (After an invitation by the Portuguese king to start deaf education in Lisbon, Borg spent the period 1823–1828 there and introduced his manual alphabet, to which today's Portuguese alphabet can still be traced back.)

The position of sign language at the Manilla school was weakened in 1862, when the oral method was introduced as a result of a visit to Germany by one of the teachers. In 1874, training of teachers of the deaf was initiated at the Manilla school, and when more schools were founded in the 1870s, they adopted the oral method. Thus the Swedish schools for the deaf had already adopted the oral method before the resolution in favor of the oral method in 1880 at the congress for teachers of the deaf in Milan. However, other methods coexisted with the oral method in writing classes and sign classes.

4.3   The SDR and the fight for sign language in education

The first deaf club in Sweden was founded in Stockholm in 1868, and in 1922 fourteen Swedish deaf clubs joined to form a national association, today's Sveriges dövas riksförbund, (Swedish National Association of the Deaf, SDR). It was not until the mid-1960s that the SDR managed to enter into a dialogue with the government, due in no small part to the election of a member of the Riksdag (Swedish Parliament) as president of the SDR. Since the 1970s, the government consults the SDR, especially in issues relating to education and culture.

Owing to the technical advances in the 1950s, which created new possibilities for sound amplification, and the (false) conclusion that all deaf people had some residual hearing, the position of sign language in education was further weakened. The official view of sign language at this time is clearly expressed in a report from the government in 1955: "Sign language differs from the speech of the hearing through great deviations in syntactic structure and is therefore a strong hindrance in the child's acquisition of speech. [Sign language should be used] only in the teaching of children with very low ability" (Swedish Government survey 1955:20; our translation).

The great expectations for the results of the oral-auditory method of the 1950s were not realized. In 1958, a SDR's congress decided that speech alone was not sufficient in the communication with deaf pupils and that speech should therefore be accompanied with signs, a view still supported in the early 1970s.

In order to make it possible for deaf adults to receive education in sign language, the SDR founded Västanviks's folk high school in 1969. At the same time, the SDR intensified its efforts to have sign communication used in the education of deaf children. It invited parents of deaf and hard-of-hearing children to a conference in Uppsala in 1970, where, among others, the Norwegian psychiatrist Terje Basilier and the Swedish psychologist Göte Hanson talked about the importance of early communication between child and parents and recommended the use of speech and signs for this purpose. The meeting turned out to be a milestone in the history of deaf people in Sweden in that it was the beginning of a fruitful cooperation between the SDR and the parents' organization.

Encouraged by the SDR, hearing parents of deaf children began to take sign language lessons. However, the fast-growing number of courses advertised as "sign language courses" did not teach the language used by deaf people, but rather a form of communication that deviated strongly from the indigenous sign language, consisting of spoken Swedish accompanied by signs according to the principle "one word – one sign." Some new signs were created, in particular signs for Swedish grammatical morphemes, such as conjunctions and tense suffixes. This way of using signs spread rapidly and was referred to within the deaf community as "the new sign language" or "sign language with grammar." Native signers, deaf as well as hearing, began to feel that they did not know sign language well enough and participated in "sign language" courses.

4.4   Research and official recognition

Linguistic research into sign language started in Sweden in 1972 at the Department of Linguistics of Stockholm University with financial support from the National Board of Education. The first study, "Linguistic status of sign language" conducted by Brita Jonsson (later Bergman), resulted in a description of Signed Swedish (Bergman 1979) and concluded that it is, in fact, not a manual representation of Swedish. Consequently, a child exposed to Signed Swedish cannot automatically acquire Swedish, but is dependent on formal instruction.

Another research project, "Cognitive linguistic development in deaf and hard-of-hearing children" (also supported by the National Board of Education), began in 1976 with Inger Ahlgren as the principal investigator and followed the development of children of both deaf and hearing parents. In order to enhance the communication between the hearing parents and their deaf children, the parents were offered sign language instruction, i.e., instruction in Swedish Sign Language. This was to become the start of similar courses all over the country. The "Saturday School," which was a kind of monolingual sign language preschool for the children in the project, also became the impetus for other municipal, sign language pre-schools for deaf and hard-of-hearing children.

Sign language research continued with studies of the structure of the indigenous sign language used by deaf people (the first doctoral dissertation on Swedish Sign Language: Bergman 1983) and provided linguistic arguments for the recognition of Swedish Sign Language as a language. Lars Kruth, who was president of and active in other positions of the SDR between 1951 and 1989 and was awarded a honorary doctorate at Stockholm University (1980) for his work for Swedish Sign Language, acknowledges in his book *En tyst värld – full av liv* (A Silent World – Full of Life) (1996) the crucial importance of the research at Stockholm University for the recognition of Swedish Sign Language as an independent language. At the annual meeting of the SDR in 1980, the representatives agreed on a declaration about Swedish Sign Language as a language in its own right. This marked the end of the association's advocacy for Signed Swedish.

Sweden was the first country in the world to give official recognition to a sign language used by deaf people. After many decades of advocacy by the SDR in close cooperation with sign language linguists and the organization of parents of deaf and hard-of-hearing children (for details, see Bergman & Wallin 1994), Swedish Sign Language was officially recognized by the Riksdag in 1981 in a declaration stating deaf people's right to be bilingual: "The commission on integration points out that the profoundly deaf to function among themselves and in society have to be bilingual. Bilingualism for their part, according to the commission, means that they have to be fluent in their visual/gestural Sign Language and be fluent in the language that society surrounds them with: Swedish" (Government Bill 1980/ 1981:100, supplement 12, quoted in Bergman & Wallin 1994:318).

Two years later, a new national curriculum for the Special Schools for the deaf and hard-of-hearing (Skolöverstyrelsen 1983) was issued. In accordance with the declaration of the Riksdag, it set a bilingual goal for deaf education and stipulated that Swedish and Swedish Sign Language be studied as two separate languages. It also prescribed that the language of communication in the classroom and the language of instruction in all subjects should be Swedish Sign Language.

4.5   Swedish Sign Language in the present education system

There are six special schools for deaf and hard-of-hearing students in Sweden and a unit for deaf and hard-of-hearing children at a municipal school in Gothenburg. After elementary school, the majority of the students continue at the Swedish National Upper Secondary School for the Deaf in Örebro.

Because children with cochlear implants now attend these special schools, Swedish Sign Language is no longer the only language of instruction. The special schools offer instruction in Swedish Sign Language and in spoken Swedish, with the possibility of choosing different instructional languages for different subjects and changing the choice during the course of schooling. The special schools have deaf, hard-of-hearing and hearing teachers.

The first university course in which Swedish Sign Language was the language of instruction was an introductory course on sign language at Stockholm University in 1979. Today there is a Master's program and a PhD program in Swedish Sign

Language and sign language linguistics. The first doctor in sign language was Lars Wallin (see Wallin 1996), who thereby also became the first deaf person in Europe to get a PhD degree.

4.6 Swedish Sign Language in Swedish society

Swedish Sign Language can be studied in courses of varying lengths, organized by adult education associations and at folk high schools. Parents of deaf children have a right to 240 hours of sign language instruction free of charge during the child's preschool years. Siblings to deaf children and hearing children of deaf parents are offered one-week courses at the special schools. Swedish Sign Language is one of the languages offered in the regular school system for hearing pupils, and it is the third most popular choice among language options after French and Spanish, English being obligatory for all children. The universities in Malmö and Stockholm have two to three semester programs in Swedish Sign Language as a "foreign" language.

Swedish Sign Language seems to have a fairly stable position in Swedish society and is no longer a concern of only deaf people. The Swedish Association of Hard of Hearing People (HRF) also strongly advocates sign language, although a majority of its 37,000 members do not use sign language. The Swedish National Association for Children with Cochlear Implants and Children with Hearing Aids writes in their information brochure: "Children with cochlear implants (CIs) are differently predisposed for understanding speech and sign language, and differently predisposed for speaking or using sign language. It is therefore not possible to recommend one pedagogical method which would suit all children and young people with CI" (Barnplantorna n.d.:4; our translation).

Unlike Sweden's officially recognized minority languages (Finnish, Sami language, Romani, Yiddish and Meänkleli), Swedish Sign Language has not been declared as a minority language in the sense of the convention of the European Council. According to a law that took effect in 2009, "[p]ublic institutions have a particular responsibility for protecting and promoting Swedish Sign Language. Every person who is deaf, hearing-impaired or needs sign language for any other reason has to be given the opportunity to learn, develop and use sign language" (Government Offices of Sweden 2009).

4.7 Interpreter services

The first official support for interpreter services dates back to 1947 when the National Board of Education set up a register of persons who could interpret for deaf persons in court. In 1969, interpreter services were set up at a regional level, and in 1974, the system became permanent through a law stating that it is the county councils' duty to provide interpreter services, free of charge. The right to interpreter services includes all kinds of situations in everyday life, such as meetings at work, educational settings, family-related issues and recreational activities.

The training for sign language interpreters is a four-year full-time program offered at five different folk high schools spread over the country. Since 2004, the national office that authorizes interpreters and translators (the Legal, Financial and Administrative Services Agency) has included interpretation between Swedish Sign Language and spoken Swedish.

4.8   Religion, theatre and television

In the early days at the Manilla School, the subject Religion and the preparation for confirmation were taken care of by ministers of the Church of Sweden (an Evangelical Lutheran church). In 1906, the first minister working exclusively for the deaf was employed and today, the staff of the deaf church comprises thirty-five persons, mainly ministers and deacons. In addition, the Catholic Church, the Pentecostal Church and the Salvation Army also have various activities in Swedish Sign Language.

In 2001 the Swedish Bible Society published a translation into Swedish Sign Language of the Gospel according to St. Mark (first in the form of video cassettes, and later, 2006, on DVD).

The Government Commission on Handicapped Persons proposed in one of their reports the establishment of a touring theatrical company performing in sign language. As a result, the already existing theatre group Tyst teater (Silent Theatre) (est. in 1970) was affiliated to Sweden's Nationwide Theatre. Tyst teater is a professional group of deaf, and occasionally hearing, actors, performing in Swedish Sign Language for both hearing and deaf audiences and is well known nationally as well as internationally.

As early as 1966, the first program – informing about the coming transition from left- to right-hand driving in Sweden – was broadcast in Swedish Sign Language. In 1987, the Swedish public television (SVT) began broadcasting weekly news programs in Swedish Sign Language, and in 1993, daily news programs five days a week. Since the early 1980s, political debates before general elections have been interpreted into Swedish Sign Language as well as the counting of votes on election day.

5   The three sign languages compared

There are many similarities in the transmission of the three Nordic sign languages described here. The first school for the deaf was officially founded in Denmark in

1807 and in Sweden in 1809, but for political reasons somewhat later (1858) in Finland. In all three countries, the oralist method became influential before the Milan Congress in 1880 as there was much interaction among Nordic teachers of the deaf, and the German influence was strong in general, and specifically in deaf education. Moreover, all three countries were influenced by the trend away from oralism toward acceptance of sign language in deaf education beginning in the 1960s. But there are also differences between the three countries.

The Finnish Constitution recognizes Finnish deaf persons' right to Finnish Sign Language – or a sign language; a Swedish government bill recognizes Swedish deaf persons' need to be bilingual in Swedish Sign Language and the language of society, Swedish. No such official recognition of Danish Sign Language exists, partly because there is no tradition of recognizing languages in this way in Denmark. Recognition of a language gives its users a means of pressure for their civil rights, but official recognition may be an empty gesture if it is not followed by sufficient means to comply with the needs of deaf people. In all three countries, there is a lack of teachers sufficiently qualified to teach sign language and to teach in sign language.

In Finland and Sweden, there are sign language programs in universities, but not in Denmark. Again, this can partly be explained historically. In Finland, sign language programs seem to have gained a foothold in the universities through teacher training and interpreter programs, which themselves engendered research on the two sign languages. In Denmark, teacher training and interpreting programs are not found in the universities, but in separate colleges and schools. When the government established an interpreter training program, the Center for Total Communication of the Deaf was the most prominent institution giving courses in Danish Sign Language, so it was an obvious choice to involve the center in the program. In Sweden, the linguistic research on Swedish Sign Language was established independently of any programs aiming at professions.

How strongly related then are these sign languages? In a comparison of 300 signs from Swedish Sign Language, British Sign Language (BSL), the Sign Language of the Netherlands (NGT) and Finnish Sign Language, Mesch (2006) identified *identical*, *similar* and *different* signs between Swedish Sign Language and each of the other sign languages. She found that there were considerably fewer completely different signs in Swedish Sign Language and Finnish Sign Language (40 percent) than between Swedish Sign Language and the other two sign languages: BSL – Swedish Sign Language: 65 percent different signs, NGT – Swedish Sign Language: 67 percent different signs. Moreover, 37 percent of the Finnish and the Swedish signs were identical, in contrast to only 16 percent and 19 percent of the signs in the comparisons between Swedish Sign Language and the other two sign languages.

Mesch mentions as possible explanations for the greater similarity between Swedish Sign Language and Finnish Sign Language the historical relations between deaf education in the two countries, the physical proximity of the two countries, the contacts between deaf people from the two countries especially within deaf politics and sports events at the end of the nineteenth century, and iconicity, without elucidating why iconicity would only increase the similarity of the Swedish and the Finnish signs. She is skeptical about the postulation of a genetic relation between the two languages, although she acknowledges the potential influence in terms of borrowing from Swedish Sign Language on Finnish Sign Language because of the Finnish children attending the Manilla School in Stockholm in the nineteenth century.

We are equally skeptical about postulates concerning the genetic origin of Danish Sign Language and Swedish Sign Language in French Sign Language. Signing is attested in Sweden already in 1759, before l'abbé de l'Epée founded the school in Paris. The founder of the first school in Denmark, Castberg, did indeed visit the Paris school but was extremely sensitive to Danish deaf people's own signing. He may have imported a few French signs, but if so, they should rather be described as loans than as the origins of Danish Sign Language.

The situation is somewhat different with respect to the relations between Danish Sign Language and the sign languages of Iceland, Greenland and the Faeroe Islands as deaf children from these parts were sent to the schools in Denmark for longer periods. However, the relationship between Norwegian Sign Language and Danish Sign Language may be one of borrowing rather than genetic relatedness, similar to the relationship between Finnish Sign Language and Swedish Sign Language.

5

Transmission of sign languages in Mediterranean Europe

Josep Quer, Laura Mazzoni and Galini Sapountzaki

1   Introduction

This chapter aims at presenting an overview of sign language transmission and use in three Southern European countries in the Mediterranean area: Greece, Italy and Spain. As will become clear, the reality of signers and the vicissitudes of deaf education and sign language recognition are roughly comparable in the three countries, which is mainly amenable to the social and political similarities among them. In some aspects, the shared features differentiate them from Northern European countries, but at the same time the evolution observed is parallel to those of Western countries, albeit at a different pace at times.

The sign languages present in these countries are the following: Greek Sign Language (GSL; Ελληνική Νοηματική Γλώσσα, ΕΝΓ/Eliniki Noimatiki Glósa, ENG) in Greece; Italian Sign Language (LIS, Lingua dei Segni Italiana) in Italy, Spanish Sign Language (Lengua de Signos Española, LSE) in Spain and Catalan Sign Language (Llengua de Signes Catalana, LSC) in Catalonia. Here we will adopt the established acronyms in the spoken languages of the respective countries, except for the Greek case, where we use the English acronym for typographical unification.

Research about different aspects of these languages is relatively recent and it often covers partial areas.[1] The results presented in this chapter are mainly obtained from the existing literature, but also from interviews and observations collected in the contact with the respective Deaf communities.

First we introduce the current demolinguistic situation of the different signing communities, and we review the legal status of the respective languages in each of the three countries. Next, the core means of language transmission are examined, namely education for the deaf and social organizations within the Deaf communities. We also offer an overview of other means of dissemination that indirectly contribute to the transmission of these sign languages (artistic forms in sign language, sign language use in the media, sign language interpretation and second language teaching of sign language).

2   Status of sign languages and the signing communities

There exist no official statistics for the number of signers in these countries, because no specific question about sign language use had been included in the national census or a question was only posed about audiological status. Obviously, this does not correlate with the number of sign language users. Consequently, the figures that are available at present amount to estimates provided mainly by Deaf associations or federations, who make projections on the basis of the number of members of Deaf associations and clubs. Usually, a second figure is provided that includes hearing signers that have acquired sign language as a second language.

In the case of Spain, the rough figure is 120,000 Deaf signers of LSE, not including CODAs (children of deaf adults) or hearing signers that learned a sign language as a second language (L2 learners).[2] For LSC, the Catalan Federation of Deaf People (FESOCA) estimates that there are 12,000 Deaf signers, and up to 25,000 users if all LSC users are included. In Greece, 42,600 are estimated to be signers of GSL, of which 12,600 would be deaf children. No L2 signers are included in this total, although the numbers for this group grow steadily. For LIS, according to the statistics of the national association of the deaf (Ente Nazionale Sordomuti, ENS), there are about 40,000 deaf signers and a considerably increasing group of LIS L2 learners.

Although full legal recognition of sign languages has only been granted in Spain very recently (and maybe in Italy as well, as a draft bill for the recognition of LIS is going through parliament), partial legislation in all three countries had indirectly recognized the status of sign language in education or in public media, for instance. This is the case in Greece, where a Special Education Law from 2000 recognized GSL as the language of deaf and hard-of-hearing students. Sign languages in Spain were legally recognized in 2007, when a Spanish State law concerning sign languages was passed. However, several autonomous regional goverments had already passed bills during the 1990s that aimed at promoting accessibility in LSE in different areas, featuring education as one of of the central ones. It should be pointed out that legal recognition is not equivalent to official status, because the Spanish Constitution from 1978 grants official status to only four spoken languages (Spanish, Catalan, Galician and Basque).

The new Catalan Autonomy Law from 2006 includes the right to use LSC and promotes its teaching and protection. At present (2009) a bill has been passed by the Catalan Parliament in order to regulate LSC use in all areas of public life. However, the Catalan Parliament had already passed a non-binding bill in 1994 promoting the use of LSC in the Catalan education system and research into the language.

An indirect recognition of sign languages and the rights of signers has taken place through recognition, professionalization and funding of sign language interpreters, which will be dealt with in section 4.3.3 below.

The general ignorance of the surrounding hearing society about sign language and signers has been rapidly overthrown by the impact of deaf and sign language right movements and by the discussion of deaf demands in the media, often linked to law initiatives. A bigger presence of TV programs in sign language or with sign language interpretation has raised consciousness among a broader section of the population in the three countries. Despite the current differences in the degree of legal protection of sign languages and signers, a general advancement has been observed in this area during the last decades of the twentieth century and in the twenty-first century. Deaf communities have used the goal of legal recognition of their languages in order to put the issue of civil and linguistic rights of signers on the political agenda. However, such attempts have often been counterbalanced by oralist lobbies that argue for spoken language as the basic communication system, if not the only one. This situation has led policymakers to adopt a compromising, complementary approach to the linguistic and social needs of signing and non-signing deaf populations.

3   Sign language varieties and influences

Despite the first attempts in this direction, none of the languages under consideration has been systematically standardized, and diatopic variation is often reported. However, among signers of the relevant linguistic community there is a shared sense that a common sign language is being used. This is a relatively recent situation, as the older generation of signers and deaf signers with a weaker link to the deaf community and deaf associations used to identify their language as "mimics," "hands" or "signs," and not as "language"; the use of a national adjective to describe it was far from a reality (see, for instance, Morales-López *et al.* 2002 for LSC). The emancipatory movements that took place in the deaf communities in the last decades of the twentieth century contributed to the identification of the sign languages as such by their users and to the establishment of a name for them, mirroring American Sign Language (ASL) and other sign languages that had followed the same path.

As is often the case in many sign languages, differentiation results from having attended different schools in the country. But even for signers from the same area, minor lexical or phonological differences emerge as a consequence of having attended a male or a female school, when such divisions played a role in the organization of education. In addition, major urban centers (Rome for LIS,

Athens and Thessaloniki for GSL, Madrid for LSE and Barcelona for LSC), where the most influential deaf schools were located, had a bigger impact in the development of a national variety of sign language. This process was intensified from the moment that materials on the language were produced (dictionaries, teaching materials, etc.), broadcasting in sign language started and population mobility and contact became easier, and research into sign language started to produce results.

For GSL no major dialectal variation has been documented; still, deaf individuals belonging to the Gypsy ethnic minority are reported to use a different sign language. Research on GSL agrees that the language has roots in ASL and French Sign Language (LSF) as well as in various indigenous sign languages, which came together in the 1950s (Kourbetis 2005, Gordon 2005). An older form may have been used long before that time among deaf pupils of Asia Minor, and it might have come into contact with preexisting varieties, as in 1923 ten deaf orphan children from Asia Minor moved to the first school for the deaf in the island of Syros (Lambropoulou 1994a).

In the domain of LIS, there are two main varieties that differentiate themselves from the form shared at national level: the one used in the Trieste area and the one in the Turin area. According to Corazza (1997), the former features both spoken and signed Austrian, Slovenian and Croatian influences. Till twenty to thirty years ago important lexical differentiation existed even within Venezia Giulia. Younger Triestian and Friulian signers are now abandoning the Triestian variety in favor of the LIS variety used in the Veneto, which is closer to the common LIS form. The other identifiable variety, the one from Turin, has less marked features, and it has French and Swiss influences in the lexicon.

There is little known about differences among sign language varieties in Spain. The only piece of research so far consists in a preliminary study based on limited lexical comparison, mutual intelligibility and language attitudes (Parkhurst & Parkhurst 2001), which confirms that LSC is the variety that differentiates itself most from the rest. Still, comparative in-depth lexical and grammatical research is lacking, and superficial comparison does not shed much light, as LSE and LSC are clearly related and in addition linguistic contact is playing a visible role mainly at the lexical level. There is no research on dialectal variation within the domain of LSC, but it is implicitly recognized that in Western Catalonia (Lleida) some lexical variants are used that differentiate themselves from the main variety, the one centered in Barcelona. However, beyond the connection to the LSF group of European sign languages, little is known about the diachronic development of LSC, LSE and LIS.

Nowadays, many signers have been exposed to foreign sign languages, mainly ASL, but also other European sign languages and International Sign (IS). In Spain,

Catalan signers have at least passive knowledge of LSE. This does not mean that there is a sign language bilingual situation in Catalonia, as LSC is the sign language used by Catalan signers almost exclusively. This is, for instance, reflected in the curriculum for interpreter training in Catalonia, which devotes most of the sign language proficiency hours to LSC, with some additional LSE and IS learning.

It has been observed that Spanish signers show some degree of insecurity about their proficiency in the language, although they are clearly more proficient in LSE than in spoken Spanish (Gras 2006:187). The degree of insecurity is much higher with respect to the command of the oral language, and speaking is the oral language skill that they score best in. The younger section of the signing population is the group that feels most comfortable about their spoken language proficiency. Few individuals, though, characterize themselves as balanced bilinguals.

With the spread of sign language use to a wider variety of formal contexts beyond the informal ones, it is going through a process of register and lexicon widening. Neologisms are created by groups of specialists and disseminated in contexts of formal interpretation or in education. The register of the language used on those occasions also develops into new forms of discourse partially determined by the interaction with spoken language discourse. However, a large section of the signers is unaware of that process and feels that language is being created without enough consensus and collaboration with the Deaf community.

4   Language transmission

As for most sign languages, the transmission in Mediterranean Europe relies on the pillars of deaf education and Deaf associations because most deaf infants are born into hearing families, being thus deprived of native exposure to sign language during the critical period of language acquisition. In this section we will devote special attention to the evolution of educational policies and practices for the deaf. Let us mention here that as long as residential and special schools for the deaf existed, they contributed to sign language preservation and transmission, as well as to Deaf community building. Nevertheless, since mainstreaming was imposed in the 1980s for deaf children, this means of language transmission has been seriously jeopardized.

4.1   Education of the Deaf

Perhaps the oldest record about institutional provision for deaf children in the area under review can be traced to Greece. According to Lazanas (1984), during the Byzantine period there was provision for deaf children by social programs of the time such as those implemented in asylums, but there is no evidence for educational settings or language policies. There is no readily available evidence for the status of sign language in Byzantine years. However, evidence from St. Markos's life gives two important hints: St. Markos was deaf and communicated through signs (or gestures) with the other monks in his monastery. Also, he was assigned full sainthood regardless of the fact that he could not use words in the sense that his monk peers could.

The first reports about the education of deaf infants date back to the sixteenth century in Italy and Spain. Even though Bartolo della Marca d'Ancona (1314–1357), in his *Digesta Nova*, already mentioned the possibility of a deaf person being able to express him- or herself with signs and use lip-reading to understand other people's speech, Girolamo Cardano (1508–1576) was the first scientist in Italy to support the possibility and the social duty of educating deaf people, although he was not involved in this specific field himself. He was reproducing the position sustained by the early humanist Rodolphus Agricola, in his *De inventione dialectica* (1479), where it was narrated that a deaf had been trained to understand and to communicate with everyone through writing. Cardano invented a code of teaching for which, unfortunately, no evidence remains. Later, Fabrizio Acquapendente (1533–1619), borrowing and sharing the statements of Cardano, argued, in his two essays devoted to the matter, that there is a difference between mimics and the use of signs by deaf people and that muteness was mere consequence of the lack of hearing.

In sixteenth-century Spain, the pioneering experiences of teachers of the deaf are documented.[3] The Benedictine monk Pedro Ponce de León (around 1508–1584) is the first one about whom there is information. He taught several deaf children to write and to represent words manually, although little is known about his teaching method. Juan Pablo Bonet (1573–1633), with his *Reduction of Letters and Art to Teach the Mute to Speak* (1620), is the next important character in the development of methods for deaf instruction. He taught noble children to speak with a method that would become known in deaf education throughout Europe in the following centuries. In his work he included a version of the one-handed manual alphabet that has become the base for the international one used in most sign languages connected to a Latin alphabet. The later adoption of the alphabet by Abbé Charles-Michel de l'Épée's school in Paris was decisive for its further spreading. The first record of this type of alphabet dates back to the one by Melchor Sánchez de Yebra, published posthumously in 1593. Contemporary with Pablo Bonet, Manuel Ramírez de Carrión (1579–1652) was later active as educator of the prince of Carignano.

While much pioneering work had taken place in Spain, during the sixteenth and seventeenth centuries the lead in deaf education was taken by the Spaniard Jacob

Rodríguez de Pereira (1715–1780), who followed Juan Pablo Bonet's method, although not much is known about his implementation. The French school of de l'Épée (1712–1789) and Sicard (1742–1822), with its methodic signs, was much more influential. Deaf education in Italy remained, however, limited to the wealthy families up to 1784, when Father Tommaso Silvestri, trained as educator at de l'Épée's school in Paris, opened the first public school for the deaf in Rome thanks to the financial contribution of a lawyer, Pasquale Di Pietro. Initially the school was established in Di Pietro's house and it was attended by a small number of students. After the deaths of Silvestri and Di Pietro, it became a school under the control of the Church. The school directed by Father Silvestri followed a bilingual model of education in which written and spoken Italian were used together with sign language; this is documented in the posthumously published manuscript entitled "On the way to make speak and expeditiously instruct the deaf mute from birth."

In eighteenth-century Spain, special mention must be made of the multifaceted Jesuit scholar Lorenzo Hervás y Panduro (1735–1809). Among his enormous production, the work entitled *Spanish School of Deaf-Mutes or Art to teach them to write and speak the Spanish language* (1795) should be highlighted. The publication of this work certainly influenced education of the deaf at that time, as we will see. He had written it during his exile in Rome, where he came into contact with the school founded by Silvestri. His ideas were quite revolutionary, as he acknowledged the existence of "grammatical ideas" in the signing of the deaf and he recommended the use of the actual signs they used, next to the manual alphabet. He was involved in the creation of the first deaf school in Barcelona in 1800.

In 1795 a royal decree was issued that required the creation of the first classroom for deaf pupils. It was called Real Colegio de Sordomudos de San Fernando, in Madrid, and was hosted at the Colegio de los Padres Escolapios del Avapiés under the direction of José Fernández Navarrete, a disciple of Tommaso Silvestri. Unfortunately, the enterprise did not succeed. A new project was approved in 1802, but it was not until 1803 that the first steps toward actually opening the school were taken. Roberto Prádez (1772?–1836) became one of the deaf teachers of the deaf at Spain's first official school for deaf students.

Meanwhile, Joan Albert i Martí had opened the first school of the deaf in Barcelona. It was first private, but later received the support of the city council, and that is why it is known as the first Barcelona Municipal School of the Deaf-Mute (1800–1802). It was quite an unprecedented experience, as it was open to as many deaf children as necessary, irrespective of their social and economic status. In 1857 a law on public instruction led to the creation of different schools for the deaf and the blind in the second half of the nineteenth century. In addition specific training for teachers of the deaf was set up at the Colegio de Sordomudos de

Madrid. In 1904 Emilio Tortosa Orero founded the Instituto Catalán de Sordomudos, a private school. The City Council of Barcelona also supported the Municipal School of the Deaf-Mute, where the phonetician Pere Barnils was appointed in 1918.

In the nineteenth century, other institutes were founded in various Italian cities based on the model founded by Father Silvestri. They were managed by members of the clergy who maintained a good network of contacts among the institutes (Zatini 1993), and since then the history of deaf people has mirrored the history of their institutes. In 1889 the Roman institute moved to the site of Via Nomentana, a site that still exists today as a center of culture and research of great relevance for the Italian Deaf community.

In Italy more generally, before the 1880 Milan Congress, there was a widespread awareness of signs, their value and the importance of their use in the education of deaf children, and in fact many deaf people succeeded in reaching a "bilingual" linguistic competence.[4] Sign language was also used in didactic circles, and some deaf persons had an important role in the educational field, among them Basso, Carbonieri and Minoja (Folchi & Mereghetti 1995).

Giacomo Carbonieri (1814–1879) in particular was a bright deaf psycholinguist who had grasped, before Saussure, that the language faculty was independent from its modality and in his work as a deaf trainer he mastered, used and defended sign language in a bilingual approach to education. He also tried to promote a not merely clinical perception of deafness. Among his production, the 1895 book, *Osservazioni sopra l'opinione del Sig. Giovanni Gandolfi Professore di Medicina Legale della R. Università di Modena*, has become the most famous, as he referred to the gestural system of communication used among the deaf as "Italian sign language." In 2000 the deaf writer and researcher Renato Pigliacampo devoted a book to Giacomo Carbonieri recognizing his profoundness of intuition and retracing the cultural and social debate, still actual, between oralism and sign language.

Paolo Basso (1806–1879) grew up in Genoa, where he attended the Institute for the Deaf-Mute created by Father Assarotti. Noted for his intelligence, he was able to learn and write several languages, which contributed to his renown. Although his stance on sign language is rather controversial (it seems he had criticized the wide use of sign language that Father Assarotti made in his institute), after his training he worked as instructor for deaf pupils first at the institute in Genoa and later at the Royal Institute of Deaf-Mutes in Turin.

Giuseppe Minoja (1812–1871) became a trainer for the deaf almost by chance: he was trained at the Royal Institute for Deaf-Mutes in Milan and once back home he began sharing his knowledge with other deaf boys of his town. He was extremely successful and, thanks to the support of Father Don Gelmini, founded a school for the deaf in Villanova, close to Milan, where he started working as a deaf trainer. He was author of several books about instruction and deafness, among which *On the need for education of the deaf*[5] in 1852 and the *Compendium of Religious, Scientific and Moral Doctrines to be used by Deaf-Mutes*[6] in 1858.

Despite recommending the use of the oral method in teaching the deaf, the use of signing continued to exist outside the classroom in deaf schools during the twentieth century. It has even been reported that in Greece, for charity reasons, some of the child-care workers at schools were deaf: some of the cooks in boarding schools, gatekeepers and bus drivers were deaf, and although they had usually only received primary education, they served as role models for the children, who could "hear" the daily news from them, do some homework under their supervision, and even be told off in sign language, by someone who would not consider them as handicapped.

In Greece, Andreas Kokkevis, Member of Parliament and later Minister of Health and Welfare (1964–1974), who had a deaf daughter himself, supported legislative and educational means in favor of deaf children. After 1956, the tuition fees for deaf children were to be paid by the public social security system. The first private school for the deaf was established by Iro Kokkevi in 1956. Amalia Martinou, the owner and life director of this school, was very much in favor of oral-only communication. In 1986 the school was transferred to the public system, as the Primary and High School for the Deaf and the Hard of Hearing in Argyroupolis. Another private school establishment was founded by Sofia Starogianni, mother of two deaf sons, in 1973, under the direction of the devoted language teacher Victoria Daoussi. This school was also transferred to the public sector in 1982. Graduates of the Martinou–Argyroupolis school, even employees, use a form of GSL that is slightly more influenced by Greek than graduates of the Starogianni, EIPK school.

In 1984 Total Communication was officially adopted in Greek deaf schools, and as of 1995 we find deaf teachers active in deaf schools (Lambropoulou 1994a, 1999). In 1986 the first infant program that could introduce sign language to families of deaf children was established in the three largest cities in Greece.

In Italy and Spain, deaf education in the last quarter of the twentieth century made the shift to mainstreaming, under the assumption that all children with any sort of handicap should be integrated in regular schools with provision made for their specific needs. The consequences of such policies for deaf children are well known: lag in language development (both in sign language and in spoken language), lack of Deaf models, poor academic results, and isolation leading to social and psychological difficulties.

In 1977, National Law 517 specified Italy's strategies for school integration, making it possible for families to enroll their deaf children in the schools of their choice, whether special or mainstream. This law triggered the closing of special schools, since the majority of parents chose to insert their deaf children in the "normal" schools (Caselli, Maragna & Volterra 2006). This chimera of a new and more effective integration has, as a matter of fact, isolated deaf individuals who often find that they are the only deaf persons in their class and, sometimes, the whole school. This new situation of linguistic isolation has brought the deaf population to a state of heavy cultural impoverishment, depriving it of its primary means of linguistic and cultural transmission – the institutes – where values, behaviors, traditions and ideals were learned (Jacobucci 1997). The deaf institutes have become progressively smaller and emptier and, as Caselli, Maragna and Volterra (2006:34) point out, "so they have come to lack, with a lowered number of pupils, the communicative, linguistic and of cultural transmission context that existed in the past thanks to the existence of a widened deaf community."

Since the 1990s, the special schools in Italy that somehow had survived the diaspora of deaf pupils have also decided to accept hearing pupils, offering experimental programs and, in some cases, a bilingual educational program, of which the more "famous" experience is represented by the Cossato school in Biella. In Biella's school the bilingual program provides teaching of different subjects in LIS or Italian, although only a few deaf students are present in each classroom as the number of deaf students is about a tenth of the total. This peculiar and unusual situation influences sign language transmission in two ways: on the one hand it guarantees LIS access to deaf pupils born in hearing families who otherwise would never be exposed to sign language but, on the other, considering the differences in numbers, it exposes sign language to the risk of modification and improper use because the number of hearing signers using it is considerably larger than the number of deaf ones. The teachers working in Biella, however, are firm in their assurances that the linguistic competence reached by deaf and hearing students at the end of their schooling is analogous and native-like. Finally, in 2000, some special schools still active merged into a unique institute denominated ISISS (National Institute of Specialized Education for the Deaf).

The developments in Spain in this domain were very similar. In 1982 a new Law for Social Integration of the Handicapped (LISMI) was issued. The educational regulations deriving from that law were deployed in a Royal Decree about Special Education Planning dating from 1985. As in the Italian case, it implied the inclusion of deaf children in regular classrooms with some special support. Specifically for deaf pupils, it made possible the provision of a supporting teacher, a teacher in Special Education and a speech therapist, meant for speech rehabilitation. In a further reform of the overall educational system in 1990 (Ley de Ordenación General del Sistema Educativo, LOGSE), a modified perspective was introduced whereby the school obtained more freedom to organize its resources in order to meet the needs of its pupils with special educational needs. So there will be no specific curricula for those pupils, but just adapted ones. The goal of this new move is to become more inclusive and less homogenizing. Given that many autonomous regional governments have powers in the arrangement of education, the reality of education for deaf students is very varied. One of the developments observed has been the progressive incorporation of interpreters in educational settings. This has been favored for instance in regular schools with preferential enrollment of deaf pupils, where small groups of deaf are present. At the same time, Deaf coaches or teachers have been recruited on some of the bilingual projects.

As a consequence of the pressure of associations of parents of deaf children in favor of sign language (e.g. APANSCE in Catalonia) and professionals specializing in deaf education, some bilingual projects were set up around the mid-1990s: in Catalonia (Col·legi Públic de Sords Josep Pla, CEIPM Tres Pins-Escola Forestier, CEE de Sords CRAS Sabadell-IES Sabadell, IES Consell de Cent) and in Madrid (Instituto Hispanoamericano de la Palabra and Centro Público de Educación Especial de Sordos Ponce de León, Colegio Público El Sol, Escuela Piruetas). Only a few of those are implemented at secondary school educational level. A shared characteristic is that these bilingual programs are still experimental, as not all the needs have been met for fully bilingual education and they have been functioning for quite a short time. One of the main difficulties of the programs for effective bilingual education is the limited and varying sign language proficiency of the professionals involved. Moreover, little specific instruction about sign language is being offered (Morales-López 2004).

The new LSE and LSC laws both recognize the right to full-fledged bilingual education, so important and rapid changes are expected as a consequence of their deployment.

The presence of sign language in tertiary education is scarce, as most of the few deaf students that enroll for university studies rely on spoken language. Small-scale provision of interpreters is present, though. A different situation arises in specific postgraduate programs for deaf teachers, where sign language is used.

4.2   Social groups and families

The other pillar for sign language transmission in the twentieth and twenty-first centuries has been Deaf associations. Associations and clubs constituted not only the center of socialization and leisure activities for deaf individuals, where the sense of Deaf community took root and sign language was used naturally as a default, but they were also the cradle of Deaf activism in defense of the status of sign languages and the rights of Deaf citizens. Deaf families, when they exist, have played an important role in some of these associations, as they tend to constitute the elite of the community, and have provided leaders that play a crucial role in Deaf emancipation. During the few past decades, there seems to have been an ongoing change in the way deaf individuals relate to Deaf associations and clubs. As a consequence of the possibilities offered by the new communication technologies (chat, videoconferencing, videophone, etc.), as well as the different schooling situations, the younger Deaf generation seems to be less inclined to join Deaf clubs. In addition, the expansion of cochlear implants at earlier ages is reducing the number of children who might be candidates to follow specific education for the deaf, as there is almost no support for the idea that even implanted children should be exposed to sign language as well. Gras (2006) has pointed to another factor that has contributed to the reduction of the deaf population in Spain and that is the eradication of German measles, which was a principal cause of deafness before the introduction of the relevant vaccine in the 1960s.

In Greece, the first club to be established was the Greek Union of Deaf-Mutes, in 1948. It is now named Greek Union of the Deaf. This club also started publishing a newspaper in 1956 (*The Problems of the Deaf-Mutes*), but it was soon discontinued for funding and organizational reasons. In 1954 Iro Kokkevis and Sofia Starogianni (see above for her involvement in the establishment of deaf schools) formed the Organization for the Welfare of the Deaf and coordinated a series of educational and social activities. In 1963 the club Prophet Zacharias, Friends of the Deaf Mute, was founded, where the first sign language lessons and first GSL dictionary were organized (presented by a Deaf man). It started as a group of deaf boys and a hearing one, Nikolaos Grekos, who would become Bishop Nikodimos of Thiva and Livadia. During World War II about twenty-five young men and women studied the Bible every Friday, and this was informally established as the first gathering of adult deaf people who used sign language as their preferred means of communication for social purposes. At the same time, not only young adults but also schoolchildren had an opportunity to socialize with one another in sign language in an environment where this was not banned. A group of about 120 Deaf pupils of the National Institute for the Protection of Deaf Mutes (Maroula Katsibra, personal communication, January 2007) were accompanied by their teachers to attend the monthly liturgies in Greek sign language, although paradoxically sign language was not allowed at their school officially. Girls groups followed a similar path, and a group of up to forty young post-teenage deaf girls also started similar Bible study and social activities, accompanied by nineteen-year-old hearing Maroula Katsibra. It should be noted that Bishop Nikodimos was the first to bless weddings of Deaf couples, which were forbidden at the time. This was the beginning of transmission of GSL from one generation to another through biological families.

The Greek Federation of the Deaf was established in 1968. It now has nineteen member Deaf clubs. The two associations of Parents of Deaf Children were founded in 1965 and 1980 and made a significant contribution to the improvement of deaf education, by assisting the deaf organizations and pressing the government.

The main Italian institution that represents and defends the rights of deaf people is the ENS, acronym for the National Deaf Association. It was founded in Padua in 1932 during the First Unitary National Meeting of Italian Deaf people, thanks to Antonio Margarotto's involvement and to the unwavering desire of Deaf people (Zatini 1993). The ENS is currently the only association of Deaf people recognized by the laws of the Italian government. It has over 101 provincial offices, 21 regional committees and numerous local headquarters. In every provincial office and in the local headquarters, there is a recreational club that represents a place of meeting, information, socialization and enjoyment for the Deaf population.

In Spain the first first Deaf association was created in 1906 in Madrid, followed by the Sociedad de Socorros Mutuos entre los Sordos de ambos sexos de Cataluña, in Barcelona, in 1909. The latter was followed by the Centro Familiar de Sordomudos (currently Casal de Sords) in Barcelona in 1916. Valencia, Zaragoza, Oviedo, Seville and other cities followed within some years. At the National Assembly of Deaf-Mutes celebrated in Barcelona in 1935, Juan Luís Marroquín was asked to set up the National Federation of Deaf Associations in Spain. The associations existing before the Spanish Civil War met in 1936 in order to create the federation, and Marroquín was appointed as its president. He stayed in charge till 1992. It is now called Confederación Estatal de Personas Sordas de España (CNSE) and represents the regional federations and associations across Spain. It has had a very active role in the legal recognition of sign languages in Spain, and it also leads many social and educational initiatives for the Deaf community.

Despite the different chronologies in the establishment of Deaf clubs and organizations, it is clear that they played a central role in the twentieth century in community building through socializing and activism, and, more importantly for the purposes of this chapter, in the consolidation and transmission of the national signed languages. Nowadays, though, there seems to be a change in the way Deaf individuals from younger generations relate to such organizations, partly because of the impact of new communication technologies. In addition, current policies concerning cochlear implantation do not tend to offer sign language to the implanted infant after the intervention. Some of these implanted individuals join the Deaf community only at a later stage in their lives, thus becoming late signers and members with a less clear-cut Deaf identity.

4.3   Sign language dissemination

In this section we briefly review the means by which sign language gets disseminated within the signing communities and across the whole of the societies in which
they are integrated in: art, media, interpretation and second language courses.

4.3.1   *Artistic manifestations in sign language*

Theatre has been the most traditional way of sign language artistic expression and
dissemination in Western Deaf communities. Along with it, Deaf cinema and
visual poetry have contributed to Deaf art conveyed in some form of artistic
sign language. In Greece the Greek Theatre of the Deaf was established in 1983.
Its impact on the development of GSL was immense, as this was the first time that
Deaf people used their language in order to express themselves artistically and in
public. The Greek Theatre of the Deaf held many performances all around
Greece. For Italy it is not known when exactly the first theatre company was
created, organized and run by deaf actors.[7] According to some reports from the
most elderly people, it seems that at the beginning of the twentieth century there
were already deaf actors that realized and staged performances and shows in the
Deaf clubs of their cities. Today there exist festivals devoted to Deaf theatre and
thanks to the new means of recording, shows can have widespread diffusion and
popularity, both among the deaf and hearing public, which was unthinkable
before. Together with the staging of famous works, an original repertoire is
proposed in which central themes of Deaf culture are represented: the recognition
of the language, the traditions and the inherent cultural values, the shared school
experiences, the sometimes painful educational background, the sense of exclusion
and ostracism, the desire for approval, etc. Currently a large number of theatre
companies exists, formed by deaf people acting in LIS, among which
"Laboratorio 'Zero'" of Rome, "Maschera Viva" of Turin, "Gestum" of
Salerno, "Senza parole" of Milan, "Ciclope" of Palermo, "David" of Florence.
In Spain theatre in sign language by and for the Deaf also has a solid tradition,
and festivals are organized periodically.

   Deaf cinema is an artistic genre of the latest generations where Deaf people are
perceived and represented as "the cultural and visual linguistic minority using sign
language."[8] Inside this genre short films have great success. In Italy a national
festival is devoted to such short Deaf films whose second edition took place in 1996.
The company DeafMedia (www.deafmedia.eu) is very active in this domain. In
Catalonia the association Cercle d'Artistes Sords Units (ASU) produced over a
hundred films in sign language, many of which are adaptations of well-known
movies played by deaf actors.

As for poetry, in Italy the first literary work of poetry was the CD-ROM *Sette poesie in LIS* (Seven LIS poems) containing some pieces of Rosaria and Giuseppe Giuranna (Giuranna & Giuranna 2003), refined poets and experts in the language. This work is known and appreciated at national level, so much as to be considered the first official documentation of LIS poetry. This study has also made possible the first study of the key aspects of LIS poetry (Giuranna & Giuranna 2000) and its comparison with spoken language poetry (Russo, Giuranna & Pizzuto 2001). In Spain, translations of spoken language poetry into LSE are also available through the Internet.[9]

4.3.2   *Sign language in the media and Deaf press*
Television provided the first means for incorporating sign language in the media. In Greece a single newspaper of the Deaf was established and then discontinued after only some issues. TV news slots in GSL were transmitted through only one national television channel in Thessaloniki. This news slot was less than a minute long and transmitted once daily, in some form of Signed Greek. After 1998, GSL registered interpreters started appearing in all major TV channels, transmitting in the low commercial zones (very early in the morning) and for very few seconds at a time. In the following years, and after pressure by GFD and the Interpreters' Association, this improved significantly. As of 2007, news in GSL is several minutes long and appears daily in high commercial time zones (late afternoon or evening). A new cable television channel, called Prisma, addressing citizens with special needs was launched in 2005 and started transmitting programs of all kinds for more than twelve hours daily, with Greek captioning and interpreted windows.

On Italian national television no program exists that is broadcast in sign language. Only some brief news interpreted into LIS is transmitted every day. Since 1994 the President of the Republic's New Year message has been interpreted into LIS, although it is not subtitled. Many programs are subtitled in Italian. The services televideo and teletext offer some pages devoted to the deaf population. RAI 3, one of the three state networks, has also produced two documentaries about Deaf-related issues: *The Man's Brain. The Sign Language* (1990) and *The Computer in the Service of Deaf Children* (1992).

Spanish public (and some private) TV stations include some programs in sign language or interpreted into sign language. This is mostly limited to news broadcasting or to specific programs aimed at a deaf audience and about Deaf issues, such as State TVE's *En otras palabras*, which for many years was the only program realized in LSE and Spanish. In addition, captioning in spoken language has increased in the past few years. Some political broadcasts or official campaigns are now interpreted into sign language. As for printed press, CNSE has been publishing the periodical *Faro del silencio* for many years now.

Since the Internet became widespread, accessibility to information through sign language has increased considerably. In Catalonia there is an Internet TV site (Visual Web: www.webvisual.tv) in LSC. Several popular Deaf sites like Difusord (www.difusord.org), Diario Signo (www.diariosigno.com) or Minoría Sorda (www.deminorias.com/canal.php?canal=minoriasorda) provide community news by means of sign language and written spoken language. Moreover, some non-deaf-related sites have started to offer part of the information in sign language. CNSE is developing the possibilities offered by the Internet in order to establish a virtual Deaf Community, with initiatives like a virtual Deaf Town (www.ciudadsorda.org) or a Deaf Network (www.redsorda.com/presentacion.htm).

In Italy, websites and portals dedicated to deafness are still few. Certainly first among all is the site of ENS (www.ens.it) where since 2004 it has been possible to see LIS videos among which are messages of the National ENS President. Other portals of great success are the Dizlis network (www.dizlis.it) and Eurosordi (www.eurosordi.it). Various specialized periodicals devoted to the deaf population exist, some of which are managed by deaf people. The most popular periodical among Deaf people is the monthly newspaper of information, culture and politics of the Deaf Italian *Parole e segni* (Words and signs), edited by ENS. It replaced *La settimana del sordo* and the most remote *La settimana del sordomuto*. Other publications are *Il Sordoudente*, *V. S. P. Voci Silenzi Pensieri* and *L'educazione dei sordi*.

It is clear that the introduction of audiovisual technologies and the Internet have had a very positive effect on the dissemination of sign languages, making them visible to a wider section of the population, but also facilitating non face-to-face contact among signers and distant access to sign language contents, including community issues. As usual, the form of the language used in these media has some standardizing effect, even if no explicit measures have been taken with respect to that.

4.3.3   *Sign language interpretation*

Sign language interpreters have constituted the traditional link between signers and non-signing hearing individuals, and as such they are an important vehicle of sign language dissemination. In all three countries we observe a progression from CODAs and volunteer workers realizing this mediating function in the beginning towards the officialization and professionalization of interpreters. Given their public role in the signing communities, together with the fact that many of them have learned sign language as a second language, their practice can influence the form of the language, mainly in the formal contexts where they are asked to interpret.

In Spain, although the first recognized sign language interpretation took place in 1987, it was not until 1995 that professional training for sign language interpreters was legislated and consequently implemented in 1998. Before that, many interpreters were, of course, active in connection with Deaf associations or sign language interpreter associations. Training at tertiary level is limited to postgraduate programs for professionals with a basic degree in sign language interpretation or with years of experience, but since 2008–09 the first university BA degree in LSC interpreting has been offered in Barcelona. In Greece the first interpreter training program for GSL interpreters and GSL tutors was established in 1990 in Argyroupolis (Lambropoulou 1994b, 1999). In Italy, indirect recognition of LIS and the rights of Italian signers was achieved in 1982 with the introduction of a special law on disability (National Law 104/1982) that recognized deaf people's right to have sign language interpreters available to them at university and signing tutors at elementary and intermediate school. Thanks to the scientific support of the National Council for Research (CNR), the first training program for LIS interpreters was established in Rome in the 1980s and since then various training initiatives have been adopted (by private schools, Deaf associations and universities), although at present there is no unified program. In Italy there exist two national associations of sign language interpreters, both founded in 1987, which are involved in providing training programs and professional support to sign language interpreters.[10]

4.3.4 *Second language teaching of sign language*

Apart from the usual ways of sign language transmission described above, sign language teaching curricula have been established with two main purposes: sign language interpreter training and sign language proficiency for hearing parents and relatives, professionals engaged in deaf education and other people interested in learning sign language as L2.

Outside of the Italian university contexts, it is currently possible to find LIS courses organized by the ENS provincial headquarters of many Italian cities. To this end, several years ago ENS founded a department devoted to didactics and LIS research activities called FALICSEU (Formation and Updating of the Language and Culture of the Deaf-School Education University), part of whose activities are devoted to the design of programs and contents of LIS courses and teacher training. In such courses lecturing is generally commissioned to deaf teachers, while the teaching of theoretical parts is sometimes assigned to hearing teachers. Currently, there does not exist an official qualification for LIS teaching. Even in the institutional centers (schools and universities), LIS teachers are selected on the basis of experience – i.e., anecdotal linguistic and cultural competences.

In Greece the first sign language classes in various settings were offered in 1988 (Local Authority of Argyroupolis in Athens, the University of Patras, the National Institute for the Deaf and some local Deaf clubs).

In Spain teaching of LSE and LSC has traditionally taken place through courses organized by Deaf associations or cooperatives. There is no official curriculum so far, and the programs vary between three and four levels of proficiency.

5   Conclusion

In this chapter we have reviewed the general situation of the sign language communities in Greece, Italy and Spain, and we have examined the patterns of sign language transmission and dissemination in those countries. Alongside different instances of education for the deaf that go back several centuries, we find very important educational experiences and pedagogical approaches in Italy and Spain in the eighteenth and nineteenth centuries that involved sign language in teaching practice. The decisive steps towards systematic (public) education for the deaf, though, were taken in the twentieth century. After a period of schooling in specialized centers and boarding schools for deaf pupils, where different methods were applied and where sign language was transmitted basically among peers, in the last quarter of the century integration policies closed down many of those specialized schools. Mainstreaming of deaf students has weakened one of the basic sign language transmission links, but current attempts to consolidate bilingual/bicultural programs for signing pupils try to counter this trend. The other pillar for language transmission has been socialization in Deaf associations and clubs, which emerged at different points in the three countries during the twentieth century. Younger generations of signers appear to participate less structurally in those organizations, as a consequence of the new communication possibilities offered by innovative technologies. Sign language dissemination, moreover, takes place through artistic forms like theatre or poetry, through the media and the Internet, sign language interpreting and in sign language courses for non-signers.

Despite the differences encountered in Mediterranean Europe, due in part to their particular historical backgrounds, it can be safely concluded that the patterns of language transmission and dissemination present rather similar traits in the three countries examined in this chapter.

6

Transmission of sign languages in Africa

Dorothy Lule and Lars Wallin

1 Introduction

This chapter provides an overview of sign language transmission in Uganda, one of the countries in East Africa. It is hoped that this chapter will increase readers' awareness about African sign languages since there is limited documentation as compared to European sign languages. We have gathered information on a wide range of topics pertaining to how the language is transmitted, used, disseminated and preserved. To examine sign language transmission in Uganda, a combination of methods for collection of data was used, including ethnographic observation, interviews and documentary analysis.

Working definitions: It is vital to draw readers' attention to the use of different definitions and their relationship from the linguistic point of view as observed in signed languages. "Transmission" according to the *Collins English Dictionary* is "the passing or sending of something to a different person." Language transmission means a process whereby a language is passed on from generation to generation. The term "use" simply refers to the ability of language users to freely speak/sign the language for different purposes. How they use the language can reflect their feelings or attitudes toward the language. The term "dissemination" implies the situation where the language is spread to be used by other people within and outside the community. A measure employed by the language community to guard and promote the use of language to ensure its continuity in future generations is "preservation." Lastly, when a language enters an endangerment situation, it means there are so few users of the particular language that it ceases to be used as a primary language of a community.

For the purposes of this chapter, a brief background on Uganda is provided. Found in Eastern Africa, Uganda, "Pearl of Africa," is a landlocked country bordering the Sudan to the north, Kenya to the east, Rwanda and Tanzania to the south and the Democratic Republic of Congo to the west.[1] It is one of the developing countries in the world with a population of about 31 million in 2007, which is growing at a rate of 3.6 percent according to the United Nations Population Fund (UNFPA) New Vision, 2007.

Great importance has been attached to the development and social inclusion of people who are Deaf as one of the minority cultural groups in society, although this group still experiences inequality exacerbated by poverty, illiteracy and varying degrees of societal negative attitudes.

2   Status and population of signers

2.1   Status

Uganda is composed of many different cultures. Every culture portrays its special characteristics such as language, customs, history, to mention a few. The aim of this chapter is to explore the culture of Deaf people in Uganda who identify with the Deaf community and use Uganda Sign Language (USL) according to the Uganda National Association of the Deaf (UNAD) Information Handbook (2004). The term Deaf community has been used to mean a Deaf cultural group whose members share common experiences, cultural values and language (Gillian & Brook 1997). USL is the national language and the primary language, with its own grammar, vocabulary and special rules of use. The information is transmitted in a visual gestural modality rather than a vocal auditory modality similar to other signed languages worldwide.

USL is currently a cultural symbol of identity and solidarity to the members of the minority Deaf community who treasure and value it highly. As a human linguistic right, USL has an official status as the national independent language used among Deaf persons and others. Uganda was the second country worldwide to legally recognize sign language in the national constitution as the preferred language of the country's Deaf community. The preamble to the Constitution of Uganda (1995), last revised in (2005), under the cultural objectives XXIV clause (iii), states that, "The state shall promote the development of a sign language for the deaf."[2] Besides, USL is mentioned in some government policies such as the Uganda People's Defence Force (UPDF) Act amended 2005 and the Persons with Disabilities Act 2006.

However, on close examination, the legal recognition of USL in the past ten or more years since the promulgation of the constitution is no guarantee that the life of Deaf people in Uganda is effectively provided with support under this legislative provision. It is reported by Nkwangu (2006:3) that "Deaf people still live in deplorable conditions and face social barriers, which prevent their integration and full participation … in the nation" (Wrigley 1997; Oluoch 2006). Notwithstanding, the legal policy remains a useful instrument for Deaf people for lobbying the government for provision of various services. Most important of all, it is the constitutional right of Deaf people to belong, enjoy, maintain and promote their culture, and to develop USL, which they use freely.[3]

2.2   Population of signers

The estimated number of Deaf people in Uganda varies greatly, and extreme care must be taken in interpreting the available statistics as they may not reflect the correct figures. The Ministry of Gender, Labour and Social Development in Uganda estimated the number of deaf people to be nearly 30 percent of the 2.7 million of the total population of persons with disabilities (Nakagwa 2006). Wallin *et al.* (2006) put it at 528,000 deaf people, while Oluoch (2006) put it at 700,000. There is no up-to-date, accurate census statistics; hence information about d/Deaf people as a group, who they are, where they live, the extent of their hearing loss, what services they need, and what services, if any, are accessible to them, can be difficult to trace. These data serve primarily to emphasize that d/Deaf people do exist among the Ugandan population, but the estimates of the population of d/Deaf people are probably erroneous because the incidence of deafness increases with age.

The culturally Deaf people with uppercase "D" who use USL on a regular basis and have developed a stronger identity constitute the core of the Deaf communities in Uganda. It should be remembered that not all audiologically deaf people with lowercase "d," especially adults who acquire deafness late in adulthood and young deaf children of hearing parents who lack awareness of deafness and sign language, are exposed to the community of Deaf adults.

The number of signers is likely to grow as the boundaries of the Deaf communities are shifted to embrace the automatic membership of children of deaf adults (CODAs) (Lane, Hoffmeister & Bahan 1996). These are hearing and deaf children raised by Deaf adults and exposed to sign language from the earliest age. There is also a broad category of hearing people with an appropriate attitude and respect for the Deaf community under the following subdivisions: hearing parents of deaf children, relatives, teachers of deaf children, interpreters and friends who share USL with Deaf people in daily interaction. They are accepted in the community of signers, although most activities are managed by Deaf people themselves.

The plight of the minority Deaf people in Uganda was similar to that of Deaf people in different communities around the world who have been subjected to societal oppression and suppression in the past. Credit therefore goes to a variety of partners of international nongovernmental organizations that have worked together with UNAD through financial assistance to change the situation of deaf people in society through its strategic programs and activities (Mbulamwana 2004a).

Positive change has been attained during the past twelve years under the current government, where the recognition of Deaf people's linguistic right is a major achievement. This is a revolutionary step forward that has paved the way for other achievements. Examples of successful lobbying of which Deaf people in Uganda can be proud of include: an increased number of Deaf people with a stronger sense of community, increased involvement and participation in the democratization and governance process,[4] increased Deaf awareness and sign language knowledge in society, increased use of sign language in schools for Deaf, sign language research and formal training of interpreters, daily access of interpreted TV news, recent publication of the *Uganda Sign Language Dictionary* and improved secondary and tertiary educational opportunities for Deaf young people, to mention just a few.

Comparison with the other language situations of Deaf people in African developing countries would suggest an improved environment for Ugandan Deaf people to an extent. Indeed, there is opportunity for some Deaf people to participate in the social, cultural, economic and political life of the country. However, there are some challenges and grievances among Deaf people and persons with disabilities in general as regards the implementation of government policies and legislation "on the ground" (Mbulamwana 2004a, Mubangizi 2007). In spite of the many good policies and legislative initiatives that have been developed, the implementation process still excludes Deaf persons from mainstream activities in society.

This makes it difficult to predict the future of Deaf people as they still face barriers to communication, as well as to participation and access to information, which depends on a number of social-cultural, political and economic factors that influence each other. Otherwise, the growth and development of a Deaf cultural and linguistic group plays a crucial role in USL transmission. The reason being that for a number of years, Deaf people have maintained a sense of belonging to the community where sign language usage is a priority and where they are served by the good leadership of vigilant Deaf people who have carried forward the struggle for their human rights. Potential endangerment of USL or any sign language can occur if Deaf people do not come together and communicate on a regular basis. Contrary to spoken languages, these remain the most favorable conditions for the development of any sign language (Akach 1993, Serpell and Mbewe 1995, Woll, Sutton-Spence & Elton 2001).

3   The role of Deaf communities and language transmission

3.1   Acquisition of sign language and sources of exposure

Every child, hearing or deaf, has the capacity to acquire a full, natural language, provided the child is exposed to language input during the early years. However, sign language acquisition in deaf children varies from child to child because there is a great difference in parenting styles in the home environments of deaf children of Deaf parents and deaf children of hearing parents (Kyle and Woll 1993).

As noted by Meadow (1980, cited in Deucher 1984), the pattern of sign language acquisition will differ based on when it occurs – from birth, at school age or in adulthood. Language transmission within the family is possible only for deaf children of Deaf parents, who are blessed with early access to a full linguistic model and to Deaf cultural experiences (Baynton 1996, Wrigley 1997). In this way language maintenance is ensured via intergenerational transmission (Fishman 1991) in the typical way that is similar to that of spoken language communities.

A significant percentage of d/Deaf people are born into hearing families in Uganda (Lule 2001). Some hearing families raise between two to six deaf children (Mubangizi 2006, Nampala 2007). The incidence of deafness is caused mainly by illnesses such as meningitis, malaria, measles, chicken pox, mumps, as well as by genetic factors. In addition, there is evidence of a few identified cases of deaf children born into Deaf families (Iyute Deborah, personal communication, March 2008). In the former group, the problem is, of course, language incompatibility, where deaf children do not share the native (home) language spoken by the parents. Hence, the pattern of developing a language in hearing environments diverges greatly in these deaf children.

Acquisition of sign language during the early years is delayed in most deaf children as a result of the situation described above for children in a hearing environment. Many develop a gestural homesign system as a means of interactive communication with family members prior to formal education (Bonvillian & Folven 1993, Woll, Sutton-Spence & Elton 2001).[5] For many such deaf children with hearing parents, residential schools, also known as special schools for the deaf, form the foundation upon which USL, Deaf culture and a sense of belonging to the Deaf community develop. Sign language acquisition is passed down to the young deaf generation at school age through social interaction with older deaf peers. This, according to Parasnis (1998), is lateral transmission of culture (peer to peer), which differs from vertical transmission within families, which is at the center of mother tongue transmission where language is passed down from parent to child. A small number of Deaf adults working as role models to develop the sign language skills of deaf children in such schools also participate in vertical transmission, but outside the family.

At the national level, there are a few such special schools for the deaf in Uganda and two secondary schools for Deaf young people. Many Deaf people who have gone through such schools bond together as a community through USL, which offers a locus for group identity that allows for a shared means of communication and culture. The situation, however, is not homogeneous across the country as there are some places where such residential schools do not exist for economic and logistical reasons. Statistics show that more than forty districts in Uganda do not have even a unit for the Deaf (Iyute & Nkwangu 2007). Thus some deaf children and adults in rural communities are deprived of the right to access basic education. They remain at home, while others who are mainstreamed in the local schools suffer extreme isolation. In such circumstances a Deaf community does not develop because individuals lack the opportunity to associate with other Deaf children and adults (Pedersen 2004). Without such exposure, sign language acquisition is further delayed and language transmission endangered.

However, the process of learning sign language up to the level matching that of adults may continue in adulthood when such children join the adult Deaf community (Paul & Quigley 1984, Crystal 1987). Here there is a high degree and frequency of contact between Deaf persons who maintain USL fluency. Deaf communities provide centers where adult deaf learners acquire the culture and language from Deaf adult instructors who handle sign language courses.

Therefore, from the African perspective, the need for residential schools for deaf children and Deaf communities is of crucial importance to the language users. These serve as the main source for fostering language transmission, maintenance, dissemination and preservation from one generation to another. This is partly due to the fact that sign language plays the major part in developing Deaf identity.

3.2   Language contact

Language contact takes place in normal circumstances in multilingual societies, where most speakers who are in contact with each other share and borrow lexical and grammatical material from the languages surrounding them. Uganda is an example of a multilingual society with an ethno-linguistic diversity of at least forty-three languages representing the two major families, namely the Bantu and the Nilo-Saharan families.[6] The ethnologue database (1999) gives another figure of forty-seven languages but includes USL, English, Swahili, Gujarati and Hindi. This therefore means that sign language users have the potential to be multilingual themselves – in the national sign language, the majority national language and the

Figure 6.1 *ABUSE accompanied by the reduced mouth pattern 'vu' of the Luganda word* onvuma. *Palm forward O-handshape held upright in the front of body, moves sharply forward as fingers open repetitively.*

Figure 6.2 *VERY accompanied by the reduced mouth pattern 'nyo' of the Luganda word* nnyo. *Palm fist hand held in front of the body, sharply moves up and down repetitively.*

different indigenous spoken languages used by their hearing families and by those within their local vicinity.[7]

An individual's knowledge of the spoken languages will depend on the age of onset and degree of hearing loss as this can have a profound influence on communication, especially if one acquired speech during childhood prior to becoming deaf. To other members of Deaf communities, competence in these spoken languages depends in varying degrees on their job environment and social networks (Grosjean 1998) since Deaf people coexist with hearing people in different ways.

A few examples of USL signs appear in Figures 6.1–6.3; these were documented in research conducted recently that reflected the possibility of local spoken

Figure 6.3 *NOT-YET accompanied by the reduced mouth pattern 'bdo' of the Swahili word* bado. *Extended thumb makes small and quick side-to-side movements repetitively.*

languages influencing USL by means of mouthing as the consequence of language contact.

In addition, we need to focus on the educational environment that influences bilingual development in the young generation of sign language users. The majority have knowledge of USL and English (in its spoken, written or signed form) used as a medium of instruction in the Ugandan education system.[8] The educational settings of deaf children and young people show a preference for Signed English and the use of voice to teach the structure of English. This in turn has influenced the attitudes of Deaf young people toward the use of Signed English for the economic, employment, social and educational advantages attached to English as a majority and world language. This integration and deaf children's identification with the majority language is reinforced by hearing teachers who find it easier to use the English systems in schools.

Nevertheless, USL still has a role in social interaction among Deaf members. Depending on the educational level attained, the competency and fluency of spoken or written English vary greatly in individuals who are deaf. Therefore, multilingual experiences in Deaf individuals vary within Deaf communities in Uganda.

Similar to other sign languages, one of the consequences of the diffusion of spoken English is its influence on USL, which is seen in constant fingerspelling and mouthing among the young generation of sign language users. Fingerspelling is used quite a lot in the USL lexicon, and there are many initialized signs representing written English words using both the two-handed and one-handed alphabets (similar to British Sign Language and American Sign Language manual alphabets, respectively, but with minor adjustment to some letters).

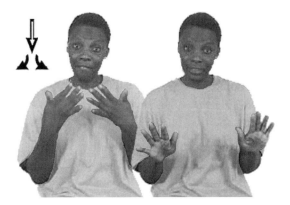

Figure 6.4 *FINISH accompanied by the reduced mouth pattern 'fsh' of the English word* finish. *Palms back spread hands held in front of the body, moves forward as hands flex backwards sharply from the wrists changing orientation to palms forward.*

Figure 6.5 *DEAF accompanied by the reduced mouth pattern 'df' of the English word* deaf. *Palm tips of extended index and middle fingers contact the right ear then move down to contact the lips.*

Mouthing (with voice or without) of spoken English mouth patterns appears to be shortened or reduced when accompanying the articulation of a sign; this is illustrated in Figures 6.4–6.5. Rarely do you find fingerspelling and mouthing patterns during interactive discourses used by the older generation or deaf people in rural areas, specifically those who did not have access to basic education.

3.3   Deaf people's attitude toward Uganda Sign Language

Historically, USL is known to have been influenced by American Sign Language (ASL) and other foreign sign languages such as British Sign Language (BSL) and

Kenyan Sign Language (KSL) in the past. This happened during the establishment of deaf education in Uganda where Church Missionary Society (CMS) teachers from the UK used BSL in the first schools of deaf children. ASL was introduced by two adult Deaf trained in Nigeria in ASL by the Deaf African American missionary Reverend Andrew Foster (Woll, Sutton-Spence & Elton 2001, Korbus, 2006, Wallin *et al.* 2006). The influence from KSL was a consequence of the fact that many Deaf adults moved to Kenya for higher education following the completion of their primary education. Deaf people by then considered the use of a foreign sign language more prestigious and advanced in status than the local sign language.

However, this attitude has changed with time as awareness of the advantages of developing a national sign language that binds signing communities geographically increased. Unlike in the past, today language consciousness and positive attitudes among the signing communities play a significant role in resisting the influence of foreign sign languages imposed on USL. Despite the influence, USL is an independent language that has adapted and assimilated some foreign sign lexical items after being in use for so long. Having said this, borrowing cannot be ruled out completely as one of the effects of language contact. Many new foreign lexical items still find their way into USL through this process. Fromkin and Rodman (1998) assert that this happens as society keeps on transforming. According to Aitchison (1991:117), a transforming society necessitates "language to alter as the needs of its users alter."

USL is widely used for social interaction among the large concentration of Deaf people living and working with hearing members of the wider society in the urban areas of Kampala, Jinja, Mbale, Mbarara, to mention a few. This is because USL is highly valued and seen as a symbol of identity. As a result, the strong signing community supports and encourages positive attitudes toward USL recognition locally, nationally and internationally, as it is being used among them and in a wide variety of settings. This is important because the survival of any language depends largely on the degree of interaction of its users. It should be noted, however, that a number of factors might influence the attitudes and views of Deaf people to switch between different communication modes – indigenous languages, Signed English or USL. These factors include the social environment, the persons being addressed and the topic of conversation.

Positive attitudes toward USL have also transformed some Deaf people (sign language teachers and researchers) into active participants who promote USL nationally. Indeed, the belief that Deaf people are the best teachers of USL has led some institutions and schools to employ Deaf sign language instructors and researchers to run sign language programs irrespective of whether they meet the standard qualification requirements. It is argued that qualifications remain a major hindrance to Deaf people in developing countries of Africa where educational achievement is lower. This explains why many Deaf instructors are paid less or fail to secure paid employment. Some Deaf instructors have broken this vicious circle, achieving high academic status after many years of dedication and developing competence in USL and English to varying degrees.

To conclude, a combination of external and internal factors sometimes results in imperfect language learning by young deaf people. This plays a central role in developing a view by Deaf people that their minority language is impoverished. These factors include the influence of foreigners, mobility of people within and between countries, and negative attitudes toward sign languages and their use. In many instances minority indigenous spoken languages in developing countries suffer the consequences of such factors. For example, many people in Uganda speak English well, but they cannot speak their local mother tongue languages. Parents attach high value to the idea of speaking a foreign language, such as English or French, to their children, even in the home, rather than the indigenous spoken languages.

3.4   Deaf association (national and local)

The UNAD was established in 1973 with the aim of fighting poverty, unemployment and social humiliation, though it is influenced by hearing people who started the Uganda Society for the Deaf (USD; Ndeezi & Ssendagire 1998).

A strong national association of Deaf people has existed since 1993 when Deaf people began to manage their activities themselves. The UNAD is affiliated to the World Federation of the Deaf (WFD), an international organization that advocates for the human rights of Deaf people worldwide. As an institution, the UNAD has played a salient role in protecting the transmission, usage and dissemination of USL by expanding to more districts throughout the country where more signers are found. Currently, UNAD is operational in forty-seven districts where District Deaf Associations (DDA) have been formed with the aim of bringing the services nearer to Deaf people in the rural areas[9] (UNAD 2004). The national and district associations advocate for improved fundamental human rights, as well for higher social and political status of Deaf people in society.

The fight that is now on is to implement strategies of sign language preservation in the future by demanding a USL policy (Oluoch 2006). This is UNAD's top priority if Deaf people are to achieve the Millennium Development Goals (Ndeezi 2006 cited by Oluoch 2006). It is hoped that the policy will receive the support and approval of the relevant lawmaking bodies to facilitate and enhance equal opportunities and fundamental linguistic rights.

The existence of other organized Deaf groups such as the Deaf women's group, sports group, youth group, the Silent Theatre (launched in 2004: Mbulamwana 2004b), and a strong Deaf church known as Immanuel Church of the Deaf provide a strong base for the growth of the Deaf community's consciousness (Okombo 1991). The groups mentioned help to maintain the use of USL through social activities shared by Deaf people and help to protect their culture. A network among Deaf people has been developed at both national and local levels.

4   Language and education

4.1   The history of deaf education

Education of the deaf plays an important role in the use, transmission and dissemination of USL. As mentioned earlier, it is the schools, Deaf communities and associations or groups, not the families, that promote and protect USL and its culture from generation to generation in terms of transmission. For years, the education of the d/Deaf in Uganda lagged behind because mainstreamed education for non-deaf children developed as early as 1898.

The idea of the need to educate deaf children was conceived in 1958 when the ENT surgeon Dr. Peter Rowland launched the USD and when other prominent Ugandans became closely involved in efforts to improve the situation of deaf people. As a result, the first school for the deaf known as the Uganda School for the Deaf, then located at Namirembe (south of Uganda's capital city Kampala), was founded. The school has since transferred to its present site at Ntinda, east of Kampala city. The British teachers from the CMS laid the foundation of deaf education in 1959. They were joined by the first trained Ugandan teacher of the deaf, Mrs. Julia B. M. Lule, upon her return from Britain. The second school – Ngora Regional School for the Deaf, Kumi – was established in 1969 in eastern Uganda. The Christoffel Blinden Mission (CBM) of Germany has funded and sustained these two schools to date.

In the past, most signers used to come from Ntinda and Ngora, but the trend has changed. There has been an increase in units/schools for the Deaf in Uganda due to an increased number of signers. The Bavarian Association of Germany, through Project Africa, has supported the development of St. Mark's School for the Deaf, Masaka. Other schools, such as the Nancy School for the Deaf, Lira, and the Kinyinya School for the Deaf, Kyaka, have been established with the technical assistance and support of international nongovernmental organizations and well-wishers from abroad.

As a consequence of the Milan Congress held in 1880, the education system adopted the oralist method imported into Uganda by CMS teachers. The introduction of the manual method in mid-1980 by Voluntary Services Overseas (VSO) teachers was mainly to reinforce the philosophy of Total Communication.

The educational services have been streamlined to a certain extent to address both deaf and hearing children so as to achieve education for all. Under the Education Act (1970), children with disabilities are entitled to educational training opportunities equal to other members of society. Since 1990, there has been some improvement in the educational opportunities for deaf children, though there are still gaps. Both the number of schools that are residential and units linked to mainstream schools have increased. In addition to these, deaf children are offered places in regular schools at different levels to utilize the available resources. More teachers are learning to sign, though they are not fluent in the grammar of USL. Employment of Deaf instructors in schools as linguistic models is an indication of increased recognition of USL. Regardless of the increased recognition of USL in education, there is no specific law/policy yet referring to the right of deaf children to learn USL as a preferred first language.

Teacher training for educators of the deaf was established in 1988 at a centralized institute of Special Needs Education known as the Uganda National Institute of Special Education (UNISE). The institute has since 2003 merged with the Institute of Teacher Education, Kyambogo, and the Uganda Polytechnic, Kyambogo, to form Kyambogo University. The institute specialized mainly in training teachers as well as other personnel working in the field of special needs education and the rehabilitation of learners who are deaf, hard of hearing, blind, and physically and learning disabled. However, the training has since been affected by the change in the curriculum in an attempt to realize Inclusive Education, one of the goals of the international Salamanca Statement (1994). Therefore, Uganda faces demands for more and better-qualified teachers of the deaf, armed with signing fluency and knowledge of Deaf culture in order to address the educational challenges and needs of deaf children.

4.2   The current educational situation of Deaf people

Even though the majority of deaf people remain uneducated in rural areas, a small percentage of deaf children have access to pre-primary (nursery), primary and higher levels of education – i.e., secondary, tertiary education and university. In order to support a sign language environment for preschool deaf children and encourage hearing parents to use USL to facilitate communication with their deaf children, early education has been provided in the form of playgroups for preschool deaf children alongside offering counseling services to hearing parents of deaf children. The current primary schools for deaf children have incorporated the nursery education program due to a lack of specialized preschools or kindergarten for deaf children. Nursery education is a stepping stone for deaf children into a bigger social world, especially for those who come from homes without the appropriate language, social and emotional skills. It provides a smooth link to the primary-level curriculum; however, challenges such as communication barriers, attitudinal barriers, lack of communication support services, and a high teacher–pupil ratio hinder the effective participation of deaf children in inclusive mainstream classes. Rarely do deaf children in mainstream classes get exposure to Deaf adults as linguistic models. The effective inclusion of deaf children still calls for increased planning so that their educational and communication needs can be met in mainstream schools.

A few Deaf young students take part in secondary education based on their academic capabilities, positive attitude and support from families. Prior to this, Deaf students accessed education in the neighboring country of Kenya. However, with the introduction of Universal Primary Education (UPE), the increased number of deaf children who lacked placement in secondary and vocational education after completing primary cycle (Mugenyi 2003) led to the recently established government-aided residential secondary schools for deaf young people. The two schools established at Wakiso in 2006 and Mbale in 2007 are the first schools to be built by the government since 1959 when education of the deaf commenced in the country. Deaf people took the lead by establishing the Makerere special secondary school for the Deaf, and they contributed toward its growth until the government took it over in 2004 and relocated it at Wakiso. Under the current Universal Secondary Education (USE) and training policy (2007), it is hoped that a good number of Deaf young people will benefit from secondary education.

The other kind of secondary education available for Deaf young people is a secondary Unit annexed to a mainstream secondary school, such as the one at Ngora High School in Eastern Uganda that has been operating since 1998 with sign language interpretation services. A few successful pioneering Deaf students have continued their higher education at university.

Provision of vocational education remains scanty in the country, with only one vocational center for young deaf students established in 1998. A good percentage of Deaf adults received vocational training in Kenya and within the rehabilitation centers for persons with disabilities at Kireka, Lweza and Ruti where they were equipped with electrical, carpentry, tailoring, building, farming, shoemaking, knitting and cooking skills.

The recent introduction of "affirmative action" (i.e., the desire to represent the proportion of students at the university according to their proportion in the general population) has led to an increase in the number of students with disabilities being admitted to public universities. Generally, institutions of higher learning (universities, colleges and technical schools) with sign language interpretation services have opened their doors to deaf students who meet the required academic qualifications. It is anticipated therefore that the number of Deaf professionals is likely to increase in the future.

In reality, access to education by d/Deaf children exists on a continuum of educational placements as mentioned, with interpreters being available in some classes but not in others. However, the right to information access in education is not regarded by many as a priority for Deaf students. They are discriminated against and denied equal opportunities in education, because currently the deaf child's families must meet interpreting costs on top of the tuition costs.

All in all, deaf education is a privilege for some Deaf children who attend established Deaf schools at primary, secondary and vocational levels. These schools for the Deaf have fostered the development of Deaf communities. The formation of Deaf culture and communities in developing countries tends to be stronger where schools for Deaf children exist, where being Deaf and the use of sign language plays a central role.

5   Sign language and Deaf communities in Ugandan society

5.1   Sign language courses

USL training has been at the core of UNAD'S activities to raise sign language awareness in society in order to eliminate communication barriers. As a result, society has developed mutual respect for Deaf people's language, culture and customs to a large extent. USL courses are part of the training programs for teachers, parents of deaf children, interpreters, interested hearing people and service providers in institutions. Likewise, UNAD has expanded the provision of sign language courses across different districts in the country to empower adult signers, parents of deaf children, service providers and interested hearing people. Significantly, there is increased and more widespread usage, preservation of USL and transmission of culture.

5.2   Sign language interpreters

Although USL is legally acknowledged, members of the Deaf communities are not offered adequate provision of sign language interpreter services. Communication support services through sign language interpreters enable the integration of Deaf people in society to access information and participate equally with the hearing people in all parts of life. However, the majority of Deaf people in rural areas barely has access to public information and is unable to participate in social life. There is formal professional education for sign language interpreters at the university level, established in 2002. As the number of qualified interpreters increases, access to information becomes available to Deaf people. Many interpreters working in the area of Kampala are self-employed, while others are employed staff of nongovernmental organizations, public institutions and universities as well as Parliament. Interpreters offer services in a variety of settings such as education, medical, politics, religion, office, meeting and conferences to improve Deaf people's access to information. Many service providers, though, are ignorant about the role of sign language interpreters in facilitating communication services. Nevertheless, the legal acknowledgment of USL in the Person with Disabilities Act 2006 supports further improvements for the integration of Deaf people living in the country.

5.3   Media and technology

The area of media and technology is still virgin territory in spite of the provision on disability under the Uganda Communication Act 1998; Act 8, part 11, section 8 that encourages, "the promotion of research into the development and use of new communications, techniques and technologies including those which promote accessibility of hearing impaired people to communication services" (Ndeezi 2004).

Few Deaf people in urban areas have access to timely interpretation services. News and weekly news summaries are available on two television stations introduced in 1998 and 2004 (Mbulamwana 2004c). Owing to lack of resources, daily sign language interpretation of the news has stopped; it has not been offered for over two years on Uganda Broadcasting Corporation (UBC), formerly Uganda Television (UTV), while many other programs for hearing people are left untouched (Ariko 2006, Mubangizi 2007). Therefore, Deaf people still miss out on vital information on politics and health issues, such HIV/Aids programs. It is not known how long it might take them to get better TV services.

Access to Internet use is limited to a few Deaf people with higher literacy levels who can work independently for personal communication and educative information since most online texts appears in written English. Similarly, accessing journals and newspapers, and the use of mobile phones for sending and receiving text messages benefit a small number of Deaf people fluent in written English.

It can be argued that Deaf people in Uganda still have a strong face-to-face tradition perhaps because the level of technology use appears to be lower than in developed Western countries. So far the communication technologies in place do not meet the visual communication needs of Deaf people. The use of advanced computer technology, video clips and DVD, for example, would not only immensely benefit Deaf adults, but also assist young deaf children in learning and using USL as they grow. In addition, it would serve as means of preserving USL for future generations since there is no recognized orthography for signed languages worldwide.

Likewise, a wide range of technology can be explored to improve the lives of D/deaf persons, such as subtitles, wire loop systems, hearing aids and flashing lights. The major challenge both D/deaf and hearing people face in developing countries is the poor economic status that hinders technological advances which would transform d/Deaf people's lives.

5.4 Societal attitudes toward sign language and Deaf communities

Fighting attitudinal change in the society has been the pivot of UNAD's activities, though still unsatisfactory. It is a pity that society still has the kind of negative perception that regards deafness as a "loss" and deaf people as "less than normal" members of the society. Deaf people are branded with discriminative titles like "deaf and dumb," "kasiru," "kiteta," "ebang" – i.e., different cultural equivalents to "deaf-mute" – considered to be politically incorrect terms to use (Mbulamwana 2005).

Rejection, neglect and isolation of deaf people in rural communities continue in Africa, denying them access to proper care and a productive quality of life. Many Ugandan cultures still view deafness as a result of misfortune, curses and witchcraft and do not easily accept and regard deaf persons as one of them.

In addition, the general attitude toward sign language among some hearing educators and hearing parents of deaf children is that it is still unacceptable. Some parents wish their deaf children to be integrated in the dominant hearing culture and acquire speech (that is, English, which is the majority language) rather than USL. The urge toward the strong identity with the majority language of the hearing culture resulted in Uganda's first cochlear implant surgery on a deafened adult being registered in March 2008.

Since the vast majority of deaf children have hearing parents, society may perceive cochlear implants as a good thing since the rationale is to make deaf people much like hearing people. Today, the cochlear implant is not felt as a threat to USL and Deaf culture in Uganda because it can benefit a certain category of hearing-impaired people. Further more, less than 0.4 percent of the Ugandan families can afford the cost of implant surgery and rehabilitation (Hon Alex Ndeezi, personal communication, April, 2008). Regardless of a modest, growing interest in cochlear implants, there are more hearing people learning and using USL and there is increased recognition and acceptance of USL in schools, on TV, on streets and in places of work in comparison with past years. These all reflect the societal attitudinal change toward sign language and Deaf communities. (Wallin *et al.* 2006).

6   Research on sign language and its dissemination

Attempts to develop USL through small-scale research were done by the UNAD and UNISE, which has led to the USL manuals. The first linguistic study into the structure of USL concentrated on variation in handshapes (Nyst 1999).

This was followed by a five-year (2001–2006) extensive linguistic research, which produced the recently published first edition of the *Uganda Sign Language Dictionary* (Wallin *et al.* 2006). It aimed at describing the structural aspects of USL, mainly concentrating on the phonological and morphological levels of analysis. This dictionary is important for Deaf communities in Uganda. It preserves the visual language and proves that USL is a language. Having the dictionary published on the Internet, CD-ROM and DVD is the next future task subject to financial support.[10]

7   Conclusion and future research

This chapter has outlined the situation of sign transmission in Uganda, examining how the image of USL has been enhanced in society over a relatively recent period under a supportive political situation. This situation, however, is not representative of other African countries. Deaf people still face a lot of challenges and are struggling to achieve political support to have sign languages recognized. This is important in order to develop self-esteem and a sense of identity. Deaf people need to know that they are Deaf in order to use sign language freely in society. Acceptance and recognition of sign languages facilitate the growth of Deaf communities, which further creates a political strength within which the language, culture, values and customs are shared, maintained, preserved and protected.

The lack of Deaf identity means continued oppression of minority sign languages, since society at large will deny Deaf people their language and the opportunity to use it. Oppression of Deaf people and their language are potential dangers to the growth of Deaf communities. Living in isolation with a lack of opportunity to communicate on a regular basis puts sign languages at great risk. Deaf people need to be supported to maintain and foster the development of sign language and Deaf culture and community. Therefore further research into sign transmission, dissemination and preservation are critical activities that need to be undertaken if minority sign languages are to survive across African countries.

7

Transmission of Polish
sign systems

Piotr Wojda

1 Introduction

This chapter will discuss the overall context in Poland in which "non hearing"[1] persons live and work, and also the modes of transmission of sign systems in Poland, including what will be referred to as the natural variety of Polish Sign Language (PJM, polski jezyk migowy), which has arisen organically from interactions from within this community. The goal of this chapter is to bring forth the specificity of the Polish condition and its dilemmas.

Non-hearing persons living in Poland constitute a unique community worthy of its own description and examination. They are a diverse group, both in terms of their functional language performance as well as their various social properties. Unfortunately, broad conclusions about the deaf community are often drawn from singular phenomenon, small non-representative samples, or even individual cases. The conclusions derived in such a matter can be quite harmful, for "individual features cannot be representative of a collective" (Babiński 1998:13); they can only be characteristic of a specific number or group of people.

The assessment of "non-hearing" environments in Poland is typically based on data derived from pedagogical and applied linguistics research, which tends to focus more on spoken rather than signed language. Moreover, scholarly works about this community tends to focus on practical applications for the education of non-hearing persons, and there is more attention on deaf education (*surdo*-pedagogy) rather than on deaf studies (*surdo*-logy). Educational concerns raise many sociolinguistic and socioeconomic issues pertaining to the deaf, and in the end, all of these elements allow for diversity among non-hearing groups, which might be an indication that life experiences and reflections are now part of an ongoing positive intellectual exchange (Perlin and Szczepankowski 1992; Perlin 1993; Krakowiak 1998, 2003; Świdziński 1998; Świdziński & Czajkowska-Kisil 1998; Szczepankowski 1999; Wojda 1999, 2000, 2001; Tomaszewski & Rosik 2002).

In light of these introductory remarks and despite some of the already existing characterizations within the literature, a linguistic and socio-educational description of non-hearing persons living in Poland and the transmission of their language will be provided. The goal is not to put forth any hypothesis that would lead to a scientific proof that Polish non-hearing persons constitute an ethnic minority. Instead, ethnological reflection on some social aspects of the non-hearing community seems necessary, because it will help to reveal its particular elements, especially its quasi-cultural and linguistic issues. Also, it will help to verify Hendzla's thesis presented in the *Polish Exact Sign Language Dictionary*, which states that "sign language is also a general concept that includes various sign systems which function among non-hearing persons in Poland" (1986:14). The goal is to present the complexity of the sign systems, their transmission in Poland, to draw out their diversity, and to assess their impact on the educational process of non-hearing individuals and the transmission of these systems across generations. Therefore, I will attempt to first present a typology of sign systems existing in Poland, delineating their genesis as well as their characteristics and applications in education (section 2). These elements will then be linked to the aspects of social functioning and awareness as they relate to the "non-hearing" community membership and identity (section 3). Finally the issue of transmission of PJM and other Polish sign systems will be directly addressed. All of these facets of the language situation within the Polish non-hearing community have a profound impact on the transmission and survival of PJM.

2   Types of sign systems and education

Based on their origin and structure, the Polish sign systems can be organized into three types of languages: *natural* (Polish Sign Language, PJM), *mixed* (Sign Pidgins and Creoles Sign Languages) and *artificial systems* also known as Polish Exact Sign Language with its two types: SJM (Speech and Gesture) and JM (Gesture) (Perlin 1993, Kobosko, Szuchnik & Wojda 2004).

Historically, the tradition of non-hearing education in Poland reaches back to the 1700s (Wojda 2001). However, it should not be assumed that this history is limited to only two centuries. Adamiec (2003) notes that it is not clear how far one would have to reach into the historical record to find the origins of the modern sign languages. In Poland, the creation of the first school for non-hearing children, the Deaf and Mute Institute (Instytut Głuchoniemych), in Warsaw during 1817, was a significant moment in the establishment of PJM. Jakub Falkowski (1774–1848), a priest and the institute's founder, favored the sign method in teaching non-hearing students (Szczepankowski 1999). The other schools, which were later established during Poland's partition by Russia, Austria and Germany, each developed regional differences in their sign languages. Today, these differences have diminished because of the social and recreational interactions among non-hearing persons (Szczepankowski 1999).

However, one can still speak of regional sign language varieties of Silesia, Wielkopolska and Pomorze. In many instances, these broader geographically based categorizations could further be broken down into sign languages endemic of large cities and their vicinities. For example, one could examine the sign language varieties of Katowice, Poznań, Wrocław, Szczecin, Warsaw, Łódź, or Lublin. Yet, these regional differences are weakening and the few indications of their presence can be typically detected only among the older generations of non-hearing people. Technological developments and the ability to communicate via Internet have allowed for increased integration within the non-hearing community. In a sense, a centralizing effect has taken place, in which the regional variations are abandoned in favor of adapting the sign language prevalent in the Warsaw region.

2.1   Polish Sign Language (PJM)

For many years, PJM was referred to as the natural, classical or traditional sign language. In more extreme instances, it was labeled as primitive or deaf and mute (*głuchoniemski*) (Wojda 1999). This "primitive" notion of the sign language was often contrasted with the "cultured"[2] sign language, in which signs accompany the spoken Polish language (see below SJM and JM). However, this bimodal approach failed to gain much traction due to its biases and simplification in depicting the complexities of the sign language both ontologically and sociolinguistically.

Written by two priests, Józef Hollak and Teofil Jagodziński, *The Sign Dictionary for the Deaf as well as Persons who Come in Contact with Them* (1879, *Słownik mimiczny dla głuchoniemych i osób z nimi styczność majacych*) is the first characterization of PJM and its grammar. Most notably, this first volume recorded significantly more gestures and facial expressions then any of the contemporary sign language dictionaries. For instance, *Polish Sign Language Dictionary* (*Słownik polskiego jezyka migowego*) edited by J. Hendzel (1986) contains only 2,138 signs as compared to around 10,000 signs in Hollak and Jagodziński's work. In the new editions, the number of signs has increased, yet the newer work remains rather poor in lexical and etymological detail (compared to, for example, Wojda 2005) due to the lexical unification of the Polish Deaf Association (PZG, Polski Zwiazek Głuchych). Based on common features, the signs from various regions, which relate more or less to the same designator, are narrowed down to a single sign and deemed as "proper" both in use and application.[3] However, the larger tension arises from the assumption that sign language varieties ought to support spoken languages, an idea that is difficult to accept since they are two incompatible and semantically different linguistic systems.

In the last decade, PJM became the subject of research in a few Polish universities. The bulk of the work is conducted at Warsaw University's Polish Language Institute and Warsaw's Institute for the Deaf. The main research goals focus on providing a grammatical description of PJM. Also, the Catholic University of Lublin continues to do research as well but focuses on the communication of people with speech and hearing disorders.

The study of the genesis of PJM should begin with the individual attempts at gesturing and facial expressions in persons who never spoke or heard. Also in some instances, it might be worth analyzing the systems of individuals who did not hear but knew the spoken language, for they acquired it before the loss of hearing. The formation of these systems can only be interpreted as the great need for communication. In the early stages, the sign codes were rather basic and limited in use to the individual non-hearing persons and a few hearing people who interacted with them (similar to "homesign" systems). There were no common sign languages as there are today. If such a situation persisted, the created sign languages would most likely perish with the passing of the individual persons using them. However, the facial and gesture expressions continued to develop as non-hearing people began to interact with each other, giving their individual signs more conventional meanings. The signs were transformed into the occasional signs shared and understood by two or more people through the mutual processing of images and activities. These newly established signs were then passed from generation to generation, gaining both a standardized meaning and a broader use with each transmission (Krakowiak 1998; Wojda 2001). Thus, it can be argued that an isolated individual with a hearing disability would not be able to create a sign language (Wojda 2001), which would imply that the sign language could only arise, develop and function within a non-hearing community such as a family or a school.

2.2   Artificial sign systems

In an effort to teach a person who cannot hear a spoken language, systems using signs superimposed on the spoken language sequence have been created. Such a system is classified as an artificial language or the so-called "language surrogate" or "language hybrid" since it consciously combines elements of two different languages. In this case, the spoken language is supplemented with signs forming a hybrid speech and gestural system, in Poland commonly known as the Speech and Signed System (SJM; system jezykowo-migowy) or Signed System (JM, jezyk migany). Both of these systems bare close resemblance to the well-known codified systems, such as those in the United States, called Seeing Exact English (SEE) or a "sign-supported speech" type of system.

The first attempts at creating hybrid systems can be found in Abbé Charles-Michel de l'Épée's (1712–1789) methodical signs. This concept also reached Poland, and its origins can be traced to a particular group of non-hearing people who were fluent in the Polish spoken language and began to use signs along with speech (i.e., sign-supported speech). This form of communicating has become a subject of in-depth analysis, leading to its application in Polish deaf education. Szczepankowski (1999) has outlined and described these artificial hybrid systems. Due to their artificial construction, they can be easily be catalogued in a dictionary, and rules of usage can be precisely stated because they are prescriptive rather than descriptive. Currently in Poland, hearing people and a small number of non-hearing people use this type of system. A special unifying committee of PZG is in charge of defining and describing the signs of this artificial language.

From the theoretical perspective, SJM and JM should be categorized as *speech and gesture hybrids*. They are distinguished by the following four elements (Perlin 1993, Kobosko, Szuchnik & Wojda 2004):

> *Signs* – Perlin (1993) and Szczepankowski (2001) define them as ideographs or ideographic signs. They are taken from PJM or are artificially created. They also must be approved by the Polish Deaf Association.
>
> *Polish manual alphabet* – an illustration of Polish morphemes.
>
> *Polish spoken language order* – a way of situating words with respect to time; the word order affects the linear composition of an utterance and should be distinguished from the syntax rules which govern how smaller units (simple words) are combined to create complex meanings based on their intended function.
>
> *Act of speaking* – an integral part of speech, which consist of *language*, *text* and *understanding* (Milewski 1993).

These elements can occur in different combinations, creating variations of these systems. The grammatical non-manual features of PJM are not included in these systems. The execution of these elements is always parallel, meaning that one timeline carries Polish spoken language while the other, parallel timeline, contains sign language signs and manual alphabet forms. Theoretically, this parallelism allows for four different such systems – two "complete" versions and the practical versions that are more commonly used in day-to-day communication.

Owing to a lack of a clear definition of PJM, SJM and JM for many years were considered as "grammatical and cultured" types of PJM. PJM was often confused with the artificial systems, which culminated in Perlin's (1993) unsuccessful attempt at their linguistic description. While his attempt was to present PJM, he ultimately showcased the artificial hybrid systems. The relative popularity of SJM and JM largely resulted from the preconceived notion that these systems were the best and most cultured ways of communicating between the hearing and non-hearing worlds since they most closely resembled normal speech communication. For a while now, SJM has been used as a tool in propagating bilingual education (Szczepankowski 1999). In the initial stages, this notion had a considerable impact on the education policy. The aim was to introduce at least some elements of the sign language to non-hearing (deaf and Deaf) education with an intention that it would gradually change attitudes about deaf studies in Poland (*surdo*-logy) and make hearing people aware that there are others who do not exclusively use the spoken language. With oralism as a predominant method of deaf education in post-World War II Poland, the language hybrids were received enthusiastically in the deaf education centers. With the support of institutions (e.g. PZG) and instructors who work with non-hearing students, SJM is still the primary tool in teaching spoken language in many residential schools. Yet despite increasing criticism, there still is no research evaluating the effectiveness of this approach. It is widely known that the language hybrids were created for purposes of "normalization" and "assimilation." The assumption that signs correspond with spoken words and can be used simultaneously was to aid non-hearing children in learning the spoken language. The prevalence of the hybrid systems remains strong and is especially noticeable on Polish television, where all the programs are translated from Polish into SJM, rather than PJM. Only non-hearing viewers who have a good command of Polish as a spoken language and have mastered lipreading can understand these broadcasts.

2.3   Polish Sign Language Pidgins (or "contact" varieties)

With only a few works in this area (Kobosko, Szuchnik & Wojda 2004; Tomaszewski & Rosik 2002), the subject of sign pidgins is relatively understudied in Poland.[4] Within these semi-artificial language varieties, there occur two fragmentary language expressions with one superimposed upon the other: spoken and signed. The two languages often interact and mix with each other on grammatical and word levels, transforming themselves into new varieties that do not fully resemble either spoken Polish or PJM. Also, brand new elements appear that are not found in either language. The use of these elements is not preplanned as in the case of artificial sign systems, such as SJM or JM, the "ideal" and the "practical" versions of the Speech and Gesture systems, respectively. In some instances, the structure of these pidgin-system sign utterances tends to be short, simplified in grammar and limited in vocabulary. In others, it can be complex and quite sophisticated.

Two types of pidgins can be distinguished in Poland, those employed by non-hearing and those employed by hearing users. The first type emerges when sign utterances typical of PJM are intentionally transformed into a Polish sign pidgin, in this case, primarily by non-hearing users. In this instance, the signs are produced in a sequence similar to Polish and are contingent on the signer's spoken language competence. Depending on the person's ability, speech also accompanies the signing. Some users employ only the signs which they can easily translate into the spoken language. When they are unsure of some signs' meaning, they use finger-spelling. If a non-hearing person is well experienced in both languages, then he or she can "code switch," which consists of a continual shifting between two languages for either short or long passages. However, if a deaf person does not know PJM very well, the sign pidgin itself becomes a form of everyday communication. This is a less conscious process. A non-hearing person can use the two languages, but in doing so at the same time they both have an incomplete grammar, making a non-hearing person a semi-lingual user.

The second type of pidgin is created among hearing persons as a result of interacting with non-hearing people; this also constitutes an interesting phenomenon. A hearing person who does not sign well will tend to model sign communication of a non-hearing person who will most likely not be a PJM user. From general observation, there emerge two subtypes of pidgins that hearing people construct and use. On one hand, when constructing pidgins, they model them on the spoken language structure, using mouthed spoken utterances along with signs. Occurring less frequently, this practice tends to resemble artificial sign systems (e.g., SJM, JM), except it uses individual signs or even entire phrases from PJM. On the other hand, a hearing person more familiar with a sign language may borrow some typical sign structures and use them to communicate with non-hearing individuals. In this instance, the hearing signer tends to use grammatical sign forms, articulating each sign with its proper verbal equivalent. This practice tends to happen most often in the residential schools for non-hearing people.

In summary, among all these various forms of communication, PJM, the one most resistant to outside influences, has become somewhat lost. It could be successfully used in bilingual education in Poland, yet despite increasing work on the subject of PJM, it is still difficult to clearly define what it is among all the variations of the sign systems. Moreover, difficulties with description make it difficult to decide which type of sign system a particular person is using and when it is being used. Such a task requires knowledge, experience, as well as linguistic expertise.

This situation tends to diminish the educational achievements and social status of non-hearing individuals and creates a dangerous relativism and pluralism of opinion, which shapes perceptions about non-hearing people as a social group. Attempts at implementing bilingual and bicultural education are made by (among others) the Deaf and Mute Institute in Warsaw. These efforts, however, are only in the early stages, which primarily focus on the study of the written form of the Polish spoken language and the simultaneous usage of PJM. As a result of common stereotypes about the Deaf, the bilingual education model still faces resistance as it is slowly introduced into the policies concerning deaf education in Poland.

3   Social aspects

In Poland, the number of people with hearing disorders reaches almost 1.5 million, yet it is estimated that the group directly influenced by the "stigma" of the sign language accounts for approximately 50,000 individuals. Yet, the quantitative approaches to this phenomenon seem insufficient, for it would be difficult or "practically impossible" to indicate the exact number of people afflicted with deafness (Szczepankowski 1999:44). Perhaps it would be more beneficial to estimate the size of this population using the readily available and reliable rehabilitation and treatment data from various institutions. Also, as a person's level of hearing loss decreases, the information about particular non-hearing individuals becomes increasingly difficult to obtain. Those with lesser hearing loss tend to integrate themselves with the hearing population and live out most of their lives outside of the exclusively non-hearing environment. Others with more severe hearing loss become a part of the non-hearing community, which is often stigmatized based on its disability status. Their group membership is often marked through such formal elements as membership in non-hearing (deaf and Deaf) organizations or ability to benefit from tax allowances for the disabled. Subsequently, looking at the internal social structure of the community with a hearing loss would allow us to determine the cultural diversity of a particular group within that community as well as that of a broader non-hearing landscape.

Relying mainly on the level of hearing loss, many authors try to categorize non-hearing people into various qualitative categories, yet their groupings often neglect the population's "ethnic" characteristics. Audiometrical classifications (e.g., BIAP – Bureau International d'Audiophonologie), which represent a purely medical approach, are quite unsatisfactory. Pedagogical methods (e.g., Gallaudet's descriptive scale) which rely on the evaluation of communicative abilities with the use of technological devices seem a bit more appropriate. Descriptions from the discipline of speech pathology that carry information about the extent of hearing loss as expressed in decibels, the level of speech comprehension with the help of hearing aids (Kirejczyk 1967, Szczepankowski 1973), the ability to acquire speech (see Szczepankowski 1999) or lip-reading skills (Gałkowski, Kunicka-Kaiser, & Smoleńska 1976) may be employed. The work of Grzegorzewska (1964), Hoffmann (1979) and Nurowski (1983) presents some cognitive and socio-logical considerations and aspects, which are more solid and precise. Krakowiak (2006) offers a complex classification, specifying 107 types of hearing damages grouped into five different categories, and scientific and technological advancements continually provide new developments in the field of hearing aids technology (Szczepankowski 1999, Skarżyński 2004), that make talking about people with a complete hearing loss impossible (Krakowiak 1995) and the term "deaf" meaningless. Yet, the richness of these categories still leaves the question *Who then is considered deaf/Deaf in Poland?*, unanswered. It is not just the regional variations or the diachronic changes within PJM that influence the structure and the social and educational qualities of the sign language, but also society's attitudes towards Deaf people, which in turn are closely related to the social identity formation of non-hearing people in Poland.

The social identity (or perhaps ethnic/cultural identity) of a non-hearing person can often be determined through self-identification, yet the subjective responses will be heavily dependent on asking the appropriate question, something that is not easily accomplished in PJM. The challenge lies in accurately interpreting the solicited response in regard to a person's primary identity. The structure of questions formed in PJM has a specific strategy and requires the use of an exact predicate: "BELONG." The subjective elements and self-identification are often sufficient to determine the social group membership of a non-hearing person. That said, the Deaf community covers a broad landscape of ethnicities. As there are hearing Poles and hearing Gypsies, there are also non-hearing Poles and non-hearing Gypsies. The issue of the objective group identity formation and the role of group consciousness within that process then becomes of primary interest. My own observations would indicate that non-hearing individuals do not deny their Polish nationality, assuming that they were previously informed of their national membership. Similarly, deaf people must become aware of their Deafness and realize that the language they use is different from the official Polish spoken language. These phenomena must be explicitly conveyed to a non-hearing person who is not born with a sense of one's "otherness." Thus, it is not completely known how the Polish Deaf community perceives itself, and if it considers itself an ethnic minority.

Szczepankowski (1999:176) notes that "hearing-impaired persons consciously create their own history, culture, art and social structure." Their cultural originality manifests itself through their active participation in cultural activity, including dance, painting, graphic art, sculpture, pantomime, sign-theatre, film and even literature (see Szczepankowski 1999). Following Padden and Humphries's (1988) comments that American Sign Language (ASL) is a distinguishable element of Deaf culture and is a factor in cultural integration, some scholars (Świdziński 1998, Czajkowska-Kisil 2005) apply the same approach to the Polish context. Szczepankowski (1999) claims that Deaf people form a "language minority." According to the cultural approach in Poland, the "natural" environment for Deaf people is the Deaf community that is culturally defined by its sign language (Świdziński 1998, Świdziński & Czajkowska-Kisil 1998, Szczepankowski 1999, Tomaszewski & Rosik 2002).

   Grabias (Krakowiak 1998) suggests "that the Deaf community is a 'language minority' and that it is entitled to the same rights as any minority of that type seems to be a myth." Continuing, he concludes that "each 'language minority'" is usually a bilingual group. Krakowiak (1998:14) claims that "PJM or any sign language is capable of matching a spoken language, both as a cognitive tool and as means of social communication" but also "to a large extent sign language in Poland can be considered natural ..., and yet the collectivities which form and use it lack cultural autonomy" (p. 56). To be recognized as a language minority, a social group must be culturally autonomous. Yet the language autonomy of the Deaf is a complex phenomenon, and it would be inappropriate to consider them an ethnic group, even in the United States where the organizational and educational level of the Deaf is the highest (Krakowiak 1998). And while PJM has been recently widely discussed (Świdziński 1998; Tomaszewski & Rosik 2002; Wojda 2006, 2005), its autonomy is still under consideration (Krakowiak 1998, 1995; Wojda 2000).

   Two aspects of this argument are worth further deliberation. First, perhaps it is an accurate statement that within the contours of American society, the Deaf form a social and cultural minority if not an ethnic minority, and this might be the reason why the promotion of "Deaf culture" is so widely accepted. As the title of the book, *Deaf in America: Voices from a Culture* (Padden & Humphries 1988) suggests, the voices of the Deaf Americans are emerging from a cultural community of the type that has simultaneously produced and sustained all other *homo sapiens*. The sign language user helps to shape that culture as much as he or she is shaped by it. Sign language is a product of human creative activity. It can present new cultures, relay cultural values, be a way of exchanging experiences, as well as being a source of inspiration for cultural transformations. Krakowiak (1998) notes that a sign language is an example of an impressive and delicate cultural artifact worthy of attention and preservation. It is the Deaf person's contribution to overall human culture (Wojda 2000).

Second, it is important to consider whether Deaf Poles – children, youth and adults – think of themselves as having a distinct culture, and if so, are they aware of its symbolic character? The popular literature written in Polish provides us with reports on notable non-hearing persons, for example, Stanisław Chraca, a dancer and a glass painter, or the painters Epifaniusz Drowniak and Jarosław Orłowski (see Szczepankowski 1999). These individuals deserve particular recognition for popularizing the important cultural and historic events of non-hearing people in their work, which help to shape and increase awareness of the symbolic and cultural Deaf context for non-hearing and hearing people alike. The Deaf cultural context is deeply immersed in a world where most of the values are derived from the surrounding spoken language community (Wojda 2000). Thus we cannot speak of distinct religious practices, corresponding cultural symbols, celebrations and rites which find their origin in sign language.

It is also worth examining the self-awareness of non-hearing people with respect to the notion of Deaf as "other," specifically, the relationship of non-hearing communities to other social groups. This relationship does not exclusively capture only the hearing vs. non-hearing dichotomy, but it can also occur among various communities of people with hearing disorders, for instance, those who do not fall into the category of "culturally Deaf." Individuals who have captured the general public's attention come from various non-hearing groups and may include those who are functionally hearing, hard of hearing, and hearing-impaired, and consider a spoken language to be their first language. This presents a paradox, because people who are completely or nearly completely competent in Polish can easily derive information from written texts. They may even be able to access English language literature that promotes "Deaf culture." Overall, this group creates an impression of having the most active and well-informed members in the Deaf community, becoming the quintessential Deaf group against which all other Deaf groups are assessed. Furthermore, some of the representatives of this group who currently are non-hearing might at some point have possessed some hearing ability which would have allowed them to access the spoken language more easily. So on one hand, the basis of the success of such individuals is derived from being raised in the oral tradition, which does not encourage others to become a part of the Deaf culture. And on the other hand, there emerges a necessity for non-hearing people to distinguish themselves from the hearing world.

4 Transmission of PJM

The transmission of sign language through various teaching practices is strongly associated with several factors that have a profound impact on the use of PJM and other forms of sign systems by various groups in Poland, both hearing and non-hearing. Some are formalized institutional factors and some informal factors. The most important issues are the type of "sign language" taught and who teaches the classes. Both PZG and Polish universities have had a strong impact on the institutionalized forms of sign language teaching. A brief description of these influences paints a very complex reality in the area of sign language teaching.

The PZG has been in charge of teaching sign language courses for hearing persons since the first course that was taught in 1961, and the PZG was the first organization which contributed to the popularization of sign language. The first class was composed of hearing employees of the Social Services Agency for Handicapped Persons. In February 1964, S. Siła-Nowicki and B. Szczepankowski (a deaf person) organized the first sign language course for sign language lecturers. In 1966 the first handbook of basic sign language was published, which was in fact the description of the complete version of SJM or JM.

The year 1985 was the turning point for deaf education, when the Department of Education agreed to use sign language as a tool for the non-hearing. At the same time the PZG had begun training the teachers, particularly those teachers who taught at the residential schools. The first sign language courses for teaching personnel began in 1986, at which time didactic materials for teaching sign language were financed by the Department of National Education (MEN). Thanks to this initiative, three sign language handbooks were published by WSiP Press (School and Pedagogical Press): *The Basis of Sign Language* (Szczepankowski 1988), *Sign Language for Educators* (Pietrzak 1992), *Sign Language at School and Boarding-School* (Prałat-Pyrzewicz & Bajewska 1994), along with 115 short didactic films for learning sign language (Szczepankowski 1999:164).

The first organized movement to teach sign language (described above) actually pathologized it, and it had serious consequences for users of this language because the primary form taught was SJM rather than PJM. "Sign language in its classic aspect [PJM] is exceptionally difficult to learn, both actively and passively" (Szczepankowski 1999:162). This statement presents the challenges of teaching for PJM as insurmountable, and this was the main reason why the participants of these early courses learnt SJM, demonstrating signs and sound speech simultaneously. This notion of choosing to teach SJM rather than PJM also reinforced the notion that "sign language" presupposed a variety of sign systems of communication. PJM was somewhere lost and treated as primitive, *głuchoniemski* (deaf and mute) variety. Graduates of SJM courses became a population of SJM signers, but they might not necessarily understand the signs produced by deaf people. This had and in fact still has enormous influence on deaf education in Poland. This trend in teaching SJM by the PZG put in place a system that closed for many years the possibility of developing a different educational approach. Now there are whole generations of non-hearing people in Poland who have been educated using this approach, and the traces of SJM remain in their signing. The postwar Soviet system was also highly in favor of artificial systems that included the structures of Polish; however, I do not wish to put too much emphasis on the political climate. Special education in Poland has always been treated more marginally, and general attitudes beyond those of the political environment are very important as well.

Hearing users of SJM are currently sign language instructors of these SJM courses – teachers of deaf children and youth, hearing children having deaf parents (CODAs), and even the priests of the deaf. These courses occur throughout the three-degree system in Poland. Some CODAs use PJM fluently and, despite the fact that they are licensed instructors, they do not participate in disseminating the idea of SJM.

The second organized movement to teach sign language is usually independent from the training activity of the PZG. It is that of post-secondary institutions, such as universities or other technical high schools in Poland. SJM is generally the variety taught, and instructors include both hearing and deaf persons that are often not licensed by PZG. Therefore, there is a wider range of sign language communication competence among these instructors. The particular research interests of these post-secondary institutions vary widely, and these interests can also play a role in the choice of sign system that is taught .

The PZG has recently become more interested in PJM, and since the 1990s, it has begun to soften its goal to make the Polish deaf more Polish. It has begun to show more acceptance of the possibility of deaf identity, and even the idea of bilingual and bicultural education is much more appreciated. This change has occurred at some universities as well (the Catholic University of Lublin and Warsaw University). As a consequence, although SJM is still taught at many residential schools, there are also some schools where PJM is taught by competent teachers.

It is very important to point out that institutionalized forms are mostly linked to the area of teaching signs, while non-institutionalized forms usually show how the sign language in different types could be acquired. The reality shows that all of it is, in fact, mixed now, and even if sometimes intellectual recognition of PJM as the system of primary importance seems to have been achieved, the final result in practice is that we still need to approach the use and teaching of it as a complex phenomenon. Higher standards for instructors and instruction are seriously needed.

On the positive side it does not appear that PJM is completely pathologized. Acceptance of being deaf and discovering that PJM is a valuable language has brought power to the Deaf community. Some deaf people become teachers of the deaf at residential schools or sign language teachers at post-secondary institutions and are able to bring much more awareness of "non-hearing" people to mainstream environments than ever before. And, thanks to sports and athletics clubs, clubs affiliated with the PZG and social gatherings after church services, deaf persons have cultivated PJM. Sign conversations via webcam also deepen the knowledge of PJM by the deaf themselves. But, while interactions among the deaf or between deaf and hearing individuals play some role in furthering the awareness of PJM, the sources of knowledge about sign language are the collective consciousness of residential schools, sports and athletics clubs or social clubs for the deaf. Yet, in spite of their great importance, these sites do not often enough make deaf people feel very proud of being users of PJM, because the reality of signing seems so obvious for deaf people that it is often taken for granted rather than becoming the object of fascination. More resources are needed (always) and it would be best if the tiny number of knowledgeable Deaf were more influential, but first and foremost the Deaf should have more faith in what they do and how they do it, and under-stand that change can take a long time. The Deaf are responsible for their future, and they should understand the process of change in which they are participating.

5   Conclusion

Currently in Poland, there is a lack of innovative solutions that could bring the non-hearing and hearing communities together, and the available options seem inadequate in the face of new challenges. The selection of a "right" type of communication with non-hearing persons still presents a dilemma (Kobosko 1999; Wojda 1999; Szczepankowski 1999, 2001). Despite many changes in Poland, the platitude "to speak or to sign" remains. It emerges from two main and opposing approaches to non-hearing education. One of the approaches relies on a priori solutions and treats all non-hearing persons in Poland as "culturally Deaf" (Świdziński & Czajkowska-Kisil 1998, Tomaszewski 2005). It promotes bilingual and bicultural education with the use of PJM as a new and primary way to educate non-hearing people and overcome "pathologizing" attitudes towards the Deaf (Czajkowska-Kisil 2005, Tomaszewski 2005). Interestingly, this approach tends to marginalize important trends in the spoken language education, treating it merely as a written form of a spoken language. Moreover, it seems to offer non-hearing Poles a predetermined lifestyle that centers around cultivating one's own "silent culture" as the only alternative. As Krakowiak (2006:259) notes, "in Poland, many non-hearing people are left to themselves upon birth, silent and illiterate (…), only the hard-of-hearing individuals and the few 'lucky ones' who mastered the spoken language can voice their opinions and speak out on behalf of all deaf people." In the search for knowledge about the "human as a *homo loquens*," "deaf education is in need of syntheses that will facilitate the application of that knowledge" (Krakowiak 2004:4) since there are still difficulties in teaching non-hearing persons the spoken language (Krakowiak 1995, 1998). For the basics of bilingual education, Krakowiak (2003) points to the presence of several unresolved issues that can only be clarified through neurobiological, neurological or psycho-linguistic research. Moreover, non-hearing people themselves realize the difficulty of mastering the spoken language and try to acquire it with great determination (see Krakowiak, Muzyka & Wojda 2002). The instances of Deaf parents wanting to raise their Deaf children using only a sign language are quite rare. From an early age, they incorporate the elements of spoken language into verbal transmission, even if only through the use of manual alphabet. Often, it is a hearing grandmother that is the primary caretaker (Wojda 2000, Tywonek 2006), and furthermore, the hearing parents of deaf children are reluctant to employ sign language as the solitary way of communicating. Attempts to incorporate sign language into the family typically tend to foster the creation of new sign systems such as contact varieties, SJM, or JM.

The structure of spoken Polish further exacerbates the issue of access to the spoken language. As a heavily inflected language, it poses a great challenge to any one who wishes to learn it, even in the most perfunctory manner. This complexity tends to breed difficulties in social interaction between hearing and non-hearing individuals. With this increased interaction, it seems inappropriate to accept a thesis that all non-hearing people are part of some specific and socially distin-guished Deaf culture. As a matter of fact, many of them are not aware of having such a possibility. At the same time, most of the social, cultural, political, scientific or religious aspects of life arise in the surrounding spoken language community, a world to which non-hearing people still have limited access.

The skepticism revealed here has a methodological character; that is, by refrain-ing from identifying a single solution, its aim is to foster a pluralistic array of perspectives relative to non-hearing Poles regarding their deafness.

The situation of non-hearing individuals in Poland remains undefined and some-what ambiguous. To sum up, here are some concluding remarks about PJM language transmission and preservation:

1. The scientific achievements of the past decade in the area of research of deaf studies have significantly contributed to increased interest in the Deaf as a social group. Although methodologically accurate, the scientific approaches lead to various conclusions that are often impractical if not impossible to apply.

2. The percentage of non-hearing individuals participating in research efforts who "genuinely" use PJM remains insufficient. Non-hearing researchers are quite rare and their already limited input is often misunderstood, misconstrued or ignored. Typically, it is non-hearing persons who are not proficient in PJM that participate; perceived as more credible, their spoken language proficiency gains them legitimacy outside of the deaf community and awards them the privilege of speaking on behalf of all non-hearing people. Such a situation seems especially disadvantageous to the non-hearing persons who are fluent PJM users and depend on signing.

3. The deaf community tends to lack group cohesiveness. The slogans about "Deaf culture" are not often reflected in everyday experiences. They are understood by only a few individuals who mainly acquire their understanding and meaning of culture from the surrounding Polish spoken language community. A "genuine" deaf person is practically removed from such currents of thought. For a deaf person in Poland, learning a spoken language is often a primary concern. Thus, dividing the Deaf community into those who are culturally Deaf vs. all others remains problematic.

4. The sign pidgin systems, which are most commonly used by Polish non-hearing people, still constitute a dilemma. In certain respects, they are a consequence of artificial sign systems in use (e.g., SJM, JM). SJM is still the most widely used method in educating non-hearing children. It is also assumed that this is a type of "language bridge" that could connect hearing with non-hearing people, breaking the language barrier.

5. The deliberation over "speaking or signing" results in unfortunate consequences not only for the education or the structure of PJM, but also on the social well-being of non-hearing people. The continued arguments within deaf education and applied linguistics tend to deprive non-hearing people of their agency, leaving them with few practical solutions.

6. The education of a child with a hearing disorder may occur within two paradigms, integrational or separationist, each having its own internal options: preschool or special schools (i.e., residential school); special educational units within a preschool or grade-school; integration units within preschools or grade-schools; therapeutic class, or individual education. This educational system tends to create a socio-educational dichotomy where an "assimilation"/"integration" approach is set

against an "ethnic"/"cultural" approach (Krakowiak 2003). The non-hearing people who go through the integration process often gain few benefits. Positive integration is rare, for its positive meaning comes strictly from a biological perspective that neglects numerous social aspects.

7. A more fitting educational methodology that would incorporate PJM has not been yet developed. This situation is especially unfavorable to people with a severe or profound hearing loss, limiting their social communication with others.

8. While in recent years, an increased number of non-hearing individuals have entered institutions of higher learning, many of them, especially persons with severe hearing damage, have had difficulty completing their degrees, even with the aid of the sign language interpreters. This perhaps is an indication of integration's less favorable effects.

9. The biological and social attempts to characterize non-hearing people as a social group reflect a reductionist perspective. Perhaps an individualist approach would be more fitting. Without neglecting the technological advancements or socializing elements, it emphasizes the personhood of a non-hearing individual, retaining the dignity and right to make informed decision about his/her life.

There is a great need for an open dialogue among Polish deaf education, deaf studies and linguistics, a dialogue that would include Deaf people fluent in PJM and, most especially, the "Deaf" (non-hearing people with a Deaf cultural approach). Such communication could culminate in fresh perspectives and ideas on language preservation and deaf education, and could lead to innovative solutions that address the social needs of non-hearing people.

PART II
Shared crosslinguistic characteristics

8

Notation systems

Harry van der Hulst and Rachel Channon

1   Introduction

Consider the following visual representations[1] for the concept number 3":

Photographs (Figure 8.1), drawings (Figure 8.2), videotapes and sound tapes are examples of *recordings* of linguistic data. Although they vary in their degree of data "fidelity" due to the fact that any recording necessarily makes a selection from all the data points present in an actual utterance and its context, these recordings stay close to the actual utterance. They can be collected, but the collection cannot be sorted into subsets nor can subsets be counted meaningfully because a recording is a *non-analytic* representation of the perceptible side or form of a linguistic utterance. For example, without a notation system, one cannot select all recordings that show all fingers extended in a corpus of American Sign Language (ASL) signs.

Figure 8.3 through Figure 8.8 are *notations* of a linguistic utterance. Figure 8.3, Figure 8.4 and Figure 8.5 show *writing systems*, Figure 8.6 and Figure 8.7 *transcription systems*, and Figure 8.8 a *coding system* we are developing for signed languages. Notations, unlike recordings, intentionally abstract away from the original linguistic events in ways not dictated by limitations of the recording process or "artistic license," but by (more or less) systematic decisions to annotate or symbolize only some (discrete) elements of the original signal. In almost all cases, they are part of an analytic system of some kind, but they differ from each other in what they represent, how they do it and their goals.

It seems relatively easy to distinguish between recordings and notations, but it can sometimes seem harder to distinguish between the purposes and characteristics of different notation systems, especially for sign languages. Are SignWriting and HamNoSys in competition with each other? Which should be used as coding systems for the analytic study of signs? We argue here that SignWriting is (primarily) a writing system and HamNoSys is a transcription system, and that they are not in competition, but that neither should be used for a coding system. We will also show that some of the confusion may be due to two unusual characteristics of notation systems for sign: they are highly iconic and feature-based.

151

Figure 8.1 *Photograph of ASL sign.*

Figure 8.2 *Drawing of ASL sign.*

Three

Figure 8.3 *English written word.*

3

Figure 8.4 *Common internationally recognized writing symbol.*

Figure 8.5 *Sutton SignWriting symbol.*

θri

Figure 8.6 *IPA (International Phonetic Alphabet) notation of English spoken word.*

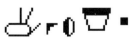

Figure 8.7 *HamNoSys symbols for ASL THREE.*

Sign Id	Stage	Field Name	Detail Level 1	Detail Level 2	Detail Level 3
1	1	Location	Neutral Space	Lateral Dimension	Ipsilateral
1	1	Location	Neutral Space	Vertical Dimension	Chest Height
1	1	Handshape	Extended Finger Set	TIM	

Figure 8.8 *SignTyp Coding System entries for ASL THREE (cf. section 6).*

We may characterize a writing system, such as written English or SignWriting, as a system used by the general population of literate speakers or signers of a language for the purpose of communicating and remembering the meaning of some linguistic event – a conversation, a contract, an order, a shopping list, a poem, etc. In contrast, transcription and coding systems are tools for a much smaller population of scientific specialists to communicate, remember and further analyze the form of some utterance. A transcription system and a coding system can be distinguished on the basis of their goals. A transcription system seeks to accurately, unambiguously and rapidly notate language samples in a variety of media, ranging from paper and pencil, print, to computer files so that they can be used as the basis for a more extensive analysis of the language and/or as illustrative examples. A coding system, as we define it, is specifically intended for use in the computerized analysis of language samples. For example, a coding system might be used to establish the frequency of coronal stops or handshapes with bent fingers in a language lexicon.

The boundaries between these types of notation systems are not always crisp, but we nonetheless discuss each type of system in turn, looking at its purpose, its requirements and characteristics. Along the way we note some significant differences between these types of systems for speech and sign. The goal of this chapter is to present some of the basic terminology and notions important in understanding and using notation systems, and to try to pin down important characteristics shared or not shared by different notation systems[2] for different modalities.

1.1   Examples of notation systems

To clarify our discussion of notation system characteristics, we refer where possible to actual examples of these systems, so we provide here a small amount of background material for each. English writing and SignWriting are examples of writing systems, the International Phonetic Alphabet (IPA) and HamNoSys of transcription systems and SignTyp of a coding system. With the exception of SignTyp, these are probably already familiar to many of our readers.

Writing systems. While written English needs no introduction, not everyone will be familiar with written sign. Perhaps the first to work out a comprehensive written sign system was Bébian (1825), discussed in some detail in Rée (1999), but no system had much public participation until Valerie Sutton proposed SignWriting in 1974.[3] SignWriting has about 500 basic graphs, although any specific sign language would use fewer than that (Sutton, personal communication, 2007). According to its inventor, it is much easier to learn than a completely arbitrary writing system (Sutton, personal communication, 2007). It has both computerized printing and shorthand hand printing forms. It is used in a number of schools for the deaf (Flood 2002), and by some deaf adults. From reports on the SignWriting listserv (www.signwriting.org), there appear to be at least fourteen schools around the world that are using it.

A second system, the ASL-phabet, which we discuss briefly, was developed by Samuel Supalla and colleagues.[4] This is a much simpler writing system with far fewer graphic units, which appear to be similar to Stokoe's symbol set (Stokoe, Casterline & Croneberg 1965) or HamNoSys. The symbols are less iconic than SignWriting symbols. This system, much more than SignWriting, acknowledges the fact (rightly, we believe) that a written representation of a word does not need to be a recipe to produce it, but only to be sufficiently unique to act as a trigger to activate the relevant words in the reader's mind.

Transcription systems. Many transcription systems for written speech have been proposed, including those by Thomas Wright Hill, Erasmus Darwin, Otto Jespersen and Kenneth Pike (see Abercrombie 1967 for more details). Some used an existing alphabet such as the Roman alphabet; others used arbitrary holistic symbols for each separate speech sound, and still others tried to capture similarities between speech sounds *in* the notation, by using symbols that are "directly iconic" in that the graphs are actual pictograms of the articulatory position and action of the vocal tract. Systems like this were devised by William Holdsworth and William Aldridge (1766), Isaac Pitman (1837), and perhaps most famously by Alexander Melville Bell (1867, 1881), who called his system "visible speech." His system was later adopted and modified by Henry Sweet. It was extremely well designed, but linguists made very little, if any, use of it. Instead, almost all linguists came to use the IPA.

The International Phonetic Association, founded in 1886, developed a phonetic alphabet that is rich enough to capture the speech sounds of all (known and studied) languages. Most IPA graphs represent "complete" speech sounds, but some (called "diacritics") represent specific properties of speech sounds. Graphs are taken from various varieties of the Roman alphabet, complemented by symbols from other alphabets (e.g., the Greek alphabet). Other graphs are mutated or inverted version of the above, while a few symbols are entirely "made up." The phonetic meaning of the IPA symbols, whose shape is arbitrary, has to be memorized. Hence serious training is required to transcribe speech into those symbols, or to read it back (especially for those whose own writing system is not some version of the Roman alphabet).

While several transcription systems have been proposed for sign (see Miller 2001 for an overview) the system we will focus on here is HamNoSys, which is perhaps the most widely used of the current transcription systems. This system was developed at the University of Hamburg (Prillwitz *et al.* 1989). It was originally based on Stokoe's 1965 notation system but has evolved to a much more comprehensive set of approximately 200 symbols with the goal of allowing for a phonetic transcription of any potentially significant characteristic of any sign in any sign language. As in SignWriting, symbols in HamNoSys correspond to features or feature groups. It uses a single symbol for handshapes (a feature group), but most of the other symbols would be considered to be single features.

Coding systems. Sign researchers have constructed coding systems and associated sign databases for a variety of purposes. The most extensive database focused on coding the form of signs is the *SignPhon* project with detailed codings for over 3000 signs from Sign Language of the Netherlands (Crasborn, van der Hulst & van der Kooij 2001). SignPhon, which uses a high number of condensed alphanumeric codes, has also been used for other sign languages. In this chapter we focus on *SignTyp*, a successor to SignPhon. SignTyp has an explicit crosslinguistic goal and is discussed in some detail in section 4.

2   Writing systems

2.1   What is being represented?

We have already referred to the notions "form" and "meaning." Here we want to consider carefully the possible relationships between them because this provides an interesting categorization of notation systems. A "sign" (in the semiotic sense) has two sides: its "form" (the signifier) and its "meaning" (the signified), with a third "player" being an actual or potential *referent*. For example, the ASL sign THREE and the spoken English word *three* are signifiers or forms for the meaning "the number that follows two." In spoken/signed languages, therefore, the form and meaning of words are "associated" (see Figure 8.9).

A notation system graph is also a sign with a form and meaning. In the IPA, for example, the form of each graph is associated with a specific speech sound, or aspect of a speech sound. (To avoid misunderstanding we could say that words, as signs, have a *semantic* meaning, while IPA symbols, as signs, have a *phonetic* meaning. From a semiotic point of view, meaning is whatever the form of the sign is associated with.)

Form ⟵⟶ meaning

Figure 8.9 *Relationship of form to meaning in speech or sign.*

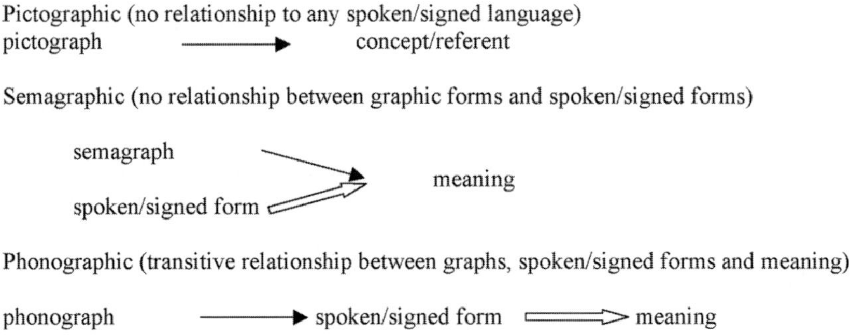

Pictographic (no relationship to any spoken/signed language)
pictograph   ⟶   concept/referent

Semagraphic (no relationship between graphic forms and spoken/signed forms)

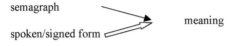

semagraph
                                        meaning
spoken/signed form

Phonographic (transitive relationship between graphs, spoken/signed forms and meaning)

phonograph   ⟶ spoken/signed form ⟹ meaning

Figure 8.10 *Possible relationships between form and meaning for writing systems and their parallel spoken/signed system (double lines represent internal spoken/signed language relationships).*

In the domain of writing systems there are three possibilities to consider: *pictographic*, *semagraphic* and *phonographic* systems. In pictographic systems, the graph has no relationship to any language but represents extralinguistic sensory-based representations, concept or referents rather than word meanings, usually in a highly iconic way. For example, the form < o > might refer directly to a meaning 'bright object in sky.' Such systems are usually considered as potential precursors of semagraphic systems, the next possibility, rather than writing systems. (The distinction can be subtle, cf. Mallery 1893.)

In a semagraphic system, graphs refer to elements of the meaning of spoken/signed words of a specific language.[5] For example, the symbol < $ > refers to (the meaning of) the English word *dollar*.

Finally, in a phonographic system, the graph refers to the form of a spoken/signed word. For example, the three graphs in < bat > refer in systematic ways to the forms (phonemes) of the spoken English word "bat."[6] In this kind of system, the written system has no direct relationship to the semantic meaning of these words, but only a transitive one, i.e., via the form of these words. (However, it is certainly possible that < bat > has, or acquires, a direct relation to the semantic meaning of the word *bat* in which case it effectively becomes part of a semagraphic system.) These relationships are illustrated in Figure 8.10.

The oldest systems for writing spoken languages appear to be semagraphic (word or morpheme-based systems) with the graphs being iconic of (sensory-based representations of) the referent denoted by (the meaning of) words. Iconic writing systems of this sort can develop in two directions. In the first, the system remains basically semagraphic, although the graphs tend to lose their iconicity due to the fact that frequent use undermines the detail required to remain iconic. They can still remain *motivated* (with graphs for semantically related words sharing graphic properties), or they can become arbitrary. In the second, the system becomes more and more phonographic. Phonographic traits enter the system when graphs are taken to represent (aspects of) the (phonological) form rather than the word meaning. This is often due to what is called the "Rebus Principle," where a semagraphic symbol for *sun* or *eye* comes to be used for other (near)homophonic words such as *son* or *I*. This tends to lead first to a syllabic system, and then, possibly (and at least once), to a system in which graphs represent speech sounds or phonemes (an alphabetic system), typically consonants at first, but with symbols for vowels in the alphabetic system that we are most familiar with. Phonographic elements may also enter a semagraphic system as *disambiguators*, i.e., symbols distinguishing two different pronunciations of an otherwise identical semagraph. For example, if < o > means both 'sun' and 'moon,' scribes might eventually start adding a small additional phonographic symbol for one or both meanings: s< o > versus m< o >.[7]

SignWriting might at first appear to be a (word- or morpheme-based) semagraphic system, but it is actually phonographic: the graphs depict aspects of the phonological form of signs. Wherever the phonological form is iconic of the semantic meaning, it *appears* that SignWriting is iconic of the semantic meaning because of the transitive nature of phonographs. The phonographic nature of its iconicity is demonstrated by the equal iconicity of the symbols for the completely arbitrary EUROPE and the highly iconic THREE (in ASL).

As for phonological or phonetic transcription systems (such as the IPA or HamNoSys), these of course are phonographic by design.[8]

The discussion so far regards what notation units represent. We also need to look at how the form of notation units represents their meaning.

2.2   Iconicity and motivation

Once the semiotic form/meaning distinction is made, we can ask what the nature is of the relationship between them. The following distinctions are usually made:[9]

1.   Symbol: the relationship between form and meaning is arbitrary
2.   Icon: the relationship between form and meaning is motivated

The prototypical "iconic" or motivated relationship claims some "resemblance" between a form and its meaning (or, rather, a sensory-based representation of its referent), as in ASL THREE. But a second, more abstract motivation, which we will call "systematic motivation," exists whenever forms correlate systematically to meanings, even without resemblance. An example is the placement of letters on the page where (in left–right/top–bottom systems) leftmost/topmost is earliest and rightmost/bottommost is latest in time, even though there is no obvious resemblance between the zigzag line down the page and temporal order.[10]

Systematically motivated phonographic writing systems have graphs that are systematically related to their (phonological) meaning, i.e., their articulatory or acoustic properties. Suppose, for example, that all letters for labial consonantal phonemes contained a "ˆ" shape, so that letters for /p/, /b/, /v/, /f/, etc. had this wedge shape in addition to other graphic elements which differentiate them. The wedge is not iconic per se, but its systematicity would make the writing system non-arbitrary vis-à-vis what it is that the graphs represent. Such a motivated system would in fact recognize the featural level without necessarily being featural all the way. (Think of the tilde for all nasal vowels.) It would be fully featural if *all* features were represented by a unique graphical element. A syllabary would be motivated in the same way if all graphs for syllables starting with a /p/ or with a voiced obstruent shared a graphical element. Such a system is syllabic while having alphabetic or featural traits.

Iconicity would exist if, for example, graphical elements resembled articulatory positions. Suppose that graphs for some or all labial sounds contain an < ( ) > like shape (resembling the two lips). Iconic systems are bound to introduce the featural level into either an alphabetic system or a syllabic system since it would be hard to select iconic graphs that uniquely resemble a single phoneme (unless, metonymically, if this phoneme had a unique feature, as in a trilled r). Thus, it would seem that motivation in phonographic systems involves introducing a lower level into a higher level system (i.e., featural graphs into an alphabetic system or alphabetic or featural graphs into a syllabic system).

Motivation typically plays an important role in another aspect of writing systems. Any writing system uses some "syntax" to place its graphemes together, i.e., to create "graphic expressions." Therefore, when considering motivation in writing systems we need to consider not only the units, but also their mode of combination. For example, in an alphabetic system, the letters are placed in some linear order (in the horizontal and vertical dimension). Such linear order can be said to be iconically motivated by the linear sequences of phonemes, no matter what the direction of writing.

If a writing system were featural *and* had iconic order, one could imagine representing the graphic feature units that jointly characterize a phoneme non-linearly in order to capture their simultaneity iconically. This is what happens in

Table 8.1 *Types and examples of writing systems*

		System examples	
System type	Linguistic form level	Phonographic	Semagraphic
Featural	Features	SignWriting, Korean (Hangul)	
Alphabetic	Phonemes	English	
Syllabic	Syllables	Cherokee, Cree, Hiragana	
Podic	Feet		
Motic	Word/morpheme		Chinese

SignWriting, where both the forms and the syntax are motivated. As Martin (2000) points out, SignWriting has symbols for handshapes, actions and orientations, but it does not have specific symbols for the location of the hands.[11] Instead, each written sign uses a two-dimensional space as a map of a human body. The symbols for the hands are placed within that space, so that the vertical and lateral dimensions of location are completely iconic.[12]

SignWriting also has examples of systematic motivation. For example, various handshape symbols use the convention that the back of the hand is black, and the front is colorless.

2.3   Unit or level of representation

Phonographic writing systems are either feature-based (subsegmental) or alphabetic (the graphs have a [loose] relationship to phonemes or segments of the language). Written English, like many or even most writing systems for speech, is alphabetic. In contrast, SignWriting expressions are decomposable into a set of basic symbols that correspond to phonological features in all current phonological analyses. Not only SignWriting, but all writing and transcription systems created for signs (including that by Bébian) appear to be feature or feature-group systems.[13]

Table 8.1 shows that writing systems in general differ with respect to the level or size of the linguistic unit that is represented by the graphic units (using the invented terms "podic" and "motic" to refer to foot and word-based systems).

The table shows interesting gaps. No system targets any semagraphic elements below the word or morpheme level (such as semantic "features" or conceivable intermediate semantic structures). No phonological system targets feet or words. Furthermore, there may be a modality difference as well, since it appears that written sign exclusively targets the feature level, which is uncommon for written speech. Only Hangul has been claimed to be based on features, but, as such, it is far from transparent or exceptionless in the way that SignWriting is. We do see, however, that writing systems frequently use feature-based diacritics (such as the tilde, umlauts) or letter doubling to indicate length.

Why do the only attested cases of semagraphic systems choose to represent whole word (or morpheme) meanings (which is why the term logographic is commonly used)? If there are semantic units below the level of morpheme meaning, i.e., a set of basic semantic features, it would be conceivable to design a writing system that targets these units. Such a system does not seem obvious as a practical writing system, probably because such smaller semantic units are not salient enough either in themselves or in comparison to competing units, such as phonemes.[14]

Also, why are there no phonographic podic or motic systems? The number of symbols required would be very large, but this objection would apply equally to semagraphic motic systems which do occur. Again, the answer may lie in what is cognitively salient. When someone creates a written system, the natural focus is the word, which must be more cognitively salient than lower phonological levels, and much more likely to be committed to memory than sentences. In turn, the meaning of words is more salient than the form, which is merely the vehicle. It is well known that it is much easier for people to invent iconic signs than to come up with something arbitrary, so the most natural starting point for a writing system would seem to be a set of iconic graphs that represent word meanings as a whole, leading to a motic semagraphic system. However, semagraphic systems raise a learnability problem because of the large number of graphs required to symbolize all the language's morphemes. In addition, the iconicity of the original invention will soon run into problems because of the variability of the referents (as well as different perceptions of them) that are the source of the iconicity. These factors may be causes (along with other factors such as the introduction of disambiguators or the use of the Rebus Principle) for the emergence of phonographic systems, both syllabic and alphabetic. Such systems, of course, pose learnability problems of their own since their use requires an awareness of the phonological structure of words or "phonemic awareness," i.e., of meaningless chunks of form like syllables and phonemes. While phonemic awareness generally requires teaching, children are clearly capable of learning these distinctions. Less clear is their ability to become feature-aware for spoken languages, which may be one reason why featural systems are uncommon for spoken languages. A second factor is that a feature-based system for speech will generally result in a set of complex or bundled symbols which are grouped and understood at the segmental level (as appears to be the case in Hangul). This type of bundled symbol readily decays into a non-decomposed unitary alphabetic symbol.

Thirdly, why are there no podic systems, either phonographic or semagraphic? We suggest that their absence is rather easily explained if we assume that feet are "phonetic" rather than cognitive-phonological units (cf. van der Hulst 2009). It is, indeed, rare if not nonexistent for writing systems to encode phonetic properties of speech.

Lastly, why are all sign writing systems based on features or feature groups? Within the phonographic category we could imagine systems that target a higher phonological level, such as a segmental/phonemic or syllabic level. That these candidate systems do not exist bears on a well-known problem of sign language phonology: there is little consensus on either the existence or definition of the various phonological levels in sign language beyond the feature or feature class (such as handshape).

Most representational systems for signs have at least one phonological unit or level smaller than the word. Candidates for this unit are the segment (phoneme) or syllable. Sandler (1989), Perlmutter (1990) and Liddell and Johnson (1989) propose *multisegmental* approaches, with most signs having two or three segments. Although these systems allow a syllabic level (explicitly or implicitly), multi-syllabic signs are usually cases where the second and succeeding syllables are copies of the first syllable. Thus, such systems, while allowing for two phonological levels, do not actually need the full power of a syllabic level. Repeating syllables might equally well be handled with a repeat feature (see Channon 2002b). The multisegmental perspective claims that there are segmental and syllabic levels that should be available for an alphabetic or syllabic system exactly like spoken languages. The fact that such systems are not attested argues that either they are (strangely) less cognitively salient than the featural level or that such levels do not exist in signs.[15]

Brentari (1998) proposes a *syllabic* model, which eliminates the segmental level in favor of the syllabic, with timing units dependent on the syllabic level. Van der Hulst (1993, 2000) and Channon (Crain 1996, Channon 2002a) propose *monosegmental* models, which establish a formal parallel between the representation of a sign and a phoneme, each consisting of a set of "class nodes" defined in terms of a set of features, and without a syllabic level of organization. The syllabic and monosegmental views converge on the notion that in addition to the phonological level of features there is only *one* further significant phonological level which comprises the whole phonological form of monomorphemic signs. A writing system that would target this level would therefore be alphabetic, syllabic and motic all at the same time. The choices for a writing system are therefore featural (attested) or motic (not attested).

If, as suggested above, in the case of spoken languages, (iconic) motic semagraphic systems tend to come first, why then do we not get analogous systems for sign languages? Why is it that, in sign, the form takes precedence over the semantic meaning in "capturing the attention" of writing units? We suggest that, contrary to what we find for spoken languages, signers have a high degree of awareness for sign features and feature bundles (class nodes), due to the visibility of sign articulation, which makes it easy to develop graph sets that are iconic of the phonological shape. In spoken languages, articulation is largely invisible. Moreover, the immediate vehicle of meaning is the acoustic effect of the articulation, not the articulation itself. Apparently, acoustic events (being auditory) do not capture the attention of a visually based writing system because a clear basis for iconicity is lacking. Finally, as mentioned above, because the form of signs tends itself to be iconic, an iconic phonographic system for signs is often also iconic of their meaning so that, if iconicity is desirable (all other things being equal), an iconic phonographic system may be the best of all possible choices for writing systems for sign languages.

2.4   Bi-uniqueness

Bi-uniqueness is another aspect of the relationship between form and meaning to be considered. Is the relationship between form and meaning one-to-one (a unique form for each meaning), or can several forms refer to the same meaning, or several meanings be referred to by one form?

The "ideal" of a one grapheme ~ one phoneme system is rare, although nearly attained in some systems such as Finnish writing, but certainly not in English, which is notorious for the extent to which it deviates from this ideal. Deviation arises when the phonological system of a language changes over time, while the writing system remains the same (in accordance with what is sometimes called the etymological principle). Due to its faithfulness to history, writing may preserve semantic distinctions between words that have become homophonic (thus, in a sense, introducing a semagraphic dimension to a phonographic system: < to >, < two > and < too > represent different meanings). But they may also find their root in other design principles. For example, the decision to write < hond > for the Dutch word for dog which is pronounced [hɔnt], with a < d > rather than a < t > is that in the plural < honden >, pronounced [hɔndə], a [d] surfaces. The relevant design principle is often called the morphemic principle. Thus, a phonographic writing system may deviate from the bi-unique goal due to historical faithfulness or faithfulness to allomorphic alternation. One might even argue that phonographic writing systems for spoken languages due to both the etymological and morpho- logical principle display a semagraphic tendency, though not a requirement, for a bi-unique relationship between graphs and (semantic) meanings.

SignWriting, unlike most or all spoken language writing systems, appears to maintain a rigid requirement for bi-uniqueness of graphic form to phonological form. For example, in ASL the signs APPLE and ONION are distinct forms, and they are equally distinct in SignWriting, but the signs GOOD and THANKYOU are not (manually) phonologically distinct, and they will not be distinct in SignWriting. The kind of mismatch seen in English *read* (present tense) and *read* (past tense), which are distinct spoken forms but the same graphic forms, could not occur in SignWriting, because it is always faithful to the phonological form.

Bi-uniqueness in semagraphic systems is difficult to maintain because it is hard to come up with (and learn) different forms for all the different morphemes. Hence, we see that in such systems the same units are used for different semantically related morphemes. To point the reader to the different morphemes, phonographic disambiguators may then be added.

2.5   Economy and redundancy

Reductionism (the strategy to break down entities into increasingly smaller primes) reduces the number of basic units, but this simplicity is counterbalanced by an increase in the complexity of the combinatorial system (i.e., the syntax). Featural writing has fewer primes than alphabetic writing, which has fewer primes than syllabic writing. Writing systems that have a separate graph for each morpheme/ word have the simplest "syntax" for writing down words, but the largest number of basic units (namely as many as there are morphemes/words). It might be that systems in general tend to increase reductionism, although, at the same time, single forms for complex meanings may be favored if, by offering shortcuts, they reduce frequent uses of complex syntax. An example of this (which we call "bundling") is the use of handshape forms (like "A") in sign notation systems.

The notion of "economy" refers to the idea that any representational system, given its primes and syntax, favors simple over complex forms to represent a given set of meanings. Economy reduces the amount of "effort" that it takes to produce a form and thus favors minimally distinct forms. However, to be resilient, sign systems typically do not go for minimal differences, and the reason is that minimal differences can easily be missed, i.e., overwritten by "noise" or by the detrimental effect of overzealous production efficiency or "laziness." To counterbalance noise and signal deterioration, signifiers tend to display *redundancy* in their form. It has long been understood (cf. Shannon and Weaver 1949) that if differences are minimal the slightest "noise" may cause confusion, wiping out the crucial difference between two forms. If there are multiple cues, in other words *redundancy*, forms will be more resistant to noise. Redundant coding can take various forms, including repetition or doubling, extra properties (enhancement) or amplification (magnification). In general, redundancy increases *dispersion*, i.e., it maximizes differences between different forms.

Any sign system that has evolved in/for humans or has been designed to be used by them will establish a balance between economy and redundancy. Depending on the goal of the system, one or the other may be given more weight. It seems obvious that writing systems for both speech and sign (as well as speech and sign in their own right) make ample use of redundancy because, after all, perceptual clarity is of paramount importance.

2.6   Summary: writing systems

To summarize, we have discussed several important characteristics of writing systems. First, writing systems for spoken languages can be phonographic (dependent on the form of another linguistic system) or semagraphic (dependent on the meanings of another linguistic system), although both types typically have ingredients of the other kind. The writing systems that we know of for sign all appear to be purely phonographic. Second, phonographic written speech, in addition to using semagraphic units (i.e., "&" in English writing), often displays a tendency for holistically matching a unique written symbol sequence to one spoken form (due to the etymological and morphological principle). Sign writing, as mentioned, seems to adhere more strictly to its phonographic basis. Third, phonographic written speech is almost always phonemic (alphabetic), but it appears more natural for written sign to be featural. Fourth, written speech generally uses symbols which, even if they are originally iconic, over time become entirely arbitrary. The order of the symbols on the page is iconic. Written sign systems seem to use primarily iconic symbols. SignWriting (but not all written sign systems) also uses iconic order.[16] Fifth, written systems in both modalities show some evidence of tendencies toward more economical syntax by using bundled symbols.

Will SignWriting succeed? It is an elegant solution to the problem of writing signs and has a natural and understandable quality about it that is appealing. Children can learn it without any difficulty greater than that involved in hearing children learning to write speech, perhaps less in fact. But just as external realities have established English as the de facto language of science instead of other languages, SignWriting may succeed or fail because of extrinsic demographic, political and technological realities. The Deaf community is small and may be shrinking (Johnston 2004). Most deaf children have hearing parents, who naturally emphasize the writing system for their native, spoken language. These children usually acquire sufficient skills in English (or another spoken language) to manage to communicate with hearing people and with other deaf people, while many hearing people do not really learn to sign, let alone use SignWriting. Additionally, most technological devices deaf people use for communication, such as email, instant messaging and Telecommunication Devices for the Deaf (TDDs), are not currently available in a form that would allow SignWriting to be used.

Regardless of whether SignWriting is ultimately successful, we suggest that the use of SignWriting by children as well as the learning process involved in it should be interesting topics for research, especially because SignWriting may be the only true example of a rigidly bi-unique, feature-level writing system, as well as the clearest example of an iconic phonographic writing system.

3   Transcription and tagging systems

3.1   How is a transcription system distinguished from a writing system?

A transcription system is usually meant to notate the form side of linguistic expressions.[17] In many cases, transcription is needed to capture phonetic details whether allophonic, free, stylistic, geographic (dialectal), pathological or characteristic of second language learners.[18]

The basic requirements for a transcription system are:

- Bi-uniqueness: no graphic unit can be ambiguous, while using two units with the same meaning should be avoided.
- Completeness: There must be a graphic unit for all phonetic properties that might be relevant for intended further analysis

Desirable characteristics would be:

- transcribable on a computer
- Appropriate documentation available
- Stable group responsible for maintaining/changing the system
- easy to learn, write and read back

Phonographic writing systems (and of course semagraphic systems as well) for speech are clearly inadequate, because (1) they do not rigidly adhere to bi-uniqueness, (2) the graph inventory of any given written language is not adequate to represent the sound inventory of all languages (lack of completeness) and (3) they are typically alphabetic or phonemic and cannot easily represent featural distinctions.

Written sign systems, however, are somewhat different. SignWriting is phonographic, but it is featural and maintains rigid bi-uniqueness between the written and signed forms. As such, SignWriting expressions can include more or less phonetic detail as desired. Furthermore, partly by design and partly because of the phonological similarity of sign languages, the symbol set is sufficient to cover all sign languages, as amply demonstrated on the SignWriting website. This makes SignWriting (and Supalla's ASL-phabet) a potential transcription system in addition to being a writing system.

The IPA, HamNoSys and SignWriting all fulfill the two most important criteria of rigid bi-uniqueness and completeness (granted that new empirical work may uncover new entities that need to be notated with new forms).We can next ask the question as to whether they equally fulfill the desirable characteristics.[19]

If we compare HamNoSys and SignWriting as transcription systems, there is one major difference. HamNoSys is a linear one-dimensional system similar in that respect to written alphabetic systems. HamNoSys uses an arbitrary linear ordering of symbols (handshape, location, movement). A HamNoSys expression has no significant internal structure that can be freely altered. Thus, while the HamNoSys symbol set is iconic, its order is not. The linear ordering is purely an artifact of the system and has no iconic resemblance to the actual temporal order. For practical purposes, a specific linear order can be (and has been) adopted as a matter of convention. (Supalla's ASL-phabet has a similar arbitrary linear order.)

In contrast, a SignWriting symbol does have internal structure. For example, one SignWriting symbol is a round circle representing the signer's head. Sub-symbols are placed within it for eye shapes (squinting, widened), eyebrows (frowning, raised) and mouth (smiling, frowning, mouthing, exhaling, etc.). This means that SignWriting is a non-linear, two-dimensional, iconically arranged symbol set that appears to circumvent at least one of the problems that Miller (2001) notes with linear systems such as HamNoSys. In sign, as has often been said, many things happen at the same time.

A system that allows non-linear or multilinear notation[20] therefore seems desirable, but there is a related drawback. While it is certainly possible to use SignWriting on the computer, it requires specialized software to manipulate the symbols to the appropriate place. While SignWriting does have decomposable symbols that can be translated or converted to a coding system, there may be potential difficulties in a conversion, especially with regard to the non-linear locations (cf. above). (The website developed by the creators of SignWriting discusses a form of the system that is intended for research purposes and does have specific location symbols.) In contrast, HamNoSys (and Supalla's ASL-phabet) can adapt easily to a computer. It is quite easy to download the fonts for HamNoSys and use them for transcription. HamNoSys may therefore have an edge as a more easily digitized system, although they seem equally good choices for manual transcription.

SignWriting appears to be well documented on its website, with manuals for teaching the system, plus children's books and other material to practice with. In contrast, the documentation for HamNoSys is somewhat difficult to obtain and seems to be still in progress.

One other issue is that while the IPA is controlled by an organization with broad support in the linguistic community, SignWriting and HamNoSys, although in competent hands, do not have this type of large organizational support.[21]

3.2   Tagging systems

While a transcription system by itself is often adequate, many researchers want and need to refer back to the original data as well. A difficulty with videotapes or other multimedia sources is that it is not always easy to find and return to a specific point in the tape and to tag it for comparison with another point in the same or a different tape. Both SignStream and ELAN focus on the important task of aligning linguistic information with original source data.

These software tools allow researchers to tag video material (frame by frame, if necessary) with information arranged on multiple lines, each line being defined (by the program or by the user of the program) in terms of some relevant linguistic property (handshape, location, etc.). There are few if any restrictions on the types of properties that can be annotated. SignStream was developed by researchers at Boston University (www.bu.edu/asllrp/SignStream/) and ELAN (EUDICO Linguistic Annotator) by researchers at the Max Planck Institute (www.mpi.nl/tools/). SignStream is primarily aimed at syntactic analysis of signs, but it allows some phonetic detail to be entered. It is available for Mac systems only. ELAN has a more phonetic focus, although it allows almost any kind of detail to be transcribed. It is available for Mac, Windows and Linux systems. Both could be considered to be counterparts in the visual realm for PRAAT, software developed by Paul Boersma and David Weenink to annotate audio material (www.fon.hum.uva.nl/praat/).

One concern with these kinds of programs is that because sign language linguistics is a relatively small, relatively low budget research area, it may not be possible to maintain complex, specialized software. It should also be noted that these annotators are intended to work with multimedia material only (not still photographs, drawings or dictionary descriptions). With these minor caveats, these tagging systems appear to be valuable tools for the examination and transcription of phonetic data on videotapes.

3.2.1   *Summary*

The crucial characteristics for a transcription system are that it observes bi-uniqueness and completeness. Both HamNoSys and SignWriting have these characteristics. HamNoSys is probably a better transcription system, however, because it appears to be more easily computerized.

Perhaps the most interesting characteristic of transcription systems for sign languages is that while it is unlikely that any written speech system could function effectively as a transcription system, it seems that SignWriting, HamNoSys and the various Stokoe-based systems are actually all potentially both writing and transcriptions systems.[22] This appears to be a joint result of their featural as opposed to alphabetic nature and their iconicity, which seems to lead naturally to rigid bi-uniqueness.

In addition, we briefly discussed two tagging systems that allow detailed notation of videotaped signs.

4   Coding systems

4.1   Requirements

A coding system is a research tool to allow linguists to research questions about various aspects of language. It requires high explicitness and simplicity for its users, and ease of data storage and retrieval.

In comparing coding and transcription systems, we can note first that both must be bi-unique and complete. The crucial distinction is that a coding system must allow computerized sorting, counting and comparing of any significant characteristic, while a transcription system need not (it may not even be computerized).

Because transcription systems emphasize writing speed, they use many *bundled* symbols that contain information about many different characteristics, such as HamNoSys 4 and 5 representing a hand with either one or two fingers extended. But bundled symbols do not allow sorting, counting or comparing the sub-units of the coded entity. For example, it would be difficult to sort the above two HamNoSys symbols simultaneously for thumb posture and number of extended fingers. The two symbols cannot be compared to determine if the number of extended fingers or the thumb postures are the same. They cannot be counted to find how many times a hand has a single extended finger. This poses a barrier to the user (although specialized software could be used to get around this). A coding system must therefore avoid bundled symbols.

A transcription system emphasizes ease and speed of use from the writer's/creator's perspective, while a coding system emphasizes ease and speed from the reader's/user's perspective. Thus, it is important that the symbols for a coding system should not only be unbundled, but as transparent as possible to reduce the reader's learning curve. Even iconic symbols such as < 4 > are not completely transparent (what is the thumb doing? Does the symbol represent the extended index or the extended pinkie (little finger)?). Character codes and abbreviations are even more difficult for a user. We therefore propose that the symbols be selected from a closed vocabulary of ordinary English[23] words. This has the additional advantage that special fonts are not needed, and it greatly reduces (though it does not eliminate) the need for system documentation. A further advantage is ease of correction: single character codes, or combinatorial codes (such as < cd > for contralateral and downward) are almost impossible to correct if errors are made, while if a data entry error is made in a word like *contralateral*, it is a simple matter to see that *contraladeral* should be corrected to *contralateral*. A related principle is to use the more common word over the more technical wherever possible: words like *pinkyside* and *thumbside* are easier to understand than *radial* or *ulnar*, and make the database language accessible to a wider audience.

4.2   A proposed database structure: SignTyp

While the above principles for choosing a symbol set are probably applicable to almost any coding system, we now turn to something more specialized: the structure of SignTyp, which apparently represents an entirely new approach to sign language databases. SignTyp is both a physical database (currently including about 12,000 signs from nine different sources) and a coding system. It is not a software system and can be used with any database software. Output from the tagging systems discussed above or data transcribed using a transcription system can become input to SignTyp.

The data structure for SignTyp is the same structure used in phonological feature trees (directed graphs).[24] However, instead of being a graphic representation, it is tabular, because graphical representations are not suitable for analytic work. (Of course, SignTyp includes a much broader range of data than a phonological tree, but this does not affect the structure.)

To understand this, consider the directed graph representations of location for the ASL signs BEAUTIFUL and FLOWER, shown in Figure 8.11 and a corresponding tabular representation in Table 8.2. (In BEAUTIFUL, the fingers move in a circular gesture over the face as a whole, while in FLOWER, the hand contacts the ipsilateral and contralateral nostrils.) For our purposes here, we are not concerned with any particular phonological theory but have simply selected a reasonable possible structure for location features. These are ordinary (somewhat simplified) phonological trees, rotated so that the root is oriented to the left instead of to the top of the page. It should be easy to see the relationship between the graphic tree in Figure 8.11 and the tabular tree in Table 8.2.

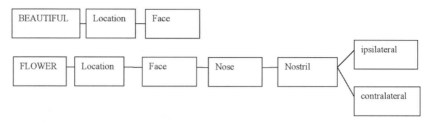

Figure 8.11 *Partial feature trees for BEAUTIFUL and FLOWER (rotated).*

Table 8.2 *SignTyp records for BEAUTIFUL and FLOWER*

			Field values detail			
SignID	Stage	Field name	Level 1	Level 2	Level 3	Level 4
1	1	Location	Face			
2	1	Location	Face	Nose	Nostril	Ipsilateral
2	2	Location	Face	Nose	Nostril	Contralateral

The graphic tree uses lines to show the relationship between the text boxes (nodes): *Face* is a dependant of *Location*. In SignTyp, the root node is the leftmost column and the terminal node is the rightmost column. Columns to the right are dependants of columns to the left. The left to right organization of the columns and the repetition of all non-terminal nodes on each row substitute for the lines in the graphic tree form.

A graphic tree has one additional convention: sister nodes to the left are temporally ordered before those to the right. In the tabular tree, the stage value makes explicit the temporal order of the data. Both graphic and tabular methods therefore provide the same information for dependency and linear order.

The SignTyp structure has numerous advantages: The structure directly mirrors the hierarchical nature of the data and shows relationships between fields. Related fields are automatically and naturally sorted together, and pivot tables or similar data summaries will always result in like material being kept together. For example, location information will sort separately from orientation.

Similar material will be aligned. BEAUTIFUL's terminal node is *face*, while FLOWER's terminal nodes are the contralateral and ipsilateral *nostrils*. Both FLOWER and BEAUTIFUL share a *face* node, which shows up in the same column for both signs. In a traditional row–column structure, *face* for BEAUTIFUL and *nostril* for FLOWER would probably be put in the same column, which would miss a generalization. Data with more detail will have more nodes, but all the data can be compared on any shared higher nodes. This also means that data from different databases that code different depths of detail can be united in SignTyp (after normalization of labels). For example, data source A might treat all locations on the chest as a single location, while data source B might distinguish upper chest, mid-chest, lower chest and so on. Both databases can be compared at Detail Level 1 where they would both have a value of chest, even though data source A has no further information available for any sign, while data source B has much more information available.

With an ordinary relational database, once the database administrator has set up the database structure, and the data structure, the analyst can add more rows at any time without needing to ask the administrator to change anything. But if the analyst wanted to add a new field, *iconic location*, the database administrator (and probably the website designer/administrator) would need to review, approve and make this change. This can be a problem in a research database, which is much more likely to add or change fields than a business database, because the analytic process frequently means that new fields will be added.

SignTyp handles the problem of changing data structure much more neatly. In the example above, *iconic location* is not a new column, but just a new possible value for a record. No database changes would be required. New kinds of data are simply new rows of data with different node names. This structure goes a long way to freeing the researcher from dependence on the database and website administrators.

SignTyp can also be used with videotapes, photographs, drawings or other source material. It is meant to be crosslinguistic and can record different historical stages of languages as well as different languages, thus allowing study of historical change and crosslinguistic typological or genetic relationships. It can also function as an archive for material from different projects.

4.3   Summary: coding systems

In this section, we have provided an overview of a new coding system for signs that uses a closed English vocabulary to describe signs in as much detail as the analyst wants and allows for simple searches and sorts on atomic data. The unusual database structure, while remaining relational, allows researchers more freedom in making changes to the data structure without involving the database or website administrator.

5   **Summary**

In this chapter we have examined three types of notation systems: writing, transcription and coding, with special attention to their use in sign languages. We discussed their properties, compared them to similar systems for spoken languages and speculated on the reasons why some conceivable systems do not exist or are unpopular.

If a writing system is phonographic, it focuses on the phonemic or syllabic level for speech, and on the feature level for sign. The success of alphabetic systems for written speech suggests that the phoneme is a central cognitive unit for speech (cf. Taylor 2006), even though phonemic *awareness* is a stage that needs considerable training. In signs, on the other hand, the featural-level system appears to be more successful and usable, suggesting that in this modality the feature or feature group is the central cognitive unit for sign. This difference in which level of analysis is salient reflects a fundamental difference between speech and sign. Both written speech and sign have iconic timelines (order of symbols), but only written sign uses iconicity systematically and, apparently, persistently. Children's use of SignWriting should be an interesting research topic because SignWriting is an unusual combination of a feature-level writing system, as well as the clearest example of an iconic, phonographic and rigidly bi-unique writing system.

Most of these differences also occur for transcription systems which, in this sense, are much like writing systems, differing mainly in terms of the bi-uniqueness and completeness requirements. Our discussion of coding systems was limited to sign language. We have proposed that a coding system for signs should use a symbol set of English words to allow for understandability and ease of sorting, and have a data structure that is a tabular version of a phonological tree.

9

Verb agreement in sign language morphology

Gaurav Mathur and Christian Rathmann

1 Introduction

Verb agreement is a topic that has received much attention in the sign language literature. Figure 9.1 shows what is often called "verb agreement" in the literature. This phenomenon has been noted in many signed languages.[1]

The two signs, taken from American Sign Language (ASL), both describe a person asking another person. The difference lies in which of the two persons is asking the other. In the absence of prior context, the first sign means *I asked someone* while the second sign means *someone asked me*. They differ only in the orientation and direction of movement; in the first example, the hand is oriented and moves away from the signer's body, and in the other, it is oriented and moves in the opposite direction, toward the body. Such changes in the orientation and direction of movement are linked to the change in meaning described above. The phenomenon has several properties in almost all of the sign languages documented to date that make it look different from verb agreement in spoken languages.

For a working definition of agreement, the chapter follows Corbett's (2006) criteria for canonical agreement. He starts with a broad definition from Steele (1978: 610): "the term *agreement* commonly refers to some systematic covariance between a semantic or formal property of one element and a formal property of another." Then, he distinguishes four necessary aspects of agreement – *controller*, *target*, *domain* and *feature* – and defines each as follows:

(1)   Corbett's (2006: 4) definitions of aspects of agreement
      controller: "element which determines agreement"
      target: "element whose form is determined by agreement"
      domain: "syntactic environment in which agreement occurs"
      feature: "respect in which there is agreement"

In addition, there may be a fifth aspect, *conditions*, which are "other factors ... which have an effect on agreement but are not directly reflected." Corbett

173

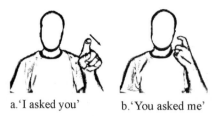

a. 'I asked you'   b. 'You asked me'

Figure 9.1 *ASK in two of its forms.*

(2006) provides a list of twenty criteria related to these aspects to determine whether agreement is canonical. His claim that verb agreement in signed languages does not meet the criterion of systematic covariance will be revisited by discussing particular criteria throughout the chapter.

Padden (1983), following previous researchers like Friedman (1976) and Fischer and Gough (1978), notes that some verbs in ASL seem to display agreement. In fact, an example from Padden (1983:14) could be said to involve verb agreement according to Corbett's criteria: $_1$INDEX $_1$GIVE$_i$ BOOK 'I gave him the book.' The pronoun $_1$INDEX (*I*) and the implicit pronoun meaning *him* are the controllers, while the verb GIVE is the target. The domain is the clause, and the features could be person and number, as in the English example. $_1$INDEX is first person singular, while *him* is non-first person singular. These features are manifested through a change in the orientation and direction of movement of the hand during the production of the verb GIVE. The change reflects locations in signing space that have been associated with the referents of the subject and the object respectively. In that sense, the verb could be said to agree with the subject and the object in person and number.

This claim remains controversial in the field of sign language linguistics. Liddell (2000), for example, rejects the term "agreement" for the phenomenon, an analysis also adopted by Johnston and Schembri (2007). Other terms that have been used to describe the phenomenon illustrated in Figure 9.1 are "directional" (Baker-Shenk & Cokely 1980, Meier 1982), "inflecting" (Padden 1983) and "indicating" (Liddell 2000). Since this chapter takes the view that the phenomenon can be understood as agreement, the chapter uses the term "agreement" to refer to the phenomenon throughout, in line with Aronoff, Meir and Sandler (2005), Neidle *et al.* (2000), Lillo-Martin (2002), Meier (2002), and Steinbach and Pfau (2007), among others.

In reviewing this literature, this chapter aims to arrive at a better understanding of verb agreement in both signed and spoken languages. The chapter begins with a detailed description of the different forms that verb agreement takes in signed languages (section 2). Then section 3 summarizes the historical and psycholinguistic data that bear on the description. Section 4 closes the chapter by revisiting the above questions in light of the preceding description. For a review of theoretical approaches to the analysis of verb agreement in signed languages, see Mathur and Rathmann (forthcoming).

2   A detailed description of verb agreement in signed languages

This section provides a detailed description of verb agreement as it appears in various signed languages. First, it reviews the distinction between "single" and "double" agreement and relates the distinction to the number of controllers. Then, it turns to the features of agreement, namely person and number. Next, the section discusses the types of verbs that participate in such agreement and considers phonological constraints on these verbs. At the end of this section, we provide a survey of the range of crosslinguistic variation that occurs with verb agreement in signed languages.

2.1   Agreement with arguments

Verb agreement forms mark arguments in a sentence, such as the subject and/or the object. When the form overtly marks only one argument, it is called single agreement, and when the form overtly marks both the subject and the object, it is called double agreement. Each kind is described in detail.

2.1.1   *Single agreement*

Single agreement occurs when the verb overtly agrees with one argument, namely the direct object of a transitive verb or the indirect object of a ditransitive verb (Meier 1982, Padden 1983). In what follows, the term "object" will be used to refer to either of these arguments. Another way to describe single agreement is to say that the verb is directed toward a single entity labelled y, which is notated as $\text{VERB}^{->y}$ by Liddell (2003b). One example is the German Sign Language (DGS) sign BEEINFLUSSEN 'influence,' illustrated in Table 9.1. If the object is non-first person, the corresponding form would mean 'someone influenced a particular person.' The form can also be used to mean 'someone influenced a certain group of people.' If the object is first person, the form would mean, for example, 'You influenced me.'

Table 9.1 *Phonological forms of agreement in DGS, ASL, Auslan and JSL*

		DGS	ASL	Auslan	JSL
Orientation and direction of movement	ENTLASSEN 'fire'	46%	31%	38%	26%
Orientation	BEEINFLUSSEN 'influence'	42%	20%	21%	19%
Direction of movement	FRAGEN 'ask'	12%	10%	17%	23%

Source: Reproduced from Rathmann and Mathur 2008.

The difference between the two forms lies in the orientation of the hand. The first form of BEEINFLUSSEN shows that the hands are oriented toward an area in signing space that has been previously associated with the referent of the object. The second form shows that the hands are oriented toward the signer's body. There are other ways to show single agreement (Askins & Perlmutter 1995, Mathur 2000). One is to change the direction of the movement of the hand, as with the DGS sign FRAGEN 'ask' in Table 9.1. Another way to show single agreement changes both orientation and direction of movement, illustrated with the DGS sign ENTLASSEN 'fire' in Table 9.1. In addition, Mathur (2000) describes other ways that occur with two-handed signs.

In a survey of four signed languages (DGS, ASL, Auslan and Japanese Sign Language [JSL]), Mathur and Rathmann (2004) found all ways of manifesting single agreement in all of the signed languages. Table 9.1 presents the frequency of each way for each signed language. The relative frequency of each way is different for each language, reflecting the phonological structure of the verbs and in turn the lexical idiosyncrasies of each language. At the same time, what all the signed languages have in common is that the change in orientation and direction of movement is the most common way, thus suggesting that this is the most proto-typical and therefore the target form of agreement in signed languages.

2.1.2 *Double agreement*

Double agreement means that the verb shows agreement with two arguments, which are the subject and the (in)direct object respectively (Meier 1982, Padden 1983). Liddell (2003b) describes this form by saying that the verb is directed toward two entities labelled respectively as x and y, notated as $\text{VERB}^{x->y}$. As with single agreement, there are three ways to realize double agreement at the phonological level: through a change in orientation, through a change in direction of movement only, or through a change in both.

Meir (1995, 1998a, 1998b) observed that in such verbs, the palm or the fingers are oriented toward the area associated with the object referent, while the back of the hand is oriented toward the area with the subject referent. Mathur (2000) observed that other parts of the hand can be oriented toward the area associated with the object referent too, such as the back of the knuckles in ASL TEASE, BLAME and CONTROL or the radial side of the hand in ASL IGNORE and CONVINCE. Henceforth, Meir's (1998b) term "facing" will be used to mean that a particular part of the hand is oriented toward the area associated with the object. Note that the relevant part of the hand always faces the area associated with the object referent and/or moves from the area associated with the subject referent to the area associated with the object referent.

There are exceptions to this order, i.e., some verbs face and/or proceed from the area associated with the object to the area associated with the subject. These verbs have been called "backwards" verbs in the sign linguistics literature. Examples from ASL are BORROW, COPY, STEAL, INVITE, TAKE-ADVANTAGE and TAKE, the last of which is illustrated in Figure 9.2. The backwards pattern does not extend to facing. The hands in backwards verbs are still oriented toward the area associated with the object. Accounting for the pattern of backwards verbs has been a major issue in the field of verb agreement in signed languages. For a review of various approaches to this issue, see Mathur and Rathmann (forthcoming).

While all these verbs have the ability to show agreement with both the subject and the object, Padden (1983) suggests that agreement with the subject is always optional, whereas agreement with the object is obligatory.

Some verbs are capable of showing only single agreement. The reason for their not being able to show double agreement is usually phonological: these verbs tend

a. Form of TAKE meaning 'I take (something) away from you'

b. Form of TAKE meaning 'You take (something) away from me'

Figure 9.2 *Backwards verbs.*

to be specified for initial contact with a part of the body, which prevents the verbs from showing agreement with the subject. For example, the ASL sign TELL starts with contact at the chin, and the hand then moves to the area associated with the object referent. However, there is a variant of ASL TELL that allows double agreement. This variant starts with contact at the chin, moves to the area associated with the subject referent and then moves to the area associated with the object referent. This variant shows that the boundary between single and double agreement is not a strict one, and that it is possible for verbs to show more forms of agreement over time, as discussed in section 3.

2.1.3   *Nonmanual forms*

All the forms of agreement described thus far involve the hands. Aarons *et al.* (1992), Bahan (1996), and Neidle *et al.* (2000) argue that there is a nonmanual component to agreement that involves eye gaze and head tilt occurring simultaneously with the verb phrase. Eye gaze signifies agreement with the object, while head tilt marks agreement with the subject. Neidle *et al.* note that the nonmanual forms of agreement are optional. In the absence of nonmanual forms of agreement, the manual form of object agreement is often realized when possible.

2.1.4 *Canonical agreement*

The verb agreement forms thus far reveal a systematic distinction between agreement with the subject and agreement with the object. The subject and the object then constitute distinct controllers; their formal features systematically co-vary with particular properties of the target, namely, the verb. In that sense, the distinction between subject agreement and object agreement can be said to be one instance of systematic covariance.

Corbett (2006) presents four criteria for the controller to determine whether agreement is canonical. The description of the agreement forms in signed languages suggests that they meet at least three of them: the controller can have overt expression of agreement features itself by being produced in a particular area of signing space, the controller is consistent (it is always the object and optionally the subject), and the controller's part of speech is irrelevant, although it is usually a noun phrase. The one criterion that the agreement forms do not meet is that the controller is present. In signed languages, the controller can be phonetically null and be recovered from prior discourse (Lillo-Martin 1991).

With respect to the domain of agreement, Corbett (2006) has given another three criteria for determining canonical agreement, all of which the agreement systems in signed languages seem to meet. The domain is asymmetric, that is, the relationship between the controller (subject/object) and the target (verb) is hierarchical. The relationship is also strictly local: the controller and the target occur in the same clause. Finally, the domain is one of a set, meaning that agreement in other domains may occur.

2.2 Agreement with features

This section describes the features and their possible values that are marked in verb agreement forms. The section shows that verb agreement marks two features, person and number. In the end, the section returns to Corbett's (2006) criteria and shows another way that the verb agreement system approaches canonical agreement.

2.2.1 *Person agreement*

Many signed languages seem to display a two-way person system in verb agreement, as Meier (1990) has argued for ASL. That is, the feature of person has two values: first person and non-first person. First person is realized as the area on the signer's chest. The realization of non-first person has received much debate in the sign linguistics literature. For now, it is assumed that non-first person is realized as a zero form, following Rathmann and Mathur (2008).

All the forms of single and double agreement illustrated thus far mark one of the person features for the object and/or the subject. Figure 9.1 shows the contrast between first and non-first person. Figure 9.1a shows the form for a first person subject and a non-first person object, while Figure 9.1b illustrates the form for a non-first person subject and a first person object. The difference lies in the orientation and/or direction of movement of the verb. For a first person subject, the hand is oriented and directed away from the signer's chest. Backwards verbs also manifest the contrast between first and non-first person: Figure 9.2a shows the form of a backward verb for a first person subject and a non-first person object, while Figure 9.2b illustrates the form of a backward verb for a non-first person subject and a first person object.

2.2.2   *Number agreement*

All of the examples seen so far show *singular* agreement, meaning that the object and/ or the subject are singular in number, as in *She saw him*. Singular agreement is not to be confused with single agreement. Single agreement means that the verb shows agreement with just one argument such as the object, i.e., there is one controller and one target. Singular agreement means that the argument itself is a single entity (in the sense of one person or one group) as opposed to a plural entity (in the sense of several people or several groups), i.e., the controller has the feature of singular number. Thus, if there is single agreement, the controller can be singular or plural. Likewise, in double agreement, the two controllers can be either singular or plural.

Some verbs in many signed languages show agreement with a plural entity. Klima and Bellugi (1979) and Padden (1983) describe several forms of plural agreement for ASL, including multiple, exhaustive and dual. They stand in contrast to the singular form which occurs when the subject and the object are singular, as exemplified above.

This section describes the plural forms. The plural forms are usually not obligatory, and as mentioned above, the singular form can be used to refer to a plural entity provided that the plurality of the entity has been established in prior discourse. At the same time, it is important to understand the different forms of number agreement, since they stand in contrast to the category of person.

2.2.2.1   *Multiple form*   The multiple form, as described by Klima and Bellugi (1979) and Padden (1983), is used in the context of a sentence like *She asked all the people in a group*. The meaning is usually collective. Kamp and Reyle (1993) analyze the collective reading as introducing a discourse referent that represents a set, in contrast to the distributive reading, which converts this set into individuals.

Suppose there is a group of six people. When the multiple form is used, it can either mean a person asked six questions, one for each person in the group, or it can mean that the person asked one question of the whole group at once. The singular form could also be used to mean 'she asked the group at once,' but the implication there is that the group receives the question as a single entity and likewise gives an answer as a single entity, whereas with the multiple form, members of the group receive the question (at the same time) and can give their own answers.

This form inserts a horizontal arc into the path movement of the verb, as illustrated for ASL ASK in Figure 9.3a.

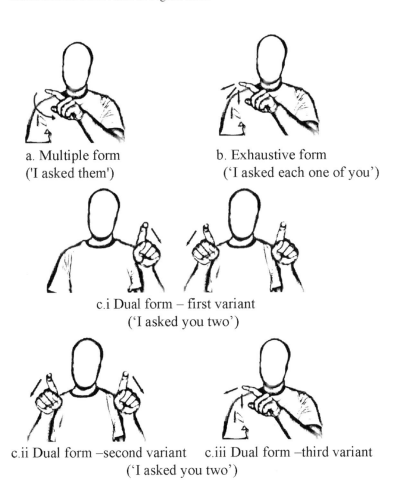

a. Multiple form
('I asked them')

b. Exhaustive form
('I asked each one of you')

c.i Dual form – first variant
('I asked you two')

c.ii Dual form –second variant   c.iii Dual form –third variant
('I asked you two')

Figure 9.3 *Plural forms of ASK.*

If there is a handshape change in the sign, it is spread over the arc (Sandler 1996a). In some cases, if the sign is one-handed, the multiple arc can be produced on both hands moving simultaneously away from the midline.

The multiple form is available only for the object, not for the subject (Padden 1983, Supalla 1997). That is, the multiple form can be used in a sentence like *She asked the group* but not in a sentence like *The group asked me*. The only way to express the latter sentence is to use the singular form of agreement for both the subject and the object. The restriction of the multiple form to the object is true for backwards verbs as well (Rathmann and Mathur 2008). For example, the multiple form is available for a sentence like *I invited them* but not a sentence like *they invited me*.

2.2.2.2   *Exhaustive form*   The exhaustive form, again described by Klima and Bellugi (1979) and Padden (1983), is used when the object (or the subject) refers to more than two entities, as in *She asked each person in the group*. The form seems to carry a distributive force, i.e., an event is distributed over each entity. The form involves reduplication of the singular form. This time, each reduplicant is directed toward several areas in signing space, each of which is associated with referents that constitute the object (or the subject). These areas are arrayed in an arc, and the hand moves along the arc rapidly. This form is illustrated for the ASL sign ASK in Figure 9.3b.

For some verbs that use only one hand (like the ASL sign ASK), the exhaustive form can be produced on both hands simultaneously, with the hands moving away from the midline.

The exhaustive form is available for both the object and the subject. The orientation and direction of movement in Figure 9.3b can be reversed to mean 'Each person in the group asked me.'

Padden (1983) emphasizes that the exhaustive form is distinct from another form in which the hand is carefully directed toward each area in signing space associated with a referent, using separate movements for each articulation. This form would mean 'She asked him, and her, and him, and her' rather than 'She asked each person in the group.' The exhaustive form can be used when the group has an indefinite number.

2.2.2.3   *Dual form*   The dual form is used when the object (or the subject) refers to two entities. Padden (1983) notes that there are three ways to produce the dual form. In a sentence like *I asked both of them*, the hand moves to one area in signing space that is associated with one of the two entities; then the hand moves to the other area associated with the second entity. The second way uses both hands: one hand moves toward one area, and then the other hand moves toward the other area. The third way is similar to the second way, except that both hands move simultaneously. These three ways are illustrated for the ASL sign ASK in Figure 9.3c.

The dual form is available for both the object and the subject. The above examples show the dual form for the object. It is possible to reverse the orientation and the direction of movement of the hands in these cases to produce a sentence like *Both of them asked me*. It is possible that the dual form is a special case of the exhaustive form and thus can be collapsed with it.

2.2.2.4   *More on plural forms*   Klima and Bellugi (1979) mention other plural forms: reciprocal, allocative determinate, allocative indeterminate, apportionative external, apportionative internal, seriated external and seriated internal. These forms await further analysis; it is very possible that some of these forms may be collapsed with one of the plural forms discussed above.

One significant constraint that holds across plural forms like the dual, the exhaustive and the multiple is that they are available only for one argument. The dual and the exhaustive are available for either the subject or the object, but not both at the same time (as in *Two people asked two people* or *Each person in one group asked each person in another group*). The multiple form is available only for the object. When both arguments are plural, the singular form is used for the subject and the plural form is used for the object.

Moreover, the exhaustive and the multiple forms follow an arc. The arc can be convex, i.e., the middle of the arc can be farther from the signer's body than the ends of the arc, or the arc can be concave, i.e., the middle of the arc can be closer to the body than the ends. See Figure 9.4a–b for an illustration of the two possibilities.

The choice of a convex or a concave arc depends on whether the argument is first person or non-first person (Mathur 2000). If the argument is non-first person, the arc is convex; otherwise, it is concave. The form of number agreement then depends on person agreement.

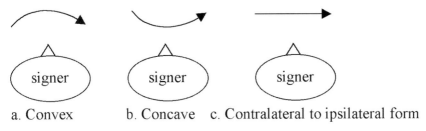

a. Convex   b. Concave   c. Contralateral to ipsilateral form

Figure 9.4 *Targets for agreement forms.*

2.2.3 *Location*

It has been demonstrated that verb agreement forms in signed languages can mark the person and number features of the subject and the object. Another feature that has been proposed in the sign linguistics literature is location. The realization of first person is fixed as the area on the signer's chest. As the preceding figures show, the realization of non-first person depends on the particular area/location in signing space that is associated with the object/subject referent. It could be said that the verb agrees with the object/subject with its assigned location in signing space. There are theoretical issues with assuming location as a feature of agreement, which are reviewed in Mathur and Rathmann (forthcoming).

2.2.4 *Canonical agreement*

The preceding subsections demonstrate that there is a two-way contrast within the feature of person for both the subject and the object, namely first person and non-first person. Within the feature of number, there is a multi-way contrast: singular, multiple, exhaustive, dual and reciprocal, among others. All of the values for the number feature are available for the object; a restricted set (singular, exhaustive, dual and reciprocal) are available for the subject.

Corbett (2006) presents three criteria for canonical agreement with respect to the features of agreement. The first criterion is whether the features are lexical or not. All the features here are lexical, in the sense that the realization of the values come from the lexicon and are thus fixed. One potential exception is non-first person; if it is treated as a zero morpheme, it can be considered lexical.

The second criterion is whether the features have matching values or not. This means that the realization of the values match the properties of the controller. In the case of signed languages, the values of number do not match the properties of the object and/or the subject. For example, the number feature of multiple is realized by a movement in the shape of a horizontal arc; this arc does not always appear in the object. It is assumed that the values of person do not match the properties of the controller either. First person is realized as an area on the signer's chest; this area does not necessarily match the area associated with the object (or subject) referent, especially in cases of referential shift when the signer takes on the role of another person. The realization of non-first person also does not have to match the controller: the controller could well be a lexical sign while non-first person is realized as a zero morpheme or as an area associated with a referent, depending on the analysis.

The third criterion relating to features is whether there is a choice of feature value in the agreement system. The description so far suggests that there is no choice: the controller has a specific value which determines the realization of the agreement form on the target, i.e., the verb. In sum, the verb agreement system meets two of three criteria for canonical agreement with respect to the features.

2.3   Verb classes

Not all verbs in signed language display these forms of agreement. Padden (1983, 1990) noted that there are three classes of verbs in ASL that differ with respect to the morphology that they can display. First are the "inflecting," later called "agreeing," verbs that display the forms discussed above, e.g., ASK and HELP. The second class contains "plain" verbs which do not display the agreeing forms; they may, however, be inflected for aspect, e.g., ACCEPT and DOUBT. The third class is called "spatial" and includes verbs that do not inflect for agreement as described above nor for aspect. Rather, this class includes verbs that convey motion or location, such as ASL MOVE, as well as many classifier constructions denoting the motion or location of an entity.[2]

One main issue in the field of sign language linguistics has been predicting the class membership of the verbs. Semantic criteria alone are not enough to distinguish agreeing from plain verbs. For example, while all agreeing verbs select for two animate arguments, so do some plain verbs like ASL LIKE and LOVE. Likewise, phonological criteria are not sufficient for predicting the class membership of the verbs. Plain verbs like LIKE and LOVE can be argued not to inflect for agreement because they are "body-anchored" – they are specified for a location on the body which blocks a potential agreement form. However, not all plain verbs are body-anchored, like ASL BUILD and CELEBRATE. Moreover, some agreeing verbs are body-anchored, like ASL TELL and INFORM.

These cases raise the issue of whether it is necessary to distinguish between agreeing and plain verbs. The above distinction may have more to do with the ability to realize the agreement forms (e.g., there is variation in whether ASL TEST displays agreement), whereas other verbs always remain plain (e.g., ASL ENJOY and SLEEP). The relevant distinction seems to lie in whether verbs select for two animate arguments. The conditions under which verbs display agreement are reviewed in Mathur and Rathmann (forthcoming). To clarify the fact that verbs do not always show agreement, one could say that verbs "participate in agreement" or that verbs are "candidates for participating in agreement" rather than talk about "agreeing verbs," which implies that there is a set of verbs that shows agreement in every case.

2.4   Phonetic and phonological constraints

There are several cases in which the realization of agreement with subject and object arguments in their person and number features can be affected by additional

a. contraHELPipsi   b. contraGET-HOLD-OFipsi
'She helped him' (acceptable)   'She got a hold of him' (awkward)

Figure 9.5 *Acceptable vs. awkward forms of agreement.*

factors like phonetic or phonological constraints. For example, in one non-first person singular subject form, the subject referent is associated with an area on the contralateral side (the side opposite the dominant hand), and the object referent is associated with an area on the ipsilateral side. The target form of verb agreement for this context must orient the hands toward the area associated with the object referent and/or move the hands from the area associated with the subject referent to the area associated with the object referent. See Figure 9.4c for an illustration of the target form.

Mathur and Rathmann (2006) have observed that two sets of verbs show the target form: those that do not require a change in orientation but only in direction of movement, like the ASL sign HELP, and those that involve a change in orientation and have a "mid" orientation (defined as when the palm faces to the side), like the ASL sign ABANDON. In contrast, signs that require a change in orientation and do not have a "mid" orientation, like GET-HOLD-OF in ASL, do not show the target form. See Figures 9.5a and 9.5b for illustrations of these signs.

The relevant constraint that prevents GET-HOLD-OF from achieving the target form is one against rotating the radio-ulnar part of the arm beyond a certain point. While this constraint is rooted in the physiology of the arm, there is evidence that the constraint has been systematicized as a phonetic-phonological one (Mathur & Rathmann 2006). For instance, the same constraint also explains why the target for the first person plural object form (meaning something like 'you verb us') is not realized for some verbs like the ASL signs RESPECT and ANALYZE. To produce the target forms for these signs, the non-dominant hand would have to be twisted at an angle that is beyond awkward.

2.5   Identification in case of unrealized agreement

When an agreement form is not fully realized, for example due to phonetic or phonological constraints, it is still possible for the addressee to identify the referents of the subject and object based on a number of cues.

First, it is possible to identify the referents of the subject and the object of a sentence if these referents have been established earlier in the discourse. For example, a signer may be talking about two people, Sue and Bob, who have been associated with areas on the signer's left and right respectively. The topic could be how Sue came to know Bob. After explaining how Sue met Bob, the signer could sign something like KNOW SINCE-THEN, meaning 'Sue has known Bob since then.' Lillo-Martin (1991) has noted such use of discourse context for "plain verbs," but the use of discourse also seems to be available for verbs that participate in the process of agreement.

Another means of identifying the referents of the subject and the object is to use nonmanual signals like eye gaze and head tilt, as pointed out by Neidle *et al.* (2000) and as described in section 2.1.3. Thus, the signer could tilt her head toward the area associated with Sue to refer to her and gaze at the area associated with Bob to refer to him.

Yet another way to identify the referents of the subject and the object is to point manually to the area associated with the referent. This kind of pointing often constitutes an overt pronoun, which usually takes the form of an extended finger. Thus in the same example above, the signer can point directly to the area associated with Sue, then point to the area associated with Bob, and then sign in KNOW SINCE-THEN, assuming that the language allows a Subject-Object-Verb (SOV) word order. These overt pronouns may be related to the head tilt and eye gaze described above, in that they represent different means of pointing.

Naming the subject and the object overtly and placing them in the language's basic word order is another way to identify the referents of the subject and the object. Thus, if the language's basic word order is SOV, the signer could sign SUE BOB KNOW. The word order makes it clear that Sue is the referent of the subject and Bob is the referent of the object.

One last cue for identifying the referents of the subject and the object is the use of an auxiliary-like element called Person Agreement Marker (PAM). The element does not carry any particular meaning and realizes the agreement form when it does not appear on the main verb (Rathmann 2000), i.e., it provides *do*-support for the main verb. In DGS, PAM is capable of realizing all the possible agreement forms described above, although the plural forms are less common (Rathmann 2000, Rathmann & Mathur 2008). PAM in DGS is illustrated in Figure 9.6.

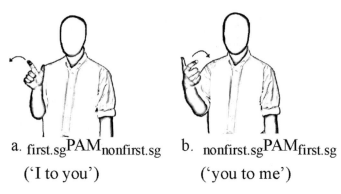

a. first.sg^{PAM}nonfirst.sg   b. nonfirst.sg^{PAM}first.sg

('I to you')   ('you to me')

Figure 9.6 *Person Agreement Marker (PAM) in DGS.*

Not all of these cues can be considered equivalent to agreement based on the criterion of systematic covariance. For example, the use of discourse context, overt pronouns and word order do not count as instances of agreement because they do not systematically co-vary in the presence of different person and number features. The use of head tilt and eye gaze in transitive sentences has been argued by Neidle *et al.* to be nonmanual instantiations of subject agreement and object agreement respectively. As pointed out in section 2.1.3, these non-manual signals are systematically associated with the subject and the object respectively, and can be considered as instances of agreement in distinguishing between the subject and the object. Less clear is whether they systematically co-vary with respect to the person and number features of the arguments. On the other hand, the use of PAM can be argued to be a substitute for an agreement form realized on a main verb, since the form of PAM systematically co-varies with the same person and number features in the same ways as those verbs that participate in agreement.

2.6   Crosslinguistic variation

This section describes the range of crosslinguistic variation with respect to the patterns that have been described regarding verb agreement. It appears that the patterns are universal across signed languages, in terms of the particular agreement forms realized, the sets of verbs that realize them, and the ways that signed languages use these patterns to identify the subject and object in cases where an agreement form is not realized.

It has been found that across a number of signed languages, including ASL and DGS, verbs vary in the particular combinations of person and number features that they can overtly realize. They show at least one of six distinct combinations in (2) (Rathmann & Mathur 2005).

(2)   Feature combination that can be overtly realized on the verb in signed languages:

    a.   First person singular subject and non-first person singular object (e.g., *I to you*)

    b.   Non-first person singular subject and first person singular object (e.g., *you to me*)

    c.   Non-first person singular subject and non-first person singular object (e.g., *you to him*)

    d.   First person singular subject and non-first person plural object (e.g., *I to y'all*)

    e.   Non-first person singular subject and first person plural object (e.g., *you to us*)

    f.   Non-first person singular subject and non-first person plural object (e.g., *you to them*)

Verbs marking (2b) always realize (2c), and similarly those marking (2e) always realize (2f). Thus the (2b) and (2c) forms are collapsed together, and likewise the (2e) and (2f) forms. There are then four distinct agreement forms, which are schematically represented below.

(3)

(2a)	(2b)	(2d)	(2e)
addressee	addressee	addressee	addressee
○	○	○	○
↑	↓	↗	↘
○	○	○	○
signer	signer	signer	signer
first sg subj, non-first sg obj	non-first sg subj, first sg obj	first sg subj, non-first pl obj	non-first sg subj, first pl obj
'I to you'	'you to me'	'I to y'all'	'you to us'

In a survey of seventy-five to eighty verbs that are potential candidates for showing agreement in DGS, ASL and JSL, Rathmann and Mathur (2005) have observed that verbs can be grouped into one of five sets. The five sets occur within an implicational hierarchy (cf. Supalla 1997 for a similar proposal). The first set contains verbs that realize all of the four forms in (3). The next set also realizes all forms, except the form for the first person plural object (i.e., 2d). The third set realizes only the singular forms, while the fourth set realizes just the non-first person singular form and the fifth set realizes none. Thus, the realization of person seems universal, while there seems to be crosslinguistic variation with respect to the realization of number. Some signed languages like DGS and ASL realize the plural feature, while this feature is not attested in JSL based on a survey from Mathur (2000). McBurney (2002) has found a similar crosslinguistic distribution with respect to the pronominal system in signed languages.

Signed languages are also similar with respect to identifying the referents of the subject and the object in case an agreement form is not realized manually on the verb. For example, the use of discourse and pragmatic conventions is attested in two of the signed languages discussed here, DGS and ASL. The use of overt pronouns and word order has been attested in ASL (Lillo-Martin 1991), BSL (Sutton-Spence & Woll 1999), DGS (Rathmann 2000) and Israeli Sign Language (Meir 1998b), among others.

It is the use of an auxiliary-like element that is subject to crosslinguistic variation. Rathmann (2000) and Steinbach and Pfau (2007) observe some signed languages use an auxiliary-like element (e.g., DGS, Sign Language of the Netherlands [Bos 1994, Hoiting & Slobin 2001] and JSL [Torigoe 1994, Fischer 1996]), while others do not (e.g., ASL, Auslan [Johnston & Schembri 2007] and BSL [Sutton-Spence & Woll 1999]).

As Rathmann (2000) and Steinbach and Pfau (2007) note, the properties of PAM differ from one signed language to another with respect to form, syntactic position and precise function. It is important to compare the properties of PAM across these languages so that additional crosslinguistic similarities and differences can be identified across signed languages with respect to verb agreement.

Regardless of the crosslinguistic similarities and differences, each signed language has its own system for realizing verbal agreement forms, and each system appears to be internally consistent, thereby meeting several of Corbett's (2006) criteria for canonical agreement.

2.7   Summary

The description of verb agreement as it appears in signed languages suggests that it is a morphological process reflecting a syntactic relationship and meets many of Corbett's (2006) criteria for canonical agreement with respect to the arguments that are agreed with, the features that are agreed in and the verbs that realize agreement. The arguments that are agreed with always include the object and optionally the subject. The features that are agreed in are person and number, and each feature is further divided into a number of values that each have a consistent form. The verbs that realize agreement seem to share a common argument structure of selecting for two animate arguments.

To round out the description of verb agreement systems in signed languages, Corbett's (2006) criteria for canonical agreement with respect to the target are evaluated. According to the description here, the target of verb agreement in signed languages is a bound morpheme, is obligatory and appears regularly, with certain exceptions. The target is alliterative in that it is based on the areas in signing space associated with the referents of the subject and object (cf. Aronoff, Sandler & Meir 2005 for a similar proposal). The marking of agreement is productive and is present even if a controller is absent. The target agrees with a single controller, namely either the subject or the object. That is, while there may be two targets on the verb, each target has a single controller. There is no choice of controller for the target; for most verbs that participate in agreement, one target is always controlled by the subject and the other by the object. Finally, the target's part of speech is irrelevant: the target is realized only on verbs, and more narrowly, a subset of verbs which is defined by a condition. These properties indicate that verb agreement in signed languages meets all of Corbett's (2006) criteria for canonical agreement with respect to the target.

3   Psycholinguistic and historical studies of verb agreement in signed languages

This section briefly summarizes psycholinguistic studies of verb agreement, including both experimental and developmental, and summarizes historical studies that shed further light on the development of verb agreement in signed languages.

3.1   Experimental studies

Experimental studies of verb agreement in signed languages to date have used repetition priming and eye-tracking. Through repetition priming, Emmorey (1991) examined the status of verb agreement as a morphological process. Repetition priming occurs when a lexical decision on a word is faster after a morphologically related word has been presented earlier in the experiment. As summarized in Emmorey (2002:132), it was found that "agreeing verbs did not facilitate recognition of the base form of the verb. That is, verbs in ASL such as ASK[dual], BEAT [multiple] and SHOOT[reciprocal] did not prime their citation forms." In contrast, aspectual modulations like the habitual and continual forms primed citation forms. This finding suggests the verb agreement is distinct from other morphological processes like aspect. It also suggests that the plural forms are less productive compared to the aspectual forms and is consistent with the lower frequency of plural forms relative to singular forms across signed languages. It would be interesting to see in future studies whether singular forms, including both first and non-first person forms, prime citation forms. If so, such a result would be consistent with the distinction between singular and plural features.

The eye-tracking study, conducted by Thompson, Emmorey and Kluender (2006), sought to evaluate the claim by Neidle *et al.* (2000) that the nonmanual component of agreement confirms that all verbs in ASL exhibit syntactic agreement. One main prediction of Neidle *et al.*'s claim is that eye gaze is systematically directed toward the area associated with the object referent with plain verbs, since that is the only way plain verbs can mark agreement with the object. To test this and other related predictions, Thompson *et al.* mounted an eye-tracking system on the heads of participants and asked the participants to tell a story based on eight pictures; retell the same story from memory; and make up a story using a list of twenty-six plain, agreeing and spatial verbs. Thompson *et al.* coded the direction of eye gaze (e.g., the addressee or a location in signing space), whether the location was associated with the referent of the subject or the object and whether the verb was plain, agreeing or spatial. One significant finding was that eye gaze was directed toward the area associated with the object referent for 74 percent of agreeing verbs but only for 11 percent of plains verbs. Thompson *et al.* conclude that eye gaze does not necessarily play a role in agreement since it does not consistently co-occur with plain verbs as predicted.

There are two reasons to reconsider this conclusion. First, Neidle *et al.* (2000) state that the use of eye gaze (and head tilt) is always optional, thus leaving room for other functions of eye gaze during the production of verb agreement. For example, eye gaze can function to mark a certain argument during discourse in a process separate from verb agreement. Second, Thompson *et al.* follow Padden's (1983) definition for a plain verb, namely, a verb that does not show overt manual agreement. The list of plain verbs in their appendix reveals a mix of verbs with different argument structures, e.g., those that select for two animate arguments (ASL HUG, LIKE) and those that do not (ASL MAKE, LOSE). It is possible that the pattern of eye gaze may be sensitive to the argument structure of the verb rather than whether it shows overt manual agreement or not.

The process of verb agreement awaits further experimental studies using other kinds of techniques such as brain imaging techniques.

3.2   Developmental studies

Another kind of psycholinguistic study has examined child (L1) and adult (L2) acquisition. Meier (2002) provides a recent review of L1 acquisition of verb agreement in a signed language. Among the major studies that have investigated this topic in ASL are Meier 1982; Lillo-Martin 1986, 1991; Casey 2003; and Quadros and Lillo-Martin 2007. There have also been investigations of verb agreement acquisition in BSL (Morgan, Barriere & Woll 2006), Brazilian Sign Language (LSB) (Lillo-Martin, Quadros & Mathur 1998), DGS (Hänel 2005), Dutch Sign Language (NGT) (van der Bogaerde & Baker 1996), Italian Sign Language (LIS, Pizzuto 2002), and Hong Kong Sign Language (Tang, Lam, Sze & Lau 2006), among others. The overall consensus is that verb agreement appears in child sign language relatively late, not until the age of three years, thus attesting to its morphological complexity. See, however, Lillo-Martin, Quadros and Mathur (1998), who claim that verb agreement emerges early by the age of two years. They take this finding to support the prominence of verb agreement in sign language structure. One possible explanation for the different findings is the criteria that researchers use to code agreement. After the coding criteria are taken into account, a clearer picture may emerge regarding the L1 acquisition of verb agreement in signed languages.

Several specific findings regarding the acquisition of verb agreement seem to corroborate the importance of features in the agreement process. For instance, Casey (2003) has found reversal errors in which children learning ASL incorrectly use non-first person forms for first person forms and vice versa, showing that they have to learn the distinction between the two values of the person feature. There also seems to be evidence that non-first person object forms are acquired before first person object forms. The order of acquisition of specific agreement forms could be a cognitive issue (it is apparently easier to produce verbs away from oneself than toward oneself), or it could be taken to support a two-way person distinction in verb agreement that must be learned.

Another finding from Supalla (1991) reveals that children must learn which arguments the verb agrees with, as pointed out by Meier (2002). Supalla followed a group of deaf children who were not exposed to ASL but rather Manually Encoded English (MCE), an artificial form of signed language that follows English grammar and that lacks the verbal agreement forms seen in signed languages. Even though these forms were absent in the input, some of these children spontaneously innovated agreement-like forms. These forms differed in one important respect from the agreement forms in signed languages: whereas the forms in signed languages reflected areas associated with the direct object of a transitive verb (as in *saw **Mary***) or the indirect object of a ditransitive verb (as in *gave the ball to **Mary***), the innovated forms sometimes reflected areas associated with the direct object of a ditransitive verb (as in *gave **the ball** to Mary*), a fact which has not been attested in signed languages. The fact that the innovated forms diverge from those seen in signed languages suggests that constraints on the process of verb agreement are real and must be acquired.

Most of the acquisition studies have focused on the mastery of single and double agreement with respect to first and non-first person forms. The forms under discussion are often singular. To date, there has been little study on the acquisition of plural agreement forms. It is possible that child production of plural agreement forms is rarer and thus harder to study. If plural forms are indeed harder to acquire, one question for future investigation is whether they are harder to learn because they are complex forms and/or because they are less frequent in the adult input.

3.3   Historical studies

In addition to the development of verb agreement within a child or an adult, there have also been studies of the development of verb agreement within a signed language over time. Engberg-Pedersen (1993) notes some verbs in Danish Sign Language go through a number of stages. First, they start out as plain, not showing any form of agreement. Then they begin to show what has been called non-first person agreement and then first person agreement. They seem to parallel the stages of child acquisition with respect to verb agreement. Similar stages have been reported for other signed languages, including ASL (Rathmann, Mathur & Meier 2003). For example, ASL TEST and TEASE at first showed only non-first person agreement. Later on, in some regions of the United States, a first person object agreement form became acceptable for these signs.

Supalla (1997) has observed from a crosslinguistic survey of various signed languages that there is an implicational hierarchy with respect to person and number features in single and double agreement. Verbs can progress up the hierarchy, going from agreement with no features to agreement with several features.

In addition, Rathmann (2000) and Steinbach and Pfau (2007) discuss different pathways for the development of PAM. In DGS, PAM is derived from the sign for PERSON, while in other languages, it is derived from a lexical verb as in Taiwan Sign Language (Smith 1990) or from a pair of pronouns as in JSL (Fischer 1996).

Another way to study the historical development of verb agreement is to compare older signed languages with younger signed languages. Most of the preceding discussion has concentrated on older, standardized, well-documented signed languages like DGS, BSL and ASL. More recently, there has been research on the emergence of verb agreement (or the lack thereof) in younger sign languages like Nicaraguan Sign Language (ISN) (Senghas *et al.* 1997), Israeli Sign Language (ISL) and Al-Sayyid Bedouin Sign Language (ABSL) (Aronoff, Meir & Sandler 2005). NSL and ISL show evidence of a verb agreement system that has emerged in stages parallel to those seen in older sign languages. On the other hand, ABSL has yet to show any kind of agreement, especially first person object agreement. That is, when signing a sentence like *He handed me a ball*, the ABSL signer would sign 'give' away from the body (instead of toward the signer, as in most sign languages) and point to herself to indicate that she is the object referent. This finding has led Aronoff, Meir & Sandler (2005) to propose that by default, the body marks the subject; over time, in some signed languages like ASL and ISL, the body then can be used to mark first person separately from the subject.

Signed languages then proceed along similar pathways with regard to the development of verb agreement. They may be found in different stages of the grammaticization of verb agreement, accounting for the crosslinguistic variation in the expression of person and number features (cf. Supalla 1997). It is difficult to account for such unidirectional progression with a lexical approach as in Padden (1983) or Liddell (2003b), who assume that verbs must be lexically specified as indicating. Rather, such progression is consistent with the view that verbs participate in agreement as opposed to the view that there is a set of verbs that show agreement in all conditions. The more frequently a verb is used, the more likely it will participate in agreement if it meets the conditions on the process. In that case, a linguistic innovation takes place, a kind of grammaticization in which an ongoing interaction emerges between a linguistic element and a gestural element (Rathmann & Mathur 2008). This kind of grammaticization differs from other kinds of grammaticization under which a linguistic element emerges from a gestural element but is ultimately disassociated from it, like modals or nonmanual markers (Wilcox 2004a).

4   Verb agreement in signed languages

This chapter has provided a detailed description of how verb agreement works in signed languages. The description has shown that verb agreement in signed languages systematically marks the features of person and number of the subject and the object, and that this process is subject to several constraints such as the restriction of some forms to the object and the restriction of agreement to verbs with a specific argument structure. Some of these properties, especially those concerning unrealized agreement, are subject to crosslinguistic variation. Otherwise, many properties of verb agreement are universal across signed languages, including emerging grammars. The uniformity of these properties can be attributed to the modality-specific property of using gestural space, a medium that is not required for spoken languages. Another possible source for the uniformity of verb agreement across signed languages comes from the relative youth of the languages, both with respect to their chronological age (Aronoff, Meir & Sandler 2005) and the number of cycles the languages go through, which repeat themselves with each generation of signers (Newport & Supalla 2000, Rathmann & Mathur 2002).

Many properties of verb agreement in signed languages meet Corbett's (2006) criteria for canonical agreement, suggesting that verb agreement in signed languages is conceptually similar to that in spoken languages and that there is a cross-modal need for a mechanism that cross-references words within a sentence with respect to a universal set of features. However, other approaches to verb agreement in signed languages may interpret Corbett's criteria for canonical agreement differently. Even other criteria such as those by Lehmann (1988) have been used by sign language researchers to reach different conclusions about verb agreement in signed languages (see Liddell 2000 and Rathmann & Mathur 2002). Thus, interpreting criteria based on spoken languages in the context of signed languages remains a challenge, and by continuing the study of verb agreement in signed languages in the directions suggested throughout the chapter, we can begin to determine whether agreement in the two modalities constitutes a unified linguistic phenomenon, or two distinct but parallel phenomena.

10

Functional markers in sign languages

Sandro Zucchi, Carol Neidle, Carlo Geraci,
Quinn Duffy and Carlo Cecchetto

1 Lexical morphemes and grammatical morphemes

It is a common observation that grammatical morphemes often develop gradually from lexical morphemes.[1] Some languages show this fact more transparently than others. For example, Sebba (1997) observes that creoles and pidgins often use lexically contentful elements with the meaning of 'finish' or 'done' as functional markers signaling that the event described by the sentence occurs *before* the time of utterance:

(1)   mo   fin   mahze (Mauritian Creole)
        I   finish eat
        'I ate.'

(2)   me   waka   kba   (Sranan Tongo)
        I   walk   finished
        'I had walked.'

(3)   mipela I   ting   olsem   i   mas   dai pinis (Tok Pisin)
        we   him think anyhow him must die finish
        'We think he must have died.'

(4)   a   don   kom   (Pidgin of West Africa)
        I   done   come
        'I have come.'

Similar examples from other spoken languages are offered by Pfau and Steinbach (2006). In Rama (a spoken language of Nigeria), the verb *aktul* meaning 'finish' is now used as a completive marker, and in Lhasa (spoken in Tibet), the verb *tshaa* meaning 'finish' marks perfective aspect.[2]

Examples of this sort are also quite common in sign languages.[3] For instance, the signs FINISH and FATTO belonging, respectively, to American Sign Language

197

(ASL) and Italian Sign Language (LIS), can both occur as lexically contentful main verbs with the meaning of 'finish' (or 'done') and as aspectual/temporal morphemes. Both signs, when acting as grammatical morphemes, also exhibit a peculiar behavior with negation and negative quantifiers.

Although FATTO and FINISH share many temporal/aspectual properties and interact in a similar way with negative items, they do so in structurally different environments: LIS is an SOV language (at least as far as the variety we are investigating goes), while ASL is SVO; moreover both FATTO and negation are postverbal in LIS, while FINISH and negation regularly occur preverbally in ASL. These similarities and structural differences provide a testing ground for analyses of FATTO and FINISH, which is why it may be interesting to try to pursue a parallel analysis.

In this paper, we propose an account of these morphemes that explains their temporal/aspectual properties, as well as their behavior with negative items. In particular, we will argue that their interaction with negators relates to other properties of ASL and LIS, as well as to a more general crosslinguistic pattern observed in Huang (2003) for negative quantifiers of spoken languages. Our account is based on Huang's and is spelled out within the theoretical framework provided by Chomsky and Lasnik (1993), Halle and Marantz (1993), Chomsky (1995) and Marantz (1994).

Although our discussion is restricted to LIS and ASL (two languages that are probably historically related through French Sign Language), our analysis may also apply to similar items in other sign languages. Future research may assess the extent to which the analysis applies and, by doing so, may help to determine how sign languages vary with respect to the behavior of their functional markers.

In section 2, we briefly introduce some temporal/aspectual notions we will use in our discussion. In sections 3 to 4, we focus on the temporal and aspectual properties of FINISH and FATTO. The behavior of FINISH and FATTO with negative items is discussed in section 5.

2   Some basic notions

Before we proceed to discuss the temporal and aspectual properties of FATTO and FINISH, let us briefly clarify how we will use certain terms.

By "perfective" marker we mean any morphological marker indicating that the event described by the predicate to which it applies is a "complete event." We explain what we mean by a complete event by providing the following illustration: in the case of a house-building event, a complete event is one that includes both the process through which the house is built and the completion of the process (or its "culmination," in Parsons's 1990 terminology).[4] An "imperfective" form is a predicate form which, from a semantic standpoint, is non-committal as to whether the event it describes is complete or not.

With the term "perfect" (not to be confused with *perfective*), we refer to a construction in which a tense is combined with some anteriority operator to the effect that the event described by the predicate is placed at a time that precedes the time referred to by the tense. Thus, for instance, the sentence *John has built a house*, uttered now, means that the event of building a house has occurred before the time referred to by the present tense form *has*. We take this to follow from the fact that, at the level relevant for semantic interpretation, the present tense has an anteriority operator in its scope which locates the event at a time prior to the time referred to by the present tense.[5]

Notice that, by our characterizations, perfect and perfective are not mutually exclusive categories. In particular, the perfect sentence *John has built a house* also carries the information that the house-building event is complete, thus it also carries perfective meaning. Following current usage, we call information concerning whether an event is complete or not "aspectual" information. Notice that morphological markers traditionally referred to as *tenses*, in addition to information of a temporal nature concerning the location of the event with respect to the utterance time, may often carry aspectual information. For instance, Italian *passato remoto* carries both the information that the event occurs before the utterance time and the information that the event is complete. Thus, the sentence *Gianni costruì una casa* (Gianni build-*passato remoto* a house) means that a complete house-building event by Gianni occurs prior to the utterance time.

3   The story about FATTO

3.1   Some basic facts

The sign FATTO in LIS may be used as a main verb with the meaning of 'finish.' In this case, it usually occurs alone, without an overt complement, as in (5).[6]

(5)   FATTO?
      'Did you finish?'

In (6), however, illustrated in Figure 10.1, FATTO occurs after the verb with the grammatical function of indicating that the action described by the verb was completed before the time of utterance.

(6)   GIANNI   CASA   COMPRARE   FATTO
      Gianni   house   buy   done
      'Gianni has bought a house.'

Figure 10.1 *Illustration of example (6)*.

In the discussion that follows, we concentrate on the postverbal use of FATTO as a grammatical marker and ignore its use as a main verb.

As (6) shows, LIS is an SOV language. Negation and modals occur postverbally, and determiners and prepositions are naturally found after their complements,[7] as one might expect in a head-final language. *Wh*-items, when not left *in situ* (a marked occurrence), occur at the right periphery of the sentence (see Cecchetto, Geraci & Zucchi 2006 for a presentation of LIS syntax).

One interesting fact about FATTO is that it cannot co-occur with sentential negation NON. Thus, (7) cannot be negated as in (8).

(7)   GIANNI   MANGIARE   FATTO
       Gianni   eat   done
       'Gianni has eaten.'

(8)   a.   * GIANNI MANGIARE FATTO NON
       b.   * GIANNI MANGIARE NON FATTO

In section 5 below, we present a more complete paradigm of the behavior of FATTO with negation. First, however, let us try to give a more precise account of the role of FATTO in sentences like (6) and (7).

3.2   Temporal and aspectual properties of FATTO

From a temporal standpoint, FATTO expresses anteriority. Thus, while (9) may be interpreted as describing an event taking place at the time of utterance,[8] (6) locates the house buying event in the past.

(6)   GIANNI   CASA   COMPRARE   FATTO
       Gianni   house   buy   done
       'Gianni has bought a house.'

(9) GIANNI CASA COMPRARE
     Gianni   house buy
     'Gianni is buying a house.'

FATTO may also express anteriority with respect to a time specified by a time adverb, as in (10).

(10) IERI   ALLE-3 GIANNI MANGIARE FATTO
      yesterday at-3   Gianni eat   done
      .'Gianni had already eaten yesterday at 3.'

From an aspectual standpoint, FATTO expresses perfectivity; namely it indicates that the event described by the verb has reached its completion and is not an open process. Thus, for instance, sentence (11) cannot be used to report that Gianni's house building was going on at a past time, but conveys the information that the house building was completed.

(11) GIANNI CASA   COSTRUIRE FATTO
      Gianni   house build   done
      'Gianni has built a house.'

The fact that FATTO carries aspectual information of this kind may also explain why it cannot co-occur with stative predicates. For instance, FATTO is anomalous with a verb like PUZZARE ('stink'):

(12) ?? GIANNI PUZZARE FATTO
          Gianni   stink   done

The restriction here is really about stativity and not agentivity, as indicated by the fact that, while (12) is deviant, (13) is acceptable:

(13) FOGLIE AVVIZZIRE FATTO
      leaves   wither   done
      'The leaves have withered.'

FATTO's restriction to nonstative predicates is expected if FATTO requires the event described by the predicate to be a culminated event: the restriction follows from the fact that states, unlike events, do not have culmination parts and thus cannot be required to culminate.

Summing up, the data presented so far suggest that FATTO carries both temporal information telling us that an event of the type described by the predicate occurs at a time preceding the utterance time (or some time referred to by a time adverb) and aspectual information telling us that the event in question is a culminated event.

In principle, these facts are compatible with different hypotheses concerning the function of FATTO. One hypothesis is that FATTO is a past tense marker which also carries perfective meaning.[9] Another hypothesis is that sentences with FATTO are present tense sentences and FATTO, besides carrying perfective meaning, is an anteriority marker indicating that the event described by the predicate takes place at a time preceding the time referred to by the present tense. According to this second hypothesis, sentences with FATTO should be analyzed on a par with Italian present perfect sentences like *Gianni ha comprato una casa* ('Gianni has bought a house'). A third possibility is that FATTO is an anteriority marker with perfective meaning, but, contrary to what the second hypothesis claims, LIS sentences with FATTO have no tense at all.

In Zucchi (2009), it is argued that LIS sentences are tensed and that, in particular, LIS sentences with FATTO, like those that have been presented above, are present perfect sentences. Let us see how the argument goes. The hypothesis that LIS sentences like (6) above are tenseless is problematic, since it fails to account for the assignment of (abstract) nominative case to the subject. Under the assumption that case is either assigned by tense or by agreement (or by both),[10] if sentences like (6) are tenseless, the only possibility is that case is assigned by agreement in LIS. Indeed, in LIS, as in many other sign languages, there is evidence that agreement is present, since for some verbs it seems to be overtly marked by spatial orientation.[11] However, in this case, we should also conclude that agreement is unable to assign nominative case in LIS, because of examples like (14), where the subject of the agreeing predicate PARTIRE raises out of the subordinate clause, presumably in order to receive case:

(14)   LUI   SEMBRA   PARTIRE$_{3p.}$ FATTO
      he   seems   leave   done
      'He seems to have left.'

Thus, the hypothesis that LIS sentences like (6) are untensed fails to account for how nominative case is assigned to the subject.

Moreover, at least in the variety of LIS spoken in the Napoli-Salerno area, tense is explicitly signaled by nonmanual marking on the verb: the shoulder's position is tilted back for past tense, tilted forward for future tense and straight (aligned with the rest of the body) for present tense. If this is correct, since in the elicited sentences with FATTO the shoulder is straight, we should conclude that these sentences are best analyzed as present tense sentences, thus favoring a present perfect analysis over a past tense analysis.

Finally, additional evidence favoring the present perfect hypothesis comes from the co-occurrence of FATTO with time adverbs like ORA ('now'):

(15) ORA   CAFFÈ   BERE   FATTO
      now   coffee   drink   done
      'Now I have drunk the coffee.'

As Zucchi shows, sentences of this sort are expected if they are analyzed as present perfect sentences with ORA under the scope of tense and with FATTO in its scope (possibly in AspP), while they are not expected if FATTO is analyzed as a past tense. Summing up, our final conclusion is then that postverbal FATTO, from a semantic standpoint, carries perfective meaning and is also a marker of anteriority indicating that the event described by the predicate takes place at a time preceding the time referred to by the tense.

Crosslinguistically, items similar to FATTO have been independently analyzed as perfect markers. Meir (1999) describes a sign of Israeli Sign Language (ISL) which she glosses as ALREADY and which seems to be the ISL counterpart of FATTO. She proposes to analyze ALREADY as a perfect marker because, among other things, it can co-occur with adverbs like NOW and future adverbials.[12] Similar claims have been made about one usage of the sign FINISH in ASL.[13] Rathmann (2005) offers a detailed proposal analyzing some occurrences of FINISH in ASL as perfect markers, an issue to which we now turn.

4   The story about FINISH

The sign FINISH in ASL, illustrated in Figure 10.2, has a wide range of distinct functions described in the literature (e.g., Fischer & Gough 1999, Rathmann 2005).[14]

Among its many possible meanings, FINISH can be used in constructions very much like those described for FATTO: (a) as a main verb with the meaning of

Figure 10.2 *Illustration of ASL sign FINISH.*

'finish' (in which case it frequently precedes an NP or VP complement), (b) as a perfect marker (in pre-VP position), and (c) as an adverbial with the meaning of 'already.' ASL differs from LIS in that the ASL versions of these three distinct constructions frequently contain FINISH in the same linear order relative to the relevant VP, resulting in sequences of signs that can be potentially ambiguous. However, there are often prosodic cues, differences in the articulation of FINISH, and semantic/pragmatic considerations to distinguish these constructions.

For example, in the sequence FINISH READ BOOK, as shown in (17) below, FINISH can function as a main verb followed by a VP complement. This would be appropriate in a context where one is relating that John started reading the book on Monday and that he finished reading the book on Saturday. Assuming that same scenario, the following Monday, it would then be appropriate to declare that John has now read the book, which could be done with the construction illustrated in (22) below, containing the same linear sequence of signs.

The examples included in this section are taken from the National Center for Sign Language and Gesture Resources (NCSLGR) database of video examples of ASL sentences and narratives collected at Boston University, annotated with SignStream™ (Neidle & MacLaughlin 1998, Neidle, Sclaroff & Athitsos 2001) and are accessible on the Internet[15] and on CD-ROM (Neidle 2003, 2004, 2007). The volume number, database file and utterance number from which each example has been taken are listed in parentheses. Glosses are conventional English (rough) translations of the ASL signs. The lines above the glosses, as in (19), show the scope of facial expressions and head gestures that occur in parallel with phrasal groupings of manual signs to convey grammatical information, in this example marking the question status of a wh-question. The symbol # at the beginning of a gloss signals a fingerspelled loan sign.

Main verb

(16)   MUST FINISH #ALL BEFORE SUNSET

                                          (NCSLGRv4, Accident, U 9)
         'We must finish everything before sunset.'

(17)   JOHN FINISH READ BOOK   (NCSLGRv1, ncslgr10a, U 1)
         'John finished reading the book.'

Perfect marker

(18)   JOHN FINISH VISIT MARY
         'John has visited Mary.'   (NCSLGRv2, ncslgr10l, U 74)

Figure 10.3 *Illustration of example (18)*.

wh

(19)   STUDENT UP-TO-NOW FINISH READ HOW-MANY BOOK

                          (NCSLGRv1, ncslgr10b, U 24)

     'How many books have the students read so far?'

Adverbial

(20)   FINISH EXHAUSTED   (NCSLGRv7, Roadtrip 1, U 25)

     'We were already exhausted …'

Clause-external use of FINISH for discourse purposes (between, before, or after sentences)

(21)   TIRED FINISH BED GET-IN-BED ALL-NIGHT

                        (ASLLRPv1, DSP Ski Trip Story, U 8)

     'I was tired. So … I got in bed for the night.'

The focus for the rest of this section will be on the construction in which FINISH precedes VP and functions in ASL as a perfect marker. As in LIS, the FINISH in examples (18) and (19) marks culmination of an event, but not past tense. This is shown by ASL examples similar to (15), such as (22).

Context: Last week, John was asked a question in class, and he didn't know the answer, because he hadn't read the book that had been assigned. But now he does know the answer. Why?

(22)   NOW JOHN FINISH READ BOOK
       'Now John has read the book.'

Furthermore, ASL FINISH in this usage is compatible with eventualities that have not yet happened, as illustrated in (23), as it can co-occur with the tense marker glossed here as FUTURE (sometimes glossed as WILL), which has a function comparable to that of 'will' in English (Aarons *et al.* 1995, Neidle *et al.* 2000).

(23)   JOHN FUTURE FINISH SEE MARY
                              (NCSLGRv2, ncslgr10l, U 77, 78)
       'John will have seen Mary.'

Thus, the perfect construction not only does not mark past tense, but also is not restricted to present tense sentences in ASL. As in LIS, FINISH can be argued to occur under the scope of Tense (perhaps in AspP) and similarly carries the information that the event culminated prior to the reference time signaled by Tense.

As in LIS, FINISH in the perfect construction is consistent only with terminated events and thus is not used with predicates that are inherently incompatible with culmination, including most states and imperfective aspectual inflections, as reported in Duffy (2007),[16] from which the ungrammatical examples in (24)–(29) are taken.

(24)   * IX-1p FINISH HUNGRY
       (on the reading where it means 'I have/had been hungry.'
       Acceptable, in an appropriate context, with the reading 'I was already hungry.')

(25)   * IX-1p FINISH WANT CAR
       'I have/had wanted that car.'

(26)   * IX-1p FINISH LIKE CHOCOLATE
       'I have/had liked chocolate.'

(27)   * IX-1p FINISH ASK[iterative] (UP-TO-NOW 4-WEEK)
       'I have been asking, over and over (for four weeks).'

(28)   * IX-3p FINISH WORK[incessant] (UP-TO-NOW 20 HOUR)
       'He has been working, incessantly (for twenty hours).'

(29)   * IX-1p FINISH LOOK[durational] (1-HOUR)
       'I have been looking at it (for an hour).'

ASL does not make use of the perfect construction for events that necessarily continue into the present (the so-called universal perfect, or U-Perfect construction), despite Rathmann's claim that it does, which was based on an example of his, presented here as (30).

(30)   IX-1p FINISH LIVE HAMBURG 10 YEAR

According to our consultants, (30) would most naturally be translated by the English sentence in (31).

(31)   I have (or had) lived in Hamburg for 10 years.

Although that terminated eventuality may – but need not – extend to the present time, it does not continue. To express an ongoing, temporally unbounded event, FINISH cannot be used, as shown in (32).

(32)   IX-1p (*FINISH) LIVE BOSTON UP-TO-NOW 5 YEAR.
         IX-1p STILL LIVE THERE
         'I've been living in Boston for 5 years. I still live there.'

Thus, ASL FINISH, like LIS FATTO, has a usage on which it simultaneously conveys perfect and perfective. FINISH in ASL can mark anteriority of event culmination with respect to present, past or future reference time.

5   Interaction of FATTO and FINISH with negation

5.1   Negation in LIS and ASL

Before we turn to the interaction of FATTO and FINISH with negation, let us briefly review some differences between LIS and ASL with respect to negation. In LIS negation occurs only after the verb, while in ASL negation occurs preverbally:

(33)   ___neg
        GIANNI   CASA   COMPRARE   NON
        Gianni   house   buy   not
        'John is not buying a house.'

(34)   _____neg
        JOHN NOT BUY HOUSE
        'John is not buying a house.'

Besides differing for the position of negation, ASL and LIS also differ with respect to the nonmanual marking of negation, which in LIS is usually confined to the

negation sign, while in ASL it can optionally spread on the c-command domain of
negation when negation is expressed by a manual sign. Negative quantifiers in LIS
do not normally occur in argument position (i. e., preverbally, since LIS is an SOV
language), but are placed postverbally, where negation occurs:

(35)

                                                                 __neg__

CONTRATTO   FIRMARE   NESSUNO
contract   sign   no one
'No one is signing the contract.'

(36)

                                                       __neg__

GIANNI   FIRMARE   NIENTE
John   sign   nothing
'Gianni is signing nothing.'

In ASL, on the other hand, negative quantifiers occur in argument position (recall
that ASL is an SVO language):

(37)

                                              __neg__

JOHN VISIT NONE/NO-ONE
'John visits nobody.'

(38)

                                              __neg__

NONE/NO-ONE VISIT JOHN
'Nobody visits John.'

For more detailed analyses of negation in ASL and LIS, we refer the reader to
Neidle *et al.* (2000) and Geraci (2006), respectively.

5.2   Distributional restrictions

The sign FATTO, when it occurs postverbally and not as a main verb, never occurs
with the sign NON ('not') or with negative quantifiers like NESSUNO ('no one'),
NIENTE ('nothing'), MAI ('never'):

(7)   GIANNI   MANGIARE   FATTO
         Gianni   eat   done
         'Gianni has eaten.'

(8)   a.   *GIANNI MANGIARE FATTO NON
         b.   *GIANNI MANGIARE NON FATTO

(39) a. *GIANNI MANGIARE FATTO NIENTE
     b. *GIANNI MANGIARE NIENTE FATTO

(40) a. *MANGIARE FATTO NESSUNO
     b. *MANGIARE NESSUNO FATTO

(41) a. *GIANNI MANGIARE FATTO MAI
     b. *GIANNI MANGIARE MAI FATTO

There is a similar restriction on the use of negation with FINISH when used to mark aspect in ASL. To negate a sentence such as (18), to express the idea that John has *not* visited Mary, or that John has *never* visited Mary, or that John has visited *no one*, the standard ASL negators cannot be used in conjunction with FINISH (on its aspectual usage). A sentence like (42) could not be used to contradict a claim made by a sentence like (18).

(18) JOHN FINISH VISIT MARY   [NCSLGRv2, ncslgr10l, U 74]
     'John has visited Mary.'

(42) * JOHN NOT FINISH VISIT MARY

(43) * JOHN NEVER FINISH VISIT MARY

(44) * JOHN FINISH VISIT NONE/NO-ONE

Note that no such restriction is found when FINISH or FATTO is used as a main verb. Compare the above ungrammatical examples with the following:

                                neg
                         ‾‾‾‾‾‾‾‾‾‾‾‾‾‾‾‾‾‾‾‾‾‾‾‾‾
(45) JOHN NOT-YET FINISH READ BOOK
                       (NCSLGRv1, ncslgr10a, U 4)
     'John has not yet finished reading the book.'

                                     neg
(46) JOHN START READ BOOK, BUT NOT-YET FINISH
     'John started reading the book, but has not yet finished.'

                         neg
(47) JOHN NOT FINISH READ BOOK
                       (NCSLGRv9, ncslgr10s, U 193)
     'John did not finish reading the book.'

                                     neg
(48) GIANNI   UOVO-ROTTURA   FATTO   NON
     Gianni   egg-break   done   not
     'Gianni has not finished breaking eggs.'

Why are negative items barred from co-occurring with FATTO in LIS and with
FINISH in ASL when they are used to convey aspectual information? Some
hypotheses are considered below.

5.3   Negation and aspect

Semantically, in simple sentences like (7) and (18) above, FATTO and FINISH
convey the information that the event described by the verb has culminated by the
time the sentence is uttered. In this sense, FATTO and FINISH act, among other
things, as markers of perfectivity (complete action). It is well known that in some
languages negation is incompatible, or dispreferred, with perfective markers. For
example, Stevenson (1969) reports that in Bagirmi, a Nilo-Saharan language, the
marker of completion *ga* cannot co-occur with negation.

(49)   ma   m-'de   ga
        1SG   1SG-come   CMPL.
        'I have come.'

(50)   ma   m-'de   li
        1SG   1SG-come   CMPL.
        'I did/have not come.'

In Russian negative sentences, imperfective aspect is preferred to perfective aspect.
Thus, for example, Matthews (1990) reports that (51) is preferred to (52) in actual
discourse:[17]

(51)   pro-chital   stat'ju
        Pfv-read   paper
        'I read the paper.'

(52)   ne pro-chital   stat'ju
        NEG Pfv-read   paper
        'I did not read the paper.'

These cases may suggest that the ungrammaticality of (8) and (39)–(41) in LIS, and
of (42)-(44) in ASL, is an instance of a more general crosslinguistic phenomenon by
which markers of complete action (perfective aspect) are reluctant to occur with
negation. Some authors have tried to account for this phenomenon by suggesting
that that there is some incompatibility between the meaning of negation and the
meaning of perfective aspect. For example, Schmid (1980) suggests that perfective
aspect and negation are incompatible because negation is aspectually stative and

thus is incompatible with perfective predicates, which are eventive in nature. Matthews (1990) seems to attribute the incompatibility of perfective aspect and negation to the fact that there is no such thing as a negative event (while there are negative states). Hagman (1977), in discussing Khoekhoe (a Khoisan language), suggests that perfective aspect marks the event described by the predicate as punctual and that negation is barred with this aspect because the non-occurrence of a punctual event cannot be located in time. If some account of the meanings of negation and perfective aspect can be worked out to derive their alleged incompatibility, then the same account may also be applied to the LIS and ASL facts in (8) and (39)–(41) and in (42)–(44).

There are at least two reasons, however, to doubt that this strategy will deliver the desired results. First, as Miestamo and van der Auwera (2006) have pointed out, by examining an extensive sample of 297 languages (and an areally balanced subsample of 179 languages), imperfective-type categories are as likely to be affected by the presence of negation as perfective-type ones: in both the larger and the balanced sample, the number of languages in which a perfective-type category, but not an imperfective-type category, is barred with negation is identical to the number of languages in which an imperfective-type category, but not a perfective type category, is barred with negation. Moreover, there are languages, like Italian, in which both perfective and imperfective forms are acceptable under negation:

(53) Gianni   non   si   muoveva
      Gianni   not   refl. move-Impfv.
      'Gianni was not moving.'

(54) Gianni   non   si   mosse
      Gianni   not   refl. move-Pfv.
      'Gianni did not move.'

(55) Gianni   non   si   è   mosso
      Gianni   not   refl. is   move-Perf.
      'Gianni has not moved.'

These facts do not show that the ungrammaticality of (8) and (39)–(41) in LIS and of (42)–(44) in ASL is unrelated to aspect. They show, however, that attempts to derive that ungrammaticality from some semantic incompatibility between negation and perfective aspect is unlikely to succeed.

The second reason why appeal to incompatibility of negation and perfective aspect is unlikely to account for the LIS and ASL facts is that characterizing (8), (39)–(41) and (42)–(44) as instances of this incompatibility is, to some extent, a misdescription of the data. While, as we saw, FATTO cannot co-occur with the negation sign NON, LIS does have some signs that, while carrying some additional presuppositions, serve the purpose of denying that a complete event of the kind denoted by the predicate has taken place. For example, if Gianni has not done his homework yet, we may report this fact in LIS with sentence (56).[18]

(56) GIANNI   FARE-COMPITI   NON-ANCORA
      Gianni   do-homework   not-yet
      'Gianni has not done his homework yet.'

If Gianni has not done his homework and will not do it, this fact may be reported by uttering (57).[19]

(57) GIANNI   FARE-COMPITI   NIENTE
      Gianni   do-homework   nothing
      'Gianni has not done his homework (and won't do it).'

Note that the sign glossed as NON-ANCORA, while it carries the presupposition associated with Italian *non ancora* ('not yet'), unlike its Italian counterpart cannot be used to state that the event described by the verb is not yet going on but conveys the information that no event of that type has been completed yet. Thus, for instance, while Italian (58) can be used to deny that Gianni is doing his homework and (59) to deny that Gianni has done his homework, LIS sentence (56) above corresponds only to (59); i.e., it can only mean that Gianni has not done his homework yet.

(58) Gianni non sta ancora facendo i compiti
      'Gianni is not doing his homework yet.'

(59) Gianni non ha ancora fatto i compiti
      'Gianni has not done his homework yet.'

Indeed, in a situation in which Gianni is doing his homework but has not finished yet, one cannot reject (56) as false. This means that (56) is the negation of (60) (in contexts in which the relevant presupposition associated with 'not yet' is satisfied):

(60) GIANNI   FARE-COMPITI   FATTO
      Gianni   do-homework   done
      'Gianni has done his homework.'

Similar considerations apply to (57), where the sign NIENTE is used to deny that Gianni has done his homework (with the additional implication that he won't do it).

The facts for FINISH in ASL are very much the same. To deny an assertion as in (18), options include (61) or (62), depending on whether or not there is an expectation that this visit will occur in the future.

(18) JOHN FINISH VISIT MARY   [NCSLGRv2, ncslgr10l, U 74]
'John has visited Mary.'

$$\overline{\hspace{4cm}\text{neg}}$$
(61) JOHN NOT-YET VISIT MARY
'John has not yet visited Mary.'

$$\overline{\hspace{4cm}\text{neg}}$$
(62) JOHN NOT VISIT MARY
'John didn't visit Mary.'

There is also a construction similar to the one illustrated in (57), with a sign traditionally glossed as DON'T (both hands palms down, initially crossing in front of the body and then moving outward) occurring sentence-finally (at least as used by some signers; one of our signers does not use this sign at all):

$$\overline{\hspace{2cm}\text{neg}}$$
(63) JOHN READ BOOK DON'T
'John hasn't read the book (and there's no expectation that he will).'

Looking at these data, it becomes clear that while FATTO and FINISH are barred from occurring with the sign NON/NOT and with negative quantifiers, this fact is not correctly described as an instance of incompatibility between negation and perfectivity. Indeed, as we just saw, LIS and ASL do have a way of negating perfective sentences. What is peculiar to these languages is not that perfective sentences cannot be negated, but that the negation of a perfective sentence like (60) or (18), instead of being obtained via the co-occurrence of the sign NON/NOT with the completion marker FATTO/ FINISH, is expressed by single lexical signs whose function is to indicate that no complete event of the kind denoted by the predicate occurred (plus the presupposition that such an event is expected to occur in the case of NON-ANCORA or NOT-YET and the implication that it is no longer expected to occur in the case of NIENTE).

If this assessment is correct, notice that the data described so far seem to show a gap in the LIS and ASL paradigms to express the negation of a perfective sentence with FATTO or FINISH. Indeed, while, as we just saw, LIS provides a specialized form for asserting that a complete event of a certain kind has not occurred yet or that it has not occurred and it will not occur, there seems to be no specialized form to convey the negation of a sentence with FATTO without some additional meaning. Thus, for instance, while it is appropriate to use a sentence like (64) also in a case in which there is no particular expectation that Gianni should call, negative sentence (65) cannot be used appropriately in the same situation and requires instead that, in the context of utterance, Gianni was supposed to call. Similarly, (66) says that Gianni has not called and implicates he will not, and cannot be used simply to convey the information that Gianni has not called.

(64)   GIANNI   CHIAMARE   FATTO
       Gianni   call   done
       'Gianni called.'

(65)   GIANNI   CHIAMARE   NON-ANCORA
       Gianni   call   not-yet
       'Gianni hasn't called yet.'

(66)   GIANNI   CHIAMARE   NIENTE
       Gianni   call   nothing
       'Gianni hasn't called (and he won't).'

When asked to negate a sentence with FATTO in a context that neither allows NON-ANCORA nor justifies use of NIENTE, our informants simply produced pairs like (67)–(68a) where the negative counterpart of the sentence with FATTO is the sentence with the simple sentential negation NON:[20]

(67)   GIANNI   CASA   COMPRARE   FATTO
       Gianni   house   buy   done
       'Gianni has bought a house.'

(68)   a. GIANNI   CASA   COMPRARE   NON
           Gianni   house   buy   not
           'Gianni has not bought a house.'
       b. * GIANNI CASA COMPRARE FATTO NON-ANCORA
       c. * GIANNI CASA COMPRARE NON FATTO

Since NON, unlike NON-ANCORA, may be used to deny the occurrence of an ongoing process, as in (69), one possibility is that NON in (68) simply expresses sentential negation and that the denial of the past occurrence of the event of buying a house in (68) is inferred contextually (as is often the case in LIS).

(69)   GIANNI   FARE-COMPITI   NON
       Gianni   do-homework   not
       'Gianni is not doing his homework.'

Another possibility, suggested by the fact that our informants naturally produced pairs like (67)–(68) when asked to provide the negation of sentences with FATTO in the absence of additional contextual information, is that NON is ambiguous between simple sentential negation and the lexical realization of FATTO + NON. Here, we leave open the question as to which hypothesis is correct.

Aside from the issue of a possible lexical gap in denying sentences with FATTO, the facts we described suggest that the relevant question in investigating the behavior of FATTO and FINISH with negation is not why FATTO and FINISH cannot be negated, but rather why negation of FATTO and FINISH can be expressed only by means of negative forms like NOT-YET or NOTHING or DON'T, and not by the co-occurrence of FATTO/FINISH with NON/NOT as in (8) and (39)–(41) and (42)–(44). A clue to answering this question is provided by the behavior of negative indefinites in spoken languages, the issue to which we next turn.

5.4   Negated existentials and adjacency

Huang (2003) observes that, while in English one has the option of using negative quantifiers like *nobody, no book*, etc. to express negated existentials, in Japanese no counterparts of negative quantifiers exist and one must use sentential negation with a separate indefinite (negative polarity item) at a distance. Thus, for instance, while in English we can use (70) to express the same meaning as (71), in Japanese only the "discontinuous strategy" corresponding to (71) is allowed, as shown in (72)–(73):

(70)   a.   I saw nobody.
        b.   Hanako read no book.

(71)   a.   I didn't see anybody.
        b.   Hanako didn't read any book.

(72)   boku-wa   dare-mo   mi-nak-atta
        I-Top   anybody   see-Not-Past
        'I didn't see anybody.'

(73)   Hanako-wa   dono   hon-mo   yoma-nak-atta
        Hanako-Top   any   book   read-Not-Past
        'I did not read any book.'

An intermediate case between English and Japanese is provided by Mandarin Chinese, in which negative NPs can occur only in preverbal position (as subjects, or as objects that have been placed in preverbal topic or adjunct positions). Thus, for instance, while a negative quantifier is acceptable in subject position in (74), it is barred in (postverbal) object position in (75)–(76).

(74) meiyou   ren   kanjian   wo
      no   person   saw   me
      'Nobody saw me.'

(75) * wo   kanjian-le meiyou   ren
        I   saw   no   person
      'I saw nobody.'

(76) * ta   tidao   meiyou   yiben   shu
        he   mentioned   not   one   book
      'He mentioned no book.'

In order to express negated existential meaning with an object in Mandarin Chinese, one must either prepose the object, as in (77), or use the discontinuous strategy, as in (78)–(79):

(77) meiyou   yiben   shu   ta   kanguo
      not   one   book   he   read
      'No book has he read.'

(78) ta   meiyou   kanjian   renhe   ren
      he   not   see   any   person
      'He did not see anybody.'

(79) ta   meiyou   tidao   renhe   yiben   shu
      he   not   mention   any   one   book
      'He has not mentioned any book.'

Huang claims that the crosslinguistic pattern exhibited by Mandarin Chinese and Japanese is explained by the theory proposed in Christensen (1986) to account for the distribution of negative NPs in Norwegian, which exhibits a pattern strongly similar to Mandarin Chinese.[21] In short, according to this theory the occurrence of a negative NP is made possible by the fact that, at some stage in the syntactic derivation, there exists an adjacent string consisting of negation immediately followed by the existential NP with which negation is construed. When they are adjacent, negation and the existential NP are reanalyzed as a single constituent and negation is "conflated" with the existential NP to yield the negative quantifier.[22]

This hypothesis accounts for the Mandarin Chinese facts. Indeed, since in Mandarin negation is preverbal, when the existential object is postverbal, as in (78)–(79), negation is not adjacent to it, thus the process that reanalyzes negation and the existential NP as a single constituent cannot occur, barring the presence of a negative NP. When the existential NP is in subject position or is a preverbal object, it is adjacent to negation, thus yielding the negative NPs in (74) and (77). Japanese, on the other hand, is an SOV language and negation is postverbal (it occupies the head of NegP to the right). As a result, again, negation is not adjacent to the subject or object; thus we should expect negative NPs, whether in subject or in object position, to be barred and only the discontinuous strategy to be available, as shown in (72)–(73). The rescue strategy adopted in Mandarin, which brings the existential NP adjacent to negation and thus licenses the negative NP, is unavailable in Japanese, since negation is to the right of the VP; in order to move to a position adjacent to negation, the NP would have to move rightward, something that is not possible in Japanese.

This account does not explain the occurrence of English negative NPs in (70) above, since in English the verb intervenes between the object NP, which is postverbal, and the preverbal negation. Huang suggests that the English facts can be made consistent with the proposed analysis of Mandarin, Japanese and Norwegian by supposing that, initially, in the syntactic derivation of (70), the object NPs *anybody* and *any book* are preposed, thus conflating with preverbal negation and yielding the negative NPs *nobody* and *no book*. Then, the VP out of which the object has been moved is also preposed (an instance of remnant movement, independently proposed by Kayne 1996, 1998), as shown in (80):

(80) a. John not [$_{VP}$ saw anybody] (underlying source)
      b. John not [anybody$_i$ [$_{VP}$ saw t$_i$]] (QP-movement)
      c. John nobody$_i$ [$_{VP}$ saw t$_i$] (not + any => no)
      d. John [$_{VP}$ saw t$_i$] nobody$_i$ t$_{V\,P}$ (VP remnant movement)

Assuming that some account along these lines is essentially correct, let us see how it works for LIS. In LIS, as we saw, negative NPs are available and negation is postverbal. The "discontinuous strategy" is also available, as shown by (68), where the indefinite NP CASA is under the scope of the negation NON:[23]

(68) GIANNI   CASA   COMPRARE   NON
      Gianni   house   buy   not
      'Gianni has not bought a house.'

In the present context, it is significant that when a negative NP occurs, as in (81)–(82), its canonical position is not preverbal, as we should expect if it occupied an argument position (recall that LIS is SOV), but is postverbal:[24]

(81) CONTRATTO   FIRMARE   NESSUNO
      contract   sign   nobody
      'Nobody has signed the contract.'

(82) PAOLO   FIRMARE   NULLA
      Paolo   sign   nothing
      'Paolo has signed nothing.'

On Huang's account, this surprising position of negative NPs is expected. Assuming that, as in Mandarin and Norwegian, LIS negative NPs are derived by conflation of negation with an existential NP under syntactic adjacency, we expect that, in order for this process to be triggered, the existential NP should move rightward to become adjacent to negation (which is postverbal in LIS), where we do indeed find the negative NP.[25] In particular, we may assume that the existential NP moves to Spec,NegP, where it is adjacent to negation, thus yielding the negative NP by conflating with negation, as shown in (83):[26]

(83)

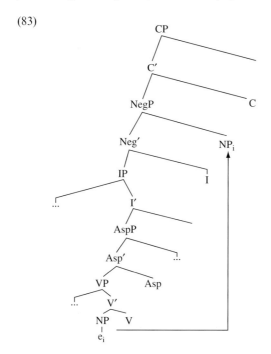

Let us now come back to our question concerning why negation of FATTO can be expressed only by means of negative forms like NON-ANCORA or NIENTE (or NON) and not by the co-occurrence of FATTO with NON. We will assume that existential items – whether NPs or items of a functional kind – when adjacent to negation must trigger reanalysis, namely, that they must combine with negation to yield a constituent with negative existential meaning ($\neg\exists$). This assumption, although not explicitly adopted by Huang, is consistent with the data he presents in his paper. Moreover, there is evidence that this is indeed what happens in LIS. Thus, for instance, while negative NPs, as we saw, do not follow the canonical SOV order but occur postverbally, positive indefinites do not occur postverbally in negated sentences but follow the standard SOV order as in (68) above.

(84) * GIANNI   COMPRARE   CASA   NON
      Gianni   buy   house   not
      'Gianni has not bought a house.'

(85) * GIANNI   COMPRARE   NON   CASA
      Gianni   buy   not   house
      'Gianni has not bought a house.'

Moreover, both LIS possibility operator POSSIBILE (arguably, an existential quantifier over possible situations) and LIS existential predicate C'È ('there is'), which occur adjacent to negation, cannot co-occur with negation but must be expressed by specialized forms with negative existential meanings. Thus, for instance, in order to negate (86) and (90), we must use the specialized negative forms NON-C'È and IMPOSSIBILE, as in (87) and (91), and we cannot use NON and C'È or NON and POSSIBILE:

(86) CASA   MIA   GIARDINO   C'È
      house   my   garden   there-is
      'My house has a garden.'

(87) CASA   MIA   GIARDINO   NON-C'È
      house   my   garden   there-isn't
      'My house doesn't have a garden.'

(88) * CASA   MIA   GIARDINO   NON   C'È
      house   my   garden   not   there-is
      'My house doesn't have a garden.'

(89) * CASA   MIA   GIARDINO   C'È   NON
      house   my   garden   there-is   not
      'My house doesn't have a garden.'

(90)   DOMANI   VENIRE   POSSIBILE
        tomorrow   come   possible
        'Tomorrow I can come.'

(91)   DOMANI   VENIRE   IMPOSSIBILE
        tomorrow   come   impossible
        'Tomorrow I cannot come.'

(92)   * DOMANI   VENIRE   NON   POSSIBILE
        tomorrow   come   not   possible
        'Tomorrow I cannot come.'

(93)   * DOMANI   VENIRE   POSSIBILE   NON
        tomorrow   come   possible   not
        'Tomorrow I cannot come.'

These data indicate that LIS existential items adjacent to negation *must* reanalyze to yield a constituent with negative existential meaning. Now, consider that FATTO, under the interpretation we suggested, introduces an existential quantifier: it says that there is a complete event of the kind described by the predicate that occurs before the time of evaluation. Given that it is structurally adjacent to negation, we should expect that the presence of negation should trigger reanalysis by causing the selection of a specialized form that negates the existence of a complete event of the relevant kind. Thus, we should expect (8) to be anomalous for the same reason (84)-(85), (88)-(89), (92)-(93) are: syntactic adjacency of existential items with negation fails to trigger reanalysis.

(8)   a.   * GIANNI MANGIARE FATTO NON
       b.   * GIANNI MANGIARE NON FATTO

The fact that FATTO cannot co-occur with negative NPs like NESSUNO, etc., may be accounted for along similar lines. Presumably, (40) should be derived by an underlying source in which negation is both adjacent to FATTO and to the existential NP moved into SpecNegP. If the existential NP conflates with negation to yield NESSUNO, FATTO cannot conflate with negation, thus, again, violating the requirement that syntactic adjacency with negation should trigger reanalysis.

(40)   a.   * MANGIARE FATTO NESSUNO
        b.   * MANGIARE NESSUNO FATTO

On the other hand, (87), (91), (65)–(66) are, respectively, the outcome of conflating the negation NON with C'È, POSSIBILE and FATTO, respectively:

(87) CASA   MIA   GIARDINO   NON-C'È
      house   my   garden   there-isn't
      'My house doesn't have a garden.'

(91) DOMANI   VENIRE   IMPOSSIBILE
      tomorrow   come   impossible
      'Tomorrow I cannot come.'

(65) GIANNI   CHIAMARE   NON-ANCORA
      Gianni   call   not-yet
      'Gianni hasn't called yet.'

(66) GIANNI   CHIAMARE   NIENTE
      Gianni   call   nothing
      'Gianni hasn't called (and he won't).'

If this proposal is on the right track, there is a further issue that needs to be addressed concerning the way conflation works. Recall that, for NON-ANCORA and NIENTE, the semantic contribution of these forms is not simply derivable from the meaning of NON and the meaning of FATTO, since NON-ANCORA and NIENTE, respectively, add the additional information that the event described by the predicate was supposed to occur and that it will not occur. Moreover, the phonological forms of NON-ANCORA and NIENTE are not derivable from the phonological form of FATTO and NON.[27] How is this possible if NON-ANCORA and NIENTE are derived from negation and FATTO by syntactic reanalysis under adjacency?

Notice that the Norwegian negative quantifier *ingen* ('no') that results from conflation of *ikke* ('not') and *noen* ('any'), like the LIS forms NON-ANCORA, IMPOSSIBILE, NON-C'È, etc., is not phonologically predictable from the phonological form of negation (*ikke*) and of the item negation conflates with (*noen*). If Christensen's proposal is correct for Norwegian, one way to make sense of forms like *ingen* is provided by the idea, proposed in Halle and Marantz (1993, 1994), that assignment of phonological features takes place after the syntax. According to this approach (Distributed Morphology, DM), terminal nodes of syntactic trees are bundles of abstract features lacking phonological interpretations. Assignment of phonological features to morphosyntactic feature bundles takes place when syntactic structure is mapped into phonological structure. In the case of Norwegian negative NPs, this means that phonological features are assigned after syntactic reanalysis occurs, thus what gets phonologically interpreted is the bundle of morphosyntactic features that corresponds to the negative quantifier.

Assuming that the phonological realization of this feature bundle specified in the vocabulary is *ingen*, we expect that the result of the syntactic reanalysis process, when it is spelled out, should yield forms like *ingen bøker* ('no books') as in (iii) from note 21:

(iii)   Jon   har   ingen   bøker   kjøpt
        John   has   no   books   bought
        'Jon has bought no books .'

The syntactic morpheme (feature bundle) corresponding to the negative quantifier in the syntactic structure of (iii) may have a unique phonological realization, namely *ingen*. However, in the DM approach, a syntactic feature bundle, in general, may be realized by different phonological expressions belonging to different vocabulary items. This is the case for those expressions whose meaning is not fully predictable from their morphosyntactic description. For example, nouns like *cat*, *dog*, *pig* have the same morphosyntactic representation (root), which may thus be spelled out by any of these forms or by other forms with the same morphosyntactic representation made available in the vocabulary of the language. Semantic interpretation is then computed from both LF and PF structures (on the basis of the meanings assigned to each form in the *encyclopedia* of the language).[28] In a similar way, we may suppose that the morphosyntactic representation of the form resulting from the syntactic reanalysis of FATTO and negation is represented by the abstract morphological feature bundle { pfv, perf, neg }, which may then be spelled out by any form matching this description made available by the vocabulary of the language, namely by NON-ANCORA, NIENTE and, perhaps, NON in LIS. In short, then, the answer to the question of how it is possible that phonologically idiosyncratic forms with idiosyncratic meanings, like NON-ANCORA and NIENTE, are derived from negation and FATTO by syntactic reanalysis under adjacency is that what is derived in the syntax are not these forms but rather an abstract morphosyntactic feature bundle which may then be spelled by any form in the vocabulary of the language that shares this morphosyntactic description. Since NON-ANCORA and NIENTE share the features { pfv, perf, neg }, they can be late-inserted at PF and contribute their idiosyncratic meanings to the meanings carried by the features { pfv, perf, neg } that they spell out.

The account may also be extended to ASL. A form like NOT-YET, for example, would express a comparable bundle of features to those proposed for NON-ANCORA. Sentence (61) is a case in which syntactic adjacency of FINISH with negation has triggered reanalysis to yield NOT-YET; sentence (42), on the other hand, is out, on a par with LIS sentences in (8) above, because syntactic adjacency of FINISH with negation fails to trigger reanalysis:

(61) $\overline{\qquad\qquad\qquad}$ [neg
      JOHN NOT-YET VISIT MARY
      'John has not yet visited Mary.'

(42) * JOHN NOT FINISH VISIT MARY

What is left to explain is why ASL sentence (44) is out, where FINISH is barred by the presence of the negative quantifier NONE/NO-ONE in postverbal position:

(44) * JOHN FINISH VISIT NONE/NO-ONE

Recall that, according to Huang's proposal, English sentence (70a) is derived from an intermediate form like *John not anybody saw*, where negation is adjacent to an existential NP and this triggers reanalysis to yield *nobody*:

(70) a. I saw nobody.

If this account is correct, then, assuming that the negative quantifier NONE/NO-ONE in ASL sentence (37) is derived along similar lines, we can account for (44) above on a par with LIS (40).

(37) $\overline{\qquad\qquad\qquad}$ neg
      JOHN VISIT NONE/NO-ONE

According to this analysis, the quantifier NONE/NO-ONE in (44) must be derived from an intermediate form in which preverbal negation NOT is adjacent to the existential NP ONE and this triggers reanalysis to yield NONE/NO-ONE. In this case, however, preverbal negation in this intermediate form is also adjacent to FINISH, which is competing with the existential NP to trigger reanalysis. It follows that, like FATTO in (40), in the derivation of (44) FINISH cannot conflate with negation, thus violating the requirement that adjacency with negation should trigger reanalysis.

It is interesting to note, by the way, that the use of distinct lexical items in LIS and ASL to spell out combinations of the morphological features of negation and perfect when they occur in adjacent strings is not found for Italian or English, as seen in (94) or (95).

(94) Gianni   non   ha   telefonato
      Gianni   not   has   telephoned
      'Gianni has not called.'

(95) John has not left.

The lack of adjacency effects between negation and perfect would follow trivially from the non-adjacency of these features. Iatridou, Anagnostopoulou and Izvorski (2001) argue that in perfect constructions involving auxiliary plus participle (found in many spoken languages), the perfect semantics is contributed by the participial morphology rather than by the auxiliary (based on the fact that the perfect meaning is retained by the participle in constructions where it can be separated from the auxiliary). If this is correct, then in Italian and English sentences such as (88) and (89), where *neg* and *perf* features are not adjacent – separated either by the auxiliary or its trace – such effects are not found: there is no incompatibility between the lexical negator and the morphological marking of perfect that occurs in VP.

6   Summary

A grammaticalization process from a homophonous lexical verb meaning 'finish' has yielded functional elements, glossed as FATTO, occurring postverbally in Italian Sign Language, and FINISH, which precedes the VP in American Sign Language. We argued that FATTO and FINISH occur under the scope of tense (possibly in AspP) and semantically carry the information that a culminated event of the type denoted by the VP occurs at a time preceding the time indicated by the tense. We argued, moreover, that this accounts for very similar semantic restrictions in LIS and ASL on the usage of FATTO and FINISH, as well as for their occurrence with time adverbs like ORA and NOW. Finally, we argued that the behavior of FATTO and FINISH with negation is explained by the fact that existential items and negation must be reanalyzed as a single constituent under adjacency. We suggested that the phonological realization of this reanalysis is best accounted for under a distributive morphology approach of the kind proposed by Halle and Marantz.

11

Clause structure

Ronice Müller de Quadros and Diane Lillo-Martin

1   Introduction

This chapter is concerned with the clause structure of Brazilian Sign Language (LSB) and American Sign Language (ASL). In order to investigate clause structure, we devote some consideration to issues of basic and derived word order. These considerations allow us to formulate a proposed structure which captures the word order possibilities.

We find that LSB and ASL share a basic word order of Subject-Verb-Object (SVO). However, other word orders are also possible due to a variety of syntactic processes including topicalization, object shift and focus.

The chapter also discusses ways in which clause structure is different for sentences with agreeing verbs versus plain verbs (cf. chapters in this volume by Mathur and Rathmann and by Padden *et al.* on verb agreement). These differences motivate distinct phrase structures for sentences of the two types.

The structures in this chapter are presented using the terminology of generative syntax (see, among others, Chomsky 1995, Bošković & Lasnik 2007). We find that the formalism of this approach allows us to ask specific, detailed questions and make explicit proposals. The observations and generalizations we make are empirically based, however, and should be of interest to linguists using other approaches as well.

Our approach contributes to the overall goal of this volume by exploring the crosslinguistic similarities and differences between two geographically distinct sign languages. LSB and ASL have many similarities in word order and clause structure, but they also show intriguing differences. A detailed study of these similarities and differences helps to reveal patterns of crosslinguistic variation in sign languages, which we compare with known patterns of crosslinguistic variation in spoken languages.

In this chapter, we will first examine the underlying word order of LSB and ASL. Then, we will look at word order changes and their derivation.

2   Overview of word order and clause structure

Word order is a basic concept related to the phrase structure of a language. The idea that languages may differ in their basic word order has played a significant role in linguistic analysis. For instance, Greenberg (1966) observed that of the six possible combinations of subject (S), object (O) and verb (V), certain word orders are much more common than others. Languages often allow several variant orders, but Greenberg observed that even though this variation exists, usually each language has a single dominant word order. According to him, the dominant order is either SOV, SVO or VSO. He observed that the ordering of the elements tended to be consistent, i.e., a VO language will have the object of the preposition after the preposition, while an OV language will have the opposite order, object then postposition.

In addition to the term "basic" word order, "canonical" and "underlying" word order are also used to describe word order in different languages. From typological studies to formal ones, we see a distinction between "basic" or "canonical" word order and "underlying" word order. The first is related to the surface word order in a language. In any particular language the decision to label a particular word order as dominant is based on the word order of unmarked simple clauses, that is, clauses in a neutral setting.

On the other hand, the "underlying" word order is that which is generated in the deep structure. "Deep structure" is the bare structure in the sense of Chomsky (1965), i.e., the structure before any transformations have been applied to it. Deep structure does not obligatorily correspond in form to what is pronounced (i.e., surface structure); it is an abstract level of syntax which relates the computational system and the lexicon, and thus, it is an "internal interface." Variation in word order will be expressed by the phonological component, in which the elements in the structure are pronounced. At this level of the computational system of language, we observe the result of the transformations in different derivations. This gives us the possible word orders allowed by the language.

The underlying word order, in this sense, is related to a parameter, known as the "head parameter". "Underlying" order(s) is(are) the one(s) that the operations will apply to. For example, the underlying word order of a topicalized sentence will be one in which there is no topicalization. Variation in word order is the result either of different derivations being allowed by different languages, or of different settings of the head parameter.

3   Clause structure in LSB and ASL

There are numerous works that mention the flexibility of word order in ASL (Fischer 1974, Fischer 1975, Liddell 1980, Padden 1988, Brennan & Turner 1994,

Table 11.1 *Distribution of word order in ASL and LSB*

Word order	Yes	No	With restrictions
SVO	X		
OSV			X
SOV			X
VOS			X
OVS			X
VSO		X	

Wilbur 1997, Neidle *et al.* 2000); LSB (Felipe 1989, Ferreira-Brito 1995, Quadros 1999, Quadros 2003) and other sign languages (for example, Deuchar 1983 and Sutton-Spence & Woll 1999, for British Sign Language; Engberg-Pedersen 1994 for Danish Sign Language; see also papers in Brennan & Turner 1994). The word order possibilities for ASL and LSB are summarized in Table 11.1.

Research on word order points out that these languages have different possibilities for ordering the words in the sentence, but even with this flexibility, there seems to be a basic order SVO. We will review empirical support for the conclusion that SVO is basic in ASL and LSB in section 3.1. The evidence comes from simple sentences, sentences with embedded clauses and sentences with adverbs, modals and auxiliaries. The varied word orders allowed in ASL and LSB result from movement operations leading to structures with topicalization, object shift and focus. We discuss these constructions in section 3.2. LSB clause structure reveals that there are important differences between sentences with and without verb agreement. In section 3.3, we propose a representation of phrase structure capturing both the basic and derived orders.

3.1   Evidence for clause structure

3.1.1   *Basic sentences*

Sentences like (1) are very natural in LSB and ASL, and examples using SVO order as in these examples are very generally considered grammatical. The sentence in (1a) contains an "agreeing verb," i.e., a verb which displays person or location inflection.[1] The sentence in (1b) has a "plain verb," i.e., a verb that does not mark overt agreement. We present sentences with both kinds of verbs, because the agreement asymmetry that distinguishes these verbs in LSB and ASL can have, and probably must have, different behavior in the syntactic structure (to be discussed in section 3.3). Also, these examples have in common the special non-manual marker that can be associated with the subject and object of the sentence, i.e., eye gaze toward the object (cf. Bahan 1996). For our purposes, we are considering only eye gaze with agreeing verbs.

(1)   eg:a   eg:b   (LSB;[2] also ASL)

   a. IX < det > JOÃOa   a ASSISTIRb b TV.
   'John watches TV.'

                                     hn

   b. IX < det > JOÃO GOSTAR FUTEBOL.
   'John likes soccer.'

Fischer (1974, 1975) presented an analysis of word order in ASL considering syntactic and semantic aspects. Her analysis indicates that SVO is the basic word order in ASL, since it is the order that is found with reversible subject and object, and the one that appears in embedded clauses with any two full NPs (as shown in (2a–b). She observed that we cannot have SOV word order when the object is an embedded clause (whether this order is base-generated or derived by extraction), as shown in (3). This is true for both LSB and ASL.

(2)   a. MAN NOTICE CHILD   (ASL; also LSB)
       'The man noticed the child.'

                                         (Fischer 1975:5)

    b. ME THINK ED FINISH PAY JOHN
       'I think Ed has paid John.'

                                     (Fischer 1974:200)

(3)   eg:loc

   a. IX < 1 > THINK [$_{IP}$ IX < det > MARYa   aLEAVEloc].
   'I think that Mary left.'

                                       eg:loc

   b. * IX < 1 > [$_{IP}$ IX < det > MARYa aLEAVEloc] THINK.

Based on these facts and others to be presented in this chapter, we assume that SVO word order is the basic order in LSB and ASL. Having determined the basic word order, we turn now to the goal of identifying the sentential phrase structure. We need to know what positions are occupied by each element in the sentence. We will discuss the distribution of adverbs and modals, as well as that of the LSB auxiliary sign glossed AUX, since it is very important to identify the position of these elements to be able to define the phrase structure. Also, we will show that these elements can give additional support for the conclusion that the basic word order in LSB and ASL is SVO.

3.1.2 *Clause structure and adverbs*

It is interesting to analyze examples with adverbs because they can normally be adjoined to different parts of the sentence, although observing some restrictions. If there are restrictions in some cases, these may provide suggestions about the phrase structure. Also, adverb distribution in the sentence has been used as evidence to show movement of constituents. Therefore, we present some examples considering the placement of adverbs in sentences with the basic word order SVO.

The first case that is analyzed includes temporal adverbs.

(4)   a. IX < det > JOHN BUY CAR YESTERDAY.   (ASL; also LSB)
       'John bought a car yesterday.'
    b. * IX < det > JOHN YESTERDAY BUY CAR.
    c. * IX < det > JOHN BUY YESTERDAY CAR.
    d. YESTERDAY IX < det > JOHN BUY CAR.

(5)   a. IX < det > JOÃOb a ENCONTRARb MARIAb JÁ.
                            (LSB; also ASL)
       'John already met Mary.'
    b. * IX < det > JOÃOa JÁ aENCONTRARb MARIAb.
    c. * IX < det > JOÃO aENCONTRARb JÁ MARIAb.
    d. JÁ IX < det > JOÃOa aENCONTRARb MARIA.

There is a clear preference for placing the temporal adverb in the initial position of the sentence, as in (4d) and (5d). In the examples in (4a) and (5a), with the adverb in final position, the interpretation is one of confirmation, but not new information. The examples in (4b) and (5b) can be pronounced with a break before and after the adverb, and "John" must be topicalized; without these markers the sentences are ungrammatical. Therefore, we will not consider this special case here (topicalization will be discussed in section 3.2.2). The most important examples for our purpose are (4c) and (5c), since they show us that there is a strong restriction against breaking the constituent VP that includes the verb and the object. This gives support to VO as the basic word order. Considering this distribution, we assume that temporal adverbs are left- or right-adjoined to Inflection Phrase – IP (or Agreement with Subject Phrase – AgrSP).

Adverbs of frequency have a different distribution from temporal adverbs; however, they observe one restriction in common. It is not possible to insert a frequency adverb between the verb and the object. This is observed in (6c) and (7c).[3]

(6)   a. IX < 1 > BEBER LEITE AS-VEZES.   (LSB; also ASL)
        'Sometimes I drink milk.'
       b. IX < 1 > AS-VEZES BEBER LEITE.
       c. * IX < 1 > BEBER AS-VEZES LEITE.
       d. ? AS-VEZES IX < 1 > BEBER LEITE.

(7)   a. IX < 1 > ASSINAR IX < det > DOCUMENTO NUNCA.
                                   (LSB; also ASL)
        'I've never signed the document.'
       b. IX < 1 > NUNCA ASSINAR IX < det > DOCUMENTO.
       c. * IX < 1 > ASSINAR NUNCA IX < det > DOCUMENTO.
       d. ? NUNCA IX < 1 > ASSINAR IX < det > DOCUMENTO.

The initial position of frequency adverbs can be acceptable only with a break between the adverb and the rest of the sentence, or with special intonation (head nod above the sentence after producing the adverb). Given the facts in (6) and (7), we assume that the frequency adverb is adjoined to the left and right of the VP (as Braze 2004 assumes for ASL).

In sum, the distribution of temporal and frequency adverbs suggests that there is a constituent VP in LSB and ASL that includes the verb and the object: [$_{VP}$ [V NP]]. This relation cannot be interrupted by an adverb, providing another argument that VO word order is the basic one in these two languages.

Moreover, we assume that temporal adverbs are right- or left-adjoined to IP (AgrSP) and the frequency adverbs are right- and left-adjoined to VP. This distribution can be used to show the position of different syntactic categories.

3.1.3 *Clause structure and modals*
In both LSB and ASL, modals can occur between the subject and the verb, as in (8).

(8)   DADa MUST PAY B-I-L-L.   (ASL; also LSB)
      'Dad must pay the bill.'

In previous research on ASL, Padden (1988) concludes that modals are verbs which take clausal complements (like modals in Italian). Petronio (1993) argued against Padden's conclusion and argued that modals in ASL occupy the position of Infl (or T), the same conclusion arrived at independently by Neidle *et al.* (2000) (a common analysis for many spoken languages including English). However, Matsuoka (1997) proposed that modals in ASL head a separate projection (ModP). Given the distribution of modals with respect to negation and adverbs in ASL and LSB, we adopt Matsuoka's analysis here.

Cinque (1999) proposed that for each position occupied by an adverb and/or modal, there is a different functional projection, and the interpretation of these elements depends on their hierarchical position. Modals can be interpreted as having root modality or as having epistemic modality. "Root modals typically denote permission, obligation, or ability, specifying characteristics of the subject of the sentence. Epistemic modals typically indicate possibility or entailment" (Braze 2004:45). Root modals are considered to be in a syntactically lower position than epistemic modals (Butler 2003).

Cinque observed a different distribution between root and epistemic *can* in Italian, as illustrated in examples where the modal interacts with an adverb. Such examples from LSB are given in (9) and (10).[4] The sentences in (9a) and (10a) must be interpreted with root modality and the sentences in (9b) and (10b) must be interpreted with epistemic modality.

(9) a. IX < det > MULHER AS-VEZES PODE BEBER CERVEJA
      (LSB)
      (Context: The woman is taking medicine which allows her to drink alcohol only sometimes.)
      'That woman is sometimes permitted to drink beer.'
      *'That woman is sometimes able to drink beer.'

   b. IX < det > MULHER PODE AS-VEZES BEBER CERVEJA.
      (Context: The woman has a stomach condition which makes her unable to tolerate alcohol sometimes.)
      *'That woman is sometimes permitted to drink beer.'
      'That woman is sometimes able to drink beer.'

(10) a. IX < det > MULHER SEMPRE PODE SUBIR-MONTANHA.
      (LSB)
      (Context: The owner of the mountain gives out special permission for certain climbers.)
      'That woman is always permitted to climb the mountain.'
      *'That woman is always able to climb the mountain.'

   b. IX < det > MULHER PODE SEMPRE SUBIR-MONTANHA.
      (Context: The woman works out regularly and is in very good health.)
      *'That woman is always permitted to climb the mountain.'
      'That woman is always able to climb the mountain.'

We conclude that in LSB, frequency adverbs must follow the modal when it has a root reading, and precede the modal when it has an epistemic reading. Such a distribution can be best accounted for by assuming that the modal heads its own projection. This projection must be located between IP and VP, as illustrated in (11).

(11)

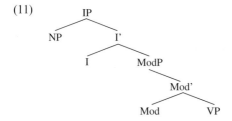

There are several other positions in which modals appear, which we will only briefly mention here. First, it has been observed that modals may occur in the sentence-initial position. However, Braze (2004) and Quadros (1999) observe that such a position for modals is permitted only in particular discourse contexts, so it will not be considered further here.

Modals may also occur in both the preverbal and sentence-final position. These examples are related to focus, which will be discussed in detail in section 3.2.4.

3.1.4   *Clause structure and auxiliaries*

In LSB and some other sign languages, but not ASL, there is an auxiliary (glossed here AUX) as shown in examples (12b–c).

(12)

              eg:a   eg:b   (LSB)

a. IX < det > JOÃOa GOSTAR IX < det > MARIAb.
'John likes Mary.'

              eg:a   eg:b   hn

b. IX < det > JOÃOa   IX < det > MARIAb aAUXb GOSTAR.
'John likes Mary (aAUXb).'

                  eg:b   eg:a   eg:a-b   hn

c. IX < det > MARIAb IX < det > JOÃOa   aAUXb GOSTAR.
'John likes Mary (bAUXa).'

AUX in LSB is a pure expression of agreement by movement from one point to another point (these points are those of the subject and the object of the sentence). Mathur and Rathmann's chapter on verb agreement in the present volume uses the expression "area in signing space associated with the referent of the subject/object" to refer to these points in the signing space. AUX cannot occur alone, but must be signed together with a plain verb, a verb that lacks overt agreement. Through its direction of movement, AUX expresses the relation established between the arguments of the sentence.

Following Lasnik's (1995) proposal for auxiliaries in English, in LSB it seems that the auxiliary AUX is the head of IP (or the head of TP, considering the split of IP into AgrSP, TP and AgrOP). AUX in LSB establishes a relation between the subject and object in sentences with plain verbs. It seems to compensate for the lack of agreement in these sentences. AUX is required only when the word order differs from the canonical one and has no way of identifying the subject and the object in a sentence with a plain verb. This context is observed in (12b–c), in which we have a sentence with reversible arguments (JOÃO and MARIA) and we can have the word order SOV or OSV.

3.1.5   *Summary*

We have seen several types of evidence that SVO is the basic word order in LSB and ASL. After Fischer's analysis, many other studies investigated word order in ASL. Basically, all of them conclude that ASL has SVO word order as the basic order. One exception is Friedman (1976), who argues that the flexibility of word order in ASL is the result of a lack of any fixed word order. A similar conclusion was reached for Quebec Sign Language by Bouchard and Dubuisson (Bouchard & Dubuisson 1995, Bouchard 1996), and some researchers looking at other sign languages have also come to a similar conclusion (cf. some papers in Brennan & Turner 1994). We mention this position just to show the potential alternative possibilities of analysis that might be considered to explain the apparent flexibility of word order. Liddell (1980) provided arguments against Friedman's analysis, and further discussion of the derivational alternative is given by Kegl *et al.* (1996) and by Sandler and Lillo-Martin (2006). We turn now to an examination of derivational analyses of word order changes in LSB and ASL.

3.2   Clause structure with movement operations

When we discuss complementizer, topic and focus positions, we are looking at derivations that project functional categories above IP (or AgrSP), i.e., A'-positions. Usually, the arguments (phrases) found in these positions were not base-generated there but moved there from A positions. Alternatively, elements in A'-positions are base-generated there but are not arguments. Arguments that move to a non-argument position do so for specific reasons. Linguistic theory is concerned with these specific reasons. What motivates an element to move to another position in a specific derivation? In this section, we discuss several such

Figure 11.1 *Topic nonmanual marking (tm1)*.

movements, which are motivated by grammatical and discourse-related considerations (topicalization, object shift and focus).

3.2.1   *Topicalization*

Since Fischer (1975), there has been an analysis of topicalization in ASL to explain
the < O > SV and < VO > S word orders. Fischer observes that there is a break
between the element topicalized and the rest of the sentence, and Liddell (1980:84)
notes that there is "a change in the facial expression and head position from that
indicating topic to some other expression." A set of nonmanual markings often
including raised brows is associated with topics in ASL, LSB and other sign
languages (to name a few: Argentine Sign Language, Massone & Curiel 2004;
Australian Sign Language, Johnston & Schembri 2007; Danish Sign Language,
Engberg-Pedersen 1993; Israeli Sign Language, Rosenstein 2001) (see Figure 11.1).

An important point observed by Liddell is that the topic nonmanual marker is
separated from the negation nonmanual marker in sentences containing both. This
is an indication of the position of Topic in ASL, at least over Negation Phrase. The
following example illustrates this aspect in ASL, which also holds for LSB.[5]

(13)   _____t_____   _____neg_____   (ASL; also LSB)
CAT   DOG CHASE.
'As for the cat, the dog didn't chase it.'   (Liddell 1980:84; original (22))

Following Chomsky (1977), Liddell assumes that topics in ASL are adjoined to
the main clause. This assumption is in agreement with Fischer's (1975) analysis.
Liddell also observes the same distribution for sentences with the entire VP topicalized, i.e., < VO > S, or the subject only, i.e., < S > VO. Another interesting fact
observed by Liddell is that topics cannot be indefinites in ASL, as expected on

semantic and pragmatic grounds, if we make the common assumption that topics express given/old information.

There is another interesting case in which elements not constituents of the rest of the sentence are topics, as observed by Padden (1988). This is shown in the following example.

(14)   <u>top</u>   (ASL; also LSB)

FOOD   1INDEX ONLY-ONE V-E-G.

'With respect to food, I eat only vegetables.'

(Petronio 1993:21; original (4))

This kind of topic is also observed by Saito (1985) in Japanese. He uses this kind of construction as evidence for base-generated topicalization in this language, since the topic does not bind any argument position in the sentence. The following example illustrates this fact.

(15)   Sakana-wa [tai-ga   oisii]

        fish-top   red snapper-nom tasty

        'Speaking of fish, red snapper is tasty.' (Saito 1985:282; original (6))

Petronio (1993) assumes that there are two kinds of topics in ASL: those which move to adjoin to CP and those which are base-generated in this position.

The first type includes topicalization of object, subject or VP. The second type includes topics as shown in (14). Petronio assumes that Topic position must be higher than CP based on evidence such as that shown in (16) below. In this kind of construction, there is a clear restriction against topics following a *wh*-word in CP (16a), while topics preceding the *wh*-constructions are grammatical (16b). The same distribution holds for LSB.

(16)   <u>wh</u>   <u>top</u>   <u>wh</u>   (LSB; also ASL)

      a. * ONDE   CAFÉ   COMPRAR

     <u>top</u>   <u>wh</u>

      b. CAFÉ ONDE COMPRAR.

      'Where do you buy coffee?'

Aarons (1994) investigates topics in ASL further and argues that there is more than one type of topicalization in ASL. In agreement with Petronio (1993), Aarons assumes that there are moved topics and base-generated topics. According to Aarons, topics occur in a structural position called Topic Phrase adjoined to the left of CP. Aarons also notes that there are different sorts of nonmanual markers associated with different topics. She identifies three nonmanual markers, described

Figure 11.2 *Topic-comment tm2 (left) and tm3 (right) nonmanual markers.*

in (17). The marker commonly considered to be the typical topic nonmanual marker is what Aarons calls the tm1 marker, illustrated in Figure 11.1, and what she calls tm2 and tm3 are given in Figure 11.2.

(17) (i)   tm1: raised eyebrows and chin, with a slight pause between the signing of the topic–marked item and the rest of the sentence
      (ii) tm2: movement of the head back and to the side then forward, eyes very wide
      (iii) tm3: head forward, widening of the eyes, rapid head nods

The moved cases include subject, objects and adjuncts (locatives) associated with the typical nonmanual marker: raised brows, head tilted slightly back and to the side (17i). The base-generated topics analyzed by Aarons include the one pointed out by Padden (1988) and Petronio (1993), and others using the two kinds of nonmanual markers listed in (17ii) and (17iii).

Lillo-Martin and Quadros (2008) noted that the different types of topics described by Aarons includes some focus constructions. Although Aarons (1994) claimed that tm1 topics are used for emphasis or contrastive focus, we have found two different means for expressing these information types. We discuss this further in section 3.2.4.

Lillo-Martin and Quadros also proposed that the base-generated topics and the moved topics occupy different positions in the hierarchical structure. In particular, since the base-generated topics are always highest in the structure (Aarons also notes this ordering restriction), this would follow if there is a higher position for base-generated topics (called "topic-comment topics" because they are associated with clauses without a gap).

(18) <u>   t-c   </u> <u>   top   </u>   (ASL; also LSB)
FRUIT,   BANANA,   JOHN LIKE MORE
'As for fruit, bananas John likes t̲ best.'

Neidle (2002) also proposed that base-generated topics and moved topics occupy different structural positions; see Lillo-Martin and Quadros (2008) for discussion. An example showing this interaction was given in (18), and the structure proposed by Lillo-Martin and Quadros is given in (19).

(19)   T-CP

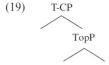

3.2.2 *Object shift*

In addition to basic sentences and sentences with topics, both ASL and LSB permit other types of word-order variation. We focus here on various cases in which the object occurs before the verb (but not as a topic), which we group together as cases of "object shift."[6] The general idea is that some feature of the verb, such as its agreement marking, aspectual marking or use of a classifier, allows the object to move to a position between the subject and the verb, resulting in SOV order, or to a position above the subject, resulting in OSV order.

We start with cases having verbs with aspect marking. Liddell (1980) observed that OSV order is possible in examples such as (20).

(20)   TOMATO GIRL EAT[durative aspect].   (ASL; also LSB)
'The girl eats tomatoes for a long time.'

                                        (modified from Liddell 1980:103)

Liddell analyzed this kind of structure as derived from SVO, having the object moved to initial position. Liddell speculates that this movement is related to the "heaviness of the verb." As he observed, the verb is inflected for durative aspect and takes longer to sign. However, Liddell does not provide an explicit analysis.[7]

Matsuoka (1997) and Braze (2004) proposed that in examples such as (20), the verb moves to a projection headed by Aspect. On both of their accounts, this projection is right-headed in ASL, leaving the verb in the sentence-final position. This movement licenses the movement of the object to a position above the subject. This position is the specifier of the Object Agreement phrase on Matsuoka's account, but higher, to within the CP-domain, on Braze's.

Some authors find that SOV is also permitted with aspectually marked verbs (e.g., Matsuoka 1997, but not Braze 2004). On Matsuoka's analysis, this is derived when the object optionally fails to raise after the verb moves to the Aspect projection.

Examples similar to those discussed here can be found when the verb is marked not for aspect, but for one of two other characteristics, a classifier or agreement (person or location). For instance, Liddell (1980:89–91) shows that SOV sentences include structures that have some iconicity, such as WOMAN PIE PUT-IN-OVEN. He says that the information about the relation between the activity and the object involved is clearly expressed in some spatial, pictorial sense. Another SOV case mentioned by Liddell (1980:88) is the grammatical sentence MAN BOOK READ,[8] in contrast to the ungrammatical *MAN MOVIE SEE, *MAN NUMBER FORGET and *BOY CANDY NOT LIKE.

Both of these cases can be analyzed as sentences with classifiers. Chen Pichler (2001) agrees with Matsuoka (1997) in concluding that certain classifiers allow syntactic verb movement of a type similar to that used for aspectually marked verbs. Following Matsuoka's analysis of aspectual cases, verb movement to a higher position[9] can occur, resulting in SOV order or OSV when the object also moves, as in the examples in the next paragraph.

Finally, Liddell also observed another specific case: examples such as BALL JOHN SWING-A-BAT and FENCE CAT SLEEP (1980:91–100) allow OSV order but do not have the topic marker on the object. Liddell argues that the initial noun is related to the locative reference point used in what he calls a "complex predicate." These predicates are considered complex because with only one sign, both a locative and a noun are expressed. This locative point is part of the agreement system found in most sign languages.

ASL sentences with agreement have been discussed as examples of flexible word order since Fischer (1974, 1975). We can see that this is also illustrated in LSB through the examples in (21) and (22), as compared with (1) and (2), presented earlier. In the (a) examples below, OSV or SOV order with an agreeing verb is permitted (ASSISTIR agrees with its object's location but behaves like person agreeing verbs in this way). In the (c) examples, such word order variability with non-agreeing verbs having reversible arguments is not allowed. The (b) examples show that word order variation may be allowed with plain verbs when the arguments are non-reversible.

OSV constructions

(21)   eg:b _____ eg:a _____ eg:b   (LSB; also ASL)
         a. TVb IX < det > JOÃOa aASSISTIRb.
         'John watches TV.'

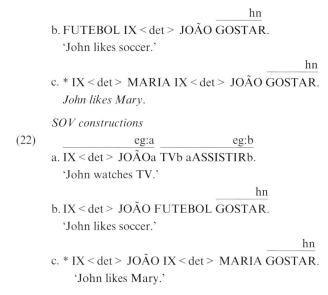

b. FUTEBOL IX < det > JOÃO GOSTAR.
    'John likes soccer.'

                               hn

c. * IX < det > MARIA IX < det > JOÃO GOSTAR.
    John likes Mary.

SOV constructions

(22)   eg:a   eg:b
a. IX < det > JOÃOa TVb aASSISTIRb.
    'John watches TV.'

             hn

b. IX < det > JOÃO FUTEBOL GOSTAR.
    'John likes soccer.'

              hn

c. * IX < det > JOÃO IX < det > MARIA GOSTAR.
    'John likes Mary.'

Thus, in both LSB and ASL locative or person agreement can sanction OSV and SOV orders. Chen Pichler (2001) collapsed these cases with the cases of classifiers and aspectually marked verbs discussed earlier. It seems that a variety of verb markings may require verb movement to a rightward position in the sentence, resulting in SOV order. Further movement of the object to a position preceding the subject results in OSV.

3.2.3 *Focus*

Both LSB and ASL allow two kinds of constructions analyzed as involving focus. One of these constructions shows "doubling," that is, the focused element appears both in its usual position and again in the sentence-final position. The second shows the focused element in the sentence-final position only. Examples are given in (23) below.[10] These examples show that modals, quantifiers, verbs, negation and *wh*-elements participate in these constructions.

(23)   E-foc   (ASL; also LSB)
a. IX < 1 > (CAN) GO PARTY CAN.
    'I really *can* go to the party.'
    (Context: There is some doubt on the part of the hearer as to whether or not the speaker can attend the party.)

            E-foc

b. IX < 1 > HAVE (TWO) CAR TWO.
    'It's *two* cars that I have.'

E-foc
c. IX < 1 > (LOSE) BOOK LOSE.
'Indeed I *lost* the book.'

neg   E-foc
d. IX < 1 > (NO) GO PARTY NO.
'I absolutely did *not* go to the party.'

wh E-foc
e. WHO BUY CAR WHO.
'Who was it that bought a car?'

Petronio (1993) analyzed such constructions in ASL as involving focus; and Quadros (1999) also analyzed them as focus in LSB, although the details of their analyses are different. Petronio noted that focus constructions in ASL display the following five properties (1993:135):

(24)   (i)   the double occurs at the end of the sentence;

        (ii) the double is an X^0, not an XP;

        (iii) there is only one double per sentence;

        (iv) the twin cannot be within a syntactic island; and

        (v) only a wh-double can occur in direct wh-questions (not a modal or verb double).

Petronio proposes that the final double element is base-generated in the sentence-final head position of a CP specified for [+Focus]. This explains why double elements are always X^0 and always occur at the end of the sentence, and why there is always only one double element per sentence. Furthermore, she proposes that a null focus operator moves to Spec of CP to check its [+Focus] feature, accounting for the inability of focused elements to occur with islands. Finally, because *wh*-elements are associated with the CP projection as well, Petronio proposed a filter which states that if CP contains a [+WH] element, only that element may be focused.

Petronio and Lillo-Martin (1997:30) restrict the "double construction" "to sentences in which a significant pause does not precede the final 'double'. When there is a significant pause, the construction has different syntactic properties." This note makes a distinction between focus constructions on the one hand, and constructions such as tag questions and use of the discourse strategies to confirm some part of the sentence on the other hand.

The analysis of focus position in LSB by Quadros (1999) starts with the research mentioned here. As Kim (1997) proposed for Korean and Kato and Raposo (1994) for Portuguese, Quadros proposes an independent projection for focus, Focus Phrase (FocP), to account for aspects similar to those analyzed by Petronio. However, her analysis makes theoretical improvements over Petronio's, including uniformity of branching and use of a phrasal position for movement of *wh*-elements.

Note that all double elements present a nonmanual marker associated with them. This nonmanual marker seems to be related to the element in final position. In LSB, this nonmanual marker is intensified after the double element is pronounced. The nonmanual marker gives a hint of the presence of a feature associated with FocP that must be checked.

Like ASL, LSB shows double constructions with modals, quantifiers, verbs, *wh*-elements, negation and adverbs.

Alongside double constructions, it is also possible to find constructions in which the emphasized element appears sentence-finally without the sentence-internal "twin." It seems that the position occupied by the double element in final position licenses the omission of the sentence-internal element. This raises some questions: What is the position occupied by double elements? Why does this position license null elements? What kind of feature is related to double constructions?

Nunes and Quadros (2006, 2008) propose an account of this using the theory by Nunes (2004) of how the string of words in an utterance is linearized. According to the Copy theory of movement, when a constituent moves from one syntactic position to another, it leaves a copy which is deleted before the sentence is pronounced. Principles of linearization determine which copy is pronounced and which is deleted. However, in certain cases the conditions determining which copy should be pronounced result in an output where both are pronounced. This gives rise to doubling constructions, which occur in certain environments in spoken languages as well as sign languages.

Putting this idea together with Quadros's previous analysis, the derivation of doubling constructions goes as follows. The doubled element moves to the head of the Focus projection (which we call here E-Foc, for emphatic focus, to distinguish it from information focus). Then, the "remnant" – the rest of the sentence including the "twin" of the focused element – moves up to the specifier of Topic Phrase (TopP), because the part of the sentence that is not focused is considered a topic. This process is illustrated in (25).

(25)

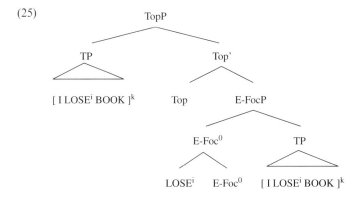

When linearization applies, the copy of the topic is completely deleted. However, it is possible for the copy of the focused element in the higher structural position not to be deleted, giving the double construction, or to be deleted, giving the final construction. See Nunes and Quadros (2006, 2008) for detailed explanation of the derivation and why this deletion is optional.

As noted by Arrotéia (2003) (for LSB), focus-final constructions also lead to the possibility of final subjects (i.e., VOS order). An example from her study is given in (26).

(26)   _____wh   (LSB; also ASL)
            Q. QUEM COMPRAR CARRO?
            'Who bought the car?'
            A.   E-foc
            (JOÃO) COMPRAR CARRO JOÃO
            '*John* bought the car.'

In addition to the focus constructions discussed here (doubling and final constructions for emphasis), LSB and ASL employ a different mechanism for information focus and contrastive focus, as discussed by Lillo-Martin and Quadros (2008). Information focus (I-focus) and contrastive focus (C-focus) are unlike emphatic focus (E-focus) because (a) they do not involve doubling and (b) they do not involve the sentence-final position. Furthermore, they employ different nonmanual marking, as illustrated in Figure 11.3 (the model is a signer of LSB; the ASL nonmanuals are the same). As discussed in Lillo-Martin and Quadros (2008), the nonmanual marker we call I-focus is essentially the same as that called tm1 by Aarons (1994); the main elements include raised brows and a

Figure 11.3 *Information focus (left) and contrastive focus (right) nonmanual marking.*

prosodic break before the rest of the utterance. The different label is used to point out the function of the signs which co-occur with this marker, based on discourse context. The main elements of the nonmanual indicating contrastive focus include brow raise and a sharp downward head movement. Examples are given in (27) and (28).

(27) <u>   y/nq</u>   ASL (also LSB)

      S1: YOU READ CHOMSKY BOOK?

          'Did you read Chomsky's book?'

                  <u>   C-foc</u>

      S2: NO, BOOK STOKOE I READ

          'No, I read Stokoe's book.'

(28) <u>   wh</u>

      S1: WHAT YOU READ?   (ASL; also LSB)

      'What did you read?'

             <u>   I-foc</u>

      S2: BOOK STOKOE I READ.

      S2: I READ BOOK STOKOE.

          'I read *Stokoe's book*.'

Combining these observations with the two positions for topic as discussed in section 3.2.2, Lillo-Martin & Quadros (2008) propose the structure in (29). I-focus and C-focus constituents occupy the FocP projection, while E-focus uses the lower projection.[11]

(29)

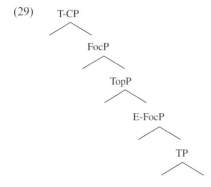

To summarize, considering focus allows us to explain a variety of structures found in LSB and ASL. These structures include double and final constructions using E-focus, where the focused material shows up in the sentence-final position, as well as information and contrastive focus, where the focused material is sentence-initial (or following a T-C topic).

3.3   Clause structure with different verb types

The structure of sentences with plain and agreeing verbs is recognizably different. One hint to the difference in structure associated with plain and agreeing verbs comes from an examination of nonmanual marking associated with agreement, as described by Bahan (1996). The asymmetry concerns the behavior of the nonmanual markers: when there is an agreeing verb in the sentence, the nonmanual marker is salient, but not with a plain verb. This is confirmed for ASL by the work of Thompson, Emmorey and Kluender (2006), who found that signers rarely produced eye gaze with plain verbs but frequently with agreeing verbs.

This asymmetry can be seen in LSB and ASL, as shown in (30) and (31).

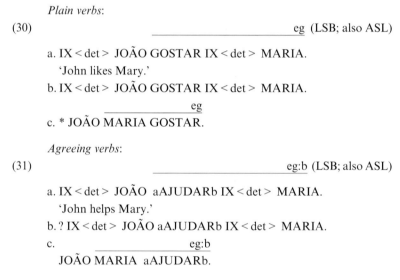

Plain verbs:

(30)   <u>   </u> eg (LSB; also ASL)

       a. IX < det > JOÃO GOSTAR IX < det > MARIA.
       'John likes Mary.'
       b. IX < det > JOÃO GOSTAR IX < det > MARIA.
                    <u>   </u>
                         eg
       c. * JOÃO MARIA GOSTAR.

Agreeing verbs:

(31)   <u>   </u> eg:b (LSB; also ASL)

       a. IX < det > JOÃO aAJUDARb IX < det > MARIA.
       'John helps Mary.'
       b. ? IX < det > JOÃO aAJUDARb IX < det > MARIA.
       c.   <u>   </u> eg:b
       JOÃO MARIA aAJUDARb.

Considering the strong evidence for a nonmanual marker with sentences that contain agreeing verbs (at least when the word order is not the basic one), in opposition to what happens with sentences with plain verbs, we assume that there is a true asymmetry between these two classes of verbs that must be explained.

In ASL and LSB, sentences with agreeing verbs seem to allow more freedom in word order than those with plain verbs. This fact was first observed by Fischer (1975). Fischer and Gough (1978) observed that when arguments are reversible the word order can be OSV, in addition to SOV (as illustrated in (31c)), with agreeing verbs, but not with plain verbs. This is true for LSB as well. The following examples illustrate this fact.

(32)   _____eg:b_____   __eg:a__ __eg:b__ (ASL; also LSB)

a. IX < det > MARYb IX < det > JOHNa aLOOKb.
'John looks at Mary.'

                                           _____hn_____
b. * IX < det > MARY IX < det > JOHN LIKE.
'John likes Mary.'

Lillo-Martin (1986, 1991) noticed another important asymmetry, the behavior of null arguments with plain and agreeing verbs. Null arguments are quite prevalent with agreeing verbs, and according to Lillo-Martin, they behave like true pronouns (*pro*). On the other hand, null arguments are more limited with plain verbs. Lillo-Martin analyzed these as similar to the null arguments of discourse-oriented languages, which require a discourse context to retrieve their reference. The same distinction is found in LSB, as argued by Quadros (1995).[12]

The examples in (33) and (34) show that the distribution of null arguments with agreeing verbs is different from the distribution of null arguments with plain verbs.

(33)   _____eg:b_____   (ASL; also LSB)

a. TOMORROW aGIVEb BOOK.
'(You) give (her) the book tomorrow.'
b. TOMORROW aGIVEb BOOK.

(34)   a. * TOMORROW TALK.   (ASL; also LSB)
a'. TOMORROW IX < you > TALK IX < a >.
'(You) talk with (her) tomorrow.'

                                 _____eg:a_____
b. * TOMORROW TALK.

The sentence in (34a) with a null subject and object and a plain verb is impossible without the appropriate context, while in (33a) with an agreeing verb the null argument is allowed. The cases in ASL in which it is possible to have null arguments with plain verbs mentioned by Lillo-Martin are similar to the example illustrated in (35).

(35)   *Speaker A*:   _____y/n_____   (LSB; also ASL)
                      BEBÊ COMER JÁ?
                      'Did the baby eat already?'
      Speaker B: _____hn_____
                      COMER JÁ.
                      'Yes, he did eat already.'

The distribution of null arguments observed in (33) and (34) is the one relevant for our purposes here. These examples confirm the asymmetric distribution of the nonmanual markers. It is clear that nonmanual markers are not related to the licensing of null arguments when plain verbs are inserted in the derivation, since if this were the case, the sentence in (34b) would be grammatical. On the other hand, agreeing verbs, with or without nonmanual marking, allow null arguments as shown in (33a) and (33b).

Another difference between plain and agreeing verbs observed in LSB but not in ASL concerns the distribution of negation. Examples (36) and (37) show the contrast between agreeing and plain verbs, respectively, with respect to the surface occurrence of negation in the preverbal position.

(36)   _____ neg   (LSB)
         IX < det > JOÃO NÃO aDARb LIVRO.
         'John does not give the book to (her).'

(37)   _____ neg   (LSB)
         * JOÃO NÃO APRECIAR CARRO.
         'John does not like the car.'

With plain verbs, lexical negation is allowed only in final position. Example (38) illustrates this case.[13]

(38)   _____ neg
         JOÃO APRECIAR CARRO NÃO.
         'John does not like the car.'

It is assumed that the underlying position of negation is preverbal for both plain and agreeing verbs in LSB, as it is for ASL. Note that although the negative item is not pronounced in the position preceding the plain verb in (38), the scope of negation is marked from the NegP position on, and it spreads over its domain including VP, through the nonmanual marker. We assume therefore that negation is associated with a negative nonmanual marker in a position between IP and VP. However, there is a clear difference between plain and agreeing verbs concerning the surface distribution of the negative sign.

Note that with agreeing verbs as with plain verbs, negation can occur in the final position, as shown in (39).

(39)   _____ neg   (LSB)
         IX < 1 > 1AJUDAR2 NÃO

For both plain verbs and agreeing verbs, the appearance of the negative element in the sentence-final position can be accounted for by using the focus/double construction discussed in section 3.2.3.

In this section, we have seen that agreeing verbs and plain verbs behave differently with respect to many phenomena in sign languages such as ASL and LSB. We summarize the relevant facts below.

(40) (i)   In ASL and LSB, sentences with agreeing verbs seem to have more freedom in word order (e.g., OSV, SOV) than those with plain verbs;

(ii) In ASL and LSB, null arguments with agreeing verbs differ in distribution from null arguments with plain verbs;

(iii) In LSB, though not in ASL, plain verbs disallow preverbal negation, while agreeing verbs allow it.

The issue, then, is to explain the differences between plain and agreeing verbs in LSB and in ASL.

Quadros (1999, 2003) proposed that the differences between plain and agreeing verbs in LSB can be accounted for by using two different phrase structures. Linguists have proposed that for some languages, the "inflection" of a sentence might be represented in separate functional projections for subject agreement, object agreement and tense (Pollock 1989, Chomsky & Lasnik 1993, Bobaljik 1995 and many others), as illustrated in Figure 11.4a. In contrast, other languages use a simple single projection for inflection, as in Figure 11.4b.

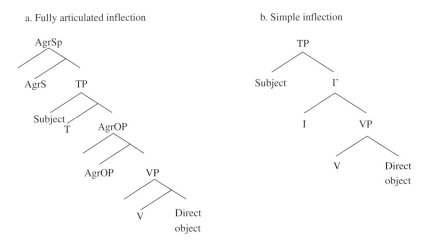

Figure 11.4 *Phrase markers with fully articulated (a) and simple (b) inflection.*

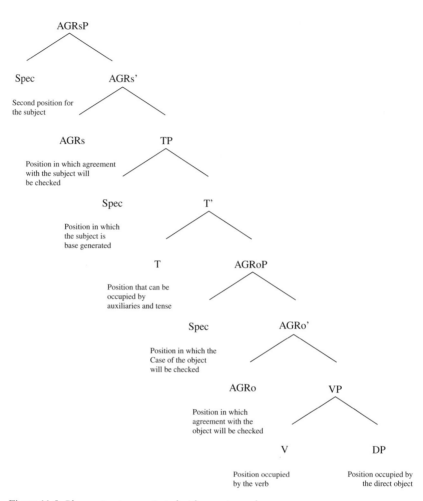

Figure 11.5 *Phrase structure projected with agreeing verbs.*

Quadros proposed that the difference between Figure 11.4a and Figure 11.4b exists not only across languages, but also within one language (LSB). On her proposal, agreeing verbs make use of the full structure, as explicated for LSB in Figure 11.5, while plain verbs use the simple structure, shown for LSB in Figure 11.6.

Verbs in either structure must check their features by moving to the inflectional projections, either overtly (thus changing their order on the surface) or covertly (thus keeping the order as it is base-generated). Quadros proposes that agreeing verbs in LSB are inserted "fully inflected" and so need to move only covertly. However, plain

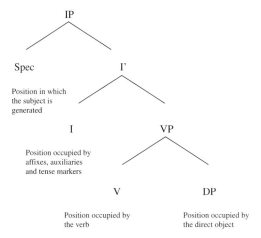

Figure 11.6 *Phrase structure projected with plain verbs.*

verbs must combine with inflection in the overt syntax. This set of assumptions explains the behavior of plain and agreeing verbs summarized in (40), as we will now discuss.

The first characteristic, greater freedom of word order with agreeing verbs, can be explained by the observation that the fully articulated structure has available slots for the movement of the object, which the simple structure does not have. In particular, when the verb is marked for agreement, the object can move to the specifier of AgrOP (this is akin to the discussion of object shift in section 3.2.3). However, there is no location for such movement in the IP structure.

The second characteristic concerns the use of null arguments with agreeing versus plain verbs. There are various analyses of null arguments in syntactic theory. Without making a commitment to one of them, we assume that the analysis of agreement-licensed null arguments must refer to the projections AgrSP and AgrOP. Since only agreeing verbs appear in structures with these projections, only agreeing verbs will have such null arguments.

Finally, LSB (though not ASL) also has another type of strong evidence for a difference in the structures used for agreeing and plain verbs, i.e., the ordering of negation with respect to the verb. Quadros accounts for this by proposing that the combination of the verb with Inflection, which is required in the overt syntax for plain verbs, is blocked when a negative sign appears in the NegP position, between the Inflection and the verb. This can be compared with the similar blocking of inflection combining with the verb in English negative sentences, as illustrated below.

Table 11.2 *Similarities and differences between LSB and ASL clause structure*

		Plain	Agreeing	Spatial
● LSB		● Simple IP		
		● Inflection affixal	● Split IP	● Split IP
		● Verbs bare	● [+person] agr	● [+loc] agr
		● No pre-verbal negation	● Verb raises to check Agr	● Verb raises to check Agr
		● No object shift	● Verbs fully inflected	● Verbs fully inflected
		● AUX		
● ASL		● Simple IP	● Pre-verbal negation	● Pre-verbal negation
		● Verbs fully inflected	● Object shift	● Object shift
		● Pre-verbal negation	● No AUX	● No AUX
		● No object shift		
		● No AUX		

Source: From Quadros, Lillo-Martin and Chen Pichler 2004.

(41)   *John not likes Mary.
         John does not like Mary.

In ASL, agreeing and plain verbs behave similarly with respect to the placement of negation. Both verb types allow preverbal negation, as illustrated in (42).

(42)   _____neg_____   (ASL)

a. JOHN NOT a HELPb MARY.
   'John did not help Mary.'

                                              _____neg_____
b. JOHN NOT LIKE MARY.
   'John does not like Mary.'

This indicates that both agreeing and plain verbs are inserted "fully inflected" in ASL, so both can check agreement covertly, as claimed by Quadros, Lillo-Martin and Chen Pichler (2004). Quadros *et al.* considered the similarities and differences between LSB and ASL with respect to the structure of sentences with plain and agreeing verbs, and summarized them as in Table 11.2.

4   Summary/conclusion

We have shown that SVO is the underlying word order in LSB and ASL, and that other word orders are derived from SVO. In particular, we have seen that these orders result from syntactic operations motivated by some additional feature, like agreement or nonmanual markers, topic and focus constructions. In both languages, the following operations are found:

- Topicalization – objects, verb phrases and subjects can be topicalized, leading to $<O>SV$, $<VO>S$, $<S>VO$ and $<S><O>V$ orders; also base-generated topic-comment structures with no gap
- Object shift – licensed by the presence of handling verbs, aspectual verbs and agreement, leading to SOV and OSV orders
- Focus – emphatic focus leading to doubling and final constructions; information focus and contrastive focus with the focused information potentially sentence-initial
- Null arguments – subject and/or object can be null with agreeing verbs because ASL and LSB are *pro*-drop languages; discourse-oriented null arguments with plain verbs

We have also shown that there is an asymmetry between sentences with plain verbs and sentences with agreeing verbs. We proposed that different phrase structures are used with agreeing (Figure 11.5) and plain (Figure 11.6) verbs. In particular, agreeing verbs employ a "split IP" structure with projections of AgrSP, TP and AgrOP; while plain verbs employ a "simple IP" structure with IP only. These structures capture the following observations:

- Word order is more flexible with agreeing verbs than with plain verbs.
- Null arguments are licensed freely with agreeing verbs but require a discourse context with plain verbs.
- In LSB, negation can precede an agreeing verb but not a plain verb.

In conclusion, we see that theoretical notions from current linguistic theory can capture facts about sign languages including similarities and differences across sign languages. Such a focus on crosslinguistic comparison is an important component of this book. Further research on these similarities and differences is anticipated.

12

Factors that form classifier signs

Elisabeth Engberg-Pedersen

1   Introduction

Since the mid 1970s, sign language researchers have debated how to analyze signs that denote an entity's motion or state of being located somewhere, signs with some similarity between the sign form and the sign meaning (for an overview of the discussions, see Schembri 2003 and papers in Emmorey 2003). One example is seen in Figure 12.1 from a Swedish signer's description of how a boy falls from a tree to the ground.[1] The signer's hands can be seen as representing the boy and some surface related to the tree, respectively, and the movement of her right hand as representing the motion aspects of the boy's fall. Within the framework of functional linguistics and its interest in motivated relations between linguistic form and linguistic meaning (Jakobson 1971, Haiman 1983, Givón 1991, Engberg-Pedersen 1996), this chapter investigates the factors that shape signs like the one in Figure 12.1 and discusses different approaches to their description in the sign linguistics literature.

In a paper on arbitrariness and iconicity in American Sign Language (ASL), Frishberg (1975) introduced the term "classifier" to describe the hands in signs such as ASL MEET, which is made with two index-handshapes (see Appendix) facing each other (see Figure 12.2): "ASL uses the index finger in a vertical orientation as a sort of classifier for human beings" (Frishberg 1975:715). She claims that

> the verb MEET has no "neutral" form; the citation form actually means "one person meets one person", or perhaps more specifically "one self-moving object with a dominant vertical dimension meets one self-moving object with a dominant vertical dimension" ... Many of these classifiers are productive and analyzable, although not strictly transparent. (Frishberg 1975:715)

Frishberg points out that the classifier denoting "one self-moving object with a dominant vertical dimension" in ASL is an arbitrary, language-specific symbol since what Frishberg calls Chinese Sign Language (identical to Hong Kong Sign

252

Figure 12.1 *A Swedish signer's description of a boy's fall from a tree (initial and final position of the hands).*

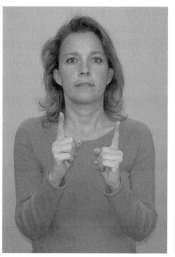 

Figure 12.2 *The ASL sign MEET as described in Stokoe, Casterline and Croneberg (1965); (initial and final position of the hands). Here both hands move. Johnson and Liddell (1984) describe the ASL sign MEET as monomorphemic and in the form represented in their paper, only one hand moves and the orientation of the hands differ from the orientation in the Figure.*

Language in this chapter) uses a different handshape to express a person classifier, i.e., the Y-handshape.

Since Frishberg's paper, classifiers have been described for many sign languages (Schembri 2003), the proper linguistic description of the signs they occur in has been extensively debated (especially DeMatteo 1977, McDonald 1982, T. Supalla 1982, T. Supalla 2003, Cogill-Koez 2000a, Liddell 2003a, Sandler & Lillo-Martin 2006), and the appropriateness of the term classifier has been questioned (Engberg-Pedersen & Pedersen 1983, Engberg-Pedersen 1993, Schembri 2003, Sandler & Lillo-Martin 2006) and other names suggested, e.g., "property marker" (Slobin *et al.* 2003).[2]

The different descriptions can roughly be categorized as belonging to one of the following three categories:

1. Descriptions emphasizing the analogy between the signs' form and their meaning (e.g., DeMatteo 1977, Cogill-Koez 2000a, Cogill-Koez 2000b).
2. Descriptions of the signs as complexes of morphemes (e.g., McDonald 1982, Supalla 1982, Benedicto & Brentari 2004).
3. Descriptions of the signs as (partially) lexicalized verbs (Liddell 2003a).[3]

Liddell (2003a) has convincingly argued against an analysis of classifier signs as multimorphemic, an argumentation that I shall summarize in section 2.1. The main part of this chapter consists of analyses of motion descriptions in nine different sign languages with the purpose of investigating whether they are best described in terms of visual analogy, as suggested primarily by Cogill-Koez, or as partially lexicalized verbs, as suggested by Liddell. If some sort of visual analogy plays a role in the formation of classifier signs, we can expect somewhat similar descriptions of the same event by signers of different, unrelated sign languages depending on whether the forms are motivated by the same visually perceptible extralinguistic forms. If, by contrast, classifier signs are lexical verbs, we would not expect the descriptions to resemble each other across sign languages, unless, of course, we could claim either a common ancestor to sign languages with systematic similarities or extensive borrowing among the sign languages. If, however, the forms are partially lexicalized forms that were originally visually motivated, then we might expect some similarity and some differences, again depending on the original motivating factors and the type of lexicalization that has taken place.

Before I turn to the data, I shall briefly introduce the three main types of descriptions of classifier signs: as multimorphemic signs, as, possibly stylized, visual analogs and as partly lexicalized signs. In section 3 I will present the data for my analysis and the foci of the analysis and in section 4 the analysis of the descriptions of two events in the same story told by signers of nine different sign languages, with the purpose of illuminating similarities and differences in the signs across sign languages. Section 5 summarizes and discusses the different factors that can be claimed to have influenced the signs used by the signers.

2   Different descriptions of classifier signs

2.1   Classifier signs as multimorphemic signs

In the first major analysis of classifier signs in a sign language, T. Supalla (1982) analyzed ASL verbs of motion and location (i.e., classifier signs) as multimorphemic. He categorized the movement of the hand as the verb's root that necessarily combined with some, if not all, of the following types of morphemes: affixes of agreement, manner, orientation, placement in relation to the signer, relation between the two hands, distance between the hands, etc.

Liddell (2003a) attempts a full morphemic description of the ASL sign UPRIGHT-PERSON$_1$-WALK-TO-UPRIGHT-PERSON$_2$ along the lines suggested by Supalla (1982) and based on the form analysis of signs that he has developed with Robert E. Johnson (Liddell & Johnson 1989). In this model, the sign is analyzed sequentially into movements (i.e., periods in the production during which some aspect of the articulation is in transition) and holds (i.e., periods during which there is no such transition of any aspect of the articulation). Each movement or hold segment is composed of segmental and articulatory features. The segmental features specify the activity of the hand (i.e., whether it is a movement or a hold segment) and the contour of the movement (e.g., a straight line or an arc), any local movement of the fingers, and timing information such as duration. The articulatory features specify the handshape, the position and orientation of the hand, and nonmanual signals. The model was developed for lexical signs, and it is not immediately clear how it can be transferred to classifier signs (cf. Brentari & Padden 2001 and Sandler & Lillo-Martin 2006 for discussions of the phonological analysis of the different parts of the sign lexicon), but I shall talk informally about the initial and final positions of such signs in this chapter.

The sign UPRIGHT-PERSON$_1$-WALK-TO-UPRIGHT-PERSON$_2$ is made with two index-handshapes, with a hold in the weak hand, which is held at a distance from the signer, palm facing the signer, while the strong hand with the palm facing the weak hand is moved from close to the signer to contact with the weak hand. Moreover, the signer looks in the direction of the weak hand. Liddell finds that according to Supalla's analysis, the sign must include four movement roots: one hold root in the weak hand, and three roots in the strong hand (hold, linear movement, hold). Both handshapes represent classifiers and, thus, a morpheme each. Their upright orientation and their orientation in relation to each other are also meaningful, as well as the distance between the hands and their relation to the horizontal plane.

By using this approach, Liddell ends with an analysis of the sign as consisting of four roots and twenty-four affixes – or fourteen affixes depending on whether each movement root is described as having its own set of affixes or identical repeated affixes are counted as single affixes. Even then the analysis does not account for all aspects of the sign's meaning. An extremely troublesome area is the location of the hands in the signing space in front of the signer. If we wish to comply with Supalla's claim that all aspects of meaning in the signs derive from morphemes, space must be treated as analyzable into discrete units, each representing a morpheme. But as Liddell writes, "it appears that signers are free to select points in the signing space guided by the actual physical relationships they are trying to depict" (2003a:207). There may be no end to the number of possible locations in space and accordingly no end to the list of possible morphemes. By isolating all meaning aspects that may change along with a change of form, Liddell makes it evident that the attempt to compile a finite list of morphemes of ASL classifier signs is bound to fail.

Benedicto and Brentari (2004) have suggested a morphological analysis of classifier signs where the number of morphemes is reduced considerably. Here the classifier itself may consist of more than one morpheme, but the verb is said to be "formed of a verbal root (represented by the movement of the sign) and the classifier itself (the handshape)" (Benedicto & Brentari 2004:748), that is, the spatial relations between the hands and between the hands and the signer's body are not analyzed in terms of morphemes. These meaningful aspects of the signs are apparently integrated into the verb roots or the classifiers (e.g., 1_{H2_static}-1 + COME_UP_BESIDE_THE_OTHER, where the plus sign indicates the simultaneity of the two morphemes, the classifier and the verb root), but we are not told exactly where in the signing space the two hands meet.

Liddell (2003a) also argues against Supalla's analysis by pointing out that the potential morphemes cannot combine productively to produce an unlimited number of classifier signs, a point to which I shall return after the presentation of analyses of classifier signs in terms of visual analogy.

2.2   Classifier signs as visual analogs

A radical alternative to Supalla's morphological analysis is DeMatteo (1977), which represents an example of analyses that emphasize the analogy between the signs' form and their meaning. DeMatteo claims that a traditional linguistic analysis of a sign such as ASL MEET (Figure 12.2) will fail to predict that from the initial position of the hands the signer may proceed in an indefinite number of ways, all distinguished by the movement of the hands in relation to each other. Like Liddell later, he points to the problem of the endlessness of meaningful units if we use a traditional linguistic analysis.

DeMatteo analyzes instead the hands in MEET as each representing a standing person. The hands "trace in the signing space an analogue of the trajectory the actors would take in the real world or some imaginal world" (1977:115). So the trajectory of each hand is "a spatial analogue of the movement in the real/imaginal world: the function is to enable the addressee in the signed communication to reconstruct the scene in order to infer the relationships between the two actors in the event" (DeMatteo 1977:115).

One objection that is often raised against an analysis of classifier signs as visual analogs is that they are not realistic depictions. In her analysis of classifier signs, however, Cogill-Koez (2000a, 2000b) rejects the idea that a representation based on visual analogy has to be realistic. A one-to-one mapping of every point in the form of a referent to every point in the form of the representation is only one form of visual analogy or visual representation. Its aim is pictorial realism, as we see it in skilled Western realistic drawing or sculpture, or in photographs. Toward the other end of a continuum of visual representation strategies, we find what Cogill-Koez describes as "a *schematized* visual correspondence between *selected, relevant* parameters of the referent and the representation" (2000b:160; author's italics). In this type of representation, objects may be represented by a fixed class of shapes such as circles, points and lines. The spatial relations and distances between the shapes may also be more or less schematized, and the ones who make the sketches may be free to select and represent only those aspects of the objects that they find important in the context. We see schematic visual analogy in maps, diagrams and models, in non-Western art and in children's early drawings. The drawing of a face in Figure 12.3 is an example of what Cogill-Koez would call a *templated visual representation* with circles, lines and dots in a recognizable, but far from realistic pattern. Cogill-Koez assumes that schematic conventions of visual representation are culture-specific, but based on principles that may be innate. Users of these

Figure 12.3 *A templated visual representation of a face. From http://tell.fll.purdue.edu/ JapanProj//FLClipart/.*

conventions may shift up and down the continuum between highly schematic and highly analog strategies. When required, they can exploit or break the conventions of the schematic representations to represent something in a more analog way.

Analyses of classifier signs as linguistic and not visual representations have focused on the fact that the signs include discrete elements with restrictions on their combinations (especially T. Supalla 1982). But identifiable elements in regular patterns of combination can be found almost everywhere where one has repetition of behavior, Cogill-Koez claims, including drawing.

Cogill-Koez sharpens the criteria for showing that classifier signs are truly linguistic in nature. We do not need to pursue her argumentation here. Suffice it to say that classifier signs differ from other signs, for instance, in changing meaning if they are made in mirror-image fashion. In classifier signs, the left–right dimension is often exploited to reflect a particular scene, for instance to indicate that someone was placed to the left or the right of a car. A further difference between lexical signs and classifier signs pointed out by Cogill-Koez is that the forms of lexical signs diverge in historically related sign languages such as British Sign Language (BSL) and Australian Sign Language (Auslan), whereas classifier signs used in the two sign languages are almost identical, as we would predict if they are a form of visual representation and as such not free to alter their form independently of their meaning.

On this background Cogill-Koez (2000a) suggests that classifier signs are a form of schematic visual representation composed largely of discrete parts, the so-called templates. Examples of templates are the index-handshape for people and the linear movement for movement toward a goal. Some of the templates contain conventional deformational possibilities, i.e., they can change form to represent something in an analog way. According to Cogill-Koez, Australian signers may, for instance, bend one finger of the V-handshape of the biped classifier to represent a one-legged person.

Liddell (2003a) criticizes analyses of classifier signs in terms of visual analogy by pointing to the fact that the ASL classifier sign UPRIGHT-PERSON$_1$-WALK-TO-UPRIGHT-PERSON$_2$ includes the lexical meaning 'walk.' The sign is made with a movement of one of the hands in a straight line, and this, Liddell finds, is not a visual analog of walking. Nevertheless, the addressee knows that the person did not saunter, shuffle, skip, trot or run, but did indeed walk up to the other person. This is a fact about the sign's lexical meaning; it is not inferred from an understanding of the sign as a visual representation, Liddell claims. Liddell finds that both morphological analyses and analyses in terms of visual analogy predict classifier signs that are unacceptable in ASL. We would, for instance, expect Supalla's morpheme "a straight path movement" to combine with the animal classifier if the signs were productively produced by morphemes – and also if the signs were visual analogs ("an animal moves in a straight line"). The straight path movement can, however, only combine with three different classifiers and not with the classifier for animals, Liddell claims.

In the National Science Foundation (NSF) project from which the data used in section 4 are drawn, Diane Brentari and her collaborators collected descriptions of drawings with a running dog, a dog running out of a dog's house and a dog running toward or away from a man. In these descriptions some of the signers, and all three ASL signers, use the animal classifier, i.e., a V-handshape with bent index and middle fingers, with a straight line. Brentari's discussions with the participants do, however, confirm that there are constraints on the combinations of classifiers and movements, but for these ASL signers, not the restriction on the use of the animal classifier mentioned by Liddell (Brentari, personal communication).

2.3   Classifier signs as partially lexicalized verbs

Like DeMatteo and Cogill-Koez, Liddell (2003a) recognizes that the meaning provided by the placement of the hands in space and part of the hands' orientation in classifier signs is expressed in an analog and gradient manner, which defies a morphological analysis. In Liddell (2003b) these analog parts of classifier signs are analyzed within a cognitive linguistics framework, but in Liddell (2003a) his emphasis is on the parts of classifier signs that, according to him, should not be subjected to an analysis in terms of visual analogy. These parts he describes as the lexical item, which must combine with gestural elements to create a full – pro-nounceable – sign. The lexical part of the ASL verb UPRIGHT-PERSON-WALK-ALONG, meaning 'person walks along (in an unhurried manner and in a normal forward orientation)' (Liddell 2003a:213), is expressed by "a 1-handshape [i.e. an index-handshape in the terminology used in this chapter], a straight path move-ment with a repeated bouncing movement from the initial location to the final location, and features orienting the base of the hand downward" (Liddell 2003a:212). The initial and final locations of the hand and the orientation of the hand toward the final location are "variable, gradient elements" (Liddell, 2003a:212), i.e., gestural in nature (Liddell 2003b, see also Schembri, Jones & Burnham 2005). With the gradient elements removed, we no longer have a full sign "because it has no features locating the hand or orienting the palm" (Liddell 2003a:212). But the formally stable part constitutes the lexical item, which can be subjected to a morphological analysis.

The verb UPRIGHT-PERSON-WALK-ALONG, meaning 'person walks along (in an unhurried manner and in a normal forward orientation),' contrasts with the verb UPRIGHT-PERSON-WALK-TO, meaning 'person walks (normal forward orientation) to a place.' The two signs differ in both meaning and form since the former includes a bouncing movement in the linear path movement. Liddell examines whether the bouncing movement of UPRIGHT-PERSON-WALK-ALONG can be given morphological status, e.g., a morpheme meaning 'move in an unhurried manner without a final goal.' It appears, however, that this hypothetical morpheme has very limited productivity in ASL. It cannot be used with the classifier for animal or vehicle, for instance. Liddell concludes that the limited productivity of the bouncing movement with the suggested meaning makes "it difficult to support the bouncing movement as morphemic. The most one could say is that, if it is morphemic, it is highly restricted" (Liddell 2003a:216).

The limited productivity of, for instance, the bouncing movement of UPRIGHT-PERSON-WALK-ALONG can be compared with the limited productivity of, for example, the affix *-ity* in English *seniority*, Liddell claims; *-ity* can be separated from *senior*, which forms an independent word, but *-ity* does not combine freely with other adjectives, for instance not with *junior* to form *juniority*. Still, because of the existence of *senior* and the similarity of *senior* and *junior*, we recognize two parts in *seniority*, and we cannot exclude the possibility that some user of English will combine *junior* and *-ity* some day, just as we cannot exclude the possibility that some user of ASL will substitute, for example, the vehicle classifier for the upright-person classifier in UPRIGHT-PERSON-WALK-ALONG to denote a personified car in a children's story.

Liddell tests the combinability of the apparently meaningful subparts of classifier signs in ASL by means of grammaticality judgments by native signers, and he finds that many meaningful parts of classifier signs have restricted distributions.[4]

There is no doubt that parts of classifier signs become more stable lexicalized items over time. In Danish Sign Language (DSL) there are three different handshapes that may represent moving human beings, which profile different aspects of their motion or location, and they cannot substitute freely for one another (Engberg-Pedersen 1993). This should come as no surprise; languages tend to have more ready-made lexical items for the activities of human beings than for animals or objects. In English, for example, the motion of a human being may be described by many different verbs such as *walk*, *go*, *run*, *skip*, *hop*, *trot*, *saunter*, etc., whereas the inventory to describe the motion of a mouse is much more restricted.

We should also expect that analog – or motivated – relations between form and meaning are not always straightforward. Liddell discusses a signer's description of a security chain on a door that was not attached. The signer used a sign in which her index finger was pointing down and swinging back and forth. The signer's point was not that the chain was swinging back and forth, but that the door was unlatched. The movement of her index finger is not a direct visual analog of the unattached chain, but it is not unmotivated either. There is a metonymic (not metaphorical, as claimed by Liddell [2003a]) relation between the chain's ability to dangle and the fact that it is not attached; the sign's form depicts the dangling chain, and the metonymic relation between dangling and the state of not being attached makes the addressee understand in an appropriate context that the intended meaning is that the chain is not attached. Thus, the swinging movement is a conventionalized way of representing the fact that something that could have been attached was not.

Similarly, one could analyze the bouncing movement of ASL UPRIGHT-PERSON-WALK-ALONG, along the lines suggested by Cogill-Koez, as a templated visual representation of the gait of many human beings, which explains why it cannot be used of animals or cars. There is of course no direct representational relation between a bouncing gait and 'move in an unhurried manner without a final goal.' The point is, however, that a bouncing gait contrasts with, among other types of motion, running or hurried walking as when one does have a goal. Metonymically, the bouncing gait may be used to indicate 'move in an unhurried manner without a final goal,' and this metonymic relation may lexicalize so that 'move in an unhurried manner without a final goal' becomes the conventional meaning of the form. In DSL, a tense bouncing movement can be used with a linear path movement and a classifier expressed by the index hand in a classifier sign meaning 'walk resolutely to a goal,' which may be a different lexicalization from the one found in ASL.

In the following sections, I will investigate the role of analogy and lexicalization in classifier signs by investigating variation in descriptions of two fall episodes in eight sign languages.

3   Data collection and foci of analysis

The data used for the analysis presented in this chapter were collected for a cross-linguistic study of classifiers by Brentari as principal investigator and her collaborators (NSF grant BCS 0112391).[5] The part of the data used here are recordings of three to five signers (named by the letters A to C/D/E) from each of nine different sign languages (see Table 12.1). The signers told stories based on the wordless picture book *Frog, Where Are You?* (Mayer 1969) about a boy who loses his pet frog and goes looking for it in the forest.[6] The signers, who were all native signers of their sign language, first looked through the book and then retold the story to another native signer. The Croatian, Hong Kong and Japanese signers did not consult the book again while telling the story; the others did.

Table 12.1 *Sign languages represented and the number of signers*

Name of sign language	Abbreviated name	Number of signers
American Sign Language	ASL	3
British Sign Language	BSL	4
Deutsche Gebärdensprache – German Sign Language	DGS	5
Deutschschweizer Gebärdensprache – German Swiss Sign Language	DSGS	5
Dansk tegnsprog – Danish Sign Language	DSL	5
Hong Kong Sign Language	HKSL	5
Croatian Sign Language	HZJ	5
NihonSyuwa – Japanese Sign Language[*]	JSL	5
Svensk teckenspråk – Swedish Sign Language	SSL	5

* Note: See Fischer and Gong, this volume, for an account of the name.

Figure 12.4 *First part of the tree event. From* Frog, Where Are You? *by Mercer Mayer, copyright © 1969 by Mercer Mayer. Used by permission of Dial Books for Young Readers, a division of Penguin Young Readers Group, a Member of Penguin Group (USA) Inc., New York. All rights reserved.*

In the story, the boy loses his foothold in two situations. First, he climbs a tree, but an owl frightens him, and in the next picture he is seen lying on his back at the foot of the tree (Figures 12.4 and 12.5). I shall refer to this episode as the "tree event." In the second instance, the boy climbs a rock and holds on to what he

Figure 12.5 *Second part of the tree event. From* Frog, Where Are You? *by Mercer Mayer, copyright © 1969 by Mercer Mayer. Used by permission of Dial Books for Young Readers, a division of Penguin Young Readers Group, a Member of Penguin Group (USA) Inc., New York. All rights reserved.*

believes to be some branches, which turn out to be a deer's antlers. When the deer gets up from lying down, the boy is hauled onto its head and ends up lying on his stomach between the deer's antlers (Figures 12.6 and 12.7). This episode will be called the "deer event." Thirty out of the forty-two signers described the tree event, and thirty-five signers described the deer event.

The tree event represents a fairly straightforward fall where someone loses control and falls from a higher to a lower level ending up on his back. In the deer event, the boy also loses his foothold but does not move from a higher to a lower level, and he ends up in a highly unusual position. Moreover, in this event there are two moving entities, the boy and the deer. If there is a contrast in sign languages between more standardized lexical signs and more iconic descriptions based on visual analogy, we may expect them to turn up in the descriptions of these two events. In general, a more standardized event can be expected to be described by a more frequent and standardized lexical item, and a less standardized, more unexpected event by means of circumlocutions and more complex descriptions, depending on the genre and on the type of focus and detail chosen by the language user.

In the description of the signs, I shall use Talmy's (1975) terms "figure" and "ground." The figure of a motion event is "[t]he object that is considered as moving

Figure 12.6 *First part of the deer event. From* Frog, Where Are You? *by Mercer Mayer, copyright © 1969 by Mercer Mayer. Used by permission of Dial Books for Young Readers, a division of Penguin Young Readers Group, a Member of Penguin Group (USA) Inc., New York. All rights reserved.*

Figure 12.7 *Second part of the deer event. From* Frog, Where Are You? *by Mercer Mayer, copyright © 1969 by Mercer Mayer. Used by permission of Dial Books for Young Readers, a division of Penguin Young Readers Group, a Member of Penguin Group (USA) Inc., New York. All rights reserved.*

or located with respect to another object" (Talmy 1975:181), and the ground is "[t]he object with respect to which a first object is considered as moving or located" (Talmy 1975:181). In (1) *The cat* is the figure (nominal) and *the mat* the ground (nominal), and in (2) *The bottle* is the figure (nominal) and *the cove* the ground (nominal).

(1)   The cat is on the mat.
(2)   The bottle floated into the cove.

More specifically I use the term "source" of the ground (nominal) that denotes the starting point of the figure's movement, and the term "goal" of the ground (nominal) that denotes the end point of the figure's movement. In (2) *the cove* is a goal.

Earlier studies have shown that the handshapes of the classifiers used of human beings may differ among sign languages (Schembri 2002, Schembri, Jones & Burnham 2005). In an analysis of the descriptions of the same two fall events by deaf children and adults signing DSL (Engberg-Pedersen 2003), I found that loss of control can be signaled by a change of the hand's orientation. I also found that in descriptions of a more typical fall such as the tree event, the weak hand is used to represent the movement's starting point (i.e., the source), but in descriptions of the atypical fall of the deer event, it was used to represent the goal.

The features that I shall focus on are the following:

1.   Which classifier do the signers choose to represent the figure?
2.   How do the signers indicate the figure's loss of control?
3.   Do the signers simultaneously represent the figure and the ground? If so, by means of which classifier do they represent the ground?
4.   Is the weak hand used to represent the source or the goal of the boy's motion?
5.   Which types of strategies do the signers use to describe an unusual, non-standard, fall, i.e., the deer event (e.g., the signer's own body to represent the boy or the deer in the deer event)?

The study might include many other features, e.g., the signers' facial expression (expressing emotions or neutral?), their mouth movements (the equivalent of a spoken language word, a conventional nonmanual signal – such as blowing out air – or part of an emotional facial expression?), or their gaze direction (eye contact with the addressee, gaze directed at their hands or gaze direction imitating the boy's gaze?). The outline, length, direction and quality of the hand's movement are also relevant. The five features listed above will, however, permit me to illuminate the factors focused on here.

4   **Analysis**

4.1   Descriptions of a typical fall

The tree event (see Figures 12.4 and 12.5) represents a straightforward fall in the sense that the boy loses control of his orientation and falls from a higher to a lower level. Moreover, the only moving entity in the event is the boy. Table 12.2 shows the different handshapes used to represent the figure in the descriptions of the fall. The majority of the European signers in this study use the biped classifier (V-handshape). Only one European signer, DSL signer B, uses a different handshape: she describes the boy's fall by means of a sign or gesture (see below) that depicts the way people may move their hands up and back when falling back (see Figure 12.8).

In the stories in Hong Kong Sign Language (HKSL), the biped classifier competes with an established classifier for human beings in HKSL (Tang 2003), and with a classifier consisting of two index-handshapes. The latter can be seen as a representation of the boy's two legs. As it appears from Table 12.2, the three HKSL signers that describe this event all use the standard classifier for human beings in HKSL. Two of them start with a different handshape, but break off and shift to the standard classifier. In Japanese Sign Language (JSL) only one signer describes the fall, and he uses a classifier expressed by the A-handshape. The general classifier for human beings in JSL is the upright-person classifier, expressed by an index-handshape; the classifier expressed by the A-handshape signifies male but is used in many signs as the unmarked human classifier (Susan Fischer, personal communication).

All signers thus choose a standard classifier in their language to describe the tree event, and all the signers of the European sign languages use a classifier expressed

Figure 12.8 *The sign or gesture used about someone falling on their back (initial and final position of the hands).*

Table 12.2 *Classifiers used to represent the boy in the descriptions of the tree event*

'boy'	biped	HKSL person	JSL person	person-by-legs
ASL – USA	AB			
BSL – UK	ABCD			
DGS – Germany	ABDE			
DSGS – Switzerland	ACDE			
DSL – Denmark	ACDE			
SSL – Sweden	ABCE			
HZJ – Croatia	ACE			
HKSL – Hong Kong	A	ADE		D
JSL – Japan			D	

Note: The letters identify the signers who use the classifier in question.

by the same handshape. This does not necessarily mean, however, that the classifiers have the same meaning in these languages. In DSL the biped classifier contrasts with at least two other classifiers for human beings, one of them expressed by the A-handshape like the JSL classifier, but in DSL this classifier does not have the meaning 'male'; it is the handshape of the number sign ONE, and it is used in classifier signs where the emphasis is on one individual as opposed to others (Engberg-Pedersen 1993). It could not be used to describe the boy's fall from the tree in DSL.

The signers use two strategies to signal the boy's loss of control in the tree event (see Table 12.3), and both contrast with a sign meaning 'jump' where the arm stays pronated with the tips of the middle and index fingers facing the ground level. The biped classifier with its typical orientation indicating an upright person can be made with the index and middle fingers more or less bent or extended (see the Appendix). If the fingers are bent in the middle knuckles, the palm faces down. A change in the person's orientation from upright to lying down can then be indicated simply by extending the two fingers, while the arm and hand are still pronated (see the second part of Figure 12.1). With this orientation and handshape, the classifier can be used in a sign meaning 'person lying on his or her back,' in DSL at least. Some signers describe the boy's position in Figure 12.4 in this way, i.e., as lying on his back in accordance with the drawing. These signers start the sign with the biped classifier in its typical orientation with the fingers more or less extended, usually at a some-what higher level and in most cases in contact with a classifier representing a surface or, more specifically, the tree (see the first part of Figure 12.1). Typically, the signers bring their hand in an arc movement to a lower level, while straightening their wrist in the movement. The boy's loss of control in the fall is here described by the combination of the arc movement and the straightening of the wrist which indicates

Table 12.3 *Signers from each sign language indicating the boy's loss of control by changing the orientation of the hand during the sign's path movement or straightening the wrist of the V-handshape of the biped classifier*

	straightening of wrist with no change of orientation	change of orientation	no indication of loss of control ('jump')	unclear
ASL – USA	A	B		
BSL – UK	ABD	C		
DGS – Germany	B	ADE		
DSGS – Switzerland	E	A	CD	
DSL – Denmark	ACDE			
SSL – Sweden	CE	B	A	
HZJ – Croatia		AE		C
HKSL – Hong Kong	(not applicable)	AE		D
JSL – Japan	(not applicable)			D
Total	12	11	3	3

Figure 12.9 *The boy's fall from the tree described by means of a sign where the strong hand ends with the arm supinated ("change of orientation") (initial and final position of the hands) (cf. Figure 12.1).*

the change in the boy's orientation from upright to lying on his back. The sign is, moreover, in most cases accompanied by a facial expression of fear or surprise.

In the second strategy the hand changes its orientation in the downward movement so that it ends with the palm up, i.e., supinated (see Figure 12.9). Some of the signers who use this strategy also extend their index and middle fingers; others use a more lax handshape in the sign's final hold. Both subtypes are classified as "change of orientation" in Table 12.3 as the crucial difference between the first strategy and the second strategy is that the arm stays pronated in the first strategy but changes from pronation to supination in the second strategy. The change of orientation of the V-handshape of the biped classifier is part of the lexical sign FALL in some sign languages, including ASL and DSL. The change-of-orientation strategy signals loss of control in a way that goes against an analog representation of the boy in the tree event as he ends on his back (see Figure 12.5): the orientation with the palm up would in other cases denote a person lying on his or her stomach. In signaling loss of control by a change of the hand's orientation, the significant value lies in the change of orientation, not in the resulting orientation of the hand after the change.

Table 12.3 presents the number of signers in each sign language that use either of the two strategies. As the three HKSL signers who describe the event use the HKSL person classifier expressed by the Y-handshape, they cannot use the first strategy (straightening the wrist of the biped classifier) to indicate loss of control. Neither can the JSL signer, who uses the A-handshape. The HKSL signers change the orientation of the hand with the HKSL person classifier, two to palm down and one to palm up. The JSL signer changes the fall sign to a sign meaning 'run' in the middle of the movement of the JSL person classifier without changing the hand's orientation. Three more signers, one SSL signer and two DSGS signers, do not use either of the two strategies; their signs rather mean 'jump' than 'fall.'

What is interesting in Table 12.3 is that so many European signers use the second strategy of signaling loss of control, i.e., by a change of the hand's orientation that forces them to describe the boy's end position as lying on his stomach, even though they do have the option of signaling the boy's loss of control by means of a handshape indicating someone lying on his or her back (the first strategy of straightening the wrist) as does the boy in the drawing.

Sign languages are made with several articulators, in particular the two hands. In many cases the two hands contribute to making one lexical sign, but in classifier signs they may represent two different entities. Two-handed non-classifier signs tend to become more symmetrical over time (Frishberg 1975), but classifier signs go against this tendency when the weak hand contributes independent meaning to the complex. In such cases, the choice of classifier determines the form of the weak hand, e.g., a classifier for the hole in the tree trunk (the C-handshape). Table 12.4 shows what the signers' weak hand represents in the descriptions of the tree event. Nine of the twenty-nine signers use only one hand; all the others use the weak hand for the source, i.e., something related to the tree from which the boy is falling.

As it appears from Table 12.4, there is some variation in the choice of handshape in the weak hand among the sign languages and among the signers within one sign language, except for DSL. Most of the signers use a handshape that represents a general surface, a more or less flat hand, palm down or toward signer (the

Table 12.4 *Representations of the source of the movement in the descriptions of the tree event*

	general surface, palm down	general surface, palm toward signer	same handshape as strong hand, palm toward signer	handshape representing the hole in the trunk	handshape representing the branch	handshape representing the tree	other (see text)	no use of weak hand
ASL – USA					B	A		C
BSL – UK			A	B			D	A
DGS – Germany	BD		E					C
DSGS – Switzerland	A	DE						
DSL – Denmark	ACDE							
SSL – Sweden	BC					E		A
HZJ – Croatia								CE
HKSL – Hong Kong		A			A			DE
JSL – Japan								D
Total	9	3	2	1	2	2	1	9

B-handshape) (see Figure 12.1). Three signers choose more specific handshapes that represent the hole in the tree trunk, the branch that the boy was sitting astride or the tree itself; two of these handshapes perseverate from earlier signs. The use of a handshape identical to the handshape of the strong hand is probably a case of handshape assimilation.

The variations in hand orientation and handshape due to assimilation demonstrate that the weak hand plays a secondary role compared to the strong hand. Even the use of semantically more specific classifiers than the general surface classifier in the weak hand is the result of perseveration from a preceding sign in two out of three cases. The ground is simply not very important in the descriptions of the typical fall.

In sum, we find the main consistent differences among the nine languages in the choice of handshape in the strong hand, i.e., the handshape that represents the boy as the figure. But even here there are striking similarities; apart from one individual, all signers of European sign languages use the handshape representing a biped; it is clearly iconic and the form of a standard classifier for human beings in many sign languages. One HKSL signer also uses this handshape, but all HKSL signers who describe the event use the HKSL person classifier (expressed by the Y-handshape), and the only JSL signer who describes the event uses the JSL person or male classifier (expressed by the A-handshape). The variation in choice of handshape for the boy is clearly a case of different conventionalization in different sign languages.

There are also differences in the choice of handshape in the weak hand, but here the context seems to play a greater role. In some cases, the handshape is a result of assimilation to the handshape of the strong hand, and even when the signers use classifiers to represent different aspects of the ground (e.g., the hole, the branch or the tree as an entity), these alternatives may be a result of perseveration from a preceding sign. Except for HKSL signer A, the signers put little emphasis on the ground, but the Western European signers tend to use a classifier in the weak hand to a greater extent than the signers of Croatian Sign Language (HZJ), HKSL, and JSL.

Finally, almost all signers indicate the boy's loss of control by either changing the hand's orientation or by straightening the wrist of the V-handshape; both strategies denote a change in the boy's body orientation. The change of the hand's orientation goes against iconicity as the back of the hand represents the boy's front, but the change of orientation signifying the boy's loss of control is here more important than the end result. Except for the DSL signers, both strategies are used with the biped classifier in all the European sign languages. All three HKSL signers who describe the tree event also change the orientation of the hand. The change-of-orientation strategy can tentatively be described as a universal way of describing a human being's loss of control of their body posture.

In the next section I shall analyze the signers' descriptions of a more unusual loss of control, an event that presented a challenge to many of the signers.

4.2   Descriptions of an unusual fall

The deer event (Figures 12.6 and 12.7) is a spectacular event in the story, and crucial since it brings the story to its climax. Thirty-six out of the forty-two signers describe the deer event; two HZJ signers and one HKSL signer leave out the episode, possibly because they tell the story without consulting the book after having leafed through it initially. One ASL signer, one DSL signer and one HZJ signer describe the boy as sitting on the deer's head, but not his movement onto it.

That this event is linguistically more challenging than the tree event appears from the fact that many of the signers use several different classifier signs to describe the boy's movement from the rock onto the deer's head. Both the deer and the boy move, and the boy moves because he holds on to a moving object, i.e., the deer's antlers. The different signs made by the same signer highlight different aspects of the event as explained below. I have concentrated on the signs where the boy is involved and left out signs that describe only the deer's movement without mentioning the boy.

All the signers who describe the tree event use a classifier of the so-called whole entity type (Engberg-Pedersen 1993, Benedicto & Brentari 2004). A whole entity classifier is one where the handshape represents the referent as an entity; examples are the different person classifiers in the descriptions of the tree event. To describe the deer event, the signers use many different classifier types (see Table 12.5), including signs with whole entity classifiers.

ASL signer A's use of two whole entity classifiers can be seen in Figure 12.10. Her right hand with the biped classifier representing the boy is moved up to contact with the left hand representing the deer. The handshape in her left hand is semantically imprecise. This is the case with many of the signs in the first column of Table 12.5, which is why I have described the strategy as a combination of a whole entity classifier and a whole entity or surface classifier. The hands representing the deer are clearly distinct from the cases where the signers represent the deer or the boy by means of their own head or body (the second most frequent strategy in Table 12.5). When ASL signer A moves up her right hand, she also moves up her left hand, and after she has made contact between the two hands, they both move down to a hold. The movement to a hold at the end has been described for several sign languages as an indication of location in a place: the boy is now lying on the deer – and he is lying

Table 12.5 *Strategies used in the descriptions of the deer event.*

	whole entity + whole entity or surface	whole entity + body	handle	"fall forward"
ASL – USA	AC	A		A
BSL – UK	CD	AB	AD	C
DGS – Germany	BCE	A	C	B
DSGS – Switzerland	ABC	ACE	ABC	
DSL – Denmark	ABCDE	ABCDE	ACE	
SSL – Sweden	ABCE	D	B	
HZJ – Croatia	AB		A	
HKSL – Hong Kong	ABCE			
JSL – Japan	ACDE	A	B	
Total	29	14	12	3

Note: All the HKSL signers, HZJ signer B and JSL signer E describe the event as the boy's jumping onto the deer's head or mounting the deer. A few strategies that were used by only one signer out of the total of thirty-seven signers have been left out. Each signer is only mentioned once for each strategy, no matter the number of signs they made.

Figure 12.10 *ASL signer A's description of the deer event with two whole entity classifiers (initial, middle and final position of the hands). The last photo is unfortunately inaccurate: in the video the back of the signer's extended fingers have contact with the radial side of her left hand.*

on his stomach: the back of the signer's extended fingers has contact with the radial side of her left hand.

All the whole entity classifiers are used to represent the boy as the figure in the deer event except in the case of one: Swiss German Sign Language DSGS signer A who combines what looks like the biped classifier (representing the deer as the figure) "hidden" underneath a very loose B-handshape with the fingers slightly bent on the weak hand (representing the boy), which is lifted up by the strong hand.

Figure 12.11 *Description of the deer event where the signers use their own head to represent the deer's head and a whole entity classifier about the boy (final position of the hand).*

The second strategy in Table 12.5 includes the signers' use of their own body to represent one of the entities. In almost all cases, the signers use their head to represent the deer's head (Figure 12.11). Very similar signs are used by one ASL signer, two British signers, three Swiss signers, three Danish signers, one Swedish signer and one Japanese signer. A few signers (i.e., DGS signer A, DSGS signer E, DSL signers D and E, and SSL signer D) use the whole entity classifier of the deer and bring their hand representing the deer or its head into contact with their chest (Figure 12.12) or in between their legs (Danish signer E) while leaning forward to describe how the deer – or its head – comes into contact with the boy's front (or in between his legs).

Handle classifiers are classifiers expressed by handshapes that imitate an agent's handling something, for instance, a sticklike object (S-handshape). The signers use one or two S-handshapes to represent the boy's holding onto the deer's antlers, and those who use two hands show the boy's movement by an upward and forward movement of the hands and their own body. One signer, DSL signer E, holds her hands with the S-handshape still to represent the boy as the ground and simultaneously moves her head from a low position upward to demonstrate the deer raising its head as the figure, i.e., she articulates backgrounded information with her hands and foregrounded information with her body (Figure 12.13). This distribution of articulators on information chunks is highly unusual and is evidence of her trouble with describing the event and her willingness to go beyond usual restrictions on signing. The preferred way of describing the deer lifting its head is by holding the hands as "antlers" on the forehead and lifting one's head, a strategy used by seven signers from four different sign languages (not included in Table 12.5).

The strategy called "fall forward" in Table 12.5 has been classified as a gesture (Emmorey 1999a). Two signers describe the boy's forward movement by means of

Figure 12.12 *Description of the deer event where the signers use their body to represent the boy and a whole entity classifier about the deer (final position of the hand).*

Figure 12.13 *DSL signer E's description of the deer event where her hands represent backgrounded information about the boy (his holding onto the deer's antlers) and her head and body represent foregrounded information about the boy (his movement upward and forward) (initial and final position of the head and body).*

their own body and flat hands, fingers extended and spread, palms facing forward; they move their body forward, holding their hands over their shoulders and bringing them forward as one might do when falling and trying to mitigate the damage (see Figure 12.8 representing a fall in the opposite direction, i.e., on one's back).

Some of the variants not listed in Table 12.5 are the use of only one hand and the combination of a handle classifier and a whole entity classifier. DSGS signers D and E

Figure 12.14 *SSL signer D's description of the deer event with a backgrounded handle-classifier and a foregrounded whole-entity classifier, both used of the boy (initial and final position of the sign).*

use only one hand (representing the boy as the figure) and leave out the ground. SSL signer D also leaves out the ground and uses instead her weak hand with a handle classifier as a sort of backgrounded information about the boy's holding on to the antlers while at the same time describing the boy's movement forward by means of a whole entity classifier (the biped classifier) (Figure 12.14).

The prototypical fall was described by means of only one classifier type, a whole entity classifier. For the unusual fall, we see signs with whole entity classifiers, handle classifiers and the use of the signer's head to represent the deer's head and the signer's body to represent the boy. In most of the sign languages more than one classifier type is used.

Table 12.6 shows the whole entity classifiers used to represent the boy in the deer event. The table can be compared with Table 12.2 with the classifiers used to represent the boy in the tree event. We see again that the European signers all use the biped classifier, but this handshape is also used by four Asian signers who might instead have used their standard classifiers for human beings (Y-handshape or A-handshape). The reason why the Asian signers are more inclined to use the biped classifier in the descriptions of the deer event may be that they wish to emphasize that the boy ends up straddled on the deer, which is easily depicted by means of the biped classifier.

All the signers who use the weak hand to represent the ground in descriptions of the tree event use it to represent the source of the movement. By contrast, in the descriptions of the deer event, the ground is the goal of the movement in all examples of the whole entity + body strategy and in twenty-nine out of the

Table 12.6 *Whole entity classifiers used to represent the boy in the descriptions of the deer event*

	biped	HKSL person	JSL person
ASL – USA	AC		
BSL – UK	ABD		
DGS – Germany	BC		
DSGS – Switzerland	ABCDE		
DSL – Denmark	ABCDE		
SSL – Sweden	ABCDE		
HZJ – Croatia	AB		
HKSL – Hong Kong	AE	BC	
JSL – Japan	CE		AD

thirty-seven descriptions altogether. A few use only one hand, some use the weak hand about the rock and some use it about an unspecified surface more or less unrelated to the movement of the strong hand. There is thus a general consensus that the emphasis should be on the goal in this case, an emphasis that is particularly clear in the use of the whole entity + body strategy, where the signers use their body to represent the goal.

To represent the deer or its head as the goal of the fall, the signers use nine different handshapes. In the European sign languages, no two signers within each language choose the same classifier or handshape. They use the handform of the biped classifier for the deer,[7] the general surface classifier (the loose B-handshape), a handshape that may resemble a deer's head (the flat O-handshape), the S-handshape to represent its head, the V-handshape with extended index and middle fingers with the tips of the fingers pointing up to represent the deer's head with antlers, an index-handshape with the index finger held horizontally, and a U-handshape with the middle and index fingers held horizontally. Three HKSL signers use one and the same handshape, the Y-handshape of the HKSL person classifier, but with three different orientations. None of the European signers use this handshape.

In sum, the focus in the descriptions of the second fall is on where the boy ends, i.e., the goal of the movement, not its source. Many of the signers use standard classifiers to represent the goal – the general surface classifier, the biped classifier and a classifier for an animal.

In the following section I shall compare the descriptions of the two events focusing on similarities and differences within one sign language and among the sign languages in an attempt to get closer to an understanding of the factors that influence the form of classifier signs.

5   Factors that Influence the form of the fall descriptions

Liddell (2003a) found that the meaning of classifier signs cannot be derived from an understanding of the signs as visual analogs, and he used the restricted and idiosyncratic distribution of many elements of classifier signs as an argument for their lack of productivity. He acknowledged the potential creativity of the elements of classifier signs but saw this creativity on a par with morphological creativity of English -*ity*, e.g., *seniority*. Apparently, he does not accept visual analogy as a factor that forms classifier signs except for certain spatial and orientational aspects of the hand.

As Cogill-Koez (2000a) points out, visual analogy in representation does not mean realistic representation. She offers an alternative analysis of classifier signs as templated visual representations, emphasizing the iconic and creative potential of the elements of classifier signs in that they can be changed or deformed to represent unusual aspects of a situation. Moreover, others have pointed out that linguistic expression may be motivated not only by iconicity or visual analogy, but also by metonymy and metaphor (Wilcox 2000, Taub 2001).

It should be obvious from the preceding analysis of descriptions of fall events in nine different sign languages, most of which are unrelated (cf. Bergman and Engberg-Pedersen, this volume), that iconicity plays a role in word formation in these languages. But the systematic variation in especially handshape to express human classifiers in the different languages demonstrates that there are language-specific, lexicalized parts of classifier signs. Even when the handshape is identical in two sign languages, the classifiers may not have the same value, as evidenced by the (male) person classifier in JSL and the individual person classifier in DSL, both expressed by the A-handshape. Such differences point to the need to examine in detail the restrictions on the use and combinability of classifiers in each sign language separately along the lines suggested by Liddell (2003a). But it is also clear that the V-handshape is used more widely than can be explained in terms of genetic relatedness or borrowing. Although they use different handshapes for human beings in general, one HKSL signer uses the biped classifier in the description of the tree event, and two HKSL and two JSL signers also use the V-handshape in descriptions of the deer event with its emphasis on how the boy becomes straddled on the deer.

There is too little evidence in the data for the use of the JSL (male) person classifier, but the handshapes that express the biped classifier and the HKSL person classifier both have an orientational dimension that permits a change in the orientation of the hand to denote a change in the orientation of the person in the event described. This change in orientation was obtained in two ways with the

V-handshape of the biped classifier: either by straightening of the wrist or by supinating the arm and hand. What we see here is a clash between two features that, taken in isolation, are motivated: (1) the back of the hand of the biped classifier represents the front of a human being when it is moved in a certain direction or is used to indicate the orientation of a lying person with focus on the person's orientation; (2) change of the hand's orientation in a downward movement signals loss of control metonymically. The term "lexicalization" may be used to indicate lack of productivity, as does Liddell (2003a), but it may also be used of a standardized norm (Lipka 1994) no matter its productive status. Standardization of the change of hand orientation may be the reason why this strategy is used in descriptions of the boy's fall from the tree in all sign languages except JSL and DSL, even though the hand's final orientation conflicts with the fact that the boy ends lying on his back. In sum, the change of the hand's orientation in fall descriptions is motivated, and motivation is not only a matter of direct visual analogy as witnessed by the following three results of the comparison of the nine sign languages: (1) orientation change is used in several non-related sign languages; (2) orientation change correlates systematically with the same handshapes' use with the same orientational aspect and the same meaning in other signs of the same sign languages (e.g., signs meaning 'move in a certain direction' or 'lie on one's back'); (3) orientation change is used in spite of the clash between the final orientation of the hand in the descriptions of the tree event and the boy's position in Figure 12.5.

The difference between templated and realistic visual representation relates to functionality: what is relevant to the story? And to cognition: what is the focus of attention? In a realistic visual representation, every feature of a scene is represented with the same detail. This is not how linguistic representation works. As Talmy points out, different linguistic expressions can "govern the distribution of attention without changing the contents" (2000:77), as we see in differences of linguistic foregrounding and backgrounding. In a commercial scene, "focal attention can either be mapped onto the seller, with lesser attention on the remainder, as in *The clerk sold the vase to the customer*" (Talmy, 2000:77), or "focal attention can be mapped onto the buyer, with lesser attention on the remainder, as in *The customer bought the vase from the clerk*" (Talmy 2000:77). In a templated representation, those aspects of the event that are most conspicuous or relevant to the purpose are foregrounded.

In the deer event, both the boy and the deer move. The deer is most active as it gets up voluntarily from its lying position and thereby hauls the boy onto its head. Because of this active status, it can be expected to be chosen as the figure. By contrast, the boy is the protagonist of the story and, for that reason, an obvious choice as the figure. Moreover, there are conventional classifiers for human beings (see Table 12.6), but it is clearly less obvious what handshape to choose for the deer or its head; the signers use seven different handshapes besides their own head to represent the deer. Most of the signers choose to describe the boy as the figure, but significantly they choose to focus on either the boy or the deer, not to describe both movements simultaneously.[8] This goes against realistic visual representation, but is in accordance with cognitive Gestalt theory and what we know about linguistic representation and foregrounding and backgrounding in spoken languages (Talmy 2000, Engberg-Pedersen 2007).

In the tree event the goal (i.e., the ground below the tree) is predictable and none of the signers mentions the goal, but in the deer event the goal is highly unpredictable and thus worthy of attention. The agreement among the signers on representing the goal rather than the source in the deer event has in itself nothing to do with visual analogy, but with cognitive factors of attention and focus. The signers attempt to represent the deer's head in many different ways and by means of two different classifier types, by a whole entity classifier or by representing the deer by means of their own head. Here we see again the importance of standardization or conventionalization: the signers were much more in agreement on the choice of classifier for the boy than for the deer, even though both forms can be seen as – templated – visual analogs.

Since the source is contextually given in both events, we may ask why so many signers nevertheless represent the source of the movement in the tree event (twenty out of twenty-nine signers, see Table 12.4). Liddell uses the term "buoy" of the weak hand "held in a stationary configuration as the strong hand continues producing signs. Semantically [buoys] help guide the discourse by serving as conceptual landmarks as the discourse continues" (2003b:223). A special group of buoys is fragment buoys where the weak hand perseverates from a preceding sign simultaneously with a one-handed sign. Liddell distinguishes fragment buoys that do not serve a semantic function from those that do. His examples of meaningful fragment buoys do not include classifiers, but it is possible that the cases of perseveration seen in this study serve the same function as fragment buoys (see also Perniss's [2007] analysis of the use of the weak hand in discourse in DGS). In descriptions of the tree event – and in a few cases also in descriptions of the deer event – we see a loose B-handshape held horizontally or vertically, sometimes clearly to represent the ground, in other cases held somewhere near the point in space where the strong hand starts its movement. This handshape may represent a general surface, which may also have the buoy function of serving as a conceptual landmark linking the classifier sign to the preceding context. However, there is a difference between the sign languages in this respect.

Most of the signers of the Western European sign languages use the weak hand in the tree event, while only one out of six signers of HZJ, HKSL, and JSL does. In a comparison of the use of the weak hand with no movement (only *hold*) and a classifier with a very general meaning (especially a general surface expressed by a loose B-handshape, palm down) in four sign languages, ASL, DSL, HKSL and Israeli Sign Language (ISL), I found that the signers of the two Western sign languages, ASL and DSL, were more inclined to use the weak hand in this way in short narratives than the signers of the two non-Western sign languages (Engberg-Pedersen 2007). In a comparison of classifier signs in ASL and ISL Aronoff *et al.* (2003) found that the ISL signers did not use two classifiers to represent two distinct entities simultaneously as often as the ASL signers, and they attribute the difference in use to a difference in the sign languages' age. Signers of the older sign language, ASL, are said to prefer "representation of the object on the hands" (Aronoff *et al.* 2003:68) to "mapping of the body of the referent onto the body of the signer, which is more motivated, or iconic." In the descriptions of the deer event, one of the two ASL signers does indeed use her body to represent the deer in my study. The strategy is also used by all five DSL signers, and DSL has as long a historical record as ASL (see the relevant chapters of this volume). There is no obvious reason for the frequency difference in the use of the weak hand for a backgrounded general classifier or buoy between the signers of Western sign languages and the signers of HKSL and possibly JSL. The age factor needs to be more thoroughly investigated as does the stability of the frequency distribution over more signers of the different sign languages.

The comparison of classifier signs in nine sign languages has demonstrated that these signs are shaped by a number of factors, not only lexicalization and visual analogy. Standardization plays a role especially in the choice of handshape used to represent a human being, but the standardized way of describing human beings' loss of their orientation by changing the orientation of the hand indicates that the handshape of the classifiers is a templated visual representation of a human being with a standard vertical orientation. The focus is on the conspicuous part of the event, the change of orientation, irrespective of visual details. That the focus is on the conspicuous parts of the events is also clear from the fact that the ground in the tree event is the source of the movement, but the ground in the deer event is overwhelmingly its goal. Here functional and cognitive factors play a role.

In sum, the factors that may influence the form of classifier signs are lexicalization in the sense of standardization, which may or may not lead to violation of visual analogy, templated visual representation, metonymy, contextually determined functionality, cognitive factors of attention focus, and processing in terms of both ease of perception (buoys as conceptual landmarks) and ease of production (perseveration of the weak hand, assimilation of handshapes). In any individual sign language, we should look for constraints on the use of frequently used classifiers and movements along the lines suggested by Liddell (2003a) without opposing such an analysis to an understanding of classifier signs in terms of templated, not realistic, visual analogy (Cogill-Koez 2000a, 2000b) and without neglecting the roles of metonymy and foregrounding and backgrounding.

Appendix

The handshapes referred to in the chapter are listed below in Figure 12.15. Some of them have acquired traditional names in linguistic research on sign languages,

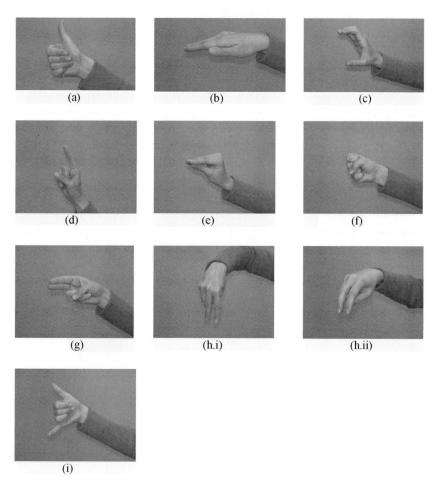

Figure 12.15 *Handshapes discussed in this chapter.*

particularly names derived from the handshapes used to represent the letters of the American manual alphabet. When looking at the figures, it should be borne in mind that the handshapes look different when made with the right and the left hand and with different orientations. Moreover, their exact form may vary within limits that are not specified here. The photos represent the handshapes with the orientation most relevant to the signs discussed in the chapter. The exemplification of how the handshapes are used is primarily relevant to the signs discussed in the chapter.

(a)   A-handshape: used to express a classifier used of male human beings or human beings in general in JSL (JSL person classifier).

(b)   B-handshape: used to express a classifier for flat surfaces in many sign languages: the general-surface classifier.

(c)   C-handshape: used to express the hole in the tree trunk.

(d)   index-handshape: used to express a classifier in several languages: the upright-person classifier. Two index hands with the tips of the index fingers pointing down can be used to represent human beings by their legs: the person-by-legs classifier.

(e)   flat O-handshape: used to represent the deer's head.

(f)   S-handshape: used to express a handle classifier: the handle-sticklike-object classifier.

(g)   U-handshape: used to represent the deer.

(h.i–h.ii)   V-handshape: used in many sign languages to represent human beings by their legs: the biped classifier. The middle and index fingers may be more or less bent. If they are bent, they may be used of human beings in, for instance, DSL, but also of animals, even animals with four legs. The neutral orientation is with the palm down.

(i)   Y-handshape: used to express a person classifier in HKSL: the HKSL-person classifier.

13

Handshape contrasts in sign language phonology

Diane Brentari and Petra Eccarius

1   Introduction

Of the five parameters of sign language structure – handshape, movement, place of articulation, orientation and nonmanual behaviors – handshape is the parameter that has been analyzed most successfully with a variety of methodologies, both theoretical and experimental. Since it is here that we find the most complete body of work to draw upon, we have chosen to examine handshape behavior as a way of better understanding the nature of phonological contrast in signed languages.[1] The goal of this chapter is twofold. First we will draw attention to the range of variation in the form and use of handshapes, and second, we will analyze the distribution of handshape properties. We will also investigate these issues both crosslinguistically and language-internally in order to determine which features are phonologically contrastive and where they are contrastive in the lexicon.

In order to achieve our goal of showing how sign languages use handshape in their phonological systems, a little background is necessary on both the organization of a sign language lexicon and the phonological structure of signed languages. After covering this introductory material and our methodology in sections 1 and 2, we will describe differences in the way that handshape feature classes are used across the three components of the lexicon (foreign, core and spatial) in three different sign languages – namely, American Sign Language (ASL), Swiss German Sign Language (DSGS) and Hong Kong Sign Language (HKSL). In sections 3–5, we analyze specific distributions of two types of handshape properties – *selected fingers* and *joint configuration* – across the lexicon and across different classifiers types. Evidence will be presented showing (1) that both selected finger combinations and joint configurations can behave differently across the lexicon, and (2) that even among different types of classifier handshapes, there are systematic distributional differences regarding these properties, due in part to the link between morphology and iconicity. In section 6, we address the theoretical consequences of our results. We begin the section by discussing recent work in

284

phonological theory (Clements 2001), demonstrating that the two most commonly held categories of phonological distribution (*distinctive* and *allophonic*) are not sufficient to represent the types of feature contrasts found in spoken or sign language data.

1.1   Handshape in a sign language lexicon

Many languages of the world – signed and spoken – have lexicons composed of words with different origins. Itô and Mester (1995a,1995b) propose a core-periphery model for Japanese that not only captures these different origins (Yamoto, Mimetic, Sino-Japanese and Foreign) but also presents an analysis of the differences in sound and constraint distribution. One example from Japanese used by Itô and Mester to illustrate their point is the distribution of [h] and [f], shown in (1). In the *core* (which includes the Yamoto, Sino-Japanese and Mimetic components), [h] and [f] are allophones of /h/, while in the *periphery* (Foreign component), /h/ and /f/ are phonemic. This is illustrated by the fact that in the core [f] does not appear before any vowels except [u] (i.e., *[fa], *[fe], *[fi], *[fo]), where [h] appears instead; in other words, they are in complementary distribution. In the periphery, however, both [h] and [f] appear more or less everywhere, showing that these two sounds – or, more specifically, these two opposing values of the feature [labial] – are distinctive in the periphery.[2]

(1)   Distribution of [h] and [f] in Japanese:
   a.   core distribution (Yamoto, Sino-Japanese and Mimetic components)
        *[fa],   *[fe],   *[fi],   *[fo],   **[fu]**
        [ha],   [he],   [hi],   [ho]   ø
   b.   foreign distribution (borrowings)
        [fa],   [fe],   [fi],   [fo],   [fu]
        [ha],   [he],   [hi],   [ho]   ø

Following Ito and Mester's model for the Japanese lexicon, Brentari and Padden (2001) proposed a three-part lexicon for ASL (see Figure 13.1). These three lexical components – core, foreign and spatial – behave differently not only because of their historical sources, but also with respect to morphological and phonological criteria in the synchronic grammar.

Figure 13.2 shows ASL examples from each component. While handshapes in all components are composed of sub-lexical structures and phonological features,

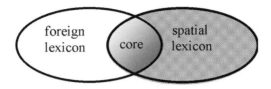

Figure 13.1 *The ASL lexicon (from Brentari & Padden 2001).*

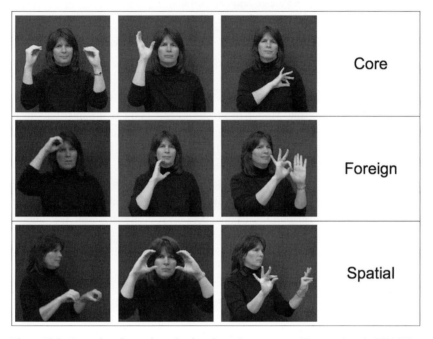

Figure 13.2 *Examples of signs from the three lexical components. Top row (core): TEACH, STRANGE, BENEFIT; middle row (foreign): O̲PINION, C̲AFETERIA, GET-AN-'F̲'; bottom row (spatial): round-pipe, hold-binocular, hold-thread.*

their morphophonemic properties differ across the lexicon. In the core, handshapes are exclusively phonological and combine with other elements to form stems – i.e., both the handshape as a whole and the features from which it is composed *have no meaning*. Examples are TEACH, STRANGE and BENEFIT. The foreign component of the lexicon has forms that have a relationship with the surrounding spoken language or another sign language. The foreign forms that we will discuss in this chapter are the initialized forms, which have a handshape of the manual alphabet as an affix and are built from stems in the core. This means that, like the core, the handshape features have no meaning, but that, unlike the core, the handshape as a whole *has meaning*. Examples are O̲PINION, C̲AFETERIA and

GET AN 'F.' The spatial component includes spatial signs (UP, DOWN, etc.) and classifier constructions. Classifier constructions are polymorphemic complexes with a verbal root – the movement – and affixes that involve place of articulation and handshape. Therefore, in classifiers, either the whole handshape or its features *have meaning*, the latter often carrying information about the size and shape of the object. Examples are 'binoculars,' 'round-pipe,' 'hold-thread.' In addition, Benedicto and Brentari (2004) show that classifier handshapes also demonstrate syntactic alternations such as transitive and intransitive; the handshapes in the other two components do not carry this type of morphosyntactic information.

The core and spatial components are considered the native components of the lexicon, with foreign forms conforming to the native lexicon to varying degrees depending on their adherence to the constraints of the core. In general, as a form gets further from the core – either in the direction of classifier forms or in the foreign vocabulary – it obeys fewer of the set of phonological constraints attested in core forms. Furthermore, just as there is asymmetry in the distribution of the sounds [h] and [f] across the lexicon of spoken Japanese, we also see an asymmetry in the inventories of handshapes that occur in the three components of ASL. The examples in Figure 13.2 show the same three handshapes being used in each component (namely 𝅘 , 𝅘 and 𝅘), but not all handshapes occur in all three components. Some examples of those that do not appear in all lexical components are given in Figure 13.3.

To summarize, handshapes and their features across the three components of the ASL lexicon have different types of phonological, morphological and sometimes syntactic relationships within different components of the grammar. In the core,

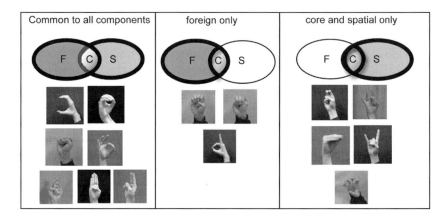

Figure 13.3 *Handshape asymmetries across ASL lexical components.*

handshapes have no morphological status. In the foreign lexicon, the whole hand-shape is an affix with its own meaning, playing a morphological role. Finally in the spatial component, handshape features can play both a morphological and a syntactic role. Although Brentari and Padden's model was developed to represent phonological behavior in ASL signs, here we apply it to the other two languages in this analysis as well, because all three languages also have the same types of lexical components.

1.2   The phonological structure of handshape

The structure of handshape is given in Figure 13.4; while there is reasonably wide consensus about the general structure of handshape among various models of sign language phonology, the one here is taken from Brentari 1998. The two main structures of handshape are the *joints* and the *selected fingers*; these are class nodes in the feature geometry. The joints structure expresses the disposition of the joints – [stacked], [spread], [flexed] (closed) or [crossed] – as well as which joints are affected by the feature – the base joints (knuckle joints) or the non-base joints (intraphalangeal joints). The selected fingers structure expresses which fingers are foregrounded in the handshape. Selected fingers typically move and/or make contact with another part of the body during the articulation of a sign (depending on orientation and other physical limitations). The number of these fingers is expressed by *quantity*, and their *point of reference* can be [ulnar] (pinkie/little-finger side) [mid] (part of the hand referencing the middle finger), or the unmarked "radial" (index-finger side). For example, $\uparrow$, $\downarrow$ and $\downarrow$ all have a [one] quantity specification but with different points of reference on the hand – [ulnar], [mid] and radial, respectively.

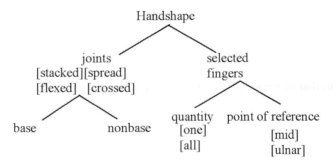

Figure 13.4 *The phonological structure of handshape (Brentari 1998).*

The handshape structure fits into the larger structure of the Articulator (which can include a second hand, the arm or the body as an articulator), and the Articulator, in turn, fits into the larger structure of the sign, including place of articulation and movement. Since none of the other structures are involved in the analysis presented here, the only one we introduce is that of handshape.

2 Methodology and description of the data

In order to describe and analyze handshape, we examined a variety of data from ASL, DSGS and HKSL. We chose these particular languages for two main reasons. First, we had access to many kinds of data in each language; phonological and/or morphological information on core and foreign forms was available to us via dictionaries and/or lexical databases (Stokoe, Casterline & Croneberg 1965, Boyes Braem 2001a, Valli 2005 and Tang 2007, among others), and classifier data was available because they are three of the languages in a larger crosslinguistic project focusing on classifier constructions. Second, we believe that these three languages are sufficiently different from each other historically to facilitate crosslinguistic comparison – HKSL shares no common linguistic ancestor with the other two languages, and ASL and DSGS are only very distantly related, if at all.

Core and foreign data were taken from the dictionaries and lexical databases mentioned above. In the case of HKSL and DSGS, information was checked with local researchers whenever possible. The classifier data used in this work are examples taken from a larger set, including signers' descriptions of 300 pictures and five short stories designed by Zwitserlood (2003). These stimuli depict a wide range of participants and events, both plausible and implausible, in hopes of eliciting both common and rare forms. (More detailed descriptions of specific stimulus items will be provided in later sections as necessary.) The dataset also included interviews with informants during which signers provided grammaticality judgments about how the articulation of classifiers could (and could not) be altered morphologically using a variety of fingers and joint configurations. For all classifier data, we used elicitations from three native signers per language.

Before presenting our analysis, a few points are worth mentioning. First, the results that we report here are qualitative. Since our data come from a wide range of sources, counting the number of tokens for any given handshape on any given task is much less relevant to our analysis than is a consistent pattern seen across all of the data we included. Second, for this work, the phenomena described consider only handshapes that do not change within a sign. We did this because we wanted to be consistent across all lexical components – since classifier and foreign handshapes occur most often without a change, we held to the static set of handshapes across all components. Third, as we discuss the handshapes in the following sections, we refer mostly to the four fingers of the hand; the thumb is largely left out of the discussion because of its vast possibility for phonetic variation and its independence from the other fingers. Finally, since certain handshapes are ubiquitous throughout sign languages (for example, those with all of the fingers or only the index finger selected, and/or those with joint configurations that are fully open and fully closed), we chose three-finger handshapes for the selected fingers analysis and stacked joints for the analysis of joint configuration (described in detail below), both of which are much less common. Sections 3 to 5 are summaries of a more detailed analysis of these forms that appears in Eccarius (2008).

3   Selected finger combinations: distribution of three-finger handshapes

In this section, we describe the distribution of three-finger handshapes (3FHSs) for each language, both crosslinguistically and language-internally. These are handshapes in which three digits other than the thumb are selected. In terms of the representation in Figure 13.4, 3FHSs are captured by a dependency relation: one-finger handshapes have a [one] feature; four-finger handshapes have an [all] feature; two-finger handshapes have a dependency relation [one] > [all] and three-finger handshapes have a relation [all] > [one] (Brentari *et al.* 1996, Brentari 1998, van der Kooij 2002). Traditionally, these handshapes are considered to be marked across sign languages due to their rare occurrence crosslinguistically and language-internally, their physical complexity and their tendency to be acquired late (e.g., Battison 1978; Woodward 1985, 1987; Boyes Braem 1990a). Because of these facts, we expected that these handshapes would not be equally distributed across the lexical components of individual languages. In particular, we expected that 3FHSs would occur more often in the foreign and spatial components than in the core within languages since according to Ito and Mester's model, core forms adhere to more constraints and are thus more limited. We also predicted crosslinguistic differences regarding the specific phonological constraints motivating this tendency.

In addition to using dictionaries and lexical databases as sources for core and foreign forms in each language, articulatory interviews and a short story were used to elicit classifier handshapes. The short story contained a three-legged boy to see whether or not such a character would be represented by a 3FHS. (See Figure 13.5 for a sample image of the story from Zwitserlood 2003 and for example handshapes used by signers to express the three-legged person.)

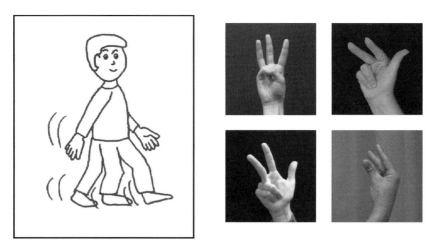

Figure 13.5 *(left) Stimuli used to elicit 3FHSs. (right) Examples of 3FHSs.*

The data indicate that there are crosslinguistic differences regarding the acceptability of 3FHSs in the various parts of the lexicon (Figure 13.6). Crosslinguistically,
HKSL appears to be more accepting of 3FHSs in core signs than DSGS and ASL
based on the available data. These handshapes are still marked in HKSL (based on
frequency), but they do occur in at least a few core lexical signs. We also see a
greater variety of 3FHSs as classifiers (i.e., variation in allowable joint configurations and in the specific fingers selected) in HKSL than in the other languages, as
well as a higher degree of certainty about using them. Our data also indicate that
within languages, the distribution of 3FHSs was not homogeneous; more (if not all)
of these handshapes tend to be found in the foreign and classifier components of the
lexicon rather than in the core. These language-internal facts are described in the
next three subsections.

3.1   ASL

Examining the entries in the two ASL dictionaries (Stokoe, Casterline & Croneberg
1965 and Valli 2005), we found four 3FHSs in use within the core or foreign
components – , , and . The first three, , and , are from the ASL
fingerspelling alphabet and were used exclusively in initialized signs (e.g.,
WEDNESDAY, DORMITORY, MUSEUM). The fourth handshape, , was
used in only one sign borrowed from a hearing gesture (BOY SCOUT). In other
words, all signs in the ASL dictionaries using 3FHSs could be categorized as

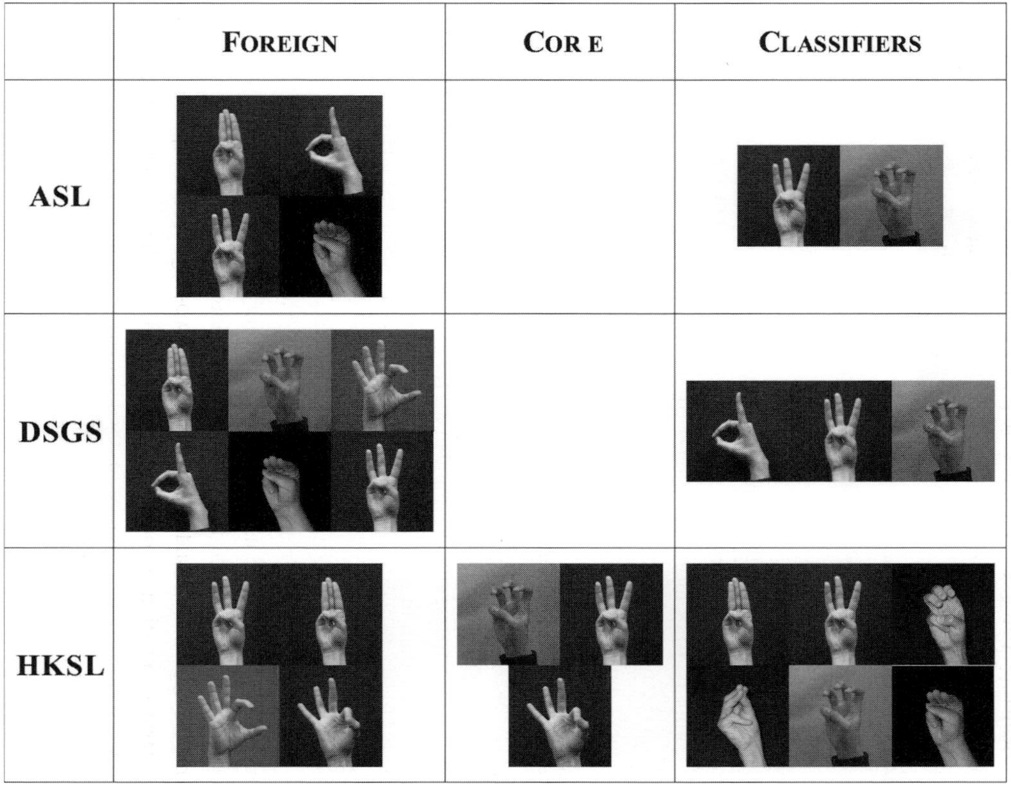

Figure 13.6 *Examples of three-finger handshapes (3FHSs) in the foreign, core and classifier components of ASL, DSGS and HKSL.*

foreign; there were no signs found that could be classified as "core" by the criteria spelled out in Brentari and Padden 2001. In the ASL classifier data, 3FHSs were used, but to varying degrees depending on the informant. For depictions of the three-legged-boy, only one of the three informants used a [handshape] handshape spontaneously, and that was only after starting with a two-fingered handshape (i.e., the 3FHS was not her first instinct). The other two informants did not use [handshape] spontaneously but thought it would probably be acceptable (although one did not allow the handshape if movement was added). In the articulatory interviews, when asked about using [handshape] to depict the thickness of an object at a gradation between what was represented by two and four fingers (e.g., a medium-sized paintbrush), all of the ASL informants declared it to be ungrammatical. One signer did say that [handshape] and [handshape] could be used for tools (e.g., fork, three-pronged rake), but only if accompanied by an extensive description of the object, adding that it would be ungrammatical if such a handshape was *used* as a rake, as in an instrumental classifier.

3.2   DSGS

In the DSGS lexical databases, we found six 3FHSs: [handshape] , [handshape] , [handshape] , [handshape] , [handshape] and [handshape].[3] Again, all 3FHSs were from components outside the core; they were either initialized (e.g., WAADT [place name], DIGITAL, MATURA [a specific kind of test]), borrowed from other sign languages ([handshape] to [handshape] in WALES, [handshape] in WC/ TOILETTE 'toilet'), or (in one case) a classifier handshape in the process of lexicalization ([handshape] in NATEL 'cell phone'; Boyes Braem, personal communication). As with ASL, there appeared to be no 3FHS in the core lexicon of DSGS. Also similar to ASL, use of these handshapes in the classifier data was infrequent and varied by informant. Two of the three informants used [handshape] spontaneously in their retelling of the three-legged-boy story; one used it spontaneously throughout but commented that it was a difficult handshape to produce, while the other used it to introduce the character but then proceeded to use two-finger handshapes (both classifier and lexical) to represent the boy in the rest of the story. The third DSGS informant did not use a 3FHS in the story at all, consistently using a handshape with two fingers and the thumb to represent the three-legged boy. When asked about the grammaticality of [handshape], she seemed uncertain and said she preferred the two-finger handshape. In response to interview questions about 3FHSs, the informants did not accept most three-fingered alterations of established classifiers (e.g., changing the thickness of an object, or representing three specific prongs of a fork), although one signer did offer a form changing from [handshape] to [handshape] to represent birds' claws grabbing something.

3.3 HKSL

The HKSL dictionary yielded signs using five 3FHSs: [handshape], [handshape], [handshape], [handshape] and [handshape].[4] The origins of many of these signs is uncertain, but while some were outside the core – either character signs (i.e., foreign signs based on written characters, e.g., [handshape] in ILLEGAL, [handshape] in JADE), borrowed signs (e.g., [handshape] in WC) or signs still closely related to the classifier system (e.g., [handshape] in FORK) – unlike in ASL and DSGS, there are also core lexical items with 3FHSs (e.g., [handshape] in CHAMPION, [handshape] in CANCER, [handshape] in TRENDY).[5] 3FHSs were also more prevalent in the HKSL classifier data than they were in the other two languages. In representing the three-legged boy, all informants used [handshape] spontaneously throughout the story. In response to interview questions about morphological alternations involving 3FHSs for thickness or size and shape, all informants allowed 3FHS in at least some situations, although answers varied regarding which classifiers could be modified using three-fingered versions (e.g., rope, paintbrush, cat's paw) and with what joint configurations (e.g., extended, bent, crossed). Interestingly, HKSL also uses 3FHSs in their number system ([handshape] and [handshape] are both acceptable variants of '3'), while ASL and DSGS do not.[6]

4   Joint configurations: distribution of the feature [stacked]

In this section, asymmetry in the distribution of joint configuration is illustrated by analyzing the joint feature [stacked]. We first address its crosslinguistic distribution, and then we describe language-internal differences. In the [stacked] configuration, each successive selected finger of a handshape becomes increasingly flexed, beginning with the index finger (Johnson 1990). In other words, the fingers are progressively spread apart from each other in a plane perpendicular to the palm. In Figure 13.4, this feature is located at the joint node. Examples of "plain" and [stacked] handshapes are shown on the top of Figure 13.7. As with the 3FHSs, we first looked at the dictionaries and lexical databases to determine the distribution of the stacked configuration in the core and foreign components forms of each language. For classifier forms, we concentrated on data from two pictures from the Zwitserlood stimuli that we felt had the strongest chance of eliciting a stacked configuration due to the leg positions of the characters involved (bottom of Figure 13.7). Although the stacked feature is attested in four-fingered handshapes as well as in handshapes with the index and middle fingers selected, here, we limit our discussion to the two-finger cases (e.g., [handshape] vs. [handshape]).

Unlike the 3FHSs, the stacked joint configuration in [handshape] was found in nearly all segments of the lexicon crosslinguistically, although the degree to which it was used varied depending on the language.[7] Crosslinguistic distributional differences included

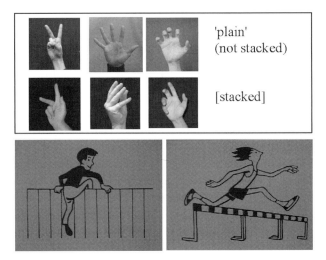

Figure 13.7 *(top) Examples of plain and [stacked] handshapes. (bottom) Stimuli used to elicit [stacked] handshapes.*

a lack of stacked handshapes in the foreign component of HKSL (likely due to the relatively small set of character signs available rather than a phonological constraint), and an apparent bias against (but not prohibition of) stacked handshapes in DSGS classifiers as compared to ASL and HKSL. The distributional analysis of [stacked] language internally is described in each of the following subsections.

4.1   ASL

The stacked configuration ↝\ is found in the foreign component of ASL in the fingerspelled letters K and P, as well as in initialized signs using those letters (e.g., KING, PRINCIPAL) and in variants of initialized V (↝\ ) signs in specific phonetic contexts (e.g., VERB). In the core component, [stacked] can be seen in signs such as BORROW, TWICE and SEE, as a variant of ↝\ , again in specific contexts. The classifier data also yielded stacked handshapes: to represent the pictures in Figure 13.7, two of the three informants used the [stacked] configuration to represent both the boy climbing over the fence and the person hurdling. (The third informant used lexical items to portray each event.) We also observed that a [stacked] variant of a ↝\ semantic vehicle classifier can be used, when, for example, a bicycle is lying on its side, but not for a two-legged ↝\ body part classifier in the same orientation, when, for example, a sunbather is lying on her back. (See section 6 for further discussion of this point.)

4.2   DSGS

As in ASL, a ⟨⟩ handshape is used to represent the letter K in DSGS, and consequently, it is seen in initialized signs with that letter (e.g., KIOSK, KLASSE). Examination of the video entries in the lexical database (Boyes Braem 2001a) suggests that in the core, a stacked variant is sometimes used in signs with ⟨⟩ handshapes in certain orientations; however, its use seems to vary across signers. In the classifier data, the stacked configuration did occur but was rarely chosen (and was sometimes actively avoided) in the depiction of perpendicular leg positions; other strategies were utilized instead. In fact, of the three informants, no one used a stacked handshape spontaneously to represent the boy climbing over the fence – leg position was either not mentioned or a two-handed form (representing one leg per hand) was used – and only one informant used stacked fingers for the hurdler, the others using a two-handed form or a non-stacked handshape with both fingers "jumping" simultaneously. When asked, one of the informants who did not use a stacked handshape admitted that it was an acceptable variant, but then went on to say that she felt representing each leg on a separate hand was the better choice.

4.3   HKSL

In contrast to ASL and DSGS, there were several core lexical items using ⟨⟩ in HKSL (e.g., BORROW, SILVER and EXPLOIT), none of which seemed restricted to particular phonological contexts. No stacked handshapes were found in known character signs, but that could be due to the small set of forms and does not necessarily mean that stacked forms are expressly prohibited in the foreign component.[8] In the classifier data examined, all three informants used stacked handshapes spontaneously in their depictions of the two picture stimuli. In addition, ⟨⟩ is the recognized semantic classifier used to represent bikes of all sorts in HKSL.

To summarize these two sections on selected fingers and joint distribution, we see that there are discernible differences both crosslinguistically and language-internally in the way that sub-lexical properties of handshapes are used. For 3FHSs our analysis shows that there are differences in the degree of acceptability across the three sign languages: 3FHSs are more acceptable in HKSL than in either DSGS or ASL, based both on the confidence and consistency of the informants and on the fact that there are core lexical items with 3FHSs in HKSL but not in the other two sign languages. Moreover, when 3FHSs were deemed acceptable in ASL and DSGS classifier handshapes, the 3FHSs were used only to alter morphologically the number of subparts belonging to the whole (e.g., three legs of a boy, three prongs of a tool, three claws of a bird's foot), while in HKSL they were used more readily overall (i.e., to alter the number of parts or the thickness of an object). These crosslinguistic variations may be explained by a different ranking placed on such factors as ease of articulation, ease of perception or iconicity (see Eccarius 2008). Regarding the distribution of [stacked] joints, our data suggest that it is an acceptable configuration in all three languages to varying degrees.[9] However, there are indications of differences in the way [stacked] is used in each component – an issue that will be discussed in more depth in section 6 in the context of the application of constraints. For the three sign languages studied here, our analysis suggests that DSGS is the language that uses these two marked properties of handshape the least, with a stronger preference for the two-finger variants over the 3FHS and reluctance to use [stacked] when another option is present, even in classifier constructions. Meanwhile, HKSL uses both of these properties much more readily, and ASL is somewhere in between the two.

5   Feature asymmetries across classifier types

Not only can the distribution and types of feature contrasts differ among the major lexical components, as illustrated above, but they can also vary across smaller segments of the lexicon. In this section, we suggest that there are asymmetries in the phonological behavior of handshape features across different classifier handshape types. In addition to the grammatical importance of the handshapes for syntax and morphology in classifiers, there is also a great deal of iconicity that is present in these forms, and this iconicity is present in the different types of classifiers to varying degrees. However, of all of the potentially iconic properties that classifiers contain, only a small subset of these is codified in a discrete way in the linguistic system (see Supalla 1982 and Eccarius 2008 for a discussion of the morphological status of handshape structures in different classifier types). Incorporating iconicity into the phonological grammar is an idea that has been argued for by others previously (e.g., van der Kooij 2002, van der Hulst & van der Kooij 2006). Brentari (in press) and Eccarius (2008) have also suggested that, rather than considering iconicity a factor that undermines the phonology of sign languages, it should be considered a unique and important element in shaping the phonology, along with the pressures of ease of articulation and ease of perception.

Here we provide a phonological analysis of four classifier types – semantic classifiers (SCLs), instrumental classifiers (ICLs), descriptive classifiers (DCLs) and handling classifiers (HCLs) – and the ways they use iconicity in a more in-depth way for the sign language we know best (ASL). The data described in the subsections below come from our ASL informants' descriptions of the Zwitserlood pictures and from the interviews eliciting grammaticality judgments about which feature classes can be altered in members of these four classifier types. Examples of the classifier types discussed in the next sections are provided in Figure 13.8.

5.1   Semantic classifiers (SCLs)

SCL handshapes represent an object as a whole via their semantic class. Their representation tends to be more abstract than other classifier types, although remnants of iconic relationships can still be apparent in some forms (e.g., ⬧ for an upright person, or ⬧ for an airplane). Within this classifier type, we have found quite a variety of possible selected finger combinations (especially considering SCLs constitute a very small number of forms), ranging from unmarked hand-shapes (⬧) to more marked ones (⬧). The selected fingers themselves are not used morphologically, that is, they cannot be used to represent the specific size or shape of a specific object, but rather they are used phonologically as in core forms. In contrast, we find only a small number of joint configurations used in these forms, with the vast majority of classifiers having extended fingers. Selected fingers are utilized more in SCLs than in any other classifier type, and joint configurations the least.

5.2   Instrumental classifiers (ICLs)

ICLs are a mixed category of classifiers in many ways. Like SCLs, these handshapes represent whole objects, but they make use of more iconicity than do SCLs and can represent more physical attributes of the individual tool being used. Also like SCLs, ICLs have an asymmetry between the distribution of their joints and selected finger possibilities – we have found multiple selected finger combinations and very few joint configurations represented (see the ICL handshapes in Figure 13.8). However, the handshapes of these classifiers appear to be restricted to finger combinations including adjacent fingers. Selected fingers are used morphologically in ICLs since they can be altered (albeit with restrictions) to indicate changes in size and shape – e.g., ⬧ , a thin paint brush vs. ⬧ , a thicker paintbrush – or the number of component parts – e.g., ⬧ a two-pronged garden tool vs. ⬧ a three-pronged garden tool. While selected fingers are utilized more than joints in ICLs, joints are also occasionally used in a restricted way. In some rare instances, while providing detailed descriptions of tools, informants were able to alter the joints morpholog-ically (e.g., a fork mangled in a dishwasher), but most of the time when this type of alternation is possible, the handshape is a description and cannot be *used* as an instrument (e.g., the mangled fork handshape cannot be used to eat with, even if the

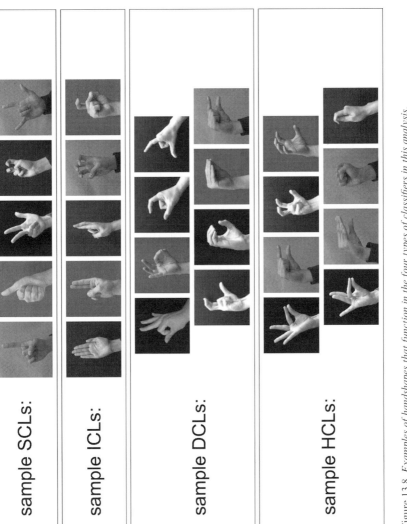

Figure 13.8 *Examples of handshapes that function in the four types of classifiers in this analysis.*

fork itself is still functional), suggesting that these classifiers behave more like DCLs in this case.

5.3   Descriptive classifiers (DCLs)

DCLs do not represent the whole object but instead represent the perimeter and the number of spatial dimensions of that object (2-D vs. 3-D) by altering the selected fingers and joints. The extent to which these features can be altered morphologically is as yet unclear. Emmorey and Herzig (2003) determined that joint alterations in this type of classifier handshape were categorical when produced by signers naïve to a specific range of sizes; e.g., using a generic 'small round flat object' classifier when referring to a shirt button without making a comparison to the full range of button sizes in existence. Perceptually, however, signers could be sensitive to gradient differences in handshape (e.g., someone describing a variety of buttons in a collection). Based on their results, they hypothesize that: "[W]ithin a contrast set, signers know that handshape size can be manipulated to indicate gradient variations in size. This gradient variation may be thought of as a gestural overlay on a morphemic representation. As noted, the analogy may be to English speakers using variations in vowel length to indicate gradations in duration or length" (Emmorey & Herzig 2003: 244).

This ability to use DCLs either gradiently or categorically makes determining specific contrasts challenging, to say the least. However, in our data thus far we have found examples of numerous potentially contrastive joint configurations.[10] For example, Supalla (1982) and new perceptual evidence by Eccarius (2008) suggest that there are at least four contrastive joint configurations used in DCLs simply for representing round objects. The selected finger possibilities, on the other hand, are much more restricted, even given the few fingers available. In our data thus far we have observed only the use of the index finger, middle finger, index and middle fingers together, and all fingers (but not 3FHSs) as shown in Figure 13.8, with change in the quantity of selected fingers frequently indicating varying widths.[11] Like the ICLs, in DCL handshapes involving more than one finger, the fingers are adjacent to one another. We conclude, based on our data, that the joints are used more frequently for contrast than selected fingers in DCLs.

5.4   Handling classifiers

In contrast to DCLs, we consider HCLs to be a representation of the shape of the hand manipulating an object rather than the dimensions of the object itself. There is some research that indicates that HCLs, at least in terms of their handshapes, are highly gestural in nature (e.g., Slobin *et al.* 2003). We agree that of all the classifier types, HCLs seem to be the closest to the gesture system, but we maintain that they are not completely void of linguistic systematicity. While HCLs represent the shape of the hand manipulating an object rather than the shape of the object itself, changes in the joints and/or selected fingers of a given HCL can result in a perceived change in an object's shape or size, although in this case it is by virtue of the way various objects are routinely held. For example, a flat, closed hand ( ) represents the handling of a thin, flat object like an envelope, while a flat-open hand ( ) represents how someone would hold a thicker, flat object like a book. There are numerous potential joint contrasts (including [stacked] joint configurations) based on differences in handling objects of various sizes, such as those shown in Figure 13.8, especially as compared to the small number of observed selected finger combinations. Changes in selected finger combinations (in conjunction with varying joints) indicate differently sized objects (e.g., light bulbs) by showing how each is manipulated. The same selected finger combinations are found in DCLs and HCLs. ASL does not permit HCLs with three fingers, despite the fact that such grips are used in the real world.[12] Hence, HCLs utilize joints more than any other type of classifier, and to a much greater degree than they utilize selected fingers.

In summary, the four types of classifiers discussed in this section vary in the distribution of joint and selected finger contrasts as well as in the type of contrasts possible, constituting a continuum ranging from the more core-like SCLs to the more gesture-like HCLs (see Figure 13.9). As you move away from the SCLs on this

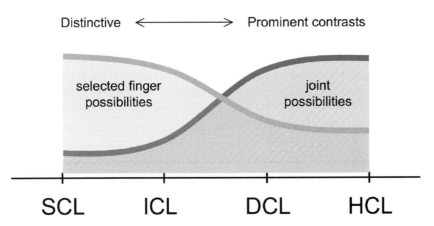

Figure 13.9 *Continuum of joint and selected finger possibilities for the four types of classifier handshapes analyzed.*

continuum, the relative number of selected finger contrasts found in each subtype decreases, while the number of joint contrasts increases. SCLs behave like lexical items in the core because handshape properties are used phonologically, while in other classifier types these properties are used morphologically.

6   Theoretical implications

In this section, we will first address how the differences described in sections 3 to 5 can be captured in a phonological system using new work on *phonological contrast*. These examples are not simply the familiar phenomena of minimal pairs and phonological rules that hold for core lexical items, yet we are claiming that they are important and useful facts about the phonological grammar of sign languages. Second, we will describe what is gained by knowing about these differences in terms of new insights and generalizations.

6.1   Theories of phonological contrast and their application to sign languages

Every theory of phonological representation has had to deal with the concept of phonological contrast, including the Prague School (e.g., Trubetzkoy 1939), Structuralism (e.g., Bloomfield 1933, Harris 1951), distinctive feature theories (e.g., Jakobson, Fant & Halle 1951), early generative phonology (Chomsky & Halle 1968) and Underspecification Theory (Archangeli 1988a,1988b; Steriade 1995). Focusing on more recent work regarding contrast (Avery & Idsardi 2001, Clements 2001, Dresher 2003), we argue that the *types of contrast* in (2) and the *distributional patterns of contrast* in (3) (discussed in section 6.2) come together to explain some aspects of sign language phonology that heretofore have been left unaccounted for.

First, in order to appear in a phonological representation, a feature or structure must be *contrastive*, but this means much more than simply participating in a minimal pair. There are different types of contrast in a phonological system. The criteria developed in the Prosodic model (Brentari 1998) for including a phonological structure or a feature in the hierarchy were: (1) use in a minimal pair (or in the absence of a minimal pair, if a change in feature value results in an ungrammatical form), (2) use in a phonological constraint or (3) use morphologically in a productive way. These criteria are quite similar to the criteria set forth for spoken languages in Clements (2001), who uses the terms "distinctive," "active" and "prominent," described in (2). These are not mutually exclusive categories, as a feature can participate in more than one.

(2) Phonological contrast types
  a. Distinctive: The presence/absence of this type of feature in a pair of segments creates a minimal pair. E.g., [voice] in English obstruents in a pair, such as '[z]oo'/'[S]ue.'
  b. Active: This type of feature is used in a phonological constraint. E.g., [voice] in German obstruents in word-final position, in a case such as 'ra/d/' > 'ra[t]', (Eng: 'advice'). A constraint prohibits voiced obstruents in codas: *CODA$_{[+\text{voice}]}$.
  c. Prominent (a subtype of active): This type of feature qualifies as an autosegmental tier because it is: (a) involved in a particular type of phonological operation (such as spreading), (b) used productively for morphological purposes, (c) a participant in long-distance effects, where a segment affects a non-contiguous segment, or (d) involved in many-to-one association.[13] E.g., [high] in Japanese palatalization used to mean 'unreliable' (Hamano 1998), as in cases of awkward or irregular movement, such as 'pʲoko-pʲoko' (Jap: 'jumping around in an uncontrolled manner') from 'poko-poko' (Jap: 'up and down movement').

In Clements's (2001) terminology, features are "distinctive" when the presence of that feature results in a minimal pair (a lexical distinction, not one where the two forms are morphologically related), "active" when involved in a phonological operation and "prominent" (a subtype of active) when used to establish an autosegmental tier (Goldsmith 1976). Active features have always been a part of the representation at some level,[14] but prominent features have not played a large role in discussions of distribution types in spoken language phonology, since often these are considered "not purely phonological." Clements's approach brings them back under the phonological umbrella. Crucially this approach allows all three types of features or feature structures to be in the phonological representation rather than allowing only distinctive features in the representation.

6.1.1 *3FHSs*
What our data in sections 3 to 4 show is that 3FHSs are "distinctive" either in the foreign component alone (in ASL and DSGS) or in both the core and the foreign components (in HKSL). They are "prominent" in classifier forms, and since they participate in historical change, they can also be "active." For example, some contrasts involving 3FHSs seem to be disappearing over time, as they move from the foreign to the core component. For instance, the ASL signs DOCTOR and THOUSAND were originally borrowed from the initialized LSF signs MÉDECIN

and <u>M</u>ILLE using M-handshapes (⟨handshape⟩), but there seems to be a diachronic move toward use of a four-finger handshape instead as these signs lose their foreign status. Similarly, in HKSL, the dictionary lists three- and two-fingered variants for one instance of a borrowed sign (⟨handshape⟩ vs. ⟨handshape⟩ in BOYSCOUT, originally from a hearing gesture), perhaps indicating that, although allowable in the core, in some cases 3FHSs are still less desirable than other alternatives.[15]

6.1.2   *Stacked handshapes*

The data show that [stacked] handshapes are distinctive in the foreign components of ASL and DSGS, and in the core component of HKSL. [Stacked] participates in a synchronic phonological operation as well, so it is also *active* (at the very least, in ASL). For two-finger forms, the relevant contexts for an unstacked handshape to become [stacked] are: (1) when the palms face inward toward the midline, as in the ASL core signs BORROW, FIGURE-OUT and CARE; (2) when the middle finger makes contact with another part of the body, as in the ASL core forms SEE and TWICE and the initialized sign <u>V</u>ERB; and (3) when an underlying palm-up orientation and/or wrist rotation to a palm-up orientation occurs, as seen in the final position of the sign FALL or the classifier construction 'vehicle-turned-on-its side.'[16] This active use of the [stacked] feature is available in all of the ASL lexical components, but it is blocked in situations where the [stacked] feature is prominent. For example, in the palm-up classifier handshape used to represent a sunbathing person lying on his/her back, a stacked configuration would be rejected unless it matched the leg position of the sunbather.

6.1.3   *Classifiers*

This approach also allows us to see more clearly the differences among classifier types – phonologically in ASL (and likely crosslinguistically), classifier handshapes do not form a homogeneous class with respect to contrast type. In SCLs (despite historical iconic links between handshape and meaning), when the fingers or joints are altered in some way, it creates either an ungrammatical form or a completely new one; hence, according to our definitions of contrast, these elements are distinctive.[17] For example, if you increase the number of selected fingers (not counting the thumb) in a 'vehicle' classifier from two (⟨handshape⟩) to four (⟨handshape⟩), the resulting handshape cannot be used to represent a larger car; the change is ungrammatical in this context, the relative size instead being shown by in the signer's facial expression (e.g., 'puffed cheeks' indicate a large truck driving past). Furthermore, changing which two fingers are selected – e.g., the index and middle fingers for a 'vehicle' classifier (⟨handshape⟩, e.g., car) to the index and pinkie (⟨handshape⟩) – results in a different SCL (in this case, 'airplane'). Further evidence for the distinctive use of features in SCLs comes from a fact mentioned in section 4.1; namely, the active use of [stacked] is possible in the ASL SCL 'vehicle lying on its side,' but not in the body part classifier 'sunbather lying on her back.' We would argue that this is because the feature specifications of the base handshape are distinctive in the SCL but prominent in the body part classifier. In ICLs, selected fingers and joints are also distinctive to some extent, since a change in feature often results in a different tool (e.g., 'toothbrush' must have one selected finger to be grammatical; and curved fingers in 'spoon' contrasts with extended in 'knife'). However, as mentioned earlier, ICLs are a mixed class, as evidenced by some instances where selected fingers can be used prominently to indicate varying dimensions of the same tool (e.g., widths of 'paintbrush' using two or four fingers). Finally, both feature types are used prominently in DCLs and HCLs to indicate differences in size and shape (e.g., varying thickness via different selected finger combinations and round vs. flat objects via joint configurations). Therefore, we see that SCLs with their distinctive feature contrasts are phonologically more similar to core items with regard to contrast type than the other classifier types which can use features prominently to varying degrees.

In summary, in making this move to allow features of all contrast types in the representation of sign languages, several insights can be made. First, contrast types and lexical affiliation are closely linked. This is true not just in ASL, but crosslinguistically for the three sign languages studied. The work in sections 3 to 4 shows that prominent contrasts are present in classifier constructions, distinctive contrasts appear primarily in the core and foreign components, and active contrasts are possible throughout the system. This pattern is quite strong, even if there are notable crosslinguistic differences in terms of degree of acceptability as we have shown. Furthermore, without a category of prominent features, the generalizations about selected fingers being associated with semantic and instrumental classifiers and joints associated with descriptive and handling classifiers would be missed, since prominent features had previously been relegated to the margins of phonology. These divisions of labor of features and their contrastive types in sign languages can be seen as potentially universal for this language family and are elements that can be followed closely in emerging sign languages and homesign systems as they change over time.

Second, we see more clearly that the elements of a handshape's phonological representation function very differently across the different components of the lexicon and among classifier types. Referring back to Figure 13.4 we see that, following Brentari (2005), the "handshape" node is phonological in core forms, but in both foreign and classifier forms this same node plays a morphological role. In foreign forms and in semantic classifiers, the handshape node itself is the site of the morphological affix; while in other classifier forms, nodes lower in the tree such as joints and quantity (under selected fingers) may be morphological.

Finally, the approach taken here also helps to explain why there are so many differences among the phonological models of sign language. The reason why some models have more features and even more types of features is, in large part, due to the lexical components from which the researchers draw their data. To take a few examples, models such as Sandler (1989), van der Hulst (1993, 1995) or Channon (2002a), have focused primarily on what is needed to capture the core lexicon, considering primarily those features that are distinctive, while others such as Liddell and Johnson (1989) and Brentari (1998) have sought to capture the spatial and foreign components as well. This is true for the handshape elements discussed in this chapter, for handshape in general, as well as for the larger representation, which includes movement and location features. One direction for future work in sign language phonology would be to take into account the type of data presented in this chapter to create representations that more transparently reflect the asymmetries among the lexical components.

6.2   Types of phonological distribution

In addition to recognizing different contrast types, we also recognize different kinds of distributions in our analysis. Goldsmith (1995) describes five distributional patterns of contrast that can hold between a feature and a phonological system; these are shown in (3). Like the constraint types, these are not mutually exclusive categories, and features can participate in more than one of these distributions within a given language.

(3)   Distributions of spoken language features within a phonological system
   a.   Allophonic: completely determined by the system (e.g., [aspiration] in English)
   b.   Barely contrastive: almost completely determined by the system (e.g., [retroflex] in English)
   c.   Not yet integrated semi-contrasts: a general move has taken place in the system but a few remnants remain (e.g., [tense]/[lax] in Florentine Italian mid-vowels)
   d.   Modest asymmetry case: the alternation is allophonic in one part of the lexicon, but distinctive in another (e.g., [±labial] in the Japanese periphery)
   e.   Distinctive contrast: the opposition creates a minimal pair (e.g., [voice] in English)[18]

Typically (3a) and (3e) are the efficient workers in the phonological workplace (albeit in different ways), and most work on spoken language phonology has focused on them. In allophonic cases, (3a), it is the *rule system* that is working; a feature such as aspiration in English is typically not in the lexicon. Instead, there is a rule that selects a set of well-defined forms to which the feature is added. This is exactly what happens in the case of aspiration in English – /p, t, k/ > [pʰ, tʰ, kʰ] at the beginning of words when followed by a vowel. In distinctive contrast cases, (3e), it is the *representation system* that is working; a feature such as [voice] in English is always in the lexicon. For example, the voiceless obstruents /p, t, k/ are distinct from the voiced ones /b, d, g/ because the feature [voice] is in the representation in the latter forms.

Cases (3b)–(3d) are the in-between cases. Barely contrastive cases, (3b), are determined largely by rule, but not completely; in the case of English [−retroflex], a redundancy rule makes all sounds [−retroflex], except for /r/ which needs [+ retroflex] to distinguish it from /l/. In the not yet integrated semi-contrasts, (3c), the feature in question is largely allophonic, but a small pocket of forms with contrast remains. For example, all vowels are redundantly [tense] in Italian except in Florentine Italian which holds onto a mid-vowel contrast /e/-/ɛ/ and /o/-/ɔ/. Modest asymmetry cases, (3d), are determined largely by representation, but there is a sizable set of forms that is handled by a rule, such as the Japanese /h/-/f/ case we saw at the beginning of the chapter. The Italian and Japanese examples in (3c) and (3d), respectively, are particularly important because they show that variable behavior in the phonological system may be due to having multiple components of the lexicon – in the Florentine Italian case the distribution is due to an historical remnant of Late Latin (Marotta 1985, van der Leer 2006), and in the Japanese case it is due to recent foreign borrowings into the language.[19]

For sign languages thus far we have focused on the specific, marked 3FHSs and [stacked] forms as a pair of case studies, but let us now widen the discussion to include selected fingers and joints, more generally. Using the categories of distribution for spoken languages described in (3), examples of the distribution of selected fingers and joints structures of handshape are given in (4).

(4)   Distributions of handshape elements
  a.   Allophonic: determined completely by the system.
    i.   Selected fingers: We found no examples of this.
    ii. Joints: e.g., [flexed] in the context of handshape change; the value of one handshape is predictable from the value of the lexically specified handshape.

    b. Barely contrastive: almost completely determined by the system.

        i. Unselected fingers:[20] These are largely predictable from aperture value of the selected fingers, but there are a few cases where unselected fingers in index finger handshapes are contrastive. (ASL near minimal pair PERFECT (　) vs. REVENGE, (　)).

        ii. Joints: flexion of the metacarpal (knuckle) joint is largely predictable (Crasborn 2001), but there are a few cases in B-handshape forms where the metacarpal joint must be bent, such as ASL SUN (　).

    c. Not yet integrated semi-contrasts: a general move has taken place in the system, but a few remnants remain. We found no examples of this.

    d. Modest asymmetry case: the alternation is allophonic in one part of the lexicon, but distinctive in another. (Numerous examples)

        i. Selected fingers: 3FHSs (i.e., the historical changes from LSF to ASL in the 'M' to 'B' in DOCTOR).

        ii. Joints: [stacked] handshapes.

    e. Distinctive contrast: the opposition creates a minimal pair.

        i. Selected fingers: one- vs. two-finger handshapes in ASL APPLE (　), vs. NERVE (　).

        ii. Joints: the feature [spread] in the SCREWDRIVER (　) vs. MEANING (　).

First of all, as (4d) shows, both of our specific examples – 3FHSs and [stacked] – are like the modest asymmetry cases of (3d). They are neither allophonic or distinctive everywhere, so they do not match the criterion of (3a) or (3e). Their contrasts are more widespread than a feature such as [retroflex] in English, so (3b) is also eliminated. We are left with (3c) and (3d). (3c) cases are in the process of being incorporated into the grammar. Notice that our specific examples of 3FHSs and the feature [stacked] fall best into the (3d) "modesty asymmetry" group because there are clear asymmetries in contrast type based on lexical affiliation.

More generally, while the examples in (4) show that selected fingers and joints have distinctive contrasts throughout the core and foreign components, phonologists working on sign languages know that minimal pairs are scarce; work by Liddell and Johnson (1989), Sandler (1989) and Brentari (1998) demonstrates clearly that distinctive contrasts exist, but there are far fewer minimal pairs in signed languages than in spoken languages. This is also true for operations that are purely allophonic.

In ASL both selected fingers and joints participate in phonological processes such as handshape assimilation in compounds in ASL (Liddell & Johnson 1986, Sandler 1989), but almost all rules/constraints are optional. To our knowledge the example of handshape change is the only example of purely allophonic alternation. Comparing the spoken language examples like those in (3) with sign language examples such as in (4), the number of cases in spoken languages in categories (3a) and (3e) is very high, and as Goldsmith (1995) notes, these have received the lion's share of attention in the spoken language literature. In sign languages, however, fewer cases exist at these extreme ends, and more cases are mixed cases (3b–3d).

We would argue that the explanation for differences between signed and spoken languages in the number of cases per distribution type is twofold. First, *articulator independence* and *iconicity* conspire to realize a different distribution of phonological elements in signed vs. spoken languages. Regarding (4e) we would argue that the small number of minimal pairs in the core lexicon is due to iconicity in movement and location because this iconicity creates a sparsely populated grid of lexical items (van der Hulst & van der Kooij 2006).[21] On the other end of the spectrum, purely allophonic distribution, we would argue that the small number of examples is due to the greater articulatory independence in sign languages with respect to spoken languages. In spoken languages, because of the confined space and the limited number of articulators in the vocal tract, most movements of one part of the tongue – e.g., the tongue tip – effect movements of other parts of the tongue as well as the length of the vocal tract. In the absence of antagonist moves to the contrary, phonological "gestures" in speech have a constellation of concomitant, phonetically motivated and potentially allophonic consequences. Some such phonetic consequences exist in sign languages, too, but in general, articulation is slower in sign language, and the articulators of the body, arms and hands in sign languages are capable of greater articulatory independence than spoken language articulators.[22] Since sign languages are freer to control the movements of the hands and body, phonological elements have fewer allophonic consequences dictated by the entire articulatory system.

This section demonstrates there are surprising consequences of modality on the distribution of feature elements for both signed and spoken languages that only come to light by juxtaposing the two types of languages and their distribution types side by side. Sign languages are excellent language cases for studying both the effects of contrast types throughout a system and how the system is changing in historical time, precisely because they have a wide range of synchronic lexical origins and evidence of historical change as well.

7   **Conclusions**

This chapter has attempted to provide a glimpse into the crosslinguistic and language-internal variation that exists in handshape. To undertake this type of study, corpora of considerable size must be employed in several languages, and in making a list of handshapes and handshape contrasts, all types of contrast must be considered – distinctive, prominent and active – as well as the lexical affiliation of the forms examined.

In sections 3 to 4, crosslinguistic and language-internal differences were described for two rare properties of handshape – 3FHSs and [stacked]. From our analysis, HKSL emerged as the language that accepted and used these marked properties the most, DSGS the least, and ASL was between them. We also determined that in terms of function and distribution, there was a similar pattern across the three languages. The spatial component used these features prominently (with the exception of semantic classifiers), the foreign and core components used them distinctively, and the entire lexicon has the potential to use them actively. In section 5, based on ASL data, we see the relationship among iconicity, morphology and phonology more clearly; that is, certain types of iconicity are abstract in the classifier system (as in SCLs) and not all iconic properties are used by the morphophonology equally in the different types of classifier handshapes.

In section 6, the theoretical implications of this work were explored. We argued that without a model that recognizes different types of contrast, several generalizations would be overlooked. First, without a comparison between distinctive, active and prominent contrasts, we would miss the different distribution of these contrasts in foreign and core forms across languages. Second, we would overlook the fact that SCLs are the classifier type most similar to core lexical items, because the distinction between prominent and distinctive contrasts would not be evident. Third, we would not recognize the iconic and morphophonological use and distribution of selected fingers and joints in the different types of classifier handshapes (at least for ASL), because prominent features are not typically considered in phonological analyses, making such comparisons impossible. By using Clements's three types of contrast, considered to be at equal levels of importance, we can begin to sharpen our gaze at exactly how morphology (and iconicity) interact in the phonology.

We also discussed how obscuring the differences between lexical components can make the phonological models of sign languages look more different than they actually are with regard to the number of features. This calls for a new type of approach to representation that accounts for differences among lexical components and across languages, while also providing an analysis of the use of contrast and iconicity for different classifier handshapes. This is a question for future research, but our work suggests that a set of ranked constraints using Optimality Theory may work well to represent FAITHFULNESS or MARKEDNESS constraints operating in perception, production and iconicity to different degrees (see Eccarius 2008).

In doing this work, we hope to encourage other researchers to include in their inventories not only handshapes whose features can be supported by a minimal pair (distinctively), but also those that are used morphologically (prominently), as well as those used in phonological operations (actively). In doing so, a more accurate tally of handshapes and their uses crosslinguistically can be made.

14

Syllable structure in sign language phonology

Tommi Jantunen and Ritva Takkinen

1   Introduction

In this chapter we will deal with the "signed syllable," a unit of increasing interest in sign language phonology since the early 1980s. In general, we aim to give an overview of the syllable's nature and role in sign languages, focusing especially on the research done on American Sign Language (ASL) and Finnish Sign Language (FinSL). More specifically, our goals are: (i) to introduce the concept of the syllable, and argue for the existence of the syllable, in signed language; (ii) to present and compare, on a general level, the main models of the structure of the signed syllable and (iii) to contrast and compare the signed syllable with its spoken language counterpart. As regards a theoretical framework, most work on the signed syllable has been influenced by "generative phonology" (Kenstowicz 1994). Consequently, all the theories and models discussed in this chapter also belong to this school.

The syllable has already been investigated in a number of sign languages, most notably in ASL (e.g., Wilbur 1991, Perlmutter 1992, Sandler 1993, Brentari 1998), but also, for example, in Sign Language of the Netherlands (van der Kooij 2002) and Israeli Sign Language (Nespor & Sandler 1999). Recently, the syllable has also begun to be studied in FinSL (Jantunen 2005, 2006, 2007). From the point of view of exploring similarities and differences between sign languages, the data from FinSL, which we will present in this chapter, adds to our understanding of the crosslinguistic nature of the signed syllable.

2   Syllable: the basics

2.1   Defining the spoken syllable

In everyday speech, a spoken language syllable is perhaps most often, and certainly rather easily, characterized as a short sequence of vowel (V) – "sonant" – and optional consonants (C); for example, CV or CVC.[1] However, empirically (i.e., phonetically) the syllable has proved to be an extremely difficult unit to define. In the history of linguistics several definitions of the syllable have been put forward (see Ladefoged 1975), but so far no single one of them has been found to be complete. Some researchers have invoked this trait of the syllable to escape empirical definition to deny its existence altogether, but the current state of our knowledge suggests that this view is overly pessimistic: the ability of most speakers to intuitively identify syllable boundaries and, for example, to assign stress to words according to these boundaries, as well as the existing syllable-based writing systems, all favor the existence of the syllable as a unit in spoken language. Further support, more linguistic in nature, for the existence of a spoken syllable is also provided by the fact that it is often the most convenient unit to refer to when one needs to make generalizations, for example, of a phonological nature.

Although there are no watertight definitions of syllable available, and although in the end it might be that the syllable is an abstract "unit that exist[s only] at some higher level in the mental activity of a speaker" (Ladefoged 1975:221), many spoken language researchers still approach and define the syllable in terms of *sonority*, that is, a property traditionally assigned to sound segments and understood as their intrinsic loudness. From this perspective it has been claimed (e.g., Blevins 1995) that the spoken syllable is a unit which includes only one "sonority peak" – that is, a segment whose inherent value of loudness is relatively high, meaning typically a vowel – and in which the segments as a whole are organized so that their sonority values first increase and then decrease. As a typological generalization, this sonority-based definition of the spoken syllable has stood the test of time well, but language-specifically there are certain well-known exceptions to it. One such exception comes from English and deals with monosyllabic words beginning (and ending) with the consonant clusters /sp st sk/: the word *spill*, for example, includes two sonority peaks since the inherent loudness, or sonority value, of segments /s/ and /i/ is higher than the loudness of the segments or the parts of the signal immediately preceding and following them.[2]

During the past decades researchers (e.g., Ohala & Kawasaki 1984, Ohala 1990) have departed from the classical view according to which sonority is simply equated with loudness and redefined the concept as an inherent property of a sound segment which contributes to the "perceptual salience" of that segment. Superficially, the change may seem to be a minor or merely philosophical one, since loudness and perceptuality are obviously related concepts. However, on the level of principle, the consequences of this redefinition have been more far-reaching: the breaking of the conceptual link between sonority and "hearing" has opened up the possibility for researchers to begin investigating sonority – and syllable – also in signed language.

2.2 On sonority

The close relationship between the syllable and sonority has been noted in most current theories dealing with the spoken syllable, and consequently sonority has become a key concept also in the study of the signed syllable. With the basic understanding that sonority has mostly to do with perceptual salience, signed language researchers – including Corina (1990), Perlmutter (1992), Sandler (1993) and Brentari (1998) – have proposed that the property which most contributes to the perception – or visibility – of a signed signal and its parts is *movement*,[3] and that movements therefore function as the sonority peaks of signed syllables. In the field of signed syllable research, this view has now become the dominant one, as has the idea which follows from it, that signed syllables are units formed around movement "pulses," identified in turn with the dynamic lexeme-internal and underspecified – i.e., phonological – parts of the signal. This latter stand is captured, for example, in the following rough criteria by Brentari (1998:6) for the identification of signed syllables (FinSL examples added; see Figure 14.1):[4]

   a.   The number of sequential phonological dynamic units in a string equals the number of syllables in that string (e.g., the sign MUSTA 'black' includes one syllable and the sign TIETÄÄ 'to know' two syllables).[5]

      i.   When several shorter dynamic units co-occur with a single dynamic element of longer duration, the longer unit is the one to which the syllable refers (cf., for example, the monosyllabic sign VÄHETÄ 'to decrease').

      ii.   When two or more dynamic units are contemporaneous, they count as one syllable (cf., for example, the monosyllabic sign KULTTUURI 'culture').

   b.   If a structure is a well-formed syllable as an independent word, it must be counted as a syllable word-internally (cf. MUSTA 'black,' VÄHETÄ 'to decrease' and KULTTUURI 'culture').

Paradoxically, there is no direct evidence available to support the view that the parts of the signed signal which include (phonological or any other kinds of) movement are indeed the most salient and therefore also the most sonorous parts of the signal. However, indirectly the claim can be supported, for example, by the studies of Allen, Wilbur and Schick (1991), Wilcox (1992) and Crasborn (2001). First, in their study of rhythm in ASL, Allen, Wilbur and Schick (1991:197) found that the rhythmical beats, that is, "those events that are felt to be more forcefully produced and around which the other events in the sequence are organized" are

Figure 14.1 *FinSL signs MUSTA 'black' (top left), TIETÄÄ 'to know' (top right), VÄHETÄ 'to decrease' (bottom left) and KULTTUURI 'culture' (bottom right). All signs are produced with a Finnish mouthing. (Original photographs from Malm 1998; by permission of FAD.)*

associated with sign-internal movements. Second, Wilcox's study on ASL finger-spelling has shown that perception is enhanced by an increase in movement velocity. Finally, Crasborn has provided phonetic evidence in support of the positive correlation between "visual loudness" and the amplitude (i.e., the size) of a sign's movement. In addition to these studies, the link between salience and movement can also be strengthened by the general research that has been carried out into visual perception (e.g., Bruce & Green 1990); the research suggests, for example, that movement enhances the possibility of perceiving the object, and that movement contributes positively also to the identification of the object.

In a coherent treatment of sonority, the question of its articulatory basis must also be addressed. With regard to this issue, it has been suggested that with spoken language the degree of sonority of a sound correlates articulatorily with the openness of the vocal tract. The main idea is that a sound generated in an open vocal tract is more sonorous than a sound generated in a closed tract since the larynx sound resonates differently in the vocal cavity depending on the degree of openness of the tract; the larynx sound going through an open tract produces a stronger – and thus better perceived – signal than one going through a closed tract. Traditionally, this view of the articulatory basis of sonority has been used to explain, for example, the greater sonority of vowels over consonants: vowels are always produced in a relatively open vocal tract whereas in the production of consonants there is always a closure of some sort.

As far as we are aware, the articulatory basis of sonority in signed language has not been investigated in a level comparable to that in spoken language. However, an exception is Brentari (1998), who uses the physiologically, socially, etc., motivated weakening and strengthening phenomena of lexical movements to argue that sonority in signed language correlates with the proximality of the joint used in the production of the movement. According to this view, movements produced from more proximal (or larger) joints of the arm are more sonorous than movements produced from distal (or smaller) joints because proximal joints are able to produce larger and thus more visible – i.e. better perceived – movements than distal joints. For the proximality hierarchy of the joints of the arm Brentari suggests the following, listed from the most proximal to the most distal (Brentari 1998:75):[6]

> shoulder > elbow > wrist > base [finger] joints > nonbase [finger] joints.

Like the proposal for the articulatory basis of sonority in spoken languages, Brentari's view of the articulatory basis of sonority in signed languages has also been criticized. For example, Sandler and Lillo-Martin (2006) take the view that connecting sonority with the amplitude of movement is to confuse sonority with another property, namely *loudness*; indeed, we think that it is not always easy to distinguish between these two properties in signed language and that their relationship should be investigated further. Jantunen (2005; see also Jantunen 2006, 2007), on the other hand, in campaigning for the phonological commensurability of manual and nonmanual movements (see section 3.2.2), points out that Brentari's view deals explicitly only with "manual sonority," that is, only with movements produced with manual articulators, hands and arms.[7] However, unlike Sandler and Lillo-Martin, Jantunen does not abandon Brentari's proposal but instead chooses to modify it. First, on the basis of FinSL signs which contain only nonmanually produced phonological movement (e.g., KYLLÄ 'yes,' ON-KUULLUT 'has heard,' and MUKAVA 'nice'; see section 3.2.2), he argues that there is also nonmanual sonority in signed language. Second, relying on the "trans-articulatory movement migration processes" – i.e., processes in which responsibility for the production of the abstract shape of a movement is shifted, for example, from a manual articulator to a nonmanual articulator, such as the upper body – he further argues that sonority in signed language also correlates with the size of the articulator, a bigger articulator entailing greater sonority than a smaller one (for additional discussion of the range of nonmanuals in sign languages, see Pfau and Quer, this volume). For the hierarchy of articulators, Jantunen (2005:56) suggests, on the basis of FinSL data, the following:

upper body & head > hands [incl. Brentari's hierarchy] > mouth.

In Jantunen's hierarchy, the upper body and the head are treated together since in FinSL – although capable of moving independently, and in certain contexts (e.g., when negating) even required to do so – they in many cases move as one (cf. Woll 2001 for British Sign Language).[8] Movements produced by the upper body and head are taken by Jantunen to be more sonorous than movements produced by the hands since, for example, the default manual movement of the FinSL sign HÄMMÄSTYÄ 'to be surprised' (see Figure 14.2) can be enhanced with a non-manual body and head movement of similar shape. Movements produced with the mouth – or to be more precise, only *mouth gestures* (Sutton-Spence & Boyes Braem 2001)[9] – Jantunen considers to possess the lowest sonority. The basis of this decision is the observation that, for example, the default movement of the sign LINNUN-NOKKA-AUKEAA 'the bird's beak opens' – i.e., the change of the handshape ⬚ to ⬚ – can be weakened to be articulated with the mouth alone (i.e., the mouth opens). The weakening analysis is based on etymological

Figure 14.2 *FinSL sign HÄMMÄSTYÄ 'to be surprised' produced with the default manual movement. The sign includes a Finnish mouthing. (Photographs from Malm 1998; by permission of FAD.)*

knowledge according to which the origin of similar descriptive signs (e.g., LEUAT-LOKSAHTAVAT-AUKI 'jaw-drop') is on descriptive nonmanual gestural activity (e.g., the opening of the mouth), and that only later that activity has come to be imitated (i.e., "enhanced") manually.[10]

Our opinion is that both Brentari's and Jantunen's claims about the articulatory basis of signed language sonority include open questions. Why, for example, is the most frequent movement in signs the straight movement articulated from the elbow joint (Brentari 1998, Jantunen 2005) and not one of the allegedly most sonorous movements articulated from the shoulder?[11] And are the upper body, head and mouth really the only nonmanual articulators whose movements contribute to sonority?[12] Such questions need exploration in the future. Consequently, this means that research into the signed syllable cannot be based solely on the relationship that seems to exist between movement and sonority – more grounding for the existence of the signed syllable is needed.

2.3   More arguments for the claim that sequential dynamic units formed around phonological movements are syllables

In the following sections we present two more arguments to support the view that sequential phonological dynamic units are syllables (cf. section 2.2). The first argument (see section 2.3.1), called here the "Minimal Word argument," is widely cited in the literature (e.g., Perlmutter 1992, Sandler 1993, Brentari 1998, Jantunen 2007) and deals with the well-formedness of prosodic words (signs). The second argument (see section 2.3.2), called here the Babbling argument (cf. Brentari 1998), is based on the functional similarities in the language acquisition process between deaf and hearing children.

2.3.1   *The Minimal Word argument*

The basis of the Minimal Word argument is in the spoken language-based generalization that all well-formed (prosodic) words must contain at least one syllable (e.g., McCarthy & Prince 1993). The argument states that sequential phonological dynamic units are syllables since no surface form of any sign is well formed unless it has a phonological movement.

If the Minimal Word argument is valid, then it can be assumed that signs which do not inherently contain a movement are given one by the grammar in their production. According to Brentari (1998) and Jantunen (2007), this is exactly what happens at least in ASL and in FinSL. In ASL, Brentari has observed that inherently movementless signs such as the numeral signs 1 to 9 are given an extra short straight epenthetic movement when used as independent words. Jantunen

Figure 14.3 *The old (left) and modern (right) form of the FinSL sign LÄMPÖ 'heat.' The old form is produced pantomimically by blowing "warm air" to the palm. The modern form includes a straight sequential phonological movement and a Finnish mouthing. (Photographs from Hirn 1910 and Malm 1998; by permission of FAD.)*

states that the same is true also with the movementless FinSL numerals 0 to 8, as well as with fingerspelled letters containing no movement in their base form.

We take the observations concerning the movement epenthesis in inherently movementless signs to be synchronic evidence to support the Minimal Word argument. Additionally, the argument can be grounded also diachronically. For example, Jantunen (2003) has shown that the origin of FinSL signs is in many cases in pantomimic gestures and postures. However, in the historical development of signs, many pantomimic features have disappeared from the system, and consequently, many originally movementless signs (e.g., the FinSL sign LÄMPÖ 'heat,' see Figure 14.3) have come to be produced with a phonological movement.

2.3.2   Babbling argument

In addition to the Minimal Word argument (and the relationship which seems to exist between movements and sonority; see section 2.2), the claim that signed syllables form around sequential phonological movements can be supported also with the "Babbling argument." This argument is based on studies which have investigated the prelinguistic development of deaf children (e.g., Petitto & Marentette 1991), and it can be formulated in the following way: a sequential dynamic unit formed around a phonological movement is a syllable because a deaf child starts to produce such units at the same time as hearing children start to produce syllabic babbling[13] (e.g., *dadadada*) and because the distributional and phonological properties of such units are analogous to the properties usually associated with syllabic babbling.

Petitto and Marentette (1991) call this developmental phase "manual babbling," which starts from the appearance of sequential dynamic movement units to a child's language, e.g., a repeating change of the handshape. According to them, manual babbling evolves at the same time as syllabic babbling with hearing children, i.e., usually by the age of ten months. Like syllabic babbling, manual babbling includes a lot of repetition of the same movement, and also like syllabic babbling, manual babbling makes use of only a part of the phonemic units available in a given language. Petitto and Marentette's research also shows that manual babbling develops without interruption into the first signs (just as syllabic babbling continues without interruption into the first words), and that manual babbling is different from other coexisting non-linguistic gestures.

We accept the evidence presented above to support the existence of syllables in signed language. However, for the proper study of the signed syllable, it is not enough simply to be able to show that syllables exist; one also needs to show that they are actually needed to describe phonological operations. This is an issue we will consider briefly in the next section.

2.4   On the need for the unit syllable in signed language

In spoken languages the need for the syllable as a linguistic unit has often been justified on the grounds that in many cases the syllable is the "simplest" unit to be referred to in phonological or morphological constraints (Blevins 1995; see also section 2.1). Following this line of argumentation, constraints which rely on the syllable unit have been presented also with regard to signed language (see, e.g., Corina & Sandler 1993, Brentari 1998, Sandler & Lillo-Martin 2006). One often cited (e.g., Brentari 1998, Jantunen 2007) example of these is the one dealing with the phonological length of lexemes in the core lexicon, according to which core lexemes may contain minimally one but maximally two syllables.

That the constraint limiting the phonological length of signed lexemes to two syllables[14] is indeed relevant in the study of signed language phonology has been demonstrated by, among others, Brentari (1998). According to her, the pressure to obey the constraint is seen, for example, in the discourse-situated ASL "local lexicalization" process, through which long sequences of fingerspelled letters reduce to independent lexeme-like forms containing only a maximum of two sequential phonological movements, i.e., two syllables. Also, the constraint is taken by her to be of importance in the description of non-nativity of certain compound-like ASL signs which include fingerspelling (e.g., SUN + B-U-R-N).

A crucial question is why the constraint on the phonological length of signed lexemes must refer precisely to the syllable and not to some other phonological unit? A recent answer to this question comes from Jantunen (2007), who claims that the other theoretically relevant units, such as the segment, are definitionally too ambiguous to meet the purpose (on the nature of segments, see also Wilbur & Petersen 1997). To back up this view in particular, Jantunen discusses the segmental representation of the FinSL sign MUSTA 'black' which, for example in the updated version of Liddell and Johnson's (1989) Hold-Movement model, consists of three segments (XMH), but in Brentari's (1998) Prosodic model of only two segments (two x-slots). On the grounds of the obvious differences in these representations, Jantunen argues that the segment cannot be accepted as the optimal point of reference in the description of lexemes' phonological length; reference to the dynamic phonological unit argued in previous sections to be a syllable is required.

According to current understanding, the syllable is a necessary unit in sign language phonology. However, consensus about the syllable dies when more specific questions about its structure are taken into consideration. These are the questions we turn to next.

3   Syllable structure

The following sections first briefly present the two most influential views about syllable structure in spoken language (3.1). After this, the structure of signed syllables is considered in more detail (3.2); it is discussed both with respect to the present main models of sign language phonology (i.e., Liddell & Johnson 1989, Sandler 1989, Perlmutter 1992, Brentari 1998) and with respect to spoken language-based views about syllable structure.

3.1   Syllable structure(s) in spoken language

Views about the internal structure of the spoken syllable have exhibited some variation (for an overview, see Blevins 1995). However, in analysis, two models have proved to be especially useful: the classic Hierarchical model (e.g., Selkirk 1982) and the Moraic model (e.g., Hyman 1985). Both models have also been applied to sign languages (e.g., Wilbur 1990 and Perlmutter 1992, respectively; see section 3.2).

The hierarchic model view of the spoken syllable is given in Figure 14.4a. In this model, the syllable (σ) is divided first into constituents *onset* (o) and *rhyme* (r), of which the latter is further divided into *nucleus* (n) and *coda* (c).

The nucleus is the phonological unit which corresponds to the syllable's sonority peak. It usually consists of one or more non-consonantal segments, that is, typically of a vowel or a short sequence of vowels (cf. section 2.2), although occasionally also consonants can be nucleic. Of the other terminal units, the onset is the consonant (cluster) which (optionally) precedes the nucleus, and the coda is the consonant

a)   b)

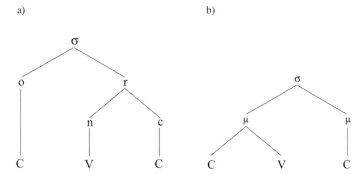

Figure 14.4 *The representation of spoken language syllable structure in the hierarchical model (a) and in the moraic model (b).*

(cluster) which (again, optionally) follows the nucleus. Functionally, with respect to their information-carrying ability, there is a disparity between the onset and the coda: in the standard case, only the onset can carry all the lexical contrast, the coda being limited in this sense to only a subset of these contrasts.

The rhyme constituent is an important unit in the analysis of metrical properties such as stress. In quantity-sensitive languages (e.g., English), the internal structure of the rhyme decides the "weight" of the syllable, that is, whether syllables are "light" or "heavy." Syllables with no coda and whose nucleus does not consist of more than one segment (prototypically CV) are interpreted as light, whereas syllables with a coda (prototypically CVC), or those whose nucleus has more than one segment (prototypically CVV), are labeled as heavy. Typologically, heavy syllables are stressed (e.g., Blevins 1995, Maddieson 2005).

In the hierarchical syllable model, an increase in syllable weight is equated first and foremost with an increase in the syllable's duration. However, the increase in weight can also be seen as the result of another type of phenomenon, that is, as a result of the increase in the number of *moras* (μ), prosodic weight units (for more on moras, see Perlmutter 1995). A model of the spoken syllable built on the concept of mora is the Moraic model. In this model, the (light) CV syllable is taken to include one mora and the (heavy) CVC/CVV syllable two moras. Hyman's (1985) view of the canonical moraic structure of the spoken language syllable is given in Figure 14.4b.

In Hyman's view, the syllable-initial CV cluster has the status of *core syllable* and it forms the first mora. The core syllable can be followed by a V or a C, the second mora. Structurally, the second mora is simpler than the first one, but its addition to the first mora makes the syllable as a whole more complex. Since moras are prosodic units, the addition of the second mora also increases the syllable's overall prosodic complexity.

The two models briefly presented above address different aspects of the spoken syllable structure. The hierarchical model approach of dividing the syllable into onset and rhyme constituents reflects perhaps most clearly the empirical fact that hearers identify rhythmical beats in between the syllable-initial consonant (cluster) and the vowel (Wilbur & Allen 1991). Hyman's moraic view, on the other hand, captures perhaps more effectively the typological generalization that, in quantity-sensitive languages, it is the CVC/CVV-style syllables, i.e., prosodically complex two-moraic syllables, which are typically stressed.

3.2   The structure of the signed syllable

As with views about the structure of the spoken syllable (cf. section 3.1), so also views about the structure of the signed syllable exhibit variation, and in some sense this variation is even more fundamental than that in spoken language. One reason for this "fundamentality" is the fact that there is no agreement among sign language researchers as to what kind of unit the phonological movement, functioning as the sonority peak of the syllable, is in phonological theory (cf. Liddell & Johnson 1989, Sandler 1989, Perlmutter 1992, Brentari 1998). Consequently, before the structure of the signed syllable can be discussed, an overview of the main ways of treating phonological movements must first be given.

Currently, there exist, in principle, two views about how phonological movement should be represented in phonological theory. According to one view, movements are dynamic segments defined by a change in articulator posture, contrasting to static segments during which the posture of the articulators does not change; this is the view taken, for example, by Liddell and Johnson (1989) in their Hold-Movement model and by Sandler (1989) in her Hand Tier model. According to the other view, movements are *autosegmental* prosodic units, analogous to the contrastive tone found in certain spoken languages, such as Mandarin Chinese; this is the view taken by Brentari (1998) in her Prosodic model. A diagram illustrating these two views and their mutual relationship is given in Figure 14.5.

Whether movements are seen as a segment or as a tone-like autosegment directly affects what kind of unit the syllable is considered to be in signed language. Accepting the segmental view of movement means that signed syllables are seen as sequences of static and dynamic segments, such as the sequence LML (i.e., Location–Movement–Location) in Sandler's Hand Tier model, that is, basically as units resembling spoken language syllables (cf. CVC). Accepting the autosegmental view, on the other hand, entails the ontological view that the relationship between a signed and spoken syllable is not so much a formal but rather a functional one, a signed syllable being perhaps most easily characterized as one sequential

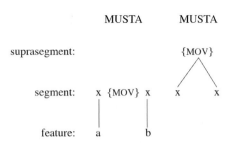

Figure 14.5 *The phonological movement {MOV} of the FinSL sign MUSTA 'black' (see Figure 14.1) represented as a segment (left) and as a suprasegment (right).*

phonological movement with a more paradigmatic internal structure. Both of these views – labeled here, respectively, as "the sequentially oriented approach to signed syllable" and "the simultaneously oriented approach to signed syllable" – are discussed further in sections 3.2.1 and 3.2.2.

3.2.1   *The sequentially oriented approach to the signed syllable*

The basis of the sequentially oriented approach to signed syllable structure is the ontological assumption that movements are segments, and that syllables are, consequently, short sequences of static and dynamic segments. Advocates of this view are, for example, Perlmutter (1992) and Sandler (1993). According to Perlmutter, the prototypical syllable in signed language is a PMP sequence, P corresponding to the Position of the articulator and M to its (path) Movement (the term "path movement" refers, in general, to movements which are produced from the elbow or from the shoulder); other syllable types recognized by Perlmutter are MP, PM and M, as well as a plain P consisting of (in contrast to a path movement) a "local movement," i.e., a movement produced from the wrist joint or from the finger joints. The trisegmental syllable is the prototypical syllable also for Sandler. However, in her framework the segments used are Ls and Ms (L is the Location, M is, again, the path Movement), the overall structural representation of the syllable prototype thus being LML. In addition to this type, Sandler also recognizes the syllable type L, which includes, like Perlmutter's P-type, a local movement. By analogy with the overall organizational principle of the spoken syllable, both Perlmutter and Sandler claim that signed syllables can also be understood in such a way that their segments form rising and falling "sonority cycles" (see section 2.1), static segments having, by definition, lower sonority value than dynamic segments (for an overview, see Brentari 1998; also Corina & Sandler 1993).[15]

In general, quite direct analogies to the spoken syllable have been drawn by the "sequentialists" also with regard to the internal structure of the signed syllable (see section 3.1). On the one hand, it has been proposed (see Wilbur 1990, Corina & Sandler 1993, Sandler 1993) that, like spoken syllables in the hierarchical model, signed syllables are also internally organized into units like onset (the syllable-initial static segment) and rhyme, the latter branching, like the spoken counterpart, into nucleus (the dynamic segment) and coda (the syllable-final static segment); models in which rhyme does not exist have also been presented. On the other hand, it has been argued (e.g., Perlmutter 1992) that the structure of the signed syllable includes moras, and corresponds to the structure proposed by the Moraic model (see Figure 14.4b).

One important observation to be made about the views held by supporters of the sequentially oriented approach to the signed syllable is, we think, that they are in many cases not built on any direct phonetic evidence as far as the structure of the syllable is concerned. In fact, in many cases phonetic research, although scarce, has even provided results which seem to contradict some of the sequentialists' claims. For example, the view that there is an onset–rhyme dichotomy in the signed syllable seems unreasonable in the light of the tapping experiment conducted by Allen, Wilbur and Schick (1991): in their experiment, rhythmical beats were not associated with any particular part of signed syllables, as they are with spoken language (i.e., with the border between onset and rhyme). Equally unlikely seems to be even the slightly modified view that the nucleus and the coda are independent constituents directly related to the syllable node: for example, the research on backward signing by Wilbur and Petersen (1997) suggests that there is no spoken syllable-like information-carrying disparity between the beginning and the end of the syllable (i.e., between the onset and the coda) but rather that both the beginning and the end of the syllable carry an equal load of information; the postulation of an intermediate level of representation between the segment and syllable (i.e., the level of onset, nucleus and coda) is thus unnecessary. The only sequentially oriented view about the structure of the signed syllable which may be taken to be directly based on phonetic evidence, that is, on the phenomenon known as the "phrase-final lengthening," is Perlmutter's (1992) mora view, according to which signed syllables are composed of one or two moras. However, criticism has also been leveled against this view (e.g., Wilbur & Allen 1991, Corina & Sandler 1993, Brentari 1998; Tang *et al.*, this volume; see also the next section).

3.2.2   *The simultaneously oriented approach to the signed syllable*
The basis of the simultaneously oriented approach to the structure of signed syllables is the assumption that movement is not a segment but a tone-like

suprasegment, and that the signed syllable is, unlike the spoken syllable, therefore more simultaneously composed – or layered – than sequentially composed – or mono-level. The main advocate of this view is Brentari (1998), and her view is now presented in more detail.

In contrast to sequentialists like Perlmutter (1992) and Sandler (1993), Brentari considers that spoken and signed syllables are not formally comparable. Instead, in the framework of her Prosodic model, Brentari argues that signed syllables are sequential phonological movements, basically corresponding to phonologically relevant dynamic sequences of the sign stream, during which the static, inherent features describing the shape and main location of the articulator (e.g., the features used to describe the static properties of the selected fingers and the major plane of articulation) remain unchanged. More formally, Brentari represents the prototypical signed syllable as a sequence of two timing units (x-slots; segments), tied together by the suprasegmental, hierarchically organized autosegmental group of dynamic – i.e., prosodic – features. In general, Brentari's view means, for example, that there are no rising and falling sonority cycles in signed syllables (cf. the stands taken by Perlmutter and Sandler), since there are no categorically different types of segments in the syllable, and since there is only one sequential suprasegmental movement per syllable.

Brentari argues that the internal structure of the signed syllable cannot be analyzed using conceptual machinery developed for the spoken language. She says, for example, in unspoken agreement with the studies of both Allen, Wilbur and Schick (1991) and Wilbur and Petersen (1997), that there is no onset–rhyme or comparable dichotomy in the signed syllable[16] and goes even further to claim that the notion of mora is also not a feasible concept for analysis. The basis for this latter position is her view that, although an abstract prosodic unit of weight, the term mora refers also to physical duration; according to Brentari, weight and duration are two separate things in sign languages.

Instead, Brentari suggests that signed syllables are composed internally of "weight units." The number of weight units correlates directly with the complexity of the syllable's nucleus, i.e., the movement: the more complex the syllable's movement, the more weight units there are per syllable. "Complex movements" are defined by Brentari as movements involving more than one co-occurring local or path movement; a movement involving a single local or path movement is "simple" in Brentari's terms. In practice, the complexity of movement correlates in Brentari's framework with the number of joints used in the production of the (phonological) movement. Basically this means that, for example, the movement in the monosyllabic ASL sign THROW is more complex than the movement in the monosyllabic sign UNDERSTAND because in the sign THROW the movement is produced

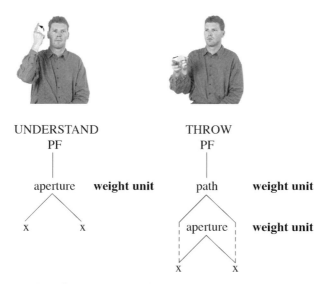

Figure 14.6 *Prosodic model representations of the syllable structure in ASL signs THROW and UNDERSTAND. (Photographs from Brentari 1998: 5–6; by permission of MIT Press.)*

simultaneously with the elbow and the finger joints (cf. the straight path movement and the handshape change), whereas in the sign UNDERSTAND the movement is reducible only to the finger joints (cf. the handshape change). Consequently, in Brentari's framework, the sign THROW is a (mono)syllable including two weight units, and the sign UNDERSTAND a (mono)syllable including one weight unit (see Figure 14.6).

In his work on FinSL, Jantunen (2005, 2006, 2007) argues that the definition of complexity given by Brentari (1998) is not sufficient, since it deals only with manual movements. In order to cover also nonmanual movements, which, it is argued, are relevant in FinSL phonology (see below and section 2.2), he suggests that the definition be expanded so that a movement is taken to be complex also when it is produced with more than one articulator. This suggestion depends on the following arguments for the commensurability of manual and nonmanual movements: (1) signs containing only nonmanual movements (e.g. KYLLÄ 'yes,' ON-KUULLUT 'has/have heard' and MUKAVA 'nice'; see Figure 14.7) are in FinSL as well formed as signs containing only manual movements; (2) in signs containing both manual and nonmanual movements (e.g. LÄHTEÄ 'to go'; see Figure 14.7), the nonmanual movements are structurally as essential as the manual ones; and (3) the production of the abstract shape of a movement does not in all cases depend upon the articulator (cf. the trans-articulatory movement migration phenomenon

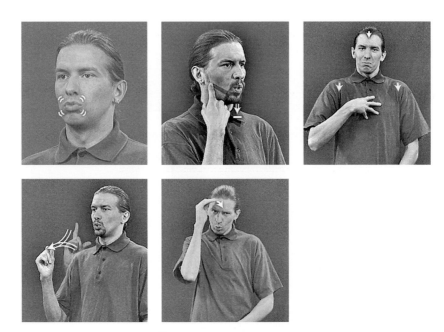

Figure 14.7 *FinSL signs KYLLÄ 'yes' (top left), ON-KUULLUT 'has/have heard' (top center), MUKAVA 'nice' (top right), LÄHTEÄ 'to go' (bottom left) and UJO 'shy' (bottom right). The sign KYLLÄ is a simple repeated mouth gesture (cf. kissing gesture). The sign LÄHTEÄ includes a mouth gesture resembling spoken sequence [viu]. All other signs are produced with a Finnish mouthing. (Original photographs from Malm 1998; by permission of FAD.)*

discussed in section 2.2). In practice, Jantunen's suggestion means that the movement in the monosyllabic FinSL sign UJO 'shy' (see Figure 14.7), for example, is more complex than the movement in the monosyllable MUSTA 'black' (see Figure 14.1), since UJO 'shy' contains both a local movement and a phonological head movement, whereas MUSTA 'black' has only a path movement. Consequently, Jantunen takes UJO 'shy' to be a (mono)syllable consisting of two weight units and MUSTA 'black' to be a (mono)syllable consisting of one weight unit.

Brentari (1998) discusses only ASL syllables with one or two weight units. However, with regard to FinSL, Jantunen (2007; also 2005, 2006), using Brentari's framework and considering manual and nonmanual movements as commensurable, has also identified syllables with three or four weight units and shown that there is a clear tendency in FinSL to prefer structurally simple syllables.[17] A summary of the frequency of occurrence of Jantunen's four FinSL syllable types among the one-handed monomorphemic monosyllables in the Basic Dictionary of FinSL (Malm 1998) is given in Table 14.1.

Table 14.1 *The distribution of different FinSL*
monosyllables in Jantunen's (2006, 2007) data

monosyllable type	n	%
one weight unit	131	57
two weight units	80	35
three weight units	19	8
four weight units	1	–
Σ	*231*	*100*

Figure 14.8 *The FinSL monosyllable EI-TUNNE 'does not know him/her' including four weight*
units. (Original photograph from Malm 1998; by permission of FAD.)

In Jantunen's data, syllables with one (e.g., MUSTA 'black') and two (e.g.,
KULTTUURI 'culture') weight units were the most typical manually produced
syllables. However, maximally the number of weight units in a manually produced
syllable could be three (e.g., MIES 'a man,' consisting of a straight path movement,
orientation change and handshape change), although in general, syllables with three
weight units tended to occur with two manual and one nonmanual movement
components, the latter type being typically a mouth gesture (e.g., LÄHTEÄ 'to go,'
including a mouth gesture resembling the spoken sequence [viu]). Syllables with
four weight units (e.g., EI-TUNNE 'does not know him/her,' consisting of three
manual components and one nonmanual component, i.e., the mouth gesture
resembling the opening *b* where the opening manifests as slightly opened mouth;
see Figure 14.8) were identifiable only if nonmanual movements were taken into
consideration and treated as commensurable with manual movements. In general,

these types of syllables were rare in Jantunen's data, which can perhaps be explained by the tendency of complex forms to reduce in complexity in their production (Jantunen 2006).[18]

With regard to nonmanually produced syllables, the type including only one weight unit (e.g., ON-KUULLUT 'has/have heard,' MUKAVA 'nice') occurred more frequently than the type including two weight units (e.g., KOVIN-PIENI 'rather/very small' containing a simultaneous head nod and a mouth movement resembling the spoken sequence [ka] or [sha]); two was the maximum number of weight units in a nonmanually produced syllable.

Analogously with the spoken language, Brentari claims that ASL syllables including one weight unit are light (cf. syllables with one mora) and those including more than one weight unit are heavy (cf. syllables with two or more moras). This light–heavy weight distinction in ASL syllables is supported by Brentari with two functional arguments. First, referring to Supalla's and Newport's (1978) study on ASL noun–verb pairs, she argues that just like only the light syllables in certain spoken languages, e.g., Nootka, so also only the ASL syllables including one weight unit can be reduplicated in order to nominalize them. Second, just like phonologically heavy material in spoken languages, also heavy syllables in ASL tend to occur sentence finally.

Again, in Brentari's framework, Jantunen (2007) has observed that also in FinSL only syllables consisting of one weight unit tend to be inputs of grammatical reduplicative processes, basically the nominalizing reduplication. However, although this tendency in FinSL corresponds to that described by Brentari (and Supalla and Newport) for ASL, Jantunen does not accept it as sufficient evidence to posit a light–heavy weight distinction in FinSL. The main reason for this is that, in FinSL (Rissanen 1998), the nominalizing reduplication is not at all the productive process it has been said to be, for example, in ASL, and therefore it cannot be used as a ground for argumentation (see also Johnston 2001 for Australian Sign Language). The syntactic behaviour of syllables consisting of more than one weight unit has not been researched in FinSL (cf. the tendency of phonologically heavy material to occur sentence finally).

In general, with respect to the views presented about spoken syllable structure, Brentari's view about the structure of signed syllables can be seen to be functionally analogous with Hyman's (1985) moraic view: both associate an increase in syllable weight with an increase in prosodic complexity (cf. section 3.1; see Brentari 1998:79–80). With Hyman, this means an increase in the number of moras (manifested by an increase in the syllable's physical duration). With Brentari, this means an increase in the number of weight units (manifested by an increase in the movement's subcomponents). Another general observation that can be made about

Brentari's view is that it is a model of signed syllable structure that seems to be most supported by syllable-related phonetic research (e.g., Wilbur & Allen 1991, Wilbur & Petersen 1997).

4   Conclusion

We consider that there are syllables in signed language, identified as short dynamic sequences of sign stream containing one sequential phonological movement. Such movements function as sonority peaks of syllables, sonority (cf. perceptual salience) in turn being the most important empirical property defining both spoken and signed syllables. Grammatical evidence (cf. the Minimal Word argument), as well as evidence from sign language acquisition (cf. the Babbling argument), further supports the interpretation of sequential phonological movements as syllables. With regard to the signed syllable's internal structure, there exist almost diametrically opposed opinions. However, regardless of these differences, the syllable, as we have applied the notion in this chapter, must nevertheless be considered an important unit in capturing phonological generalizations in sign languages. A prime example of these is the generalization that limits the phonological length of core lexemes to two syllables.

15

Grammaticalization in sign languages

Sherman Wilcox, Paolo Rossini and Elena Antinoro Pizzuto

1   Background: routes from gesture to language

In this chapter we examine the developmental routes by which gesture is codified into a linguistic system in the context of the natural signed languages of the deaf. We suggest that gestures follow two routes as they codify, and thus that signed languages provide evidence of how material which begins its developmental life external to the conventional linguistic system, as spontaneous or conventional gestures, is codified as language.

The first route begins with a gesture that is not a conventional unit in the linguistic system; these gestures enter signed languages as lexical signs and develop further to grammatical morphemes (Figure 15.1). Previously, linguists working with spoken language data have described grammaticalization, the process by which grammatical morphemes develop out of lexical morphemes (Heine, Claudi & Hünnemeyer 1991b, Hopper & Traugott 1993, Bybee, Perkins & Pagliuca 1994). We claim that the first route is as an extension of the typical grammaticalization process "backwards" in developmental time beyond the linguistic system. It identifies the gestural source of a lexical morpheme. We also claim that codification, which drives grammaticalization in spoken and signed languages (Haiman 1998, Janzen 1999), also drives the development of gesture into language (see also Janzen & Shaffer 2002, Wilcox 2007).

The second route proceeds along quite a different path. In this route, the source gesture is one of several types including the manner of movement of a manual gesture or sign, and various facial, mouth and eye gestures. We claim that this second route follows a path of development from gesture to prosody/intonation to grammatical morphology (Figure 15.2). Notably, the second route bypasses any lexical stage.

In the next sections we present data from American Sign Language (ASL), French Sign Language (LSF), Catalan Sign Language (LSC) and Italian Sign

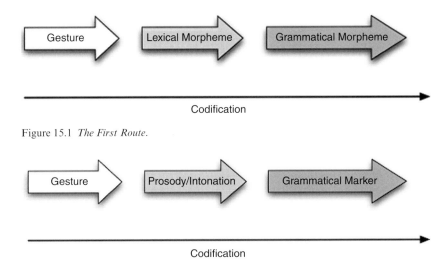

Figure 15.1 *The First Route.*

Figure 15.2 *The Second Route.*

Language (LIS) to describe the characteristics of these two developmental paths. Following that, data from LIS, specifically the LIS modal verb IMPOSSIBLE (*impossibile*) will be examined in detail. We will suggest a possible first route by which this sign, and a cognate sign meaning DEAD/TO DIE (hereafter DEAD), emerged from a commonly used and ancient gesture. We also will examine how this sign exhibits features of the second route developmental path.

In a concluding section, we will suggest that the data presented here lead to three general findings. First, we propose that previous descriptions of grammaticalization need to be revised in light of data from gesture and signed languages. Second, it appears that the strict segregation of linguistic elements into hierarchical levels of analysis, in which prosody is regarded as categorically distinct from morphology, does not hold for signed languages (see also Pierrehumbert & Hirschberg 1990 for a similar suggestion from spoken languages). Finally, we suggest that common cognitive processes and structures underlie the development of both gestural meaning and linguistic function. These processes are metonymy and autonomy/dependency (A/D) relations.

2   Route One: from gesture to lexical morpheme to grammatical morpheme

Previous research (Wilcox 2002, 2004a, 2007) has identified four sources of evidence for the developmental path leading from gesture to lexical morpheme to grammatical morpheme: futures, venitives, markers of obligation, and evidentials and epistemic modals. We will briefly examine only the first two by way of documenting the path of development from gesture to lexical morpheme and then to grammatical morpheme.

Data from a cross-section of the world's spoken languages demonstrate that there are three common sources for future markers: desire, obligation and movement verb constructions (Bybee, Perkins & Pagliuca 1994). Lexical morphemes meaning 'come,' 'go' and 'desire' are the source of grammatical morphemes used to indicate the future in a remarkable number of spoken languages. Using a corpus of historical as well as modern conversational data, Shaffer (2000) and Janzen and Shaffer (2002) have demonstrated that the grammatical morpheme used to mark future in ASL developed from the lexical morpheme 'go.' The gesture also appears in nineteenth-century LSF as the lexical morpheme PARTIR 'depart' (Brouland 1855).

A second set of examples documenting the first route comes from venitives, gestures signaling movement toward speaker. This path begins with a gesture meaning roughly 'come here' identified in De Jorio's (1832/2000) study of Neapolitan gesture as CHIAMARE, 'to call or summon someone': "Fingers extended and then brought towards the palm several times." The 'come here' gesture appears as a lexical item in a number of signed languages, especially those used in the Mediterranean region or historically related to those languages. This form appears in ASL in a variety of senses including requests for physical movement, incitement to action and requests for metaphorical movement such as the transfer of information or ideas. As an example of the latter, a signer might use an ASL lexical sign derived from the 'come here' gesture to request that more information be provided. When a deaf consultant was asked how she became interested in linguistics, she replied, "I took a beginning course and became fascinated with linguistics – I wanted more," where the phrase translated here as "I wanted more" was the two-handed ASL lexical sign COME-HERE. Higgins (1923) gives the form as NECESSITY, which although still lexical is moving toward a more grammatical meaning.

In LSC, the 'come here' form appears as a lexical sign to request physical movement or, more generally, an invitation to join or affiliate with a group. It also appears in a more specific sense as the lexical sign EMERGENCY. In LIS, the form functions to request physical movement; in addition, the 'come here' form is used in LIS to encourage action on the part of the interlocutor. For example, in one recorded LIS conversation, a deaf teacher was asked whether hearing students learning LIS could be forced to sign. She responded that students should be encouraged rather than forced to sign in class. The LIS one-handed COME-HERE form was used to mean 'encourage' (Wilcox, Rossini & Pizzuto 2001).

2.1 Cognitive processes and Route One

Metonymy is the underlying cognitive process that links chains of semantic extensions in a gesture indicating departure, the lexical morpheme expressing physical departure from/movement toward, and the grammatical marker for future. These metonymic extensions are motivated by pragmatic inferences (Traugott & König 1991, Panther & Thornburg 2003) and metaphor (Heine, Claudi & Hünnemeyer 1991b).

Pragmatic inferencing clearly motivates the extension from departure or movement toward a location to future: if one leaves a place toward a second place, he or she will naturally arrive at the second location in the future. The same metonymic extension is at work in the grammaticalization of English *going to* from its physical movement sense, *I am going to Santa Fe* to *going to/gonna* as a future marker, as in *I'm gonna fail this test if I don't study*.

Pragmatic inferencing also motivates the extension from a request for physical movement to the necessity and emergency senses. One reason that one might request that another person come is because he or she is facing an emergency and needs assistance, as in Alexander Graham Bell's famous first use of the telephone, "Doctor Watson, come here, I need you!" The extension from a request for physical movement to a request for information is metaphorically motivated by mapping the movement of physical objects toward the speaker onto metaphorical objects of communication (Reddy 1979). An inferential link motivates the extension to encouragement: one reason a teacher might request a student to perform an activity (e.g., signing in a language class) is because he or she wants to encourage the student.

3 Route Two: from gesture to prosody/intonation to grammatical marker

In order to understand the second route from gesture to language, we must first clarify our meaning of gesture. We work with a definition of gesture that is (a) not limited to movements of the hands but also includes facial gestures such as eye and mouth movements, and (b) regards type of movement and manner of movement – *what* movement is being produced and the *way* in which it is produced – as distinct types of gestures. Thus, we regard a circular movement of the hand, perhaps representing a cranking motion, as one kind of gesture. This gesture, however, may be produced with several different manners of motion – slow, fast, slow and steady, accelerating and decelerating. We regard these and other manners of movement, such as reduplicated linear movements, soft versus tense movement, speed of movement and size of movement, as gestural. For example, while speaking of some mental action that needs to be undertaken, such as thinking through a complex problem, a speaker may use a cranking gesture to refer metaphorically to the process. The gesture will be produced with some manner of movement, which will further modify the meaning of the cranking motion, perhaps signaling that the process is necessarily slow and deliberate. The meaning that these two distinct types of gestures encode is different – *I am **cranking** in a certain way*. As we will see, these distinct functions allow these two gestures to codify along different paths as they enter the linguistic system.

Manner of movement clearly plays a role in gesture. Duncan (2002), for example, has documented the role that manner of movement plays in gestures accompanying the expression of verb aspect in spoken English and Mandarin discourse. As we will describe in the next section, one way in which manner of movement functions in signed languages is as prosody. Although we will not go into detail about the role of eye and mouth movements in gestural production, they also play a significant role in signed languages, functioning both as intonation and as grammatical markers. Similar findings are reported by Parrill (2001) for English discourse.

We propose that when manner of movement enters the linguistic system of signed languages, it first appears not lexically but as prosody and intonation (Wilcox 2007). The use of manner of movement and facial gestures to mark prosody and intonation in signed languages has long been known. Friedman (1977) was one of the first signed language researchers to document the expression of prosody and intonation in signed languages. She observed that signs articulated with emphatic stress are larger, tenser, faster and with longer duration than unstressed signs. Other differences in stressed versus unstressed signs included changes in the manner of production, both in rhythmic characteristics (addition of tension, restraint or faster movement) and in the movement itself.

Wilbur and Schick (1987) noted that in spoken languages, the primary cues for linguistic stress are increased duration, increased intensity and changing the fundamental frequency. Fundamental frequency is a feature of spoken languages without any apparent analog in signed languages. Wilbur and Schick proposed that the correlates of linguistic stress in signed languages are increased duration and increased intensity. They identified markers of increased duration, including larger movement, slower movement, repetition, added movement. The markers of increased intensity included the addition of nonmanuals (for example, eye or mouth gestures); sharp boundaries between signs; higher articulation of signs in the signing space; increased tension of articulation; and more forceful articulation.

Another feature of prosody is prominence. Examining data from Israeli Sign Language, Nespor and Sandler (1999) found that the phonetic correlates of prominence included reduplication, a hold at the end of the prominent sign and a pause after the last word of the phonological phrase. Once again, we find that the phonetic correlates to prosody in signed languages predominantly lie in manner of movement: reduplication, hold (stopping the movement), speed and acceleration. Increased size is also related to movement, since decreasing/increasing the size of a sign typically results in a faster/slower movement, respectively.

Sandler (1999) maintains a distinction between prosody and intonation in signed languages, suggesting that facial articulations may be best understood as fulfilling the role of intonation. She calls these facial articulations "superarticulation" and proposes that the primitives of superarticulations are different positions of the brows, eyes, cheeks, mouth and head.

It is well documented that facial gestures such as eye widening and squinting and mouth movement play a significant role crosslinguistically in signed languages, expressing a variety of grammatical roles such as interrogatives vs. declaratives, topic makers, adverbial markers and more. Studies have also shown that facial and mouth gestures play an important role in LIS with respect to modals and aspectual modifications (Pizzuto 1987/2004).

3.1   Cognitive processes and Route Two

The primary cognitive process operating in Route Two is the autonomy–dependency (A/D) relation. The notion of autonomy–dependency as a conceptual relation was first described by Langacker (1987). A/D asymmetry applies to both phonological and semantic structures. An autonomous structure is one that exists on its own and does not presuppose another structure for its manifestation. For example, in phonological structures, vowels are autonomous relative to consonants. A dependent structure therefore is one which presupposes another for its manifestation. Phonologically, consonants are dependent on vowels. Suprasegmental structures such as intonation patterns are dependent because they require segmental content to serve as their "carrier" (Langacker 1987:308).

When we consider only semantic structures, A/D asymmetry accounts for the conceptual autonomy–dependency of elements in a relation or events and their participants. As Langacker (1991:286) notes, "an event is conceptually dependent vis-à-vis its participants. For instance, one cannot conceptualize an act of slapping without making some kind of mental reference to the entity doing the slapping and the one receiving it."

Conceptually, movement may be seen as an event. In the case of gestures or signs, the hand is a participant in the event of moving. A/D asymmetry applies to a moving hand because the hand is conceptually autonomous while the movement is dependent – it makes reference to *what* is moving. We can also observe an A/D relation solely between movement and its manner of production. What we have called the *type* of movement is autonomous, both conceptually and phonologically, while *manner* of movement is dependent. One cannot produce a *slow* circular movement without producing a circular movement. Thus, producing a *manner* of movement presupposes, both conceptually and articulatorily, some *type* of movement, which in turn presupposes that some *thing* is moving.

As we will see in the following section, this A/D relationship is maintained, both phonologically and conceptually, as items develop from non-linguistic gesture to prosody and then to grammatical markers. We use the term A/D alignment to characterize the observation that semantically autonomous structures are almost always manifest by means of autonomous phonological structures, and vice versa.

A/D asymmetry and A/D alignment are important characteristics of Route Two. When we examine manner of movement and facial gestures as phonologically dependent structures in signed languages, we can then ask what kinds of information they express semantically. The answer is that they predominantly convey conceptually dependent information. Manner of movement is commonly used to express verb aspect; to mark different adjectival predicate forms such as the ASL distinction between *sick*, *sickly* and *prone to being sick* (Klima & Bellugi 1979); and to indicate intensification along various axes, such as color as in the ASL distinction between *blue*, *light blue* and *deep blue*. In the case of color intensity, the movement type, indicating base color, is phonologically autonomous, while manner of movement, indicating intensity, is phonologically dependent. These phonological A/D relations align with the semantics of the signs because intensity is conceptually dependent on base color. We cannot conceptualize "deep" or "light" as color intensities without making mental reference to what the color is.

Although we do not specifically focus on facial gestures in this chapter, we note that they exhibit the same A/D relations and alignments. Mouth gestures, for example, are phonologically dependent structures that mark adverbial modifications to verbs, such as the mouth gestures used in ASL to mark an action as performed "carefully" as opposed to "carelessly" (Baker & Cokely 1980). In LIS, Franchi (1987/2004) and Ajello, Mazzoni and Nicolai (2001) have shown that mouth gestures may mark morphological information specifying values of intensity, modality and action state.

4   Gesture to language in Italian Sign Language

To demonstrate how the two routes operate in the development of signs and grammatical markers in a signed language, we have chosen to examine the LIS sign IMPOSSIBLE(H-fff) 'impossible' (Figure 15.3).[1]

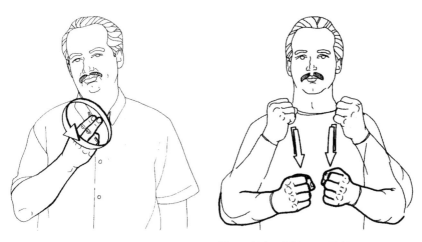

Figure 15.3 *IMPOSSIBLE(H-fff)*.   Figure 15.4 *POSSIBLE(SS)*.

Figure 15.5 *IMPOSSIBLE(SS)*.   Figure 15.6 *POSSIBLE(O)*.

IMPOSSIBLE(H-fff) belongs to a set of modal verbs in LIS described below.

- POSSIBLE(SS): a two-handed sign (both hands using the S-handshape) made in neutral space (Figure 15.4).
- IMPOSSIBLE(SS): negated variant of the above sign (Figure 15.5).
- POSSIBLE(O): one-handed sign, made at mouth (Figure 15.6).
- IMPOSSIBLE(H-pa-pa): either a one- or two-handed (H-handshape) sign, made in neutral space (Figure 15.7).
- POSSIBLE(F): an F-handshape sign made in neutral space (Figure 15.8)

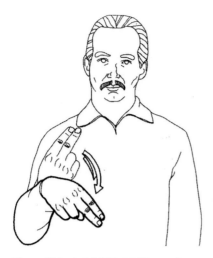

Figure 15.8 *POSSIBLE(F)*.

Figure 15.7 *IMPOSSIBLE(H-pa-pa)*.

From our analysis and consultations with native signers of LIS, both hearing and deaf, it appears to us that POSSIBLE(SS) and IMPOSSIBLE(SS) are considered more formal signs. Some consultants felt that POSSIBLE(O) and IMPOSSIBLE(H-fff) would not be appropriate for use in formal settings such as TV interpreting. In addition, contrary to previous reports, we found that IMPOSSIBLE(H-fff) is not an idiomatic expression but appears to function as a normal modal form. Register does not appear to be the only variable governing the use of these modal forms; rather, they encode semantic information concerning type of modality, such as physical ability vs. root possibility and degree of subjectivity, etc. A brief summary of the semantics of these modal forms follows.

4.1   POSSIBLE(O), POSSIBLE(F) and POSSIBLE(SS)

Both POSSIBLE(O) and POSSIBLE(F) appear to refer to the agent's ability to carry out the main verb action, but POSSIBLE(O) is more frequent in discourse and exhibits more features of modal verbs, while POSSIBLE(F) behaves more as an adjectival predicate meaning 'being capable.'

POSSIBLE(SS) functions more as a root modal referring to general enabling conditions. POSSIBLE(O) appears to be most commonly used when it is not known whether the agent has the required skill/ability to perform some action, and what is requested is whether he or she is physically or mentally capable of doing something. For example, if a person uses POSSIBLE(O) to ask a friend if he could repair a broken car, the sense is that this questions the person's knowledge or skill to carry out the repair.

(1)   CAR BROKE, FIX, POSSIBLE(O) YOU?
       'Are you capable of repairing the car?'

POSSIBLE(O) apparently cannot be used, or it would be inappropriate or impolite to use it, if the question is addressed to a competent mechanic, one who is assumed to have the required knowledge and skill. In this case, POSSIBLE(SS) would be used to question whether general conditions (e.g., time, parts availability) would allow for the repair to be made; it presumes that the agent has the capability.

(2)   CAR BROKE, FIX POSSIBLE(SS)
       'My car is broken, is a repair possible?'

The negative IMPOSSIBLE(SS) also appears to code root modality and perhaps epistemic modality. For example, in a conversation one person might say that he or she spent the weekend at the beach. An interlocutor might respond that she was there too. Not having seen her the entire time, the first person might reply, "You were at the beach too? That's impossible!" The implication is, if you were there, I would have seen you.

4.2   IMPOSSIBLE(H-pa-pa) and IMPOSSIBLE(H-fff)

IMPOSSIBLE(H-pa-pa) appears to refer to impossibility due to circumstantial inability, having little or no sense of reference to the agent's capability. IMPOSSIBLE(H-fff) expresses the signer's subjective judgment on the impossibility of the event/action ever taking place. For example, if a person were trying to send a fax and the transmission repeatedly failed, he or she might describe this using the IMPOSSIBLE(H-pa-pa) form, indicating that something is wrong with this fax machine. After numerous failed attempts, the person might switch to IMPOSSIBLE(H-fff), expressing his or her subjective evaluation that this attempt will ever succeed.

(3)   SEND-FAX IMPOSSIBLE(H-pa-pa), SEND-FAX
       IMPOSSIBLE(H-pa-pa), IMPOSSIBLE(H-fff)

5   Route One: gestural source of IMPOSSIBLE(H-fff)

We propose that gestures in common use in the local society often enter the linguistic system of signed languages as lexical signs. In this section we attempt to identify the source gesture for IMPOSSIBLE(H-fff) and track its use and semantic development prior to its entry into LIS.

5.1   From speaking to benediction

The gestural source of IMPOSSIBLE(H-fff) is perceived by LIS signers to be the benediction gesture, which is the sign of the cross made in neutral space. The gesture is commonly made either with a full hand (B-handshape) or a two- or three-finger form (H- and 3-handshapes). The *New Catholic Encyclopedia* (2003:382) summarizes the history of the H-handshape form of the benediction gesture:

> In the East the practice of making the sign of the cross with two or three fingers was introduced in the sixth century to combat the Monophysites. In this case the emphasis was on number – the numbers signifying the two natures of Christ or the Trinity, etc. The custom passed over into the West and in the ninth century we find a synod directing the priest to make the sign of the cross with the thumb and two fingers over the oblation at Mass. This gesture remains to this day in the Eastern rites and also in the papal rite of blessing.

Barasch (1987) suggests that the source of the benediction gesture lies in an ancient Roman oratorical gesture used to identify the speaking person. Reviewing Barasch's work on the Italian painter Giotto, Ladis (1992:160) concurs: "What Barasch calls 'the speaking hand,' a group of gestures that accompany and indicate speech, is thus profitably considered against the background of Roman oratory and Christian gestures of benediction."

According to Aldrete (1999:63), this Roman gesture also appears throughout the Illustrated Terence Manuscripts (ninth to twelfth centuries AD): "Overall, the most common gesture in the panels consists of the right arm being outstretched with the index and middle fingers extended and held together, while the thumb and other fingers are curled into the palm." Aldrete concludes that the gesture occurs so frequently in the panels that no one meaning can be discerned, suggesting that it "may have been used to add emphasis to narration or argument" (p. 63).[2]

Gombrich (1966) also offers an extensive discussion of this gesture in his essay on ritualized gesture and expression in art. He states that the two outstretched fingers conventionally accompany the swearing of an oath in Central Europe (Gombrich 1966:393) and notes the resemblance to the "Christian gesture of blessing" (p. 394). According to Gombrich, the gesture "originally signified neither blessing nor oath" but accompanied any "more solemn spoken announcement" (p. 394). Like Barasch, Gombrich attributes its meaning in medieval narrative art as a 'speaking gesture.'

Gombrich also attributes a more abstract meaning to this gesture. In describing an Ottonian miniature depicting Christ explaining to St. Peter the ritual of washing the feet, Gombrich suggests that the scene is meant to illustrate the account in the Gospel of St. John (13:8, 9): "Peter saith unto him, Thou shalt never wash my feet. Jesus answered him, if I wash thee not, thou hast no part with me." In the scene, Christ makes the two-finger benediction gesture, which Gombrich (1966:394) suggests is a "gesture of unambiguous non-action."

We suggest that there is a metonymic link between the secular Roman speaking gesture and the liturgical benediction gesture: they both mark speech acts. Evidence for this metonymic link can be seen in Giotto's *St. Francis Preaching to the Birds.* In this painting from the Upper Church in Assisi, Italy, dating from 1295–1300, St. Francis is depicted standing before a flock of birds on the ground. He is bent slightly at the waist as he preaches to the birds. As he speaks, he simultaneously makes the benediction gesture with his right arm.

Finally, we note that this gesture continues in contemporary use. Gombrich again provides a telling example from a 1924 poster by Käthe Kollwitz (Figure 15.9) in which a young anti-war protestor produces the gesture with his

Figure 15.9 *Käthe Kollwitz "Nie wieder Kreig!"*

fully extended right arm. The accompanying text declares "Nie wieder Krieg," "No More War" (literally "Never again war").

5.2   From benediction to death

The next link in the chain of gestural meaning leads from the benediction gesture to death. Again, this link is motivated by a natural metonymic contiguity, since the blessing spoken over a dead person is commonly accompanied by the benediction gesture. We do not know when this use of the benediction gesture to mark death first appeared in liturgical settings, but we do have evidence that by the early nineteenth century the gesture was commonly associated with death. De Jorio (1832/2000:281–83) describes a gesture he calls "Morte (Death)":

> The sign of the cross is made in the air with an extended hand. This gesture, which is also frequently done with just the index and middle fingers extended, can be used to mean physical death, but it can also refer to moral or political death, since it can be said of someone that he ceases to exist, as far as society is concerned or so far as the estimation of others is concerned. In this case, the meaning of the gesture changes, not so much according to the facial expression that accompanies it, as it does according to what the interlocutors take the topic of the discourse to be. In fact, if the benediction is accompanied by a dejected and pained facial expression, and one deals with someone who is gravely ill, physical death will be understood. If the person being talked about is someone who enjoys great favor or who has a very showy job, it will be understood that he no longer enjoys either the one or the other.

The metaphorical extension from physical to moral or political death sanctions a further metonymic link to a meaning of hopelessness and despair (de Jorio 1832/2000:283):

> *Lost hope, despairing of one's business.* It is the same as saying "I am lost, it is finished." Accordingly, if the good outcome of some activity is under discussion, and someone wishes to say that it is finished, that there is no more hope, it will be sufficient to make a cross in the air, either with the hand or with only two fingers.

It is worth noting that the two-finger gesture drawing a cross in the air and glossed as 'dead' is still widely used across Italy by hearing speakers (Poggi

2007:123), with the same metaphorical extensions noted by De Jorio. More interestingly for the present discussion, Southern Italians (e.g., Neapolitans and Sicilians) also use a variant of this gesture with the same meaning, characterized by a single, continuous circular movement (Oliveri 2000:85). Precisely this variant of the gesture has also been incorporated into LIS to mean DEAD (see Radutzky 1992, and 5.4 below). LIS signers are clearly aware of the links relating this sign, the sign IMPOSSIBLE(H-fff), and both the benediction and the "dead" gestures.

Also, there is a colloquial sign in LIS made by extending the arm horizontally in front of the torso with either the B-handshape or H-handshape, and making the sign of the cross. Regarded by deaf people as "the Pope's blessing," this sign has a complex meaning. It is used in a situation where the signer wishes to state that some person is on their own, that the signer wishes nothing further to do with this person. For example, if the signer has often helped this person in the past and has received no thanks, or even has been insulted by this person, the signer will make this sign to indicate 'I don't want any more to do with this person, he's on his own.' We might well imagine translating this sign as 'He's dead to me.'

5.3   From death to impossibility

We propose that the conceptual domain common to both death and despair is *absence of future potential*. Death, whether real or metaphorical, precludes any possible or potential future from coming into existence. This, in turn, leads to hopelessness and despair. We also suggest that this conceptual domain forms the semantic basis for the constructs of grammatical modality under discussion here.

We start by noting that death, hopelessness and despair are already in the semantic domain of modal notions. Givón (1984:321) points out that epistemic verbs include such notions as probability, possibility, uncertainty, doubt, hope and fear. This connection is easily demonstrated in a pair of sentences. If a sportscaster were talking about the last minutes of a soccer match in which Manchester United is down a goal with only a few seconds to play, but otherwise they have been strong and now have the ball, (4) might be used. If Manchester had been playing very poorly up to this point and had lost control of the ball, the sportscaster might use (5) to express his subjective judgment that victory is impossible.

(4)   It's still possible for Manchester to pull out a victory.

(5)   There's no hope for a victory now.

For a more fine-tuned analysis of the conceptual domain underlying grammatical modality, we turn to cognitive grammar (Langacker 1991). In presenting a model for the conceptual basis of modality, Langacker (1991:272) notes that lexical items often evolve into grammatical items, and that this process accounts for the rise of modal forms out of main or content verbs as well. We will not provide a full description of the model proposed by Langacker; instead, we point out relevant points of contact with our suggestion that the conceptual domain which subsumes the gestural meanings described so far, as well as the modal meaning of 'impossible,' is absence of future potential.

First, modal verbs as a class evoke the conception of some associated activity encoded in the main verb. "One does not want, know how, or have a physical capacity in the abstract – rather, one wants, knows how, or has the capacity *to do something*" (Langacker 1991:269).[3] Second, the subject of the modal verb is "the locus of some kind of **potency**" directed at the main verb (p. 270). This is clearly seen in the English expression *I can lift 100 pounds*.[4] Finally, the potency indicated by the modal verb is *potential* rather than *actual*. *I can lift 100 pounds* does not entail that *I am lifting 100 pounds*; rather, it only implies that the circumstances exist, in this case, my physical ability, to permit an act of lifting to take place (at some point in the future).

Potency plays a significant role in distinguishing root and epistemic modals. A modal is regarded as epistemic "when its sole import is to indicate the likelihood of the designated process" (Langacker 1991:272); that is, epistemic modals encode the speaker's judgment about whether the process will come to reality (in the future). In root modals, the potency is fairly salient and well defined, and it is directed toward the realization of the process, i.e., some notion of obligation, permission, desire or ability (Langacker 1991:270). In epistemic modals, on the other hand, potency is maximally vague and not associated with any person or specifiable fact of the world. Often, however, this distinction is ambiguous and tentative, suggesting that the critical distinction is strength of potency and not its specific source. As Langacker (p. 272) notes, the historical evolution of modals from main verbs through root modals to epistemic modals is probably best understood "as a matter of the locus of potency becoming progressively less salient and well-defined."

What emerges is a view of modals in which a core concept is "the likelihood of reality evolving in a certain way" (Langacker 1991:274), whether the potency that drives reality forward is a person's mental or physical ability, general conditions, the force of authority, or the speaker's subjective assessment of the likelihood of reality evolving in some particular way. This view of modality is captured by Langacker in a *dynamic evolutionary model* (Figure 15.10). In this idealized

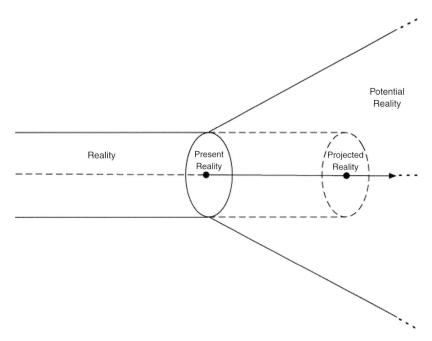

Figure 15.10 *Dynamic Evolutionary Model.*

cognitive model, reality is conceived as moving forward along a temporal axis, from the present reality into some projected future reality.

5.4   Grammaticalization in LIS: from death to impossibility

We have traced the metonymic links that lead from a Roman gesture marking the act of speaking to a particular type of speech act, that of benediction, and further to a particular type of benediction, the blessing made for one's death. We also saw that death is metonymically linked to hopelessness and despair. Finally, we have provided support for connecting the semantic domain of death, hopelessness and despair, or more generally absence of future potential, with grammatical modality through an idealized cognitive model that captures our conception of present reality evolving into a projected future reality, one of several potential future realities. Death, by eliminating the hope of any potential future reality, embodies the modal notion of epistemic impossibility.

We are now ready to explore the manifestation of these notions in LIS. If grammaticalization is taking place, we would expect to find a lexical sign, such as one meaning 'death,' developing grammatical meaning such as the

Figure 15.11 *DEAD*.

modal notion 'impossible.' The LIS sign DEAD is clearly phonologically related to IMPOSSIBLE(H-fff). Grammaticalization is characterized by phonetic reduction and semantic generalization (Bybee, Perkins & Pagliuca 1994:6). The semantic generalization from *death* to epistemic impossibility is the type of change one would expect to see in grammaticalization. The change in form between the benediction gesture and DEAD, that is, from the two movements required to make the sign of the cross to the single circular movement required for DEAD, can be characterized as phonetic reduction.

The same change in form is also found in the gesture for 'dead' commonly used by hearing Italian Southerners (see Oliveri 2000:85). Further research is needed to clarify the historical links between this gesture and the benediction gesture, and the areal distribution of both such gestures. However, these observations suggest that gestures may undergo somewhat comparable processes of changes in form and meaning, irrespective of whether they become integrated into a linguistic system such as LIS.

It is also of interest to note the following. First, as remarked by Ajello, Mazzoni and Nikolai (2001:241), facial and mouth gestures play a key role in marking the morphological difference between the two LIS signs described here. DEAD is produced with a neutral expression, optionally accompanied by a mouthing of the Italian word for 'dead.' IMPOSSIBLE(H-fff) obligatorily includes its distinctive mouth gesture, along with a negative headshake and an optional puffed cheek(s) facial gesture. Independent evidence of the distinctive role of facial and mouth gestures in encoding modal information in LIS also comes from recent work by Di Renzo (2006) who describe pairs of signs identical with respect to their manual components, but in which the difference between a form encoding modal information versus a neutral form is conveyed via mouth gestures. All these observations point out the need for exploring further the morphological role of facial gestures.

Second, we must note that the semantic generalization linking death to radical impossibility is rooted in Italian culture at large, suggesting a common cultural-cognitive construct that surfaces in different ways in the gestural and linguistic systems of LIS signers and Italian speakers. In fact, Italian possesses a widely used idiomatic expression, *manco morto* (or the equivalent, slightly more formal *neanche morto*) which, translated literally, means 'not even dead.' Speakers frequently use this expression, which is attested in written texts since at least the nineteenth century, to mean that it would be radically impossible or unlikely that they would perform a given action or make a given choice. An appropriate exploration of the historical roots and semantics of this expression remains to be done. However, its existence highlights the same conceptual, metonymic link which, in LIS, relates the signs DEAD and IMPOSSIBLE(H-fff). It is also revealing that, in Italian-to-LIS interpreting, both the Italian form for 'impossible' and for *manco morto* can be rendered with the IMPOSSIBLE(H-fff) LIS form (Franchi, personal communication, January 7, 2008).

6   Route Two: manner of movement in gesture and language

Gombrich (1966) draws an insightful distinction between symptom and symbol in examining ritualized gesture in art. We saw in section 5.1 how Gombrich analyzed the oath/benediction gesture. Gombrich classifies such conventional gestures as *symbols*. Turning again to the Kollwitz poster, Gombrich characterizes the young man's heightened muscle tone, rigid posture, raised head and forward thrust of the chin, and bristling hair as *symptoms* of the emotion that accompanies mass enthu-siasm. Symptoms are visible signs of emotion, while symbols are conventional gestures.

As useful as this distinction is, Gombrich (1966:393) acknowledges that it is an abstraction because "the symbolic ritual of oath taking is charged with all the symptoms of the emotion both in the way the upraised arm is tautened and the way it is drawn with emphatic strokes." Because of the articulatory A/D asymmetry that characterizes a movement and its manner of production, gestures necessarily embody both symbol and symptom. Symbol is suffused with symptom through the *way the gesture is made*, its manner of movement.

6.1   Manner of movement in gestural expression

Manner of movement has been recognized as an important and meaningful aspect of gesture since Roman times. According to Aldrete (1999:36–37), Quintilian taught that "by altering the speed with which a gesture was made and its range of motion, the same gesture could have multiple meanings or purposes" and that "this strategy of modulating the speed of gesture in order to express slightly different meanings was used to give versatility of denotation to several basic gestures."

From the earliest times, gesture was explicitly linked to the expression of emotion. In Roman oratorical tradition this was manifest in the concept of delivery. Delivery was defined by the Romans as having two components, voice tone and gesture. The ultimate goal of Roman oratory was to persuade an audience, "and in order to do this, it was vital to incite the emotions of the audience in a way favorable to the speaker's cause. ... Certain gestures were associated with various emotions so that as an orator spoke, his body offered a separate and continuous commentary on what emotions the words were intended to provoke" (Aldrete 1999:6).

6.2   Manner of movement: from gesture to prosody

The expression of emotion through gesture can be tied to the vocal expression of emotion by means of prosody and intonation. Bolinger (1986:195) held that intonation is historically linked with gesture, claiming that "intonation is part of a gestural complex whose primitive and still surviving function is the signaling of emotion." Intonation and gesture, according to Bolinger, are biological adaptations that allow us to read the visible and audible signals that are symptomatic of emotion.

Fónagy (1983:337) suggested that intonation plays a transitional role because it is "inherently dual, Janus-faced, a sign half-way between nonverbal and verbal communication." The linking of gesture and its manner of production to prosody and intonation suggests that manner of movement might also play a transitional role in signed language between the gestural, emotive, non-grammatical expression characteristic of prosody and intonation and its function in grammaticalized forms.

We identified A/D asymmetry as an important conceptual component underlying development in Route Two, and we also see evidence of A/D asymmetry in the interplay of gesture, manner of movement and gestures that co-occur with speech. This is manifest in two ways. First, bodily gestures that accompany oratory modulate or modify the meanings of spoken words; as Aldrete says, they provide a "separate and continuous commentary" on the meanings that the words provoke. In cognitive grammar terms, the spoken words are autonomous, while the accompanying gestures are dependent; the words form the content while the gestures modulate and change the tone of the meaning.

Second, and more importantly for our study, when gesture is considered on its own, the way a gesture is made, its manner of movement, modulates the meaning of the gesture. As Quintilian pointed out, the same gesture produced with a different speed or range of motion has different meanings. Again, we can discern A/D asymmetry and alignment. The gesture itself and its meaning are autonomous, while its manner of production and the way in which its production modifies the meaning of the gesture are dependent. Naturally, every utterance must be pronounced in a certain way, and thus always requires a manner of production; distinctions are indicated by manner of production that is "marked" in some way.

We noted in section 3 that when manner of movement enters the linguistic system of signed languages, it first appears as prosody. We also learned that prosody is commonly used to mark phonetic stress.

An example of the discourse use of stress marked by dynamic changes to the movement of the sign comes from the LIS corpus we collected in Rome (Wilcox *et al.*, 2000, Pizzuto & Wilcox 2001, Wilcox, Rossini & Pizzuto 2001). In a the following dialog between two native LIS signers discussing the possibility/impossibility of a given event, we found five different tokens of the same sign IMPOSSIBLE(H-fff), four of which were produced by the same signer. Four of these corresponded to a more neutral form of the sign, while the fifth was a markedly stronger, intensified form: the forearm was further extended from the body, the hand higher in the signing space, with the circular movement becoming tighter and faster, while a distinct facial marker was used in which only the signer's right cheek was puffed, the facial muscles involved visibly more tense than in the neutral form. In contrast, the other signer's single token of IMPOSSIBLE(H-fff) was articulated with a markedly softer movement (see Wilcox 2007:120–121 for more details).

P asks R what time the train that she will take in the evening to get back to Palermo, her home town, will arrive there. R replies that it will be around 7:00 or 8:00 a.m. P then questions R whether she thinks it would be possible to arrive at an earlier time, for example around 6:00 a.m. R replies that it would be impossible. P repeats her statement, then R further comments that arriving at 6:00 would be highly desirable, but in any case the train she will take is never on time, so it is really impossible to arrive earlier. P asks again whether there really is no chance that it might arrive earlier, and R restates two more times that this is simply impossible.

P: TRAIN YOU ARRIVE, YES, WHAT-TIME?
R: MORNING, AT-SEVEN AT-EIGHT [doubtful] ABOUT
P: EARLIER, AT-SIX, POSSIBLE?
R: IMPOSSIBLE(H-fff)
P: IMPOSSIBLE(H-fff)
R: AT-SIX, EARLIER, IF-ONLY! TRAIN NEVER ON-TIME
    (…) IMPOSSIBLE(H-fff)
P: EARLIER IMPOSSIBLE(Hpa-pa) [phatic 'ah, I see'] YES
R: IMPOSSIBLE(H-fff)
P: [phatic 'ah, I see']
R: IMPOSSIBLE(H-fff)

In this example, IMPOSSIBLE(H-fff) is produced four times by R and one time by P, each with a distinct marking of phonetic stress. The five tokens of IMPOSSIBLE(H-fff) in the example above vary with respect to several manner of movement features. In R's production, the first three instances of the neutral pronunciation are followed by a markedly stronger, intensified form: the forearm is further extended from the body, the hand higher in the signing space, the circular movement becomes tighter and faster, and a distinct facial marker is used in which only the signer's right cheek is puffed, the facial muscles involved visibly more tense than in the neutral form. In contrast, P's single token of IMPOSSIBLE(H-fff) is articulated with a markedly softer movement.

These five different productions of IMPOSSIBLE(H-fff) do not represent selections from a closed class. Rather, they are better described as different ways of expressively indicating various degrees of speaker commitment to the impossibility, more analogous to prosodic stress differences than to morphological alternations. When an interpreter who is a native user of LIS translated this conversation into spoken Italian, she rendered these instances of IMPOSSIBLE(H-fff) not with different lexical items or phrases, but with the single spoken Italian word *impossibile* pronounced with different prosodic contours.

As suggested in Wilcox (2007), we propose that this example illustrates the entry of manner of movement as a gestural quality into the linguistic system as prosodic stress. At this stage, while manner of movement marks meaningful differences in the carrier or root sign, it does not yet do so in the more codified or patterned way characteristic of grammatical markers.

6.3   Verb aspect: the grammaticalizaton of prosody

Klima and Bellugi (1979) have described alternations in the manner of movement of certain ASL signs which they claim mark verb aspect. Klima and Bellugi call these alternations inflectional morphology, implying that they are highly codified grammatical forms. Indeed, some of the aspectual categories they describe do appear to be quite productive. This would suggest that the grammaticalization of prosody results in grammatical markers expressed by manner of movement (Wilcox 2005).

Recent research, however, suggests that the situation is not so simple. In a study of verb aspect in ASL, Maroney (2004) found no evidence that aspectual categories are inflectional. None of the markers were obligatory to the degree required by inflectional morphology, and productivity was restricted to a small set of specific verb types. In Maroney's data, taken from a range of conversational sources, ASL users expressed aspectual meaning primarily by means of lexical and periphrastic expression, reduplication, movement modifications and nonmanual markers. The only category that approached high productivity was reduplication used to express iterative, continuative and habitual meaning.

Thus, while verb aspect appears to be one possible endpoint of the second route, development is by no means uniform across verb forms and in very few cases has it reached the regularity and obligatoriness characteristic of inflectional morphology. Nevertheless, we suggest that this does constitute evidence in favor of the proposal that aspects of gestural production manifest by manner of movement appear in signed languages as prosody and then begin a process of codification, the end result of which, when applied to verbs, is the grammatical marking of verb aspect.

Evidence for the grammaticalization of prosody as verb aspect also comes from data on LIS. Pizzuto (1987/2004) made some early observations on temporal aspect, saying that aside from marking temporal aspect lexically (with adverbial signs), it can be expressed in LIS via systematic alterations of the verb's movement pattern, specifying for example the "suddenness" of an action by means of a tense, fast, short movement (e.g., the distinction between 'to meet' and 'to suddenly/unexpectedly meet' someone). Conversely, a verb produced using an elongated, elliptical, large and slow movement specifies that an action is repeated over and over in time or takes place repeatedly in time (e.g., *to constantly telephone* or *to always be on the telephone* compared to an unmarked reading *to telephone*). Early observations by Franchi (1987/2004) and subsequent work by Ajello, Mazzoni and Nikolai (2001) also highlight the crucial relevance of facial gestures in marking temporal aspect.

7   Conclusions

In this chapter we have examined the development of gesture to language following the two routes previously proposed by Wilcox (2004, 2007, 2000). Specifically, we have focused on one LIS modal verb, IMPOSSIBLE(H-fff), and proposed that its gestural source can be traced to an ancient Roman oratorical gesture, which later became associated with the liturgical benediction gesture. We also demonstrated how IMPOSSIBLE(H-fff) incorporates features of the second route, by which manner of movement marks emotional modulation of the base gesture. We suggest that when manner of movement is incorporated into signed languages it enters as prosody, which can then codify into grammatical markers.

Three general findings emerge from this study. First, we suggest that the characterization of grammaticalization as described by linguists who have examined only spoken languages needs to be revised. Grammaticalization is generally regarded as a process by which "grammatical morphemes develop gradually out of lexical morphemes or combinations of lexical morphemes with lexical or grammatical morphemes" (Bybee, Perkins & Pagliuca 1994:4). The data presented here suggest that, for signed languages at least, the path to grammatical morphemes need not necessarily pass through a lexical stage or involve lexical morphemes. As we have seen, in Route Two grammatical markers develop directly out of paralinguistic prosodic contours. Although we did not focus on facial gestures in this chapter, they too are commonly regarded by signed linguists as paralinguistic, and here too we see the rise of grammatical markers directly from paralinguistic material.

Second, our findings suggest that a strict hierarchical segregation of linguistic elements into distinct levels of analysis, in which prosody is regarded as distinct from lexical and morphological, does not hold for signed languages. In Route Two, prosody and intonation are transformed into morphological markers. Sometimes these markers seem to straddle the border between the paralinguistic and the linguistic. For example, it is difficult to say definitively whether the facial gesture of raised eyebrows and wide-open eye aperture accompanying the ASL question, "You voted for Bush?!" serves purely as a grammatical marker of the polar question or prosody, a symptomatic cue to the signer's surprise. More likely, it is intermediate, functioning as both. At other times these markers are clearly on the way to becoming obligatory, as we propose is the case for certain verb aspect markers.

Finally, we have demonstrated that the same cognitive processes that account for gestural paths of development – codification through ritualization, metonymy and A/D relations – are also at work in the linguistic development of signed languages. There has been much debate in the literature about whether signers gesture and whether gesture and language share the same or different neural systems. Our findings suggest that even if gesture and language turn out to be controlled by distinct neural systems, the same cognitive and cultural processes underlie both and account for the development of gesture to language.

16

The semantics–phonology interface

Ronnie B. Wilbur

1   Introduction

The analysis in this chapter addresses the question of why sign languages look more similar to each other than spoken languages do. It is generally recognized that this has something to do with the "form–meaning mapping," but previous attempts at addressing this question have been limited in their scope. It will be necessary to take a fresh look at "form" and "meaning" so that the relationship between them can be carefully described without confusion in the uses of words like "path" and "event." Additionally, special attention will be paid to the various linguistic levels, notably "morpheme," "lexical item," "verb phrase," and "clause," in order to be clear about the claims. The model presented has been tested most extensively on American Sign Language (ASL) and Austrian Sign Language (ÖGS) (Wilbur 2003, 2005, 2008; Schalber 2004, 2006; Schalber & Grose 2006; Grose, Wilbur & Schalber 2007; Grose 2008).

Traditionally, the relationship between semantics (meaning) and phonology (form) has been taken as an arbitrary mapping into morphemes stored in the lexicon and learned individually during the acquisition process. Such arbitrariness has been considered a defining characteristic of "true" language (Saussure 1916, Hockett 1960). Onomatopoetic words have been considered to be the only exceptions to the arbitrariness requirement. Gasser (2004, Gasser, Sethuraman & Hockema 2005) argues from experimental data that "arbitrariness makes sense" to help keep large numbers of form–meaning associations separate by treating them as categories. In contrast, he concludes that iconicity makes sense with relatively small vocabularies when semantic boundaries between words are not crucial.

What has generally been ignored is that the relationship between semantics and phonology in spoken languages is arbitrary not because arbitrariness is special to "language" but because spoken languages *cannot* easily represent meaning with their phonologies. Goldin-Meadow (2008) argues that sign languages are equally good at segmentation/combination of elements and at expressing imagery. As spoken languages developed evolutionarily, arbitrary segmentation/combination characteristics were a good fit, whereas the expression of imagery remained with the use of gesture. Jackendoff (2008) speculates that direct phonology–semantics correspondences may have been an evolutionary step (a proto-lexicon) prior to the emergence of syntactic structure.

Sign language linguists have gone through attitudinal stages with respect to iconicity: it's not there; it's there but not relevant; it's there but constrained; it's everything and there's nothing else (cf., for example, Wilbur 1990, Stokoe 1991, P. Wilcox 2004; S. Wilcox 2004b). Spoken language linguists have also changed their attitudes about iconicity from "it's not there" to "it's there" (Haiman 1985) to "it's everywhere" (Allott 2000). Thus, it is not a complete surprise that a recent article (Bohnemeyer *et al.* 2007) provides an analysis of motion events in spoken language in spatial terms that translate directly into a model of event structure that I and my colleagues have been developing over the last few years primarily, but not exclusively, based on sign languages.

I present a brief description of the theoretical model for event structure, then available resources for "form" and finally "the form–meaning mapping." The explanatory story ends with a consideration of constraints on form–meaning mappings, at which point it will be clear that sign languages look more similar to each other than spoken languages do because when they obey universal constraints, they all use the same forms. I have formulated this claim as the Event Visibility Hypothesis (Wilbur 2003):

> *Event Visibility Hypothesis (EVH)*: In the predicate system, the semantics of event structure is visible in the phonological form of the predicate sign.

That is, predicate signs contain morphemes that reflect the event structure they represent and have regular phonological forms by which they are recognized. These morphemes illustrate the semantics–phonology interface and lexicon in a parallel architecture grammar (Jackendoff 2002, 2008).

2   Theoretical model

For our purposes here, we focus on meanings that are generally conveyed in English by verbs (*eat*, *break*, *go*) and prepositions/particles (*up*, *into*, *to*). Sometimes, a combination (e.g., *eat up*) carries different information from the verb alone (*eat*), and sometimes it does not. Compare (1a) and (1b).

(1) a. She climbed the ladder.
     b. She climbed up the ladder.
     c. She climbed the ladder to the roof, and climbed down again.

There appears to be little or no difference between *climb* and *climb up*, and both can be contrasted with *climb down*, as in (1c). The examples in (1) fall into the domain of "motion events." Both (1a) and (1b) describe a single event, the movement of the Figure (*she*) along a path with respect to a Ground (*ladder*) (Talmy 1991). The internal structure of this single event will be elaborated further below. What concerns us here is the question of how many events there are in (1c), which could be analyzed as a sequence of two events, or as a single "larger" event. It is this larger event that we will discuss further.

2.1   Macro-events and the role of time

When does a sequence of single events constitute a single macro-event? Traditional approaches have used syntactic and/or intonational bases for making this decision. Note that (1c) has two syntactic clauses, with "clause" defined as "having its own verb"; this analysis is supported by the intonational pattern. However, compare with (2).

(2) She climbed up and down the ladder.

Clearly (2) means the same as (1c), but its syntax contains one clause. Does (2) have one event or two? We want the answer to reflect the "event structure" and not the syntax or intonation.

Typologists have observed that languages fall into three categories with respect to how they segment motion events into clauses (Bohnemeyer *et al.* 2007). Type I languages permit the source of a motion event ("from X"), the goal of the event ("to Y") and the passing of an intermediate ground ("across Z", "by way of Z") all in a single clause (3a).[1] Type II languages permit source and goal together but require some types of passing events to be in separate clauses (3b). Type III languages require each location change with respect to each ground to be expressed separately (3c).

(3) a. Floyd went from Nijmegen across the river to Elst.
     b. Floyd went from Nijmegen to Elst, crossing the river.
     c. Floyd left Nijmegen, crossed the river, and arrived in Elst.

Bohnemeyer *et al.* (2007) introduce the notion of the macro-event property (MEP), which assesses how tightly "packaged" the sub-events are with respect to syntax.[2]

The event in (3a) is more tightly packaged than in (3b), which in turn is more tightly packaged than in (3c). Note that all three packagings are possible in English; it is the fact that (3a) is possible that puts English in Type I. If we count events, how many are in (3a), (3b) and (3c)? An expression has the MEP if temporal operators, such as time adverbials, temporal clauses and tenses, which "locate a subevent entailed by the time expression also locate all other subevents in time (p. 505)." While all the sentences in (3) have this property conceptually, only (3a) has this property linguistically (4a). Both (3b) and (3c), and their counterparts in (4), contain sequences of sub-events, each of which can have its own temporal anchor.

(4) a. *Floyd went from Nijmegen at seven across the river at eight to Elst at nine.
     b. Floyd went from Nijmegen at seven to Elst at nine, crossing the river at eight.
     c. Floyd left Nijmegen at nine, crossed the river at noon, and will arrive in Elst in an hour.

For our purposes then, *time* is a critical determinant with respect to event structure as coded in the linguistic expression. Conceptually, leaving one location, passing another and arriving at a third can be part of one large unit of movement – a path with a starting and ending point and an intermediate ground. Linguistically, if the expression contains different indicators of time (tense, time adverbials) for sub-events, the expression does not have the MEP – the sub-events cannot be counted as one unit, i.e., the "macro-event," only as separate sequential events.

It has long been known that this restriction is not limited to motion events. Fodor (1970:432) offers examples like (5) to argue against Lakoff's (1965) analysis of *kill* as derived from *cause to die*.

(5) a. Floyd caused the glass to melt on Sunday by heating it on Saturday.
     b. *Floyd melted the glass on Sunday by heating it on Saturday.

Fodor argues that verbs like *melt* are "intrinsically constrained with respect to their time adverbs" whereas verbs like *cause* are not (p. 433). He demonstrates that *melt* is not alone (6).

(6) a. John caused Bill to die on Sunday by stabbing him on Saturday.
     b. *John killed Bill on Sunday by stabbing him on Saturday.

Thus we see that the construal of events as separate or as part of a larger one is related to the way the information is coded linguistically, and that one can count "events" in the surface form but not necessarily in their cognitive conceptualization.

Bohnemeyer *et al.* (2007:527) observe that sentences like (3a–c) all reflect that "the time course of the event maps directly onto a single contiguous path connecting the three grounds in the order source-route-goal." They tentatively conclude that this results from a single underlying Conceptual Structure (CS) for all three being mapped onto different syntactic structures, rather than reflecting different CS structures for each sentence. The surface form itself is influenced by the language typology and contextual focus. With respect to this latter factor, note that all three sentences in (3) are grammatical in English, so it is not language typology that determines which a speaker chooses to use. Pragmatic discourse factors would presumably influence the speaker's choice, as well as morphological resources in a given language. Thus, we are not claiming that event structure alone generates, predicts or is responsible for syntactic structure, because event structure and syntactic structure are two different structures in a parallel architecture view of language (Jackendoff 2002), rather than one derived from, or projected from, the other.

2.2   Motion events and the role of direction

We turn now to another factor that affects motion event segmentation, namely "direction" of motion, which Bohnemeyer (2003) argues plays a critical role. In the sequential unfolding of "source-route-goal," the details of the route play an important role: any change in the direction of motion forces segmentation into multiple events. The Unique Vector Constraint (UVC) (p. 101) states that "all direction vectors *in a single simple clause* referring to a single continuous motion event must be collinear and of the same polarity. They are interpreted as holding for the entire motion event" (emphasis mine). The UVC relates the expression of a motion event (single continuous motion) to a linguistic surface form (single simple clause) by requiring that any and all direction vectors point in the same direction (polarity) and follow the same linear path (collinearity). As Bohnemeyer (2003:103) observes, there are three restrictions contained in this constraint: (1) the condition of structural simplicity, (2) the condition of unique event reference and (3) the restriction to the syntactic level of "clause."[3] Expression (7a) can be used only if there is a direct and uninterrupted route of the Figure from A to B, whereas (7b) can be used in that situation or if the Figure stops or changes direction after leaving A and before reaching B (see Van Lambalgen & Hamm 2005 for the role of continuity in event structure).

(7)   a.   The Figure moved away from A toward B.
      b.   The Figure moved away from A and then (moved) toward B.

The postulation of the UVC is based entirely on analysis of spoken languages. We shall see how it is applied in the form–meaning mapping of event structures in ASL and contributes to the general similarity among sign language structures.

2.3   Events and telicity

2.3.1   *Event typology and notation*

Generally, since Vendler (1967), analyses of event structure have identified four basic types: States, Activities, Achievements and Accomplishments. States "hold" at a Reference Time (RT). In Activities, there is something going on ("dynamic"), but there is no "goal" or "endpoint" at which the activity will be complete. Activities are terminated by arbitrary factors (friction, gravity, human decision, exhaustion). In contrast, events (Achievements, Accomplishments) "happen" at an Event Time (ET). Achievements are composed of Initial States and Final States 'not broken' → 'broken', 'not sick' → 'sick.' Accomplishments are composed of two parts – an initial activity, such as painting, that leads to a final result, as in *She painted a picture* and *He painted the house*. States and Activities are homogeneous, whereas Achievements and Accomplishments are heterogeneous (composed of different parts). Bohnemeyer *et al.* (2007:527) note that sentence (3a) is a single Accomplishment, whereas sentence (3c) is a sequence of three Achievements.

Whether homogeneous or heterogeneous, all four types of events can be coded in English as a single lexical item, or by multiple phrases and clauses. The English "word" does not permit a transparent analysis of the event structure it represents, that is, the event structure is opaque at the surface and must be demonstrated by a variety of tests. Other languages may have separate morphemes that reflect each piece.

The model Pustejovsky (1995, 2000) proposes identifies States, Processes (Activities) and Transitions (Achievements and Accomplishments together) and their corresponding argument structure. For him, the primary distinction is between static sub-event type S(tate) and dynamic sub-event type P(rocess). Transitions are composed of non-identical sub-events: either S → S (Achievements) or P → S (Accomplishments). This yields the event typology in Table 16.1.

Table 16.1 *Sub-events in Pustejovsky's framework*

Sub-event type	Sub-event notation
States	S
Processes	P
Transitions: Achievements	S → S
Transitions: Accomplishments	P → S

We have extended this typology to include inception and causation. Each dynamic event has an inception from an initial state – but these are not reflected in Table 16.1. Similarly, even though Achievements are presented as changes from initial state to final state, there is no representation of dynamicity between the two states. Pustejovsky's typology is designed to neatly capture the homogeneity of atelic events (S and P) and the heterogeneity of telic events (Transitions to end States), to which we now turn.

2.3.2 *Telicity*

The telic/atelic distinction is most clearly analyzed in terms of the internal structures of events. Within the context of event structure, "telic" is understood as the property of events containing a natural conceptual endpoint. In contrast, "atelic" events do not contain such a point and have the potential to continue indefinitely, without any change in internal structure. Events composed of a single sub-event are *homogeneous*, in that they may be divided into identical intervals, each of which is an instance of the event itself, i.e., *walking* as an instance of *walking*. Events composed of at least two sub-events, one of which is the final state, are *heterogeneous* and cannot be divided into identical intervals because the last/final interval will always be different from the others (i.e., *dying* is not an instance of *die*).

One further set of distinctions needs to be made before we continue. Telicity and atelicity hold of the *predicate*, that *syntactic* unit traditionally labeled VP, which is headed by a Verb and may contain a variety of noun, prepositional or adverbial phrases; in some analyses it is vP, the shell that contains VP. However, as we proceed, it will appear that we are talking about verbs, as though they alone incorporate event structure. This is not so. When we mention a verb, say *die* or *run*, we are loosely referring to the predicate headed by this verb – that is, VP, not V. In some cases, our VP may contain more than a verb, for example *see Bill*. But when we refer to just the verb, it is because that lexical item is the only *word* in the predicate. In languages like English, the word *die* or *run* is monomorphemic, but in other languages this is not necessarily so. There is, then, no necessary one-to-one mapping of telic or atelic event structure to morphemes or words but only to a *phrase*, the VP. If VP contains only V, it looks like we are talking about the word, but that is not the case – lexical verbs can be homogeneous or heterogeneous, but only the predicate can be assessed for telicity. Thus in (1a) *climbed the ladder* and (1b) *climbed up the ladder*, or the second conjunct of (1c) *climbed down again*, it is the full predicate that is assigned the telic reading, not the verb *climb*, which by itself is homogeneous.

This single confusion has surrounded approaches to event structure in which people argue about whether an atelic verb can be type-shifted or coerced into a telic reading by adding, for example, a quantified object or "in an hour" time adverbial. Consider (8a) and (8b):

(8)   a. Carlita ran (for an hour/for a mile/everyday).
      b. Carlita ran to the store.

In (8a), *run* is the V but also the VP (even without the optional context in parentheses) – it appears that *run* is atelic, but it is the whole predicate that is atelic. In (8b), some authors say that *run* has been coerced or type-shifted to telic by the addition of *to the store*, which delimits the activity of running and provides an end state to "make it telic." Our claim is that the notion telic/atelic holds at the full predicate, not at the word/verb level, thus there is no need for type-shifting or coercion (elaborated in Grose 2008). In (8b) the full predicate is *run to the store*. The verb *run* is not telic or atelic, the predicate is. We can say that the verb *run* is homogeneous and can be placed into atelic or telic predicates (depending on what else appears in the context). This distinction holds even when we are discussing ASL signs that appear to be single lexical items/words – it is the predicates they head that are the relevant level of analysis.

At the same time, most of the signs we discuss also qualify as core lexical items in ASL. There are several observations that can be made about this situation. We could say that these signs are lexicalized from conglomerates of morphemes, each bearing pieces of meaning and form, like the English word *learner*, or we could say that they are productively composed of separate morphemes, in accordance with the derivation of *learner* from *learn* plus the agentive suffix *-er*. Either of these approaches requires further theoretical discussions of whether, for example, the morphemes are still "productive" if the form is lexicalized or if the word formation takes place in the lexicon or on the way to the syntax (e.g., Hale & Keyser 1993, 2001; Travis 2000). However, if we follow Jackendoff (2002, in press), we can assume that "there is *no strict lexicon–grammar distinction*: words are relatively idiosyncratic rules in a *continuum of generality* with more general grammatical structure." Under such an assumption, the items in the lexicon are part of the interface between phonology, syntax and semantics. As we now see, the lexical signs we discuss reflect event structure and participants, even if they do not show agreement with specific referents involved in the event, that is, even if they appear to be "just a lexical sign."[4]

2.3.3   *Argument structure for event predicates*

Each sub-event has a relationship with some entity, or argument role. S sub-events have a Holder of the State (S_H) – this is the argument about which the state holds (is true). Telic events also have another argument which is a "Resultee," the holder of the Resultant final State (S_R). In *The sky darkened*, the sky is both the holder of the initial state (before darkening) and the resultee in the final state (after darkening), that is, $S_H = S_R$. This should not be confused with the notion of the transitive verb – in *Ellen saw Bill*, there is no change of state, no resultee; indeed, Bill is unaffected. The only argument role is S_H for Ellen. The state *saw Bill* holds of Ellen, and we could say that the state of "being seen" holds for Bill, but there is no dynamicity that would lead to a change of state to license a Resultant State argument S_R for either Ellen or Bill. Note that this differs from *Ellen hit Bill*. The argument role associated with an initial dynamic P sub-event, such as *hit*, is Initiator (P_I); all other P sub-events are associated with an Undergoer (P_U). Thus, Ellen is P_I, and Bill is P_U as well as holder of the final state of being hit S_R – that is, $P_U = S_R$. In *the sky darkened*, the sky is P_U in addition to other roles assigned by the initial and final States; thus $S_H = P_U = S_R$. In *Lee hammered the metal flat*, the metal is $P_U = S_R$, and Lee is P_I, the individual who initiated the change in state leading to the metal going from "not flat" to the resultant state of "flat."

These role assignments are independent of grammatical relations Subject and Object. This labeling system can be used in the syntax associated with this sub-event analysis (Basu 2005, Grose, Wilbur & Schalber 2007, Wilbur 2008) and is modeled after Ramchand's (2008) work. With a few additional modifications (section 1.4), we provide a complete and straightforward system that serves both spoken and signed languages.

2.3.4   The "almost" test

A useful test for examining event structure is the adverb *almost*. In English, *almost* produces a single "unrealized inceptive" (UI) reading over atelic events, indicating that an event was almost, but not in fact, initiated (9).

(9)   Sydney almost slept (during the long trip but never fell asleep).

With telic events, the same UI reading is available (10a), but there is also a second "incompletive" (IC) reading, in which case the event was initiated but did not reach its endpoint (10b).

(10)   a.   Kim almost knit a pair of mittens. (but never started the first one)
         b.   Kim almost knit a pair of mittens. (but never finished the second one)

In (9) and (10a), *almost* has (wide) scope over the event initiation, regardless of internal sub-event structure, that is, it is located above the top verbal projection. In the incompletive reading (10b), *almost* has (narrow) scope over only the endpoint of the event and therefore must be located lower in the tree (below inception and above the final State). These two readings of *almost* in English are straightforward with a sub-event analysis, which predicts two different positions in telic events for *almost* to take scope, but only one such position in atelic events.

2.4   Further details of internal event structure

Pustejovsky's specification of basic sub-event types S and P does not have sufficient detail to allow full appreciation of how event structure is reflected in surface forms of sign languages or in those spoken languages where parts of sub-event structure are represented with separate morphemes. Elaborating event structure allows us to capture semantic distinctions directly encoded by surface forms in some languages, but opaque in languages like English.

Grose (2008) tackles this problems using a feature geometry approach. Using the term "Situation" for both States (static) and Events (eventive), Grose postulates two class nodes, SF (Situation Features) and EF (Event Features), with SF dominating EF to represent the fact that Events are a subset of Situations (Figure 16.1). The head node of SF is s_α, representing simple States as well as initial stages prior to initiation of Events.

EF dominates substructures representing internal structures of Events, with two possible head nodes, e_β and s_β. The e_β node is present in all Events, whereas s_β represents the end state of telic Events. It is now possible to represent Event

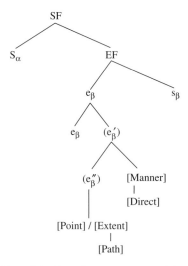

Figure 16.1 *Part of the Event Structure root tree (Grose 2008).*

inception/initiation with the transition from $[s_\alpha]$ to $[e_\beta]$. The initiator (P_I before) is the holder of $[s_\alpha]$. The undergoer (P_U before) is the argument associated with $[e_\beta]$, and the resultee (S_R before) is the argument associated with $[s_\beta]$. What this means is that the participants are identified along with the event structure, so no separate procedure of theta-role assignment is needed, simplifying the syntax–semantics interface. The event node $[e_\beta]$ dominates the head node $[e_\alpha]$, which represents internal causation ("grammatical force"). Because each head node is associated with an argument role, the presence of $[e_\alpha]$ entails the additional role "causer." The event structure also interfaces with Tense through the SF node and with Aspect through the EF node, so no movements are required in the syntax just for the purposes of making these assignments come out right. I will return to the benefits of this analysis for argument structure in section 2.2.1, and have dealt with the interface of Aspect and event structure in separate papers on reduplication (Wilbur 2005, 2009). As for the interface with Tense, as Grose (2008) observes, a fully detailed analysis still needs to be done.

Next is the distinction between Achievements and Accomplishments. Pustejovsky identifies the difference with the first sub-event, with Achievements having initial States and Accomplishments having initial Processes. If, however, there is a change from $[s_\alpha]$ to $[e_\beta]$ (initiation), then Accomplishments have initial States as well. Indeed, some authors have argued that the proper distinction is that Achievements are instantaneous, whereas Accomplishments have duration. Grose argues that temporal structure features are not sensitive to actual duration, but rather to the mapping of an Event onto one ([Point]) or more than one ([Extent]) interval in the Event Time. Achievements then map to one ET interval, and Accomplishments to more than one.

Duration of the interval(s) can be established by context, lexical semantics or temporal adverbs. This brings us full circle to the initial discussion of the role of time and temporal adverbs in the coding of motion and non-motion events, and the presence of the macro-event property (MEP). To complete our discussion of meaning and events, there is one remaining issue to address – spatial (motion) versus temporal (non-motion) interpretation of events, and the role of the UVC. The dominance of [Extent] over [Path] in Figure 16.1 allows events to have either temporal interpretation only, or both spatial and temporal interpretation, but not spatial interpretation alone. Fundamentally, all events occur over elapsing time regardless of how long the event takes. For an event to be a spatial/motion event, the spatial feature [Path] must be contributed to the event structure by a morpheme which contains it. In this way, spatial events are a subset of all events and are more marked (in the linguistic sense) than temporal events. The UVC limits the number of unique [Path] specifications in a simple clause to one. It interacts with the typology identified by Bohnemeyer *et al.* (2007), which determines whether a single morphological predicate can contain a source, a ground object being passed and a goal in its [Path] feature (Type I), or if these need to be separated into source and goal in one predicate and ground object being passed in another (Type II), or into three separate predicates (Type III). It is now possible to turn our attention to sign languages (SLs).

3   Model applied to sign languages

First, I describe the resources available for phonological representation of events, and then address the various ways in which the form–meaning correspondences occur in ASL.

3.1   Available resources for hands and mouth

In speech, the acoustic signal derives from, but is different from, the motion of the articulators. Spoken languages have a choice of articulations, hence acoustic signals, which are recruited and combined into sound patterns according to syllable structure constraints. These form the basis for the construction of morphemes. In signing, the visual signal is the motion of the articulators, that is, what is seen is the dynamics of hand, head, face and body movement. Readers are referred to Brentari (1998) for further phonological details.

The resources available from spatial geometry include point, line and plane. From physics (dynamics of motion), we also have distance (d) from $point_a$ to $point_b$, elapsed time (t), velocity (v) = d/t, acceleration/deceleration (change in the value of velocity over time) and direction of movement (vectors).

At a single point in space, the hands may be static (hold), or may change their orientation, setting or aperture, or may tremor/oscillate/vibrate (trilled movement [TM]). Or the hands may move between two points, in which case there are "geometric" options of lines with different shapes (straight, curved or tracing the outline of a figure), and "physical" options of different distances (long, short), durations (long, short) and velocities (fast, slow). These options are recruited for semantic purposes in the predicate system.

The mouth can contribute to the representation of event structure with its shape – what we call "posture (P)," and/or abrupt change of shape, which we call "transition (T)." If the mouth adopts a posture (e.g., any one in Figure 16.2) and holds it during the manual articulation of one or more signs, we have a P-NM. If the mouth changes its posture (close → open, or open → close), then we have a

23: Lip tight 25: Lip part 26: Jaw drop

Figure 16.2 *Some mouth positions and their Action Unit (AU) numbers (Eckman, Friesen & Hager 2002).*

T-NM (Schalber 2004, Schalber & Grose 2006). Like event structures, the contribution of mouth is to represent either *change* or *no change*.

3.2 Form–meaning mappings

From event structure, we have static (S) and eventive (E) sub-events, and the participants associated with them. From geometry, we have points, lines of various shapes and planes. From physics, we have distance, velocity, changes in velocity (acceleration and deceleration) and direction of movement vectors for the hands. For the mouth, we have postures (P-NMs) and transitions (T-NMs). We turn our attention now to the grammaticalized recruitment of these available resources for representing components of event structure, that is, how the form–meaning mappings are linguistically encoded. For features identified in the Situation/Event structure above, I argue that there are systematic mappings to morphemes in ASL (and probably other SLs) that contribute to the construction and interpretation of lexical items and novel forms.

To effect a form–meaning mapping, the phonological root node (root_p) and the morphological verb root node (root_v) are associated with each other, just as form and meaning are paired and stored in the lexicon for any morpheme or lexical item. The root_v in predicates contains information about event structure that the root reflects. When there is a systematic mapping between such information and the phonological components in root_p, we have instances of the EVH.

Brentari's (1998) Prosodic model of phonology works perfectly for the distinctions that are relevant to these mappings. She posits Prosodic Features (PF) for *features that change* during sign formation and Inherent Features (IF) for *features that persist* throughout the sign. For PF features, because they change, two distinct phonological timing slots (x-slots) are needed, one to show the initial specification and the other to show the final specification. A simple example is the sign DEAF, which has two different contact locations on the face, what Brentari calls a "setting change." The first setting position is given as the specification for the first x-slot, and the second setting position is the specification for the second x-slot. Because these two specifications are different, they represent setting changes during formation, that is, there is movement between contact locations (but no [Path]). Similarly, two different aperture specifications for handshape result in a handshape change, and two different orientations give an orientation change.

Obviously, two location specifications yield a change of location. However, the nature of the movement between these two locations is important for distinctions in event structure. The standard way to refer to this movement is "path," but this term is also used for semantic and morphological functions. Borrowing terminology instead from geometry, movement between locations (points) is a line. In signs, the movement along this line *within a single plane* can assume a number of shapes – straight, arc, circle or outline an object. In Brentari's model, this movement has the phonological form "path specification in PF," represented by the feature [tracing], which can combine with different shape features. When the movement has contact at a body part or reference plane perpendicular to the direction of movement, Brentari uses the feature [direction]. End contact is written [direction: > |] and initial contact is [direction: | >]. Movement along a line, represented with [direction], is compositional at the Event Structure level and multimorphemic in the predicate system in ASL. The final "contact" provides the final state for telic events. Similarly, predicate signs with changes of setting, aperture, or orientation are also compositional, representing telic events.

We begin with the observation that heterogeneous events associate different information from root$_v$ with the first and second x-slots. In contrast, homogeneous events will map information from the root$_v$ onto the first x-timing slot. The specification for the second x-slot in homogeneous signs cannot be distinctive from the first x-slot specification and hence can be treated as spreading from the initial x-slot. For example, if the sign is RIDE-BICYCLE, the first timing slot has IF specifications for handshape for both hands (fist), movement (path movement in a circle: [tracing: circle]), orientation (symmetrical: analogous parts of the hand facing each other) and POA (neutral space in front of signer in the midsagittal plane); these features spread to the second timing slot. Higher in Brentari's tree is the feature [alternate], which indicates that the movement of the two hands with respect to each other will be out of phase (i.e., when one is at peak height of its circle, the other is at bottom of its circle). The specifications for handshape, movement, orientation and POA do not change between the first slot and the second. In order to put this homogeneous sign into a telic predicate, an additional sign indicating the goal (e.g., 'to the park') must be added. By itself, RIDE-BICYCLE has both spatial ([path]) and temporal ([extent]) interpretation. It contrasts with another verb STAND which has only temporal interpretation. For STAND, the dominant hand has a V-handshape with the fingertips resting in the upward-facing palm of the non-dominant hand. When STAND occurs in the durative, the two hands cycle around together without losing contact. In this case, the circling movement can only be interpreted as extent, and not that someone stood around *in circles.*

3.2.1   *Telic predicates headed by heterogeneous lexical verbs*

The first x-slot carries information about the initial State [s_α] and the second carries information about the final State [s_β]. For simplicity, I focus on [s_β]. In the Prosodic model, the phonological movements that reflect [s_β] are change of aperture (Figure 16.3a), orientation (Figure 16.3b), setting (Figure 16.3c) or location (Figure 16.3d).

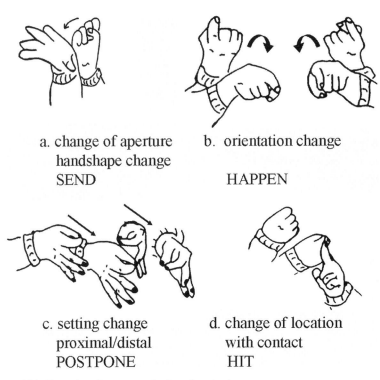

a. change of aperture
   handshape change
   SEND

b. orientation change

   HAPPEN

c. setting change
   proximal/distal
   POSTPONE

d. change of location
   with contact
   HIT

Figure 16.3 *Examples of movements in signs denoting heterogeneous events.*

The signs without movement along a line, SEND, HAPPEN and POSTPONE, are single interval telic events. The absence of [Extent] accounts for their punctual interpretation. In contrast, HIT contains movement along a line and a final specification for s_β: [contact] between the two hands (which each represent a participant in the event), that is, [direction > |]. HIT is a sign that fits Brentari's Direction-of-Transfer Principle, that is, HIT is a transfer verb (something is transferred from source to goal). As such, HIT has a *spatial* interpretation for the line movement in addition to the temporal interpretation that accompanies spatial events. The spatial interpretation is lexically specified: HIT contains the event structure feature [Path]. The *default* interpretation of the line part of predicate sign movement is temporal, that is, [Extent] is the elapsed time of an event.[5] Contrary to the general claim that temporal structure is metaphorically based on spatial structure (Clark 1973), the claim here is that spatial interpretation is actually marked (presence of [Path]) and temporal is unmarked (absence of [Path]). Indeed, in sign language linguistics spatial verbs have been identified as a separate verb category at least since Padden (1983), confirmed by Janis (1995) and discussed further in Brentari and Padden (2001).

Given these regularities, I have posited several morphemes for ASL (Wilbur 2003, 2005, 2008). Two have been mentioned above: (1) [Extent] (the default temporal interpretation of movement along a line as *duration*) and (2) [Path] (lexically specified spatial interpretation of movement). An adverbial morpheme "Extra" can modify either [Extent] or both [Extent] and [Path] (since [Extent] dominates [Path]). Extra is represented phonologically as the shape [Arc],[6] which can combine with [Extent] or [Path] to give the meaning 'more.' For [Extent], this is interpreted with respect to the "duration" of the event, whereas for [Path], it is interpreted with respect to the "distance" covered/traveled during the event and the duration of the event.

As noted, for telic events, the specifications for the two PF timing slots are phonologically distinctive. These two x-slots are available to provide an initial specification for semantic interpretation as "not the EndState" and a second specification for "EndState." In this respect, the phonology mirrors the semantic opposition. Telic events contain one more morpheme than atelic homogeneous events, which I have dubbed "EndState" because of its primary function as marking the end s_β of telic events. EndState is signaled by a *rapid deceleration of the movement to a stop*. This observation is empirically supported by phonetic evidence. Preliminary data from motion capture indicates that in isolation and in carrier phrases, the deceleration of telic signs is 1.5 to 2 times steeper than that of atelic signs (Wilbur & Malaia 2008). Within the EVH, Brentari's feature [direction > |], which is defined as entailing "contact," is the phonological representation of the *combination* of the morphemes [Extent] and [EndState]. Similarly, [| > direction] phonologically represents [InitialState] and [Extent].

These same phonological x-slot specifications provide the basis for identification of points in space for agreement with verb arguments. For example, the final x-slot of SEND can be co-indexed with an antecedent individual (the recipient). Given the absence of [Extent] in SEND, the hand is instead *oriented* toward the point denoting the co-indexed antecedent.[7] With HIT, the non-dominant hand may be placed at a point in space to show that it is co-indexed with an antecedent argument indicating the undergoer, and the dominant (moving) hand (agent, cf. Kegl 1985) will move toward it and make contact (assuming a *completed* event). POSTPONE only takes events as internal arguments, thus the Initial State and the EndState can only be mapped semantically to the time of the events. The initial point in space at which the sign starts indicates the "old" scheduled/expected time of the event, and the final point in space, shown by where the movement stops, indicates the "new" time of the event with respect to the "old" time. All of this argument information is a direct result of the event structure and its correspondences with the phonological representation, and does not require further derivation, movement or feature checking.

In summary, telic events have a significant EndState (but not necessarily [Extent] or [Path]). Supalla and Newport (1978:103) observed the correlation between the presence of EndState and the movement of the sign: "while hold manner corresponds to an action with specified spatial end-points, the continuous manner is used for actions with unspecified spatial end-points."

3.2.2 *Homogeneous roots, atelic and telic predicates*

In contrast to the above representations of telic events in sign formation, the phonological specifications for the second phonological x-slot in Process and State signs *must* be identical. For Processes, there is path movement, that is, movement over a line (regardless of geometric shape), and therefore [Extent] represented by Brentari's feature [tracing]. Also, when the Process stops, the movement simply ceases, as there is no EndState. This corresponds to Supalla and Newport's (1978) "continuous" movement, which they describe as "continuous, with no interruption, smooth and loose."

An example of [tracing], further specified as having a [straight] shape, is given by RUN in Figure 16.4a. That PLAY (Figure 16.4b) has [tracing] movement was established by Supalla and Newport (1978:101), who identify it as "continuous unidirectional repeated." Here, the repetition is captured phonologically by [TM] "trilled movement." Finally, the sign READ (Figure 16.4c) is similar in PF features to PLAY, but obviously the IF features are different.

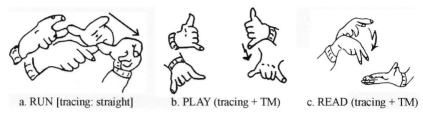

a. RUN [tracing: straight]   b. PLAY (tracing + TM)   c. READ (tracing + TM)

Figure 16.4 *Atelic predicates (phonological descriptions from Brentari 1998).*

Figure 16.5 *The lexical sign 'sick.' Used by permission from Ursula Bellugi, The Salk Institute for Biological Studies.*

In Brentari's model, either States have no PF branch, and hence no movement, or they have an empty PF branch, which is the docking site of [TM]. A State with only IF specifications needs movement in order to appear as an independent sign, which is that of the hands getting to, and moving away from, the configuration indicated in the IF (SICK in Figure 16.5).

The event representation of lexical SICK as a State is $[s_\alpha]$ dominated by SF; the phonological representation is just IF. The movement of the hands to and from the IF specifications are epenthetic, that is, they depend on the previous and following signs.

The same state SICK can be predicated of an individual who becomes sick (the Resultative), in which case SICK functions as $[s_\beta]$ in the predicate event structure. The presence of $[s_\beta]$ entails the presence of $[e_\beta]$, which in turn entails the presence of $[s_\alpha]$. Morphologically, the Resultative construction in ASL requires $[e_\beta]$ to have [Extent]; phonologically, a PF branch with [direction] is added; the meaning is then 'finally become/get sick' with one argument $(S_I = S_U = S_R)$ (Wilbur 2008). However, the added [Extent] by itself is insufficient to carry the full meaning of the Resultative to distinguish it from the meaning *get sick*, which does not carry the implication of the *becoming* taking a while to happen. Thus, there is a further phonological specification – change of speed of movement from slow to fast – specified by the ASL Resultative inflection. In our analysis, the homogeneous lexical root SICK can occur in an atelic State predicate or, as in the Resultative, in a telic [Extent] predicate (Accomplishment). No procedures of type-shifting or semantic coercion are necessary because of the transparency of the pairing between phonological form and the meaning.

3.2.3   *"Almost X" as a test for telicity*

In ASL, the equivalents of the wide and narrow scope readings of *almost* occur in different syntactic positions and are morphologically distinct (Smith 2007). In the unrealized inceptive (UI), the phonological movement of the sign is halted imme-diately after it is initiated (in the case of SIT-DOWN, the path movement down-ward is not articulated; in general, the initiation of the event is immediately followed by rapid deceleration that terminates the movement), indicating that the event does not take place (Liddell 1984, Smith 2007).

(11)   I   SIT-DOWN + (UI)
       1SG sit-down-UI
       'I almost started to sit down; I started to sit down but didn't.'

In the incompletive (IC), the phonological movement of SIT-DOWN is halted before the sign is completed (its path movement downward ends before the moving hand makes contact with the non-dominant hand, but after some portion of the phonological line has been produced; Liddell 1984), corresponding to the narrow scope of *almost* in English.

(12)   I SIT-DOWN + IC
       1SG sit-down-IC
       'I almost sat down (but stopped myself before contacting the seat).'

The different locations of the UI and IC morphemes in the event structure are shown in Figure 16.6.

   In various two-handed lexical verbs, such as CLOSE, ARRIVE and HIT, the non-dominant hand marks the location of [s_β]. In the IC, the dominant hand stops short of making contact with the non-dominant one (Figure 16.7a). Figure 16.7b

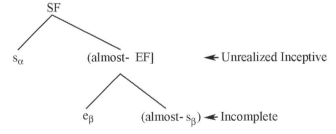

Figure 16.6 *The UI and IC Readings of "almost" (from Grose 2008).*

(a) (garage door) CLOSE-IC   (b) two versions: (CL:car) HIT(-CL:tree)-IC

Figure 16.7 *Incompletive of CLOSE and HIT(-tree).*

shows forms composed of two one-handed classifiers, and again the dominant hand stops short of contact with the non-dominant hand. The event requirement for combination with IC is the presence of $[s_\beta]$. In contrast, what UI needs is an inception, that is, $[s_\alpha] \rightarrow [e_\beta]$. In English, these differences are opaque, yielding two readings with telic predicates and only one with atelic predicates. In ASL, however, the transparency of the correspondences between event structure and form eliminates possible ambiguity of interpretation.

3.2.4   *Other form–meaning mappings*

The model proposed here proves itself in other ways as well. Consider the sign DIE, which has a change of palm orientation in PF. By itself, such a change is punctual [Point] rather than [Extent]. However, to indicate 'take a long time to die,' a curved path [tracing] movement is added between the initial palm orientation and the final one. With this added path, it is also possible to terminate the movement before the final orientation position is reached, providing the IC meaning 'almost die,' e.g., does not reach the final state.

Reduplication is also a regular source of atelic predicates from either homogeneous or heterogeneous lexical verbs and changeable state predicates. All of the temporal aspectual inflections (incessant, habitual, iterative, durative and continuative) produce atelic predicates. The first three apply only to heterogeneous verbs, the last two only to homogeneous verbs (Wilbur 2005, 2009).

It is also clear that there is a relationship between event structure and the behavior of the mouth. Schalber (2004; Schalber & Grose 2006) analyzed the correspondence between ASL and ÖGS mouth behaviors and the event structure with which they occurred. In both languages, there were P(osture)-NMs and T(ransition)-NMs. P-NMs are associated with situations containing $[e_\beta]$, where they function as manner adverbials. The NMs can spread over multiple manual signs and can contain more than one prosodic word. Note that the example in Figure 16.8, (from Schalber 2004), contains a single P-NM over several hand movements.

<u>   pursed lips</u>
(FRAU IX) BLUME GIESSEN:[supination]
   'Woman waters a plant'

Figure 16.8 *P-NM over multiple hand movements in ÖGS (Schalber 2004).*

That this is not simply spreading of the nonmanual articulator position over the prosodic word can be seen in Figure 16.9, which shows an atelic predicate containing multiple occurrences of the heterogeneous verb *give* (presumably in multiple prosodic words) but a single mouth posture.

T-NMs correspond to transitions in event structure and only occur with inceptive or completive (telic) events. In Figure 16.10, three examples of T-NMs are given. It is coincidental that these examples are closed → open, as the reverse also occurs. T-NMs can occur only on a single syllable and thus do not spread across multiple manual signs like P-NMs. They can, however, serve as the onset or offset of P-NMs. For example, in a production of EAT produced with the Allocative Indeterminate (Klima & Bellugi 1979; Wilbur 2009), one signer produces a T-NM open → closed on the first occurrence of EAT and then keeps the mouth in closed posture over the remaining reduplicated occurrences.

3.2.5 *ASL motion events and the Unique Vector Constraint*

How does the Unique Vector Constraint translate into ASL? The analysis of event structure presented here makes it clear that to have a motion event, that is, an event involving changes of location in space, the event must contain [Path]. [Path] is lexically specified, and entails movement along a line (regardless of shape). We need to consider both [tracing] and [direction] movements. Understand first that the tracing of the shape of an object is describing a "property of the Holder of the State," and is not a motion event. Thus, drawing (e.g., rectangles or triangles in descriptive classifier constructions) is not relevant to the behavior of motion events. But motion of a Figure along a tracing [Path] is. It is clear that the UVC allows [tracing] to have any *single kind of shape* (zig-zag, arc, circle) as long as there is no change in the kind of shape (e.g., from zig-zag to circle) and no stopping (no arrival at a location). Schalber and Grose (2006) observed that for both ASL and ÖGS, the representation of a cat pacing *back and forth*, that is, [tracing: zig-zag] was

Figure 16.9 *P-NM over GIVE+ Distributive (repeated a total of 5 times) in ASL.*

accompanied by a single P-NM. Figure 16.11 shows a [tracing] representation of a car swerving off the road, straightening back upright and then heading forward toward a tree. The mouth is open with tongue visible until the car changes direction to move forward toward the tree. Then there is a [direction] representation of the car moving toward the tree, with a different mouth shape at the inception of this event and an open mouth at the end of the event. In the first nine pictures, the hand

a. ASL   FIND T-NM

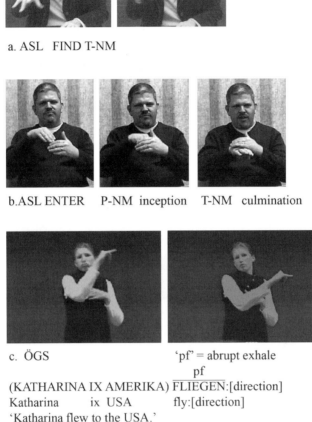

b.ASL ENTER   P-NM inception   T-NM   culmination

c. ÖGS   'pf' = abrupt exhale

$$\overset{\text{pf}}{}$$

(KATHARINA IX AMERIKA) $\overline{\text{FLIEGEN}}$:[direction]
Katharina   ix USA   fly:[direction]
'Katharina flew to the USA.'

Figure 16.10 *Two examples of T-NMs.*

moves in different directions, but the [tracing] movement is treated as a single vector, perhaps best translated as 'the car swerved off the road.' Certainly we would not expect to have each direction change translated separately into English. On the other hand, the last three pictures must be translated separately 'the car headed toward/hit the tree,' as there is a separate direction vector.

With [direction] movements, which entail contact with a body part or plane perpendicular to the direction of motion, a direction vector is defined between

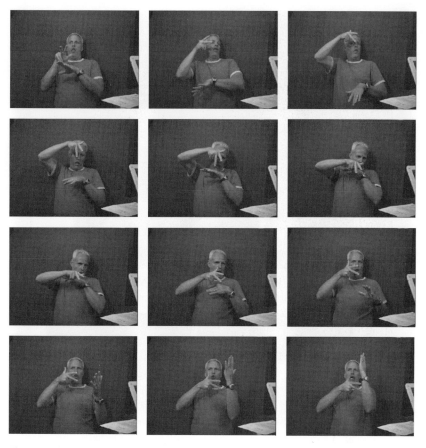

Figure 16.11 *Car swerves off road, straightens up, and then heads toward tree (change mouth shape before third picture from end and open mouth in last picture).*

where the movement starts and ends, and each change in direction requires a separate direction of motion vector, a separate sign, a separate VP, a separate prosodic unit. Compare the [tracing] event above with the three separate events in Figure 16.12. Here the bus hits the car three times (which is what causes the car to swerve off the road), and there are three mouth changes (cheeks puff), one for each hit.

4 Conclusion

Using our event-based analysis, Brentari's Prosodic model and the EVH, we can provide explanations for a number of otherwise inexplicable facts. For example, in

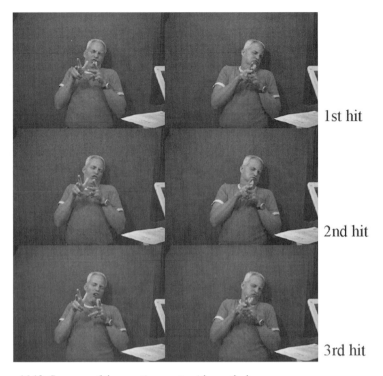

1st hit

2nd hit

3rd hit

Figure 16.12 *Sequence of three motion events with mouth changes.*

Klima and Bellugi (1979), "end marking" was a contributing factor to the phonological forms of aspectual modulations. However, no linguistic function for its presence or absence was identified. We provide a straightforward explanation of the meaning of "end marking" as EndState, and, from that, can predict its presence or absence in the different aspectual forms.

We provide a correlation for Brentari's phonological movement inventory with the event structure of predicate signs. Handshape (aperture) changes, orientation changes and setting changes are used in telic predicate signs that contain [Point] and lack event [Extent]. The difference between [tracing] and [direction] path movements is correlated with atelic and telic [Extent] events, respectively, with [direction] mapping onto two event features [Extent] and [s$_\beta$], represented by a point in space. The argument structure associated with each predicate type falls out naturally, including the number of arguments (based on the number of head node States) and type of arguments (individual, event, location). The analysis provides a consistent explanation of the phonological forms of [unrealized inceptive] and incompletive modifications, and is applicable to both core lexical items and classifier predicate constructions.

Spatial verbs contain the feature [Path], which contributes to their motion event interpretation. To learn a sign language, one must learn that in predicates phonological path (along a line in space) is most often interpreted as [Extent] (time); as some would say the metaphor TIME IS SPACE has been grammaticalized. Those items (e.g., DRIVE-TO) that retain space as [Path] are exceptions to this generalization and presumably have to be learned separately (hence "lexically specified"). Note that this situation is completely counter-iconic.

Given that these options are based on the physics and geometry of the real world and hence potentially universal, it is expected that other sign languages will recruit these options and assign them various meaningful functions. This grounding may provide the fundamental basis that makes sign languages look more similar to each other than spoken languages do (Newport & Supalla 2000).

17

Nonmanuals: their grammatical and prosodic roles

Roland Pfau and Josep Quer

1   Introduction

There are numerous popular misconceptions about sign languages. One of these misconceptions has it that sign languages are "languages on the hands," that is, that sign language lexemes as well as morphologically and syntactically complex structures are articulated entirely by the hands (and possibly the lower arm).

In the course of this chapter, we will show that this statement is far from appropriate. Surely, the hands play an important role in the articulation of signed utterances, but other articulators – the body, the head and (parts of) the face – are just as important. All linguistically significant elements that are not expressed by the hands are referred to as "nonmanual markers" or just "nonmanuals." Actually, it has been shown that signers, while communicating, do not focus their attention on each other's hands but rather on the face, where essential grammatical information is encoded nonmanually (Siple 1978, Swisher, Christie & Miller 1989).

Linguistically significant nonmanuals have to be distinguished from purely affective nonmanual markers such as facial expressions or head movements expressing disgust, disbelief or surprise, which are used by signers just as they are used by speakers. Differentiating between the two types of markers is not always straightforward, but certain distinguishing criteria have been suggested. The scope and the timing of linguistic nonmanual behaviors, for instance, is linguistically constrained relative to the manual sign(s) they accompany in a way that affective markers are not (e.g., Baker-Shenk 1983, Reilly & Anderson 2002). The examples discussed in this chapter will make clear that this is indeed the case.

The chapter is divided into two parts. In section 2, we will address various grammatical functions of nonmanual markers. In this section, the grammatical nonmanuals are grouped together according to their role at different linguistic levels. We will consider phonological (section 2.1), morphological (section 2.2), syntactic (section 2.3) and pragmatic (section 2.4) markers in turn. Section 3 looks at prosodic functions of nonmanuals. Here, we will make a distinction between edge markers (section 3.1) and domain markers (section 3.2). We will see that occasionally, a syntactic nonmanual may also function as a prosodic domain marker. Note that in both section 2 and section 3, it is not our goal to describe the repertoire of nonmanuals as found in a single sign language. Rather, we present data from various sign languages and, wherever relevant, point out similarities and differences found among sign languages. Section 4 concludes our survey of linguistic nonmanual markers in sign languages.

2   Grammatical functions of nonmanuals

2.1   Phonological nonmanuals

Phonological (or lexical) nonmanuals are assumed to be an essential part of a sign's phonological description. That is, just like manual parameters such as handshape, movement and location, these nonmanuals have to be specified in the lexical entry of a sign. Here, we will consider three distinct types of nonmanual articulation, head and body movements, facial expressions and mouth patterns (section 2.1.1 to 2.1.3), and we will briefly consider their interaction with the manual part of a sign (section 2.1.4).

2.1.1   *Head and body movements*

Signs may be lexically specified for a particular head or body movement. In many sign languages, for instance, in the sign for SLEEP, one hand or both hands are brought to the side of the head as if supporting the head and the head tilts toward the palm of the hand(s). In connected signing, the head tilt may be minimal, but it has to be present.

Head movements also commonly accompany negative particles and interjections. In both American Sign Language (ASL) and German Sign Language (DGS), the signs meaning NOT/NO, though different in all manual parameters, are signed with a single sideward head movement. This movement is usually synchronized with the manual movement, a wrist rotation at the chin in ASL (resembling a nod of the fist) and a straight path movement in neutral signing space in DGS (see section 2.1.4). While it is likely that these negative signs are lexically specified for a head movement, we will see below (section 2.3.1) that negative headshakes also fulfill a syntactic function.

Lexically specified body movements are attested in signs that involve a semantics of inclusion or exclusion (also see section 2.4). The ASL signs for AVOID and REJECT, for instance, involve a slight backward lean, while INVOLVE and ENCOURAGE are accompanied by a forward lean (Wilbur & Patschke 1998).

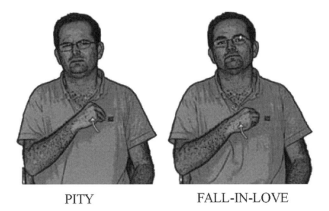

PITY   FALL-IN-LOVE

Figure 17.1 *Two LSC signs differing only in facial expression.*

2.1.2   *Facial expressions*

Just like head and body movements, lexically specified facial expressions are closely related to the semantics of a sign. In DGS and Sign Language of the Netherlands (NGT) (and probably most other sign languages), adjectival signs like HAPPY, ANGRY and SURPRISED are usually accompanied by an expression that reflects the respective emotional state. Besides emotions, sensations can also motivate the presence of a particular facial expression. This holds, for instance, for the NGT sign SOUR in which the facial expression is related to the sensation of sour taste (imagine yourself biting a lemon).

The lack or presence of a facial expression may define a minimal pair, as in the Catalan Sign Language (LSC) examples in Figure 17.1: the two signs PITY and FALL-IN-LOVE have identical manual articulation (flat O-hand at contralateral side of the chest) but differ in facial expression: as expected based on the lexical meaning, PITY is accompanied by a negative facial expression (furrowed brows and pursed lips), while FALL-IN-LOVE has a positive, relaxed one. Examples like this are good evidence for the assumption that the nonmanual marker has phonological significance.

2.1.3   *Mouth gestures vs. mouthings*

Let us now turn to the role of the mouth. In the literature, two different types of lexical mouth patterns are usually distinguished (Boyes Braem & Sutton-Spence 2001): mouth gestures (also referred to as oral components) and mouthings (also labeled spoken components or word pictures). While mouth gestures are not related to or influenced by the surrounding spoken language, mouthings are derived from spoken words.

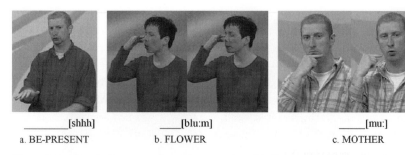

_____[shhh]   ____[blu:m]   _____[mu:]

a. BE-PRESENT   b. FLOWER   c. MOTHER

Figure 17.2 *Three NGT signs with mouth gesture (a), full (b), or reduced mouthing (c). Reprinted with permission from Schermer et al. (2006). Illustration copyright © Nederlands Gebarencentrum.*

In mouth gestures, the mouth pattern may either change or remain constant during the articulation of the sign. In the Norwegian Sign Language (NSL) sign GO-AWAY, for instance, the initial mouth position is open and neutral while the final mouth position is closed with lips pressed together (Vogt-Svendsen 2001). Crucially, the sign also involves a handshape change from open (-hand) to closed (-hand). In contrast, in the NGT sign BE-PRESENT, the hand (-hand) executes a forward and slightly downward movement ending in an abrupt stop and the accompanying mouth gesture is [shhhh], see Figure 17.2a.

As opposed to mouth gestures, mouthings are silent articulations of (a part of) a corresponding spoken word of the surrounding language. If only part of the corresponding word is articulated, it is usually its first syllable. For illustration, consider the two NGT examples in Figure 17.2: FLOWER in (b) has full mouthing, MOTHER in (c) has reduced mouthing in that only the first syllable of the Dutch word is articulated (Schermer 2001). Note that the Dutch word for 'flower' is *bloem* [blu:m] and the word for 'mother' is *moeder* [mu:də]. While these mouthings could be considered redundant in that they do not add anything to the meaning of the respective manual signs, other mouthings disambiguate the meaning of a manual sign with a more general meaning. A general sign like, for instance, the NGT sign SMALL-OBJECT can take on specific meanings such as 'pea,' 'pearl' or 'detail' by virtue of the accompanying mouthings.

It has to be pointed out that, especially for the group of redundant mouthings, it is a matter of debate whether they really constitute an integral part of a sign language. Based on the observation that there is considerable inter- and intra-signer variation in the use of mouthings, some researchers have argued that many if not most mouthings should be considered a language contact phenomenon. Following this line of argumentation, mouthings are not linguistically significant and are not part of the lexical description of a sign (e.g., Hohenberger & Happ 2001).

Moreover, sign languages may differ from each other with respect to frequency of mouthings. Obviously, the use of mouthings depends on a subject's exposure to the spoken language, which implies that the educational background has an important influence. Also, it has traditionally been argued that, in comparison to many European sign languages, the use of mouthings in ASL is very restricted because ASL signers do not consider mouthings a part of "real ASL" (e.g., Padden 1980). A recent study by Nadolske and Rosenstock (2007), however, challenges this traditional view by showing that mouthings contribute significantly to the formal and semantic aspects of ASL.

2.1.4 *Echo phonology*
Some of the above examples have already made clear that there is a strong tendency for nonmanual markers to be synchronized with the manual part of the sign. For instance, a head movement is executed in parallel with a manual path movement, and opening and closing hand-internal movements tend to be accompanied by opening and closing mouth movements, respectively. This characteristic synchronization pattern is referred to as "echo phonology" (Woll 2001).

Similarly, mouthings, especially reduced mouthings, can be synchronized, for instance, by means of reduplication. The NGT sign HOLIDAY (the Dutch word is *vakantie* [vakantsi]), which is signed on the cheek and involves an inherent repetition, is commonly accompanied by the reduplicated syllable [vava]. Given that in this case the mouthing matches the syllabic structure of the sign, it could be argued that the synchronization of the reduplicated pattern is prosodic in nature.

2.2 Morphological nonmanuals
Nonmanuals that serve a morphological function come in two different types. On the one hand, such markers may fulfill an adjectival function when modifying nouns (section 2.2.1); on the other hand, they may fulfill an adverbial function when modifying verbs (section 2.2.2). In addition, it has been claimed that occasionally a nonmanual marker may be a free morpheme, that is, appear on its own without accompanying manual material (Dively 2001, Vogt-Svendsen 2001). We shall not consider this last type in the present context.

2.2.1 *Nonmanual adjectives*
Above we have pointed out that some adjectival signs are lexically specified for a particular nonmanual. Moreover, certain adjectival meanings can be realized by a nonmanual configuration alone, which is articulated simultaneously with the nominal it modifies. This is a common strategy, for instance, for expressing the

diminutive ('small x') and the augmentative ('big x'). Consider the DGS examples in (1). In (1a), in order to express that the object (a house) is smaller than usual, the signer sucks in his cheeks (represented by ')(' in the gloss), while in (1b), he or she blows his or her cheeks to indicate that the object (a tree) is of considerable size (represented by '( )'). Note that neither of the two examples contains a manual adjective. At least in (1a), however, the manual articulation of the respective noun will also change according to the intended meaning.

$$\overline{\qquad\qquad})($$

(1) a. POSS$_1$ FRIEND HOUSE BUY   (DGS)
         'My friend bought a small house.'

$$\overline{\qquad\quad}()$$

     b. TODAY MAN TREE INDEX$_3$ CUT-WITH-SAW$_3$
         'Today the man will cut down the huge tree.'

It is worth noting that the same nonmanuals can also function as intensifiers when combined with manual adjectives. That is, the nonmanual in (1a) might as well combine with the sign SMALL yielding the meaning 'very small' and the nonmanual in (1b) could accompany the sign TALL to express the meaning 'very tall.'

For NSL, Vogt-Svendsen (2001) points out that in combination with a noun, mouthings occasionally function as nonmanual adjectives, in particular, color adjectives. In one of her examples, the nominal sign PULLOVER is accompanied by the mouthing [rœd] ('red') to express the meaning 'red pullover.' She refers to such signs as simultaneous compound signs.

2.2.2 *Nonmanual adverbials*

Mouth gestures may modify not only nouns but also verbs; in this case, the superimposed nonmanual functions as an adverbial expressing how a particular action is executed. For instance, in order to express that a particular action has been done in a relaxed manner, ASL signers may make use of a nonmanual that is glossed as 'mm' (2a). The significant part of this nonmanual is the configuration of the lips: the lips are kept together and pushed out a little bit (Liddell 1980:42).

$$\overline{\qquad\qquad\qquad}\text{mm}$$

(2) a. MAN FISH[continuous]   (ASL)
         'The man was fishing with relaxation and enjoyment.'

$$\overline{\qquad\qquad\quad}\text{th}$$

     b. INDEX$_1$ GO-ACROSS. WRONG, ACCIDENT
         'I crossed the street carelessly. Whoops! There was an accident.'

Another nonmanual adverbial from ASL is illustrated in (2b). According to Liddell, the nonmanual glossed as 'th' contributes the meaning of lack of control, unawareness and inattention. It is the last of the three meanings that is expressed in (2b) (Liddell 1980:52). Clearly, the fact that the action expressed by the verb GO-ACROSS was performed carelessly is essential for the interpretation of the sentence. This nonmanual is characterized by a slight head tilt and protrusion of the tongue through the lips.

2.3   Syntactic nonmanuals

At the level of syntax, nonmanuals can fulfill numerous functions. They may change the polarity of a sentence (section 2.3.1), determine the sentence type (section 2.3.2) and mark topicalized constituents (section 2.3.3). Moreover, they accompany different types of embedded clauses (section 2.3.4 and 2.3.5) and are capable of expressing agreement (section 2.3.6) and person distinctions in pronominals (section 2.3.7).

2.3.1   *Negation and affirmation*
The expression of sentential negation has been investigated for a vast number of sign languages. The available studies show that basically all sign languages have at their disposal manual and nonmanual means to negate a sentence. As far as the latter is concerned, the most common marker is a side-to-side headshake (hs). While these similarities are certainly striking, more recent research has shown that there are also subtle differences between sign languages with respect to the distribution of the headshake.

Let us illustrate the common pattern with ASL examples (Neidle *et al.* 2000:44f). In the presence of the manual negative particle NOT, the headshake can either be co-articulated with the particle only, or it may optionally spread over the VP, as indicated by the square brackets in (3a). The particle, however, is optional, that is, headshake alone is sufficient to negate a proposition. In this case, the headshake *must* spread over the entire VP (3b).

$$\text{hs} \quad [\qquad\quad \text{hs}]$$
(3)   a.   JOHN NOT BUY HOUSE   (ASL)

$$\underline{\qquad\qquad\ \text{hs}\qquad}$$
       b.   JOHN BUY HOUSE
            'John didn't buy the house.'

The example in (4a) indicates that LSC, despite differences in word order, patterns with ASL when the manual negator is present. As in ASL, the particle NOT is optional. In the absence of NOT, however, the spreading pattern is different from the one in ASL. In LSC, it is possible (and actually common) for the headshake to accompany only the predicate. In contrast, in (3b), headshake on BUY only would be ungrammatical. Optionally, headshake may spread onto the direct object (4b) (Pfau & Quer 2002).[1]

      [[ ]] hs

(4) a. SANTI MEAT EAT NOT   (LSC)

[   ] hs

      b. SANTI MEAT EAT
        'Santi doesn't eat meat.'

While nonmanual-only negation seems to be the favored option in many sign languages, there are still some sign languages where a sentence cannot be negated by a negative headshake alone, as illustrated in the ungrammatical Hong Kong Sign Language (HKSL) example in (5) (Tang 2006:217). Other sign languages that have been claimed to require a manual negator are, for example, Italian Sign Language (LIS) and Jordanian Sign Language. Zeshan (2006b) refers to such sign languages as being "manual dominant," while sign languages of the ASL- and LSC-type are considered "nonmanual dominant" sign languages.

hs (over YESTERDAY NIGHT FATHER FAX FRIEND)

(5) * YESTERDAY NIGHT FATHER FAX FRIEND   (HKSL)
      'Father didn't fax his friend last night.'

In addition to the headshake and to the lexically marked head turn (see section 2.1.1), we find a third type of nonmanual marking: a backward head tilt. This is attested only in a few languages (e.g., Greek Sign Language, Turkish Sign Language, Jordanian Sign Language), and it appears to be an areal feature resulting from the grammaticalization of the isomorphic gesture used in the speaking community of that area (Zeshan 2004a). Interestingly, this nonmanual coexists with a negative headshake.

Just like negation, the positive polarity of a clause can be marked nonmanually when required by emphatic affirmation. This is typically realized by co-articulation of a headnod (hn) on the emphasized constituent, as in the following LIS example (Geraci 2005).

hn

(6) SOMEONE ARRIVE   (LIS)
    'Someone *did* arrive.'

2.3.2 *Interrogatives*

Across sign languages, different types of questions are marked by distinct eyebrow positions (Zeshan 2004b). Typically, in yes/no questions, the eyebrows are raised (re). In addition, the head and shoulders are often moved forward. In yes/no questions, it is usually the entire clause that is accompanied by the nonmanual marker, as shown in the ASL example in (7a) (Liddell 1980:20). In fact, in most sign languages, the nonmanual is the only indication that we are dealing with a question, since the word order does not change. In addition to the nonmanual marker, some sign languages employ optional question particles. In NGT, for instance, the particle PALM-UP may appear in sentence-final position (7b).

			re	

(7) a. WOMAN FORGET PURSE   (ASL)
        'Did the woman forget the purse?'

			re	

     b. YESTERDAY INDEX₂ BIKE BUY PALM-UP   (NGT)
        'Did you buy a bike yesterday?'

In contrast, in most sign languages, *wh*-questions are accompanied by lowered eyebrows (le), often in combination with a slight backward head tilt. While in the LIS example in (8a), the nonmanual accompanies the entire clause (Geraci 2005), it has been claimed for ASL that nonmanual marking on the *wh*-sign alone is possible when it appears in sentence-final position (8b) (Neidle *et al.* 2000:113). Still, in ASL, too, the nonmanual may optionally spread over the entire clause.

			le	

(8) a. TOMORROW HOUSE BUY WHO   (LIS)
        'Who will buy a house tomorrow?'

			le	

     b. TEACHER LIPREAD YESTERDAY WHO   (ASL)
        'Who did the teacher lipread yesterday?'

An exception to the general pattern that *wh*-questions are marked by lowered eyebrows is found in Indopakistani Sign Language (IPSL); in this sign language, *wh*-questions are marked by raised eyebrows in combination with chin up and a forward head movement (Aboh, Pfau & Zeshan 2005). In Figure 17.3, we illustrate the nonmanual markers accompanying yes/no- and *wh*-questions in Flemish Sign Language (VGT; Van Herreweghe & Vermeerbergen 2006) as well as the marker attested in IPSL *wh*-questions.

a. VGT yes/no-question   b. VGT wh-question   c. IPSL wh-question

Figure 17.3 *Nonmanuals accompanying VGT interrogatives (a,b) and IPSL wh-questions (c).
Figures (a) and (b) reprinted with permission from Van Herreweghe and Vermeerbergen
(2006). Illustration copyright © Ishara Press.*

2.3.3   *Topics*

In this section, we introduce a nonmanual marker which is related to information
structure: topicalization. While information structure has to do with the discourse
function of a constituent and is therefore clearly pragmatic in nature, topicalization
also has an impact on the constituent order; it can therefore be located at the
syntax–pragmatics interface.[2] Nonmanuals related to information structure that
can be considered purely pragmatic will be discussed in section 2.4.1.

Sign languages are sometimes claimed to be topic-prominent languages – just
like, for example Chinese. Sentence topics are characteristically realized as constituents at the left edge of the clause and are co-articulated with specific nonmanual markers. The basic marking of topics is raised eyebrows, but since the
information structure status of topics can vary, other nonmanuals can be layered
with the raised eyebrows.

In the LSC example in (9a), the direct object occupies a topic position where it
receives nonmanual marking. Example (9b) is different in a number of respects.
First, it involves topic stacking, where the first topic relates to the subject position
and the second is a temporal adjunct. Second, the subject topic is resumed by an
indexical sign in the clause. It has been argued for ASL that different types of topics
are accompanied by slightly different nonmanual markers such as eyes wide open,
backwards movement of the head, mouth open or head jerked up and down
(Aarons 1994). In the gloss, these are usually lumped together as "t." However,
for LSC (and other sign languages) such subtle differences have not yet been
identified.

$$\overline{\quad\quad\text{t}\quad\quad}$$

(9) a. ONION, INDEX₁ HATE   (LSC)
        'Onions, I hate.'

$$\overline{\quad\quad\quad\quad\quad\text{t}\quad\quad\quad\quad\quad}\quad\overline{\quad\quad\quad\quad\quad\text{t}\quad\quad\quad\quad\quad}$$

     b. INDEX₁ BROTHER INDEX₃, TOMORROW MORNING,
         INDEX₃ CAR BUY
         'As for my brother, tomorrow morning he will buy a car.'

The topicalized constituent is usually followed by an intonational break, which is marked by a change of different nonmanuals simultaneously (see section 3.1.3) and possibly an eye blink (see section 3.2).

2.3.4   *Conditionals*

Just like topics, conditionals involve raised eyebrows, possibly in combination with other nonmanual markers (such as raised chin). In fact, similarities between topics and conditionals have been the topic of studies on spoken (Haiman 1978) and signed (Coulter 1979) languages. In the sign languages that have been investigated to date, it is always the protasis, that is, the clause that describes a hypothetical situation, which is accompanied by the nonmanual marker. Just like topics, this clause appears in sentence-initial position; it may be followed by an eye blink (see section 3.1) and by a change in head orientation. In addition, Liddell (1986) argues that in ASL the predicate in the conditional clause is frequently accompanied by a head thrust (ht), see (10a). ASL also has the manual conditional markers I-F and SUPPOSE; the use of one of these markers, however, is optional.

$$\overline{\quad\quad\quad\quad\text{ht}\quad\quad\quad}$$
$$\overline{\quad\quad\quad\quad\quad\quad\text{re}\quad\quad\quad\quad\quad}$$

(10) a. TOMORROW RAIN, PICNIC CANCEL   (ASL)
         'If it rains tomorrow, no picnic.'

$$\overline{\quad\quad\quad\quad\quad\quad\quad\quad\quad\quad\quad\quad\text{re}\quad\quad\quad}$$

     b. IF INDEX₃ INVITE-ME BIRTHDAY-PARTY OF-HIM,
         INDEX₁ GO   (ISL)
         'If he invites me to his birthday party, I will go.'

$$\overline{\quad\quad\quad\quad\quad\text{re \& squint}\quad\quad\quad\quad}$$

     c. IF INDEX₃ STOP SMOKE, INDEX₃ LIVE   (ISL)
         'If he had quit smoking, he would be alive.'

It has been defended that nonmanuals systematically distinguish between factual (neutral) and counterfactual conditionals in Israeli Sign Language (ISL): while

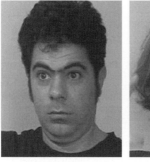

factual/neutral   counterfactual
conditional (10b)   conditional (10c)

Figure 17.4 *Nonmanuals accompanying ISL conditionals. Reprinted with permission from Dachkovsky (2008). Illustration copyright © Signum Press.*

brow raise marks the former type of conditional (10b), the combination of the brow raise and eye squint flags the latter (10c) (Dachkovsky 2008). See Figure 17.4 for illustration of the respective nonmanuals.[3]

2.3.5 *Relative clauses*

In the area of relativization, sign languages have been shown to be subject to typological variation. Just as in spoken languages, an important distinction concerns the use of head-internal versus head-external relative clauses; the former type has been described for ASL (Liddell 1980), while the latter has been identified in DGS. Irrespective of this typological distinction, and similar to topics and the protasis of conditionals, relative clauses are marked by raised eyebrows.

LIS relative clauses usually appear in sentence-initial position. As can be seen in (11a), borrowed from Branchini and Donati (2009), the time adverbial TODAY preceding the head noun MAN has scope over the relative clause predicate. Moreover, the nonmanual (re) extends over the head noun and the adverbial, thereby defining a prosodic constituent (see section 3.1). Note that PE is an obligatory clause-final marker that is accompanied by the mouth gesture [pǝ] (Cecchetto, Geraci & Zucchi 2006, Branchini & Donati 2009).[4]

                                                                     re

(11)   a.   [TODAY MAN₃ PIE BRING PE₃] YESTERDAY (INDEX₃)
            DANCE   (LIS)
            'The man that brought the pie today danced yesterday.'

$$\text{b.}\quad \overline{\text{body lean-3a}}$$

$$\overline{\text{re}}\quad\quad\quad [\overline{\text{re}}]$$

b.   TOMORROW [MAN (INDEX$_{3a}$) [RPRO$_{3a}$ TIE BUY]]
     CONFERENCE$_{3b}$ GO-TO$_{3b}$ (DGS)
     'Tomorrow the man who is buying a tie will go to a conference.'

Things are different in DGS. Note that in (11b), the adverbial TOMORROW scopes over the main clause predicate and, crucially, the head noun MAN is outside of the domain of the nonmanual marker, which either marks only the clause-initial relative pronoun RPRO or spreads over the entire relative clause. It has therefore been suggested that DGS relative clauses are externally headed (Pfau & Steinbach 2005). In addition, DGS relative clauses may be accompanied by a body lean toward the locus of the antecedent of the relative, i.e., locus 3a in (11b).

2.3.6   *Agreement*

It has long been realized that in most sign languages, the movement and/or orientation parameter of certain verbs can be modulated to express agreement with the subject and the object of the verb (Padden 1988). That is, agreement can be realized manually (see Mathur and Rathmann, this volume, and Padden *et al.*, this volume, for discussion). More recently, it has been claimed that, at least in ASL, agreement can also be expressed nonmanually (Bahan 1996, Neidle *et al.* 2000). The important observation is that in transitive sentences, head tilt toward the subject locus may be used to express subject agreement while eye gaze toward the object locus may mark object agreement. These markings are found both in clauses containing agreement verbs (like BLAME in (12a)) and in clauses containing plain verbs (like LOVE in (12b)). Note that head tilt is argued to begin slightly prior to eye gaze (examples adapted from Neidle *et al.* (2000:64).

$$\overline{\text{head tilt-3a}}$$
$$\overline{\text{eye gaze-3b}}$$

(12)   a.   ANN$_{3a}$ $_{3a}$BLAME$_{3b}$ MARY$_{3b}$ (ASL)
            'Ann blames Mary.'

$$\overline{\text{head tilt-3a}}$$
$$\overline{\text{eye gaze-3b}}$$

b.   JOHN$_{3a}$ LOVE MARY$_{3b}$
     'John loves Mary.'

However, the assumption that eye gaze systematically targets the locus of the object referent is challenged in a study by Thompson, Emmorey and Kluender (2006).

Making use of eye-tracking equipment, they show, amongst other things, that only eye gaze accompanying agreement verbs frequently targets the object location. In contrast, with plain verbs, eye gaze is rarely directed toward the object; rather, it targets the addressee or some other location. They therefore conclude that there is no nonmanual object agreement in plain verbs.[5]

2.3.7   *Pronominalization*

The pointing sign glossed as INDEX in the previous examples has been argued to fulfill various functions: it is used to localize a referent in signing space (as in (11b)), it may function as a definite determiner or a spatial adverbial, and last but not least, it may serve to pronominalize an argument. In particular, the latter use of INDEX is debated (see Coppola & Senghas, this volume). While the first person pronoun INDEX$_1$ has a fixed location (the signer's chest), the same does not hold for second and third person pronouns, which can be articulated anywhere in the signing space (the "listability problem"). It has therefore been argued that sign languages, in contrast to spoken languages, distinguish only between first and non-first person in their pronominal systems (Meier 1990).

This proposal has been challenged on the basis of meticulous analyses of the pronominal systems of Brazilian Sign Language (LSB; Berenz 2002) and Croatian Sign Language (HZJ; Alibašić Ciciliani & Wilbur 2006). In both studies, it is argued that nonmanual properties systematically distinguish second from third person pronouns. Taking into account not only the direction of pointing, but also the direction of eye gaze and degree of head turn, the authors find that all three parameters align with each other in second person pronouns but tend to be in disjunction in third person pronouns. That is, when pointing to the addressee, the face and the eye gaze follow the direction of the hand. For the sake of illustration, we give two representative HZJ examples in Figure 17.5. Note that in the right picture, the nonmanual features eye gaze and head turn are not aligned with the hand.

The evidence from HZJ and LSB suggests that at least these sign languages distinguish between first, second and third person in their pronominal systems, thereby conforming to a universal that has been suggested on the basis of spoken language evidence.

2.4   Pragmatics

2.4.1   *Focus: body leans*

In section 2.1.1, we already pointed out that certain verbs may be lexically specified for body leans. Besides this phonological function, another important function of

second person   third person
pronoun   pronoun

Figure 17.5 *HZJ pronouns distinguished by nonmanuals. Reprinted with permission from Alibašić Ciciliani and Wilbur (2006). Illustration copyright © John Benjamins.*

body leans lies in marking pragmatic distinctions. In this use, leans interact with the discourse notion of focus. Broadly, forward leans are associated with inclusion and affirmation, while backward leans are associated with exclusion and negation.

Wilbur and Patschke (1998) distinguish various focus functions of leans, some signaling completive focus, some indicating contrastive focus. Here, we will consider only one example of the latter type: replacing (corrective) focus whereby a specific item of the previous discourse is rejected and replaced by another item. In the ASL example in (13), we observe a backward lean on the rejected (i.e., excluded) item but a forward lean on the replacing (i.e., included) item (Wilbur & Patschke 1998:296).

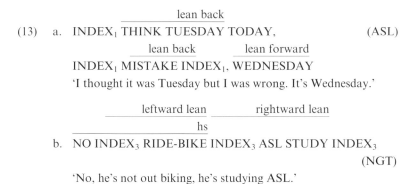

contrast is more common. The sentence in (13b) is a response to the question "Is your brother riding his bike?" Note, however, that the left–right contrast in NGT is not used systematically to indicate inclusion/exclusion, as has been suggested for the forward/backward contrast in ASL by Wilbur and Patschke.

2.4.2   *Role shift*

Role shift (also known as role taking and referential shift) plays two, sometimes overlapping, roles in the grammar of sign languages. First, in its quotational use, it is used to directly report the speech or the unspoken thoughts of a character (also known as constructed discourse). Consider the LSC sentence pair in (14). Example (14a) involves indirect speech; $INDEX_{3a}$ in the embedded clause targets the locus in signing space that has been assigned for ANNA. In contrast, in (14b), we observe a slight body shift toward the locus of ANNA (bs-3a) following the main clause predicate SAY. Crucially, in this example, the signer uses the first person pronoun $INDEX_1$ to refer to the referent producing the reported utterance. In addition to body shift, role shift may be marked by a change in head position, and a break in eye gaze contact with the addressee (Quer 2005).

(14)   a. $ANNA_{3a\ 3a}SAY_1\ INDEX_{3a}$ FED-UP LOSE + + +   (LSC)
'Anna told me that she was fed up with losing so often.'

$$\overline{\qquad\qquad\qquad\qquad\qquad\text{bs-3a}\qquad}$$
b. $ANNA_{3a\ 3a}SAY_1\ INDEX_1$ FED-UP LOSE + + +

Second, in its non-quotational use, role shift expresses a character's action, including facial expressions and non-linguistic gestures. That is, the signer embodies the event from the character's perspective. This embodiment is also referred to as constructed or reported action. The DGS example in (15) is part of a retelling of a *Canary Row* episode. The signer first takes on the role of the cat by means of facial expression and eye gaze; the referent is projected onto the signer's body and the action is reported as seen in the cartoon. He then switches to the role of the bird, again by adapting the nonmanual features to those of the cartoon character. Note that the adverbials in the translation are inferred from the nonmanual features.

		tongue out	pursed lips
		squint	eyes open
	t	eye gaze up	eye gaze down

(15)   DRAIN-PIPE, CAT CLIMB-UP(2h), FLAT-SURFACE BIRD LOOK-DOWN
(DGS)

'The cat (eagerly/slyly) climbs up through the drain pipe while the bird (curiously) looks down from the roof.'

There is some overlap between both uses of role shift since in quotational role shift, signers frequently take on affective facial expressions of the character whose utterance they report (e.g., an annoyed or frustrated expression in (14b)). Moreover, non-quotational role shift may also involve body shift to a character's locus in signing space.

3   Prosodic functions of nonmanuals

The intention of the previous sections was to convince the reader that nonmanual markers are indeed an essential part of the grammar of natural sign languages. Although the story so far certainly does not suffer from a lack of complexity, we shall now add to our investigation yet another domain in which nonmanuals have been claimed to play a crucial role, thereby making the plot yet more complex. The domain that we are referring to is prosody.

Besides the various grammatical functions set out above, it has been shown that nonmanuals also participate in structuring an utterance prosodically. In sign languages, just as in spoken languages, utterances are organized in chunks that are characterized by intricate patterns of stress, rhythm and intonation. These patterns are referred to as prosody. The relevant prosodic chunks are hierarchically organized according to the Prosodic Hierarchy in (16) (Selkirk 1984).

(16)   syllable > foot > **prosodic word** > phonological phrase > **intonational phrase (IntP)** > phonological utterance

While it has been argued that the syllable (see Jantunen and Takkinen, this volume) and the phonological phrase (Sandler 1999b) are also relevant prosodic constituents in sign languages, in the following we shall be concerned only with the prosodic word and the intonational phrase (IntP). Two distinct groups of nonmanual markers will be discussed: domain markers (section 3.1) and edge markers (section 3.2).

3.1   Domain markers

The ability to be co-articulated with a sequence of adjacent signs is a hallmark of domain markers. The reader will remember that, actually, most (if not all) of the syntactic nonmanuals introduced in section 2.3 are also capable of accompanying complex constituents, i.e., syntactic domains. At the same time, however, non-manuals can also accompany prosodic domains. We therefore have to start our discussion of domain markers with a note on the relation between syntactic and prosodic phrasing (section 3.1.1). Following these preliminary remarks, we will show how nonmanual domain markers can be employed to mark prosodic words (section 3.1.2) and intonational phrases (section 3.1.3).

3.1.1   *On the relation between syntactic and prosodic phrasing*

What complicates the search for specifically prosodic nonmanual markers is the fact that prosodic structure frequently aligns with syntactic constituency. The apparent isomorphism though is not complete, which suggests that the two grammatical components are autonomous (Nespor & Vogel 1986). Still, given that there is a tendency for prosodic constituents to be isomorphic with syntactic ones, the same nonmanual marker could potentially be interpreted as fulfilling a syntactic and/or prosodic function. In other words, one nonmanual marker might play multiple roles in grammar. For instance, since a topicalized constituent forms its own IntP, it cannot be decided with certainty whether the nonmanual marker accompanying the topic (see example (9)) marks a syntactic or a prosodic domain.

Sign language examples where syntactic and prosodic structure do not fully overlap are difficult to come by. The DGS example (11b), repeated in (17), is a possible candidate. While syntactic structure groups the antecedent noun MAN with the relative clause material (17a), intonationally the head noun and the preceding adverbial form a prosodic constituent which is independent of the relative clause (17b), as indicated by the nonmanual marking.

$$\overline{\phantom{\text{TOMORROW}}\text{re}\,[\text{re}]}$$

(17)   a.   Sy: TOMORROW [MAN (IX$_{3a}$) RPRO$_{3a}$ TIE BUY]
              CONFERENCE$_{3b}$ GO-TO$_{3b}$ (DGS)

$$\overline{\phantom{\text{TOMORROW}}\text{re}\,[\text{re}]}$$

         b.   Pr: [TOMORROW MAN (IX$_{3a}$)] [RPRO$_{3a}$ TIE BUY]
              [CONFERENCE$_{3b}$ GO-TO$_{3b}$]

              'Tomorrow the man who is buying a tie will go to a conference.'

In addition, nonmanuals associated with a specific syntactic construction are often lumped together into a single marker, although it might well be the case that the different components of the complex (layered) nonmanual marker have specialized functions, i.e., syntactic vs. prosodic. This hypothesis awaits further investigation. We will come back to the layering of nonmanuals in section 3.1.3.

In current theorizing on nonmanual phrasing, there are opposing views as to whether domain markers are ultimately determined by syntactic or prosodic structure. According to the first view, all grammatical nonmanuals spell out morpho-syntactic features (e.g., [+wh], [+top], [+neg]) in dedicated positions in the sentence structure (Wilbur & Patschke 1999, Neidle *et al.* 2000). In contrast, proponents of the second view claim that "grammatical facial expressions in sign language are best understood as intonational 'tunes'" (Sandler & Lillo-Martin

2006:259). Obviously, a more fine-grained account of the interaction of syntax and prosody is needed to resolve the tension between these domains of grammar and to do justice to the complexity of the facts.

3.1.2 *Mouthings and the prosodic word*

Occasionally in connected speech, two free words may be merged into one prosodic word. This process generally affects adjacent lexical and functional elements (e.g., English *haven't*) and is referred to as cliticization. For ISL, Sandler (1999b) describes a number of manual indicators of cliticization, such as phonetic weakening by handshape assimilation and coalescence, whereby halfway through the production of a symmetrical two-handed lexical sign, the dominant hand signs a pronominal sign, while the non-dominant hand completes the lexical sign. In coalescence, the pronoun loses its own syllabicity (see Jantunen and Takkinen, this volume, for discussion), but in assimilation, too, the lexical and the functional sign are often merged into one movement contour.

Besides that, nonmanual markers can also be indicative of cliticization. Frequently, mouthings spread from the lexical sign with which they are associated onto a neighboring functional sign. In a comparative study on NGT, British Sign Language (BSL) and Swedish Sign Language (SSL), Crasborn *et al.* 2008 found that all three sign languages make similar use of mouth patterns (mouth gestures and mouthings) and that in all three sign languages, mouth patterns are capable of spreading (which they compare to tone spreading in spoken languages). Spreading characteristics of mouthings, however, turned out to differ between sign languages. In NGT and BSL, the spreading direction was almost without exception rightward. In the NGT example in (18a), we observe three instances of spreading of mouthing, two from lexical sign onto a right-adjacent INDEX, one from lexical sign onto a classifier (the Dutch words for 'village,' 'boy' and 'live' are *dorp* [dorp], *jongen* [joŋən] and *wonen* [vo:nən], respectively).

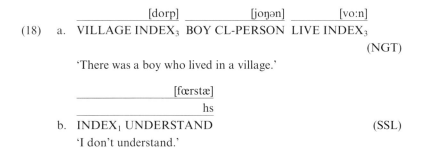

                            [dorp]   [joŋən]   [vo:n]

(18)   a. VILLAGE INDEX₃ BOY CL-PERSON LIVE INDEX₃

                                                                 (NGT)

          'There was a boy who lived in a village.'

                              [fœrstæ]

                                    hs

       b. INDEX₁ UNDERSTAND   (SSL)

          'I don't understand.'

In contrast to NGT and BSL, SSL also allows for leftward spreading of mouthings, that is, spreading from a lexical sign onto a preceding functional element. In the corpus compiled by Crasborn *et al.* (2008), in almost a third of the SSL examples that involve spreading, spreading proceeds leftward, as, e.g., in (18b), in which the mouthing spreads onto a left-adjacent first person pronoun ('understand' in Swedish is *förstå* [fœrstæ]).[6]

It has to be pointed out that spreading of mouthing, while being a possible indicator of cliticization, is also observed in other contexts. Crasborn *et al.* 2008 report cases in which mouthing spreads from one lexical sign onto another lexical sign and even cases where mouthing spreads over more than one adjacent sign. Therefore, in order to determine whether an instance of spreading flags cliticization, movement and handshape characteristics of the sequence also have to be considered.

3.1.3 *Layered nonmanuals and the intonational phrase*

As pointed out above, nonmanual markers – in contrast to prosodic signals in spoken languages (tones) – can be layered in a complex fashion. Sandler (1999b) refers to this phenomenon as superarticulation, which should be understood as the sign language equivalent of suprasegmentals.

As far as the intonational phrase is concerned, Nespor & Sandler (1999) and Sandler (1999b) conclude that superarticulatory arrays of nonmanuals systematically change at IntP boundaries. For the sake of illustration consider the ISL example in (19), which is given in a detailed score notation (adapted from Sandler 1999b:206). The example consists of two IntPs, the first one containing a topic, the second one the main (adjectival) predicate.

(19)   [[BOOK-THERE]$_P$ [INDEX$_3$ WRITE]$_P$]$_{Int}$ [[INTERESTING]$_P$]$_{Int}$ (ISL)

brows	_____ up	_____ down
eyes	_____ squint _____	_____ droop
mouth	_____ 'O'	_____ down
head	_____ tilt	
mouthing	___ 'book' ___	'interesting'
torso	_____ lean	

It is worth pointing out that within the first IntP, some of the nonmanuals (eye and mouth position) also change, presumably marking smaller intonational units, namely two phonological phrases (P) corresponding to a head noun and a relative clause. However, it is only at the IntP boundary that all nonmanuals change. Besides the nonmanual signals coded in (19), Sandler also describes a number of manual cues, such as repetition of sign, signing speed and size. Again, in this example, the prosodic structure reflects syntactic constituency.

3.2 Edge markers

In contrast to domain markers, prosodic edge markers signal the edge of a prosodic domain. They are punctual in nature, that is, they do not spread. The two types of edge markers that we want to briefly discuss are head thrusts and eye blinks. As pointed out by Wilbur (2000), there is an important difference between these two markers: while head thrusts occur on the last sign of a prosodic domain, eye blinks follow the last sign of a prosodic domain, that is, they occur during a pause (during which the last manual sign may be held).

A head thrust is articulated with the lower jaw thrust forward. Above, we have already illustrated that head thrusts tend to co-occur with the last sign of an 'if' clause in ASL (10a). Wilbur (2000) adds to this observation that head thrust is also observed on the last sign of "when" clauses (see note 3).

Eye blinks are a highly complex matter since there are different types of blinks: startle reflex blinks, involuntary periodic blinks and voluntary blinks. According to Wilbur (1994a), the last two types can serve linguistic functions: periodic blinks serve as boundary markers and voluntary blinks occur on lexical signs. Here, we will only consider periodic blinks. In particular, Wilbur argues that one of the functions of periodic blinks is to mark the edge of an IntP. For HKSL, Sze (2008) also argues that periodic blinks can function as prosodic edge markers ("boundary-sensitive blinks" in her terminology). In (20a), for instance, the blink (bl) occurs on a pause following a conditional antecedent which constitutes an IntP.

<pre>
                         bl
</pre>
(20) a. SUBSIDY HAVE,   RESTRICT-ONE'S FREEDOM   (HKSL)
         'If you receive a subsidy (from government), your freedom will be restricted.'

<pre>
                           bl
</pre>
   b. INTERPRETER STAND SIGN, INDEX₁ INDEX DEAF WATCH
<pre>
                              bl
</pre>
   UNDERSTAND CONVENIENT
         'The interpreter stood (in front of the deaf person) and signed. That deaf person and I watched her signing and understood; it was very convenient.'

In addition, Sze (2008) reports boundary-sensitive blinks that overlap entirely or partly with the co-occurring sign. In other words, these blinks behave just like the head thrust in that they occur on the last sign of a prosodic domain, thereby weakening the distinction made by Wilbur (2000). In (20b), two blinks overlap with SIGN and CONVENIENT suggesting that they serve as boundary markers. Sze also points out that blinks frequently occur at other grammatical boundaries that do not overlap with an IntP boundary, for example between a subject and its following predicate (see also Tang *et al.*, this volume).

4   Summary

In natural signed discourse, nonmanual markers are all over the place. Actually, it is quite likely that if one blackened the face of a signer on a video recording, a good part of the meaning of the message would be lost because important lexical distinctions, morphological modifications and syntactic structures could no longer be detected. Surely, pragmatic information conveyed by body leans would still be visible and (part of) the prosodic structure could probably be inferred from manual cues such as pauses and holds. Claiming that nonmanual markers are an essential part of sign languages at the level of grammar and prosody is therefore certainly no exaggeration.

Much work remains to be done in identifying and analyzing relevant nonmanual markers. Obviously, this is a challenging task given that such markers may have very subtle properties. Once a potential candidate has been identified, its actual function has to be investigated. A prerequisite for an accurate classification is a thorough understanding of the grammatical structure of the sign language under investigation. Interesting avenues of research are opened by recent psycholinguistic and neurolinguistic studies that investigate the acquisition of linguistic nonmanuals (e.g., Reilly & Anderson 2002) or the selective impairment of nonmanual processing (Corina, Bellugi & Reilly 1999; Atkinson *et al.* 2004).

PART III
Variation and change

18

Sign languages in West Africa

Victoria Nyst

1   Introduction

Little is known about the sign languages used on the African continent. This chapter considers the distribution, use and history of sign languages in the western part of this continent. Studies pertaining to these topics are very rare, and for a number of countries information is completely lacking. For others only bits and pieces of information are available. A radical increase of research efforts in this area is necessary. At present, some basic information on the sign language situation and structure is available for Ghana, Mali and Nigeria. A typical feature of the sign language situation in these and other countries is the coexistence of local and imported sign languages. The most widespread sign language of foreign origin is beyond doubt American Sign Language (ASL), which was introduced in many countries together with deaf education in the past five decades.

The sign language situation in West Africa is as diverse as it is undocumented. A non-exhaustive list of sign languages used in West Africa is found in Table 18.1. Their places of use are indicated on the map in Figure 18.1. The list of sign languages is partly based on information in the Ethnologue (www.ethnologue. org), partly on Kamei (2006) and partly on my own information.[1]

This chapter starts off with an inventory of basic facts about deafness in West Africa in section 2, followed by a short history of deaf education in the region in section 3. The impact of language policies in deaf education on the current sign language situation is considered, most notably visible in the extensive use of ASL-based varieties. An overview of sign languages reportedly found in West Africa is given in sections 4 and 5, including their vitality and origins. Also, factors contributing to variation in the social setting and transmission are discussed. Case studies of the sign language situation in three countries, Ghana, Nigeria and Mali, are presented in section 5.3.

The data presented here were in part observed during several periods of fieldwork in Ghana and Mali between 1999 and 2004 and travels through Burkina

Table 18.1 *Sign languages used in West Africa*

English name	Acronym	Alternative names	Origin	Where used in West Africa
Adamorobe Sign Language	AdaSL	Mumu kasa	Local	Village of Adamorobe, Ghana
American Sign Language	ASL	Ameslan, Langue des Signes Franco-Africaine	Foreign	Benin, Burkina Faso, Cote d'Ivoire, Ghana, Liberia, Mauritania, Mali, Nigeria, Togo
Bura Sign Language			Local	Bura land in Nigeria
French Sign Language	LSF	Langue des Signes Française	Foreign	Togo
Gambian Sign Language		–	Foreign, ASL based	Gambia
Ghanaian Sign Language		–	Foreign, ASL based	Ghana
Guinea-Bissau Sign Language		Lingua Gestual Guineense	Local	Guinea-Bissau
Guinea Sign Language		–	Foreign, ASL based	Conakry, Guinea-Conakry
Hausa Sign Language	HSL	Maganar Hannu	Local	Kano state, Nigeria
Mali Sign Language	LaSiMa	Langue des Signes Malienne, Langue des Signes Bambara	Local	Bamako, Mali
Mbour Sign Language		–	Local	Town of Mbour, Senegal
Burkina Faso Sign Language		Langue des Signes Mossi	Local	Ouagadougou, Burkina Faso
Nanabin Sign Language		–	Local	Deaf family in village of Nanabin, Ghana
Nigerian Sign Language		–	Foreign, ASL based	Nigeria
Portuguese Sign Language	LGP	Lingua Gestual Portuguesa	Foreign	Cabo Verde
Sierra Leone Sign Language		–	Foreign, ASL based	Sierra Leone
Tebul Ure Sign Language		–	Local	Village of Tebul Ure, Mali

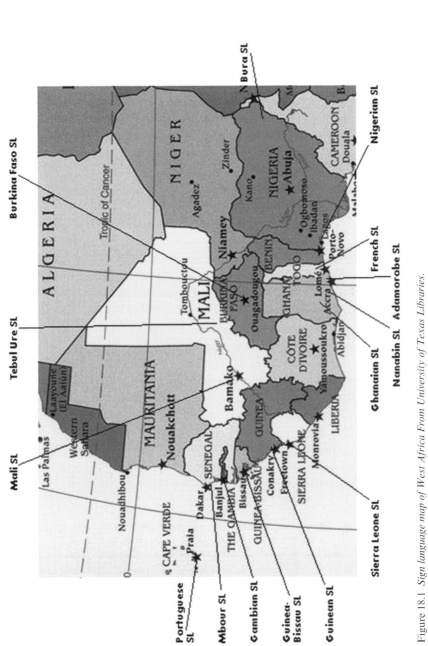

Figure 18.1 *Sign language map of West Africa From University of Texas Libraries.*

Faso, the Ivory Coast and Benin. Information on other countries is based on literature and personal communications of visitors and inhabitants of the relevant country, as indicated between brackets.[2]

2   Deafness and signing populations

Hard figures on the prevalence of deafness in West Africa are not available at present. Figures are based either on general estimates for the incidence of deafness in developing countries or on counts for specific regions within a country. UNICEF (1985) gives an estimate of 0.5 percent for the incidence of moderate to severe hearing loss in developing countries.

Although different assessment methods and hearing loss criteria have been used, studies on smaller groups, typically concentrating on child populations, tend to confirm the UNICEF estimate.

Investigating the prevalence of disabilities in 2,556 children in the Central Region in Ghana, Biritwum *et al.* (2001:252) find that 0.46 percent of the children "had difficulty with hearing and speech." Based on a study of 259 children, McPherson and Swart (1997) extrapolate a national prevalence of 0.27 percent for Gambian children. In Sierra Leone four out of every 1,000 children were found to have bilateral profound hearing impairment (Seely *et al.* 1995). However, the group of children with a mild to greater hearing loss was found to be much larger, as more than 9 percent of the 2,015 children tested fell in this category.

Evaluating the studies done on deafness in West Africa, McPherson and Swart (1997) conclude that the prevalence of severe and profound bilateral hearing loss in this region is about three to four times the prevalence rate in industrialized nations. This suggests that the number of people mainly relying on visual language is much higher as well. In fact, when taking into account the restricted access to hearing aids, we may expect the percentage of children that mainly depend on visual language to be higher than the percentage of children diagnosed with profound bilateral hearing impairment.

3   The influence of Andrew Foster on deaf education in West Africa

One person, the Deaf African American missionary Reverend Andrew Foster (1927–1987), has been of major importance for the establishment of deaf education in West Africa. In the majority of West African countries, deaf education was introduced by Foster, the first African American to graduate from what is now Gallaudet University. In 1956, Foster established the Christian Mission for the Deaf (CMD) in the United States (Kiyaga & Moores 2003). The CMD established the first school for the deaf in Ghana in 1957, the year of Ghana's independence. Eight more schools were to follow in Ghana, which are now all government schools. In addition to the nine schools in Ghana, the CMD established twenty-two more schools in seventeen other countries, including Nigeria, the Ivory Coast, Togo, Senegal, Benin and Burkina Faso (Caroll & Mather 1997). Foster also established teacher training colleges in Ghana, Nigeria and in the Democratic Republic of Congo, where deaf people were trained to become teachers of the deaf to enable them to establish schools in their home countries. Foster died in 1987 at the age of sixty when his aircraft dropped from the radar above Rwanda.

Foster has become a legend in the African history of the Deaf and rightly so. It seems hard to overstate his significance for the education of the deaf in West Africa. He has been likened to key figures in the Deaf history of other countries, such as Laurent Clerc and Thomas Hopkins Gallaudet in the United States of America, but as Kiyaga and Moores comment (2003:20): "In reality, however, Foster surpassed both of these leaders. In the sheer numbers of schools he established by himself, Foster is unrivaled by anyone, hearing or deaf, in the history of education of the Deaf." Accounts of Foster's role in deaf education emphasize his manifold virtues, including his charisma and his talent for public relations. He convinced authorities of the urgent necessity to provide deaf children with basic education and not to wait for fully equipped schools and trained personnel (Foster 1975). The CMD continues its activities in deaf education in Africa, under the direction of Foster's wife (www.cmdeaf.org) and is currently responsible for six schools. Most other schools have become government schools or have closed down for various reasons.

Foster advocated for the use of Total Communication in the education of deaf children. Although the manual method has been predominant in West African deaf education with the rapid spread of CMD schools, the oralist method of educating deaf children certainly did not miss out on West Africa either. However, the oralist schools were not orchestrated by one large organization and, as a result, much less documentation is available about this type of education in the region. At least two issues complicate the application of oralist methods in the West African context as compared to the Western context. First, West African societies are much more multilingual than Western societies. This makes the selection of a spoken language for the instruction and training of oral skills of deaf children much more difficult, as the linguistic home situation of the deaf pupils is typically very diverse. In many countries, the official language is selected as the spoken language to instruct deaf children. However, the language of the home situation is typically another one and relatives may not be conversant in the official language. Thus, deaf children may face communicative problems when going home. An additional complication concerns the distinctive role of tone in many West African languages. Foster (1975) argued that differences in tone are very hard to perceive through speechreading.

In short, Reverend Andrew Foster played a key role in the establishment of deaf education in many West African nations from 1957 until his death in 1987. His missionary institution has continued his work after his death. Foster advocated for the use of Total Communication in deaf education and used ASL signs in his schools.

4   Foreign sign languages

The activities of the CMD in deaf education in West and Central Africa have had an enormous impact on the sign language ecology in these regions. The possibility of deaf education in the form of boarding schools brought together deaf individuals who would not have met otherwise. Boarding schools not only bring together deaf children, they also significantly reduce the contact of the deaf children with their home environment, which consists of hearing people in most cases. Little information is available on the presence of Deaf communities prior to the establishment of deaf education. It is likely that the continuous concentration of deaf children resulted in new Deaf communities in places where none existed prior to deaf education. In places where Deaf communities were already present, as, for example, in Northern Nigeria and Mali (see sections 5.3.2.1 and 5.3.4.1), these are likely to have grown and changed in character due to the establishment of deaf education. For example, Deaf communities that arose in the context of deaf education typically have a National Association of the Deaf and contacts with the World Federation of the Deaf.

In Foster's CMD schools, Total Communication was used, which entailed the use of a form of Signed English, using lexical items from ASL and artificial signs representing functional elements in English (Oteng 1997). It is likely that Foster was using forms of ASL less influenced by English as well in his daily interactions with teachers and pupils.

As a consequence, forms of ASL rapidly spread throughout the region. ASL-based sign languages are the first language of educated deaf adults in most countries. They are the sign language used and advocated for by the National Associations of the Deaf. They are typically considered the official sign language of a country and are referred to as such as well, e.g., Ghanaian Sign Language (GhSL), Nigerian Sign Language and so on. These sign languages figure in vocabularies, interpretation on television and sign language courses organized by the associations.

An interesting question is to what extent these ASL-based sign languages are similar to ASL. Forms of ASL were introduced to West Africa several decades ago

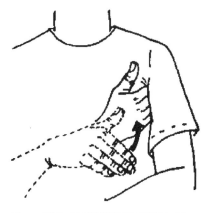

Figure 18.2 *AKPETESHIE (GSL). Signs reprinted with the kind permission of the authors from GNAD (n.d.).*

Figure 18.3 *ODWIRA (GSL).*

with limited access to native performance in this language. Thus, significant divergence can be expected.

Moreover, signs of local origin have been added to the lexicons of the languages. Foster (1975) encouraged the use of so-called "natural signs," conventional gestures or signs already used by deaf adults in a given country or region.

Such local or "natural" signs include signs for culture-specific notions, such as particular dishes and drinks, ceremonial activities and objects, names for places and ethnic groups. An example of a local sign included in the ASL-based sign language of Ghana, GhSL, is given in Figure 18.2. This is the sign for AKPETESHIE, a locally brewed alcoholic beverage. Another example from GSL is given in Figure 18.3. This is the sign for ODWIRA, a festival celebrated annually by some large ethnic groups in Ghana.

However, local signs are used not only when no ASL sign is available for a given concept. There seems to be a growing awareness of the value of a distinct national sign language and an acknowledgment of pre-existing local signs. As a result, local signs are also adopted or given a higher status even when a conventional ASL sign is available. Thus, in GhSL, the local signs, illustrated in Figures 18.4 and 18.5, respectively, are given for WICKED and BEAT in the dictionary for Ghanaian Sign Language (GNAD, n.d.).

No comparisons have been made between the lexicons of an African and an American ASL variety as far as I know, nor of two African varieties. Resources for a reliable comparison of African varieties are lacking at present. Only a very limited number of dictionaries of West African varieties of ASL has been published so far. The above-mentioned dictionary for GSL contains little over

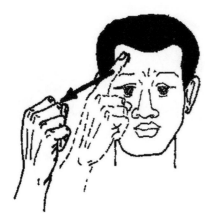

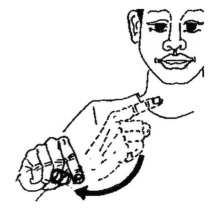

Figure 18.4 *WICKED (GSL)*.

Figure 18.5 *BEAT (GSL)*.

900 signs and was published in around 2001 by the Ghana National Association of the Deaf. This dictionary tends to render only one sign per concept and thus gives little information on variation. Other dictionaries on ASL-based sign languages are Ajavon (2003) for Nigerian Sign Language, GADHOH (2002) for Gambian Sign Language and Tamomo (1994) for ASL in francophone African countries, published in Benin. Avajon's dictionary for Nigerian Sign Language seems to be a prescriptive one, aiming at the inclusion of local signs in Nigerian Sign Language, but the criteria used for choosing or identifying local signs is not sufficiently clarified to use the dictionary as a reliable source of actual language use. I have not had the opportunity to lay hands on the other two dictionaries mentioned.

It would be interesting to assess the level of lexical similarity between African varieties of ASL and varieties of ASL used in the United States by using the lexicostatistical method as developed for sign languages (Woodward 1987, 1991, 1993, 1996; McKee & Kennedy 2000; but also Padden and Al-Fityani, this volume and Schembri *et al.*, also in this volume). Obviously, more – and more representative – data are needed for such a study to be reliable.

As for the structural level, it is harder to generate any expectations other than very general ones, which take into account the structural variation found in the sign languages studied so far. Whereas the signs introduced by Foster were tagged to a spoken language structure, following the Total Communication philosophy, this no longer seems to be case for the ASL-based sign languages I have seen in Ghana, the Ivory Coast and Burkina Faso. Nevertheless, there appear to be significant differences between ASL-based sign languages in anglophone and francophone countries. Kamei (2006) has made an extensive study of the ASL-based sign languages in francophone countries in West and Central Africa. He notes considerable adaptations made to the ASL-based sign languages in francophone countries, reflecting the intensive contact with spoken and written French. Thus, initialized signs may be modified to reflect the corresponding French word, rather than the English equivalent. English mouthings are replaced by French ones. Finally, these sign languages use calques or loan translations from French, such as compounds and idiomatic expressions. The adaptations of ASL signs to reflect features from spoken French, as well as the integration of a considerable number of local signs, result in sign languages that are unique for the African, francophone context. Consequently, Kamei (2006) argues that they are African creoles of ASL. He coins the term "Langue des Signes Franco-Africaine" as a generic term to refer to the group of sign languages that have arisen in francophone countries in Africa, leaving open the possibility that the generic term may turn out to cover a group of distinct but related sign languages.

From Kamei's account, it seems clear that enough restructuring has happened to consider the ASL-based sign languages in francophone African countries to be distinct from standard ASL. However, the restructuring described only pertains to the lexical and the sub-lexical level and thus seems to concern relexification. Relexification is a process described in the literature on contact linguistics as the replacement of lexical items of one – usually low-prestige – language by the lexical items of another – usually high-prestige – language (cf. Arends, Muysken & Smith 1995). In this case, the relexification has not been brought about by a difference in prestige, but by a difference in the languages in contact. Relexification is a very useful notion in describing sign languages as it provides a useful perspective on sign-supported speech, signed forms of spoken language like Signed English, but also manifestations of language planning, in particular with respect to the lexicon, to which I will turn later.

Observations of GhSL indicate that African varieties of ASL may also differ from North American varieties of ASL at the phonetic level. The articulation of GhSL is notably more lax than standard ASL, particularly in the handshape parameter. As such, GSL shows interesting parallels with Adamorobe Sign Language, a Ghanaian sign language of local origin (Nyst 2007).

In addition to the ASL varieties introduced in West Africa several decades ago by the CMD, there is also continuous input of North American varieties of ASL at present in some places in West Africa. Notably the presence of ASL-signing teachers sent out by the American volunteer organization Peace Corps guarantees continuous contact between American and African varieties of ASL.

An interesting question that will remain unanswered here is the extent to which the African varieties of ASL differ from each other. Kamei (2006) speculates that the different varieties of ASL-based sign languages in francophone African countries may turn out to be different enough to be considered distinct languages. However, signers of ASL-based varieties can communicate without problems across national borders, suggesting a – unsurprisingly – considerable amount of lexical overlap. Vocabularies produced for an ASL-based variety in one country may be used in other countries as well, which raises the degree of lexical similarity between these varieties. Notably, the dictionary published by Tamomo (1994) in Benin seems to aim at an international public, as suggested by its title, *Le Langage des Signes du Sourd Africain Francophone*. Indeed, this vocabulary was found to be in use in Mali in 2000.

Clearly, the most influential foreign sign language in West Africa is ASL. Little documentation is available on the use of other sign languages of non-African origin. As noted in section 5.3.4, French Sign Language (LSF) has been used in Mali for some time but is now replaced by an ASL-based sign language. However, contacts with LSF signers remain. According to the Ethnologue: Languages of the World website (www.ethnologue.org), LSF is taught at one school for the deaf in Togo as well, but it is not clear whether this information is up to date. Interestingly, no other sign language is mentioned as in use in this country.

The position of ASL-based sign languages in individual countries and possibly the degree of similarity between these varieties is enforced by the strong international position of ASL in and outside West Africa. As in other places in the world, deaf people in West Africa, especially those who are active in Deaf associations, have active international contacts with each other at the regional, i.e., West African, level. One type of activity leading to international contacts is peddling, that is, going around selling cards with the manual alphabet or pretending to collect contributions for the Association of the Deaf. Peddling has its own dynamics in West Africa and brings together peddlers from diverse nationalities who may travel long distances together. They may pass through several countries, where they are lodged by local deaf people. Although peddling is an activity not judged positively by most deaf people, the contacts with international peddlers also brings news and entertainment from other countries. This facilitates their acceptance by and integration in the local Deaf communities. The exchange between peddlers and the local Deaf communities leads to contact between various ASL-based sign languages and possibly to convergence or to maintenance of existing similarities.

In short, African varieties of ASL are found to differ from North American varieties of ASL in their lexicons, the languages they are in contact with and the reflections thereof (i.e., mouthings, loan translations and initialization) and in their articulation. Despite these differences, signers of North American ASL tend to immediately recognize these varieties as being ASL-based. To what extent the ASL-based varieties have diverged from each other remains to be determined.

5   Local sign languages

When one looks at the sign language situation in West Africa, focusing on language use in the National Associations of the Deaf and in education, it is dominated by foreign sign languages, most notably varieties of ASL.

This raises questions with regard to locally evolved sign languages. Have deaf people formed Deaf communities and consequently sign languages prior to or in the absence of deaf education? How do these local sign languages relate socio-linguistically to the ASL varieties? What are their linguistic features? Based on the available literature, these questions raised above will be discussed in the following three sections respectively.

5.1   Social settings

Sign languages have evolved in a variety of social settings in West Africa. At least in some urban areas, the number of deaf people interacting on a regular basis has been large and stable enough to give rise to the evolution of a conventional and expanded sign language. Examples of such urban sign language centers are the relatively large Deaf communities in Bamako, the capital of Mali (see section 5.3.4.1) and Kano, an old Hausa city in Northern Nigeria (Schmaling 2000; see section 5.3.2.1) and probably Mbour, a fishing town in Senegal (Jirou 2000). In other places a heightened incidence of deafness has resulted in the formation of stable signing communities with a conventional and expanded sign language, such as in Adamorobe, Ghana (Nyst 2007; see section 5.3.1.1). In rural areas, the majority of deaf people have no access to deaf education, nor to an urban Deaf community. As a consequence, they are likely to use "homesign" as their main means of communication.

However, the major part of signed communication in West Africa may turn out not to fit in the neatly formulated categories of "full-fledged sign language" and "homesign." In the Western world, these differences between the sign languages of the large national Deaf communities and the sign languages of deaf children not in contact with these Deaf communities are very large and the categories of full-fledged sign language and of homesign are quite straightforward. In West Africa, there seems to be more diversity in the settings in which deaf (and hearing) people sign. The types of sign languages distinguished in the literature so far do not adequately reflect this diversity. In fact, local sign languages often seem to be used by small groups of deaf signers, who are part of the larger hearing community and who also sign with hearing community members, as e.g., in Tebul Ure in Mali (Blench, personal communication; see section 5.3.4), or in Bura, Eastern Nigeria (see section 5.3.2.2). The influence of hearing signers, considered minor in the case of the sign languages of large Deaf communities in the Western world, is likely to be significant in these smaller African communities. In other places, families with hereditary deafness in several generations may develop a sign language that is so expanded and stable, and used by such a large number of deaf people, that the label homesign no longer seems to be in place, as, e.g., in Nanabin, Ghana (Nyst 2007; see section 6.3.1.1), where a family with three generations of mainly deaf members has developed a stable and extensive family sign language.

The large grey area between the conventional and expanded sign languages of large Deaf communities on the one hand and the functionally more restricted homesign languages on the other has remained virtually unstudied, seemingly because we do not really know what to do with them. They do not represent a kind of "pure" or "native" sign language like the sign languages used by native signers of large Western sign languages, nor do they hypothetically offer answers to the question of how language emerges in the absence of linguistic input, as in the case of homesign in its strict sense. However, the diversity of sign language types and uses found in West Africa presents a complex, but realistic picture of how sign languages emerge and develop naturally, in the absence of artificial sign systems and language planning.

One of the factors that may turn out to be of significant influence in the formation of local sign languages in the gray area, is communication with hearing people. This influence may take at least two forms, in structure and in lexicon that is. First, the number of deaf signers of these sign languages in the gray area is typically limited and the lives of hearing and deaf people are integrated to a relatively large extent. As a result, a strong sense of Deafhood or a distinct Deaf community is generally lacking. Hearing people tend to have a relatively good command of signed communication. However, their signing is likely to be influenced by the structure of their spoken language. Since a strong sense of cultural Deafness is lacking, the deaf varieties of the signed communication are not perceived as being superior or a target for hearing signers. The high proportion of hearing signers, in combination with the equal status of hearing and deaf varieties of signed communication, facilitate the presence of contact-induced features in sign languages in the gray area.

Second, the use of conventional gesture in (West) Africa seems to be relatively extensive. A similar observation is noted in the chapter on sign languages in the Arab-speaking world (Al-Fitiyani and Padden, this volume). Quantitative studies are lacking, but descriptive studies as well as casual observation suggest that hearing people use conventional gestures relatively frequently and that the lexicon of these gestures is quite extensive. Describing the conventional gestures of hearing Mofu-Gudur people in Cameroon (Central Africa), Sorin-Barreteau (1996) has published an impressive collection of drawings of an estimated 1,500 conventional gestures. In a short newspaper article, Cheikh (2007) describes the initiation rites of young men in Mbour, Senegal. He mentions that in addition to learning about the flora, fauna and hunting, they learn "un certain nombre des langages et gestes importants pour eux"[3] (Cheikh 2007:2). Jirou (2000), commenting on the surprising degree of similarity in the lexicons of isolated signers in Senegal finds that hearing people have a considerable command of gestures with abstract meanings, such as 'god,' 'refusal' or 'death.' Speculating, at least two factors can be thought of as motivating the greater use of conventional gestures in West Africa. As for its spoken languages, the area is highly heterogeneous, typically with a lot of contact between the various spoken languages. As a result, multilingualism is the standard, rather than the exception. Possibly, the high degree of multilingualism contributes to the use of (conventional) gestures. One of the environments where language contact is typical is trade. There is a centuries-old tradition of trans-Saharan trade, which survives till today, that brings into contact people from various linguistic backgrounds. Conventional gestures may play a significant role in the trans-Saharan trade (Ramada Alghamis, personal communication, December 2006; Frishberg 1987). The context of trade over long distances across West Africa indeed suggests that the conventional gestures used in it may show a certain degree of consistency throughout this region.

The presence of a relatively extensive lexicon of conventional gestures is likely to influence the formation of sign languages by isolated and less isolated deaf people in West Africa. Homesigners do not start from scratch when creating their language, as part of the lexicon can be acquired, rather than needing to be created. Moreover, the size of the user community is often claimed to influence the formation of a sign language. With a large set of conventional gestures in the wider hearing community, the size of the community sharing (part of) the homesign vocabulary is considerable.

Although local sign languages are found to be used by large Deaf communities as well as by isolated deaf homesigners, the majority of sign languages of West African origin may be used in settings that do not resemble the settings found in the Western world. Typically, local sign languages may be used by a small group of deaf signers with regular signed interaction with hearing people, which accounts for the significant influence of spoken language structures. As conventional gestures seem to have a relatively important place in the communication of hearing people, the gestures influence the lexicons of local sign languages as well.

5.2   Sign language endangerment

The rapid decrease in linguistic diversity worldwide has alarmed both linguists and non-linguists. Linguists have estimated that each week, one or two languages cease to exist. This implies that out of the estimated 6,000 languages spoken at present, only about 600 may still be spoken in 2061. Large-scale initiatives have been taken to counter this tendency or to at least document and preserve as much of the linguistic heritage of mankind as possible. So far, these initiatives have largely overlooked the diversity in sign languages and threats to their vitality.

   In some respects, sign languages are exposed to the same threats as spoken languages. Thus, in West Africa and other parts of the continent, the difference in prestige between sign languages of local and foreign origin diminishes the vitality of local sign languages. At the same time, there are additional threats specific to sign languages. In technologically advanced countries, the decreasing incidence of deafness in combination with the widespread use of a the cochlear implant pose a threat. Across the globe, through the central role played by deaf schools in the formation of many signing communities, language policies in deaf education tend to have a relatively strong impact on sign language usage. Local sign languages are often compared to sign languages imported from abroad and discarded as being inferior. The attitudes toward sign languages of local and foreign origin largely parallel the attitudes toward spoken languages of local and foreign origin in West Africa. Speakers of West African languages may refer to the former colonial (spoken) languages as "languages" and to local languages, including their mother tongue, as "dialects." In the same vein, signers in West Africa tend to perceive ASL-based sign languages as being superior to sign languages of local origin. Asked for an explanation for this evaluation, signers may indicate that the lexicon of the local sign language is insufficient. Also, the iconic nature of some local signs is mentioned as being shameful, such as the sign for WOMAN, whereby the fist touches the chest twice. In places where the foreign sign language is the only sign language used in education, using the local sign language may be perceived as a sign of not having had formal education. Also, communities using a local sign language are often restricted in size. A higher status for foreign sign languages among deaf people (and hearing people in contact with deaf people) motivates educated and non-educated signers to shift to the foreign sign language. In short, foreign sign languages tend to have a higher prestige than local sign languages, threatening the vitality of the latter languages.

Kamei (2006) does not ascribe to the view that local sign languages are endangered due to the introduction of foreign sign languages, notably ASL-based sign languages. Stressing the African character of ASL-based sign languages in francophone countries, Kamei claims that they should not be considered "killer languages," arguing that they were not introduced in their entirety from a foreign country, but rather creolized in the respective African countries. He states (2006:4):

> The spread of this sign language was not a process of oppression, but rather, a creative one, constructed by African Deaf educators and communities over a span of many years. Referring to it as "LSFA" and not "ASL" will provide new perspectives for researching this language and its relationship to African Deaf history.

Kamei claims a creole status for ASL-based sign languages in francophone African countries because of (1) the integration of French elements and (2) the integration of local or "natural" signs. It is an interesting perspective to look at the ASL-based sign languages in West Africa as African languages and not imported languages. This perspective seems to be supported and promoted by the Deaf communities in the various countries as reflected by the renaming of most ASL-based sign languages and by the presentation of the ASL-based sign language as the national sign language. Also, Deaf communities may strive to "purify" their national sign language, replacing ASL signs with signs of local origin, as happened in Uganda (Sam Lutalo, personal communication, March 2007). However, as the major part of the lexicon as well as the spoken language elements involved were imported, it is not clear whether the degree of restructuring is sufficient to consider these languages local languages. The ASL-based sign languages urgently need to be researched in order to get a clearer picture of these issues.

The origin of the ASL-based languages, however, is irrelevant with respect to the threat they pose to the vitality of (other) local sign languages. Indeed, the literature on language endangerment in Africa shows that "killer languages" in most cases are not imported from foreign countries but are local languages with a high prestige. In Tanzania, for example, large numbers of smaller languages are endangered because their speakers shift to the national and official language of the country, Swahili, a language that originated along the coast of East Africa (Brenzinger, Heine & Sommer 1991). So, despite Kamei's claim that ASL-based sign languages should be considered African sign languages, their relatively high status weakens the position and development of sign languages without foreign elements.

Another facet of endangerment specific to sign languages results from the central role of education in the formation of Deaf communities. Sign language development depends on the presence of a Deaf community and Deaf communities often evolve around Deaf schools or receive a considerable impetus from it. Depending on methodological insights, educators and decision-makers in Deaf education may decide to offer various forms of signed communication to their pupils. Deaf children often have limited contacts with the adult Deaf communities. School policies therefore tend to affect the sign language ecology of the larger Deaf community on a relatively short term. As deaf children largely depend on their school environment for their linguistic input, language planning seems to have a much more pervasive effect in the education of deaf children than of hearing children. Ironically, the influence of deaf education in the oralist tradition on the existing sign language situation typically remains limited. In East Africa, oralist schools for the deaf have been established or supported on a larger scale by Catholic missionaries, notably by the White Fathers associated with the institute for the deaf in St. Michielsgestel in the Netherlands. In West Africa, the use of the oralist method has remained limited, probably as a result of the strong influence of Reverend Andrew Foster who propagated Total Communication in the education of deaf children in the region. The lack of academic information about the linguistic status of local sign languages or scientific information about sign languages in general leaves educators and policymakers in the dark about the directions to be taken in the language use in deaf education. The lack of resources in combination with the availability of teaching material in ASL and other foreign sign languages is an important motivation to use foreign sign languages in education (Manteau & Thivilliers-Goyard 2002). The use of Total Communication based on ASL in deaf education in West Africa has had a significant impact on the sign language situation, undermining the position of local sign languages in the region.

Issues of spoken language endangerment equally apply to sign languages. The lower prestige of local sign languages relative to imported sign languages, notably ASL-based sign languages, weakens the position of the former languages. This tendency is independent of whether or not ASL-based sign languages are to be considered foreign sign languages, as Kamei claims (2006). The history of deaf education has given a central place to ASL-based sign languages in West Africa, which hampers the development and emancipation of local sign languages. The lack of resources and linguistic know-how contributes to the marginal position of locally evolved sign languages.

5.3   Case studies

Studies on local (West) African sign languages are very rare. At present, only two local sign languages have been described in considerable detail, Hausa Sign Language (Schmaling 2000) and Adamorobe Sign Language (Nyst 2007). For others only very basic information is available. In several places, people involved in deaf education have compiled small vocabularies with local signs (Kafando 1990, in Ouagadougou, Burkina Faso; IDCS, n.d.,[4] Guinea-Bissau). In her Master's thesis, Jirou (2000) presents an analysis of the sign language used by a group of deaf fishermen in Mbour, Senegal. The case for most local sign languages however, is that even the basic information of their existence is lacking.

In this section, I will present a summary of the information available for Adamorobe Sign Language and Nanabin Sign Language (both used in Ghana), Magannar Hannu or Hausa Sign Language and Bura Sign Language (both used in Nigeria), and two sign languages from Mali; Langue des Signes Malienne and Tebul Ure Sign Language (Mali). The localities of these languages are indicated on the map in Figure 18.1.

5.3.1   *Ghana*

Ghana was the country where Reverend Andrew Foster established his first school for the deaf in 1957. GhSL is ASL-based but has come to include local signs as well (see Figures 18.2 and 18.3) (GNAD, n.d.). At least two, but likely more, local sign languages are used in the country. Adamorobe Sign Language is used in the village of Adamorobe, Nanabin Sign Language in the village of Nanabin.

5.3.1.1   *Adamorobe*   One exceptional local sign language is Adamorobe Sign Language or AdaSL. AdaSL is used in a small village of about 1,400 inhabitants and has known a high incidence of hereditary deafness for many generations. Deaf and hearing use the locally evolved sign language, which is entirely unrelated to GhSL. Compared to the sign languages studied so far, AdaSL has a number of features that structurally sets it apart from other sign languages. The information here is based on Nyst (2007). Striking features of AdaSL are the absence of entity classifier handshapes in verbs of motion, an unusual system for the expression of size and shape, and language-specific features in the use of iconicity, notably in the types of spatial projections allowed. Some of these language-specific features seem to correlate with the relatively large number of hearing AdaSL signers.

Classifier constructions expressing motion and location have been reported for almost all large sign languages studied so far. Whereas handle classifier constructions typically express externally controlled motion, entity classifier constructions typically express internally controlled motion. A striking feature of AdaSL is that classifier handshapes in signs expressing motion are rare in general. AdaSL uses handle classifier constructions in verbs of motion infrequently. Moreover, AdaSL appears not to make use of a system of entity classifiers. Instead, the common way to express motion in AdaSL is by using "directionals," such as FROM, TOWARD, ABRUPT and ENTER. These motion signs (which can be spatially modified) each express a basic motion pattern, e.g., 'move towards a reference point' in the case of TOWARD or 'move into an enclosed space' in the case of ENTER (see Figures 18.6 and 18.7, respectively).

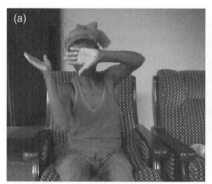 

Figure 18.6 *TOWARD – (AdaSL)*.

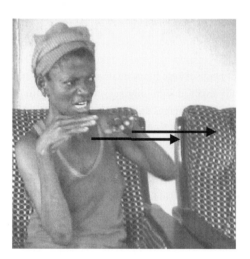

Figure 18.7 *ENTER (AdaSL)*.

These directionals are not specified with respect to the cause of motion, which may be either internally (intransitive motion) or externally (transitive motion). In other words, FROM may mean 'to go away from location X' or 'to take something or somebody away from location X.' The transitivity of the directional sign or the lack of it can be specified by adding a separate sign. Signs expressing manipulation or manner of motion may precede the directional to specify the cause of the motion. Thus, adding the sign TAKE to a directional generates a transitive reading of the motion pattern expressed by the directional, as in (1). In that example, the directional FROM – neutral with respect to transivity – is preceded by the verbal sign TAKE, which expresses a particular type of manipulation. As a result, the movement expressed by FROM is interpreted as being externally motivated. In the example below, the relevant signs are printed in italic.

(1)   MAN SEARCH FINE MARRY *TAKE FROM*- right-up CHILD-
       rep TOWARD-left
       'A man, looking for a nice (woman), marries her and takes her away,
       while her children stay.'

However, the sign FROM may also be preceded by a manner sign, showing the neutrality of this directional with respect to the cause of motion, i.e., internal or external. When FROM is preceded by WALK, which expresses a manner of motion, then the series of WALK FROM is interpreted as having no external cause of motion, i.e., as expressing an intransitive motion. The relevant signs refer to the motion of the first person singular.

(2)   *WALK FROM* SEE PATH-from-left-to-right
       'I walked away and then I just saw (the bird) flying away.'

Where most sign languages studied so far typically use classifier predicates to express motion, AdaSL instead uses directionals that have no classifying handshapes, optionally preceded by manner or manipulation signs. This results in series of verbal signs (manner/manipulation sign + directional sign) that closely resemble verb series found in Akan (Niger-Congo, Kwa), the dominant spoken language in Adamorobe.

AdaSL also differs from the sign languages so far described in the expression of size and shape. To show the size and shape of objects, AdaSL may use so-called "measure stick" (MS) signs. This type of sign is used by deaf and hearing people both within Ghana and in neighbouring areas. Rather than outlining the length of an object in space, in these signs the length of an object is indicated on the arm or hand. Thus, the sign MS:ARM, illustrated in Figure 18.8, indicates a long and thin object

Figure 18.8 *MS: ARM (AdaSL). Reprinted from Nyst 2007 with the kind permission of the publisher.*

Figure 18.9 *MS: HAND (AdaSL). Reprinted from Nyst 2007 with the kind permission of the publisher.*

of about 70 centimeters. The sign MS:HAND, in Figure 18.9, illustrates an oblong object of about 20 centimeters. Whether the length indicated using this measure-stick technique is to be considered big or small for the object under discussion may be indicated by the mouthing superimposed on the sign. These are the mouthings normally accompanying the fixed signs for relative size, i.e., BIG, SMALL, TALL and SHORT.

One way in which this size and shape system differs from equivalent systems in other sign languages is that it presents the size and shape of an object through entity depiction (Mandel 1977) and not through depiction of the outline. Thus, the arm or part of it represents the size and shape of the object directly, whereas systems indicating a size and shape in space generally do so by representing the outline of that size and shape. This difference in iconic strategy seems to be part of a wider tendency in the language to use entity depiction rather than outline depiction. Entity depiction was the most common depiction type (39 percent) in a database of about 500 AdaSL signs and tracing the least common (4 percent) (Nyst 2007:38).

AdaSL uses iconicity in a language-specific way in other contexts as well. Thus, it has a strong preference for "real-scale" spatial projections and hence the projection type typically associated with character perspective whereby the signer is part of the projection (McNeill 1992). Observer perspective, employing "reduced-scale" projections are not used in AdaSL. Also, the language appears to have strong restrictions on the use of simultaneous constructions.

AdaSL has evolved in the village of Adamorobe. There is some contact with deaf people in Aburi, the closest nearby town, which seems to have a slightly heightened incidence of deafness as well. To what extent AdaSL is similar to other local sign languages or, more generally, to other forms of gestural communication in Ghana is not clear. About 200 kilometers away from Adamorobe lies the Akan village of Nanabin.

5.3.1.2 *Nanabin Sign Language*   A family with three generations of mainly deaf members lives in this village. The family consists of about twenty-five to thirty people of all ages. The family has developed its own sign language. Some of the deaf people of the second generation, now adults, have attended a school for the deaf. As a consequence, they are fully bilingual in the ASL-based Ghanaian Sign Language as well as in the family sign language. Nanabin Sign Language (NanaSL) is not mutually intelligible with AdaSL. However, comparing NanaSL and AdaSL reveals similarities in articulatory features, the lexicon and lexical strategies, and in the use of space. Like AdaSL, NanaSL has lax handshapes. Some lexical items are identical, like the sign for WATER. To some extent, similarities in lexicon result from similarities in the conventional gestures for these concepts in Akan culture. In other cases, the similarity may be driven by the iconic motivation of the sign. Also, similar lexical strategies are employed. Thus, the signs for the months of the year refer to typical activities associated with them, such as the Akan festivals. An interesting similarity is the preference for character perspective of both NanaSL and AdaSL. Like AdaSL, NanaSL hardly seems to make any use of observer perspective.

5.3.2   *Nigeria*

5.3.2.1   *Magannar Hannu*   Magannar Hannu or Hausa Sign Language (HSL) is used in Kano State, Northern Nigeria. Schmaling (2000) gives a detailed description of the sociolinguistic setting, phonology, morphology and lexicon of Maganar Hannu. In addition to deaf people, many hearing people have a basic competence in Maganar Hannu as well, which they learn informally from deaf people. Maganar Hannu is not the only sign language used in Kano State. In the school for the deaf, Nigerian Sign Language is used. This language is based on ASL but includes Maganar Hannu signs. Through bilingualism in Nigerian Sign Language and Maganar Hannu, ASL signs have been adopted in the latter language.

Schmaling (2000) proposes a set of thirty-five distinctive handshapes and describes their occurrence. In her description of the morphology of Maganar Hannu, Schmaling does not focus on the extent to which it patterns like the sign languages studied so far. The general impression, however, is that the degree of language-specific features is moderate, as compared to the sign languages studied so far, but this may be a result of the perspective of the study. One of the few remarks Schmaling makes concerns the use of the 1-handshape (index extended) as a person-classifier; this appears not to be a very productive classifier in HSL. However, no information is given on the productivity of other (entity) classifiers.

With regard to the lexicon, Schmaling devotes ample attention to the historical and cultural context and resulting links between form and meaning. She shows how the lexicon iconically reflects sociocultural habits and knowledge. Signs for food and drink, crafts and occupations, and religious concepts reflect visual or motoric elements associated with these concepts. As in many sign languages, name signs for prominent public people depict personal traits. Signs for places often iconically refer to events associated with these locations. Signs denoting ethnic groups refer to features of these groups typically associated with these groups, such as ethnic scarifications, hairdo and clothing. The signs used for traditional titles, politicians and ethnic groups depict prominent physical features or other characteristics associated with the referent(s). Thus, the sign for FULANI MAN is the same as the sign for whipping or flogging, which refers to the Fulani initiation rites which involve flogging. Schmaling discusses some iconic signs as being universal because they are similar to those in other sign languages, e.g., TREE, SEE, BICYCLE and CAR. Other signs are described as being iconic, but not universal, such as the signs for FATHER/MALE, MOTHER/FEMALE and WATER. This distinction may not be as clear-cut, however. The sign BICYCLE in Maganar Hannu is a symmetrical sign with two alternating, circling fists in the neutral signing space in front of the body. In AdaSL, the signs for BICYCLE is similar, but has two B-handshapes (i.e., flat hands with all fingers extended and adducted). The sign for TREE in Maganar Hannu is like the ASL sign for TREE and consists of the elbow of the dominant hand, which has a 5-handshape with all fingers extended, placed on the back of the non-dominant hand. The AdaSL sign for TREE is a symmetrical sign with two 5-handshapes moving upward in a rotating, alternating movement. Thus, the Maganar Hannu signs for these concepts are not universal. Conversely, the signs for FATHER, MOTHER and WATER appear to be widely used in West Africa, by both deaf and hearing people.

Schmaling also discusses variation in the lexicon as a function of region, educational background, pattern of deafness and age. Variation in the lexicon pertains to lexical signs and the influence of spoken Hausa in the form of loan translations and mouthings.

At present, Maganar Hannu is one of the two local West African sign languages that have been studied to some extent, AdaSL being the other. Compared to the sign languages studied so far, AdaSL shows a number of language-specific features. From Schmaling's description, Maganar Hannu seems to pattern more like the sign languages described so far within the field of sign linguistics.

Maganar Hannu is in intensive contact with ASL at the school for the deaf in Kano, the Tudun Maliki school (Schmaling 2001). In this school, the teachers communicate with the pupils using Total Communicating. At the Tudun Maliki school, this involves using elements from Maganar Hannu, ASL, English and Hausa. Thus, signs from both ASL and Maganar Hannu have become part of the lexicon of these pupils. ASL signs are used not only for concepts for which no Maganar Hannu sign is available but also for basic vocabulary items like WORK, HOME and HELP. Some ASL signs have undergone modifications in form or meaning. For example, the sign OFFICE in standard ASL is made with an O-handshape (all fingers curved and forming a circle), but the Tudun Maliki form has an F-handshape (the index and thumb forming a circle, while the remaining fingers are extended). An example of semantic modification is the semantic extension of the sign RED to mean 'blood' in addition to 'red.' Coining new signs through initialization, using ASL letters, is also done at Tudun Maliki. Thus, signs for towns and places have been created, even though Maganar Hannu signs for these places already existed. Evaluating the threat the use of ASL at Tudun Maliki poses to the continued use of Maganar Hannu, Schamling (2001) finds that the use of ASL is mainly limited to the time deaf people spend at school. Once they finish school, they enter into the adult Deaf community, where the use of Maganar Hannu is the standard to which they

Figure 18.10 *The AdaSL sign EUROPEAN. Reprinted from Nyst 2007 with the kind permission of the publisher.*

quickly adapt. Schmaling thus concludes that ASL does not endanger the vitality of Maganar Hannu.

5.3.2.2   *Bura Sign Language*   In the Bura-speaking area of Eastern Nigeria lives a small group of signing people, some of whom are deaf. Preliminary observations of their sign language indicate that it bears some resemblance to Hausa Sign Language, notably in some of its lexical strategies and that it bears resemblance to other local sign languages in that it has a very lax articulation and a large signing space. As for its lexicon, Bura Sign Language has signs for all bank notes. As in HSL, these signs iconically refer to the person depicted on the bank note. As in other local West African sign languages, signs for ethnic groups refer to physical properties typically associated with these groups. Thus the sign for MARGHI refers to the double tribal marks on each cheek. The sign for EUROPEAN consists of a "smooth hand over hair (suggesting combing), then stroke inside of right fingers against inside of left forearm (suggesting 'skin')" (Blench & Warren 2005:3). Interestingly, the first part of the sign for EUROPEAN is identical to the AdaSL sign for it, which is illustrated in Figure 18.10.

5.3.3   *Senegal*

5.3.3.1   *Mbour Sign Language*   Jirou (2000) has investigated the sign language used by a group of deaf people in the fishing town of Mbour in Senegal. The analysis of Jirou takes a developmental perspective as developed by Cuxac (2000). Jirou focuses on the iconic strategies and the spatial projections used in this language. She finds that the projection of an event space on a limited plane in front of the signer, using observer perspective, is "rare or simplified" (Jirou 2000:5).

She did not witness the use of entity classifiers in observer perspective. In contrast, the use of referent projections (the enacting of a character) is used extensively. In this respect, Mbour Sign Language resembles AdaSL and Nanabin Sign Languages as discussed in sections 5.3.1.1 and 5.3.1.2 respectively.

5.3.4 *Mali*

5.3.4.1 *Langue des Signes Malienne*   Langue des Signes Malienne (LaSiMa) is used by the Deaf community in Bamako, Mali. The number of users is unknown. Like other local West African sign languages, it has arisen outside of a school context, as a result of regular interaction between deaf people in the streets of Bamako. As late as 1993, the first school for the deaf was established in Bamako. This school initially used Malian Sign Language, then switched to Langue de Signes Française and then to ASL at the end of the nineties. The second school for the deaf was established around 1995 by a Canadian linguist, Dominique Pinsonneault, who also published a vocabulary of about 570 LaSiMa signs (Pinsonneault 1999). The second school used the local sign language as the medium of instruction. The difference in the language of instruction prevented full cooper-ation between the schools. Around 2001, it was decided by the Ministry of Education that both schools should use a Total Communication approach based on ASL and elements of spoken and written French. To this end, the schools use a dictionary that was developed for this variety by Tamomo (1994).

A comparison of the lexical items in the dictionaries of Pinsonneault (1999) and Tamomo (1994) shows the embeddedness of LaSiMa in the Malian culture in contrast with the francophone African variety of ASL. For example, the sign for TOMATO in the former dictionary (see Figure 18.11) iconically reflects the

Figure 18.11 *TOMATO in LaSiMa. Reprinted from Pinsonneault 1999 with the kind permission of the publisher.*

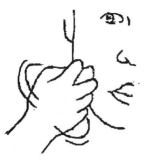

Figure 18.12 *TOMATO in francophone African ASL. Reprinted from Tamamo 1994 with the kind permission of the publisher.*

processing of the tomato in the Malian kitchen, i.e., squeezing it by hand. The sign in the latter dictionary is initialized and has the ASL T-handshape as illustrated in Figure 18.12.

The decision to use ASL and French in deaf education may negatively impact the usage of LaSiMa. Deaf schools are a crucial factor in the transmission of a sign language. Although LaSiMa has arisen outside of an educational context, present and future deaf children in Bamako will grow up using an ASL-based variety. Adult deaf signers too are eager to learn and use ASL and are often bilingual. Having virtually no child users and a lower status compared to ASL, it is likely that ASL will gradually replace LaSiMa in the Deaf community of Bamako. At present, it is not clear to what extent LaSiMa is used by Deaf communities outside of Bamako. It is more than likely that groups of LaSiMa signers are found in other parts of Mali. Indeed, Roger Blench (personal communication) has encountered a group of deaf and hearing signers in Tebul Ure, a village in the Dogon region of Mali and filmed their signing. His video recordings of this sign language again show features found in other local West African sign languages, including lax hand-shapes, a large signing space and similar signs in the lexicon, among others the signs for WATER, WORK and WOMAN. The degree of similarity of the local sign language of Bamako and Tebul Ure remains to be established.

The question of how local sign languages in Mali relate to each other can be extended for the whole of West Africa. In addition to the accounts of the sign languages above, I have had the chance to incidentally observe and record local signing in Cape Coast in Ghana, in Ouagadougou and Bobo Dioulasso in Burkina Faso and to view recordings of Bura Sign Language and Tebul Ure Sign Language. An exceptional documentary portraying a deaf magician from Ouagadougou communicating in a local sign language is *Adama, the Fulani magician* (Roselinni 1998). The general impression I gain from my own analysis of AdaSL and Langue des Signes Malienne, the accounts of Hausa Sign Language and Mbour Sign Language, and the casual observation of other local signing in different parts of West Africa, is that there are similarities between local sign across West Africa that set them apart from the imported sign languages in this region as well as from the sign languages studied so far. That is, they have a quite uniform manner of articulation, with relatively lax handshapes and a relatively large signing space. Also they share lexical items, which probably reflects similarities in the conventional gestures used by hearing communities across the region. Thus, the same sign for the verb GO is found in AdaSL, Nanabin Sign Language and Bura Sign Language. The same sign GO is found as a co-verbal gesture with hearing Malians, Ghanaians and Nigerians. Other signs or gestures that are found in several places in West Africa in signers and non-signers include the signs/gestures for 'sweat' (with the meaning 'to work'), 'refuse,' 'woman,' 'man,' 'water' and 'dead.'

Similarities in strategies of word formation are also found, but these do not necessarily differ in the West African local sign languages as compared to other sign languages. Finally, at least some local sign languages appear to have a use of space that is quite different from what has been observed for non-African sign languages, as they display a strong preference for character perspective.

The similarity between the different types of signing and gesturing in parts of West Africa, and especially the similarities in lexicon, may point at the existence of a regional gesture system. This supports Frishberg (1987), who suggests that AdaSL may be related to the "gestural trade jargon used in the markets throughout West Africa." Although the existence of such a gestural trade language has been observed by Alghamis (personal communication), a linguist from Niger, studies confirming its use are not available at present.

In short, there seem to be particular similarities that are typical of local sign languages in West Africa at the levels of phonetics/phonology, the lexicon and the use of space. More research is needed to clarify the relation between the different sign languages found in West Africa, as well as their relationship to the hearing gestures they are in contact with.

6   Summary

Foreign sign language, most notably varieties of ASL, dominate in deaf education and Deaf associations in West Africa. This is the direct result of the immense effort made by Reverend Andrew Foster in the field of deaf education in West and Central Africa between 1957 and 1987. In addition to an ASL-based sign language, most countries in West Africa also have local sign languages that are used in less formal contexts. Both the foreign and the local sign languages in West Africa are heavily under-studied.

The relative status of foreign and local sign languages parallels values attached to spoken languages of former colonial origin and of local origin, respectively. The relatively high status of foreign sign languages threatens the continued use of local sign languages, for example, in the case of HSL (Schmaling 2000) and Langue des Signes Malienne.

Descriptions and observations of local sign languages are scarce but show a certain amount of similarity. The similarities found pertain to phonetics/phonology, the lexicon and the use of space. Thus, most local sign languages seem to have relatively lax handshapes and a relatively large signing space. Also, at least some sign languages show a preference for character perspective. Similarities in the lexicon are likely to be due to similarities in the "lexicon" of conventional gestures of the surrounding hearing communities, possibly as a result of trade and/or extensive interaction in multilingual settings. However, these observations are all preliminary as very little information is available for a small number of sign languages, and for most sign languages no information is available at all at present. A large-scale survey is needed to inventory the signing communities and their languages in West Africa.

19

Sign languages in the Arab world

Kinda Al-Fityani and Carol Padden

1   Introduction

Every evening, the Al Jazeera satellite channel features a one-hour, comprehensive newscast of world events. Superimposed in the corner of the television screen is a box containing a sign language interpreter who translates the spoken Arabic of the newscaster. The interpreter is one of a team of Jordanian Sign Language (LIU)[1] interpreters who regularly interpret the newscast. However, the sign language they use is not strictly LIU. Heavily influenced by LIU, it is a newly devised sign language which uses vocabulary drawn from different Arab sign languages, including Egyptian Sign Language and Saudi Sign Language. The vocabulary was compiled in a dictionary by the Council of Arab Ministers of Social Affairs (CAMSA), a committee within the League of Arab States (LAS).

The effort by CAMSA to encourage a standard pan-Arab Sign Language (ArSL) has been met with wide resistance, in large part because deaf viewers say they cannot understand the language. In this paper, we describe the geography of sign languages in Arab countries. As we explain, there already exists a number of sign languages used by Arab deaf communities. Some are designated as nation-state sign languages and are used in the instruction of deaf students in their educational systems. The adoption of ArSL by Arab countries potentially threatens the future of these nation-state sign languages as well as an unknown number of smaller sign languages existing within this region. If ArSL were to substitute for any of these sign languages, it could potentially take on a colonial face and delimit the expression of the community's identity.

CAMSA's rationalization for the creation of the new ArSL is "to meet the needs of integration of deaf persons into society" (Council of Arab Ministers 2004). One way to achieve that goal according to CAMSA is to provide deaf people in the Arab world with a comparable language situation that exists for hearing people, namely a common language.

More than 200 million inhabitants of twenty-two countries across the Middle East and North Africa speak Arabic.[2] However, should a Yemeni and a Tunisian meet, it is unlikely that their Arabic would be intelligible to the other. The Arab world is characterized by pervasive "diglossia," a language situation in which regional dialects are spoken alongside a highly codified written language. Of the Arabic dialects, the Egyptian dialect is most widely understood by Arabs, since Arab cinema and other entertainment media is largely Egyptian-based and typically uses Egyptian actors. If a Yemeni and a Tunisian meet, they can resort to the dialect of movie stars to understand each other or they could use the highly codified language of Modern Standard Arabic (MSA) which is used by newscasters and public officials in Arab countries. Although it is the mother tongue of no one, MSA is the official literary standard of Arab countries and is the form of Arabic taught in schools at all stages. Indeed, spoken colloquial Arabic, as the regional varieties are often called, is rarely found in a written form. In addition to education, MSA is prevalent in government and news media, allowing Arabs to communicate with and understand each other across nations despite varying regional dialects. It is commonly said that the Arabic language is what unites the different members of the Arab community, despite the different geographies and cultural traditions that can be found throughout the region (Suleiman 2003).

Studies of sign languages in other areas of the world show that they do not map entirely onto the geography of spoken languages. Sign languages in English-speaking countries such as the United States and Canada on the one hand, and Australia, New Zealand and the United Kingdom on the other, have distinct histories. McKee and Kennedy (2000) describe Australian Sign Language (Auslan), British Sign Language (BSL) and New Zealand Sign Language (NZSL) as dialects of a single parent language, BANZSL (British, Australian and New Zealand Sign Language; see also Schembri *et al.* this volume). Using a lexicostatistical analysis of random vocabularies, they conclude that the three languages belong to the same family tree but are dissimilar enough to qualify as dialects. In other research, Mexican Sign Language (LSM) and Spanish Sign Language (LSE) are described as distinct languages despite a common spoken language shared between the two respective countries (Guerra Currie, Meier & Walters 2002). With respect to Arab sign languages, Abdel-Fattah (2005) suggests that the presence of a standard Arabic spoken language has led to the expectation that there should be a shared common sign language.

This paper explores the geography of sign languages of Arab countries by examining relationships among selected sign languages in the region. The method used is lexicostatistics, which compares similarity of vocabulary across sign languages to determine either the type and extent of a language relationship between two or more languages, or, as might be the case, that no such relationship exists.

1.1   Sign language communities in the Middle East

At least three ongoing circumstances affect the distribution of sign languages in the broader Middle East region. First, as Walsh *et al.* (2006:203) describe below, certain marriage traditions are common in the region:

> The unique demographic history of the Middle East has led to many [endogamous] communities. For more than 5,000 years and continuing to the present, the eastern shores of the Mediterranean have seen immigration of people from a wide variety of cultures. Villages were often established by a few extended families and, despite their geographic proximity, remained demographically isolated. For centuries, marriages have been arranged within extended families in these villages, leading to high levels of consanguinity and consequently high frequencies of recessive traits.

The common practice of endogamy has resulted in a high incidence of genetic deafness in this region compared to exogamic societies where deafness is more likely the result of disease than of genetic inheritance. Shahin *et al.* (2002) report that while approximately one in one thousand infants worldwide are born with hearing loss, communities with high levels of consanguinity have especially high frequencies of inherited childhood deafness. They state: "prelingual hereditary hearing impairment occurs in the Palestinian population at a frequency of approximately 1.7 per 1,000 and is higher in some villages" (p. 284). This means that in Palestine, the frequency of deafness is 70 percent higher than the global average.

From the few reports of sign languages in such communities, they are not confined in usage to places where deaf people are brought together by social institutions, such as schools for the deaf or local clubs for the deaf; instead, they are also used within family and community settings. As Groce (1985) illustrates in her history of nineteenth-century Martha's Vineyard, where there was a high incidence of recessive deafness, sign languages are likely to flourish in such communities as deaf people and hearing people use signed communication on a regular basis. Kisch (2004) describes the case of the Al-Sayyid Bedouin community in the Negev, where consanguineous marriage is common and frequencies of hearing loss is high at 3 percent of the population due to genetically recessive traits of profound prelingual neurosensory deafness. Sandler *et al.* (2005:2662) also write of this community:

> Members of the community generally recognize the sign language as a second language of the village. Hearing people there routinely assess their own proficiency, praising those with greater facility in the

language ... One result of [recessive deafness] is that there is a proportionately large number of deaf individuals distributed throughout the community. This means that hearing members of the community have regular contact with deaf members and that, consequently, signing is not restricted to deaf people.

Recently, Landesman and Meir (2007) have begun to describe a minority sign language in Israel used by Jewish emigrants from Algeria whose families once lived in an insular Jewish community within the old trading city of Ghardaia. Following a pattern common to the region, members of the community married within extended families, and deaf individuals began to populate the Jewish community (Briggs & Guède 1964).

Second, cultural and social circumstances in the Middle East provide somewhat more opportunity to learn sign languages from birth. With higher incidence of genetic deafness, sign languages are able to survive across generations within a family, compared to other regions of the world where genetic deafness is less frequent. Where deafness is a result of disease, a deaf person's chances of learning a sign language are more dependent on having access to organizations or institutions organized for deaf people. In the Middle East, sign language survival is not dependent on formal institutional policies.

Third, cultural, social, political and economic circumstances lead sign languages in the region to be more likely to be isolated from one another. Within the Arab world, marriage customs give preferential treatment for partners from the same region as they are more likely to share a common dialect and customs. Moreover, political factors of immigration regulations within Arab countries make it difficult for nationals of one region to travel to another. For these reasons, a Jordanian woman is more likely to marry a man from the Levant region (eastern countries of the Middle East) as opposed to one from a Gulf state. This is because she would need a visa to travel to Dubai, for example, but not one to travel to Damascus or Beirut. Moreover, the proximity of Damascus and Beirut to Jordan makes it more economically feasible for a Jordanian woman to meet a man from these cities as opposed to meeting a Qatari man. Inasmuch as cultural, social, political and economic factors restrict such contact, sign languages in the Arab world would arise within boundaries that possibly isolate them and allow them to develop independently of each other. Research on sign languages in the Arab world may reveal interesting findings on the geographic distribution of sign languages that are used on a daily, familial and tribal social basis, as opposed to those found on a more state formalized, institutional basis.

1.2   Lexicostatistical analyses of sign languages

The methodology of comparative lexicostatistics is used to develop hypotheses on possible historical relationships among spoken languages (Crowley 1992). This is done through a quantitative study of cognates among the vocabularies of the languages being studied. Cognates are defined as vocabulary from two different languages that are homogeneous enough to be considered as having similar linguistic derivation or roots. A comparison among spoken languages involves identifying similarities in syllable and segmental structure; in sign languages, cognate similarity is based on comparing handshapes, movements, locations and orientations of the hand in the vocabulary of two different sign languages.

Many spoken language linguists use basic 200-word lists as the basis of their lexicostatistical research as opposed to longer lists, as a convenient and representative way of subgrouping languages. The higher the lexicostatistical percentage among spoken languages' cognates, the closer the historical relationship among the languages as it points to a more recent split from a common parent language (Black & Kruskal 1997). Within the lexicostatistical methodology, Crowley (1992) defines languages to be dialects if they share 81–100 percent of cognates in core vocabularies. They are considered as from the same language family if they share 36–81 percent of cognates, and families of a "stock" if they share 12–36 percent of cognates. By "stock," lexicostatisticians do not identify the languages as descending from one common ancestor language, instead, the term recognizes that languages within a region can have opportunity for contact with one another. Greenberg (1957) provides four causes of lexical resemblances across languages, only two of which are historically related: those are genetic relationship and borrowing. The other two are shared symbolism, where vocabularies share similar motivations either iconic or indexic, and finally, by chance.

Woodward (1978) is one of the first sign linguists to conduct lexicostatistical research on sign languages. He compared the lexicon of French Sign Language (LSF) from a sign language dictionary with ASL, where one set of signs were elicited from an older deaf man and another set from younger ASL signers. He began with a list of 200 core words from the Swadesh list, a common tool among anthropologists for eliciting a basic vocabulary, but excluded numerals, pronouns and body parts because they are indexical and highly iconic. With 77 words remaining on his list that had counterparts in the LSF dictionary, he found 61 percent cognates for both sets of comparisons of LSF with the older deaf man and with the younger signers. Substituting the modified core vocabulary list for all 872 available signs in the LSF dictionary, he found that cognates dropped slightly to between 57.3–58 percent for both sets of ASL signs. Woodward concludes that, contrary to popular belief that ASL descended from LSF, it is more likely that some number of sign language varieties existed in the United States before contact with LSF was made, after which a creolization process took place leading to what is now ASL. Woodward (1991) also carried out lexicostatistical analyses of several sign language varieties found in Costa Rica. With results ranging from between 7–42 percent cognates, he concluded that there are at least four distinct sign languages in Costa Rica. In a third study, he compared sign language varieties in India, Pakistan and Nepal with results ranging from 62–71 percent cognates (Woodward 1993). He finds that these varieties are separate languages but belong to the same language family. When comparing Modern Standard Thai Sign Language and ASL, Woodward found that the languages share 57 percent cognates, which reflects recent long-term contact between American deaf educators and deaf Thai Sign Language users (1996). Unfortunately, in these studies Woodward does not identify how many or which parameters are taken into account when determining cognates.

Using Woodward's modified core vocabulary list of 100 concepts, McKee and Kennedy (2000) examine three historically related sign languages: NZSL, ASL, Auslan and BSL. The researchers then compared these sign languages with ASL. The vocabularies used for analysis were drawn from dictionaries and CD-ROMs of the respective sign languages. They identify signs as cognates if all phonemic parameters (handshape, location, movement and orientation of the palm) are *identical* or if one parameter is different. Vocabulary that falls in the latter category is designated *related-but-different*, that is, similar enough to have a common origin. They found that between 79–87 percent of the vocabularies of NZSL/Auslan and BSL are cognates, which would designate them as dialects of a parent language. The researchers were not surprised by a high degree of similarity, as both Auslan and NZSL have colonial origins in common, when deaf educators and other immigrants brought BSL to Australia and New Zealand from the United Kingdom. Moreover, there has been frequent contact between deaf people from Australia and New Zealand. This is in contrast to ASL, which has no historical linkage with these three sign languages. As expected, the researchers found that only 26–32 percent of ASL vocabulary was identical or similar to NZSL, Auslan and BSL, confirming that ASL is unrelated to the other three.

McKee and Kennedy (2000) acknowledge that some linguists criticize the method of using a selection of "core vocabularies" as a basis for comparing vocabularies. Because such vocabulary often consists of high frequency words, this method may overestimate the similarities among the sign languages in the sense that such words are likely to persist as languages change over time. Instead, random vocabularies should be used for comparative purposes. After altering

Woodward's methodology to double the vocabulary being compared and to include more random vocabulary as opposed to core vocabulary from the Swadesh list, McKee and Kennedy found that the number of cognates between NZSL and each of Auslan and BSL dropped dramatically to 65.5 percent and 62.5 percent respectively. As expected, cognates between NZSL and ASL remained low at 33.5 percent. The researchers reason that the slightly higher rate of commonality between NZSL and Auslan than that between NZSL and BSL is related to geographical proximity and to educational policies in which the New Zealand Department of Education adopted the Australian Total Communication Signed System in 1979, which continued to be used until the early 1990s. Their first analysis supported the conclusion that NZSL was a dialect of Auslan and BSL because it fell within the lexicostatistical range of 81–100 percent, but after altering the vocabulary set, the conclusion was weakened somewhat, suggesting instead that NZSL belongs to the same language family as Auslan and BSL with significant divergence having occurred between them.

Guerra Currie, Meier and Walters (2002) counted cognates in their lexicostatistical comparison of LSM with French Sign Language (LSF), Spanish Sign Language (LSE) and Japanese Sign Language (JSL). LSM is compared with LSF as there is reason to believe they are historically related. A deaf French educator came to Mexico in 1866 when he first learned of a deaf school being established there. Consequently, some believe LSF may be a source of borrowing for sign language(s) in Mexico. With Spanish being a shared spoken language in Mexico and Spain, LSM and LSE may have a basis for similarity. Finally, because they have no known historical relationship, the comparison of LSM and JSL is used as a control to approximate the possible degree of similarity between two unrelated sign languages.

Data for the analysis was retrieved from videotaped elicitations. Word lists ranged from 89 signs for the LSM–LSE comparison to 112 for the LSM–LSF comparison and 166 for LSM–JSL. Signs from different vocabularies were designated as cognates if they shared two out of three parameters. Unlike McKee and Kennedy 2000, Guerra Currie, Meier and Walters 2002 exclude the fourth parameter of orientation. They report 38 percent cognates for LSM–LSF, 33 percent cognates for LSM–LSE and 23 percent for LSM–JSL. While there is history of contact between LSM and LSF, it is clear that their historical development is non-genetic. They attribute the similarity between LSM and LSF to borrowing. Their findings also do not support similarity between LSM and LSE even though they exist in communities that share a spoken language, Spanish. Finally, the LSM–JSL comparison provides a base level of the degree of similarity between any two sign languages that may have shared iconicity. They argue that the visual-gestural modality of sign languages and their capacity for iconic representations support, at the very least, a minimal level of similarity among unrelated sign languages.

1.2.1   *Lexicostatistical analyses of sign languages in the Arab world*

Genetic relationships among major sign languages in the United States, Western Europe and the British colonies are mapped onto the history of deaf education in these regions, but relationships among sign languages of the Arab world may follow an entirely different pattern given that schooling for deaf children was introduced much later in the region. Brother Andrew, a pioneering educator of deaf people in the Arab world, credits Father Andeweg, a fellow Dutch Anglican missionary, with the establishment of the first school for deaf people in the region in Lebanon in the late 1950s. Brother Andrew came first to Lebanon in the capacity of a teacher and later, in 1964, moved to Jordan to resuscitate a deaf school that had also been established by Father Andeweg (Holy Land Institute for the Deaf 2004).

The Holy Land Institute of the Deaf (HLID) in Salt, Jordan, is now considered a model school for deaf people in the Arab world. Schools for deaf people in other Arab countries did not open until several years later. These schools were established by their respective governments and largely without influence from Europeans. HLID being a rare exception, most schools for the deaf in the region emphasize oral methods of communication, preferring it to sign language. Given the youth of such institutions for deaf people and their continued advocacy of oral methods for communication, we would expect sign language development in the region to exhibit a different geography from that in Europe and North America.

The following section explores similarities and differences among sign languages of the Arab world through the method of lexicostatistics. The sign languages being compared are: Jordanian Sign Language (LIU), Kuwaiti Sign Language (KuSL), Libyan Sign Language (LSL) and Palestinian Sign Language (PSL). LIU will also be compared with Al-Sayyid Bedouin Sign Language (ABSL),[3] a sign language used by a community of deaf and hearing Bedouins in southern Israel. Hearing members of this community speak Arabic. Finally, as a baseline, LIU will be compared with ASL, with the expectation that percentage of cognates will be low due to no known historic relationship between the two. However, as there are Jordanian professionals working with deaf people who have studied in the United States as well as a few deaf Jordanians who have studied at Gallaudet University, there may be lexical borrowings from ASL to LIU.

2   Methodology

Vocabulary used for comparison was drawn from published dictionaries of the respective sign languages, with the exception of ABSL where the vocabulary was elicited through an interview with a deaf member of the Al-Sayyid community on video.[4] All vocabulary in the LIU dictionary and each of the other four dictionaries were used for the comparisons. The reason for such an extensive comparison was that using a modified core list of randomly selected vocabularies would have resulted in a smaller set of comparison vocabulary from the Kuwaiti and Libyan dictionaries, or a lack of comparison vocabulary as was the case with the Palestinian dictionary which was targeted toward high school and university students in the math and sciences, or one more focused on local references such as names of organizations and royalty as was the case with the Jordanian dictionary.

Individual signs of different languages were compared based on four phonemic parameters (handshape, movement, location and orientation of the palm), following McKee and Kennedy's 2000 criteria. Non-manual differences such as facial markers were not included in the comparison.

3   Results

Following McKee and Kennedy (2000), two signs from different sign languages were termed "identical" if they shared all four parameters, as in Figure 19.1.[5] They were termed "related" if they differed on only one of four parameters, as in Figures 19.2 and 19.3.[6] They were termed "different" if they differed on two or more parameters as in Figures 19.4, 19.5 and 19.6.[7]

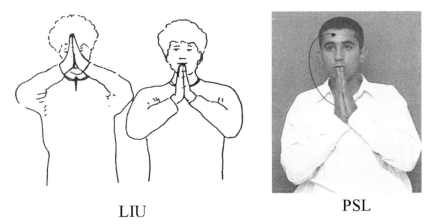

LIU   PSL

Figure 19.1 *KORAN – The LIU sign is identical to its PSL cognate (4 shared parameters).*

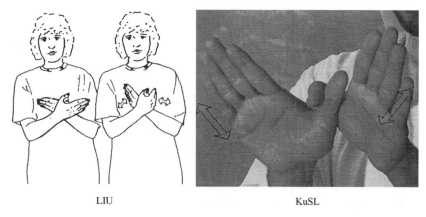

Figure 19.2 *BUTTERFLY – The LIU sign is related to its KuSL cognate (3 shared parameters; orientation differs).*

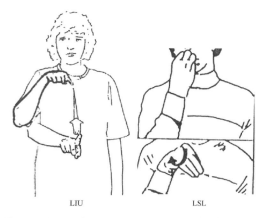

Figure 19.3 *ELEPHANT – The LIU sign is related to its LSL cognate (3 shared parameters; handshape differs).*

As Table 19.1 illustrates, between 165–410 vocabulary items were used for the different comparisons, depending on the available vocabulary for the languages. The numbers of vocabulary items are similar to past comparative research on sign languages.

Figure 19.7 shows that the sign languages being compared in this study probably are not dialects, despite the presence of a common spoken language, Arabic. As predicted, LIU–PSL had the highest number of identical and related cognates at 58 percent, reflecting their geographic proximity. Next in number of

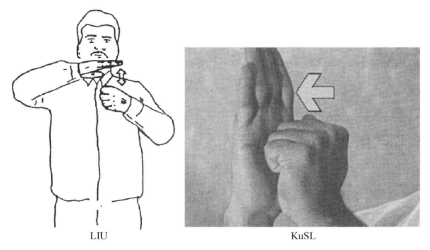

LIU   KuSL

Figure 19.4 *HOUSE – The LIU sign is different to its KuSL cognate (2 shared parameters; movement and orientation differ).*

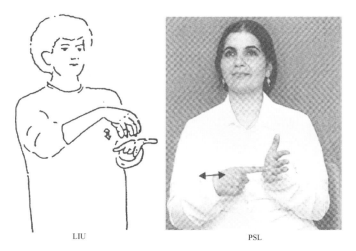

LIU   PSL

Figure 19.5 *UNIVERSITY – The LIU sign is different to its PSL cognate (1 shared parameter; handshape, movement, and orientation differ).*

similar cognates is LIU–KuSL with 40 percent, then LIU–LSL with 34 percent cognates, and finally LIU–ABSL was the lowest with 24 percent cognates. The final result is striking given that the two languages exist in neighboring countries, yet they are quite dissimilar when compared to LIU and PSL and LIU and KuSL.

Table 19.1 *Number of vocabulary items used for comparison among*
LIU and PSL, KuSL, LSL, ABSL and ASL

	PSL	KuSL	LSL	ABSL	ASL
Total signs	167	183	267	165	410

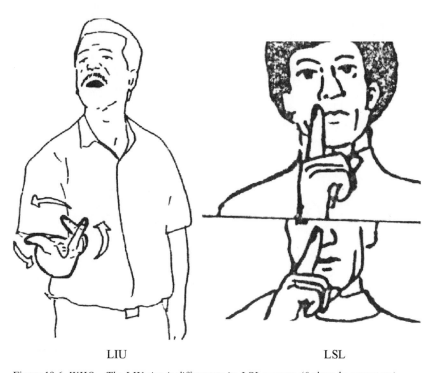

LIU	LSL

Figure 19.6 *WHO – The LIU sign is different to its LSL cognate (0 shared parameters).*

4   Discussion

From the data illustrated in Table 19.1 and Figure 19.7, we conclude that LIU–
PSL and LIU–KuSL are related but likely not dialects of the same language, as
their cognates lie within the 36–81 percent range. As for LIU–LSL, LIU–ABSL
and LIU–ASL, they are most likely not related since they share only 12–36
percent of cognates. These results demonstrate first and foremost that the geography of sign languages in this region does not map onto that of spoken

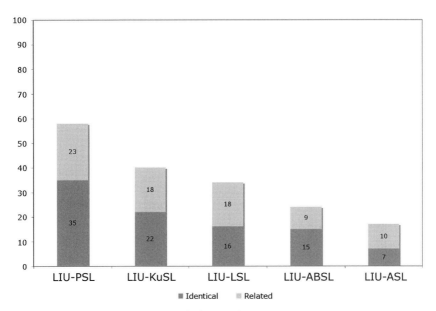

Figure 19.7 *Cognates between LIU and other sign languages.*

languages. Although ABSL, KuSL, LIU, LSL and PSL are languages existing in Arabic-speaking communities, they are distinct sign languages. Furthermore, geographic proximity does not always predict similarity; LIU and PSL are separated by the Israel/Jordan border, as are ABSL and LIU, but in the former case, the languages are more similar than in the latter case. Clearly there are cultural and economic factors in play that influence the mobility of communities of signers within this region, which in turn influences how much contact sign languages have with each other. On the whole, these results contradict anecdotes that sign languages of the Arab world are mostly similar or are dialects of a common sign language. Instead, the results suggest that at least with respect to the sign languages in this study, they do not share common origins, or if they did at one time, they have since diverged greatly.

As expected and demonstrated in Figure 19.7, LIU and PSL share the most cognates of any two languages examined in this study. This is not unexpected as the Palestinian and Jordanian communities are tightly knit in terms of custom and marriage traditions. When we juxtapose the results of lexicostatistical studies of sign languages around the world, as we do in Figure 19.8, it can be seen that LIU–PSL are as lexically similar to each other as are ASL–LSF. Woodward (1978) concludes that ASL and LSF do not share roots, but that sign language

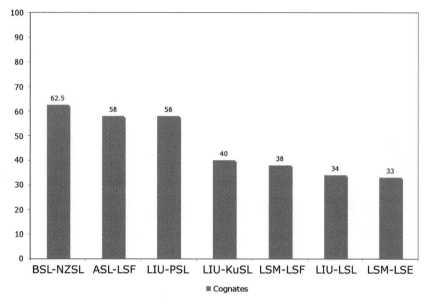

Figure 19.8 *Vocabulary similarities between pairs of sign languages.*

varieties existed in the United States before any contact with LSF was made, after which a creolization process took place. Perhaps the same could be said of LIU–PSL, where they do not share roots, but similarities develop through contact.

Returning to sign languages of the Arab world, we find from our study that KuSL and LSL have a lower number of cognates with LIU. Lexical similarity between LIU–KuSL and LIU–LSL lie within the same range as LSM–LSF and LSM–LSE. Guerra Currie, Meier and Walters (2002) note that while LSM and LSF have come into contact, their historical development is non-genetic. They also note that while Spanish is a common spoken language between Mexico and Spain, their sign languages are unrelated due to little opportunity for contact. While KuSL and LSL may have come into contact with LIU, they are probably not historically related. Also, that they share a similar spoken language may account for a degree of lexical similarity, as is the case with LSM–LSE.

Finally, LIU and ABSL share the fewest cognates of all the sign languages studied. This confirms ethnographic reports that signers in the Al-Sayyid Bedouin community have little or only sporadic contact with signers in Jordan and other Arab countries. Only 24 percent of their signs were cognates with LIU of total vocabularies compared. Figure 19.9 shows that LIU–ABSL are within the same range of similarity as are ASL–NZSL and LSM–JSL, the latter being

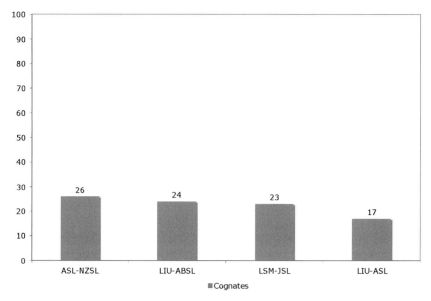

Figure 19.9 *Base level similarities between unrelated sign languages.*

considered by Currie, Meier and Walters (2002) as a base level of similarity that can
be expected between any two unrelated sign languages. . This degree of difference
falls just below the baseline of 26–32 percent that McKee and Kennedy (2000) give
for ASL–NZSL. In fact, LIU–KuSL and LIU–LSL at 40 percent and 34 percent
cognates are not significantly higher than that base level. This suggest two things:
(1) LIU, KuSL and LSL are probably unrelated historically, (2) the slightly raised
level of similarity may be due to the fact that these sign languages exist within the
Arab world where there are many common emblematic gestures. It is indeed said
that speech, gesture and culture are so intimately related to Arabs that to tie an
Arab's hands back while he or she is speaking is tantamount to tying his or her
tongue (Barakat 1973). It is not unlikely then to surmise that deaf Arab communities with little or no contact with each other can still have similar signs due to a
shared gestural repertoire.

Least similar are LIU–ASL with 17 percent cognates. This is a lower rate than
the 24 percent shared by LIU–ABSL. While these results fall within the unrelated
category, the slightly higher base level for ABSL than for ASL may be due to the
fact that LIU and ABSL share the same culture. Sharing a similar cultural stock
may account for higher lexical base levels among sign languages. It should also be
noted that the difference might also be due to the discrepancy in vocabularies

compared. In the LIU–ASL comparison, more than twice the vocabulary was available than with LIU–ABSL. Possibly if a larger vocabulary were compared, the degree of similarity would drop even further.

4.1   Why lexical comparisons from dictionaries?

Deeper language comparisons such as those that judge similarity of not just vocabulary but also morphology and sentence structure are likely to provide a more accurate measure of the degree of similarity among sign languages. A more extensive comparison may also take into account regional variations where similar vocabularies between two languages might exist in one region of a country but not in another. However, lexical comparisons remain useful, as they provide a basis by which initial evaluations can be made before proceeding to delve deeper into the vocabulary and grammar of any two comparison languages. When compared side-by-side with lexical studies of other languages, rough boundaries for sign language geographies on a global scale can be drawn that would not otherwise be possible.

For similar reasons, dictionary entries are used instead of live elicitations. While live elicitations are superior in making available three-dimensional and temporal aspects of individual signs, they nonetheless have inherent limitations. The selection of representative signers can be problematic for an investigator, because signers and their vocabularies will vary depending on age, gender, region and other individual factors such as fluency and competence. Since dictionaries (at least those that are developed within a community) are meant to be consensus points resolving disagreement within a language community, their use for lexical comparisons seems appropriate. Studies that work with very large sets of vocabulary rather than a representative set, as was the case with the lexicostatistical studies described in this paper, will necessarily involve more time and funding. These may be difficult to obtain for sign language researchers working in different parts of the world. Finally, the current trend toward CD-ROM storage of sign language dictionaries would eliminate some limitations of lexical comparisons in the future, and most certainly benefit studies of sign language geography around the globe.

5   Conclusion

Given the tradition of endogamy in the Arab world, which leads to high rates of genetic deafness, most likely there has been a long history of sign languages in the region. As the results of this study show, many of these sign languages are likely to be distinct languages, not dialects, and are unrelated historically. Similarities in their vocabularies may be attributed to sharing similar cultural values and gestural repertoires. These results follow from the historical pattern of sign languages in the Arab world, which develop largely in familial institutions as opposed to educational ones as is the Western pattern. Indeed, organized educational systems in the Arab world are relatively young. With cultural, social, political and economic circumstances restricting contact among communities, numerous sign languages may develop within families and tribes. Our results show quite clearly that the geography of sign languages in the Arab world does not map onto that of spoken MSA.

The recent trend toward standardization of sign languages on a national basis in Jordan, Kuwait and Libya suggests that a creolization or pidginization is now actively in place, where children from different families and tribes are converging and beginning to share a common sign language. This common sign language is then documented as the standardized, national one. The history of sign languages in this region presents a geography of sign languages unlike the situation in the West, where creolization and standardization has been underway since the nineteenth century. The Arab world situation can, however, be paralleled to Woodward's (1991) findings on sign languages used in Costa Rica, where he found several distinct languages among the numerous indigenous pueblos.

There is at least one implication of these findings in terms of a project to unify sign languages of the Arab world. The underlying assumption that sign languages of the region are similar enough to be standardized may in fact be erroneous. It may be risky to engineer a "standardized" sign language in the Arab world, given the difficulty of standardizing languages that are historically unrelated.

Further research could examine more deeply the patterns of mobility among deaf people in the region, particularly gender differences in the region. Such research could investigate how social and cultural traditions of gender segregation and restriction of mobility of women limit the possibility of convergence of languages. This would differ from spoken Arabic where both genders have similar access to the spoken word through broadcast media to which deaf people have little to no access. Research may also take into account other linguistic features, such as grammar, to investigate further the nature and relationship of sign languages in the Arab world. A more ambitious research project should include other sign languages from the region that have recently documented their language in dictionary form such as in Egypt, Lebanon and Yemen.

Finally, a key question in lexicostatistics of sign languages is whether two unrelated sign languages will turn out to have more vocabulary in common than any two unrelated spoken languages. The results of our comparison of five different sign languages in the Arab world show that two geographically distant sign languages can have a somewhat higher base level of similarity when compared to two unrelated spoken languages. Our results suggest that there is something inherent in the visual-gestural modality of sign languages that predispose their vocabulary to similarity. At the same time, the iconicity of tokens in the visual-gestural modality can be misleading in the sense that a casual observer might believe two sign languages are more similar than they really are. In our study, we show that while there are some similar signs among sign languages in the Arab world, the languages in fact have quite large vocabularies *not* in common. Finally, we believe that lexicostatistical analyses of sign languages are valuable as a means of addressing two important observations about sign languages: that two unrelated sign languages can have similar vocabulary, and conversely, that two sign languages in the same region can have *dis*similar vocabulary. In doing so, they can shed light on the history of sign languages in a region, but more broadly, they can address the remarkable history of sign language creation and development time and time again, all around the world.

20

Variation in American Sign Language

Ceil Lucas and Robert Bayley

1   Introduction

Even casual observation reveals that language users sometimes have different ways of saying or signing the same thing. Variation may be realized at all different levels of a language. English, for example, contains numerous examples of variation in the lexicon. Some American speakers use the word *couch*, while others say *sofa* or *davenport*. American Sign Language (ASL) also exhibits many well-known examples of lexical variation. For example, a number of signs exist for the concepts BIRTHDAY, PICNIC or HALLOWEEN.

At the phonological level, variation exists in the individual segments that make up words or signs or in parts of those segments. For example, speakers of a wide range of English dialects sometimes delete the final consonant of words that end in consonant clusters such as *test, round* or *past*, the result being *tes', roun'* and *pas'* (Labov *et al.* 1968, Guy 1980). In ASL, phonological variation can be seen in all of the parts that make up signs – in the handshape, movement, location and palm orientation, and sometimes even in the nonmanual features that are part of sign production. The basic structure of these parts is discussed in other chapters of this volume.

Variation may also occur in the morphological and syntactic components of a language. For example, in African American Vernacular English (AAVE), the copula *be* is variably deleted, and the sentences *He is my brother* and *He my brother* both occur. The example of consonant cluster reduction given earlier also concerns morphological variation because the final consonant deleted may be a past tense morpheme (i.e., a meaningful unit). For example, the phonetic realization of the English word *passed* is [paest], and the [t] is the realization of the past tense morpheme that may be variably deleted, although at a lower rate than when it is part of a monomorphemic word.

In ASL, the variable realization of the subject pronouns may serve as an illustration of syntactic variation. The ASL verb FEEL can be produced with an

451

overt subject pronoun, as in the sentence PRO.1 FEEL, 'I feel.' ASL, however, is what is known as a "*pro*-drop language," and verbs that can take overt subject pronouns are sometimes produced without them so that the preceding sentence can be produced simply as FEEL, '(I) feel.' That is, the production of subject pronouns is variable and is likely to be an interesting area for research, as it has been in languages such as Chinese, Portuguese and Spanish (see, e.g., Flores-Ferrán 2007, Jia & Bayley 2002, Naro 1981, Otheguy, Zentella & Livert 2007).

Sociolinguistic variation takes into account the fact that the different linguistic variants may correlate with social factors including age, socioeconomic class, gender, ethnic background, region and sexual orientation. For example, older people may use a given variant more frequently than younger people; women may use a given variant less often than men; a given variant may occur more frequently in the language of working-class people than in the language of middle-class users. In addition, there are some social factors that are unique to Deaf[1] communities, such as the language policy of the school attended by signers (e.g., was ASL allowed or disallowed as the medium of instruction?) or the make-up of the signer's family (e.g., a Deaf ASL-using family or a hearing family that might or might not have used ASL).

This chapter will review the history of the study of sociolinguistic variation in ASL, describe the ways in which sign language variation parallels spoken language variation and discuss some ways in which modality differences may show up in variation.

2   Perspectives on variation in sign languages

2.1   Early perspectives on sign language variation

The formal education of the deaf in the United States began in 1817 with the establishment of the American School for the Deaf (ASD; originally called the American Asylum for the Deaf and Dumb) in Hartford, Connecticut. Classes were taught through signing. The first teacher at the school was Laurent Clerc, a young deaf Frenchman who had been recruited by Thomas Hopkins Gallaudet. Clerc used "manual French adapted to English" (Lane, Hoffmeister & Bahan 1996:56) along with the so-called "methodical signs" invented to represent the morphemes of spoken French or English that did not have counterparts in signing. (The use of these methodical signs was abandoned fairly early on.) Lane, Hoffmeister and Bahan state that Clerc instructed the school's hearing teachers in the use of this manual French adapted to English and also gave private lessons "to nearly a dozen hearing teachers from as many eastern cities" (1996:56). In addition, some of the students brought their own sign systems to the school, such as the one used by both hearing and deaf people on Martha's Vineyard. The signing used at the school was not yet referred to as ASL, but as "the language of signs" (ASD 1818).

The establishment of the ASD was followed very quickly by the establishment of residential schools for deaf children in a number of states. Most of these schools were established by teachers and graduates of ASD, a development that is crucial to understanding the development of sociolinguistic variation in ASL. Lane, Hoffmeister and Bahan (1996:58) state:

> In America, as in France, the mother school sent its teachers and Deaf graduates throughout the country to teach in various Deaf schools and to found new ones. *As early as 1834, a single signed dialect was recognized in the schools for Deaf students in the U.S.* [emphasis added]. By the time of Clerc's death in 1869, over fifteen hundred pupils had graduated from the Hartford school, and there were some thirty residential schools in the United States with 3,246 pupils and 187 teachers, 42 percent of them Deaf. Most such pupils and teachers married other Deaf persons and had children. This, too, helped to disseminate ASL.

Thus, the establishment of the residential schools – which until fairly recently have been powerful crucibles of Deaf culture and language use in the United States – led to a de facto standardization in ASL. But the establishment of these schools in the vast geography of the United States in the nineteenth century also led fairly quickly to regional variation that was noticed by educators of the deaf. For example, in the proceedings of the fourth Convention of American Instructors of the Deaf held at the Staunton, Virginia, school in 1856, J. R. Keep (1857) describes how "teachers of the Deaf and Dumb" should acquire knowledge of signing:

> It is answered in this inquiry that there is a language of signs; a language having its own peculiar laws, and like other languages, natural and native to those who know no other ... *There may be different signs or motions for the same objects* [emphasis added], yet all are intelligible and legitimate, provided they serve to recall those objects to the mind of the person with whom we are communicating. As a matter of fact, however, although the Deaf and Dumb, when they come to our public Institutions, use signs differing in many respects from those in use in the Institutions, yet they soon drop their peculiarities, and we have the spectacle of an entire community recalling objects by the same motions. (p. 133)

In response to Keep's remarks, Dunlap (in Keep 1857) compares the signs used at the Indiana School for the Deaf with those used at the Ohio and Virginia schools and notes a need for uniformity "not only in Institutions widely separated but among teachers in the same Institution" (p. 138). In another response to Keep's remarks, Peet (in Keep 1857) refers to Deaf signers as "those to whom the language is *vernacular*" [emphasis added] and in a discussion of a class of signs described in current theory as classifier predicates or depicting verbs, states "Here is room for difference of dialects. One Deaf Mute may fall upon one sign and another upon another sign, for the same object, both natural" (pp. 144–146).

These writings provide a clear indication of early awareness of sign structure and variation, even though formal research in these areas did not begin until the 1960s.

2.2   Variation in the *DASL*

Following Stokoe's 1960 paper on the structure of sign languages, *A Dictionary of American Sign Language on Linguistic Principles* (known as the *DASL*), published in 1965 by William Stokoe, Dorothy Casterline and Carl Croneberg, was the first comprehensive attempt to describe ASL signs from the standpoint of sign language structure. The signs appear in the dictionary not in the alphabetical order of the English words to which they correspond, but in order of the handshapes, locations and movements from which the signs are constructed. A comprehensive list of possible handshapes, locations and movements is provided along with a notation system for transcribing signs. The notion that the language used by Deaf people was a "real language," analyzable in the same way that spoken languages are analyzed, was of course groundbreaking and even controversial for both hearing and deaf people. The notion was controversial because, after the 1817–1880 period that some have referred to as the Golden Age of ASL,[2] over eighty years of severe and harsh oralism followed during which the use of sign language as the medium of instruction for deaf education was largely forbidden (Baynton 1996). ASL and other sign languages had of course endured in Deaf communities around the world, but their status as real languages on a par with spoken languages was seriously damaged, in the case of ones that had been allowed to emerge, such as ASL, and totally unrecognized in the case of dozens of others.

Not only did the authors of the *DASL* claim that ASL was a real language, but the volume also included two appendices by Carl Croneberg entitled "The linguistic community" (1965a) and "Sign language dialects" (1965b) that provide an introduction to ASL as it was actually used in the Deaf community. In "The linguistic community," Croneberg describes the cultural and social aspects of the Deaf community and discusses the issues of economic status, patterns of social contact and the factors that contribute to group cohesion. These factors include the extensive networks of both a personal and an organizational nature that ensure frequent contact even among people who live on opposite sides of the country. Croneberg stated in 1965 that "there are close ties also between deaf individuals or groups of individuals as far apart as California and New York. Deaf people from New York on vacation in California stop and visit deaf friends there or at least make it a practice to visit the club for the deaf in San Francisco or Los Angeles ... The deaf as a group have social ties with each other that extend farther across the nation than similar ties of perhaps any other American minority group" (1965a:310). And these ties of a personal nature are reinforced by membership in national organizations such as the National Association of the Deaf (NAD), the National Fraternal Society of the Deaf (NFSD), the National Black Deaf Advocates (NBDA) and the National Congress of Jewish Deaf (NCJD).

In "Sign language dialects," Croneberg (1965b) deals with the issue of sociolinguistic variation as it pertains to the preparation of a dictionary. While the terms he chose were not precisely the ones that linguists working on spoken languages were using at the time, the constructs are analogous. He states that, "One of the problems that early confronts the lexicographers is dialect, and this problem is particularly acute when the language has never before been written. They must try to determine whether an item in the language is *standard* [italics in the original], that is, used by the majority of a given population, or *dialect*, that is, used by a particular section of the population" (1965b:313). He outlines the difference between what he terms "horizontal" variation (regional variation) and "vertical" variation (variation that occurs as a result of social stratification) and states that ASL exhibits both. He then describes the results of a study of lexical variation based on a 134-item sign vocabulary list that he undertook in North Carolina, Virginia, Maine, New Hampshire and Vermont. He finds that for ASL, the state boundaries between North Carolina and Virginia also constitute dialect boundaries, in that North Carolina signs are not found in Virginia and vice versa. He finds the three New England states to be less internally standardized (that is, people within each of the three states exhibit a wide range of variants for each item) and the state boundaries in New England to be much less important, with a lot of overlap in lexical choice observed among the three states. He points out the key role of the residential schools in the dissemination of dialects, stating, "At such a school, the young deaf learn ASL in the particular variety characteristic of each local region. The school is also a source of local innovations, for each school generation comes up with some new signs or modifications of old ones" (1965b:314). Finally, in the discussion of vertical variation, he mentions age, ethnicity, gender, religion and social status as factors in variation. He views social status as a composite of economic level, occupation, educational background and relative leadership within the Deaf community. Croneberg's focus is on lexical variation and he does not explicitly mention the possible role of modality in the observed variation.

Croneberg's appendices should be considered within the context of other variation research being undertaken at the same time. The years between 1958 (the year of publication of Fischer's pioneering study of sociolinguistic variation) and 1977 were very busy for spoken languages and sign languages alike. Labov's study of vowel centralization on Martha's Vineyard was published in 1963 and his pivotal study of New York City speech followed in 1966. Shuy, Wolfram and Riley completed their study of sociolinguistic variation in Detroit in 1968 and both Wolfram's dissertation on AAVE in Detroit and Labov's seminal article on the AAVE copula appeared in 1969 (see Hazen 2007 for a review). It was in this context that Georgetown University established a doctoral program in sociolinguistics in 1971. James Woodward, one of the program's first students, had worked with Stokoe, and his 1973 dissertation was the first to explore variation in a sign language. As Woodward states in the abstract, "This study attempts to utilize recent developments in variation theory in linguistics to analyze variation that occurs on the deaf diglossic continuum between American Sign Language and Signed English." His committee included Roger Shuy, Ralph Fasold and William Stokoe and his analysis of morphosyntactic variation in ASL was done within the framework of implicational scales developed by C. J. Bailey (1970, 1971).

2.3   After the *DASL*

The years following the publication of the *DASL* witnessed a number of studies of variation in ASL. In addition to Woodward's dissertation, phonological variation in the form of thumb extension was explored by Battison, Markowicz and Woodward (1975). Woodward, Erting and Oliver (1976) looked at signs that are produced variably on the face or the hands, and Woodward and DeSantis (1977) examined signs that are variably one-handed or two-handed. DeSantis (1977) looked at location variation in signs variably signed at the elbow or on the hands, and while called a historical study, Frishberg (1975) looked at processes such as centralization still seen in ASL today, that is, signs usually produced at "high" locations (such as the face) or "low" locations (below the waist) being produced in the more central space in front of the signer. Morphological and syntactic variation have also been explored, as has lexical variation. As Patrick and Metzger (1996) note, however, until recent years most studies of variation in ASL, in contrast to the numerous community-based studies of spoken languages, involved very small samples. Indeed, fifteen of the fifty studies that they reviewed were based on only one or two signers. Only nine of those fifty studies included data from fifty or more signers, and several of the larger studies drew the same database.

All of the early studies of phonological variation in ASL explore both linguistic (internal) and social (external) constraints on the variation. Of particular relevance to the discussion here is that all of the linguistic constraints on the phonological variables are what Wolfram (personal communication, 1993) would call "compositional," that is, phonological features of the signs themselves that may be playing a role in the variation. For example, Battison, Markowicz and Woodward (1975) identified six internal constraints on thumb extension. Signs such as FUNNY or CUTE are produced in citation form with the index and middle fingers extended and all other fingers including the thumb closed, but the thumb may be variably extended. The six constraints identified were: (1) indexicality (i.e., is the sign produced contiguous to its referent, as in a pronoun or determiner); (2) bending of fingers (i.e., do the other fingers involved in the sign bend, as in FUNNY); (3) middle finger extension (i.e., is the middle finger extended as part of the sign); (4) twisting movement (i.e., does the hand twist during the production of the sign, as in BORING); (5) whether the sign is produced on the face, as in BLACK or FUNNY; and 6) whether the sign is made in the center of one of the four major areas of the body. These studies had studies of spoken language variation as models and naturally looked for the same kinds of linguistic constraints that had been identified as operating in spoken language variation.

3   Variation in signed and spoken languages

In fact, as can be seen in Table 20.1, the same kinds of variation found in spoken languages can also be found in sign languages. Specifically, the features of individual segments of signs can vary, individual segments and whole syllables can be deleted or added, and parts of segments or syllables can be rearranged. There can be variation in word-sized morphemes (i.e., lexical variation) or in combinations of word-sized morphemes (i.e., syntactic variation). Finally, there can be variation in discourse units.

Two kinds of variation in sign languages, however, seem to be artifacts of a language produced with two identical articulators (i.e., two hands as opposed to one tongue). That is, sign languages allow the deletion, addition or substitution of one of the two articulators. Two-handed signs become one-handed (CAT, COW), one-handed signs become two-handed (DIE), and a table, chair arm or the signer's thigh may be substituted for the base hand in a two-handed sign with identical handshapes (RIGHT, SCHOOL). In addition, one-handed signs that the signer usually produces with the dominant hand (i.e., the right hand, if the signer is

Table 20.1 *Variability in spoken and sign languages*

| | Example | |
Variable unit	Spoken languages	Sign languages
Features of individual segments	Final consonant devoicing, vowel nasalization, vowel raising and lowering	Change in location, movement, orientation, handshape in one or more segments of a sign
Individual segments deleted or added	-*t,d* deletion, -*s* deletion, epenthetic vowels and consonants	Hold deletion, movement epenthesis, hold epenthesis
Syllables (i.e., groups of segments) added or deleted	Aphesis, apocope, syncope	First or second element of a compound deleted
Part of segment, segments, or syllables rearranged	Metathesis	Metathesis
Variation in word-sized morphemes or combinations of word-sized morphemes (i.e., syntactic variation)	Copula deletion, negative concord, *avoir/être* alternation, lexical variation	Null pronoun variation, lexical variation
Variation in discourse units	Text types, lists	Repetition, expectancy chains, deaf/blind discourse, turn taking, back-channeling, questions

Source: Reprinted with permission from Lucas, Bayley and Valli 2001:25.

right-handed) can be signed with the non-dominant hand. Variation is also allowed in the relationship between articulators, as in HELP, produced with an A-handshape placed in the upward-turned palm of the base hand. Both hands can move forward as a unit, or the base hand can lightly tap the bottom of the A-handshape hand.

Perhaps more important to the examination of possible modality differences in sign language variation are the internal constraints that operate on variation. Table 20.2 compares the constraints in spoken and sign variation.

As mentioned previously, early studies of variation in ASL focused on compositional constraints, that is, the variation was seen to be conditioned by some feature of the variable sign itself. Sequential constraints are those that have to do with the immediate linguistic environment surrounding the variable, such as the handshape, location or palm orientation of the segment immediately preceding or following the target sign. Functional constraints pertain to the role that the sign's grammatical category plays in the variation, while the constraint of structural incorporation has to do with the preceding or following syntactic environment surrounding the

Table 20.2 *Internal constraints on variable units*

Constraint	Example	
	Spoken	Signed
Compositional	Phonetic features in nasal absence in child language	Other parts of sign in question (e.g., handshape, location, orientation)
Sequential	Following consonant, vowel, or feature thereof	Preceding or following segment or feature thereof
Functional	Morphological status of -*s* in Spanish -*s* deletion	Function of sign as noun, predicate, or adjective
Structural incorporation	Preceding or following syntactic environment for copula deletion	Syntactic environment for pronoun variation
Pragmatic	Emphasis	Emphasis (e.g., pinkie extension)

Source: Reprinted with permission from Lucas, Bayley and Valli 2001:29.

variable. Finally, pragmatic features such as emphasis may help explain the variation observed.

Analyses of variation in sign languages subsequent to those undertaken in the 1970s continued to look to spoken language analyses for models of how to account for the variation. And they looked to explanations in which sequential constraints are the focus of the explanations. Liddell and Johnson, for example, explain variation in two forms of the sign DEAF (ear to chin and chin to ear) as a process governed solely by phonological constraints: "A number of signs exchange an initial sequence of segments with a sequence of final segments in certain contexts that appear to be purely phonological. The sign DEAF is typical of such metathesizing signs" (1989:244). They also describe the central role of the location of the preceding sign, such that the first location of the sign DEAF in the phrase FATHER DEAF would be produced at the ear, close to the forehead location of the sign FATHER, while in MOTHER DEAF, the first location of DEAF would be produced at the chin, the same location as the sign MOTHER (p. 245).

Liddell and Johnson (1989) also comment on the variable lowering of signs (e.g., KNOW) that are produced at the level of the forehead in citation form: "[T]he phonological processes that originally must have moved them are still active in contemporary ASL. The rules which account for [these signs] appear to be variably selected in casual signing, and like the vowel reduction rules in spoken languages, have the effect of neutralizing contrasts of location" (p. 253). In addition, they attribute variation in signs produced with a 1-handshape (index finger extended, all other fingers and thumb closed) to phonological processes, again with a focus on constraints of a sequential nature: "There are numerous instances of assimilation in

ASL. For example, the hand configuration of the sign ME (= PRO.1) typically assimilates to that of a contiguous predicate in the same clause" (p. 250).

4   Quantitative sociolinguistics and ASL

4.1   Multivariate analysis of variation

Studies of variation in spoken languages have long been based on the assumption that variation is likely to be the result of not one, but multiple factors, both internal (or linguistic) and external (or social). For example, the "*-ing*" variable in English (whether a speaker says *workin'* or *working*) is constrained by the grammatical category of the word in which the variable appears (e.g., progressive participle or nominal) as well as by the social class and gender of the speaker (Trudgill 1974, Houston 1991), while studies of variable *-t,-d* deletion in English have typically considered the grammatical category of the segment subject to deletion as well as the preceding and following phonological environments and syllable stress, among other factors. The majority of studies of linguistic variation have used VARBRUL, a specialized application of the multivariate statistical procedure known as logistic regression (Bayley 2002, Tagliamonte 2007). VARBRUL is specifically designed to handle the kind of data collected in studies of variation. It provides factor values (loosely called probabilities) for each contextual factor specified and a numerical measure of the strength of each factor's influence, relative to the other factors in the same group, on the occurrence of the linguistic variable. If, for example, the variable being investigated is pinkie (little finger) extension as in the signs YESTERDAY or BORING, VARBRUL allows the researcher to identify factors such as the handshapes of the preceding and following signs as possible factors in the variation, along with other factors such as the grammatical category of the variable sign, the kind of discourse it occurs in and so forth. In addition VARBRUL includes procedures for determining which factors contribute significantly to the observed variation and which do not.

Lucas (1995), an investigation of variation in the sign DEAF that served as the pilot for the larger study reported in Lucas, Bayley and Valli (2001), is among the earliest studies to adapt the multivariate methods of analysis developed to study spoken languages to the study of signed languages. The pilot study of DEAF was based on 489 tokens collected in 1993. The results were surprising in at least two respects. First, contrary to her expectation that there would be two variants, the citation ear to chin form and the metathesized chin to ear variant, Lucas found numerous instances of a third variant: DEAF produced as a simple contact of the tip of the index finger on the cheek. All three variants were included in the database and, following Liddell and Johnson (1989), coded for the location of the preceding and following signs. In addition, Lucas coded for the grammatical category of the sign DEAF itself. The sign DEAF of course functions as an attributive adjective, as in the phrases DEAF CAT or DEAF MAN. However, it can also function as a noun, as in the sentence DEAF UNDERSTAND ('The deaf understand') and as a predicate adjective, as in the sentence PRO.1 DEAF ('I am deaf'). In addition, it occurs in a number of compound nominals such as DEAF^PEOPLE, DEAF^WORLD, DEAF^WAY, and DEAF^INSTITUTION (meaning residential school for the deaf). Finally, the data were coded for the relative informality or formality of the context.

The second surprise came in the quantitative analysis. Even though she coded for the grammatical category of the sign DEAF, Lucas fully expected the VARBRUL results to confirm earlier claims that the metathesis was due to the location of the preceding or following sign. As it turned out, however, the phonological factors – the location of the preceding and following signs – failed to reach statistical significance, as did formality or lack thereof. What was significant was grammatical category, whether the sign was an attributive adjective, a noun or predicate adjective, or part of a compound (referred to at that time as a "fixed phrase"). Thinking that this might be the result of a small number of tokens, plans were made to replicate the analysis with a larger dataset. But it was intriguing, to say the least, that the statistically significant, key factor in explaining the variation was grammatical category rather than the expected phonological factors.

4.2   Variation in ASL reconsidered

In 1994 Lucas and Valli began a study of variation in ASL with large-scale spoken language studies as models. They were joined by Bayley in 1997. The overall goal of the study was to describe phonological, morphosyntactic and lexical variation in ASL as used throughout the United States, and to document the correlations of variation with external constraints such as region, age, gender, ethnicity, socioeconomic status and also factors pertaining specifically to the Deaf community such as school language policies and language use in the home. The data collection methodology and the findings of the study have been widely reported and will not be reviewed here. The part of the study that we will focus on here concerns the behavior of specific linguistic constraints and what their behavior might reveal about modality differences between spoken language and sign language variation.[3] (See Lucas *et al.* 2001 for a full account of the linguistic and social constraints.)

The constraints of concern here relate to the three phonological variables analyzed: the sign DEAF, the location of a class of signs represented by the verb

KNOW and signs made with a 1-handshape. As shown in Figures 20.1a, 20.1b and 20.1c, DEAF has three main variants. In the citation form, DEAF is signed from ear to chin. DEAF may also be signed from chin to ear or reduced to a contact of the index finger on the cheek. As illustrated in Figures 20.2 and 20.3, signs represented by KNOW and FOR are produced in citation form at the level of the forehead but can be produced at the level of the cheek, jaw or even in the space in front of the signer. 1-handshape signs exhibit a wide range of variation, from thumb open to all fingers and thumb open and variants between these two. Lucas *et al.* (2001) examined 1,618 tokens of DEAF, 2,594 of signs in the KNOW class and 5,195 1-handshape signs. And following both spoken language studies and earlier analyses of variation in ASL, the linguistic constraints included in the analysis pertained to the linguistic environment immediately surrounding the variable sign. For DEAF, this meant the location of the preceding and following signs, as in the example discussed earlier – FATHER produced on the forehead as opposed to MOTHER produced on the chin. For signs like KNOW, since the focus is on variability in location, this meant the location of the preceding and following signs and also whether or not the preceding or following sign had contact with the head or the body. For 1-handshape signs, this meant the handshape of the preceding and following signs. Other linguistic constraints were also included and the motivation for their inclusion requires some historical background.

Based on the results of Lucas (1995), all three phonological variables examined in the large-scale study – DEAF, signs like KNOW and 1-handshape signs – were coded for grammatical category, and once again this emerged as the most significant factor, confirming the 1995 results. In VARBRUL, the values of the factors range between and 0 and 1.00. A factor value, or "weight," between .50 and 1.00 indicates that the factor favors the use of a variant relative to other factors in the group. A factor value at .50 indicates that the factor is relatively neutral toward the use of the variant, while a factor value under .50 indicates that the factor disfavors the use of the variant. Table 20.3 shows that compound forms with the sign DEAF favor a non-citation form, predicate adjectives disfavor non-citation forms, and nouns and adjectives constitute a nearly neutral reference point. The other significant factor, discourse genre, shows that non-citation forms tend to occur more in narratives than in conversation. (It should be noted that when the two non-citation forms of DEAF are compared, the phonological factor of the location of the following sign is significant.)

The VARBRUL results for location variation in signs like KNOW are seen in Table 20.4.

Once again, while the phonological factors preceding location and following contact are significant, grammatical category emerges as the most important

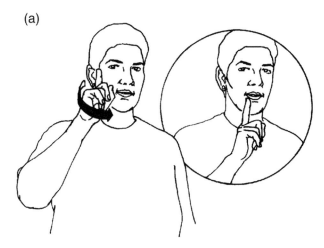

Figure 20.1a *DEAF: Citation form.*

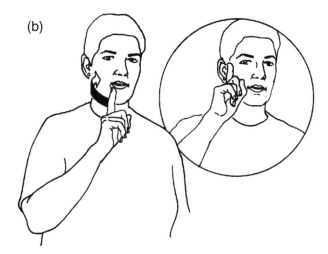

Figure 20.1b *DEAF: Chin-to-ear variant.*

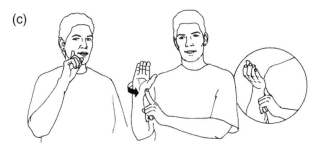

Figure 20.1c *DEAF: Contact cheek variant, in the compound DEAF^CULTURE.*

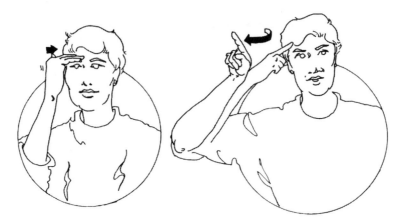

Figure 20.2 *KNOW and FOR: Citation forms.*

Figure 20.3 *KNOW and FOR: Non-citation forms.*

factor, with prepositions and interrogative signs favoring lowered forms, and nouns, verbs and adjectives disfavoring them. Table 20.5 summarizes the rankings of the linguistic constraints for all three variables and shows that grammatical category is the most powerful factor for all three.

The influence on variation of factors other than features of the preceding and following signs discussed here has also been found in other studies of ASL. Hoopes (1998), for example, completed a small-scale study of signs such as THINK, WONDER and TOLERATE. In citation form, all of these signs are signed with the pinkie closed. However, they are sometimes produced with the

Table 20.3 *Variation in the form of DEAF: + cf vs. –cf (application value: –cf)*

Factor group	Factor	Weight	5	n
Grammatical	Noun, adjective	.515	71	1063
category	Predicate	.370	58	361
	Compound	.660	81	194
Discourse genre	Conversation	.489	69	1489
	Narrative	.628	74	129
Total	Input (corrected mean)	.743	69	1618

Note: χ^2/cell $= 1.2952$, all factor groups significant at $p < .05$; the application value is the form of sign that counts as an application of the "rule" being investigated, in this case, the –cf, non-citation form.
Source: Reprinted with permission from Lucas and Bayley (2005:56).

Table 20.4 *Variation in the location of signs represented by KNOW: linguistic factors*

Factor group	Factor	Weight	%	n
Grammatical category	Preposition, interrogative	.581	59	485
	Noun, verb	.486	52	2052
	Adjective	.316	35	57
Preceding location	Body	.503	53	1648
	Head	.452	48	614
Following contact	No contact	.525	55	1323
	Contact	.466	48	991
Total	Input (corrected mean)	.518	53	2594

Note: χ^2/cell $= 1.1702$; all factor groups are significant at $p < .05$; results for preceding location and following contact do not include pauses, which were tested in separate factor groups that proved not to be significant.
Source: Reprinted with permission from Lucas and Bayley (2005:56).

pinkie extended. While we might expect pinkie extension to be governed by the handshape of the preceding or following sign, based on earlier claims, pinkie extension appears to be a prosodic feature of ASL that adds emphasis or focus to the sign with which it co-occurs. In another study, Mulrooney (2002) investigated variation in fingerspelling with the goal of determining what governs the production of non-citation forms of the individual signs that make up a fingerspelled word. Again, one might expect the immediate phonological environment to play some role, specifically the handshape of the immediately preceding or immediately following sign. However, neither of these turned out to have a significant effect. The immediately preceding and

Table 20.5 *Summary of linguistic constraints on phonological variation in ASL*

Variable	Analysis	Constraint ranking
DEAF	+ cf vs. –cf	Grammatical category > discourse genre
	Chin-to-ear vs. contact-cheek	Grammatical category > location of following segment (assimilation)
Location of KNOW, etc.	+ cf vs. –cf	Grammatical category > contact with body of following sign > location of preceding sign
1-handshape	+ cf vs. –cf	Grammatical category > features of preceding and following handshapes (assimilation)
	L-handshape vs. all others	Features of preceding and following handshapes (assimilation) > grammatical function
	Open hand vs. all others	Grammatical category > features of preceding and following handshapes (assimilation)

Source: Reprinted with permission from Lucas and Bayley (2005:61).

following locations had modest influence, but once again the strongest role was played by the grammatical category of the fingerspelled word in which the target form occurred, with proper nouns favoring citation forms, common nouns neither favoring nor disfavoring citation forms, and verbs favoring non-citation forms. Finally, as discussed in this volume, the influence of grammatical category on phonological variation has also been observed in Australian Sign Language (Auslan) (Schembri, Johnston & Goswell 2006), so this phenomenon is not limited to ASL.

For the social factors, we will look at the results for a class of signs made at the forehead in citation form (e.g., KNOW). Table 20.6 shows that gender, region, age, language background and ethnicity were found to significantly affect the location of the signs in the analysis. The results show that older signers disfavor the lowered forms (.416), signers in the middle group neither favor nor disfavor the lowered forms (.517) and the younger signers favor the lowered signs (.602). Signers in the relatively rural data collection sites of Washington State and Virginia, all of whom were White, disfavor the lowered signs, while signers in the other five areas favor them. Signers from deaf families who acquired ASL natively disfavor the lowered signs, while signers from hearing families are neutral. Female signers tend to be conservative and disfavor lowered signs, while male signers slightly favor them. African American signers also disfavor the lowered signs. So, in sum, we see that social factors clearly play a role in explaining the variation, including a factor – language background – that is unique to Deaf communities. Of these social factors, gender, region, age and ethnicity have also been found to have significant roles in explaining spoken

Table 20.6 *Effect of social factors on variation in the location of signs like KNOW (application value: –cf)*

Factor group	Factor	Weight	%	n
Age	15–25	.602	61	554
	26–54	.517	54	1,133
	55+	.416	46	907
Language	Hearing parents	.519	53	1940
background	Deaf parents	.444	52	654
Region	CA, LA, MD, KS/MO	.529	54	2055
	Washington State	.461	56	259
	Virginia	.334	40	280
Gender	Male	.544	56	1376
	Female	.451	49	1218
Ethnicity, SES	White middle and working class	.555	56	1882
	African American middle class	.445	55	257
	African American working class	.314	40	455
Total	Input (corrected mean)	.518	53	2594

Notes: χ^2/cell = 1.1702; all factor groups significant at $p < .05$; no African Americans participated in Virginia and Washington State. African American middle-class signers include persons aged 15–54.

language variation, so this gives us important perspective on variation in human languages, be they spoken or signed. And given the distinct history of the education of deaf children in the United States, the fact that language background has a role in explaining variation in ASL is not at all surprising. We found that social factors also played a key role in the sign DEAF and 1-handshape signs, the other variables that we examined.

5   The role of modality in variation

Spoken languages have been the focus of most studies of sociolinguistic variation, but the work that has been accomplished on sign languages has given rise to a basic theoretical question: "In what way, if any, is modality reflected in variation?" That is, does sociolinguistic variation in sign languages exactly parallel what has been described for spoken languages? Or is the fact that sign languages are produced with the hands, face and body as opposed to with the vocal apparatus manifested in the sociolinguistic variation that sign languages exhibit? Do visual-gestural sign languages and oral-aural spoken languages differ in fundamental ways when it comes to sociolinguistic variation? And what of the constraints, both linguistic and social, on this variation? The main question emerging from Lucas *et al.* (2001) is why do grammatical and prosodic constraints seem to have a more important role than the features of the preceding and following signs in conditioning phonological variation in ASL? The first answer is simply that, as in spoken languages, phono-logical variation in ASL is not constrained exclusively by phonological factors. The focus heretofore may have been on features of the preceding and following signs, but large data-based quantitative studies such as the one undertaken by Lucas *et al.* show that grammatical factors must also be considered.

A second answer concerns differences between spoken and sign languages. Having established that sign languages are indeed "real" languages, research on all aspects of sign language structure has begun to show some fundamental and most likely modality-related differences between spoken and sign languages. Of most relevance to the present discussion are the basic differences in how morphol-ogy functions and how the differences manifest themselves in variation. In many of the spoken languages in which phonological variation has been extensively explored, morphology is a "boundary phenomenon." That is, meaningful segments are added to the beginning or end of other units in the language in the form of plural markers, person and tense markers, derivational affixes and so forth. These units are essentially added to an existing phonological environment. It stands to reason that when variation occurs, a good place to look for the cause of this variation is the immediate environment to which units have been added (i.e., the preceding and following segments). In fact, many studies of spoken language variation have demonstrated the key role of the immediate phonological environ-ment in governing variation.

However, as seen in other chapters in this volume, morphology in sign languages is by and large not a boundary phenomenon, at least not to a great extent. There exist very few sequential affixes. Morphological distinctions are accomplished by altering one or more features in the articulatory bundle that makes up a segment or by altering the movement path of the sign. For example, segments are not usually added to other segments to provide information about person or aspect. Rather, the location feature of a segment (e.g., near or away from the signer) indicates person, and movement between locations indicates the subject and object of the verb in question. Similarly, a particular movement path indicates continuative or inceptive aspect. As Emmorey (1999b:173) states with specific regard to aspect marking in ASL:

> In many spoken languages, morphologically complex words are
> formed by adding prefixes or suffixes to a word stem. In ASL and
> other signed languages, complex forms are most often created by

nesting a sign stem within dynamic movement contours and planes in space ... ASL has many verbal inflections that convey temporal information about the action denoted by the verb, for example, whether the action was habitual, iterative, continual. Generally, these distinctions are marked by different movement patterns over-laid onto a sign stem. This type of morphological encoding contrasts with the primarily linear affixation found in spoken languages. For spoken languages, simultaneous affixation processes such as template morphology (e.g. in Semitic languages), infixation, or reduplication are relatively rare. Signed languages, by contrast, prefer nonconcate-native processes such as reduplication; and prefixation and suffixation are rare. Sign languages' preference for simultaneously producing affixes and stems may have its origins in the visual-manual modality.

The results presented in Lucas *et al.* 2001 indicate that these fundamental differences manifest themselves in the variable components of the language. That is, the immediate phonological environment turns out not to play the major role in governing phonological variables, in part because the variables themselves are not affixes. The grammatical category to which the variable in question belongs is consistently the first-order linguistic constraint. (In this regard, see also Brentari 2002.)

This finding has important implications for our understanding of variation in spoken and signed languages. As the modality differences between spoken and signed languages manifest themselves in the basic phonological, morphological and syntactic components of the language, so they also seem to appear in the patterns of linguistic variation. As the phonological and morphological processes go, so apparently goes variation.

The question arises as to the parallels between ASL and spoken languages (e.g., Chinese) that, like ASL, do not use inflectional morphology to any great extent. The gist of the question is whether the variation in these spoken languages resembles that in ASL, specifically with respect to the prominent role of grammat-ical factors in governing the variation. Or do other features, such as the extremely widespread compounding that characterizes Chinese and the resulting tone sandhi lead to patterns that differ from those of inflected spoken languages on one hand and signed languages on the other? In the absence of a substantial number of studies of sociolinguistic variation in Chinese and other languages that have no or only minimal inflectional morphology (see, for example, Bourgerie 1990, Zhang 2001), we cannot rule out modality differences as a contributing factor to the patterns reported here. At this point, the role of grammatical factors in conditioning phonological variation in ASL seems to be best described as a matter of degree. There clearly are grammatical constraints on spoken language phonological variation, and features of the preceding and following signs obviously influence variation in sign languages.

The analyses of Lucas *et al.* (2001) suggest that modality differences may play a role in accounting for a difference in the relative importance of the constraints. In the variation in phonological features observed thus far in sign languages, grammatical constraints are consistently more important than phonological ones. Ironically, it may be the visual nature of sign languages that reinforces the impressions and hypotheses that phonological variation in sign languages is governed by constraints having to do with the features of the preceding and/or following segments. That is, we can actually *see* the lower and higher locations that precede and follow DEAF and signs such as KNOW; we can *see* the handshapes that precede and follow 1-handshape signs. Being able to see the phonological environment surrounding the variation easily leads to hypotheses about this environment accounting fully for the variation, but these hypotheses are simply not supported by the data. However, recent work suggests that it is too early for large-scale generalizations about the role of grammatical category. Goeke (2006), for example, examined two-handed ASL signs that can become one-handed, such as DEER, WANT and SURPRISE. She coded 611 tokens from eighteen female signers in Kansas, Louisiana and Maryland extracted from the corpus collected for Lucas *et al.* (2001). Goeke examined the possible influence of presence of internal movement in the target sign, contact of the target sign with the body (or not), grammatical category of the target sign, handshape of the target sign (unmarked or marked), and handedness of the preceding and following sign (two-handed or one-handed). Only contact and handedness of the preceding and following sign were found to be significant. To wit, one-handed signs were favored by a contact with the body and one-handed signs or pauses preceding and following the target. The relevant linguistic influences were purely phonological, as the grammatical category of the target sign was not found to be significant. In addition, Goeke found that younger signers (under 55) were more likely to use the one-handed variant than were signers over 55.

On the basis of Goeke's (2006) results, we expanded the investigation of variation between two-handed and one-handed variants with additional data from Lucas *et al.* (2001). Multivariate analysis of 2,258 examples from California, Kansas/Missouri, Louisiana and Massachusetts confirmed Goeke's findings for the significance of contact of the target sign with the body and the preceding and following signs (Lucas, Goeke, Briesacher & Bayley 2007). With a larger dataset, however, grammatical category also reached statistical significance, although it

Table 20.7 *Variation in 1-handed and 2-handed signs (linguistic constraints only, application value = 1-handed variant)*

Factor group	Factor	Weight	%	n
Following sign	pause, 1-handed	.564	54	1547
	2-handed	.393	35	711
Preceding sign	pause, 1-handed	.552	53	1416
	2-handed	.388	35	842
Contact of target sign with head or body	Contact	.613	67	628
	No contact	.456	43	1630
Grammatical category	Other (e.g., WH-, THAT, WOW)	.664	62	151
	N, V, Adj, Adv	.488	46	2107
Total	Input (corrected mean)	.468	47	2258

Note: χ^2/cell = 1.1899; all factor groups are significant at $p < .05$; factors that did not differ significantly from one another have been combined where there was linguistic justification for doing so.

was the least important of the linguistic constraints selected. Content signs (verbs, nouns, adjectives and adverbs) slightly disfavored the one-handed variant, while signs indicating grammatical function and exclamations (e.g., WH-, THAT, WOW) strongly favored the one-handed form. In addition, results showed that African American signers used significantly fewer one-handed variants than White signers. Finally, the results provide evidence of a change in progress. Signers under 55 chose the one-handed variant at a rate of 51 percent, compared to only 36 percent for signers over 55. Results for Lucas *et al.* (2007) are shown in Table 20.7.

The results from Lucas *et al.* (2007) may be interpreted in at least two different ways. First, the results suggest that we need to be cautious in discussing modality differences as they affect phonological variation in sign languages. To date, relatively few phonological variables have been systematically examined using the kind of large corpora typically found in studies of variation in spoken languages, and only two signed languages have been studied, ASL and Auslan. Further studies of ASL, Auslan and other sign languages may reveal findings that more closely resemble our study of alternation between one-handed and two-handed variants of ASL signs than the results found in Lucas *et al.* (2001) (cf. Schembri *et al.*, this volume). Note, however, that the variables examined in Lucas *et al.* (2001), where grammatical category did play the major role in conditioning variation, varied in a single parameter, e.g., location or handshape. In contrast, alternation between one-handed and two-handed variants involves the deletion of an articulator. A second explanation may well be that the influence of the preceding and following signs is stronger in cases where an articulator is deleted. It may point to how quantity behaves differently than quality. That is, the number of articulators involved (two-handed signs vs. one-handed) may be more subject to phonological constraints, while what the articulators are doing in terms of their handshape, location, palm orientation and movement may be more subject to grammatical constraints.

6   Where do we go from here?

One area that definitely warrants more investigation is the definition and description of distinct subsystems or varieties, that is, sets of linguistic features that co-occur predictably – also referred to as dialects – as opposed to the description of individual variable linguistic features across communities. Two such varieties are currently under investigation. Collins and Petronio have examined Tactile ASL, the variety of ASL used by Deaf–Blind people, specifically those with the genetic condition, Ushers Syndrome I. Individuals with this syndrome are born deaf and later, usually in their teens, start losing vision in varying degrees due to retinitis pigmentosa. Crucially, most Deaf–Blind people in this category grow up using ASL and are fluent signers by the time that they begin to lose their sight. A variety of ASL has emerged in this community that accommodates the loss of sight at all linguistic levels: phonological, morphological, syntactic and discourse. One of the consequences of the loss of sight is that Deaf–Blind people no longer have access to the numerous ASL grammatical and discourse markers produced on a signer's face. Remarkably, these nonmanual (facial) markers are produced on the hands in Tactile ASL. For example, the raised eyebrows required for yes/no questions or the nodding required for back-channeling are produced manually (see Collins & Petronio 1998 and Collins 2004 for fuller accounts). As mentioned, features of Tactile ASL are manifested at every level of the language, and there is a substantial community of Deaf–Blind signers who use Tactile ASL. Tactile ASL qualifies as a clear example of a variety of ASL. In addition, research has demonstrated the existence of tactile varieties of other sign languages such as Swedish Sign Language (Mesch 2000) and Norwegian Sign Language (Raanes 2006).

Another such variety is what is commonly referred to as Black ASL. While there is a widespread perception in the American Deaf community of the existence of Black ASL and mostly anecdotal reports that it is as distinct from the ASL used by White signers as AAVE is from middle-class White English, empirical descriptions of Black ASL based on natural language use data do not yet exist. Hairston and Smith (1983:55) comment that there is "a Black way of signing used by Black deaf people in their own cultural milieu – among families and friends, in social gatherings, and in deaf clubs." Based on lexical data, Woodward (1976) described a variety of ASL, used by Black Deaf adults in the South, that arose in part in the schools for Black Deaf children and existed before desegregation. However, no data exist to document empirically its structure and use in any way comparable to the extensive data collected for AAVE. Over forty years of research findings have documented the structure and use of AAVE in rich detail. AAVE has been shown to be a rule-governed and systematic variety of English distinct in its structure from other varieties of English, a variety that acquired its distinctiveness over a long period of time and as a result of the interaction of many historical and social forces (see Mufwene *et al.* 1998 and Green 2004 for reviews of the AAVE literature). Furthermore, not only linguists but also both Black and White laypersons recognize AAVE as distinct from other English varieties. While laypersons may use different labels from linguists to identify this variety (e.g. "Ebonics"), they nevertheless easily and clearly perceive it to be distinct from middle-class White English as well as from other varieties of English. Moreover, laypersons' perceptions of distinctiveness are solidly confirmed by many empirical descriptions of AAVE structure and use.

The same kind of research needs to be conducted on Black ASL. Differences between Black and White signing have been noticed by researchers for at least forty years. Linguistic descriptions of the differences between Black and White signing focus primarily on Black signers in the South. For example, in his appendices to the 1965 *DASL*, Croneberg discusses these differences as a consequence of the segregation of deaf schools in the South. Based on responses to a 134-item sign vocabulary list, he reports "a radical dialect difference between the signs" of a young North Carolina Black woman and those of White signers living in the same city (1965b:315). In comparing signs that can be produced on the face or on the hands (e.g., RABBIT, LEMON, COLOR),[4] Woodward, Erting and Oliver (1976) claimed that White signers produced more variants of these signs on the face than did Black signers. They also noted a regional difference within the South. In New Orleans, both Black and White signers produced more signs on the face than did signers in Atlanta. In their study of two-handed signs that can be signed one-handed (e.g., CAT, CHINESE, COW), Woodward and DeSantis (1977) claimed that Black signers produced more two-handed variants of these signs than did White signers. More recently, aspects of Black ASL have been examined by Aramburo (1989), Guggenheim (1993), Lewis, Palmer & Williams (1995) and Lewis (1998). Aramburo and Guggenheim observed lexical variation during the course of structured, formal interviews. Lewis *et al.* studied the existence of Black ASL and attitudes toward it. They described the increases in body movement, mouth movement and the larger use of space in the signing of one Black female signer who code-switched from more standard ASL to Black ASL during the course of a monologue. In addition, they explored how sign language interpreters handled the code-switching, that is, what the interpreters said in English when the signer code-switched between Black ASL and more standard ASL. They found that the interpreters produced the shifts in posture and eye gaze that accompany role-shifting in ASL, features not unique to Black ASL. Lewis (1998) continued the examination of Black signing styles and described parallels between the communication styles of hearing and deaf African Americans. He focused on kinesic and non-verbal features, in particular, body postures and rhythmic patterns that accompanied the production of signs by one Black adult female. He specifically mentioned the lengthening of the movement in signs, the addition of side-to-side head movement and change in body posture.

Differences between Black and White signing were also examined in the large-scale by Lucas *et al.* (2001) discussed earlier and in greater detail in the Louisiana data from the same study (Bayley & Lucas, in press). They found variation between Black and White signers in the responses to a vocabulary elicitation task: for twenty-eight of thirty-four stimuli, the Black signers used signs that the White signers did not. However, signer ethnicity was found to be significant with only one of the three phonological variables produced during free conversation, with the class of signs exemplified by the sign KNOW, usually produced at the forehead but subject to lowering. Black participants in the study favored the non-lowered citation form of these signs (the form of the sign appearing in dictionaries and taught in sign language classes). It may simply be that ethnic variation does not manifest itself in the phonological variables selected for detailed study, but the explanation may also have to do with methodological issues and with perceptions of and attitudes toward the users themselves, independent of linguistic units.

As can be seen, much of the prior work on Black ASL was undertaken almost thirty years ago. A current study being undertaken by the authors of this chapter in collaboration with Carolyn McCaskill is collecting free conversation, interview and lexical elicitation data at six sites in the southern United States, sites chosen according to when the schools for Black deaf children were founded: Raleigh, North Carolina (1869), Little Rock, Arkansas (1887), Houston, Texas (1887), Talladega, Alabama (1892), Hampton, Virginia (1909) and Baton Rouge, Louisiana (1938). Signers in two distinct age groups – "over 55," people educated during the time of segregation and "under 35," people who went to school in integrated settings – are being filmed in free conversations and interviews, the goals being a re-examination of earlier claims about the structure of Black ASL and a more comprehensive description of this variety.

7   Conclusion

In the past decade, we have made considerable progress in understanding variation in ASL and other sign languages. However, a great deal of work remains to be done. Here we offer suggestions for what we see as some of the most critical areas. First, although the work reported in Lucas *et al.* (2001) covered seven different cities in the United States, as is true of any early study, it did not examine any particular city or region in the depth that is customary in studies of variation in spoken languages. Much more can be done to understand in detail the patterns of variation even in the areas that Lucas *et al.* examined, to say nothing of the many regions that could not be covered in a single study. Second, Lucas *et al.* examined four variables, the three phonological variables discussed in this chapter, and null pronoun use in narratives, as well as lexical variation. However, many other variable features obviously merit our attention. Hoopes's (1998) small-scale study of pinkie extension suggests one such variable, while Mulrooney's (2002) study of variation in fingerspelling suggests another candidate. Third, changes in the demographics of the Deaf population merit our attention. As is the case with the United States generally, the Deaf population is affected by increasing levels of immigration. Indeed, Latino children are among the fastest-growing segments of the school-age Deaf population (Gerner de García 1995). Immigrants bring with them a variety of sign languages, many of which are mutually unintelligble with ASL. Clearly we can expect contact between ASL and other sign languages to affect patterns of variation, and perhaps to lead to new dialect formation. Although research has begun in this area (Quinto-Pozos 2002, 2007, 2008), contact among sign languages in immigrant communities presents many more opportunities for research. Fourth, changes in the education of Deaf children may be expected to affect variation in ASL. As we have seen, for many years state schools for the Deaf served as crucibles of Deaf culture and as a standardizing influence on ASL. However, in the United States, Deaf children are increasingly placed in public schools where there are no more than a few Deaf children (Ramsey 1997). The effects of the decline in enrollment in state schools for the Deaf remain to be seen, but clearly it is a subject for investigation, including the effect on variation in ASL.

We have outlined only a few of the areas where research in sociolinguistic variation in ASL would be most productive. Doubtless there are other areas of equal or even greater potential interest. Research in the sociolinguistics of ASL and other sign languages will, we suggest, provide important insights that may benefit linguistics generally and at the same time provide useful information for the Deaf community.

21

Sociolinguistic variation in British, Australian and New Zealand Sign Languages

Adam Schembri, Kearsy Cormier, Trevor Johnston,
David McKee, Rachel McKee and Bencie Woll

In this chapter, we will examine the historical relationship between signed languages used in the United Kingdom (British Sign Language, or BSL), Australia
(Australian Sign Language, or Auslan) and New Zealand (New Zealand Sign
Language, or NZSL), as well as work on sociolinguistic variation and language
change in all three sign language varieties. Following Johnston (2003), we will
adopt the acronym BANZSL here (i.e., British, Australian and New Zealand Sign
Language) to refer to all three signed languages as a group. We will begin by
outlining the history of BSL and its transmission to the former British colonies of
Australia and New Zealand, before discussing studies that have compared similarities in the lexicon of BSL, Auslan and NZSL. We will then explore the relationship
between phonological, lexical and syntactic variation and change in these three
related languages and social factors such as a signer's regional origin, age and
gender.

1   The deaf communities in the UK, Australia and New Zealand

The prevalence of deafness in developed societies has long been estimated to be
about 0.1 percent of the population (i.e., one in one thousand people) (Schein 1968,
Schein & Delk 1974). If this were the case, one would expect the deaf communities
of the UK, Australia and New Zealand to number 60,000, 20,000 and 4,000
individuals respectively, based on the national populations of each country. The
precise number of signing deaf people in all three countries is, however, unknown.
Published estimates vary from 30,000 (Sutton-Spence & Woll 1993) to 70,000
(Ladd 2003) for BSL, although higher figures sometimes appear on the Internet
(e.g., at the time of writing, the British Deaf Association's website gives a figure of

250,000 deaf BSL users). Similarly, estimates for the size of the deaf community in Australia range from 6,500 (Johnston 2004) to 30,000 (Deaf Society of New South Wales 1989). The New Zealand deaf community is estimated to be between 4,500 (Dugdale 2000) and 7,700 (Statistics New Zealand 2001). Recent research indicates that there may be fewer people with severe and profound deafness in the populations of developed nations than has previously been assumed (Johnston 2004), so the lower figures are likely to be the most accurate ones in all cases.

Regardless of the numbers, the deaf populations in the United Kingdom, Australia and New Zealand each form thriving, cohesive communities. A representative organization exists in each country: the British Deaf Association was established in 1890, the New Zealand Association of the Deaf in 1977 and the Australian Association of the Deaf in 1986. National and local deaf social and sporting clubs and associations are active in the major urban centers in all three countries, along with a range of welfare organizations specifically offering services to signing deaf people.

2   The history of BSL

The origins of BSL are unknown, as there are relatively few early records of signed language use in Great Britain (although many in comparison with other sign languages). BSL, and thus the related varieties, Auslan and NZSL (see section 3 below), nevertheless may be assumed to be relatively "old" languages when compared to many of the signed languages that have been identified in other parts of the world. For example, Taiwan Sign Language dates back to only the late nineteenth century (Smith 1989), and Israeli Sign Language from the early twentieth century (Aronoff *et al.* 2003). In contrast, there is some evidence of links between BANZSL and varieties of signing used in Great Britain during the seventeenth century, as we explain below.

The earliest references to signing in Britain date from the fifteenth century, although there is no evidence to link these with BSL as it subsequently developed (Jackson 2001). For example, Princess Joanna of Scotland (1426–1486), who was born deaf, is described in contemporary records as using signs. There is also a report of signed communication used between deaf friends Edward Bone and John Kempe in Richard Carew's *History of Cornwall* (1602). None of these early references, however, provide any formational descriptions of signs or of sign language grammar.

The earliest actual description of the signs used by a deaf Briton is found in the 1575 parish register of St. Martin's Church, Leicester (Sutton-Spence & Woll 1999). It mentions that in February of that year, a deaf man by the name of

CONGRATULATE   BAD

Figure 21.1 *Two signs described by Bulwer (1648) that are still used in BSL, Auslan and NZSL today.*

Thomas Tillsye was married to a woman named Ursula Russel, and that Thomas made his wedding vows in sign. This record, however, provides very little detail about the signed language used. It is therefore impossible to know whether Tillsye used a homesign system, or an older variety of a signed language related to modern BSL.

Among the earliest records which describe the signed language(s) in use in seventeenth-century Britain are two books by John Bulwer, *Chirologia* and *Philocophus*, published in 1644 and 1648 respectively. The latter book was dedicated to a baronet and his brother, both of whom were deaf. Bulwer (1648) provided mostly written descriptions of the signs used by the deaf brothers, and some seem to closely resemble signs with a related form and meaning used in BANZSL today, such as GOOD, BAD, WONDERFUL, SHAME, CONGRATULATE and JEALOUS (see Figure 21.1).

A number of other written sources make it clear that some deaf people were using forms of signed language before the first schools and institutions for the deaf opened in Britain. In the novel *The Life and Adventures of Mr. Duncan Campbell, Deaf Mute*, Daniel Defoe described signs and fingerspelling as being widely used by deaf people in the early eighteenth century (Woll 1987). The famous diarist, Samuel Pepys, described an encounter with a deaf servant who signed to his master, George Downing, to tell him of the Great Fire of London in 1666 (Stone & Woll 2008). This reference has been used as the basis of the claim that an older BSL variety (referred to as "Old Kent Sign Language") was a possible influence on the sign language of Martha's Vineyard (Groce 1985). Groce herself reports that she was "unable to discover any direct references to deafness in the Weald [of Kent] during the seventeenth century" (1985:29–30), and no deaf people are known to have emigrated to Martha's Vineyard. Nevertheless she conjectures on the basis of the Pepys' diary entry that because Downing is known to have attended school in Kent in 1630, Downing had learned the local signed language. Although a full discussion of this issue is beyond the scope of this chapter, there appears to be no evidence to confirm Groce's conjecture.

The more widespread use of signed communication among British deaf people, however, most certainly began with the advent of the industrial revolution from the 1750s and its accompanying social and economic changes. The resulting population explosion and the mass migration to cities led to a significant increase in the number of deaf children in urban centers, and this seems to have played a significant role in the introduction of public education for deaf children (Johnston 1989). The first British school for deaf children (and perhaps the first school of its kind in the world) was opened in 1760 by Thomas Braidwood in Edinburgh, a few months before de l'Epée's institution (Jackson 2001). The school moved from Scotland to London in 1783, later becoming the London Asylum for the Deaf and Dumb in Bermondsey in 1792 (Lee 2004). It is likely, in a similar way to recent reports of the impact of the establishment of deaf education on deaf people in Nicaragua (Kegl Senghas & Coppola 1999), that these educational institutions created the first environment for a British deaf community and BSL to develop.

Joseph Watson (1809), Braidwood's grandson and the head of the London school visited by Thomas Gallaudet in London in 1815, provides a detailed description of the Braidwood approach, describing the use of signed languages as the means of instruction. The Royal Commission's report (1889), which followed the Milan Congress, supports this view: "The first school for the deaf and dumb in Great Britain was started on the combined system in 1760 by Braidwood in Edinburgh." The "combined" or "English" system used both speech and signing. Francis Green (an American who sent his deaf son to Braidwood's school in Edinburgh) testifies that signing was used in that school (1783:152):

> observing that he [Green's son] was inclined in company to converse with one of his school fellows by the tacit finger language, I asked him why he did not speak to him with his mouth? To this his answer was as pertinent as it was concise: "He is deaf."

From the eighteenth century onward, there are more records, including drawings and descriptions in English, of BSL signs and BSL syntax, which provide a relatively rich resource for researchers. The British anthropologist E B. Tylor (1874:27), for example, discussed the order of BSL signs as "1. object; 2. Subject; 3. Action," explaining that the signs 'door key open' are used to express 'the key opens the door,' and 'I found a pipe on the road' is translated by 'road pipe I find.'

By 1870, some twenty-two schools for the deaf had been established in the UK (Kyle & Woll 1985). Most of these were residential. The existence of these schools supported the creation and consolidation of the British deaf community and of modern BSL. Many schools were set up by former pupils and teachers (who were themselves deaf) at the older established schools, and this pattern of expansion was repeated in Australia, where the first schools were opened by former pupils and teachers from Britain, as we outline in the following section.

3   From BSL to Auslan and NZSL

Historical records clearly indicate that Auslan and NZSL developed from the varieties of BSL that were introduced into Australia and New Zealand by deaf immigrants, teachers of the deaf (both deaf and hearing) and others concerned with the welfare of deaf people from the early nineteenth century (Collins-Ahlgren 1989, Johnston 1989, Carty 2004).

Prior to the establishment of the first schools for the deaf, a number of signing deaf people from Great Britain had emigrated to Australia. The earliest known signing deaf person was the Sydney engraver John Carmichael who arrived in 1825 on the *Triton* (Carty 2000). There is a great deal of evidence that Carmichael used BSL and was indeed a talented storyteller in signed language. He was educated at the Edinburgh Deaf and Dumb Institution with Thomas Pattison, who later founded the first school for the deaf in Australia.

In New Zealand, the hearing teacher Miss Dorcas Mitchell arrived in New Zealand in 1868 with the family of a Reverend R R. Bradley (Collins-Ahlgren 1989). Mitchell was a tutor to Bradley's deaf children and had worked as an educator of deaf children in London. By 1877, she had taught a total of forty-two deaf pupils in New Zealand, using signed communication in all cases.

Thus, historical records suggest that signed languages were in use among deaf and hearing immigrants in Australia and New Zealand prior to the establishment of schools for deaf children. The recorded history of the distinct Australian and New Zealand sign language varieties is, however, closely bound up with the education of deaf children and the establishment of schools for the deaf which began in the middle of the nineteenth century. The first two schools for the deaf in this part of the world were opened within a few weeks of each other in 1860, first in Sydney and then in Melbourne. As mentioned above, Pattison founded the Sydney school, while another deaf man, Frederick J. Rose (a former pupil of the Old Kent Road School for the Deaf and Dumb in London), opened the Melbourne school (Flynn 1984). The method of instruction in both schools seems to have involved the use of fingerspelling and BSL, but more details are not known.

The first school for deaf children in New Zealand was opened in Christchurch in 1880 (Collins-Ahlgren 1989). Mitchell applied for the position of school principal, but this post was given instead to Gerrit van Asch, an ardent oralist who believed in an exclusive focus on the development of speech and lip-reading skills. It is said that he did not allow deaf pupils with any knowledge of a sign language into his school, and thus only fourteen deaf pupils were admitted. Strictly oralist methods prevailed when additional schools for deaf children opened in Titirangi in 1940 and Kelston in 1958. Despite oralist policy imposed by the government department of education, it seems that in the Catholic St. Dominic's School (which opened in Wellington in 1944), some use of Irish Sign Language (ISL) by Dominican teachers trained overseas may have occurred in the early years.

Some deaf children from New Zealand traveled to Australia or Britain to attend deaf schools in these countries before, and even after, the establishment of the first school for the deaf in Christchurch (Collins-Ahlgren 1989). In the oral schools, however, some signing developed naturally among the school children in New Zealand and was used in the school dormitories, but it is difficult to know how much this school-based signing was influenced by BSL. Certainly, a number of signs developed in NZSL that do not appear related to anything documented in BSL (e.g., variants of MOTHER, FATHER, NINE, ELEVEN and TWELVE).

Unlike NZSL, the history of Auslan reflects a relatively smooth transition from BSL, with an uninterrupted pattern of transmission of signed language from Melbourne and Sydney to schools for the deaf in Adelaide (1874), Brisbane (1893), Perth (1896) and Hobart (1904). It appears that deaf children from Queensland were sent to the Sydney school until the opening of the Brisbane institution, and that children from elsewhere in the country were initially sent to the Melbourne school. This pattern appears to have formed the basis for the northern and southern dialects mentioned below.

4   BSL, Auslan and NZSL in the twentieth century

Unlike in New Zealand, the use of signs and fingerspelling continued for some students in Australian and British schools for the deaf through the late nineteenth century and into the twentieth century, but many other students were also taught to speak and lip-read (Kyle & Woll 1985, Carty 2004). This was increasingly true after the Milan Congress in 1880 where the majority of educators called for a ban on the use of signed communication in the classroom and demanded purely oral methods of instruction. School records from this period in Great Britain show falling numbers of deaf teachers of the deaf, and a decreasing reliance on signs in teaching (Brennan 1992). In all three countries, however, signed language certainly continued to be used in dormitories and playgrounds (Collins-Ahlgren 1989, Johnston 1989).

In the early to mid-twentieth century, educational methodologies in the United Kingdom and Australia became increasingly focused on the sole use of spoken

English as a medium of instruction. Following changes in educational philosophies in the 1960s, the emphasis shifted to "normalising" the education of deaf children as much as possible, and residential schools began to scale down or close. By the 1980s, deaf children were increasingly integrated into classes with hearing children or attended classes in small units attached to regular schools. The use of signed language came to be seen only as a last resort for those who failed to acquire spoken English. The increase in mainstreaming and closure of centralized, residential schools for deaf children meant that many deaf children did not have children from deaf families or deaf ancillary staff as linguistic role models (Johnston 1989, Smith 2003). Furthermore, from the 1960s, manually encoded forms of English were increasingly introduced into deaf education. This was particularly true in Australia and New Zealand where Australasian Signed English was introduced from the late 1970s. This highly standardized sign system was based on Auslan vocabulary from the Australian state of Victoria, supplemented by contrived signs created by a committee of educators of deaf children.

Despite the many changes in approaches to the education of deaf children in the last 145 years, it seems that BSL, Auslan and NZSL have remained the primary or preferred language of the British, Australian and New Zealand deaf communities throughout much of that time. There can be little doubt, however, that the various educational philosophies which dominated deaf education over the last century – all of which have variously emphasized skills in signed, spoken, fingerspelled and written English (with different degrees of success) rather than the use of natural signed languages – have had considerable impact on the transmission of BANZSL varieties.

5   Comparative studies of the BSL, Auslan and NZSL lexicons

Native signers of Auslan and BSL report only lexical differences between the two languages, not grammatical ones. Indeed, it is part of the linguistic folklore of these communities, and perhaps justifiably so, that there are no major grammatical differences between the signed language used in Britain and Australia. This issue, however, has not yet been the focus of any empirical research, and there may be subtle differences in the grammars of the two varieties (e.g., differences in the marking of perfective aspect). In contrast, comparative studies of the lexicons of BSL and Auslan show clearly that these two varieties have developed many distinctive signs of their own.

Woll, Sutton-Spence and Elton (2001) suggested that Auslan retains a significant number of older BSL signs that are no longer in use in the British deaf community. This claim may be accurate, but the reverse may also be true. Signers of all ages in the British deaf community, for example, continue to use signs for the numbers six (using the pinkie [little finger] extended from the first), seven (the pinkie and ring finger extended), and eight (the pinkie, ring and middle fingers extended) that are primarily used only by older signers of Auslan. The processes of language change in both BSL and Auslan appear to have resulted in some older signs disappearing in one community, while being retained in the other.

Accounts of the degree of lexical similarity between BANZSL varieties have varied depending on a number of factors (Woll 1983, Johnston 2003). Studies have used word lists or samples of different size and composition and have involved different numbers of native signers in the research. The type of criteria applied to categorize signs as identical, similar or different has differed from one investigation to the next. The nature of the lexicographical work that produced the dictionaries consulted by the researchers, especially in regard to the recording of regional variants, has also varied between studies. Furthermore, because of iconicity, identical or similar signs may or may not be cognates (e.g., Woll 1983, Guerra Currie, Meier & Walters 2002). Similar signs may have developed completely independently in different signed languages. All of these issues explain why the various studies discussed below report different figures for the percentage of similar lexical items in BSL, Auslan and NZSL.

Woll (1987), for example, reported a similarity score of 90 percent for the 257 core lexical items in her study comparing Auslan and BSL. In lexicostatistical work of this kind, it has traditionally been accepted that a result of 36 percent to 81 percent identical or related lexical items indicates that two languages belong to the same family, while languages with above 81 percent shared vocabulary are considered dialects of the same language (e.g., Crowley 1992). Figures such as those reported by Woll (1987) would thus tend to suggest that Auslan and BSL are most appropriately considered dialects of the same signed language. However, "core" signs (such as those for family relationships, common actions, basic descriptions of size and shape, etc.) are likely to have a high degree of stability over time due to their high frequency of use and thus may not represent the overall lexicons of the languages well. In order to study a more representative sample of lexical items, the comparison of randomly selected signs from published dictionaries, rather than just the comparison of the signs for a limited set of core vocabulary, is required. However, prior to the publication in the 1980s and 1990s of the first linguistically informed and comprehensive dictionaries of British, Australian and New Zealand signed languages, it was difficult to make even lexical comparisons between the three languages with a degree of confidence. The first Auslan dictionary was completed in 1989 (Johnston 1989), the first BSL dictionary appeared three years later (Brien 1992) and the New Zealand dictionary followed in 1997 (Kennedy *et al.* 1997).

Studies by McKee and Kennedy (2000) and Johnston (2003) used both a list of basic vocabulary items prepared by James Woodward (this list was originally designed by the American linguist Morris Swadesh but was later modified by Woodward for use with signed languages, see Woodward 2000), and a second, random method of comparison. The comparisons between each set of signed languages indicated that the percentage of identical and similar or related signs in each pairing was consistently high. For NZSL and Auslan, this ranged from 87 percent to 96 percent and for NZSL and BSL from 79 percent to 96 percent depending upon how criteria were applied and consideration given to regional and phonological variants in each language.

For random-based comparisons of the lexicons, the degree of similarity is, not surprisingly, lower. Nonetheless it is only as low as 59 percent between BSL and NZSL, and as high as 82 percent between Auslan and the two other signed languages.

Despite the high percentages of similarity in core vocabulary described above, they are not identical. Indeed, though the divergence in the core vocabulary of the three languages may be small, it might still be considered higher than one would expect for three dialects of the same language having only recently diverged from a common parent language. For example, a comparative study of thirteen spoken languages with a long tradition of written records showed an average vocabulary retention of 80.5 percent for every thousand years (Crowley 1992). In the case of identical signs between NZSL and BSL, to retain "only" 69 percent of core

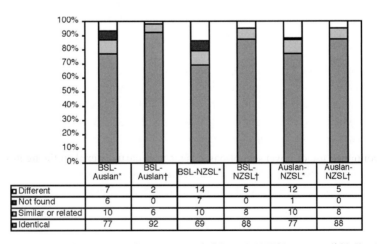

	BSL-Auslan*	BSL-Auslan†	BSL-NZSL*	BSL-NZSL†	Auslan-NZSL*	Auslan-NZSL†
Different	7	2	14	5	12	5
Not found	6	0	7	0	1	0
Similar or related	10	6	10	8	10	8
Identical	77	92	69	88	77	88

Figure 21.2 *The similarity of signs in a Swadesh list in BANZSL varieties (*McKee & Kennedy 2000, †Johnston 2003).*

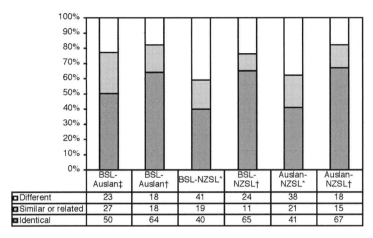

	BSL-Auslan‡	BSL-Auslan†	BSL-NZSL*	BSL-NZSL†	Auslan-NZSL*	Auslan-NZSL†
□ Different	23	18	41	24	38	18
□ Similar or related	27	18	19	11	21	15
□ Identical	50	64	40	65	41	67

Figure 21.3 *The similarity of randomly selected signs in BANZSL varieties (*McKee & Kennedy 2000, †Johnston 2003).*

vocabulary in common (the lowest score by the McKee & Kennedy study) after less than two hundred years of separation may, therefore, imply a relative rapid divergence. It certainly appears to have created greater differences in core vocabulary than one might find between the varieties of English spoken in the UK, Australia and New Zealand (Crystal 1995).

The exclusive use of speech and the absence of deaf adult role models in deaf education between 1880 and 1979 may have resulted in a comparatively disrupted transmission of signed language in New Zealand from one generation of deaf children to the next. This was compounded by the relatively small size of the deaf community in New Zealand, and the smaller resulting number of deaf families. The use and knowledge of fingerspelling in New Zealand may reflect this history: research suggests that NZSL signers make significantly less use of fingerspelling than appears to be true of signers from the Australian and British deaf communities (Schembri & Johnston 2007). Indeed, many elderly NZSL signers reportedly only use "aerial spelling" (i.e., spelling out words by tracing the shapes of the letters with an index finger in the air) (Forman 2003).

The continued use of novel school-based signs may partially explain the figures that suggest that NZSL shares fewer lexical items with both Auslan and BSL than these two languages do with each other. Nonetheless, it is clear that NZSL is part of the same signed language family as BSL and Auslan. A recent suggestion that NZSL is entirely an indigenous creole language that developed from the spontaneous school-based signing without significant influence from either Auslan or BSL appears implausible in the light of the reported lexical comparisons (Forman 2003).

6   Other signed languages with some BSL contact

One might expect that just as the spoken and written language of Britain (i.e., English) was spread around the world, its signed language – BSL, or at least the varieties of British-based signing used at the time – may likewise have spread. However, apart from some varieties of ASL and South African Sign Language, one can find only the remnants of a possible influence from BSL in some isolated lexical signs and a residual knowledge of the two-handed manual alphabet in some countries of the former colonial empire such as India and Pakistan (Woll, Sutton-Spence & Elton 2001). For example, in a dictionary of the Bangalore variety of Indo-Pakistani Sign Language (Vashista, Woodward & Desantis 1985), there are a few signs that are identical in form and meaning to BANZSL signs (e.g., SAVE, SCHOOL, SEE, SWEAR and TOMORROW). Of these signs, a small set clearly derives from the British two-handed manual alphabet (e.g., YEAR, IF, MONDAY and QUESTION).

Maltese Sign Language also shows evidence of contact with BSL (the Mediterranean island of Malta was once a British colony). Signs such as SISTER, BROTHER, WOMAN, GOOD, BAD and the numbers ONE to NINE are the same as BSL signs (Bezzina, n.d.).

Overall, however, the long-term impact of some of the schools for the deaf established in the days of the British Empire was minimal because the overwhelming majority of deaf children of school age in countries like India did not in fact receive an education. The numbers of deaf children who did attend the special schools of the time were insufficient to have a lasting impact on the signed language of emerging deaf communities, even if some of those schools employed British teachers, or teachers trained in Britain, who may have been familiar with BSL or BSL-related signed language.

In Ireland, many of the signs and the manual alphabet used there appear to result from contact with French Sign Language introduced by French nuns who

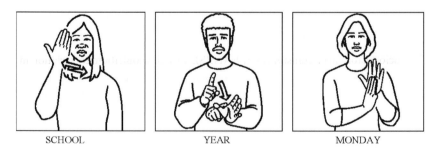

SCHOOL   YEAR   MONDAY

Figure 21.4 *Some Indo-Pakistani Sign Language signs that are identical to signs in BANZSL.*

established Catholic schools for deaf children, but there has also been contact with BSL (Matthews 1996). The first school for deaf children in Ireland was opened in Dublin, in 1816, and the first headmaster was trained in Edinburgh at the Braidwood school. It thus seems likely that some form of signing and fingerspelling may have been used at the Dublin school, perhaps influenced by BSL. This school later became the Claremont National Institution for Education of the Deaf and Dumb, which taught many Protestant deaf children for most of the nineteenth and twentieth centuries until its closure in 1971. Some elderly Irish deaf people who attended this school still use the British two-handed manual alphabet (Matthews 1996).

In North America, lexical similarities exist in only regional varieties of ASL, especially that used in the Atlantic, or maritime, provinces of Canada. Recorded in *The Canadian Dictionary of ASL* are a number of signs such as ALIVE, ANNUAL, ASK, BAD, BEFORE, BOY, BREAD, BROTHER, BROWN, EASY, FATHER, GOOD, MOTHER, SLEEP and TRAIN (Bailey & Dolby 2002). These are identical in form and meaning to existing signs in BANZSL. Others, such as AGE, APPLE, MORE, SISTER, SURE and NOT-YET, closely resemble variants of signs found in BSL.

In South Africa, it appears that the influences were many and varied (Herbst 1987). Like elsewhere, schools were established by the Catholic Church (e.g., Grimley Dominican School for the Deaf was established in Cape Town in 1874 by Irish Dominicans who used ISL-based signing). Other schools reportedly used BSL-based signing. A school for children from Afrikaans-speaking homes was established in 1881. However, South Africa has long been extremely culturally and racially diverse. There appear to be many varieties of signed language in South Africa which are quite unlike or unrelated to BANZSL (Penn *et al.* 1992), and those varieties in White English-speaking communities that have had contact with both BSL appear to share much lower levels of vocabulary with BSL than Auslan or NZSL (Woll 1987).

7   Sociolinguistic variation and change in BANZSL

The socio-historical circumstances of BANZSL varieties contribute to variation in usage, and this has served as the focus of a number of past and current studies of sociolinguistic variation in BSL (Deuchar 1981, Woll, Allsop & Sutton-Spence 1991), Auslan (Schembri, Johnston & Goswell 2006, Schembri & Johnston 2007) and NZSL (McKee, McKee & Major 2008). Each of these projects has focused on specific phonological, lexical and syntactic variables that will be explored in the following sections. Variation in these linguistic features has been quantitatively correlated to social characteristics of age, region, gender and, for New Zealand, ethnicity (Pakeha/Maori).

7.1   Lexical variation and change

Lexical variation is significant in all BANZSL varieties and appears primarily to reflect signers' region of origin and age, as we will explore in the following sections.

7.1.1   *Region*

Regional lexical variation in BSL is well known in the British deaf community. Research carried out at the University of Bristol by Woll, Allsop and Sutton-Spence (1991) involved the collection of lexical variants from BSL signers living in Glasgow, Newcastle, Manchester, London and Bristol. Flashcards with written English equivalents were used to elicit a set of signs from specific semantic fields including signs for color terms, days of the week and numbers. Signs for these concepts were known to vary greatly, and in fact, the study showed that signs used in Glasgow for the days of the week MONDAY to SATURDAY are all completely different from signs used elsewhere. In Bristol, for example, these same signs are all lexicalized fingerspelled loans (e.g. -M-M- for MONDAY), whereas in Glasgow, signs completely unrelated to fingerspelling are used. Some of this regional variation has been documented in the *Dictionary of British Sign Language/English* (Brien 1992) and in other publications (Edinburgh & East Scotland Society for the Deaf 1985), but compared to the lexicographic projects undertaken in Australia (Johnston 1998) and New Zealand (Kennedy *et al.* 1997), lexical variation and its relation to region in BSL remains relatively poorly described.

Regional lexical variation also exists in Auslan and NZSL. Johnston (1989) proposed that there are two main regional varieties of Auslan – a northern dialect (the states of New South Wales and Queensland) and a southern dialect (all the other states). Most noticeably, these two dialects differed (like BSL) in the signs traditionally used for numbers, colors and certain other concepts, such as temporal information (e.g., YESTERDAY, LAST-WEEK) and question signs (e.g., WHO). Indeed, there are important core sets of vocabulary in certain semantic areas (e.g., color signs) in which every basic term is different in the northern and southern dialects (Figure 21.5). The relationship between these variants and BSL lexical variation is not yet well understood, but it must be pointed out that the southern dialect color signs for RED, BLUE, GREEN and BLACK in Figure 21.5 appear to be identical or similar to those signs traditionally used in London BSL (Royal National Institute for the Deaf 1981). This is particularly interesting

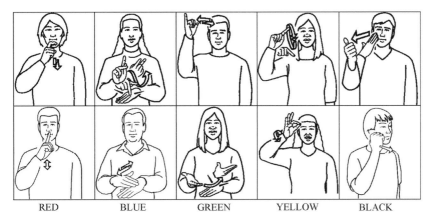

Figure 21.5 *Color signs in the northern (top) and southern (bottom) dialects of Auslan.*

Figure 21.6 *The sign AFTERNOON in various states of Australia.*

given the historical links between the first deaf schools in Melbourne and London (see above).

There are also a number of state-based specific lexical differences that cut across this major dialect division, such as AFTERNOON (see Figure 21.6). Relatively few concepts, however, have more than four distinct state-based sign variants in Auslan. Work is currently underway as part of a large-scale sociolinguistic variation project to better describe lexical variation in Auslan and to correlate regional influences with other social factors, such as age, gender and social class.

In attempting to account for regional lexical variation within BANZSL, it should not be assumed that there was a single homogeneous signed language (an "Old BSL") from which the current lexical variants in British, Australian and New Zealand varieties are historically derived. The variation is much more likely to be due to the fact that residential deaf schools were set up independently from each other in different parts of Britain, Australia and New Zealand during the nineteenth and twentieth centuries. When these schools were established, there was no single, centralized training program for teachers who wanted to use sign language in the classroom; thus the signs used within each school (by the teachers and by the students) must have varied from school to school. Furthermore, in some schools, signed communication was forbidden, leading to the creation of new signs by deaf children while using their signed communication outside the classroom. Because sign languages must be used face to face, and because opportunities for travel were few, each variant tended to be passed down from one generation to the next without spreading to other areas. In a 1980 survey (Kyle & Allsop 1982), for example, 40 percent of people surveyed in the Bristol deaf community claimed that they had never met a deaf person from farther than 125 miles away. As a result, around half of the individuals said they could not understand the varieties of BSL used in distant parts of the UK.

Of course, the situation is very different today. Travel within the UK, Australia and New Zealand (and indeed between these three countries) is much easier, and so signers more commonly come in contact with other regional variants. There is also regular signing on broadcast television in the UK. Thus deaf people are now exposed to many more lexical variants of BSL than they once were. It appears that this is the reason deaf people now report much less trouble communicating with those from distant regions of the UK (Woll 1994). Indeed, it is possible that this greater mixing of the variants may lead to dialect leveling (Woll 1987). There is in fact much controversy among sign language teachers surrounding the issue of dialect leveling and standardization, with conflict arising between preserving traditional diversity within BSL, Auslan and NZSL and the notion of standardizing signs for teaching purposes (e.g., Elton & Squelch 2008).

7.1.2   *Age*

As is well known, the vast majority of deaf people have hearing families, and the age at which they acquire signed languages may be very late. Thus the intergenerational transmission of BANZSL varieties is often problematic. This can result in some fairly extreme differences across generations, such that younger BSL and NZSL signers sometimes report difficulty in understanding older signers. A study reported in Woll (1994), for example, showed that younger signers (i.e., those under forty-five years of age) recognized significantly fewer lexical variants in BSL than older signers. An earlier study of the Bristol community showed that the BSL color signs BROWN, GREEN, PURPLE and YELLOW and numbers HUNDRED and THOUSAND used by older deaf people were not used by younger deaf people from hearing families in Bristol (Woll 1983). New signs had replaced these older forms, with the color signs having an identical manual form that was differentiated solely by mouthing the equivalent English words for 'brown,' 'green,' etc.

Sutton-Spence, Woll and Allsop (1990) conducted a major investigation of sociolinguistic variation in fingerspelling in BSL, using a corpus of 19,450 fingerspelled items collected from 485 interviews with BSL signers on the deaf television program *See Hear*. They analyzed the use of the British manual alphabet in relation to four social factors: sex, region, age and communication mode used. There were no significant effects due to gender on the use of fingerspelling, but age was significant. Sutton-Spence and her colleagues found that over 80 percent of all clauses included a fingerspelled element in the data from those aged forty-five years or older. In comparison, fingerspelling was used in fewer than 40 percent of clauses in the data from participants aged under forty-five. Region was also an important variable: the most fingerspelling was found in the signing of individuals from Scotland, Northern Ireland, Wales and central England, with the least used by signers from the southwestern region of England. Data from signers in northern England and in the Southeast included moderate amounts of fingerspelling. Deaf individuals who used simultaneous communication (i.e., speaking and signing at the same time) also used significantly more fingerspelling than those who used signed communication alone.

A much smaller study of fingerspelling use in Auslan by Schembri and Johnston (2007) found that that deaf signers aged fifty-one years or over made more frequent use of the manual alphabet than those aged fifty or younger. This was particularly true of those aged seventy-one years or older.

In both Auslan and BSL, these age-related differences in fingerspelling usage undoubtedly reflects the educational experiences of older deaf people, many of whom were instructed using approaches that emphasized the use of fingerspelling. Language attitudes may also play a role here, with older people possibly also retaining relatively stronger negative attitudes toward sign language use, although this has not yet been the focus of any specific empirical study. Language change is important here too, as many older signers appear to prefer the use of traditionally fingerspelled items rather than the "new signs" used by younger people. For example, signs such as TRUCK, SOCCER and COFFEE were used by younger signers in the Schembri and Johnston (2007) dataset, whereas only older individuals fingerspelled T-R-U-C-K, S-O-C-C-E-R and C-O-F-F-E-E. In NZSL, the changing status of sign language manifests itself in generational differences in the extent of English mouthing, rather than fingerspelling, as a contact language feature. A preliminary analysis of variation in mouthing in NZSL shows that signers over the age of sixty-five years accompany an average of 84 percent of manual signs with mouthing components, compared to 66 percent for signers under forty (McKee 2007).

One of the first studies to emerge from a large-scale investigation into socio-linguistic variation in NZSL has revealed that variation in the NZSL numeral signs ONE to TWENTY is systematically conditioned by social characteristics, espe-cially age (McKee, Mckee & Major 2006). Like the sociolinguistic variation in the Auslan project mentioned above, the NZSL sociolinguistic variation project rep-resents a replication of quantitative research into variation in ASL conducted by Lucas, Bayley and Valli (2001). The study draws on a corpus of NZSL generated by 138 deaf people in conversations and interviews; the sample is balanced for region (Auckland, Palmerston North/Wellington and Christchurch), gender and age group. All participants acquired NZSL before the age of twelve years, and the majority of these before the age of seven. Multivariate analysis of this data revealed that age has the strongest effect on variation in the number system, followed by region and gender. With respect to region, signers from Auckland (the largest urban center) are slightly more likely to favor less common variants forms than those from Wellington and Christchurch, who are more likely to favor the more standard signs that are used in Australasian Signed English. Overall, men are slightly more likely than women to favor less common forms, although gender has the weakest effect of the three social factors.

Variation in numeral usage reveals diachronic change in NZSL and increas-ing standardization in this subset of the lexicon: all 15- to 29-year-olds pro-duced the same forms for numerals ONE to TWENTY, except for numbers NINE, ELEVEN, TWELVE and NINETEEN which exhibited minor variation. Apart from these exceptions, they uniformly favored signs introduced from Australasian Signed English. Signers over thirty years of age, and especially above forty-five years, exhibited more in-group variation (using a greater range of lexical variants), reflecting the fact that they were not exposed to a conven-tional signed lexicon at school. These results confirm the powerful standardiz-ing impact of introducing total communication approaches into deaf education in 1979.

Distinctive forms produced by the youngest and oldest age groups show that numerals in NZSL (particularly numbers above FIVE) have been partly re-lexified, mostly because Australasian Signed English forms (themselves based on Auslan signs) replaced older variants. For certain numbers, such as EIGHT, the change is complete, in that none of the youngest age group uses older forms of this numeral. In other cases, alternate variants still coexist, or in some cases, a change is appa-rently in progress toward a standard form.

7.1.3   *Gender*

Although anecdotal reports suggest that a small number of Auslan lexical variants may be used differently by woman and men (e.g., the different signs HELLO or HI described in Johnston & Schembri 2007), there have not yet been any empirical studies demonstrating systematic lexical variation in any BANZSL variety due to gender. There have, however, been studies reporting the existence of other types of gender variation. In terms of conversational interaction, for example, Coates and Sutton-Spence (2001) showed that female BSL signers in their dataset tended to set up a collaborative conversational floor, while males signers generally take control of the floor one at a time and use fewer supportive back-channeling strategies. Furthermore, deaf women appear to be leading a language change currently in progress in Auslan (Schembri *et al.* 2006), as discussed below.

7.1.4   *Ethnicity and religion*

Generally, there are no clearly identifiable distinctions in the signed language used by various ethnic groups in the UK and Australia, unlike what has been identified in deaf communities elsewhere (e.g., lexical variants used predominantly or exclusively by deaf African American signers of ASL; see Lucas *et al.* 2001), partly because the education of deaf children in these countries has, for the most part, never been segregated by ethnicity. Many deaf people in the UK from minority ethnic backgrounds are, however, increasingly forming social groupings which combine their deaf and ethnic identity (e.g., social groups formed by deaf people with south Asian backgrounds), and thus we might expect some sociolinguistic variation reflecting these identities to develop over time. This is true of the Jewish Deaf Association, for example, many of whom were educated in a separate Jewish deaf school that existed in London from 1866 to 1965 (Jackson 2001). A book of BSL signs used to represent key elements of Judaism was published by the Jewish Deaf Association in 2003.

It has been reported in Australia that the signed communication of some deaf Aboriginal people from regional areas (such as far north Queensland) includes signs that differ from Auslan signs (O'Reilly 2005). This lexical variation in Auslan due to ethnicity remains to be properly documented, however.

More work on this issue has been undertaken for NZSL. NZSL exists in contact with both the dominant host language of English and Maori as the spoken language of the indigenous people of New Zealand. A colonial history of cultural contact means that "the most unmistakably New Zealand part of New Zealand English is its Maori element" (Deverson 1991:18). There is no empirical evidence yet that Maori signers' use of NZSL varies systematically from that of non-Maori deaf people, whose social networks and domains of NZSL use substantially overlap. It could be expected, however, that the NZSL lexicon would reflect some degree of contact with spoken Maori, albeit constrained by modality difference and by the minority status of both languages in society. Since Maori concepts constitute a local feature that potentially distinguishes the NZSL lexicon from close relatives Auslan and BSL, editors of the dictionary of NZSL sought to record all existing signs in NZSL that represent Maori referents through consultation with Maori NZSL users in 1993 (Kennedy *et al.* 1997). Twenty-five signs with Maori primary glosses (headwords) were recorded in the 1997 dictionary, and these signs are in general usage in the deaf community rather than specific to Maori deaf people. A project was undertaken in 2003 to expand the dictionary database, including documenting further usages with Maori reference which had observably increased in number since the dictionary data was collected a decade earlier. Recognition of NZSL and the training of some Maori-speaking NZSL interpreters from the mid-1990s have enabled Maori deaf people to participate more in hearing Maori domains of cultural activity and to develop a stronger Maori consciousness. Contact between hearing speakers of Maori and the Maori deaf community over the last decade has led to the coinage of signs and translations of Maori concepts that are in the process of becoming established "borrowings" into NZSL – used for both referential purposes and to construct Maori deaf ethnic identity. A total of seventy-two signs or usages with Maori reference were recorded by 2005, and more have entered the language since. These borrowings (locally referred to as "Maori signs") are constructed by several processes: semantic extension of existing NZSL signs by mouthing Maori equivalents, loan translations of Maori word forms and coining of neologisms (McKee *et al.* 2008).

As is also true of New Zealand, separate schools for Catholic deaf children were established in Britain and Australia. In 1875, a deaf nun, Sister Mary Gabrielle Hogan, came from Ireland to open the Rosary Convent school for Catholic deaf children near Newcastle, Australia (Fitzgerald 1999). In the later half of the nineteenth century and early twentieth century, additional Catholic schools for the deaf were opened in other parts of Australia (St. Gabriel's school in Castle Hill, New South Wales, and the St. Mary's Delgany school in Portsea, Victoria). Catholic schools for deaf children were also established in Great Britain, such as St. John's school in Leeds and St. Vincent's school in Glasgow. Most of these institutions employed ISL as the language of instruction until the 1950s. As a result, an older generation of signers in the UK and Australia make some use of ISL signs and the Irish manual alphabet, particularly when in the company of those who share their educational background. Some ISL signs have been borrowed into regional varieties of BSL (e.g., READY, GREEN) and Auslan (e.g., HOME, COUSIN) (Brennan 1992, Johnston & Schembri 2007).

7.2   Phonological variation and change

There has been only a little work on phonological variation in BANZSL varieties. Deuchar (1981) noted that phonological deletion of the non-dominant hand in two-handed signs was possible in BSL (sometimes known as "weak drop," e.g., Brentari 1998). Deuchar claimed the deletion of the non-dominant hand in symmetrical two-handed signs, such as GIVE and HOSPITAL, was frequent, as in ASL (Battison 1974). She also argued that weak drop in asymmetrical two-handed signs appeared most likely in such signs where the handshape was a relatively unmarked configuration, such as B or S. Thus, variants without the subordinate hand seemed more common in her data in signs such as RIGHT (with subordinate B) than in FATHER (subordinate H). Furthermore, she undertook a pilot study to investigate what social factors might affect the frequency of weak drop. Deuchar predicted that signers might use more deletion in less formal situations. She compared thirty minutes of BSL data collected under two situations: one at a deaf club social event and another in a church service. Based on a small dataset of 201 tokens, she found that only 6 percent of two-handed signs occurred without weak drop in the formal situation, whereas 50 percent exhibited deletion of the non-dominant hand in the informal setting. She also suggested that this weak drop variation may also reflect language change in progress, based on Woll's (1981) claim that certain signs (e.g., AGAIN) which appear to be now primarily one-handed in modern BSL (and indeed in all BANZSL varieties) were formerly two-handed.

Glimpses of diachronic change in phonological structure emerged in the study of NZSL numeral signs discussed above: McKee, McKee & Major (2008) noted that variants consistently favored by the younger generation for numerals SIX to TEN utilized only the dominant hand, whereas older signers are more likely to use a two-handed "base 5" (weak hand) plus "additional digits" (dominant hand) system for these numerals (e.g., signing FIVE on the non-dominant hand simultaneously with TWO on the dominant hand for 'seven,' similar to the number gestures sometimes used by hearing people).

The Auslan sociolinguistic variation project also investigated phonological variation, focusing specifically on variation in the location parameter in a class of Auslan signs that includes THINK, NAME and CLEVER. In their citation form, these signs (like signs in the same class in ASL investigated by Lucas, Bayley & Valli 2001) are produced in contact with or in proximity to the signer's forehead, but often may be produced at locations lower than the forehead, either on other parts of the signer's body (such as near the cheek) or in the space in front of the signer's chest. Schembri, Johnston and Goswell (2006) reported an analysis of 2,446 tokens of signs collected from 205 deaf native and fluent signers of Auslan in five sites across Australia (Sydney, Melbourne, Brisbane, Perth and Adelaide). Their results indicate that variation in the use of the location parameter in these signs reflects both linguistic and social factors, as has also been reported for ASL. Like the American study, their results provided evidence that the lowering of this class of signs reflects a language change in progress, led by younger people and individuals from the larger urban centers. This geolinguistic pattern of language change (i.e., from larger to smaller population centres) is known as "cascade diffusion," and is quite common crosslinguistically (Labov 1990). Furthermore, the results indicated that some of the particular factors at work, and the kinds of influence that they have on location variation, appear to differ in Auslan and ASL. First, the Auslan study suggested relatively more influence on location variation from the immediate phonological environment (i.e., from the preceding and following segment) than is reported for ASL. This may reflect differences in methodology between the two studies (i.e., unlike the ASL study, the Auslan study did not include signs made in citation form at the temple or compound signs in which the second element was produced lower in the signing space). Second, the Auslan data suggested that location variation in this class of signs in Auslan is an example of language change led by deaf women, not by deaf men as in ASL (Lucas, Bayley & Valli 2001). This is typical of a language change known as "change from below" (i.e., one that is occurring without there being much awareness of this change in progress among the community of speakers or signers, see Labov 1990). Third, the Australian researchers showed that grammatical function interacts with lexical frequency in conditioning location variation (i.e., they found that high-frequency verbs were lowered more often than any other class of signs), a factor not considered in the ASL study.

7.3   Syntactic variation and change

There has been little research into syntactic variation in BANZSL varieties, and there have not yet been empirical studies demonstrating whether there are consistent differences between individual signers due to gender, age, social class or region (although see the discussion above about the work of Johnston & Schembri 2007). Many authors have, however, noted the existence of English-influenced varieties of signed communication in the British, Australian and New Zealand deaf communities (Deuchar 1984, Johnston 1989).

Deuchar (1984) suggested that BSL and signed English varieties exist in a diglossic relationship, building on a similar account first proposed by William Stokoe (1969) for ASL, with signed English as the high-prestige variety used in formal situations. Deuchar's research was conducted in the deaf social club and church in Reading in the 1970s and involved the collection of data both from hearing and deaf participants, native and non-native signers. She identified a more English-like variety of signing used in the church services, primarily found in the signing of the hearing missioner but also among some deaf individuals. This variety used a lot of fingerspelling, and lexical items followed English word order. It also lacked typical BSL morphosyntactic patterns, such as extensive topicalization, exclusively nonmanual marking of negation and interrogatives, and spatial modifications of signs. While recognizing that such variation exists and that it may be partly situational in nature, there has been some debate about whether it is best characterized as a diglossic situation, and indeed whether this model is at all appropriate for the current social situation in deaf communities (e.g., Lee 1982, Deuchar 1984, Lucas & Valli 1992). English is no longer tied exclusively to some social situations – BSL has become the language of instruction in some schools for deaf children, for example, and is used in nationally broadcast television programs. Woll, Allsop and Sutton-Spence's (1991) work showed a dramatic shift away from simultaneous communication (spoken English together with sign) among deaf people appearing on the *See Hear* program during the 1980s: from 52 percent of all communication in 1981 to only 12 percent in 1987. More formal varieties of BSL appear to exist, although how they structurally differ from more informal varieties has not yet been the subject of any specific research.

As part of the sociolinguistic variation in Auslan project described above, variation in the presence of subject noun phrases has been investigated in Auslan narratives (Schembri & Johnston 2006). Like other signed languages, BANZSL varieties exhibit significant variation in the expression of subject. Based on the study of a corpus of 976 clauses collected from spontaneous narratives produced by twenty deaf Auslan signers, Schembri and Johnston found that almost two-thirds (63 percent) of clauses had no overt subject noun phrase. Factors that conditioned an increased tendency to omit subject arguments included the use of a subject that identified a referent that was the same as the one in the immediately preceding clause, the subject having a non-first person referent, the use of role shift and a spatial/depicting verb in the clause, and the presence of some degree of English influence in the clause. These linguistic factors are similar to those reported to be at work in other *pro*-drop languages such as ASL (Lucas, Bayley & Valli 2001), Spanish (e.g., Bayley & Pease Alvarez 1997) or Bislama (Meyerhoff 2000). Unlike ASL, however, multivariate statistical analysis suggested that social factors such as the signer's age and gender were not significant.

Interestingly, some 15 percent of all clauses in Schembri and Johnston's (2007) dataset showed some example of English influence (e.g., non-nativised fingerspelling, English morphosyntactic patterns and the use of mouthing unaccompanied by signing), highlighting the need for a greater understanding of contact signing in BANZSL. There has been some speculation that increased access to English (e.g., in the provision of captioned television) and growing influence from hearing, non-native signers in the British deaf community may, for example, be leading to an attrition of heritage BSL signing (Turner 1995), but no work has as yet been conducted on syntactic change in any BANZSL variety.

8   Conclusion

Much remains to be learned about the synchronic and diachronic relationship between the signed language varieties in the UK, Australia and New Zealand, and about sociolinguistic variation and language change in all three deaf communities. Major projects currently underway on BSL (Schembri *et al.* 2007) and Auslan (Johnston & Schembri 2006) using corpus-based approaches, together with ongoing work on NZSL (e.g., McKee, McKee & Major 2008) are sure, however, to teach us much more in the near future.

22

Variation in East Asian sign language structures

Susan Fischer and Qunhu Gong

1   Introduction

In this chapter, we shall discuss the history, transmission, and grammars of the two major sign language families in East Asia: the Chinese Sign Language family and the Japanese Sign Language family. We shall not be covering the rest of Asia; for South Asian sign languages, see Zeshan (2000). Neither will we be discussing Southeast Asian sign languages (e.g., the Indochinese peninsula, Malaysia, Indonesia, or the Philippines). Relatively little has been published on the grammars of these languages, and we have neither the space nor the expertise to comment on them. In our discussions of East Asian sign languages, we shall concentrate on those aspects that differ from what is found in Western sign languages.

The Chinese Sign Language family includes the northern and southern dialects of Chinese Sign Language (CSL) and Hong Kong Sign Language (HKSL), historically a variety of the southern CSL dialect. The Japanese family includes Japanese Sign Language (JSL), Taiwan Sign Language (TSL) and Korean Sign Language (KSL).[1] Unless otherwise indicated, what we are reporting here is based on our own ongoing or published research on CSL, JSL and TSL.

1.1   The two families and their histories

1.1.1   *Chinese Sign Language family*
It is difficult to discuss the history of a national sign language without also talking about the history of deaf education; China and Japan are no exceptions. As far as we know, there was no deaf education in China, and no opportunity for deaf people to congregate and foster the development of a sign language until 1887, when a former teacher from the Rochester School for the Deaf established the first school for the deaf in Shandong, China. Although this school used an oral approach, it provided the opportunity for deaf people to congregate, leading to the development of sign language in China (Callaway 1998, cited in Yang & Fischer 2002). A second

deaf school was founded in Shanghai in 1892. The northern dialect, used in places like Beijing, appears to be more heavily influenced by spoken language: for example, the northern dialect uses more Chinese pronunciation pun signs (see section 2.3.2 and Gong 2005b:76 for examples). This is due perhaps to a relatively stronger oral tradition in deaf education in Beijing (Gong 2005a: 54; 2005b:76). CSL and signed Chinese were regarded as identical before the publication of Fu and Mei (1986); that is, there was no recognition of CSL as a distinct language.[2]

The southern dialect, used, for example, in Shanghai, shows somewhat less influence from the spoken language. HKSL lexicon and structure appear to be similar to the southern variety of CSL, which is not surprising given their geographical proximity and the large influx of Shanghainese to Hong Kong in the early twentieth century.

In China, schools for the deaf in the late nineteenth and early twentieth centuries employed manual alphabets such as the Lyon manual alphabet and manual Zhuyinzimu, an early Chinese pronunciation alphabet using simple Chinese characters or parts of Chinese characters as well as CSL to teach Chinese characters (Fu & Mei:12–19). Most schools in Shanghai used CSL as the medium of instruction; most of the teachers were deaf, since the schools could not afford to hire hearing teachers (Mu Dai, personal communication, 2007).

Since the 1950s, deaf education in Mainland China has used "spoken language as major means, and sign language auxiliary " as recorded in the National Guideline for Deaf Education, that is, oralism but with tolerance of CSL. This guideline was influenced by the former Soviet Union; the wording will soon be replaced by "employing all means suitable to deaf students" (Yiji Cheng, personal communication, 2007). While sign language has not played an important role in classroom teaching or teacher training, China has not enforced the kind of strict oralism practiced in Hong Kong and some schools in the West.

There may be some influence of CSL on a few of the Southeast Asian sign languages; in Singapore, a Shanghainese couple founded the first school for the deaf in 1954; the Shanghai variety of CSL was used as the medium of instruction.[3] A few Thai Deaf people have informed us that Thai Sign Language has similar morphological processes for forming negatives as in CSL. These processes also occur in British Sign Language (BSL: Sutton-Spence & Woll 1999), which may in fact be the source for the process in Asian sign languages; BSL is the older language, and the point of contact was probably Shanghai, where there was a strong foreign presence (Bencie Woll, personal communication, May 2007).

1.1.2   *Japanese Sign Language family*

There are now about 361,000 deaf persons in Japan according to a recent white paper.[4] Deaf schools in Japan began in the Meiji Era as part of a push toward universal education, starting in the late 1870s (Nakamura 2006). Extrapolating from nineteenth-century census data,[5] one can estimate that there were approximately 100,000 deaf people at that time, though probably not all attended school or signed. Data are incomplete, but there are records of deaf teachers in the late nineteenth century; their numbers peaked in the early 1920s, but in 1932 educational policies changed and, as in China, deaf schools in Japan all became officially oral, and the number of deaf teachers declined precipitously (Okamoto 1997; see also Nakamura 2006). Most Japanese deaf schools permit the use of sign language only in middle or high school, but a few, notably in Osaka, have maintained a tradition of signing in elementary schools despite central government prohibitions.[6] Currently, there are several elementary schools using JSL or signed Japanese as the medium of instruction, including a newly accredited school in Tokyo founded by a Deaf group. Except for borrowing and adapting ASL fingerspelling, JSL appears to have evolved independently of any other sign languages.

For about fifty years, 1895–1945, Japan occupied both Taiwan and Korea (Korea for a bit less), and teachers were sent from Japan to establish deaf schools in those places. In the case of Taiwan, two schools were initially established, one in the north and one in the south, and two dialects of TSL also developed, reflecting the Tokyo and Osaka dialects of their respective founders (Smith, 1989, 2005). TSL is still by and large mutually intelligible with JSL. In 1951, a deaf person from Nangtong, near Shanghai, established a school for the deaf in Kaohsiung, Taiwan; the southern variety of CSL was used at the school. Through this conduit, as well as the influx of Nationalists from Mainland China into Taiwan over the last fifty-seven years, TSL has borrowed some vocabulary as well as some morphology from CSL. According to Sasaki (2003), TSL and JSL share approximately 60 percent of their vocabulary; however, this percentage may under-represent the similarities between the two languages, due to the grammatical processes that they share. Sasaki also reports that JSL signers have little difficulty in communicating with signers of TSL and KSL. Smith (2005) reports that TSL is used by approximately 30,000 deaf people in Taiwan.

Sign language has been in use in Korea since 1889, thus predating the Japanese occupation; KSL has been used in Korean schools since 1908 (Gordon 2005). Like TSL, KSL also shares many JSL lexical items and grammatical features, including the gender-marking indexical classifiers discussed below (section 3.3).

The Japanese Federation of the Deaf (JFD) is active in promoting the teaching of JSL to both hearing and deaf persons. JSL is also taught on educational television, and sign language news (previously largely in signed Japanese, now in JSL) airs several times a week. Other deaf organizations, many supported by the government, include athletic associations, women's associations and associations for elderly deaf.

1.2   Shared features with other sign languages

With the exception of so-called village sign languages as discussed by Marsaja (2008) or Sandler *et al.* (2005), the Chinese and Japanese sign language families have similar grammatical characteristics to those investigated in Western sign language families (see Brentari, this volume, for discussion). In the next sections, we shall touch on some of the differences we and other researchers have found between Western and East Asian sign languages.

2   **Phonology**

2.1   Handshapes

In ASL, there are marked handshapes used only in fingerspelling, numbers or initialized signs. In CSL, KSL and JSL, some marked handshapes are used only in fingerspelling or numbers (HKSL and TSL do not have fingerspelling); Pinyin, the Romanized Chinese pronunciation alphabet system, is widely used in Mainland China and has a manual counterpart. CSL examples include ⍟ (z in horizontal orientation), extended forefinger, middle finger and pinkie (little finger) (zh), (sh-) and ⍟ ⍟ (the M- and N-handshapes).[7] Examples in JSL include the symbol for the numeral 8 (all fingers except the pinkie extended), and the handshapes for the syllables E, TI, TU and HE (in its upside-down orientation).[8] See Figure 22.1a–e. KSL also has a couple of handshapes used only in fingerspelling.[9]

Some handshapes in both the CSL and the JSL families are either not present or not common in Western sign languages. In addition to handshapes used only in numbers, fingerspelling or kinship terms, some handshapes are used in only one or two signs in TSL, CSL or JSL. For example, in both JSL and some varieties of CSL, the handshape ⍟ is used only to sign 'toilet' (a simultaneous representation of 'WC'). The handshape ⍟ is used only in kinship terms in JSL and TSL. The handshape used only in the sign for 'ginger' in CSL is an imitation of the shape of ginger root using a lax fist with raised hooked pinkie. In the Beijing variety, the curling of the fingers decreases gradually up to the pinkie. A very marked handshape of extended ring finger formerly used in kinship signs in JSL remains in TSL, but again, only for kinship signs. TSL also has the handshape ⍟.

Of particular interest in terms of locations is the marked handshape ⍟ , which appears on the *non*-dominant hand in the sign for 'quality,' in the Shanghai variety of CSL. Marked locations such as the armpit are also used in the CSL family for days of the week.

In addition to the special handshapes mentioned above, there are special hand-shapes and configurations used only in signs representing Chinese characters. See section 2.3 below.

2.2   Movements and points of contact

The marked movements that we find in Asian sign languages are local rather than path movements. Some marked movements or secondary movements in Western sign languages' perspective occur in CSL too; for example, the productive CSL sign and root morpheme for things or objects involves bouncing two forefingers together and then immediately or simultaneously flicking the middle finger off the thumb. The JSL sign MIKAN ('clementine') has an interesting local movement consisting of sequentially extending the fingers starting with the pinkie, effectively the converse of ASL SEVERAL. Some JSL signers sign OOI ('many') with the thumb tucked in and the other fingers closing in sequence. Another example of a marked local movement is the sign DOOZI ('simultaneous'), in which a fist opens up to a G/1-handshape with no flicking, and hence no pre-selected fingers, involved. See Figure 22.1 (lower left).

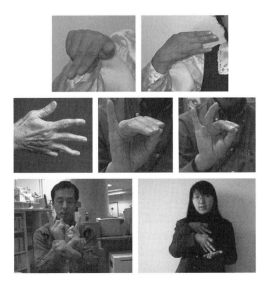

Figure 22.1 *Atypical sign configurations: (a) CSL Z, (b) CSL ZH, (c) JSL 8, (d) JSL TI (chi), (e) JSL TU (tsu), (f) JSL DOOZI (simultaneous), (g) CSL BAOMING (*报名*, register).*

Restrictions on point of contact of both dominant and non-dominant hands are quite different in East Asian sign languages from their Western counterparts. In the ASL F-handshape, only the thumb and forefinger are selected, but in CSL (and HKSL), the selected fingers include the remaining three extended fingers. This results in fewer phonotactic restrictions on the F-handshape in CSL. In the CSL sign for 'name,' the forefinger of the dominant hand moves down the distal joints of the extended fingers of an F-handshape; in the sign for 'register,' the tips of the three extended fingers of the F-handshape come into repeated contact with the palm of the non-dominant hand. In the CSL character sign for 'task,' based on the character 业, the non-dominant hand is in a 4-configuration, and the forefinger of the dominant hand moves down the back of the four extended [selected] fingers: see Figure 22.1g.

2.3   Chinese character signs

There is a special class of signs many of which present, as mentioned above, some exceptions to phonological constraints in all East Asian sign languages. These are signs representing Chinese characters, which following general practice in Asia, we will refer to as character signs. The interaction of character signs with morphology will be discussed in section 3. Here we shall concentrate on their formational properties.

Everyone, hearing and deaf, in China, Taiwan, Japan and Hong Kong draws Chinese characters, often quite complex ones, in the air or on the palm of the hand, using a forefinger for the strokes. This also used to be the case in Korea, but Korean writing is now almost exclusively in Hangul as is evident in modern Korean printed matter. The drawing of characters in the air or on the palm is analogous to ordinary fingerspelling in Western sign languages; it is used for words for which there is no sign, e.g., proper names. In addition, because there is so much homonymy in these spoken languages, characters serve as disambiguating devices, and again even hearing people with no knowledge of a sign language will write characters in the air in order to show which meaning they intend. This use of Chinese characters constitutes a separate subsystem, like fingerspelling in Western sign languages.

In contrast, *character signs* are analogous in both number and function to fingerspelled loan signs (Battison 1978). There are a few dozen frozen character signs in both the CSL and the JSL families, apparently more numerous in CSL and TSL than in JSL or KSL.[10] Frozen character signs in these sign languages are usually restricted to visually simple characters with relatively few strokes or components. Phonologically exceptional features are also present in some of these. Their morphological characteristics are discussed in section 3.

2.3.1 *Tracing and depicting*

The two major ways of forming character signs are *depicting* and *tracing*.[11] Most depicted character signs are static visual representations of Chinese characters; however, for character signs containing several identical components, such as CSL 昌 ('prosperity') or CSL/JSL 品 ('product, virtue'), movement is employed to indicate the placement of the components.[12] Other examples of depicted Chinese characters are 中 ('middle': CSL/JSL), 田 (rice paddy: CSL/JSL), 介 ('introduce': CSL/TSL), 日('day,' JSL), 入('enter': JSL).[13] As with fingerspelling, character signs utilize handshapes and/or configurations that do not occur in other signs. The sign that depicts 昌, in fact, appears to violate Battison's (1978) symmetry constraint, in that two different handshapes both move without touching or impinging on each other, in contrast to ASL signs like LEAD, HELP or SHOW, which permit two different handshapes because one hand is seen as affecting the other. See Figure 22.2b–j.

Tracing, as previously mentioned, consists of writing the character in the air, usually with the forefinger. It is interesting to note that the sign for person (人) is a character sign in both CSL and JSL, and in both languages it is grammatically active; however, the character is depicted in CSL but traced in JSL. There are more depicted character signs in the core lexicons of CSL and JSL than traced ones.

Some character signs are formed by using a combination of depicting and tracing: in the CSL character sign for 干 ('dry'), in contrast to the pure depicting sign for 工 ('work'), for instance, the two horizontal strokes are depicted in the non-dominant hand, while the vertical stroke is traced with the index finger of the dominant hand on the depicting fingers. Similarly, the JSL character sign for 川 ('river') is made by moving a 川 hand downwards.

Most depicted character signs are two-handed, e.g., the CSL sign for person (人 Figure 22.2g) or the JSL configuration for "enter" (入, Figure 22.2f) (the two signs are in fact made identically), but there are a few one-handed depicted character signs as well, such as the Shanghai and Beijing signs for '10' (十), 🖐 and 👋, respectively. Traced characters all follow the stroke order of written Chinese characters.

Most character signs are made in neutral space, but in CSL the character signs for 'stomach' (胃, depicting the upper component 田), and 'liver' (肝, showing only 干) are signed close to the body part location, with or without a point to the location.

2.3.2. *Pronunciation pun signs*

All varieties of CSL have signs based on similar spoken pronunciation of a Chinese character, though such signs are more frequent in northern varieties of CSL. A

Chinese pronunciation pun sign is a sign whose spoken Chinese equivalent shares the same or similar pronunciation with the Chinese word for another sign, whose meaning is usually simpler or more concrete. For example, the sign for 'active, enthusiastic' is the same for the sign for 'chicken'; the Chinese word for 'active' (jıjí 积极) sounds like a repetition of the Chinese word for 'chicken' (jı 鸡).

2.3.3.   *Visual metonymic signs*

Visual metonymic signs are based on a partial visual resemblance between a simpler and a more complicated character. For instance, the left part of the character for a

Figure 22.2 *Initialized and depicted Chinese character signs, from top left: (a) JSL REPOOTO ('term paper'), (b) JSL & CSL* 中 *('middle'), (c) CSL* 田 *('rice paddy'), (d) JSL* 田 *('rice paddy'), (e) CSL*介 *('introduce'), (f) JSL* 入る *('enter'), (g) CSL* 人 *('person'), (h) CSL* 业 *('task'), (i) CSL* 品 *('product'), (j) CSL* 昌 *('prosperity').*

common Chinese surname 彭 is identical with the left part of the character 鼓 for 'drum'; the sign for 'drum' is used to sign this surname as well. There are also metonymic character signs that depict part of the character; such metonymic character signs also appear in tracing: e.g., the CSL sign for '10,000' is the tracing of the 7-like last stroke of the character for '10,000' (万).

The use of Chinese characters or character components results in homonymy, especially in the CSL family; for example, the signs depicting '(water) well' (井) and 'public, communist' (共) are the same in CSL due to the visual similarity of their corresponding Chinese characters.

In JSL signs for place-names, sometimes the second character in a compound is not signed. So the sign for 'Chiba' (千葉) is based on a depiction of the first character 千. In CSL, sometimes a sequence of signs is used to express one character. For example, for the surname 'Gong' (龚), a signer might sign the two parts separately to indicate how the character is formed: first signing LONG 龙, ('dragon') to show the top part of the character and then signing the character sign GONG 共 ('public'), to show the bottom part.

2.4   Nonmanual markers

Like other established sign languages, members of both the CSL and the JSL families use nonmanual markers with overlaid affective, lexical and syntactic or discourse functions. The types of nonmanuals occurring in the literature and also that we have observed include brow raises, brow furrowing, frowns, headshakes, headnods, body leans and body shifts (see Fischer & Osugi 1998 and Tang 2006 for examples). We shall discuss the syntactic role of nonmanuals in section 4.2.

3   Word formation

3.1   Interaction with spoken/written language

3.1.1   *Fingerspelling and initialized signs*

JSL had a fingerspelling system in the nineteenth century that has all but disappeared (Nakamura 2006). In the 1930s, the ASL fingerspelling system was adapted and added to in order to accommodate the Japanese syllabary. Thus, ASL vowels were borrowed intact; KA, SA, NA, MA, HA, YA and WA use ASL K, S, N, M, H, Y, and W respectively (ASL T is not used for TA because ASL T is taboo in Japanese culture, as it refers to sexual activity). Other symbols were invented or adapted for the rest of the syllabary (Yutaka Osugi, personal communication, January 1992). Syllables beginning with voiced obstruents (GA, ZA, BA, etc.)

are formed by moving the signing hand ipsilaterally. The H series (HA HI HU HE HO) has both voiced (BA BI BU BE BO) and voiceless (PA PI PU PE PO) counterparts; the P series is formed by raising the signing hand.

Only relatively recently, however, have Japanese signers used fingerspelling with any regularity; many elderly Japanese never learned fingerspelling, hence the proliferation of signs for proper names that would be spelled in many Western sign languages.[14]

In China, starting in the late nineteenth century, a number of invented or adapted (based on Bell's Visible Speech or Zhuyinzimu) manual alphabets were used, but these alphabets also fell into disuse. In 1963, an official manual alphabet system based on Pinyin, the Romanized Chinese pronunciation system, was introduced in Mainland China. CSL has both fingerspelled abbreviations and initialized signs. One example of a fingerspelled abbreviation in CSL is YW (🖐🖐) for 'because' (*Yīnwèi*), analogous to the use of b/c for 'because' in instant messaging in English. As far as we know, JSL does not have such fingerspelled abbreviations.

Initialized signs are generally based on existing signs, and some have been coined for the "official" version of CSL (*Zhongguo shouyu* 2003). Examples of initialized signs in CSL include *HEI* 'black' and *HÓNG* 'red,' which used to be signed with the forefinger respectively touching the hair and lips. For these signs it has become common to use a CSL H-handshape (✌) reflecting the first letters of the Romanized Chinese words.

JSL has relatively few initialized signs, but some new ones have appeared, such as ARERUGII, 'allergy,' using an A-handshape in the sign for 'scratch,' REPOOTO ('term paper,' using a RE-handshape [= ASL'L'] for KAKU, 'write'), shown in Figure 22.2a, IMEEJI 'image,' and SAAKURU 'club,' using the SA-handshape [= ASL 'S'] in the sign for 'circle.' One interesting and unusual form of initialization is PASOKON ('personal computer'), which is made with the non-dominant hand performing a keyboarding gesture, while the dominant hand is held in or moves to the final shoulder-high position of the fingerspelled syllable PA. Thus, PA on the dominant hand provides the initialization, while the non-dominant hand provides the meaning.

KSL fingerspelling is structured like hangul, the Korean writing system based on phonological principles in which each syllable symbol comprises several ordered alphabetic subcomponents (Kang-Suk Byun, personal communication).[15]

TSL and HKSL have no fingerspelling and hence no initializations or abbreviations, although they do contain some character signs (see below). Pinyin and its fingerspelled counterpart were introduced at a time when Taiwan and Hong Kong were separate from Mainland China. (Hong Kong was a British colony for a hundred years before the Chinese takeover in 1997; Taiwan was occupied by

Japan for decades and continued separate from Mainland China after 1949 when the Nationalist government moved there.) A further complication is that in Taiwan and Hong Kong, Zhuyinzimu and older Romanizations have been used; further-more, in Hong Kong, Cantonese rather than Mandarin is the dominant dialect, and it is rarely written phonetically, so fingerspelling would not be straightforward.

3.1.2   *Chinese character signs*
TSL and HKSL have no fingerspelling; CSL, KSL and JSL have fingerspelling but use it much less frequently than in languages like ASL. In East Asian sign lan-guages, Chinese characters and signs based on them serve the same function. We have already discussed their phonological properties in section 2.3. Here we shall focus on their participation in morphological processes.

Character signs can be morphologically active both inflectionally and deriva-tionally. In both CSL and TSL, the sign for 'introduce' (based on the character 介) is an agreement verb with a movement from the locus of the person being intro-duced to the locus of the person receiving the introduction.[16] In the Beijing variety of CSL, a new sign meaning 'who' is formed by rotating the forefinger of the dominant hand of the sign for 'person' (人) (Yang 2004). This movement is itself a general *wh*-question morpheme meaning 'which' or 'what' in the Beijing variety. The traced JSL character sign for 人 permits simple numeral incorporation (i.e., with no changes in handshape so that the sign meaning '30 people' is acceptable with incorporation, but to express the notion of 35 people, it would be necessary to use two separate signs). In both CSL and JSL, the sign for 1,000, based on the cursive way of writing 千, is traced with an index finger, but for 2,000–9,000, handshapes for corresponding numerals are substituted for the forefinger.

Figure 22.3b shows the incorporation of the numeral 2 into the JSL sign for 'person.' Figure 22.3d and 22.3e shows the depicted JSL sign meaning 'enter,' 入, inflected spatially for goal.

In CSL, signs for words such as 'who,' 'what,' 'when,' 'where' and 'how' share different local movements and sometimes handshapes to convey information indeterminacy. In addition to the twisting motion to form *wh*-questions Yang (2004) mentions a substitute 5 handshape with wiggling fingers to show 'how many people.' These modifications constitute productive morphemes, so for example, the sign for 'how old' substitutes the wiggly 5 handshape for the original sign for 'old.'

In JSL, *wh*-signs differ from indefinites only by nonmanuals: thus, the sign NANI ('what') will generally be accompanied by a *wh*-question facial expression (whqfe), but the sign NANIKA ('something') has the same manual formation but lacks the whqfe.

Figure 22.3 *Traced and morphological active Chinese character signs, from top left: (a) CSL 千 (1000), (b) JSL FUTARI (人 incorporating the numeral 2), (c) CSL/TSL 介 (introduce), (d) JSL 入る (enter [a business]: citation form), (e) JSL 入る (enter:1st person goal agreement), (f) JSL SYOUKAI (introduce: plain verb), (g) JSL auxiliary showing agreement between direct and indirect object, (h) CSL (Beijing dialect) SHUI (谁, who, based on 人), (i) CSL (Beijing dialect) DUOSHAOREN (多少人, how many people).*

3.2   Inflectional morphology

Although inflectional morphology in CSL and JSL mostly parallels what has been described for Western sign languages, a few notable differences arise, especially with regard to the JSL family. First is the interaction between verb agreement and what Fischer and Osugi (2000) call "indexical classifiers" (ICs). In the JSL family, the two handshapes 𝄇 and 🖐 are used respectively for male and female. These ICs take the place of the referential locus for both subject and object agreement for almost any one-handed third person agreement verb involving a human definite argument (also discussed in Smith 1989). ASL and many other sign languages, including the CSL family, have ICs for object agreement, but the alternation between locus and IC use is not systematic, does not show gender and generally inflects only for object, not subject. For example, the ASL sign CONVINCE can be signed either toward a referential locus or toward an index finger IC. A few other signs have this alternation between referential locus and IC, but most signs containing ICs are frozen: examples would include FLATTER, HIT or PATRONIZE/FREQUENT (an establishment). JSL also has some frozen ICs as in the signs meaning 'rear a child', 'invite' or 'help'. Although the unmarked gender is male, some of these frozen signs can be partially thawed to permit object agreement with a female. However, since they are two-handed, they cannot participate in subject agreement (i.e., where the IC is the reference point for the subject). Languages in the JSL family are the only cases found so far where gender is overtly marked in a sign language[17] or where subject is marked using an IC.

Figure 22.4 shows the sign IU ('say') in its citation form, agreeing with a first person object, agreeing with a female third person IC object and agreeing with a female third person IC subject.

According to Hong (2006), KSL also has ICs; indeed, Hong mentions ICs first as the (apparently) predominant means of showing agreement in KSL. One-third of KSL agreement verbs require ICs. As in JSL, in KSL some signs are frozen and always require the default male handshape; a few can be partially thawed to allow the female handshape, though apparently not as many as either JSL or TSL (Smith 1989), and some permit the kinds of alternations we have described above. Since so few verbs permit the female classifier, Hong refers to the thumbs-up handshape as a person rather than as a (default) male classifier. Many of the verbs discussed by Hong are also used in JSL, though in one case, the sign meaning 'feed' in KSL means 'take care of' in JSL. KSL ICs also permit subject agreement as in JSL (Kang-Suk Byun, personal communication, February 2008).

One difference between the use of ICs in JSL vs. KSL is that in KSL it is apparently possible to use some ICs to represent first and second person arguments.

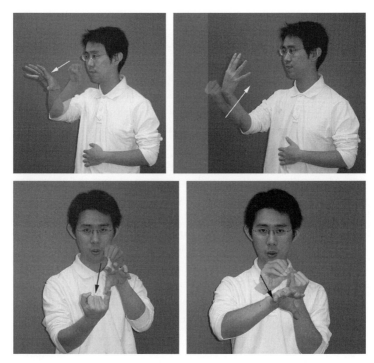

Figure 22.4 *Agreement with and without indexical classifiers: (a) IU (say), citation form, (b) IU inflected for first person object, (c) IU inflected for female object, (d) IU inflected for female subject.*

In JSL this is possible only with frozen ICs. We would like to suggest, following Fischer and Osugi 2000, that ICs are in some sense more abstract than the use of referential loci, since those loci are spatially neutralized.

In contrast to KSL, TSL has fewer verbs that permit IC agreement with objects, and consultants do not generally accept ICs in subject position. There may also be dialects of JSL where subject agreement is less acceptable (Fischer, in preparation).

3.3   Derivational morphology

3.3.1   *Hands as morphemes*

In CSL, as in JSL, the handshapes 𝄞\ and 🖐 have morphological status; in CSL 𝄞\ is used for signs with positive connotations and 🖐 is used for signs with negative connotations. Examples of pairs with substituted handshapes include the signs for good/bad (thumb or pinkie extended), hearing/deaf (thumb or pinkie strokes mouth and ear), and clever/stupid (head + good/bad). See Yang and Fischer 2002 for further discussion. BSL uses the same ⅍ and 🖐 handshapes for some of the same positive and negative pairs (Sutton-Spence & Woll 1999), including identical sign pairs such as HEARING vs. DEAF, but this process of negative incorporation appears to be more productive in CSL.

As mentioned above, in the JSL family ⅍ and 🖐 respectively represent male and female; they are used productively in kinship terms: e.g., OTOOSAN ('father') = OYA + OTOKO ('parent + male'). They can be used in isolation as pronouns usually meaning 'he' and 'she.' They can be used in honorific clitics immediately after name signs: thus NAKA-MURA^ONNA means 'Ms. Nakamura,' while NAKA-MURA^RAISED-ONNA could mean 'Professor' or 'Princess Nakamura.' Interestingly, the male and female shapes can occur on one hand simultaneously (🤟) to refer productively, for example, to a heterosexual couple. This handshape has been lexicalized in signs like HITOBITO ('people'), KAZOKU ('family = people under a roof'), and RYOUSIN ('parents' = OYA^OTOKO + ONNA). See also Smith 1989 and Byun 2004. According to Byun (2004), KSL name signs incorporate simultaneous rather than sequential gender markers.

Influenced by cultural values, both the JSL and CSL families distinguish between older and younger siblings; JSL and TSL have specific signs for these terms, using a gender-marked handshape for brother vs. sister overlaid on an upward or downward movement for older vs. younger; CSL has sequential compounds of one sign meaning younger or older sibling followed by a gender marker to indicate whether the younger or older sibling is male or female. The corresponding Chinese and Japanese words are at least synchronically monomorphemic.

Although the kinship system in the JSL family is not markedly different from those in use in other sign languages, the ways in which kinship terms interact is different from what we have come across in either Asian or Western sign languages, due to the existence of the one-handed gender markers. Although there are signs for grandparents, there are no signs (only fingerspelling) for grandchildren (this is also true for ASL). In order to talk about grandchildren, signers will sign, e.g., MUSUME ('daughter'), hold the 🖐 handshape in place, and using that handshape as a reference point (similar to Liddell's (2003b) buoy), sign MUSUME (female) or MUSUKO ('male'). When the end of one sign becomes the reference point for another, the signer switches hands. One can show very complex kinship relations in this way, for example, describing one's mother's younger sister's husband's older sister's daughter's son's wife's mother's younger sister, etc. See the slightly simpler example (1), where the subscripts A and I refer respectively to the male and female gender markers.

(1) RH: WATASI ANI$_A$ ⎯⎯⎯⎯> IX$_1$ $_1$MUSUME $_1$MUSUME$_1$ ⎯⎯⎯⎯> IX$_Z$ GENKI
     LH: TUMA$_1$ ⎯⎯⎯⎯⎯⎯⎯⎯> $_A$KEKKON$_1$
       Me elder brother wife   her daughter   daughter   marry   they healthy
'My older brother's wife has two daughters; one is married and she and her husband are thriving.'

In this example, dominance alternates successively between right and left, but each time the dominance switch occurs, the gender marker of the previous sign remains as the reference point for the next sign, as shown in Figure 22.5.

3.4   Compounding

Compounding occurs very frequently in CSL (see *Zhongguo shouyu* 2003 for examples); this is probably influenced by the fact that spoken Chinese words are mostly

Figure 22.5 *Morphological use of thumb, pinkie and middle finger handshapes: (top) CSL HEARING, thumb handshape, vs. CSL DEAF, pinkie finger handshape; (middle and bottom) JSL 'older brother's wife's daughter's husband', a sequence of middle, pinkie and thumb handshapes.*

bimorphemic disyllables. Many of these are borrowed directly into CSL via loan translation, resulting in many two-sign compounds. Sino-Japanese words in spoken Japanese also tend to be bimorphemic, but borrowing via loan translation into JSL appears to be less frequent, perhaps due to the existence of native monomorphemic Japanese words alongside their bimorphemic Sino-Japanese equivalents.[18]

4 Syntax

Relatively little has been published in English on the syntax of either TSL or KSL. We therefore concentrate on JSL, HKSL and CSL, with a few remarks on TSL based on ongoing research.

4.1 Constituent order

It seems that, like spoken Chinese, CSL is predominantly head-initial, though with shorter phrases such as 'white dog' and 'dog white,' two orders are apparently possible for the same meaning. That said, some head-final structures exist, possibly due to topicalization of postverbal constituents. SOV ordered construction such as [glossed] I MOVIE SEE, CHILDREN TOYS LIKE, I APPLE EAT NOT are abundant. However, modals always precede verbs, and sentential complements generally follow verbs, especially in complex sentences, thus providing evidence for CSL being head-initial. Smith (2005) has argued that TSL is also underlyingly head-initial, or at least SVO.

By contrast, although in the same family as TSL, JSL is quite strictly head-final, more so than spoken Japanese. For example, in general not only do verbs follow objects and auxiliaries follow verbs, but determiners usually follow nouns (Fischer, ongoing data collection).

(2) IKU SUKI/TAI NAI
     go like/want   not
     'not want to go'

(3) SENSEI
     teacher
     ANO(INDEX)
     'that (that teacher)'

There are other consequences for the typological differences between TSL and JSL. Smith (1990) was the first to describe auxiliaries in Asian sign languages. He demonstrated that a certain kind of auxiliary carries agreement, generally when the verb does not.[19] Fischer (1996) found the same kind of auxiliaries in JSL. However, the predominant order of auxiliary and main verb is different in the two languages: in TSL, it usually precedes the verb, but in JSL it generally follows the verb. Although neither spoken Chinese nor spoken Japanese has auxiliaries of this sort, the spoken languages have probably had some overall influence on the typology of the respective sign languages.

4.2   The role of nonmanuals

It is in the use of nonmanuals that we see some of the most striking differences between East Asian sign languages and Western sign languages.[20] These differences occur prominently in topic-comment constructions, negation and interrogation.

Both the CSL and JSL families are generally topic-prominent. This cannot simply be due to the fact that Chinese and Japanese are also topic-prominent languages, since many Western sign languages also have frequent topic-comment structures. A topic occurs at the beginning of the sentence in both JSL and CSL. What is somewhat unusual about CSL is that topics are not usually marked by a nonmanual behavior.[21]

In all Western sign languages that we know about, a nonmanual signal marking a negative or interrogative operator, once begun, must extend until the end of the domain of the operator; it cannot just stop. For example, in ASL in order to express the meaning 'I never go to the movies,' one could sign (4), where the nonmanual negative headshake must extend all the way to the end of its clause; it is not possible to sign (5), in which the negative headshake does not spread:

    _____neg_____
(4)   IX$_1$ NEVER GO-TO MOVIE

      ____neg____
(5) *IX$_1$ NEVER GO-TO MOVIE

The same holds for polar and content questions. Even though the logical structure of a sentence like WHO YOU LIKE ('whom do you like') in ASL is such that 'YOU LIKE' is not really being questioned, if YOU LIKE follows an overt or covert *wh*-sign, the whqfe must spread over the rest of the sentence (Fischer 2006). However, in East Asian sign languages this does not seem to be the case. In both CSL and HKSL, it is possible to have a negative nonmanual that does not spread. In example (6) from HKSL (Tang 2006), the negative headshake does not spread to the following verb phrase, as would be required in ASL:

       ___neg___   __y-no-q__
(6)   IX$_2$ MAI SHU
      you not   buy book
      'Didn't you buy the book?'[22]

Similar phenomena occur in interrogatives in the CSL family. Compare HKSL (6) with (7):

<u>   y-no-q   </u>
(7)   BABA ZUOTIAN MAI   SHU
       father yesterday   buy   book
       'Was it yesterday that father bought the book?'

In (6), the polar question nonmanual spreads across the verb phrase, but in (7) it does not. A sentence like (7) would be totally impossible in ASL; even though it functions as a cleft and only YESTERDAY is being questioned; in ASL, YESTERDAY would indeed be stressed, but the question facial expression would continue from at least YESTERDAY to the end of the sentence.

In JSL, there are also cases of sentences where a negative nonmanual does not spread; in (8) the negation operator, being head-final, applies to the previous clause:

                      <u>neg</u>
(8)   YUUMEI NABE WARU   DAIJI
       famous   bowl break   no   important
       'Don't break that famous bowl; it's valuable.'

One can argue that the typological characteristics of JSL explain the lack of necessity of spreading, in that the negative nonmanual follows rather than precedes its operator domain; it may be the case that the spreading of nonmanuals is obligatory only in a forward, not backward, direction.

Yang and Fischer (2002) also showed that in CSL a nonmanual cannot be the only simultaneous marker of negation. A negative nonmanual must either be accompanied by a manual negation sign or occur by itself after the item being negated.

Unlike polar questions, where JSL patterns like other sign languages, JSL content (*wh*-) questions differ in several ways from what we find in Western sign languages.[23] First, there are two, not one, different whqfes. One of them looks and functions like the whqfe in ASL: it spreads to the domain of the *wh*-operator, as in (9). The other is different from what occurs in Western sign languages (10–11). Consider, for example, three JSL equivalents of 'what color do you like?'

                          <u>wh</u>
(9)   IX$_2$ IRO   NANI SUKI
      You color   what like

                          <u>wh'</u>
(10)   IX$_2$ IRO SUKI NANI

$$\overline{\text{wh}'}$$
(11)   IX$_2$ IRO SUKI

The whqfe in (10) and (11) appears to be more focal than the usual one. It must occur at the end of the question. If the item to which it is associated is a real *wh*-word such as NANI 'what,' that *wh*-word must also occur at the end. If the item is questioned only by virtue of the whqfe, that is, if it is what Lillo-Martin and Fischer (1992) refer to as a "covert" *wh*-question, then the whqfe can occur at the end, leaving the item being questioned without any whqfe, as in (11). In addition, this whqfe, which Fischer and Osugi (1998) call *wh'*, can cliticize to the last element of the sentence, even if that is not the one being questioned, as in the following:

$$\overline{\text{wh}'}$$
(12)   ASITA   TAME IKU
       Tomorrow purpose go-wh
       'For what purpose are you going tomorrow?'

$$\overline{\text{wh}'}$$
(13) UTI   KIREI OK KEDO KABE NAI, YANE   DAKE WC HOOHOO IX$_2$
     House pretty ok but   walls none roof   only toilet way   you-wh
     'The house is lovely, but with no walls, and only a roof, how do you use the toilet?

In (12), the whqfe is separated from TAME, its original site, and attaches to IKU. In (13), the original site of whqfe is HOOHOO, but it attaches to the tag INDEX at the end of the sentence. The two different *wh*- nonmanuals are also discussed in Kimura and Ichida (1995).

5   Concluding remarks

Compared to the study of Western sign languages, the study of Asian sign languages is still in its infancy. Many structures and constraints seem to operate under similar principles, but there are differences as well, differences that can enlighten linguists about the possibilities available to sign languages. We naturally expect to see differences in the lexicon, but it is surprising to Western linguists to see the effects of the written language in the environment on the structure of the sign language, as well as to see the real differences in the uses of nonmanuals. We hope to have shown here the value of studying a diverse array of sign languages.

23

Crosslinguistic variation
in prosodic cues

*Gladys Tang, Diane Brentari, Carolina González
and Felix Sze*

1 Introduction

Sign languages share a common inventory of properties that are used to mark
prosodic constituents (e.g., nonmanuals of the face or properties of movement and
rhythm; see Quer and Pfau, this volume). This chapter investigates whether there is
crosslinguistic variation in the use of one prosodic cue – eye blinks – to mark
prosodic constituents in sign languages. We will compare the prosodic use of blinks
across four sign languages – Hong Kong Sign Language (HKSL), Japanese Sign
Language (JSL), Swiss German Sign Language (DSGS) and American Sign
Language (ASL). In the last fifteen years there has been significant work done in
sign language phonology with regard to prosodic structure. Miller (1996), Wilbur
(1994a), Boyes Braem (1999), Wilbur and Patschke (1999), Nespor and Sandler
(1999), Sandler (1999a, 1999b), Brentari and Crossley (2002), Sandler and Lillo-
Martin (2006) and Eccarius and Brentari (2007) have worked on various prosodic
constituents, including the Intonational Phrase, the Phonological Phrase and the
Prosodic Word (also called "Phonological Word" in Nespor & Vogel 1986). The
studies presented here are built upon these earlier analyses, expanding our knowledge of crosslinguistic variation of the blinks.

The following research questions are addressed in this chapter. First, how much
variation exists among sign languages in their use of a prosodic cue, such as blinks?
Second, if crosslinguistic variation exists, what factors condition it? Third, are
blinks always associated with intonational phrases crosslinguistically? After presenting introductory material, the results of three studies will be reported, each
taking a slightly different vantage point on these questions. The first study is
presented in section 2. It is an analysis of the potential areal influences on blink
rates across both signed and spoken languages. The second study is presented in
section 3. It examines the Intonational Phrase in four sign languages and addresses
whether blinks are a good diagnostic for this constituent. After determining that

HKSL has a unique status based on the results of the first two studies, we examine this language in detail in a third study (presented in section 4) in order to determine the distribution of blinks in this language across prosodic constituents. In section 5, we summarize our findings and discuss their relation to the literature on prosody in sign languages more generally.

Study 1 is a quantitative study, while Studies 2 and 3 are qualitative. One point that becomes clear in this chapter is that both methodologies are essential for this type of analysis and neither is sufficient on its own. In all studies register, task demands, presence of an interlocutor and linguistic context were controlled for so that these could be ruled out as confounding factors.

1.1   Prosodic cues in spoken languages

In spoken language phonology, various proposals for a prosodic hierarchy have been put forward. Our study adopts the one first proposed in Nespor and Vogel (1986:16), shown in (1).

(1)   Prosodic Hierarchy
Utterance $\rightarrow$ I(ntonational) Phrase $\rightarrow$ P(honological) Phrase $\rightarrow$ P(honological) Word[1]

We make three assumptions in this work. First, we assume that the prosodic hierarchy is present in all natural languages, signed and spoken, and that prosodic cues have the same role in signed languages as they do in spoken languages. They assist infants in segmenting linguistic strings into meaningful units (e.g., sentence, phrase, word, etc., Jusczyk 1997, Seidl 2007) and assist adults in parsing the linguistic signal, especially in ambiguous cases. For example, in '[John approached] [the man with a puzzled expression],' the man had the puzzled expression, while in '[John approached the man] [with a puzzled expression]' John had the puzzled expression (cf. Nespor & Vogel 1986). Second, we assume that the prosodic hierarchy is subject to well-formedness constraints commonly known as the "Strict Layer Hypothesis," meaning that "a category of level i in the hierarchy immediately dominates a (sequence of) categories at level i-1" (Selkirk 1984:26). In (1) above, an I-Phrase is parsed exhaustively into P-Phrases, and P-Phrases into P-Words.[2] Third, we assume that there is no strict isomorphism between the morphosyntactic and prosodic levels of analysis, but rather the syntactic and prosodic components of a grammar are mediated by means of a phonology–syntax interface. We do not take a position on which interface proposal is the correct one from among those proposed in the literature (Selkirk 1982, 1984, 1995, 2005; Truckenbrodt 1999; and Seidl 2001).

1.2.   Prosodic cues in sign languages

In the following sections, descriptions of common cues used in P-Words, P-Phrases and I-Phrases across sign languages are described.

1.2.1 P(rosodic) Words

Previous work on prosody in sign languages has demonstrated that a lexical sign is analyzed as a P-Word if it contains a maximum of one contrastive value in each of the phonological components: handshape, place of articulation (POA), movement, orientation and nonmanuals (Brentari 1998, Sandler & Lillo-Martin 2006). Further

Figure 23.1 *Examples of P-Word constraints: coalescent assimilation of handshape in HKSL compounds (top); coalescence of clitics in ISL (middle); assimilation of the non-dominant hand in ASL compounds (bottom).*

evidence comes from compounds and cliticized forms, where processes of assimilation and coalescence conspire to create forms that more closely conform to this general word-level prosodic constraint. For example, in the HKSL compound TASTE^GOOD ('tasty'), the two stems have different handshapes – $\diamond$ in TASTE and $\diamond$ in GOOD (Figure 23.1a). The compound undergoes a process of "handshape assimilation" (Sandler 1986). By adding the thumb node to the initial $\diamond$ handshape configuration of TASTE, the new handshape is $\diamond$. This creates a more well-formed P-Word because the two handshapes are now more similar to one another. Another example, the ASL compound BLACK^NAME ('bad reputation') demonstrates "non-dominant hand (H2) spread" in compounds (Liddell & Johnson 1986; Figure 23.1b). If the first sign in the compound is one-handed and the next two-handed, the H2 of the second sign regressively assimilates to the first, resulting in a well-formed P-Word with one H2 value for the compound. A third example, from ISL, shows cliticization of a pronominal index to a two-handed host sign, resulting in an output with one movement instead of two, again achieving a more well-formed P-Word (e.g., SHOP-THERE; Figure 23.1c; Sandler 1999b).

1.2.2   *P(honological) Phrases*

The P-Phrase is the next higher level. It is composed of one or more P-Words and also defines the domain of application of specific phonological rules, such as "phrase-final lengthening" of the final sign of the P-Phrase (Brentari 1998) and "H2-spread," a bi-directional phonological process of assimilation (Nespor & Sandler 1999, Sandler & Lillo-Martin 2006).[3] In the syntax, P-Phrases are generally correlated with XPs such as DP/NPs and VPs. Prosodic cues for P-Phrases in sign language are shown in (2) for Israeli Sign Language, which has been studied at length for its prosodic characteristics (Nespor & Sandler 1999 and subsequent work). In (2), one P-Phrase is marked by a hold and the other two by reduplication at the right P-Phrase boundary.[4]

(2)   Prosodic constituency in Israeli Sign Language (Sandler 1999a:199)

[[BOOK THERE]$_{PP}$ [HE WRITE]$_{PP}$]$_{IP}$ [[INTERESTING]$_{PP}$]$_{IP}$
      hold   redup   redup'
'The book he wrote is interesting.'

1.2.3.   *I(ntonational) Phrases*

I-Phrases are the next higher level in the prosodic hierarchy, independent from the syntax but mediated by a phonology–syntax interface (Seidl 2001, Selkirk 2005). Following Wilbur (1994a), we take their syntactic correlate in sign languages to be an "ungoverned maximal projection," most often realized as clauses, parentheticals and topic (or topicalized) structures. Different sign languages appear to employ different strategies to mark these prosodic constituents. In ASL, I-Phrases are optionally marked by blinks, and longer pauses are also observed, the latter of which are indicated by holds and lengthening of the final sign, as reported in Wilbur (1994a). In ISL, besides optional blinks, I-Phrases are consistently marked by a change of head position or an across-the-board change of facial expressions (Sandler 1999a). The example in (3) from HKSL is from the data elicited for the analyses in Studies 2 and 3. It illustrates how our naturalistic data including both lexical signs and classifier constructions will be described in Study 3 (see Introduction, this volume, for more discussion about classifiers, and see Appendix for notational conventions). It was elicited as a description of the picture in Figure 23.2. There are four P-Words in the passage organized into three P-Phrases and two I-Phrases.[5] The two I-Phrases exhibit both blinks and lengthening. Notice there is also a blink after ROCKET, which is not a topic structure (i.e., there is no brow raise). As you will see later in the chapter, blinks can mark P-Phrases in HKSL.

(3)   Prosodic structure of a Hong Kong Sign Language utterance[6]

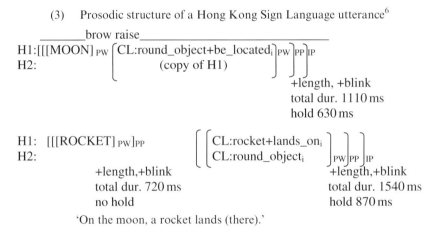

'On the moon, a rocket lands (there).'

Blinks are a good choice for a study on crosslinguistic variation or cross-modal comparison in prosody because they have been observed to be a prosodic boundary cue in numerous sign languages (e.g., ASL, DSGS, ISL, HKSL), but they do not assume this role in spoken languages. Baker and Padden (1978) conducted the first study of blinks, which included ASL signers and speakers of English. They observed that signers' blinks were more strongly correlated with linguistic structure than those of speakers. This was confirmed in Wilbur (1994a). Wilbur also identified two types of blinks in ASL: lexical blinks, which were longer in duration and overlapped at least 75 percent with the sign co-occurring with the blink, and periodic, inhibited eyeblinks, which we will henceforth call "boundary blinks."

Figure 23.2 *Stimulus for the signed descriptions given in (3), (8), (9) and (10).*

Boundary blinks were shorter in duration and, when they overlapped with a sign, did so for less than 75 percent of the sign co-occurring with the blink. More recently, Sze (2008) analyzed HKSL based on a taxonomy of five blink types; a slightly modified version of this taxonomy, given in (4), is used throughout this chapter.

(4) Blink types:

    a. *Boundary/prosodic*: blinks realized at the left- or right edges of IP; not necessarily correlated with signs ($\leq 75\%$ overlap with a sign).

    b. *Lexical*: blinks that overlap with a sign $\geq 75\%$, or which co-occur with every instance of the same sign, regardless of position.

    c. *Physiological*: blinks involving movements of the hand(s) near the face, and blinks co-occurring with head movements (e.g., nodes) and eye gaze changes.

    d. *Hesitation and self-correction*: blinks produced while thinking or correcting oneself.

Using clauses and topics as syntactic means to find candidates for I-Phrases, Sze found that only 59 percent of the I-Phrases in her corpus were marked by a blink and that boundary blinks also occurred at the edge of other constituents 41 percent of the time. She therefore speculated that blinks might be indicative of smaller prosodic constituents in HKSL, but she did not venture into analyzing the identity of these constituents. This issue is pursued in Study 3.

The properties outlined in the preceding sections are used in the subsequent analyses. The notion of "sign count" referred to in Study 1 is based on the P-Word criteria described in section 1.2.1. The boundary cues for I-Phrases and P-Phrases are employed in Studies 2 and 3, respectively. The syntactic structures associated with I-Phrases and P-Phrases are used to provide us with a set of candidates for a particular prosodic constituent (e.g., using clause, parenthetical or topic boundaries as a place to look for I-Phrase boundaries); however, the prosodic constituents themselves are defined by the prosodic cues presented in this section.

2 Study 1: Blink rate in signed and spoken languages

In this study the blink rates were compared among four sign languages – HKSL, JSL, DSGS and ASL. Then two groups of signers – HKSL and ASL signers – were compared with two groups of speakers – Cantonese and English speakers. Our goal was to determine whether the blink rates of these groups were primarily due to *areal linguistic features* shared by sign languages or *areal cultural features* shared by the surrounding spoken language community and the sign language community. Subjects were asked to watch the *Canary Row* Tweety and Sylvester cartoon and retell each of the seven episodes of the story in their native language to another native language user. Two native signers from each of the four sign languages, six American English speakers and four Cantonese speakers from Hong Kong participated in this study.[7] The sessions were recorded, captured in iMovie and then transcribed using ELAN (Eudico Linguistic Annotator, Version 3.5).[8] The three longest episodes were chosen for the current investigation.[9] For all signed productions, the modified version of Sze's taxonomy of blinks given in (4) was adopted. For speakers, we measured only blink rate (blinks/minute) and noted where blinks occurred.

2.1 Results (a): Differences among the four sign languages

The narratives of the two native signers for each of the four sign languages were compared with respect to the properties in (5).

(5) Properties transcribed for signers
  a. *Total blinks*: Total number of blinks (all types) per signer based on the three episodes
  b. *Total signing time*: Total signing time for each signer based on the three episodes
  c. $\bar{x}$ *Sign rate*: Average number of signs per minute
  d. $\bar{x}$ *Blink rate*: Average number of blinks per minute

The data are given in Table 23.1. An ANOVA done on the means in Table 23.1 reveals a significant effect between sign languages for blink rate (F = 29.5; p = .003). After

Table 23.1 *Raw data of Study 1: sign languages (ASL, HKSL, DSGS and JSL)*

	Total blinks	Total signing time	Sign rate Signs/min	Blink rate Blinks/min
HKSL-1	140	4′27″	67	31
HKSL-2	186	6′23″	72	29
HKSL	326	10′50″	**70**	**30***
JSL-1	68	3′02″	83	22
JSL-2	88	3′50″	76	23
JSL	156	6′52″	**80**	**23**
DSGS-1	68	3′14″	83	21
DSGS-2	106	4′47″	72	22
DSGS	174	8′01″	**78**	**22**
ASL-1	51	2′26″	63	21
ASL-2	97	5′09″	72	19
ASL	148	7′35″	**68**	**20**

a Tukey test, HKSL was found to have a significantly higher blink rate than the other sign languages ("*" in Table 23.1 indicates significance), but the other three sign languages showed no significant differences among them. From these results we can conclude that the difference in blink rate is not a shared areal effect for the sign languages, because in terms of blink rate JSL behaved like ASL and DSGS, not like HKSL.

Wilbur (1994a) found that articulation rate affected blink rate – that is, the faster the signing the lower the blink rate. To control for this, three measurements were taken in this project: sign rate, sign duration with pauses and sign duration without pauses.[10] These measures each yielded the same result, which we call "signing speed." Table 23.1 reports sign rate. The ranking of languages from fastest to slowest signing speed is JSL, DSGS, HKSL, ASL. Following Wilbur, one might predict that the highest blink rate should occur in ASL and the lowest in JSL; however, this is not what we found. Ranking the languages from the highest to lowest blink rate yields the following: HKSL, JSL, DSGS and ASL. ASL signers blinked, on average, approximately once for every 3.5 signs, while HKSL signers blinked, on average, once for every 2.3 signs.[11] From these results we can conclude that HKSL's high blink rate was not due to signing speed.

2.2   Results (b): Differences between signed and spoken languages

ASL and HKSL were found to have the most extreme difference in the blink rate study above; therefore, we investigated these two languages further in order to determine if there is a cultural factor related to the surrounding spoken language

Table 23.2 *Average blink rates: signed and spoken languages*

	Production time (total)	Blink rate (Blinks/min)
HKSL (N = 2)	10′50″	30
ASL (N = 2)	7′35″	20
Cantonese (N = 4)	11′12″	40
English (N = 6)	13′36″	35

Table 23.3 *T-test results: signed and spoken languages*

Languages	t-value	p-value
Signed vs. spoken	2.44	.03*
HKSL vs. ASL	6.61	.02*
Cantonese vs. English	−.31	.77
HKSL vs. Cantonese	−1.05	.37
ASL vs. English	3.54	.01*

communities – English and Cantonese respectively – that might be responsible for the blink rate difference between the two sign languages.[12] We asked a group of four native Cantonese speakers and six native English speakers to perform the same task as the one described above. As in Study 1, each participant narrated each of the seven episodes of the *Canary Row* Tweety and Sylvester cartoon to a second native speaker of the language. The same three episodes were analyzed in terms of blink rate. The results are provided in Tables 23.2 and 23.3.

ASL and HKSL were compared to the spoken languages (English and Cantonese) using a t-test to determine if the modality of communication was a significant factor. Indeed, there was a significant difference in blink rate as a function of language modality (signed vs. spoken languages; $t = 2.44, p = .03$). As seen in Table 23.3, comparisons for all pairs using t-tests revealed a significant difference between ASL and HKSL ($t = 6.61, p = .02$) and between ASL and English ($t = 3.54, p = .01$). However, the differences between English and Cantonese speakers ($t = −.31, p = .77$) and between HKSL and Cantonese were not significant ($t = −1.05, p = .37$).

The data also revealed that speakers and signers had different blinking patterns, confirming Baker and Padden's (1978) and Wilbur's (1994a) ASL–English results. Speakers of both English and Cantonese performed similarly in two important ways. First, their eye blinks were not correlated with I-Phrase or P-Phrase boundaries; they occurred both at phrase boundaries and phrase-internally, and both on and between words. Their appearance was not correlated with a particular grammatical category. Second, the Cantonese and English speakers' mean blink rates were not statistically different. This suggests that speakers as a whole were using a similar motivation for their blinking behavior, one that was of physiological origin, as reported in previous work. An example each from Cantonese and English are given below:

(6) Examples of Cantonese and English placement of blinks

    a. Cantonese

        bl

      $_{IP}$[gan1-zyu6   zek3   maau1   le1]$_{IP}$

        then   cl   cat   SFP

      'Then as for the cat, ...

          bl   bl

      $_{IP}$[zau6 kam4 soeng5 seoi2 keoi4 hai2 leoi5-min6 jap6 laa3]$_{IP}$

        adv   climb up   water pipe loc in-side   enter SFP

      ... it climbs up through the water pipe.'

    b. English

        bl   bl   bl

      $_{IP}$ [So instead of climbing up the drain]

      $_{IP}$[he wants to climb in the drain]$_{IP}$

                           bl

      [so he starts climbing up the drain] $_{IP}$

Taken together, these findings suggest that there are language-particular differences among sign languages in terms of their blinking rate. First, HKSL showed a higher blink rate than the other sign languages. Second, there was a significant difference between the blink rates in signed and spoken languages, but there was no significant difference between Cantonese and HKSL; therefore some influence of the surrounding spoken language community on HKSL blinking behavior cannot be ruled out.

3   Study 2: Identifying I-Phrases and the role of blinks

This study had two goals. The first was to identify the I-Phrase units using independent criteria (i.e., not the placement of blinks). The second goal was to test the hypothesis that blinks were primarily associated with the domain of an I-Phrase, as has been shown to be the case in ISL (Nespor & Sandler 1999), DSGS (Boyes Braem 1999) and ASL (Wilbur 1994a). Thirty still pictures were used as stimuli for eliciting descriptions about motion and location events. We used pictures as stimuli for this study instead of the Tweety and Sylvester cartoon because picture descriptions are shorter, making it easier to compare productions within and across signers as well as within and across languages. We also wanted to neutralize differences based on storytelling/narrative abilities, which can become an issue in longer passages.[13] The signers' productions were videotaped in digital format, imported and then transcribed using ELAN. The elicited productions included both lexical items and classifier constructions.

3.1   Identifying I-Phrases

The first task was to independently identify I-Phrases, and to do so using a set of criteria independent from blink placement. We looked for candidates for I-Phrases using the morphosyntactic constituents associated with them – clauses, parentheticals and topic (or topicalized) structures. These I-Phrase candidates were then counted as an I-Phrase if at least two "boundary cues" of the ones listed in (7) were present at the left or right edge. As mentioned, all of these cues have been attested as linguistic markers in previous work. Therefore, in the current study, not only blinks, but also the three other cues listed in (7) were transcribed for analysis. We purposefully chose criteria for broad inclusion of I-Phrases for two reasons. First, we wanted to clearly distinguish cases that could be explained by previous analyses from those that still required an explanation. Second, I-Phrases have been shown to have a larger set of prosodic cues than P-Phrases or P-Words, so we wanted to allow for any two plausible boundary cues to count.

> (7)   Prosodic cues transcribed: definitions and values
>   a.   *Lengthening (x2)*: a sign that is twice the length of its phrase-internal instantiation.
>   b.   *Change in head position*: (i) head nod, or (ii) a change in head position to neutral after a tilt sideways, or tilt backwards.
>   c.   *Change in brow position*: Raising/lowering of the brows to or from neutral position.
>   a.   *Blinks*: Placement with respect to the sign (left- or right-edge), duration (ms) and type (described in (4)).

"Lengthening" was based on final hold time and total sign duration; both hold and duration are indicative of phrase-final lengthening, based on the different syllable types of signs (Perlmutter 1992, Brentari 1998). Other mechanisms were also used to lengthen a sign, such as adding repetitions to the final syllable, or by simply adding duration to a single movement. Syntactic structure was used as an

Table 23.4 *Average duration of phrase-internal signs based on syllable count and type*

Syllable count	Syllable type		
	Path	Trilled	Local
Simple movements			
a. Single (1σ)	300	300	250
b. Repeated (2σ)	350	350	300
Complex movements (path + ...)	none	550	none

independent criterion, in addition to prosodic cues, to identify signs that were likely to occur at an I-Phrase boundary, and these signs were compared with those thought to be phrase-internal. These I-Phrase "candidates" (based on syntactic structure) were categorized as I-Phrases only if they exhibited two of the cues in (7), following the methodology of primarily defining prosodic units in terms of prosodic cues (Pierrehumbert 1980). For cases where no such pair existed of the same sign, a set of sign-length averages was prepared, based on syllable count (one or two) and the syllable type. Syllable types were based on the different movement/syllable types in the Prosodic model (Brentari 1998) – syllables based on "local" movements, which are the relatively smaller movements due to handshape changes and orientation changes, "trilled" based on uncountable small repetitions and syllables based on "path" movements, which are the relatively larger movements of the elbow and shoulder. In a different project (Brentari *et al.* in press), ASL signers' productions at the end of sentences were twice the length of the same signs when produced phrase-internally; therefore for lengthening to be "present" a sign had to be twice as long as its phrase-internal counterpart.[14] The phrase-internal averages for common syllable types in our data are given in Table 23.4.[15] Complex movements consisted of a path plus one of the other three types of movement – path, trill or local. Holds were seen primarily at the end of single movements, either local or path and were less reliable than sign duration as an indicator of sign lengthening.

With regard to "head position" and "brow position," we were interested in changes of these articulators to or from neutral position, since these changes are often correlated with I-Phrase boundaries (Wilbur 1994a, Nespor & Sandler 1999) or sentence boundaries (Padden 1988). We, therefore, included these properties as well.

Blinks were coded for their "placement" with respect to the co-occuring sign (left-edge or right-edge), "duration" in milliseconds (ms) and "type" (prosodic, lexical, physiological, or self-correction/hesitation (see (4)). A boundary blink was judged to be at the left edge if it occurred during transitional movement while the handshape of the hand was forming or during the first half of the sign.[16] A boundary blink was judged to be at the right edge if it occurred during the second half of the sign or during the transitional movement to rest or while the handshape was disintegrating.

3.2   Use of blinks

The second task of this study was to determine whether blinks consistently and exclusively mark I-Phrases. That is, are I-Phrases always marked by a blink ("consistency"), and are blinks used only to mark an I-Phrase ("exclusivity"). Table 23.5 displays a profile of each signer's prosodic blink productions. Blinks were divided into (U)tterance (those at the start or end of the production), I-Phrase ($\geq$ 2 cues) or "other." For both I-Phrase(R) and I-Phrase(L) boundaries, those attributed to Utterance boundaries are given in square brackets in Table 23.5 – that is, those at the beginning and end of the production. Table 23.5 shows the total number of blinks, total number of I-Phrases, percentage of right and left edges of an I-Phrase marked by a blink, and total number of "other" blinks (those that did not meet the criteria for an I-Phrase). For this analysis only boundary blinks were used; the lexical and physiological blinks have been removed.

While the number of occurrences here are not sufficient to do quantitative measures, a number of qualitative generalizations can be drawn from the data presented in Table 23.5. Considering these results in terms of consistency and exclusivity, I-Phrases are *consistently* marked by a blink in all four sign languages. In other words, it is clear from the data in Table 23.5 that when there are two or more cues present, a blink is almost always one of the cues. However, I-Phrases are marked *exclusively* by blinks only in three of the sign languages – ASL, JSL and

Table 23.5 *Profile of prosodic blinks in four sign languages*

	Total blinks	Total IPs	IP(R) blinks / Total IPs	IP(R) blinks / Total blinks	IP(L) / Total blinks	Other / Total blinks
HKSL	132	71	63/71 (.89)	63/132 (.48) [17 U(R)]	16/132 (.12) [all U(L)]	53/132 (.40)
JSL	83	61	61/61 (1.00)	61/83 (.73) [17 U(R)]	20/83 (.24) [19 U(L)]	2/83 (.02)
DSGS	48	46	42/46 (.96)	42/48 (.88) [15 U(R)]	2/48 (.04) [all U(L)]	4/48 (.08)
ASL	57	48	48/48 (1.00)	48/57 (.84) [22 U(R)]	9/57 (.16) [all U(L)]	0/57 (.00)

Table 23.6 *Blinks and their concomitant cues in four sign languages.*

	Blink + Length	Blink + HN	Blink + BP	HN + Length	Total
HKSL	52 (.83)	2 (.03)	9 (.14)	0 (.00)	63 (1.00)
JSL	16 (.26)	40 (.66)	3 (.05)	2 (.03)	61 (1.00)
DSGS	23 (.50)	8 (.17)	7 (.15)	8 (.17)	46 (1.00)
ASL	37 (.77)	0 (.00)	11 (.23)	0 (.00)	48 (1.00)

DSGS. It is not the case in HKSL that if you see a blink, you can infer that it is an I-Phrase boundary. In HKSL 40 percent of the prosodic blinks in HSKL were categorized as "other," while the percentage of "other" blinks in ASL, JSL and DSGS was quite low (0%, 8% and 2%, respectively).

In terms of edges, there was a tendency for blinks to occur at the right instead of the left edge of an I-Phrase in these four sign languages. We did not observe the occurrence of left edge in the absence of right-edge marking. In other words, any left-edge marking of a prosodic constituent implies right-edge marking for the same constituent. However, to what extent this observation provides a basis for us to formulate an implicational universal about edge marking in sign language requires further investigation. Some tokens of blinks occurring at the left edge were observed. All were U(L) boundaries except for one instance of an I-Phrase(L) blink in JSL. Most of the left-edge tokens were in HKSL and JSL; far fewer from ASL and very few from DSGS.

The data shown in Table 23.6 focus exclusively on I-Phrase boundary cues – i.e., the co-occurrence of the four cues studied – lengthening, head nods and brow position (i.e., return to neutral position after a brow raise). Crosslinguistic variation was found here as well. Among all the cues analyzed in the data, phrase-final lengthening most frequently co-occurred with blinks at I-Phrase boundaries in ASL, DSGS and HKSL, while in JSL the presence of head nods was the most frequently co-occurring cue in this position. Examples in (8) demonstrate this crosslinguistic prosodic difference.

(8) Examples of language particular differences in concomitant cues
     (1 = blink, 2 = lengthening, 3 = head nod)[17]
     a.   HKSL
          __topic_____
          [MOON CL:round_object + be_located]$_{IP(1,2)}$ [ROCKET CL:rocket
             + lands]$_{IP(1,2)}$
          [CL:'person exits and walks weightlessly']$_{IP(1,2)}$

b. JSL

__topic_____
[CL:earth + be_located]$_{IP(1,3)}$ [CL:rocket + takes off] $_{IP(1,3)}$

__topic_____
[CL:moon + be_located]$_{IP(1,3)}$ [CL:rocket + lands] $_{IP(1,3)}$

__topic_____
[CL:person_in_a_space suit]$_{IP(1,3)}$ [CL:person + exits_and jumps_around
_weightlessly]$_{IP(1,3)}$

c. DSGS

[MOON UP-THERE]$_{IP(1,2)}$ [MAN LIGHT CL:person_walks
_weightlessly]$_{IP(1,2)}$
[CL:person_in_a_space suit]$_{IP(1,2)}$

d. ASL

[ROCKET CL:rocket + takes_off_and_lands] $_{IP(1,2)}$ [S-P-A-C-E-M-A-N
CL:person + exits_and_walks_weightlessly]$_{IP(1,2)}$

In summary, this study revealed crosslinguistic similarities and language-specific differences concerning blinks at I-Phrase boundaries. First, blinks occur at I-Phrase boundaries in all four languages consistently, but only in three of these languages are blinks a marker of I-Phrase boundaries exclusively. Blinks consistently appear at I-Phrase boundaries in HKSL, but blinks occur in many other locations as well; therefore, we cannot use this cue as a crosslinguistic diagnostic of I-Phrases. Second, language-particular differences in the cues that co-occurred with blinks were also found.

Now that we have determined that HKSL behaves differently in rate and use of blinks, the next study analyzes the use of blinks in this language more closely.

4   Study 3: blinks and prosodic constituents in HKSL

The goal of this study was to analyze the distribution of blinks and their concomitant cues in HKSL, primarily those in the "other" category from Study 2; that is, those marking prosodic constituents other than the I-Phrase. Sze (2008) suggested that in HKSL blinks might mark smaller prosodic constituents than I-Phrases, at different grammatical junctures; however, she did not venture into identifying what these prosodic constituents were or how they interacted with each other.[18] The same thirty pictures used in Study 2 were used to elicit descriptions from two native HKSL signers, using the same taxonomy of blink types listed earlier in (4). As in Study 2 we focused on the boundary-sensitive blinks.

534   *Sign Languages*

As we shall see, the results suggest that HKSL is prosodically similar to ASL, JSL, DSGS, except for the distribution of eye blinks. A large percentage of blinks marked I-Phrases, but some marked P-Phrases internal to an I-Phrase, albeit to a lesser extent, and sometimes even P-Words internal to a P-Phrase were marked by blinks to a limited extent. The results confirm Sze's conclusions, but the analysis here also provides a way to distinguish I-Phrases from P-Phrases on the basis of strong vs. weak lengthening.

4.1   Identifying I-Phrase and P-Phrase constituents

The first task was to assign I-Phrase and P-Phrase constituent boundaries independently from the placement of blinks. The following procedure was used, similar to that used in Study 2. For this analysis the morphosyntactic units associated with I-Phrases were used to provide us with a set of candidates for this prosodic constituent – clauses, parentheticals and topic (or topicalized) structures – and those morphosyntactic structures associated with P-Phrases were used to provide a set of candidates for P-Phrases – XPs such as DP/NPs and VPs. However, just as in Study 2, prosodic units were ultimately defined by prosodic criteria. From the sets of candidates for I-Phrases and P-Phrases provided by the syntax, I-Phrases were defined as those units containing at least two "boundary behaviors" of the ones listed in (7). P-Phrases were defined using a weaker criterion; namely one of the boundary behaviors listed in (7) had to be present.

4.2   Use of blinks

The second task was to determine which cues were used to mark I-Phrases and P-Phrases for each signer, and particularly, whether blinks were the most relevant cue. A summary of the distribution of blinks over the three types of prosodic constituents is presented in Table 23.7 (i.e., I-Phrase, P-Phrase and P-Word).

Table 23.7 *Distribution of HKSL blinks by prosodic constituent boundaries*

	I-Phrases				P-Phrases				P-Words	
Sgr	Total IPs	IP (R)	IP (L)	No(R) Blink	Total PPs	PP (R)	PP (L)	No(R) Blink	Total PW	PW (R)
1	71	63 (.89)	16 (.23)	8 (.11)	89	35 (.39)	0 (.00)	54 (.61)	336	18 (.05)
2	66	49 (.74)	16 (.24)	17 (.26)	72	38 (.54)	0 (.00)	34 (.46)	304	5 (.02)

Table 23.8 *HKSL blinks and concomitant cues for I-Phrase boundaries*

Sgr	Total IPs	+ Length + Blink	− Length + Blink	+ Length − Blink	− Length − Blink	x̄ SignDur PW (R) of IP
1	71(1.00)	50(.71)	13(.18)	2(.03)	6(.08)	977 ms
2	66(1.00)	35(.53)	14(.21)	9(.14)	6(.12)	1043 ms

There were seventy-one and sixty-six I-Phrase(R) boundaries respectively for Signer 1 and Signer 2; those for Signer 1 were already reported in Study 2. The remaining blinks were intermediate P-Phrases within the I-Phrase and a handful of P-Word boundaries within a P-Phrase. Signer 1 was more meticulous in describing the pictures, hence producing more P-Phrases than Signer 2 (160 vs. 138 total). Despite similar backgrounds, there was individual variation with the two native signers in terms of the number of prosodic constituents produced.

4.2.1   *Blinks at I-Phrases*

Table 23.7 shows that of the I-Phrases present, most were marked by a blink (Signer 1, 89%; Signer 2, 74%).[19] Even though Signer 1 signed at a faster rate than Signer 2 and fewer blinks might be expected, Signer 1 systematically produced a blink at the right edge of I-Phrases and even more often than Signer 2. This confirms our finding in Study 1 that the speed of signing did not influence overall blink rate. Note also that some I-Phrases were not marked by a boundary blink (Signer 1, 11%; Signer 2, 24%), but they contained at least two of the other boundary behaviors listed in (7).

As in Study 2, lengthening was defined relatively, rather than absolutely, requiring that a form be double in length to count as I-Phrase lengthening. Table 23.8 shows concomitant cues for I-Phrase boundaries; lengthening occurred frequently at I-Phrase boundaries (74% and 67% in Signers 1 and 2, respectively),[20] and a high proportion of I-Phrase boundaries exhibited " + Length, + Blink" (71% for Signer 1 and 53% for Signer 2).

Because of the picture description task that was used, many sentences containing classifier constructions were elicited. These typically contained one or more nominal categories for subject, object or locative, followed by a classifier construction involving a verb of motion or location. Both I-Phrases in (9) demonstrate this. In the first I-Phrase, the nominal subject UP^WORLD 'moon' precedes a locative predicate 'CL: round_object_be_ located_here.' In the second, ROCKET precedes the motion predicate 'CL: rocket + lands_on_round_objectᵢ.' The initial nominals form their own P-Phrases (discussed in the next section).

(9)   HKSL (description of the picture in Figure 23.2 by Signer 1)[21]

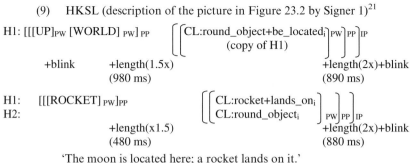

H1: [[[ROCKET] PW]PP   ⌈⌈CL:rocket+lands_onᵢ⌉   ⌉
H2:   ⌊⌊CL:round_objectᵢ ⌋ PW⌋PP ⌋IP
                    +length(x1.5)   +length(2x)+blink
                    (480 ms)   (880 ms)

'The moon is located here; a rocket lands on it.'

As in other sign languages previously studied, topics often form their own I-Phrase. The first I-Phrase in (10), (repeated from (3)) is a topicalized structure; it contains a brow raise, a blink and double lengthening.

(10)   HKSL (description of the drawing in Figure 23.2 by Signer 2)

_____brow raise_____
H1:[[[MOON] PW ⌈CL:round_object+be_locatedᵢ⌉PW⌋PP⌋IP
H2:   (copy of H1)
                                                    +length(2x), +blink
                                                    (1110 ms)

H1: [[[ROCKET²²] PW]PP   ⌈⌈CL:rocket +lands_onᵢ⌉   ⌉
H2:   ⌊⌊CL:round_objectᵢ ⌋PW⌋PP ⌋IP
        +length(x1.5),+blink   +length(2x),+blink
        (720 ms)   (1540 ms)

'On the moon, a rocket lands (there).'

Table 23.9 summarizes the distribution of nominal and verbal categories with respect to how they interact with blinks to mark P-Phrase and I-Phrase boundaries. In this analysis, those P-Phrases with a boundary blink are assigned to either I-Phrase final or intermediate P-Phrases. Given the syntactic structure discussed previously, blinks marking an I-Phrase boundary are usually mapped onto the verbal categories, and this result is consistent with both Signer 1 (87 percent) and Signer 2 (76 percent). But note that in most of these cases, this is an artifact. These verbal categories are basically P-Phrases; they become candidates for I-Phrases because they occur in sentence-final position, creating a potential I-Phrase boundary, in line with the "Strict Layer Hypothesis."

Table 23.9 *Distribution of HKSL blinks and syntactic categories*

Syntactic Categories	Signer 1			Signer 2		
	Total PPs 160	#IP Blinks 63	#PP Blinks 35	Total PPs 138	#IP Blinks 49	#PP Blinks 38
Nominal	71	8	23	66	12	30
	(.44)	(.13)	(.66)	(.48)	(.24)	(.79)
Verbal	89	55	12	72	37	8
	(.56)	(.87)	(.34)	(.52)	(.76)	(.21)

4.2.2 Blinks at intermediate P-Phrases

The data in Table 23.7 show that 39 percent of Signer 1's and 54 percent of Signer 2's intermediate P-Phrases (i.e., those internal to an I-Phrase) are marked by a blink, but a large number are not (61% for Signer 1 and 46% for Signer 2). So for the first time in our data, we see a trade-off between speed and blink rate in Signer 1, not at the I-Phrase but at the P-Phrase level. In other words, when the speed of signing is fast, the P-Phrase may get re-bracketed, affecting the alignment of the syntactic constituents within the prosodic constituent.

In (11) we see an example showing that the verbal complex may consist of a series of P-Phrases, one of which is the VP 'take the rabbit's ears' and a classifier predicate which expresses the manner of taking the rabbit by holding its ears. The picture eliciting the description is given in Figure 23.3. Many of the I-Phrases include more than one classifier predicate, each of which forms its own P-Phrase.

Figure 23.3 *Stimulus for the signed description given in (11).*

(11) HKSL (Signer 1)

[[[FATHER]$_{PW}$]$_{PP}$]$_{IP}$ [[[TAKE]$_{PW}$]$_{PP}$ [[RABBIT]$_{PW}$[EARS]$_{PW}$]$_{PP}$
+ blink + length(2x), + blink,   + blink   + blink
(710 ms)

[[CL:agent^{23} + take_rabbit_by_the_ears]$_{PW}$]$_{PP}$[[CL:agent +$_i$transfer_object$_j$]$_{PW}$]$_{PP}$]$_{IP}$
+ blink   + length(2x), + blink
(710 ms)

'As for father, he takes the rabbit by the ears and gives it [to his son].'

As a first approximation, an intermediate P-Phrase(R) boundary was defined as such because it exhibited a single cue of those in (7). On closer inspection, we realized that there was a weaker form of lengthening operating in P-Phrases, given in (12).

(12)   P-Phrase Lengthening:
Lengthening (x1.5): a sign that is at least one and one-half times the length of its phrase-internal instantiation.

We also tested the weak form of lengthening with the "other" category of HKSL blinks in Table 23.5 from Study 2 that did not qualify as special P-Word cases. In doing so, we found that the average sign duration for these structures was consistently longer than that of the phrase-internal forms, but less than the I-Phrase(R) forms. These data, showing the percentage of blinks and weak lengthening, is shown in Table 23.10. An example exhibiting the weak form of lengthening and a blink at a P-Phrase boundary appears in [ROCKET]$_{PP}$ in (10), and in (11) there are three instances of intermediate phrases with blinks alone.

In general, P-Phrases are more difficult to characterize than P-Words and I-Phrases, precisely because they are intermediate structures. Their juncture is stronger than a P-Word, but not as strong as an I-Phrase. H2-Spread has been proposed as a marker for P-Phrases in ISL (Nespor & Sandler 1999) and ASL (Brentari & Crossley 2002), but because the non-dominant hand was used

Table 23.10 *HKSL blinks and concomitant cues for P-Phrase boundaries, using the weaker version of lengthening*

Sgr	Total PPs	+ Length + Blink	− Length + Blink	+ Length − Blink	− Length − Blink	x̄ SignDur PW (R)of PP
1	89	30(.34)	5(.05)	31(.36)	23(.25)	613 ms
2	72	29(.40)	10(.14)	21(.30)	12(.16)	704 ms

morphologically in our data, H2-Spread was not a reliable P-Phrase cue here (Brentari & Crossley 2002).[24]

In summary, a P-Phrase could be marked only by a blink, only by a relatively weak form of lengthening (x1.5), or by both a blink and a lengthening (x1.5). To function reliably, lengthening must be measured relative to signs of the same syllable structure in phrase-internal position (preferably from the same discourse and the same signer). This analysis, which includes a weaker form of lengthening along with blinks, accounts for the P-Phrases of 74 percent of Signer 1's and 84 percent of Signer 2's P-Phrases (see Table 23.10).

4.2.3 *Blinks within P-Words*

Sometimes a blink with no other cue was also observed between two lexical elements of a compound. These forms were determined to be single P-words based on the criteria given in section 1.2. The examples in (13a) are nominal compounds, and those in (13b) consist of a manner verb plus a classifier predicate or a series of classifier predicates.

(13) P-Word blinks

    a. BLACKˆBELT 'blackbelt'   adjˆN
        UPˆWORLD 'moon'   advˆN
        RUNˆROAD 'running-track'   VˆN

    b. CRAWLˆCL:person + crawls 'crawl-to'   verbˆCL
        CL: handle + lifts_a_rollˆCL: handle +   CLˆCL
            puts_roll_on_shoulder
        'lift and put a roll of fabric on shoulder'

The examples in (13b) seem to suggest that some verbal groups in HKSL form verbal complexes like 'CRAWLˆCL:person_crawls,' which were marked in a special way with respect to ordinary P-Words in HKSL. These were first observed in Eccarius and Brentari (2007) in their study of two-handed classifier constructions, but here the phenomenon occurred in both one-and two-handed forms. A few P-Word blinks also occurred at syntactic boundaries, such as in a DP domain between a lexical N and its associated functional morphemes such as determiner, number and quantifier. In the VP domain, they were found between the V and its object complement. These blinks are not lexical but boundary blinks by definition, because they did not span the lexical signs and occurred at the right edge of the sign. To what extent such blinks bear linguistic consequences in these cases is still uncertain, but the fact that they occur in these positions warrants investigation in the future.

5   Discussion and conclusions

In this chapter several contributions have been made to our understanding of variation in the expression of prosodic cues of sign languages; some previously held views about prosody have been confirmed and some challenged. Methodologically, the studies employed different dimensions of analysis and emphasized the importance of having converging independent sources of evidence in order to draw conclusions about prosody in sign language. By having comparative data on blinks in surrounding spoken languages, we were able to determine that blinks function linguistically in sign languages but not in spoken languages, confirming the results of Baker and Padden (1978) and Wilbur (1994a). By comparing a range of sign languages in Study 2 with respect to some common cues, we found crosslinguistic variation with respect to the distribution of these cues. Lastly, by having a detailed description of the non-conforming language, in this case HKSL, we discovered a more precise way of measuring phrase-final lengthening to distinguish between I-Phrases and P-Phrases. For these four unrelated sign languages, a similar set of cues were used to mark prosodic constituents, but the distribution of at least one cue (i.e., blinks) may be language-specific, as we have seen from the analysis of the HKSL data.

With regard to how much variation exists in the use of blink rate, the results of Study 1 demonstrate that there is language-particular variation in blink rate among the sign languages that were studied. HKSL signers had a higher mean blink rate than that of the other sign languages. With regard to the factors that condition this variation in blink rate, we cannot rule out the possibility that the high rate of blinks in HKSL is, in part, due to an influence from the surrounding cultural community, because the rate of blinks is statistically similar between HKSL and Cantonese. Speakers of both English and Cantonese showed similar blink rates and no correlation between prosodic constituency and blinks, while ASL, JSL and DSGS had a significantly lower rate of blinks; all sign languages had more systematic boundary blinks than spoken languages.

With regard to how much variation exists in the use of blinks to mark I-Phrases and the concomitant cues that accompany them, in Study 2 we confirmed that if I-Phrases are identified independently from blinks, as they were here, blinks are still highly correlated with this prosodic category (at least 74 percent). But, while blinks consistently mark I-Phrases in the four sign languages studied, blinks do not exclusively mark I-Phrases in HKSL; that is, blinks cannot be used as a diagnostic for I-Phrases in this language. We also found that crosslinguistic variation exists in the concomitant cues that occur with blinks. In three of the four sign languages analyzed (ASL, HKSL and DSGS), lengthening was the strongest concomitant cue, while in JSL it was head nod.

In Study 3, we analyzed HKSL for the placement of the blinks that did not fit into an I-Phrase analysis in order to establish the pattern employed in this language. Blinks more consistently marked I-Phrases than any other constituent, but also P-Phrases to a lesser extent, and there were some exceptional cases of a boundary blink in the middle of a compound and between a head and its complement. The results show that the frequency of blinks decreases when the prosodic constituent gets smaller (Sze 2008). We found that except for blinks, HKSL had a prosodic pattern similar to other sign languages that have been studied to date.

An additional finding was that total sign duration, including holds, repetitions and duration of the movement, when measured in a relative way among the three types of prosodic constituents, is predictive of prosodic constituency. P-Words exhibit no lengthening; P-Phrases exhibit a weakened form of lengthening (one and one-half times that of phrase-internal forms) and I-Phrases exhibit a strong form of lengthening (twice that of phrase-internal forms). Since lengthening was sensitive to prosodic boundaries, we were able to propose an analysis of HKSL based on this cue in order to differentiate P-Words, P-Phrases and I-Phrases. This analysis argues that lengthening will vary by prosodic position, a proposal that first appeared in Miller 1996 with regard to repeated movements (i.e., that the number of repetitions is closely tied to the prosodic position of a sign). The analysis of P-Phrases in HKSL can be applied to other sign languages, and it suggests an explanation for why P-Phrases are so difficult to characterize in a unified way. They form intermediate constituents, one with a stronger juncture than at a P-Word but with a weaker juncture than that of an I-Phrase.

There are still many open questions concerning prosody in signed and spoken languages that are beyond the scope of this chapter – such as which elements of prosody are truly contrastive, which ones have a role in other components of the grammar, such as syntax, morphology, etc., and which ones are purely prosodic. But given the important role that prosody plays in parsing the linguistic signal into meaningful constituents in all natural languages (in both adults and infants), understanding prosody and its crosslinguistic variation is important for work on constituent structure generally and on sign language constituent structure in particular.

Appendix   Notational conventions specific to this chapter

carat symbol '^': e.g., RUN^ROAD 'running-track.' This indicates a compound, either lexical or classifier.

   H1: e.g., 'FATHER, ROCKET, MOON, CL: rocket + lands_on.' one- and two-handed lexical signs, or elements of classifier constructions on the dominant hand.

H2: e.g., 'CL:round_object$_i$.' Elements of classifier constructions on the non-dominant hand. If a classifier element on H2 is a copy of that on H1, this is indicated as '(copy of H1)' or

$$\textbf{bracketing: } \text{e.g., } \begin{array}{l} \text{H1:} \\ \text{H2:} \end{array} \left. {}'\left[\left[\begin{array}{l} \text{CL: rocket+lands\_on}_i \\ \text{CL: round\_object}_i \end{array} \right]_{\text{PW}} \right]_{\text{PP}} \right]_{\text{IP}} {}'$$

a. If the dominant and non-dominant hands are articulated at the same time, they are considered part of the same P-Word, following the analysis of two-handed classifiers given in Eccarius and Brentari (2007).

b. 'subscripted PW, PP, IP' indicate that the elements contained in the brackets are a Prosodic Word, a Phonological Phrase and an Intonational Phrase, respectively.

Addition symbol '+': e.g., 'CL: rocket + lands_on.' The '+' separates the handshape from the movement of classifier elements encoded simultaneously. This representation appears on H1 usually. Sometimes there is no phonological movement on H2 when it is used to express an existential predicate (Wallin 1996). Existential predicates are not indicated in the notation.

24

Deixis in an emerging sign language

Marie Coppola and Ann Senghas

1 Introduction

If you look closely at any sign language, you will soon discover familiar local gestures – nods, hand signals, even facial expressions – embedded within the language stream. At least, these signs appear familiar. However, their meanings, and the way they are combined with other signs, differ in many ways from their gesture lookalikes. Evidently, the first signers of these languages adopted everyday gestures as raw materials and used them to build the language. Once the gestures became part of a language, their functions changed.

These functions go beyond basic vocabulary. Many researchers of sign languages have suggested that gestures from the ambient culture were a source of grammatical elements too (Newport & Supalla 2000, Casey 2003, Wilcox 2004). Studies comparing gestures with contemporary signs support such an account. For example, a Jordanian hand gesture meaning 'wait a second' appears to have been co-opted as a negative completive marker in Jordanian Sign Language (Hendriks, 2004), and a French gesture meaning 'to go' is the likely source of a future marker in American Sign Language (ASL) (Janzen & Shaffer 2002). There are nonmanual examples too: the raising of eyebrows often seen on the faces of English speakers when they produce conditional sentences appears to be the origin of the eyebrow raise required with conditional expressions in ASL (Pyers & Emmorey 2007), and common American head movements and body postures have apparently been reshaped into ASL markers of negation and role shift (McClave 2000, 2001).

1.1 Grammaticalization

The emergence of new grammatical elements is not limited to sign languages, nor to language in its earliest stages. All languages undergo historical changes, referred to as grammaticalization, in which lexical forms, over time, can be reshaped into grammatical elements, which, over more time, can be again reshaped into other

543

grammatical elements (Traugott & Heine 1991, Hopper & Traugott 1993). For example, the English verb *will*, meaning 'to want,' has grammaticalized into a future auxiliary. Thus the modern English expression *I will eat* says nothing about one's desire to eat; it indicates only that the eating will happen in the future. These changes appear not to be random, as common patterns of grammaticalization have been observed across languages and elements, and across various times in languages' histories.

Pfau and Steinbach (2006) argue convincingly, based on data from a wide variety of sign languages, that the typical paths taken by lexical items as they are transformed into grammatical elements are the same in sign languages as in spoken languages. That is, these pathways are modality-independent, and not the result of the particular way that words are spoken or heard. Indeed, Aronoff, Meir and Sandler (2005) have documented changes from lexical items to morphological affixes in ASL and Israeli Sign Language, and observe that the age of a language predicts its degree of sequential morphology, in signed as in spoken languages. However, sign languages have the additional possibility of developing grammatical markers directly from the gestures produced in the surrounding community, even gestures such as facial expressions and body movements that are never adopted as lexical items (Janzen & Shaffer 2002, Rathmann & Mathur 2004, Wilcox 2004, Pfau & Steinbach 2006). This unusual source is evidently due to the particular way that signing is produced and received, through the visual-manual modality, a modality also exploited by the gestures that accompany speech.

These patterns of historical change in mature languages lead us to new questions. Are such changes the source of the first linguistic elements that arise when a new language emerges? How, exactly, do forms progress from non-linguistic to linguistic elements? Most likely, such a process entails several steps, with every step representing a deviation from the surrounding language model. Why doesn't each new generation simply learn all the available forms faithfully, using them as they are used by the previous generation? Why change anything? We are not talking about lazy or inattentive learners here – note that the changes described above represent gains in the grammar rather than just the loss or degradation of elements. Evidently learners creatively change a language as they inherit it. Do their learning mechanisms play a role in reassigning the function of elements as they acquire their language?

1.2   The present studies

In this chapter, we follow the changes in the use of a form as it progresses from its gestural origins through the early stages of an emerging sign language. We take as our case study the indexical point. A close look at this one form reveals the path taken as a basic deictic gesture, often produced along with speech to indicate real locations and objects, is being re-purposed and given new linguistic functions in a sign language. To foreshadow our findings, we observe a steady increase in the production of points to locations that refer not to locations but to entities. With this shift, points (and other common deictic gestures) are taking on certain grammatical functions, including indicating subjects, serving as pronouns and possibly determiners, and even participating in anaphoric constructions that track and switch reference.

We hypothesize that the pointing behavior of Spanish speakers has been reanalyzed by deaf Nicaraguans into pronominal and agreement systems similar to those found in other sign languages around the world. That is, a process of reanalysis has led to the creation of grammar. In this case, the transformation of pointing gestures into grammatical elements involves the loss of their locative content, allowing points to take on grammatical functions. Because this series of changes occurs as new child learners are confronted with the task of learning language, we argue that children's natural language-learning abilities underlie the specific nature of the reanalyses that take place. To the degree that the developments described here resemble historical changes observed in other, more mature languages, we speculate that the same learning mechanisms may underlie both kinds of change.

1.3   From Nicaraguan homesigns to Nicaraguan Sign Language

The recent emergence of a new sign language in Nicaragua allows us to observe the very earliest stages of a language in present-day individuals. The Nicaraguan Deaf community, and its language, have come into existence only since the late 1970s (Kegl & Iwata 1989, Kegl, Senghas & Coppola 1999, R. Senghas 2003, Polich 2005). Before that time, deaf Nicaraguans had little contact with each other. Societal attitudes kept most deaf individuals at home, in contact only with neighbors and family members who were not deaf. The few day schools and clinics available for deaf children before the 1970s served very small numbers of children (Polich 2005). Now adults, individuals who participated in such programs as children report that they did not continue to have contact with their classmates outside of school hours, or after leaving school. Furthermore, the programs actively discouraged gestural communication, training children instead in verbal articulation and reading lips, at which they were generally unsuccessful (R. Senghas 2003). As evidenced by the lack of sign language and the lack of a Deaf community among individuals over the age of forty-five today, these early conditions were apparently not favorable for the development of a sign language.

Research across a number of cultures indicates that in this situation, deaf children often develop "homesigns" to communicate with the hearing people around them (Morford 1996, Goldin-Meadow 2003b). Homesigns are systems of gestural communication, typically limited to a single family household and the few other communication partners of a single deaf individual. Various homesign systems developed by young children in places as different as the United States and Taiwan have been found to include certain common fundamental characteristics of language, including a basic lexicon, consistent word order frames that allow recursion (Goldin-Meadow 1982) and the ability to discuss referents displaced in space and time from the here and now (Morford 1993).

Homesigners who remain separated from other deaf people will continue to use their homesigns as their primary language into adulthood, and the systems can develop language-like characteristics. An examination of the homesign systems used by three different Nicaraguan adults found that each had developed a way to indicate the grammatical subject of a sentence (Coppola & Newport 2005). However, the fact that homesigners are not part of a larger signing community, and are therefore unable to pass their system along to new learners, seems to limit the complexity of homesign systems. Their lexicons, sentence patterns and use of the signing space, while internally consistent, are idiosyncratic and vary widely from one deaf homesigner to another (Coppola 2002, Coppola & So 2005).

The opportunities for deaf children in Managua expanded dramatically in 1977, when a new center for special education opened, including primary school classrooms for deaf students. The school's initial enrollment of fifty deaf students rose to a hundred within the first few years, and continued to increase throughout the 1980s. Instruction followed an oralist philosophy that emphasized speaking, writing and lip-reading Spanish, again without much success. However, the children were free to communicate gesturally on the way to school (for many, an hour-long bus ride) and during free periods, and these interactions served as the starting point of a new sign language and a new social community. What started as a hodgepodge of different homesign systems must have begun to reshape itself at this time, eventually converging into a single, common system. In 1981, a vocational school was established for adolescents, and many of the alumni of the primary school program enrolled. By 1983 the two programs served more than 400 deaf students altogether.

Every year since, a new wave of children has entered school (typically at the preschool level) and learned to sign by socializing naturally with the older children there. Graduates of these programs have maintained social contact into adulthood, establishing social and athletic programs for deaf adults, celebrating major holidays together, even marrying other deaf people and starting new families together.

Today, members of the community range in age from birth to forty-five, and number over a thousand. The language of communication is Nicaraguan Sign Language (NicaSL), the language that emerged through their social contact, and most of them have used it as their primary (indeed, only) language throughout their lives.

Because children entered this group steadily throughout the 1980s and 1990s, the community today provides a snapshot of a continuum of language experience. Recall that those who arrived in its earliest years encountered a new, fledgling system of signing, while those who arrived more recently encountered a richer, more developed language. This social situation has led to a somewhat topsy-turvy language community, in which the richest, most fluent signing is produced by the youngest members. It provides us with the rare opportunity to track the historical development of a new language by comparing different age cohorts of signers, progressing "forward" in time from older to younger signers.

To capture different periods in the language's emergence, we have divided the community into three cohorts, based on the period in which individuals first arrived. Children who arrived in the late 1970s and early 1980s (now adults) form Cohort 1, those who arrived in the mid- to late-1980s (now adolescents) form Cohort 2, and those who arrived in the 1990s (now children) form Cohort 3. In the present study, we compared signed stories narrated in NicaSL by four Deaf signers from each of these three cohorts. At the time these narratives were elicited (in 1998 and 2001), the Cohort 1 signers ranged from 23 to 30 years of age, the Cohort 2 signers ranged from 12 ½ to 17, and the Cohort 3 signers ranged from 10 to 12 ½. All of the participants are fluent signers who have used NicaSL as their primary language from the age of 5 ½ or earlier (with a mean of 3 ½ years of age). Two of the participants, one from the first cohort and one from the second, had been exposed from birth to an older deaf family member who had acquired the sign language.

To complete the picture of language emergence, we also included four deaf homesigners who never entered the programs in Managua as children. As adults, they have had, at most, sporadic contact with signers of NicaSL; none of them has a regular communication partner who signs NicaSL, none uses NicaSL vocabulary (aside from those signs that share forms with common Nicaraguan gestures) and none has even rudimentary knowledge of NicaSL grammar. The homesigners ranged from 20 to 30 years of age at the time their narratives were elicited. These participants should give us a view of the initial state of the communication systems of deaf Nicaraguans before NicaSL developed.

To collect comparable language samples from all of the participants, we showed them each an animated cartoon entitled *Canary Row*, involving the character

Sylvester the cat chasing down Tweety the bird.[1] (These cartoon characters often appear on Nicaraguan television, so most of our participants were familiar with them.) Participants watched the cartoon a few times on a monitor and then told the story to someone else. NicaSL signers told the story to a peer from the same cohort, and homesigners told the story to a communication partner familiar with their homesign system. All of the narratives were videotaped for later analysis.

By laying these narratives out in order, across the continuum from home-signers through the three cohorts of NicaSL signers, we can create a record, like rings on a tree, of the progression of the emergence of a language. However, keep in mind that there is a factor that blurs this record. To the degree that adults are able to change the language, or acquire new developments, the groups will resemble each other. For example, if adults (as well as children) can easily acquire some form or use, it will spread to members of every cohort. (We have seen such a pattern in many lexical signs as they are coined and then spread throughout the community.) In contrast, a form or use that is initiated and learnable only by children will be observed only in that cohort that was still young when it first emerged, and subsequent cohorts. What this means, in terms of the living "fossil record" of NicaSL among present-day signers, is that the differences that we do observe between cohorts represent only those develop-ments that were contributed by children. For this reason, differences between cohorts today highlight the specific effect of children's ability both to learn and to create language.

1.4   Indexical pointing

The form that we track here, pointing, has many characteristics that make it a likely candidate to be taken up and integrated into a new sign language. Pointing gestures are ubiquitous. Their use has been extensively documented in the gestures that accompany speech (McNeill 1992, Kita & Özyürek 2003, Kendon 2004, and many others), in mature sign languages (Sandler & Lillo-Martin 2006), and in homesign (Goldin-Meadow & Mylander 1984, Morford 1996, Coppola 2002, Fusellier-Souza 2006). They are typically produced with an extended finger or an open hand directed away from the body, though you can also point by using other handshapes or other parts of the body, such as jutting an elbow or pursing the lips in the direction of the intended referent (Kita 2003). Hearing children (Bates *et al.* 1979) and deaf children (Hoffmeister 1978, Bellugi & Klima 1982) start producing points at a very young age, along with their very first utterances.

Points are so pervasive that it is easy to overlook their complexity, and the cognitive machinery required to interpret them. Even the most basic use of a point, to direct someone's attention to an object in the immediate environment, requires that both communication partners understand that the person who produces the point has the intention to refer to something. Try producing a point for your cat, and you will find she is more likely to sniff your finger than follow its trajectory across the room. Most of the points that hearing people produce are integrated with a spoken sentence (McNeill 1992, 2005), and the listener must coordinate the non-linguistic action with the spoken words and the greater context of the utterance in order to arrive at the full meaning of the sentence (Kendon 2003). Among other uses, co-speech points often provide information about the location or identity of a referent, as in points that accompany expressions like *over there* or *that tablecloth*. Even without being able to hear the speech, one can often infer the intent of these gestures to indicate places and objects in the world, a use referred to as "direct deixis." For this reason, it is perhaps unsurprising that points can be used in sign languages for the same function. Researchers have proposed that the pointing gesture entered the grammar of sign languages as a marker of location (Pfau & Steinbach 2006), though their use in mature sign languages has expanded to include many other functions, to which we now turn.

1.4.1 *Pointing in sign languages*

Pointing movements take on a range of grammatical applications in sign languages: they indicate the arguments of verbs (Padden 1988, Meier 1990, Engberg-Pedersen 1993, McBurney 2002 and others) and serve as determiners (Zimmer & Patschke 1990, Bahan *et al.* 1995) and locatives (Shepard-Kegl 1985, Padden 1988, Emmorey 2002). Some recent accounts propose that points in ASL are not linguistic, and are better analyzed as a gestural component of the language (Liddell 1995, Liddell & Metzger 1998). Because the language in this case is produced using the same articulators as gesture, it can be difficult to determine whether certain uses are better categorized as part of the language or part of its accompanying gesture, so this distinction has been the focus of some debate. While we cannot resolve this question here for all uses of pointing, we will argue that many of the uses we document entail the incorporation of points into the grammar of NicaSL.

Different forms of pointing have been conventionalized within sign languages to correspond to different functions. For example, in ASL, a point with the index finger can serve as a nominative or accusative pronoun, such as *he* or *him*, while an open hand, palm forward, is used as the possessive form, such as *his* or *yours*. As Taub (2001) notes, "sign languages incorporate pointing into their grammar and vocabulary in conventionalized ways: There are many kinds of signs that consist basically of pointing in a specific way at a meaningful location or thing." What makes these locations "meaningful" is a wealth of context, usually in the signing that precedes a point. Of course, points can be used for direct deixis while signing, in much the same way as in co-speech gesture (Liddell 1996). But when the referent is not in the immediate here and now, the use is a more abstract one. As Liddell (1995) describes it, "Pronouns can be directed at non-present but *projected* referents as well as at present ones, which can be seen as being derived from direct deixis – once the image of the referent has been projected onto signing space, it is available to be pointed at."

Sign languages make extensive use of the three-dimensional space in front of the signer, and the use of pointing in a mature sign language must be fully integrated into these complex systems of spatial grammar. In one type of use found in many sign languages, certain locations in the signing space become associated with particular referents (Klima & Bellugi 1979, Supalla 1982, Padden 1988, Meir 1998a, Meier 2002). The signer can then incorporate those locations into other signs in order to refer back to the referent, or to link other signs grammatically with the referent. For example, a signer might associate a man with a location on the right and later produce the sign PAY toward the right, indicating that the man was paid. In this way, signers can link verbs with their arguments, and nouns with their modifiers. Locations in the signing space can also be associated with particular places, or points along a timeline (Frishberg & Gough 2000, Taub 2001).

All mature sign languages that have been documented take advantage of the signing space for these kinds of functions, though the specific devices that are available differ from language to language. Any use of pointing that is part of a grammar must be compatible with its other devices. Within the structure already established in the particular sign language, points can then be used to refer to locations in the signing space that are meaningful, thereby taking on meaning themselves.

Some of the uses of pointing that are common to sign languages have been documented in homesigns as well. Deaf homesigning children in many countries, including the United States, Taiwan, Nicaragua and Spain, all use a point to refer to objects and locations (Goldin-Meadow 2003b). Two elderly Japanese sisters who are homesigners were also found to use points for these functions, and to indicate non-present persons and objects. They also used points as prosodic markers for phrases and clauses (Torigoe 2000). Previous work with four adult homesigners in Nicaragua found that each had developed a preferred means of indicating non-present participants and their roles in simple events; the devices they used included points to the chest to indicate the agent of an event, points to other people who are present and points to fingers to represent arguments of events, and points to empty spatial locations to indicate both locations and persons (Coppola & So 2005).

1.5   Deixis

As we follow the use of points in the emergence of NicaSL, we pay particular attention to how their use fits into a system of "deictic expressions." Deictic expressions are expressions that "point" beyond the utterance in order to have meaning. As Diessel (1999) defines them, deictics are "linguistic elements whose interpretation makes crucial reference to some aspect of the speech situation," such as when an utterance is spoken, where it is spoken, or by whom it is spoken. For example, the expression *yesterday* does not refer to any one particular day. In order to interpret it, the listener needs to know when the speaker said it. Similarly, to interpret deictic expressions like *here* and *there*, the listener needs to know the speaker's location. Personal pronouns are also deictic expressions; the words *I* and *you* depend on the identity of the speaker and listener in order to determine their reference.

Deictic expressions can be used to refer to the immediate environment; this is referred to as "direct deixis." By using "indirect deixis" a speaker can move beyond the here and now to indicate non-present people, places and times. In such cases, the source, or *origo* (Bühler 1990), used as a reference point for the deixis, is displaced from the place and time of the utterance. For example, in the expression *The boy saw a plane **up above***, the origo is the location of the boy, and the deictic expression *up above* refers to the location above the boy, not above the speaker of the utterance. Similarly, in the expression, *The boy cut his arm **here***, accompanied by a touch on the elbow, the origo is not the speaker's arm, but some other arm, namely, that of the boy, and it is to his elbow that the deictic expression *here* refers. In sign languages, pointing can be used for both direct and indirect deixis. A point to a tablecloth to refer to that very tablecloth would be an example of direct deixis, as mentioned in the example above. A point to a tablecloth to refer to some other tablecloth would be an example of indirect deixis. In spoken and sign languages, many of the same words and gestures are used for both direct and indirect deixis, so a listener will often need to refer to the spoken and gestural context to interpret an expression.

Deictic expressions are "exophoric"; they link an expression to an aspect of the real world, outside of the utterance itself. These contrast with "anaphoric" expressions, which link an expression to another expression that appeared previously in the discourse (Diessel, 1999). For example, consider the discourse "My grandmother had a hand-embroidered tablecloth that she brought with her from Italy. I still have *that tablecloth* today on my dining room table." In this case, the *that* in the expression *that tablecloth* is anaphoric. Rather than directing the listener to some object in the world, it points to a noun phrase of the previous sentence. Again, the same forms within a language (such as *that* in English) are often used for both exophoric and anaphoric reference. Pointing is used for both functions in many mature sign languages, and it seems reasonable to hypothesize that the anaphoric use, which is more abstract and linguistically embedded, derived from the exophoric use, which is more concrete and free.[2] This is another trajectory that we will explore in our analysis of points in NicaSL.

2   Analyses and results

2.1   Pointing observed in Nicaraguan signed narratives

The goal of the present study is to follow a specific case in which elements start out as para-linguistic forms, that is, co-speech gestures, to see if they become linguistic, and possibly grammatical[3] elements that are part of an emerging language. To this end, we systematically compared the deictic gestures, mostly points, produced by participants drawn from a single culture, but from groups situated at four different moments along a proposed continuum of language emergence: adult homesigners who have not acquired a conventional sign language, and NicaSL signers from each of three sequential age cohorts that acquired the language at three successive periods during its emergence. How does the form and function of pointing change as we progress along this continuum?

We tabulated every instance of a manual deictic gesture in each narrative. These included points with a hand or finger,[4] either toward some location, or with an outward arc movement (the common ANOTHER gesture, described in more detail below). We then determined whether the deictic gesture was directed toward some aspect of the immediate real-world environment, a part of the signer's body (typically the chest) or empty space. The deictics toward empty space were further categorized into those that referred to locations (such as *overhead* or *to the left*) and those that referred to persons or objects (such as *Tweety the bird* or *the cage*). We refer to these functions as "locative" and "nominal" uses.[5] They are described further in section 2.5 below.

Note that each category, in turn, reflects a greater displacement of the referent from the real world and real objects, resulting in a higher degree of abstractness and indirectness. Such displacement is a fundamental characteristic of language that allows reference to entities and locations that are not part of the here and now (Hockett 1966). As the deictic signs took on more abstract functions, we examined how they combined into strings with other words in the language. We were interested in whether these functions became syntactically differentiated as the elements became part of the emerging grammar of NicaSL.

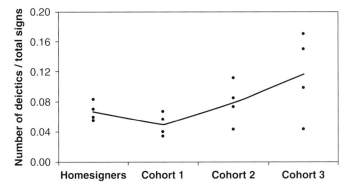

Figure 24.1 *Proportion of signs produced that are deictics. Dots represent individual participants; the solid line indicates the mean for each group. Note that the use of deictics increases across groups.*

2.2 Overall use of deictics

Figure 24.1 shows the proportion of signs that were deictic produced by each participant. To compute the proportion, we first totaled all of the deictic signs produced by each participant in the eight stories that make up the *Canary Row* narrative. This is our numerator. We then calculated the signing rate of each participant for one of the stories. We extrapolated from this calculation to estimate the number of signs produced in the narrative. By using this second figure in the denominator, we effectively control for variation in the signing rate and length of narratives. (However, note that a similar pattern of results obtains if we plot raw frequencies of deictics instead.)

As can be seen in the figure, the proportion of deictics increases as we move along the continuum. On average, deictics represented 7 percent of the signs produced by homesigners (a mean of 26 out of 393 signs per narrative), 5 percent of the signs produced by Cohort 1 signers (26/501), 8 percent of the signs produced by Cohort 2 signers (38/501) and 12 percent of the signs by Cohort 3 signers (50/421). A linear regression analysis indicates that the proportion of deictics increases significantly across groups ($t = 2.23, p = .04$). Evidently, over the past thirty years, deictic signs have been increasingly taken up as referring devices in NicaSL.

2.3 Points to the real-world environment

Points to real-world persons or objects can function to indicate those real persons or objects (such as pointing to a nearby tablecloth to mean exactly that tablecloth). Such direct deixis uses are very frequent in both spoken and sign languages, and we have certainly observed them in everyday NicaSL. Unsurprisingly, because the participants were asked to describe a situation that was not in the here and now, we did not observe any deictics of this type in the elicited narratives. We did, however, observe a few examples of indirect deixis. These included pointing to a real-world object to refer to a similar object; for example, pointing at a nearby tablecloth to refer to a tablecloth in the cartoon, as well as pointing to a real-world object to refer to some characteristic or property it possesses; for example, pointing to a nearby black tablecloth to indicate the property *black*.

Homesigners pointed to objects in the environment to refer to entities or attributes more frequently than did signers in the other groups, though even they did not do this very often. Three of the four homesigners produced this type of deictic expression (with a total of six instances), compared with one Cohort 1 signer (one instance), one Cohort 2 signer (two instances) and one Cohort 3 signer (one instance).

2.4   Points to the signer's body

Parts of the signer's body can be used to represent other entities (such forms are often referred to as "classifiers"; for an overview, see Emmorey 2003) and these forms, themselves, are then available to be pointed at. For example, the left forearm can be held up vertically to represent a telephone pole, and then pointed at with the right hand to refer to the pole. Additionally, a particular location on the forearm can be pointed at to refer to a location on the pole; for example, a point to the mid-forearm could refer to a location halfway up the pole. Twelve such uses were observed in the narratives altogether, distributed equally among the groups. So, while this is not a frequent type of deictic, it is one that is shared by homesigners and NicaSL signers.

However, a second type of pointing to the signer's body was much more frequent and showed a different pattern. This was a point to the signer's own chest (glossed as *IX:chest*), generally used to refer to a character in the story.[6] As we span the continuum, we observe a dramatic increase in the use of the IX:chest deictic (see Figure 24.2). (Because the proportions are small, we have multiplied the values on the y-axis by 1,000 for ease of presentation.) The mean proportion of IX:chest signs produced by homesigners was $0.75/393$ (0.2 percent); by Cohort 1 signers, $5.5/501$ (1.1 percent); by Cohort 2 signers, $6.5/501$ (1.5 percent); and by Cohort 3 signers, $14.3/421$ (3.4 percent). A linear regression analysis indicated that the proportion of IX:chest deictics increased significantly across groups ($t = 2.52$, $p = .02$). IX:chest was produced by only two of the homesigners (a finding consistent with previous work with the same participants (Coppola & So, 2005), three of the Cohort 1 signers, and all of the Cohort 2 and Cohort 3 signers.

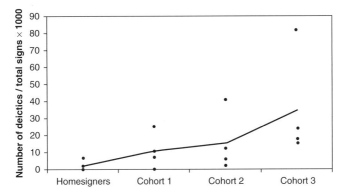

Figure 24.2 *Proportion of signs that are points to the chest. Dots represent individual participants; the line indicates the mean for each group. Note that the use of IX:chest increases across groups.*

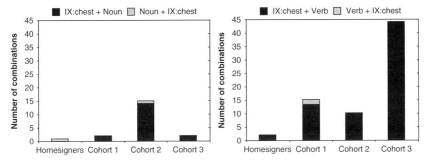

Figure 24.3 *Orders of IX:chest in combinations with nouns (left) and verbs (right). Note that the combinations with IX:chest are predominantly point-initial. Indeed, Cohort 3 produced solely point-initial combinations. They also produced these combinations much more frequently than the other groups, and almost exclusively with verbs.*

2.4.1   *Ordering patterns of points to the chest in combination with other signs*
IX:chest was nearly always combined with another sign to form a string, appearing alone in only 2 of 108 instances. It was combined with verbs, nouns, adjectives, other deictics, classifier-movement constructions and reported action sequences. The combinations produced by NicaSL signers tended to be point-initial (in 93/96 instances, or 97 percent) rather than point-final, or in what we call "sandwich" constructions (prosodic units in which one sign appears before and after another, e.g., X Y X).

By considering the patterns of use across NicaSL cohorts, we see that this deictic has changed dramatically over a short period (see Figure 24.3). Grouping the verbal elements together (verbs, classifier-movement constructions and constructed actions), we find that Cohort 1 signers predominantly combine IX:chest with a verbal element (eighteen instances) rather than a nominal element (three instances). In their narratives, these were often expressions in which the agent had been identified and the signer was continuing to narrate from the perspective of that agent. For example, having already assumed the role of the cat, the signer might produce IX:chest, followed by a constructed action of climbing, to indicate that the cat climbed.

In contrast, Cohort 2 signers combine IX:chest with both nominal (fifteen instances) and verbal elements (ten instances). In the combinations with nominals, they almost always placed the IX:chest point immediately before the nominal element to identify the character that they were about to describe (fourteen of the fifteen combinations with nominals). So, in a typical Cohort 2 use of this device, the expression *IX:chest CAT* would indicate that the signer was shifting into the role of the cat as the agent of subsequent actions (Pyers & Senghas 2007).

Cohort 3 signers used IX:chest combinations much more than any of the other groups (48 instances), but rarely in this nominal construction (2/48 instances). They were much more likely to combine IX:chest with a verbal element (44/48 instances, including classifier constructions, a combination not used in the other groups). (In the remaining two instances, the IX:chest was combined with another deictic.) This development may reflect that these signers have fully nominalized the IX:chest and are constraining it to a nominal position, such as immediately before, or simultaneous with, a verbal element. This is the typical subject position (Senghas *et al.* 1997); thus the expression *IX:chest CLIMB* would mean 'he climbs.' It is particularly striking that Cohort 3 signers appear to have abandoned the use of the IX:chest to establish a new agent, given that the device was used this way fairly frequently by the second cohort. As we will see, Cohort 3 signers have established other patterns of deictic use to introduce and switch referents, possibly freeing up IX:chest to take on the more specific use as a nominal, agentive element.

2.5   Points to empty space

The majority of points in the narratives are directed at empty space. Many of these points are used to refer to locations, what we refer to as locative uses. Of course, pointing can be used to refer to real-world locations, but, as mentioned above, such direct deixis uses were not attested in the narratives. However, there were many instances of indirect deixis, used to refer to analogous locations in the cartoon. An example is given in Figure 24.4, in which a homesigner points above his own head to refer to a location above the head of the cat in the story. Note that his eye gaze

Figure 24.4 *Example of a locative point. A homesigner points above his own head to refer to the location above the cat. Note that his eye gaze follows the point.*

Figure 24.5 *Example of a nominal point. A Cohort 1 signer points to her left to refer to the bird, who has been previously associated with that locus. Note that the movement is constrained within the signing space, and that her eye gaze does not follow the point.*

follows the point; this use of eye gaze is highly typical (possibly obligatory) with locative deictics for all four groups.

Points to empty space were also used to refer to entities, serving a nominal function. An example is shown in Figure 24.5, in which a Cohort 1 signer points to her left to refer to Tweety. These uses are quite different in appearance from the locative uses. They are articulated more quickly, and with a reduced movement, or no movement. Eye gaze, in these cases, does not follow the point; in Figure 24.5 you can see that the signer closes her eyes as she shifts her gaze away.

2.6   Ordering patterns of locative and nominal points in combination with other signs

We set aside for the moment the striking differences in the frequency of locative and nominal points, which will be considered with another deictic form below, and turn to the word order patterns in constructions with points. Locative points are produced alone (14 instances) and in combination with other signs (138 instances). When combined with other signs, the ordering preferences are not strong, though they appear to depend partly on whether the other sign is a noun (Figure 24.6a) or a verb (Figure 24.6b).[7] For the NicaSL signers, combinations with nouns are somewhat more likely to be point-initial (40 instances, or 67 percent) rather than

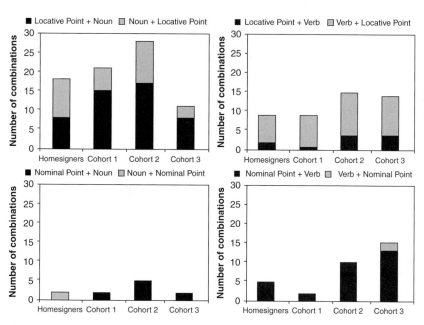

Figure 24.6 *Orders of locative points in combinations with nouns (6a) and verbs (6b), and nominal points in combinations with nouns (6c) and verbs (6d). Noun refers to all nominal elements, including lexical nouns and nominal deictics. Verb refers to all verbal elements, including verbs, constructed actions and classifier constructions. Note that combinations with nominal points, unlike locative points, are almost exclusively point-initial (6c and 6d). Note also that the use of the nominal point + verb constructions increases over cohorts (6d), suggesting the emergence of a new semantic function for that form.*

point-final (20 instances, or 33 percent); homesigners show no ordering preference (8 instances of point-initial vs. 10 of point-final). Combinations of locative points with verbs are a bit more likely to be point-final, for all groups (36/47 instances, or 77 percent). Thus, a common combination of a point with a noun would be the point-initial expression *IX:up BIRD*, meaning 'the bird (is) overhead'; while a common combination with a verb would be the point-final expression *CLIMB IX:up*, meaning 'climb up.'

Nominal points differ from locative points in their combination and ordering patterns as well as in their form. They almost never appear alone (2/53 instances). When combined with other signs, the nominal point is almost always placed initially, whether with nouns (Figure 24.6c) or verbs (Figure 24.6d). It appears initially in 42/51 combinations (82 percent), finally in 7/51 combinations (14 percent) and twice embedded in a "sandwich" construction.[8] Thus, typical NicaSL combinations using nominal points would include the point-initial constructions *IX:left BIRD* meaning 'the bird' (associated with a locus to the left) and *IX:left FALL* meaning 'he falls.' The use with a noun may constitute a determiner construction, and the use with a verb appears to be pronominal, in line with analyses of similar constructions in other sign languages (though a complete analysis of such constructions is beyond the scope of this chapter). All of the groups show this point-initial ordering preference with nominal points, though it is weaker in the homesigners (5/7 instances, or 71 percent) than in the NicaSL signers (34/36 instances, or 94 percent).

Note that there is a change in frequency across groups in the use of nominal points, depending on function. While no systematic pattern across groups is apparent in the combinations of nominal points with nouns (Figure 24.6c), the frequency of combinations with verbs appears to be increasing across the continuum (Figure 24.6d). Further, while both point-initial and point-final orders are attested for all groups in combinations containing locative points (Figures 24.6a and 24.6b), combinations containing nominal points are almost exclusively point-initial (Figures 24.6c and 24.6d). There are only four exceptions: two produced by a single homesigner, and two produced in the same sentence by a Cohort 3 signer. (This particular sentence includes three deictics, only one of which could logically appear in initial position. The other two are not the subject, appear in reported speech, and are part of a question. Clearly this sentence is too complex to be captured by our simple index-initial vs. index-final scheme.)

2.7 The ANOTHER sign

We observed a second deictic form that differed in appearance from the simple indexical point. This form, which we gloss ANOTHER, is derived from a common

Figure 24.7 *Example of a locative form of ANOTHER. A homesigner produces the sign to the left, to refer to a new location different from the one she has been discussing. Note that she bends both the elbow and wrist as she produces an arced movement with her forearm and hand. Her eye gaze follows the sign, to the left.*

Nicaraguan gesture used to mean 'over there' or 'another one' (Coppola 2007). The gesture generally occurs with the spoken Spanish word *otro* ('other'). Both the gesture and the sign are produced with an arced outward movement, with an extended index finger or a loosely open hand, ending palm-up. Like the indexical point, the sign ANOTHER can be used for locative or nominal deixis. Figure 24.7 shows a locative use of ANOTHER, produced to the left, by a homesigner about to describe an event in a new location. As in the locative point, her eye gaze follows the direction of the gesture.

2.7.1   *Locative ANOTHER*

The ANOTHER sign is not as frequent as the point, but it is clearly established in the signing of all of the groups. The locative form was produced alone (16 instances), as well as in combination with nouns and verbs (13 instances), almost always appearing initially (10/13 instances). There were two instances of deictic-final constructions, both produced by a single homesigner, and one instance of a "sandwich" construction (*house ANOTHER:left house*) produced by a Cohort 1 signer. Thus, a typical NicaSL construction using the locative ANOTHER would be *ANOTHER:left BIRD*, meaning 'in another location is the bird' or 'over there is a bird.' This new location would contrast with the location of the immediately preceding event. There were not enough instances to determine a change in use across the groups, though very few locative ANOTHERs were produced by the third cohort – two instances, by a single signer.

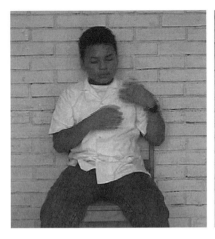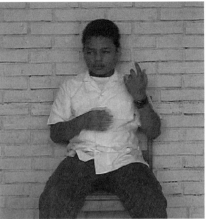

Figure 24.8 *Example of a nominal form of ANOTHER. A Cohort 3 signer uses the sign to switch reference from the cat to the bird. Note that the movement of the sign is constrained, involving a twist of the wrist as the index finger turns outward, and that his eye gaze does not follow the sign.*

2.7.2   Nominal *ANOTHER*

As was found with the indexical point, the nominal form of ANOTHER appears to be a phonetically reduced version of its locative form. It is produced more quickly than the locative ANOTHER, and with a more closed handshape, often with only the index finger, and occasionally the thumb, extended. Rather than an arced path of movement, it consists of a rotation of the wrist and forearm. In this way, it is non-spatial, not making reference to any particular location in the signing space. Figure 24.8 shows a Cohort 3 signer producing ANOTHER as he switches the agent of action from the cat to the bird. As with the nominal point, and in contrast to the locative form of ANOTHER, his eye gaze does not follow the sign, but instead shifts away.

Nominal ANOTHER differs from the locative, and from the nominal point, in more than form. It appears alone about half the time (in 27/53 instances); recall that the nominal point rarely appears alone. In combinations with adjectives, nouns and verbs, it is always in initial position (26/26 instances). Thus a typical use would be *ANOTHER BIRD*, meaning 'the bird' (as a change in subject); or *ANOTHER FALL*, meaning 'he falls' (*he* being a different subject than in the previous clause).[9]

2.8   Locative versus nominal deictics

The most striking difference between the nominal and locative uses of ANOTHER parallels that of the indexical points: the nominal uses, and not the locative, increase dramatically across the continuum of language groups. This development can be seen in Figure 24.9, which combines the two deictic forms (indexical points

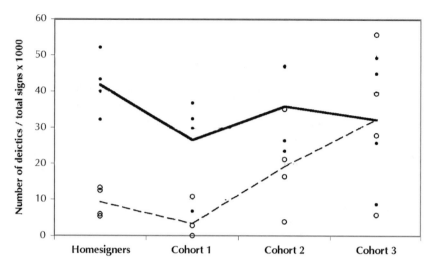

Figure 24.9 *Deictics with locative uses (filled circles, solid line indicates mean) and nominal uses (open circles, dashed line indicates mean). In contrast to locative deictics, which do not differ systematically across groups, nominal deictics exhibit a linear increase across the language continuum, suggesting the emergence of a new semantic function for these forms.*

and ANOTHER signs), separating the locative and nominal functions. The locative deictics (which are also common in co-speech gesture) are frequent in the signing of all four groups, and relatively constant. The mean proportion of locative deictics produced by homesigners was 16.8/393 (4.3 percent); by Cohort 1 signers, 14/501 (2.8 percent); by Cohort 2 signers, 18.8/501 (3.8 percent); and by Cohort 3 signers, 14/421 (3.3 percent). A linear regression analysis did not detect a change in the proportion of locative deictics across groups (t = -0.62, p = .54).

In contrast, while the nominal deictics are present in the signing of all of the homesigners, two of the Cohort 1 signers did not produce any of these forms, and as a group Cohort 1 produced the fewest. From there, they increase significantly in the signing of the members of Cohorts 2 and 3, all of whom produced them. Homesigners produced 3.5/393 (0.9%); Cohort 1 signers, 2/501 (0.4 percent); Cohort 2 signers, 9/501 (1.8 percent); and Cohort 3 signers, 14.3/421 (3.4 percent). A linear regression analysis indicated that the proportion of nominal deictics increased across groups (t = 2.91, p = .01).

2.9   The changing patterns of signing across groups

To summarize, we find an increase in the use of deictic signs as we progress from homesigners through the first three cohorts of NicaSL signers. This increase is due entirely to an increase in non-spatial, referential uses (what we call "nominal" uses) of deixis. Though locative uses are quite frequent – they are more frequent overall than nominal uses – their rate of use remains steady across the continuum.

A smaller, but probably also real change that we observed is that homesigners make more points to objects and locations in the immediate environment than NicaSL signers. This is not surprising. Presumably due to their sparser vocabulary, homesigners are more apt to take advantage of their physical surroundings to indirectly identify and describe referents.

The use of the point to the chest (*IX:chest*) is also increasing across the continuum. Note that this sign is spatially neutral from the outset and has only a nominal use; thus, it follows the larger pattern of increased use of nominal deixis. Additionally, the function of IX:chest appears to be changing as it is taken up by the third cohort, from a role-shift marker, followed by the identity of a new character, to a marker of semantic agency (possibly a subject pronoun) followed by a verb. This change could be due to a reanalysis of its typical position at the beginning of a sentence, a common position for subjects in NicaSL.

The change also represents an interaction with the changing use of the ANOTHER sign. By the time it was taken up by the third cohort, this sign appeared to have almost entirely lost the spatial, locative function of its gestural counterpart. Rather, it is used almost exclusively as a device for switching to a new referent, replacing some of the previous uses of IX:chest.

It is interesting to note that both the IX:chest and the nominal ANOTHER sign, with their functions of indicating referents, are non-spatial forms, that is, they "point" to characters in the discourse without associating them with a particular locus in the signing space. The nominal indexical point (*IX:locus*), in contrast, does make such an association. That is, the sign itself has spatial content in its form, as it points to a particular location in the signing space. However, even in this case the meaning is a non-spatial one; the point refers to a person or entity and not its location.

Considered together, these three signs, the IX:chest, ANOTHER and the nominal IX:locus, represent an emerging system of reference, possibly pronominal reference, in NicaSL. The picture that seems to be emerging is one in which ANOTHER is typically used to introduce a referent, the IX:chest is used to mark a referent as an agent (or at least the topic or perspective of an event), and IX:locus is used to refer to more kinds of referents (including agents and patients), as well as to associate referents with abstract locations in the signing space. These locations can then interact with other uses of space in the language, for example, to link arguments with verbs.

Future analyses will confirm whether this picture is an accurate one. It would be particularly useful to conduct a reference-tracking analysis across the discourse to see how abstract locations in the signing space are initially established (whether with points, nouns, classifiers or verbs) and whether these locations are then re-used with indexical points to indicate coreference. Such coreference would be an anaphoric use of space, derived from an exophoric deictic use.

As the system of spatial pointing and reference unfolds, one conclusion becomes quite clear. While there is vigorous debate regarding the appropriate characterization, gestural or grammatical, of the spatial modulations used in established sign languages, it is clearly the case that this use of space differs strikingly from that of gestures accompanying speech. Indeed, it is the relative *lack* of spatial meaning attributed to deictic forms that characterizes their increasingly grammatical uses by Nicaraguan signers. A crucial step in the transformation of pointing gestures into forms that can function as grammatical elements seems to be the loss of their locative content. Thus, as we move along the continuum from the earliest to the most developed form of NicaSL, we observe a steady increase in the production of points to loci that refer not to locations but to entities.

3   Discussion

We have referred to homesigning as the starting point for NicaSL, and indeed it is in the historical sense. When the earliest members of the Nicaraguan Deaf community first began to gather and develop a common system of communication, many of them must have had years of experience using homesigns with their families. One might expect to find minimal evidence of deictic and other referential devices in homesign, followed by more in the language's initial stage, continuing to develop and becoming more frequent with each successive cohort. This is not the picture that emerges from these data. What we find instead is that the homesigners' productions include the seeds of all of the structures that eventually emerge, including points to the chest to indicate agents, points to empty space to reference non-present entities and use of ANOTHER to switch reference. However, these devices are used sporadically and not integrated into the grammar of homesigns. They are not used by all homesigners, and do not have regular patterns of combination with other elements; that is, they are not syntactically differentiated. The same forms may also be applied to other functions, even by the same individual. The uneven profiles across homesigners reflect their lack of opportunity to conventionalize a system with others who also use it as a primary means of communication.

The effect of such individuals coming together, then, is somewhat unpredictable. The data suggest that this initial stage, when the first cohort of signers attempts to converge on a single system, is subject to two opposing forces. First, there is the loss of some relatively sophisticated functions (such as more abstract devices for nominal reference) that are unlikely to map onto the same form across the group. Second, there is a rapid convergence on those form–function mappings that are most likely to be shared; that is, those that are closest to their gestural origins, such as pointing at locations to refer to those locations. After this initial stage, once convergence on a single system has occurred, new cohorts of learners can begin to build the more complex functions back in, this time with forms that are conventionalized across the group.

3.1 Parallels to grammaticalization processes

The changes that we observe in NicaSL resemble certain changes documented in the grammaticalization of spoken languages. Three interrelated processes that underlie such changes have been proposed (Heine, Claudi & Hünnemeyer 1991a, Hopper 1991): "desemanticization," or "semantic bleaching," in which a lexical item loses its meaning as it acquires a grammatical function; "decategorialization," in which a lexical item loses properties characteristic of its category (for example, a verb losing the ability to constitute a predicate, and to take arguments); and "erosion," or "phonetic reduction," in which a lexical item loses its phonetic substance.

Reminiscent of grammaticalization, we observe in the Nicaraguan data changes in deictic points from a universal, concrete, locative meaning to a language-specific and abstract function. At the same time, they have become reduced phonetically, losing some or all of their movement across space. These forms may not yet be fully grammaticized or may yet become other grammatical elements. Nevertheless, they already participate in constructions that have a more categorical, language-like, less context-bound flavor than their original form. In the most developed form of NicaSL, represented by the signing of Cohort 3, we observe differentiated forms of the point and the ANOTHER sign being used to link arguments with verbs, indicate subjects, serve as pronouns and possibly determiners, possibly differentiate subjects and objects, and to track and switch reference.

3.1.1 *Input to grammaticalization processes*
Grammaticalization processes need original forms on which to operate. It has been noted that the sources for grammar are drawn from the most universal, concrete and basic aspects of human experience, particularly the spatial environment and parts of the body (Heine, Claudi & Hünnemeyer 1991a, Bybee 2003). Over time and use, linguistic elements become emancipated from their concrete origins. For example, in an extensive crosslinguistic survey of spoken languages, Svorou

(1994) found that words for human body parts were the most frequent sources of relational terms, such as the preposition *behind* in English deriving from the words *be* (indicating *at* or *on*) and *hind* (indicating *back* (plus an adverbial suffix)). Svorou also notes that environmental landmarks can serve as sources for spatial grammatical elements. Given that even spoken languages tend to take the spatial environment as a grammatical source, and given that the visual-gestural modality affords the ability to point directly at one's own body and at the physical environment, it is unsurprising that sign languages are particularly (and perhaps universally) inclined to exploit this source of forms and meanings, and eventually develop a rich repertoire of abstract spatial grammatical devices.

To take the argument further, the particular privilege that the visual-gestural modality provides, namely this direct way to refer to the external, physical spatial environment, may enable sign languages to take a shortcut down the path of grammaticalization, occasionally bypassing the lexical stage altogether (Janzen & Shaffer 2002, Pfau & Steinbach 2006). Wilcox (2004) notes that certain aspects of gestures are bound, that is, they must appear as part of gesture or sign. For example, a movement can never appear alone; it must be attached to some base sign, co-occurring with some handshape, in order to be produced. Since they never appear by themselves, such bound components never lexicalize. Nevertheless, they are still available as sources for grammaticalization, which in this case proceeds directly from a gestural source to a functional element.[10] It is usually tricky to argue that a stage has been bypassed in the history of a language. There is always the possibility that the particular stage did occur but left no fossil record. The real-time nature of the Nicaraguan data allows us to observe the leap as it happens, directly from a gestural point to a functional sign.

3.1.2   *De-spatialization as emancipation*

Certain words, repeated consistently in the appropriate context, can eventually become free of their contextual, instrumental associations through a process called "emancipation" (Haiman 1994). Bybee (2003) argues that the change from a lexical to a grammatical function in grammaticalization involves a process that is quite parallel, that could also be considered emancipation. We argue for the same parallelism in the changes we have observed across groups in the emergence of NicaSL, namely from the use of a point as a deictic to indicate a location (its original instrumental function) to its use as a nominal (a more symbolic, abstract, and displaced function).

Coppola and So (2006) argue for a similar process of emancipation at an even earlier moment in the grammaticalization path, from gesture to homesign. They compared the productions of adult homesigners with those of hearing gesturers

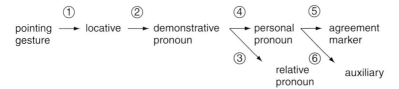

Figure 24.10 *Hypothesized grammaticalization path of pointing gestures in sign languages (from Pfau and Steinbach 2006). The current data provide support for portions of this continuum, including the development of pointing gestures to locatives, and later to more nominal forms (such as pronouns).*

asked to describe stories without speech, that is, using gesture alone. Hearing gesturers tended to spatially modulate (i.e., produce in a non-neutral location) their gestures for both entities and actions at high rates; in contrast, adult home-signers were far less likely to spatially modulate their gestures referring to entities. Coppola and So suggest that hearing adults' use of space is consistent with a holistic, pictorial representation of the event. In contrast, the homesigners' lack of spatial modulations on entity gestures reflects a process of de-spatialization that allows the gestures to function as linguistic elements, with language-like constraints on form.

3.2   Grammaticalization paths for pointing in sign languages

We have established that spatial gestures, such as points, are particularly attractive grist for sign languages as they create grammatical elements, and, furthermore, that these gestures are likely to lose their spatial content in the process. So, what do they become? Figure 24.10 shows the grammaticalization cline proposed by Pfau and Steinbach (2006), in which points progress to locatives and demonstrative pronouns, to personal and relative pronouns, to the even more grammatical forms of agreement markers and auxiliaries. While this proposal is not uncontroversial, the changes observed in the Nicaraguan data provide support for portions of it; namely, that pointing gestures first become locative, and that locatives become (pro)nominal. It remains to be seen whether pronominal forms become markers of verb agreement in NicaSL. Consistent with this possibility, younger cohorts of NicaSL signers are starting to spatially modulate their verbs consistently (A. Senghas 2003).

We did find that homesigners produce points that function as both locatives and pronouns, which might appear to violate this path. However, these uses were far less frequent than in Cohort 3 signers, and with less (apparent) systematic integration with the grammar. That is, there do not appear to be grammatical criteria in homesign for distinguishing these uses. Thus, the sporadic uses available in home-sign foreshadow some of the ultimate functions that will appear, but do not show the formal progression observed across the three cohorts of NicaSL.

The path from the spatial to the grammatical is not particular to sign languages and appears to be based on basic metaphors of physical movement and transfer. Anderson (1971) proposed a theory of grammatical cases based on such spatial relations, such as the dative marker *to* in English (as in *Alex gave a house to Adrian*), which derived from the locative term *toward*. It may be that the spatial nature of exophoric expressions sends them easily down a path to become particular types of non-spatial "pointing" expressions as they become semantically bleached. Specifically, they become anaphoric, pointing to the content of the discourse itself rather than to the world. For example, the English word *that* can have spatial content, meaning relatively far from the speaker (in contrast to *this*, which is relatively near), but when we use the expression *that tablecloth* to refer to a table-cloth mentioned in the previous sentence, *that* has lost all spatial meaning.

The case in sign languages seems exactly parallel; the movements embedded into signs to indicate grammatical relations appear to be metaphorically linked to physical spatial relations (Taub 2001). For example, the movement of a verb toward a locus in the signing space can indicate the recipient of a transfer of possession, even when the transferred object (such as a house) does not move anywhere.

Similar metaphorical extensions evidently guide the development of spatial modulations in NicaSL. Elsewhere, we have proposed that concrete uses of space served as a precursor for the more abstract use to indicate coreference relations between signs (A. Senghas 2003). Here, we argue for a process in which the development of a point into grammatical elements similarly requires a transforma-tion of its spatial content: its locative component must be separated out from a holistic package that includes its immediate physical context, leaving its form and a bit of associated semiotic content. Once segmented, the point can be combined with other linguistic elements to form more complex constituents. (See Senghas, Kita & Özyürek 2004 for a description of this segmentation process in the domain of path and manner of movement.)

It is children learning the language who do this reanalysis, which, in this extreme case, results not only in historical changes in a grammar, but the creation of a grammar. Over several iterations, as NicaSL has been passed from one cohort to the next, its grammatical elements have emerged. By comparing homesigners and signers of different ages today, we have been able to capture how the humble, "simple" point has progressed over the span of thirty years: from a concrete, deictic gesture intended to draw attention to a real-world object, to an abstract point at empty air, intended to refer to some non-present referent at some non-present time, and serving a particular linguistic role in the sentence, such as its syntactic subject. This use is more abstract, more displaced from the here and now, and more grammatical in function, and its emergence reveals the transformative power of natural processes of human language acquisition. Gesture in, grammar out.

25

The grammar of space in two new sign languages

Carol Padden, Irit Meir, Mark Aronoff and Wendy Sandler

Sign languages use space because they can.[1] In previous work on verb agreement in sign languages, we have discussed "the ability of a language produced in space to represent certain spatial and visual concepts iconically" (Aronoff, Meir & Sandler, 2005). We resolved in that work what we called "the paradox of sign language morphology." Although all sign languages that had been well studied up to that point showed a particular form of complex simultaneous non-affixal verb agreement that has no simple parallel in the morphology of spoken languages, they did not show much "run of the mill" sequential affixal morphology. Why should a language acquire complex morphology before it acquires simple morphology, why sign languages and why this particular sort of morphology? We argued that the agreement morphology of sign languages is based on an iconic use of space, which sign languages accommodate readily, and that this iconicity is what leads to the quick development of the system. Linear affixal morphology, by contrast, is much slower to emerge and much more varied, precisely because it is not iconic.

In this chapter, we will focus a much finer lens on the iconically based grammatical use of space in sign languages. Specifically, we will look at the actual production of verb forms where we expect space to be used. We will compare forms produced across two or three generations of signers of two young sign languages, Al-Sayyid Bedouin Sign Language (ABSL) and Israeli Sign Language (ISL). ABSL is a village sign language that has emerged in a socially insular community in the last seventy years and which we have been documenting for several years (Sandler *et al.* 2005; Aronoff *et al.* 2008). ISL has a similarly short history, but it is widely used by many Deaf people in Israel of different language backgrounds. To our own surprise, the use of space in the utterances we elicited diverges quite dramatically from what we had always taken to be the norm among sign languages, in ways that we will discuss in detail below. We also found interesting differences between the two languages and also generational differences within each language.

We learn from this study that not even a highly motivated grammatical system like agreement in sign languages emerges overnight, but rather that it may unfold gradually over generations and may take different courses of development. This is not to say that the use of space in ABSL and ISL is unsystematic. To the contrary, we find systematicity in the use of space at all stages, but not in the same way that we had previously found in certain other well-studied sign languages. We propose that early systematicity in a new sign language is powerfully influenced by the signer's own body. Specifically, the signer exploits the iconicity of his or her own body in the structure of verb forms in the new sign language. Both ISL and ABSL use this iconicity, but they differ from one another in how they balance the iconicity of the signer's body against other "competing iconicities," notably spatial directional movement, also emerging in the sign language. These differences may help us to understand how the emergence of a language in a village differs from the way a language develops in a less homogeneous community.

1   Background

Broadly, verb forms in many established sign languages divide between those that move in space in front of the signer's body (agreement and spatial verbs) and those that do not, but instead are anchored to the body (plain verbs). Plain verbs lack the complex morphosyntactic marking that characterizes verbs involving movement in space, though they do inflect for aspect. Semantically, plain verbs are typically cognitive, emotional or stative in nature. Verbs that exploit space are further divided between those that mark for person and number of the subject and object (agreement verbs), and those that do not (spatial verbs) (Liddell 1977, Padden, 1988). The distinction between the two verb classes is grounded in their semantics: agreement verbs denote transfer events, whereas spatial verbs denote the motion of an entity in space (Meir 2002). In a recent study, Thompson, Emmorey and Kluender (2006) used an eye-tracking device to locate signers' eye gaze during the production of verbs. They identified distinctive eye gaze behavior for each of the three classes of verbs, supporting the view that no two classes can be collapsed into one archetype.

Padden (1988) and Liddell (2003b) treat agreement and spatial verbs as distinct subtypes because of different grammatical behavior. For example, person marking on agreement verbs in American Sign Language (ASL) is not specifically indexical but "in the general direction of," resulting in more gross indexical differences between first person and second and third in agreement verbs. In comparison, spatial verbs have more fine or "gradient" locative distinctions in space. The two subtypes also differ with respect to number inflection. Multiple plural inflection adds a sweeping movement at the end point of agreement verbs, but spatial verbs cannot employ this form. Because spatial verbs do not mark person and number inflections, they are ostensibly more free to exploit space in front of the signer's body, having more distinctive locations and movements available to them.

The two types also differ in that there are apparently no "backwards" spatial verbs. In backwards agreement verbs like TAKE, COPY, CATCH, RECEIVE and STEAL, the direction of the verb is reversed: the subject is goal rather than source as is the case with regular agreement verbs, and consequently the verb's path moves from the object's referential location in space, or the R-locus, to that associated with the subject, the recipient of the transfer event (Padden 1988, Meir 2002). Because spatial verbs do not involve "transfer," they also do not have recipients. The spatial verb MOVE can have directional movement inward toward the body, but it does not change the thematic role of the subject from agent to recipient, only the referential interpretation of the source and goal. MOVE with an inward movement toward the signer's body can mean 'to move near my location (as opposed to another more distant location).'

Morphology aside, agreement and spatial verbs can look very much alike. Both agreement and spatial verbs have directional movement from source to goal.[2] In ASL as well as other sign languages, there are pairs of verbs such as GIVE (agreement) and CARRY-BY-HAND (spatial) that are formationally identical and become distinct only when inflections are added. In a psycholinguistic experiment, Cormier (1998) performed detailed measurements of signers' movements and hand placements when producing agreement and spatial verbs and found less distinctiveness in the referential interpretation of their initial and final points than their grammatical analysis would suggest.

Another grammatical system of sign languages that exploits space and iconicity is the system of classifier constructions. While these constructions share many characteristics with spatial verbs (Padden 1988, Sandler & Lillo-Martin 2006), they have subcategories and properties of their own, and we will not be dealing with them in any detail here.

2   Spatial morphology in new sign languages

The divide between spatial and non-spatial verbs, and more specifically the system of Plain-Agreement-Spatial verbs, is widely found in sign languages of the world (Sandler & Lillo-Martin 2006). The existence of such a system in sign languages outside Europe and North America, such as Japan (Fischer & Osugi 2000b) and Taiwan (Smith 1990), supports the idea that the system is general across sign languages, rather than being a typological feature of a set of historically related sign languages.

As mentioned earlier, we have argued that the tripartite system of verbs is pervasive in sign languages because it is motivated by their visuo-spatial properties (Aronoff, Meir & Sandler 2005). At the same time, we showed that sign language verb agreement is a constrained grammatical system, so the question of how it originates and develops is not a trivial one. In this chapter we examine to what extent the division into two types of verbs that exploit space can be found in a new sign language. Three hypotheses arise quite naturally:

1. All three classes are present from the beginning of any sign language.
2. Spatial verbs develop early because they are more iconic than agreement verbs and do not involve abstract grammatical categories like person, number and syntactic role.
3. Grammatical use of space in sign language develops gradually.

The strong crosslinguistic similarity of verb systems across sign languages, and the semantic basis of the tripartite classification, seems to lend support to Hypothesis 1. The different verb classes are related to fundamental semantic, and perhaps cognitive, categories, such as motion, location, transfer and states. Since these categories are expressed by all sign languages that have been linguistically analyzed to date, and since the iconicity of sign languages can reflect the relevant semantic distinctions among the classes, it seems reasonable to expect that any visual language will have all three classes from the initial stage. They come with the territory.

Other observations, however, suggest otherwise. While spatial verbs encode locations and motions, agreement verbs encode grammatical arguments and their syntactic roles. Agreement verbs inflect for person and number, while spatial verbs do not. These similarities and differences support Hypothesis 2, that spatial verbs develop early in the history of a language, before agreement verbs, since spatial verbs involve analogous spatial mapping, but no morphosyntactic categories. Spatial verbs can also be regarded as more iconic, and therefore can be expected to arise very early in the development of the language.

While Hypotheses 1 and 2 are mutually exclusive, the third hypothesis, that grammatical use of space in sign languages develops gradually, is compatible with Hypothesis 2. Both agreement verbs and spatial verbs may be absent in the early stages of a language, but when a language starts developing grammatical use of space, spatial verbs could still develop before agreement verbs. The third hypothesis relies on two assumptions. First, languages in the visual modality will use space to organize their grammars. This assumption is reasonable, since a variety of sign languages report spatial organization for verbs and for classifier constructions, as we have said. Second, studies of gestural use that is not systematized, such as home-sign (Goldin-Meadow 2003b), co-speech gesture (Iverson & Goldin-Meadow 1998,

McNeill 2000) and the signing of deaf children exposed only to Manually Coded English (S. Supalla 1991) all describe use of space to represent relations among participants in an event.

Hypothesis 3 rests on the assumption that linguistic systems take time to develop. This view is supported by our comparative studies of the morphology of ASL and ISL (Aronoff *et al.* 2003, Aronoff *et al.* 2004), and our work on ABSL (Aronoff *et al.* 2004, Meir *et al.* 2007). In the first set of studies, we examined three categories of classifiers commonly found in sign languages: size-and-shape specifiers, handling classifiers and what Schembri (2003) calls "entity classifiers." We found that while both ASL and ISL make full use of the size-and-shape specifiers and handling classifiers, the classifier system of ASL includes more abstract entity classifiers, such as UPRIGHT-OBJECT and VEHICLE, than ISL, which relies more on size-and-shape specifiers and handling classifiers. These entity classifiers are less iconic and tend to be determined more by semantic category (T. Supalla 1985) than by physical appearance of the object. We also found that ISL signers are more likely to use the whole body as a referent projection (Engberg-Pedersen 1993), in which they take on the characteristics of the participant in the event in contexts in which ASL signers will use lexically specified classifiers on the hands. In both cases, the older language is using more abstract and arbitrary forms, a tendency we attributed to language age (Aronoff *et al.* 2003). Another feature we attributed to language age was the relative dearth of sequential affixation, as we mentioned briefly at the beginning of this paper. Sequential affixation comes about through grammaticalization, often involving function words that become affixes on content words, such as the –ZERO negative suffix in ASL (Aronoff *et al.* 2005). Such processes are documented for ASL and ISL, but they are very sparse in both languages. As in spoken languages, grammaticalization takes time, and even ASL is young for such processes to arise. This view of things assigns a role to language age in the development of grammatical means.

What we did not expect when we first began to study ABSL is that even morphology that exploits visuo-spatial cognition takes time to develop, a finding we report in Aronoff *et al.* 2004 and recently in Meir *et al.* 2007. In the latter study, we find that ABSL signers strongly prefer the Z axis (in a straight center axis away from or toward the body) for verbs of transfer. In these forms, ABSL signers do not vary the axis of the directional movement. Specifically they do not produce a path movement that moves to either side or from side to side for third person subject or object as is often found in established sign languages such as ASL and other European and Asian sign languages. Instead, signers direct movement outward or inward from the signer's body. On the basis of these data, we concluded that ABSL does not have the category of person, at least not in its verb system. Grammatical subject, on the other hand, is clearly evident in ABSL, first with respect to word order (Sandler *et al.* 2005), which is consistently subject first, and second, in the strong preference for the body to represent properties of the grammatical subject (Meir *et al.* 2007).

In the present study, we conduct a much more fine-grained assessment of spatial morphology and evaluate in greater detail the idea that time is a factor as Hypothesis 3 predicts.

3   Two new sign languages

ABSL arose in a small, insular and endogamous community with a high incidence of nonsyndromic recessive deafness (Scott *et al.* 1995). The Al-Sayyid Bedouins settled about two hundred years ago in present-day southern Israel, and after five generations (about seventy-five years ago), four deaf siblings were born into the community. In the next two generations, deafness appeared in a number of other families resulting in what today is estimated at about 150 deaf adults, teenagers and children.[3] The data we describe in this paper are based on deaf signers of the second and third generation as all signers from the first generation are deceased. As described elsewhere (Kisch 2000, 2004), ABSL is used widely in the community by both deaf and hearing members and is seen as another language of the village in addition to spoken Arabic. The prevalent use of ABSL in the village has led to widespread exposure to the language by deaf signers and many of their hearing siblings and relatives from birth or a very young age.

The nine ABSL signers included in this study are divided into two groups: five are from the second generation, ranging in age from about 28 to 45 years, and four are of the third generation, ranging in age from about 16 to 25 years. As is common in the village, the signers in the second generation do not have deaf parents, but have deaf siblings and have had interaction in sign language from early childhood, with relatives such as aunts, uncles and cousins.[4] In the third generation group, three of the four younger adults have a deaf mother as well as deaf siblings, and the fourth has one deaf sibling. All of the younger adults interact with deaf signers of the second generation, including those in this study.

ISL is likewise a comparatively young sign language, which evolved along with the Israeli Deaf community about seventy-five years ago, but unlike ABSL, ISL developed in a pidgin-like situation. The members of the first generation of the Deaf community came from different backgrounds, both in terms of their country of origin, and in terms of their language. A small number of the first generation were born in Israel, and some of them went to the school for the deaf in Jerusalem that was founded in 1932. But the majority were immigrants who came to Israel from Europe (Germany, Austria, France, Hungary, Poland), and later on from North Africa and the Middle East. Some of these immigrants brought with them the sign language of their respective communities. Others had no signing, or used some kind of homesign.[5] Today, four generations of signers exist simultaneously within the Deaf community, which numbers about 10,000 members: the very first generation, which contributed to the earliest stages of the formation and development of the language, to the fourth generation, that has acquired and further developed the modern language as a full linguistic system (Meir & Sandler 2008).

For the purpose of this study, ISL signers were divided into three age groups.

1. *Older signers*: eleven signers aged 65 years and older.[6] People from this age group acquired ISL when it was still in its inception. They were not exposed to a unified linguistic system, but rather they created this system through interaction with each other. Some of the young members of this group (people in their late 60s and early 70s) were exposed to the linguistic system of ISL when they joined the community, but the language was very much in its initial stages, with great individual variation. Members of this group came from a variety of linguistic backgrounds. There are no ISL native signers among them, as the language was too young to acquire native users then, but seven of the eleven group 1 signers had deaf older siblings or other family members. Therefore, some have used a sign language or some sort of a signing system from an early age.

2. *Younger signers*: nine signers aged 45–65. Members of this group can be considered second generation signers, since they had linguistic models when they joined the Deaf community. Either they were born in Israel or immigrated to Israel at an early age and had at least several years of schooling with other deaf children. The daily interaction with other deaf children over a long period gave most members of this age group the opportunity to use signing from childhood. Three of the signers in this group have deaf siblings.[7]

3. *Youngest signers*: four signers aged 30–40. Members of this age group were exposed to an already unified linguistic system. All of them had formal schooling, where they learned Hebrew. Hence, all members of this group can be considered bilingual. Three of the four are native ISL signers, and the fourth signer was exposed to ISL from early childhood (age 2–3).

4   Method

As part of our study of language production in ABSL and ISL, we asked signers to view thirty short video clips. Each clip depicts a single action of either a human or inanimate entity by itself or involving another entity. To check for comprehension, each signer is paired with another signer who views the signed production and then is asked to identify one of three pictures best corresponding to the action just described. One of the three pictures correctly depicts the action and entities involved, the second has a different subject but the same action and the third shows the same subject performing a different action from that shown in the video. If the viewer chooses an incorrect picture, the signer is asked to repeat the description.

For our investigation into verb forms in new languages, we selected a subset of fourteen video clips which involved an action in a straight motion across space. Five of these were actions of transfer between two human entities: giving, showing, taking, feeding and throwing (Figure 25.1a). Nine other clips also depicted movement in a straight motion but were not acts of transfer between two people. One set involved either a human or inanimate object in motion: a ball rolling, a woman

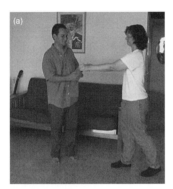

Figure 25.1 *a (top) Frame from video clip showing a woman giving a man a shirt. (b) (bottom left) Frame from video clip showing a ball rolling. (c) (right) Frame from video clip showing a woman rolling a ball.*

rolling a ball, a man putting a book on a shelf, a woman running and a woman walking (Figure 25.1b, Figure 25.1c). A second set involved humans with another object or human in motion: a girl pulling a man, a girl pulling a suitcase, a woman pushing a girl and a woman putting a box on a table. We excluded the remaining video clips from the present analysis as they do not involve straight motion in space, e.g., a girl crying, a girl running in a circle, a man washing a plate.

A total of 169 verb tokens were elicited from ABSL signers with the fourteen clips, 68 from the younger adults and 101 from the older adults. The total number of responses for ISL was 412: 212 from the older group (age 65–90 years old), 140 from the younger (age 45–65) and 60 from the youngest adults (age 30–40).

The signers' responses were transcribed in glosses with a notation identifying the direction of the verb sign movement, if any, representing the main action in the clip. If the movement of the verb sign was from the signer's body straight outward or inward, it was coded as along the sagittal or Z axis. If the movement was parallel to the front of the signer's body, from one side to the other, and not involving the center axis (toward or away from the body), it was coded as on the horizontal or X axis. This is the axis observed for the description of transitive actions involving two third person referents in many well-studied sign languages like ASL. If the movement was from the signer's body diagonally outward to the right or to the left, it was coded Z + X. In a few cases, the sign was produced with no horizontal path movement, and these were coded as None. Examples of movements along the three axes appear in Figure 25.2. Two transcribers independently reviewed the coding of the signers included in the study.

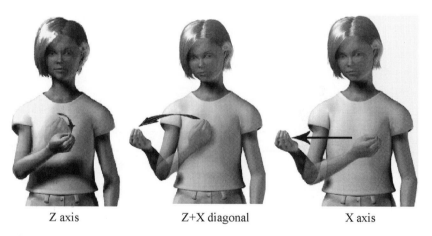

    Z axis   Z+X diagonal   X axis

Figure 25.2 *Types of path movement directions.*

5   **Results**

5.1   ABSL signers

What is striking about ABSL signers is that they strongly favor path movement along the Z axis, outward from the signer's body, for spatial as well as transfer verbs. This preference for the Z axis holds despite the fact that, in all video clips depicting actions, the individual or the object moves horizontally from one side of the screen to the other. But as Figure 25.3 below shows, when verbs are produced, ABSL signers strongly prefer to orient the movement relative to their own body. Of 169 verbs coded, 109 or 65 percent moved along the Z axis. The X axis accounted for 26 percent (44) and Z + X movement diagonally from the body to one side or the other was the smallest set, at 9 percent (16) of total forms produced by ABSL signers. In our work (Meir, Padden, Aronoff & Sandler 2007), we refer to this pattern as "body as subject," a concept we explain in more detail in section 6.

When we compare younger to older signers, we see a lessening in preference for the Z axis. Younger signers use the X axis 50 percent more often than older signers. But the overall pattern of younger and older signers remains similar: a preference for the Z axis over all other directions. Interestingly, signers overall do not appear to use the Z + X diagonal line. It is used less often than the two axes for both groups of signers.

When we examine older adult signers' verb productions by verb type, we find little difference between spatial verbs and verbs of transfer with respect to use of the X axis. Overall, older signers use the X axis and the Z + X line very seldom,

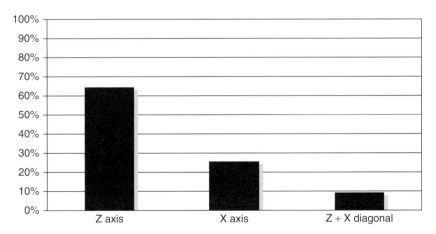

Figure 25.3 *Path movement direction in ABSL verbs as a percent of total number of verbs.*

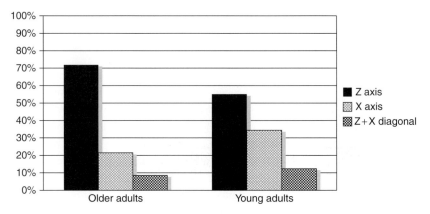

Figure 25.4 *Percent use of path movement direction in three ABSL age groups.*

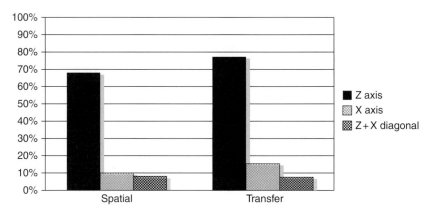

Figure 25.5 *Percent use of path movement direction by verb type in older adult ABSL signers.*

preferring the Z axis by over 68 percent for both types of verbs, as shown in Figure 25.5.

Among younger adults, we see more variation in verb forms with respect to axis, reflecting what would seem to be greater use of space (Figure 25.6). Though younger adults still prefer the Z axis for spatial verbs, they show use of the X axis to a greater degree than older adults, almost three times more. Furthermore, they show greater use of the X axis in spatial verbs than in transfer verbs, a pattern which favors Hypothesis 2, that spatial verbs develop earlier than verbs of transfer. The Z + X line is preferred for transfer verbs (19 percent) over spatial verbs

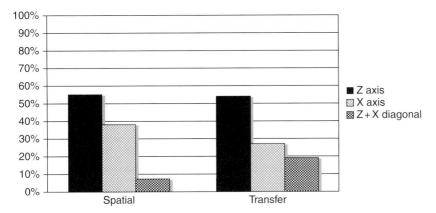

Figure 25.6 *Percent use of different axes by verb type in young adult ABSL signers.*

(7 percent), which could be seen as a means of continuing to use the body as subject regardless of person, but to use points in space to mark objects.

In ASL, it is common, but not obligatory, to establish third person referents in sentences with verbs of transfer. Typically such structures begin with establishing R-loci (such as by pointing to specific locations in space) of the subject and the object in third person space (on either side of the signer's body), followed by a path movement between these two R-loci. These are the clearest cases of agreement, where the loci of nominals is the same as that of the loci of agreement markers.

In sixty-five sentences with verbs of transfer, neither younger nor older ABSL signers established referential loci 71 percent of the time (n = 46). Of the remaining 29 percent of sentences where they did establish referential loci (n = 19), sixteen sentences contained what could be termed single (object only) or double (subject and object) agreement as the path movement in the verb form corresponded to the loci of referents. In eight cases, the loci of the referents were established along the Z axis, as was the verb form itself. In the cases with transitive actions involving two referents, the subject R-locus was located near the signer's body, and the object R-locus was placed further out along the same axis. If this small number of cases can be interpreted as "emergent agreement," It would seem that ABSL signers resolve the potential conflict between third person referents and the preferred body-out axis of verb movement by establishing referential loci for third person subject and object along the Z axis.

The choice of either Z or X axis for movement in ABSL verbs reveals interesting differences across age groups with respect to whether the event involved an animate subject or not. Two video clips differed in terms of whether the action was instigated by a human or involved action by an inanimate entity alone: a woman rolling a ball, or a ball rolling. In contrast to the older signers who used the Z axis to depict both types of rolling, two of the younger signers produced 'a ball rolling' along the X or Z + X diagonal, suggesting a human-inanimate subject difference. The body remains subject in 'a woman rolling a ball,' but younger signers can sign 'a ball rolling' along the X axis, in effect, moving off the body, in order to show motion of inanimate entities with an unknown cause.

Older signers, however, use another means to show the human–inanimate subject distinction: handshape. For 'a woman rolling a ball,' they used a cupped hand to show a human holding a ball, then releasing it. For the inanimate version, all of the older signers used instead a tracing handshape, either with an index finger or a flat palm rotated to the side, indicating the direction in which the ball rolled. This suggests that ABSL signers of different age groups recognize animacy differences but encode them in different ways. Younger signers build on the handshape distinction between human–inanimate subjects but also add the spatial distinction described above.

Taken together, we see a noticeable shift in younger signers' choices of axis with respect to the forms of verbs involving directional movement. Where older signers strongly favor the Z axis, younger signers show more flexibility and a tendency to use the signing space broadly. Disengaging from the body and using verb forms that move from side point to side point is somewhat more evident in spatial verbs than in verbs of transfer. Still, both younger and older signers favor the Z axis, the latter group by twice as much.

5.2   ISL signers

5.2.1   *Use of space*
As with ABSL signers, the overall preference of ISL signers is to use the Z axis when depicting straight path motion and transfer events. The Z axis was used in 54 percent of the responses, while the X (horizontal) axis was used in only 28 percent of the responses. The diagonal line was used in 14 percent of the responses, and in 4 percent no line was used at all. These results are presented in Figure 25.7.

However, when comparing the use of the different axes across the three groups of signers, we find interesting differences between them (Figure 25.8). Let us compare the two older groups first. These two groups look very much alike in terms of the use of the Z and the X axes (and very similar to ABSL signers): the Z axis is used in almost 60 percent of the responses, and the X axis in fewer than 30 percent of the responses. That is, the Z axis is used twice as much as the X axis in both groups. But a main difference between these groups is in the use of the diagonal: the older group

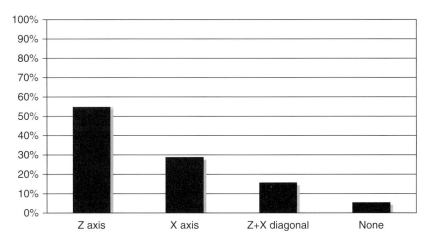

Figure 25.7 *Path movement direction in ISL verbs as a percent of total number of verbs.*

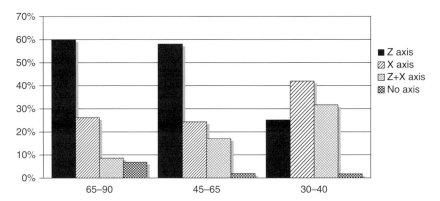

Figure 25.8 *Percent use of path movement direction in three ISL age groups.*

(age 65–90) uses it in only 8 percent of the responses, while it appears in 16 percent of the younger (age 45–65) group's responses. Additionally, the younger group hardly ever uses verb forms with no directional movement at all, while the older signers had such forms in 6 percent of their responses. The 45- to 65-year-old subjects, then, show a slightly more varied use of space than the signers of the oldest group, but the basic pattern of use of axes is very similar.

The youngest ISL signers, 30–40 years old, show a very different pattern of axis use: the Z axis is the least used one (25 percent), the X axis is used extensively (42 percent), and the Z + X diagonal also becomes quite prevalent (32 percent).

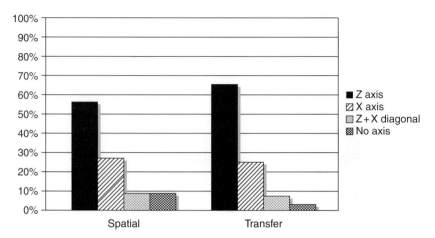

Figure 25.9 *ISL older signers' percent use of path movement direction by verb type.*

When looking at the use of axes in different types of verbs – spatial vs. transfer – we again find that the two older groups exhibit a very similar pattern, while the youngest group differs markedly. In the older and younger groups (Figures 25.9 and 25.10 respectively), there is a slight preference for using the Z axis in transfer verbs over spatial verbs, and a slight dispreference for using the X axis in transfer verbs compared to spatial verbs. The main difference between the two groups is that in the younger group, verbs of transfer employ the diagonal axis three times as much as in older (21% vs. 7% respectively). The diagonal is used more than the X axis in the younger group's verbs of transfer.

As shown in Figure 25.11, the youngest group presents a very different pattern of axis use: in spatial verbs, all three lines are used almost to the same extent. In transfer verbs, in contrast, there is a strong preference for the X axis: it is used in 50 percent of the responses. The diagonal is used in 35 percent of the responses, and the Z axis only in 15 percent. (One form, which constitutes 5% of the responses, was signed with an upward movement and was coded as having no directed path movement.) This group differs, then, from the two older groups in two respects: first, the Z axis is not the most preferred axis. Second, there is a noteworthy difference in the use of the axes between the two verb types (verbs of transfer and spatial verbs) in the youngest group, but not in the two older groups.

5.2.2   *Agreement inflection*

Since the youngest group shows a marked distinction between spatial verbs and transfer verbs, the question of whether ISL has developed verb agreement by its

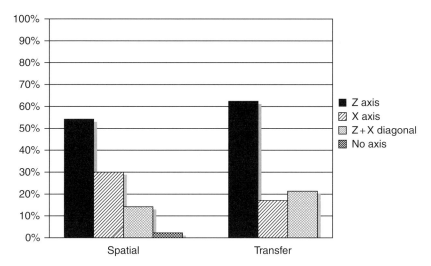

Figure 25.10 *ISL younger signers' percent use of path movement direction by verb type.*

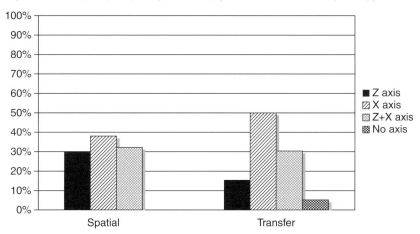

Figure 25.11 *ISL youngest signers' percent use of path movement direction by verb type.*

third generation naturally arises. Five of the clips that involve a directed movement denote an event of transfer. The responses for these clips were analyzed according to whether the verb forms indicate agreement with one argument, agreement with two arguments or no agreement at all. A verb was coded as agreeing if a referential locus was set in the signing space, and the path of the verb moved with respect to that locus. The results are summarized in Figure 25.12.

Once again, we find that the youngest group shows a very different pattern from those of the two older groups. In the youngest group, almost half of the responses

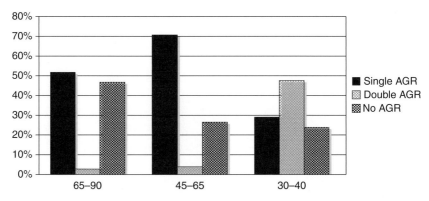

Figure 25.12 *Percent use of verb agreement type in three ISL age groups.*

had double agreement forms. In these sentences, the two third person referents were set up at locations in space, and the verb forms moved between these two points. Additionally, 24 percent of the responses marked agreement with one argument. In other words, almost 75 percent of the verb forms produced by signers in this group mark agreement. In the two older groups, more than half of the forms do not inflect at all, and there are very few forms that mark double agreement (two tokens in each group). Interestingly, older signers used more single agreement forms than the younger signers. This is somewhat unexpected, since we hypothesized that developing verb agreement in a language takes time, and a reasonable prediction is that younger generations produce more forms inflected for agreement and not fewer. A closer inspection of the single agreement forms produced by the older signers reveals that most of these forms (34 out of 42 forms) were produced by three signers. The other eight forms were produced by the eight remaining signers. The three signers who produced these forms used a special technique for encoding argument structure in some of the clips. They overtly identified themselves with the subject argument of the event, then they localized the recipient argument right in front of them, sometimes explicitly identifying that referent with the addressee, and then moved the verb path from their own body to that second person location. In other words, instead of establishing abstract referential loci in space, they use their own body and that of the addressee as loci for the participants in the event to be described.

For example, in a response to a clip showing a man throwing a ball to a girl, one signer signed: I MAN I, YOU FEMALE CHILD$_2$, I THROW. Interestingly, this technique was used almost exclusively by these three signers. Two other ISL signers

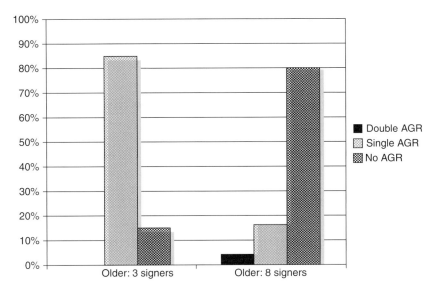

Figure 25.13 *Variation in use of verb agreement among ISL older signers.*

(one from the older group, one from the younger group) identified themselves with the subject but did not localize the other argument in space, and therefore these forms were not counted as agreement forms. This strategy was never used by any ABSL signer. Such verb forms do inflect for agreement, according to our definition, but look more like agreement forms with first and second person rather than with two third person referents. If the responses to the transfer clips of these signers are not included in the count, the picture is quite different: there are eight single argument agreement forms (16 percent), two double agreement forms (4 percent) and forty non-agreeing forms (80 percent). These results are presented in Figure 25.13.

As the results show, the use of space in ISL, both for verb agreement and for spatial verbs, does not emerge spontaneously from very early stages of the language but rather takes time to develop. Verb forms inflected for both subject and object are very rare in the two older groups. Verb forms that inflect for one argument are more common, but still, most of the verbs denoting transfer are not inflected. Spatial verbs also show a marked preference for using the Z axis. Despite the fact that the signing space is three-dimensional, and despite the iconicity of the path movement in such verbs, signers show preference for using the less iconic form along the center-out/in axis, rather than selecting points in space and exploiting the three dimensionality available to them.

The youngest signers show a very different pattern for these parameters. These signers do not confine themselves to one axis but rather make use of a much richer inventory of lines in the signing space. They use forms inflected for agreement in almost 75 percent of the transfer verb forms. And they favor double agreement forms, forms which are almost entirely missing in the two older groups.

These results show that it takes at least two to three generations for a sign language to develop a productive and consistent verb agreement system. The developmental process, though, is not linear; there is a very minor difference between the first two groups, and then a great leap forward in the youngest group. It might be that it takes time for a language to converge on one particular mechanism, but once such a mechanism is singled out, it spreads quickly in the community.

But the fact that even the youngest signers use double agreement, single agreement and no agreement forms in verbs of transfer indicates that in ISL, at least, marking of verbs for agreement is less robust than agreement systems usually found in spoken languages. In spoken languages, if a language has verb agreement, then marking these forms for agreement is obligatory; the use of the agreement morpheme is not optional. An uninflected form in a context that requires an inflected form is ungrammatical. In ISL, in contrast, verbs of transfer can be inflected for agreement, but a non-inflected form is also possible, and both single agreement and double agreement forms are acceptable.

6   Discussion

The results obtained from signers of the two new sign languages show that the body is a central reference point for all types of verbs. Signers prefer to move the path movement component of verbs from or toward the body, rather than from one side of the signing space to the other, whether they describe motion in space or a transfer event. From this perspective, all verb types behave like plain verbs since they do not vary according to person of the subject or object. We developed elsewhere (Meir *et al.* 2007) the notion of "body as subject," as a basic lexicalization pattern in sign language plain verbs.

We argue that in iconic or partially iconic verbs articulated on the body, the so called "body-anchored verbs," the signer's body is not merely a formal location for the articulation of signs, but rather is associated with a particular meaning or a particular function: the body represents the subject argument. Take, for example, verbs such as EAT or DRINK. In various sign languages, the location of these signs is the mouth of the signer. This is no accident, though: the mouth, constituting one of the formational components of the sign, also represents one particular argument in the event, the agent. Other plain verbs show the same pattern. Verbs of mental activities, such as THINK, KNOW, REMEMBER, LEARN, are often signed on the temple or the forehead, which represents the site of the mental activity of the experiencer argument. Verbs of saying, e.g., SAY, ASK, ANSWER, TELL, EXPLAIN, are signed near the mouth, which corresponds to the mouth of the agent argument. Many psych verbs, such as HAPPY, LOVE, SUFFER, UPSET, are signed on the chest, which corresponds to the metaphorical location of emotions of the experiencer or patient argument.

As the above list shows, the argument represented by the body and corresponding to specific features of the body can be associated with a variety of thematic roles: agent, patient, experiencer, recipient. However, the choice of the particular argument to be represented by the signer's body is not random. In case of a one-place predicate, the body naturally is associated with the sole argument of the predicate, the subject. In case of transitive events, we find that the argument associated with body features is the highest ranking argument: the agent in < agent, patient > verbs (e.g., EAT, DRINK, LOOK) or < agent, patient, recipient > verbs (such as ASK, INFORM, EXPLAIN), and the experiencer or perceiver in < experiencer, theme > verbs (e.g., SEE, HEAR, LOVE). According to general principles of mapping between thematic structure and syntactic structure (Fillmore 1968, Grimshaw 1990, Jackendoff 1990, Falk 2006), the argument associated with the highest ranking thematic role is the subject argument. The correct generalization, then, is that the body is associated with the subject argument of the verb rather than with a particular thematic role. An implication of our analysis is that the basic lexicalization pattern when representing a state of affairs in sign languages is body as subject.

It is useful to think about the development of verb systems in signed languages in terms of competing iconicities. The two iconicities that compete in sign language verb systems are that of the body as animate subject and that of the spatial location of the entities involved in a scene. Contrary to our previous expectations (Aronoff *et al.* 2005) that verb agreement emerges quickly in sign languages, we find here that the iconicity of the body as subject appears first and full-blown in the history of the languages under investigation, while the iconicity of spatial location required for verb agreement unfolds much more gradually.[7]

We have discussed the iconicity of the body as subject at some length above and more extensively in Meir *et al.* (2007). For the moment, what the reader must keep in mind about this iconicity is that it identifies one pole of the Z axis (the speaker's body) with the grammatical subject of a sentence. Discussion of the iconicity of space has a much longer history in sign language linguistics, but we would like to conceptualize it in a somewhat new way: in terms of the classic dramatic notion of scene, defined as "a division in a classical Roman or French drama in which there is no change of persons."[8] A scene in these terms consists of actors on a stage participating in a sequence of actions. The difference between language and drama is that the primary actors in a language scene are the signer/speaker and the addressee. These two have fixed places (or loci) in any scene: the speaker's place is his or her own body, while the addressee's place is directly opposite the signer/speaker's body. The signer/speaker (first person) and addressee (second person) thus occupy the poles of the Z axis, while the other actors in the scene (third persons) are placed in the two-dimensional space defined by the Z and X axes together. What is grammaticalized in the iconicity of two-dimensional space in sign languages is thus not just reference (in the form of referential loci) but just as importantly, grammatical person.

This depiction of the iconicity of space reveals immediately what the competition is between the two iconicities: both use the body pole of the Z axis, but to represent distinct grammatical notions: subject and first person. Thus, the iconicity of space can function grammatically with all persons only at the expense of the iconicity of the body as subject, by moving the subject off the body.

The iconic use of the body as subject emerges very early in the life of a sign language and remains a significant factor in the signing of plain verbs (Meir *et al.* 2007). For spatial and transfer verbs, this iconicity pervades the responses of all the ABSL signers in our study as well as in those of the two older groups of ISL signers (Figures 25.3, 25.4, 25.7 and 25.8). These four (out of five) groups show a strong preference for using the Z axis (which originates at the body) in representing all spatial and transfer actions, even in representing movement along the horizontal X axis (such as a ball rolling from one side of the screen to the other).

By contrast, the iconic use of space to represent location and movement appears to emerge much more slowly, and it emerges first in cases where the competition from the body is not strong. We thus see the very beginnings of space being used by younger ABSL signers, not for transfer verbs but only to represent the spatial movement of inanimate entities and then only when the movement involves no human intervention (a ball rolling vs. a woman rolling a ball). Why not in the latter cases? Because in WOMAN BALL ROLL there is a competition between using the body to represent the animate subject (WOMAN) and using space to locate the actual position of this same animate subject along the horizontal X axis. The WOMAN argument cannot be represented simultaneously on the body and at the locus of the referent on the X plane. In the case of BALL ROLL, because the subject is not animate, the iconicity of the body as subject is not as powerful, permitting space to win out, so that the locus of the ball can lie on the X axis.

Thus, between the older and younger ABSL signers, verb signs become some-what displaced from the body: a progression from no use of space in verb forms to a limited use of space, mostly for spatial verbs. Similarly, the younger group of ISL signers exploits the horizontal X axis more than the older group, specifically in their use of the Z + X diagonal, which appears in twice as many responses for the younger group, though still in a limited fashion.

The youngest group of ISL signers is very different from all other groups. This is the first group to use both the Z and the X axis fully, showing verb agreement in more than 70 percent of their responses, in contrast to 25 percent for the middle group and 20 percent for the older group. For the youngest group only, the subject has moved off the body, thus allowing for the beginnings of a full-blown agreement system of the sort that we are used to in older and more established sign languages.

The results obtained from the responses to the clips indicate that older signers of both languages hardly use space at the sentence level, when describing a single event. But it is important to point out that they *do* use space at the discourse level. A common use of space in both languages is for contrast and comparison between two discourse topics, for example, when talking about events that happened in another town and events that took place at home; or when talking about two people, or two groups of people. ABSL signers often use space to refer to specific people; they direct pointing signs to the real-world location of the house of a particular person, and this location serves to identify that person. In addition, signers of both languages often also localize referents, by signing verbs such as SIT or STAND in a specific locus in space. However, they often do not incorporate these locations in the forms of the verbs of transfer. For example, when describing a video clip showing a woman giving a shirt to a man, some signers (in both languages) localize the man as standing on one side and the woman as standing on the opposite side; but the verb's path movement is not from one locus to the other, but rather on the Z axis, from the signer's body outward.[9] Such construc-tions show that, although the language might utilize space for various purposes from early on, the incorporation of space into the grammar takes time.

7   Conclusion

To a great extent, language is determined by our physiology: phonological features are determined by our articulatory system (features become grammaticalized within a phonetic space) and the way we conceptualize events is determined by our body. The body is an important resource that new languages can rely on. But they may use it in different ways (for example, ABSL does not seem to have role shift, but ISL does). Leaving the body and developing grammatical categories in the verb system takes time. The fact that, even after a language has developed such a system (ISL), the signer can still fall back on the body point of view highlights the centrality of the body in sign language linguistic systems, and maybe in other cognitive systems as well. This study finds compelling evidence for a diachronic trend from lack of agreement toward a full agreement system such as that described for ASL and other sign languages. However, we do not imply that all sign languages will ultimately pattern like ASL. Specifically, we do not rule out either the possibility that a sign language may not develop this particular system or the possibility that the ASL system is not as regular and pervasive as is commonly assumed.

Studying new sign languages provides novel evidence for a richer view of grammar than can be obtained from the investigation of spoken languages alone, as the latter are all old or descended from old languages. The gradual emergence of a verb agreement system, one that is a robust phenomenon among the youngest group of ISL signers studied here but yet still not fully consistent among them, requires us to understand language fundamentally as a social system, characterized by the establishment and spread of a linguistic convention through interaction, both inter- and intra-generational, within a community.

NOTES

1 Introduction

In addition to the contributors and the staff of Cambridge University Press, I would also like to thank Arnold Davidson, Petra Eccarius, Donovan Grose, Ashley Jung, Marie Nadolske and Robin Shay for their comments on earlier drafts of this chapter. I would also like to thank Katie Kupski for her work in preparing the bibliography of this book.

1. See Lee 2004 for British Sign Language and Lane 1984 and Lane, Hoffmeister and Bahan 1996 for French and American Sign Languages.
2. Sign languages do not share the same genealogy, so the term "family" is used loosely, due to their shared linguistic structures that identify them as a group.
3. For a more in-depth discussion of the use of iconicity in the construction of sign language grammars, see Brennan 1991, 2005; Russo 2005; Taub 2001; Liddell 2003b and Brentari in press.
4. Throughout this volume the term "Deaf" is used to mean culturally Deaf (Padden 1980), and "deaf" is used to mean biologically deaf. The authors of each chapter have made a conscious decision about which term to employ. Some authors, such as Wojda, have expressed ambivalence about using either of these terms, since they imply an awareness of these categories, an awareness that may not exist in their particular environment.
5. The characteristics of sign language transmission discussed here are true for "deaf community" sign languages. There is another type of sign language, "village sign languages," in which the processes that shape Deaf identity are less understood. In village sign languages, there is a higher incidence of deafness and transmission takes place primarily in the family or closed village community (see Meir *et al.*, in press).
6. In the minimal space here, I cannot discuss the wider meaning of Deaf identity or Deaf culture. I refer the reader to Ladd 2003, which is an excellent introduction to a post-colonial, post-structural approach to talking about "Deaf culture" and "Deaf community," to Padden and Humphries 1988, 2005 and to Lane, Hoffmeister and Bahan 1996 for further discussion of these issues. See Mitchell *et al.* 2006 for complications in calculating the number of "signing home environments."
7. I wish to thank Arnold Davidson for translating this quote into English from the French.
8. These internal and external factors are very similar to those described in the UNESCO 2003 document, entitled *Language Vitality and Endangerment*, discussed at length in Grenoble and Whaley 2008.
9. The chapters by Boyes Braem and Rathmann and Quer and colleagues describe other areas of Europe with complex but favorable environments for sign language transmission. The constellation of factors in these cases is varied and unique, and space prevents further elaboration on them here.

10. A work of theatre circulated about the founding of the Paris Deaf school, and Abbé Charles-Michel de l'Épée and subsequent superintendents traveled widely with students demonstrating the success of the method of teaching deaf children using signs.
11. In many countries, there has been a natural sign language which has evolved within the Deaf community (in this case Swedish Sign Language) and also a form of artificial, manually coded spoken language (in this case Signed Swedish), where the grammar of the spoken language is primary, and signs are superimposed on this spoken language grammar. Throughout this volume, "Signed 'x'" refers to the hybrid form, while "'x' Sign Language" refers to the natural language of a Deaf community.
12. Constitution of Uganda (Ugandan Government 1995:8).
13. See the list of notational conventions for representing sign language glosses at the front of this volume.
14. The term "classifier construction" may call to the mind of some readers a set of spoken language structures, which actually share few properties with this set of forms in sign languages. Some researchers refer to these forms as "polycomponential" forms, in order to keep the spoken and signed forms distinct from one another.
15. See Brentari 2002 and Meier 2002 for in-depth discussions of this issue.

2 Transmission of sign languages in Northern Europe

We would like to thank the following persons, who contributed invaluable information and very helpful comments concerning the transmission of sign languages in their countries. For Switzerland: Benno Caramore, Martin Chapuis, Fanny Conod, Catherine Delétra, Anne-Claude Prélaz Girod, Alain Huber, Michael Laubacher, Tiziana Rimoldi and Donald Shelton; for the Netherlands: Trude Schermer, Beppie van den Bogaerde and Onno Crasborn; for Germany: Jochen Muhs, Christian Peters and Helmut Vogel. And finally, our thanks to Elisabeth Engberg-Pedersen and François Grosjean for their helpful comments and criticism on the entire chapter.

1. Swiss Parliament Press Release, May 27, 1994; Postulate WBK-NR 94.3227.
2. In the Suisse romande: Yverdon, Moudon and Geneva. In German Switzerland: Bern, Zurich, Hohenrain-Lucerne, Zofingen, Riehen-Basel and Aarau.
3. Gehörlosen und Sprachheilschule Riehen (www.gsr.ch). Zentrum für Gehör und Sprache Zürich, ZGSZ (www.zgsz.ch).
4. Sekundarschule für Gehörlose, Zurich (www.sek-gehoerlose.ch).
5. Berufsschule für Hörgeschädigte, Zurich (www.bsfh.ch).
6. Ausbildung für Gebärdensprachausbilder, AGSA, at the Hochschule für Heilpädagogik, Zürich (www.hfh.ch/content-n98-sD.html).
7. The Swiss National Deaf Association: Schweizerische Gehörlosenbund – Fédération Suisse des Sourds – Federazione Svizzera dei Sordi (www.sgb-fss.ch).
8. GS-Media (www.gs-media.ch) and SGB-FSS Schweizerischer www.sgb-fss.ch/product/.
9. Lautsprachlich Kommunizierende Hörgeschädigte Schweiz (LKH) and l'Association Suisse pour le langage parlé complété (ALPC).
10. The interpreter training program for LSF-SR is currently carried out in cooperation with the School of Translation and Interpreting of the University of Geneva (www.aiic.net/ViewPage.cfm/page1522.htm). The interpreter training program for DSGS is currently at the University of Applied Sciences, HfH, in Zurich (Hochschule für Heilpädagogik (HfH) Interpreter Training Program (www.hfh.ch/content-n34-sD.html).
11. Information on the DSGS web lexicon project can be found at www.hfh.ch/projekte-n70-sD.html. The LSF-SR health explanations at www.pisourd.ch and the SignWriting for both languages at www.signbank.org/signpuddle.

12. Research on Swiss sign languages includes Boyes Braem 1990b [1995], 1996, 1999, 2001a and 2001b, 2003–2005, Boyes Braem *et al.* 1990; research comparing Swiss sign languages and gesture systems includes Boyes Braem, Pizzuto and Votterra 2002.
13. Caramore 1988, Stocker 2002, Niederberger 2004.
14. The different language versions of "The right of the deaf child to grow up bilingual" as well as his many other publications on sign language can be found on the website www. francoisgrosjean.ch.
15. Owing to the lack of systematic sociolinguistic research, it is a little premature to estimate the number of regional dialects. For the purpose of this chapter, it suggests that there are six regional sign dialects in Germany: Bavarian, the West (including Cologne), the North (including Hamburg), Berlin and the East.
16. For further information on the history of deaf education in Germany, please see the following references, among others: List 1993; Fischer and Vollhaber 1996; Beecken *et al.* 1999; Vogel 1999, 2002a, 2002b; Wolff 2000a, 2000b, 2000c, 2008; and Feige *et al.* 2001.
17. For detailed information on Fürstenberg, see Muhs 1994 and on Pacher, see Fischer *et al.* 1995. For further resources on Deaf history in the eighteenth and nineteenth centuries, consult Feige 2006 and the website managed by *Kultur und Geschichte Gehoerloser e. V.*, KUGG (Deaf Culture and History Association) www.kugg.de.
18. See eight resolutions in the complete version at www.milan1880.com/milan1880congress/eightresolutions.html.
19. See further information at www.sign-lang.uni-hamburg.de/Projekte/index.html.
20. See www.uni-frankfurt.de/fb/fb10/KogLi/Lehrstuhl_Leuninger/Deutsche_Gebaerdensprache/index.html.
21. See further information at http://desire.isk.rwth-aachen.de/deutsch/CD_Demo_aktuell/index.html.
22. See further information on interpreting training programs at: www.hs-magdeburg.de/fachbereiche/f-sgw/studium/Gebaerden/; www.fh-zwickau.de/pflege/html/gebarden sprachdolmetschen.html; www.reha.hu-berlin.de/dolmet/.
23. See further information at www.gehoerlosen-kulturtage.de.
24. Two examples are the Berliner Gebaerdensprachfestival (Berlin Sign Language Festival) and DEGETH (Deaf Theater Festival). See further information at www.glvmu.de/degeth/ and http://www.goldene-hand.de/.
25. These groups include but are not limited to GGKG (Society of Sign Language and Communication of the Deaf), KUGG (Culture and History of the Deaf), DGJ (German Deaf Youth), IGJAD (Interest Group of Deaf Jewish Descendants in Germany), DKT (German Culture Society of Partially-Sighted Deaf and Deaf-Blind), among others.
26. See www.wdr.de/themen/homepages/webtv.jhtml?projekt = -2.
27. See two examples: www.dgs-filme.de/GWHomepage/referenzen.htm and www. spectrum11.de/, www.dgs-im-job.de/index_dgs.htm.
28. These laws include but are not limited to the following: the Federal Disability Equality Law / *Behindertengleichstellungsgesetz* §6 BGG (http://bundesrecht.juris.de/bgg/__9. html); disability equality laws in various states (www.netzwerk-artikel-3.de/wsite/laand. php), the Sozialgesetzbuch §17 Abs. 2 SGB (http://bundesrecht.juris.de/sgb_1/__17.html) and the Federal Code of Social Law, §19 Abs.1 SGB X (http://bundesrecht.juris.de/sgb_10/__19.html).
29. Available at http://ec.europa.eu/education/policies/lang/languages/langmin/files/charter_en.pdf.
30. See www.policy.hu/flora/ressign2.htm.

31. See http://gehoerlosenbund.de/download/pdf/CI-Flyer.RZ.pdf, http://gehoerlosenbund.de/download/pdf/Broschuere_Hoerbehinderte_Kinder.pdf, www.kestner.de/n/elternhilfe.
32. See http://stopeugenics.org/about-us/.
33. See www.ynetnews.com/articles/0,7340,L-3590158,00.html.
34. These individuals are most notably Jochen Muhs, Helmut Vogel and Mark Zaurov, and the Deaf associations KUGG and IGJAD[0])
35. Dutch Sign Center (Nederlands Gebarencentrum, www.gebarencentrum.nl).
36. Instituut voor Gebaren, Taal & Dovenstudies, Utrecht.
37. Slobin (2006) further argues that NGT, like all sign languages, is typologically a "head-marking" type of language, with the consequence that sign language researchers should be wary of linguistic notions such as "subject," "agreement" and "*pro*-drop" which are more appropriate to "dependent-marked" languages.
38. Dutch websites with information on cochlear implantation include one for adults (www.nvvs.nl) and a general forum that is also for children (www.cochlearimplants.yourbb.nl).
39. Information on the three main organizations for young children with an auditory or communicative problem can be found at www.auris.nl, www.kegg.nl and www.viataal.nl.
40. The traditional schools are in Zoetermeer (Effatha, www.effatha.nl), Rotterdam (now Polano, www.polanoschool.nl), Amsterdam (now fused with Effatha Guyot), Groningen (Guyot) and St. Michielsgestel (Viataal).
41. For further information on these institutes, see the Effatha Guyot Groep (www.kegg.nl) and Viataal (www.ivd.nl).
42. For more information on signed supported Dutch courses, see www.nvvs.nl.
43. See www.handtheater.nl. and also Julien 1991.
44. See www.deafinthepicture.nl/.
45. Information available at www.gebarencentrum.nl/publicaties.asp.
46. The interpreters' professional organization, Nederlandse Beroepsvereniging Tolken Gebarentaal, NBTB (www.nbtg.nl) and the registry (www.stichtingrtg.nl).
47. See www.let.ru.nl/sign-lang/.
48. The KOMVA project (1982–1990), which was followed by the Standardization of Basic Lexicon (STABOL) project (1999–2002). See Stroomberger and Schermer 1988, KOMVA, Schermer, Harder and Bos 1988, Schermer 2003.
49. Web-based NGT lexicons: www.gebarencentrum.nl/gebarendatabank, www.woordenboekgebaren.nl and www.kegg.nl/egg_gebaren.php.
50. Name signs: Nyst and Baker 2003; databases and variation: Schermer and Harder 1985, Schermer, Brien and Brennan 2001, Schermer 2004.
51. Brugman, Crasborn and Russel 2004, Crasborn *et al.* 2006.
52. Crasborn and van der Kooij 2001.
53. Discourse project at Radboud University Nijmegen: www.let.un.nl/sign-lang/; adult sign discourse: Schermer 1985.
54. Phonology studies: Harder and Schermer 1986, Baker and Hulst 1996, Crasborn 2001, Kooij 2002, Crasborn and van der Kooij 2003, Vermeerbergen, Leeson and Crasborn 2007.
55. Morphological and syntax studies: Verbs (Bos 1993, 1994), Classifiers (Slobin *et al.* 2003, Zwitserlood 2003), Pronouns, Person and location marking (Bos 1990, 1995; Kooij 2002), Nonmanuals (Coerts 1992), Mouthings (Schermer 1990, 2001), Time lines (Schermer & Koolhof 1990), Syntax (Coerts 1994, Slobin & Hoiting 1994, Thrift 2003, Van Gijn 2004), Interrogatives and negations (Coerts 1990), Pluralization (Zwitserlood & Nijhof 1999, Harder 2003), Syntactic Dependency (Van Gijn & Baker 2003), General introductions to NGT grammar (Baker, van den Bogaerde & Woll 2005).
56. Prosody: van der Kooij, Crasborn and Emmerik 2006.

57. Acquisition: Knoors 1992, 1994; Van den Bogaerde & Mills 1994a; Van den Bogaerde, Knoors & Verrips 1994b; Hoiting and Slobin 1998; Coerts 2000; Van den Bogaerde 2000; Fortgens 2003; Van den Bogaerde and Baker 2005.
58. Sign Language Assessment: Jansma, Knoors and Baker 1997.
59. Research on interpreting: Crasborn and De Wit 2005, Van Gils 2007, as well as an ongoing study of the efficacy of interpretation by Van Dyk and Hermans at Radboud University Nijmegen.
60. A good overview of the "Renaissance" of sign languages in Europe in the 1990s can be found in the Dänzer Hemmi and de Marco (1997) video.

3 Transmission of sign languages in Latin America

There are various individuals who have provided invaluable information for this chapter, and we would like to acknowledge their contributions. Among them are: Carmen Aguilar, Julio Roberto Bámaca, Boris Fridman Mintz, Barbara Gerner de García, Antoinette Hawayek, Ronice Múller de Quadros, Alejandro Oviedo, Yolanda Pérez, Paulina Ramirez, Benigno Ruiz, Fabiola Ruiz Bedolla and Anne Senghas.

1. Maya village sign languages are also attested in Mexico (e.g., Shuman 1980, Johnson 1991). Although many are undescribed, various indigenous sign languages occur through-out Latin America (e.g., the sign language of the Urubu-Kaapor Indians in Brazil [Brito 1984] and Providence Island sign language off the coast of Colombia [Washabaugh 1979, Woodward 1979]). These languages may interact with national sign languages like LSM. However, to date this topic has not been examined and though intriguing is beyond the scope of this chapter.
2. This includes Romance-speaking nations, and former Dutch, French and British colonies.
3. As of 2008 they are Instituto Pedagógico para Problemas del Lenguaje, Centro Clotet and Grupo Tessera. Information about various services in Mexico for families with deaf children is available on this site: www.emexico.gob.mx/work/resources/LocalContent/88 92/4/Audicion.pdf.
4. As recently as the late 1990s, INCH personnel referred to the deaf preschoolers whom Ramsey was teaching as her patients.
5. Ironically, however, in April 2005, LSM received recognition in federal law as one of Mexico's national languages, a status which would permit its use in education.
6. One ENS signer moved to the United States in 1956. His hearing children sign ASL since they were raised in the United States without contact with LSM.
7. Early reports from SIL linguists suggested that within Mexico City LSM variation was extreme, to the degree that the language used in the Iztapalapa neighborhood was a separate language. Later reports correct this claim. There is no current extant linguistic evidence that there is a separate Iztapalapa sign language.

4 Transmission of sign languages in the Nordic countries

1. Deaf people in the Nordic countries do not distinguish audiological deafness from cultural deafness in writing. For this reason, and because we do not always find it possible to make the distinction, we use only *deaf* with a small *d* in this chapter, except of course in names of organizations.
2. See www.sdrf.se/sdr/dnr/ENG/index.html.
3. We would like to acknowledge Ritva Takkinen's substantial contributions to section 3 on Finnish Sign Language and thank Rannveig Sverrisdóttir and Valgerður Stefánsdóttir for information on Iceland, Edny Poulsen for information on the Faeroe Islands, Birthe Petersen for information on Greenland, Britta Hansen, Jan William Rasmussen (who

more or less singlehandedly has built up *Historisk Samling* (Historical Collection), a marvellous library and exhibition of teaching materials, etc., documenting the history of the deaf in Denmark) and Palle Vestberg Rasmussen for help with the section on Danish Sign Language, and Penny Boyes Braem for reading everything and sharing her critical remarks with us. Needless to say, we are wholly responsible for any mistakes.

4. A folk high school in Denmark is a boarding school for primarily young people. It does not offer any kind of degree or certificate but gives people a possibility of expanding their creative talents and their knowledge of the arts, society and all subjects that evoke interest at a given time. The first folk high schools were founded in the middle of the nineteenth century for the benefit of young people in the country who rarely had had the opportunity of much education besides basic schooling. Courses are from one week up to six to eight months.

5 Transmission of sign languages in Mediterranean Europe

1. As is usually the case, the initial efforts of research into sign language focused almost exclusively on the elaboration of lexicons, as it seemed the most urgent need to be covered for deaf education. In many cases the first researchers came from the psychology of education departments at universities, or from Deaf organizations. Nowadays, more researchers with a linguistic background are active. Research on grammar has always lagged behind, but particular aspects of the respective grammars have been described in depth. Educational needs, as well as computational applications in sign language, require comprehensive descriptions of the grammar. In addition, research is being carried out in the field of bilingual education and learning processes in deaf children, as well as in sociolinguistics, psycholinguistics (mainly acquisition) and neurolinguistics (sign language processing).

2. A much smaller estimate is suggested in Gras (2006:79, 101) on the basis of data projections obtained from a partial census and questionnaire surveys among Deaf association members: approximately 15,685 deaf signers and 22,675 hearing and deaf signers (67% deaf, 12% CODAs, 21% hearing L2 signers).

3. For the history of the education of the deaf in Spain, see Plann (1997) and Gascón Storch de Gracia y Asensio (2004).

4. The influence of the French gestural method is proven by the existence of a grammar book for deaf-mutes, written by Father Ciro Marzullo in Palermo in 1857, containing some methodical signs in the way they were intended by de l'Épée.

5. *Sulla necessità di dell'educazione dei sordomuti* is the original title.

6. *Compendio di dottrina religiosa, scientifica e morale ad uso dei sordomuti* is the original title.

7. More detailed information about LIS theatre is available at www.istc.cnr.it/mostralis/pannello22.htm.

8. See www.lightkitchen.com/deafcinema.html.

9. For more information, see www.cervantesvirtual.com/seccion/signos/psegundonivel.jsp?conten = literatura.

10. For more information, see www.anios.it and www.animu.it.

6 Transmission of sign languages in Africa

We wish to acknowledge Penny Boyes Bream and Christian Rathmann for their guidelines in gathering information about the transmission and use of Uganda Sign Language. In addition, we are grateful to Diane Brentari and Victoria Nyst for their invaluable suggestions and feedback on the first draft of this chapter. A special thanks is also extended to the people who made valuable comments and who proofread this chapter.

1. Winston Churchill wrote about Uganda in his documentary *My African Journey*, published in 1908.
2. Constitution of Uganda (2005:8).
3. Article 37 of the Constitution of Uganda.
4. Uganda has had a Deaf member of parliament since 1996.
5. These gestures are ritual requests like touching the hands of an adult, showing, holding an object out for someone to view; giving, surrendering an object voluntarily and communicative pointing, pointing to an object (Volterra 1981, Bonvillian *et al.* 1985, Bonvillian and Folven 1991).
6. See http://en.wikipedia.org/wiki/language.
7. For more information, see www.sil.org/ethnologue/.
8. English, the language of the former colonial power, is the official language of Uganda. Uganda's linguistic diversity made it impossible to use the local languages. However, the introduction of a local languages policy (2006) led, in 2007, to the use of local languages in education.
9. With the establishment of new districts, Uganda is made up of eighty-two districts.
10. The research was the product of the Danish Deaf Association, through the Ministry of Foreign Affairs, the Danish International Development Agency (DANIDA) and Kyambogo University in collaboration with UNAD.

7 Transmission of Polish sign systems

1. Only with great caution will the terms "Deaf" and "deaf" be occasionally used in this chapter as they are in other countries and in most other chapters of this volume. To better reflect the circumstances of the Polish deaf, the terms that will primarily be used to make a distinction between those who hear and those who do not will be "hearing" and "non-hearing," respectively, recognizing the fractured character of "non-hearing" people as a social group, a topic that will be further explored in this work.
2. In this case "cultured" means "high-culture"; its point of reference is the hearing world.
3. For example, PJM contains a number of signs that can represent a mobile phone. Each one of them is expressed with a single sign. Through the efforts of the Unification Committee, a new sign was created which consisted of two gestures: PHONE and DIAL-THE-NUMBER. Unfortunately, this sign is not known to PSL users who do not attend the appropriate training seminars or consult a sign language dictionary.
4. A great deal of work on the topic of pidginization, contact signing, and sign language varieties has been conducted on ASL and British, Australian and New Zealand Sign Language (BANZSL) (see Lucas and Bayley, this volume, and Schembri *et al.*, this volume), and it appears that many similar motivations for the proliferation of sign varieties exist in Poland.

8 Notation systems

This material is based upon work supported by the National Science Foundation under Grant No. 0544944 to both authors. Any opinions, findings and conclusions or recommendations expressed in this material are those of the authors and do not necessarily reflect the views of the National Science Foundation. We would like to acknowledge the very helpful feedback from a number of people, especially Jean Ann, Diane Brentari and Valerie Sutton.

1. In this chapter, where necessary to disambiguate, we will use the convention of italic to refer to a spoken/signed word as a linguistic expression or meaning (e.g., *three*), < > to refer to a written form (e.g., < three >) and single quotes to refer to the spoken form

(e.g., 'three'). As in the rest of the volume, uppercase is used to refer to signed expressions (e.g., THREE) and double quotes are used for theoretical terms and concepts.

2. Missing from this chapter, for reasons of space and because discussions are available elsewhere, is a survey of a fourth type of notation, namely (linguistic) feature systems. Indeed feature models are also notational systems in which the forms (the feature names) are either descriptive labels or taken as cognitive units that represent phonetic "meanings." For explicit discussions of analogues and difference between feature systems for spoken and signed languages, we refer to van der Hulst (1993, 2000). In a way, coding systems are feature systems, while differing in that they have been designed to capture phonetic details that go beyond what a (phonological) feature system would want to capture. In a sense, then, coding systems lie halfway between transcription systems and feature systems.

3. Examples and explanations of the system can be seen online at www.omniglot.com/writing/signwriting.htm and http://www.signwriting.com/.

4. See Supalla, Cripps and McKee 2008; also described by Supalla and Blackburn at http://clerccenter.gallaudet.edu/kidsworldDeafnet/e-docs/keys/learning.html.

5. Often, the term "logographic" is used where we use semagraphic. However, we take the term logographic to refer to the size of the unit that is referred to, *logo(s)* standing for a unit that has the size of a word. As we will see, semagraphic systems always appear to be logographic, while conceivable phonographic systems that use graphs for whole word (forms) do not seem to exist.

6. Writing systems for speech usually mix phonographic and semagraphic units; English writing, for example, has many semagraphs (such as @, &, %, etc.).

7. As a matter of necessity, semagraphs that started life as (referentially) iconic will, when used phonographically, be entirely arbitrary. It is noteworthy that people tend to make any type of sign system iconic at the time that they actually invent it, but, at the same time, they have no problem in learning or handling signs that are arbitrary, nor do alphabetic systems that are rooted in semagraphic origins show any signs of "re-iconizing" with reference to (articulatory or acoustic) properties of phonemes.

8. A semanticist might, however, use a semagraphic "transcription system" with symbols for (elements of) the meaning of words. In effect, notations used in logic (when linked to natural language expressions) are semagraphic transcription systems, whereas mathematical notation systems can be thought of as being pictographic, or, when non-iconic "ideographic".

9. Another kind of relationship is that of an Index, which is not further discussed here.

10. Note that systematicity presupposes "compositionality" of the sign forms and meanings because we speak of *properties* that different entities have in common.

11. There is a special version of SignWriting for transcription which does have specific symbols for locations.

12. Because SignWriting is two dimensional and is representing something that is three-dimensional, even location cannot be completely iconic, because conventions are needed to establish the placement in the forward-back dimension.

13. Some (including Stokoe 1960) refer to graphs that represent feature complexes (such as the graph < A > for a certain handshape) as "alphabetic," taking handshapes as analogous to phonemes. But in all current analyses of signs, handshapes are subsegmental, and their graphs therefore are featural, not segmental.

14. As mentioned earlier, logical and mathematical notations (think especially of Frege's Begriffsschrift; Frege 1879) might be regarded as aiming at the representation of (submorphemic) basic concepts. Also, semantic theories that decompose meanings into basic concepts employ submorphemic semagraphic notation systems, which usually use

invented symbols for logical operators and connectives, while using "words" in bold or capital for the larger set of semantic primitives. We think of such systems as semantic transcription systems.

15. This being said, we should perhaps pay more attention to the fact that all sign phonologists, starting with Stokoe, recognize feature groups for handshape, location, movement and orientation as intermediate levels, which Stokoe designated as analogous to phonemes in spoken languages, whereas van der Hulst and Channon compare them to "class nodes" (the units for place, manner and laryngeal properties of speech sounds). Clearly, the salience of class nodes in signs is much higher than class nodes in speech phonemes, which explains why sign writing systems sometimes have holistic graphs for, in particular, handshapes, which are, perhaps, the most essential aspect of signs, or at least have some kind of special status (van der Hulst 1993).

16. Supalla's ASL-phabet does not have iconic order.

17. Notating meanings is certainly possible as well, as in the Berkeley Transcription System (Hoiting & Slobin 2002, Slobin *et al.* 2001), which we would call a semantic transcription system.

18. Even though transcriptions are meant to be accurate renderings of the perceptible form of linguistic expressions, transcription, like any analytic process, always involves abstraction. The gestures of language are largely continuous, both at the phonemic and word level, apart from pauses when people breathe or rest, but transcriptions normally slice this stream as though there were discrete phonemes and words. Paralinguistic properties of the sign (properties that depend on factors such as gender, size, age, mental state or mood, physical abnormalities, amount of alcohol and so on) are usually excluded.

Furthermore, as is well known, transcriptions differ in terms of the amount of phonetic detail that is acknowledged, depending on the goal of the transcription. If the goal is to arrive at a phonological analysis of normal speech, the transcription will anticipate the phonemic analysis by mostly notating phonetic distinctions that are, at least, potentially contrastive (i.e., have been shown to be contrastive in at least one language). For example, a broad transcription system would register aspiration in English consonants because this property is contrastive in languages such as Hindi or Thai, but the difference between released and unreleased final obstruents would not. For signs, a phonologist might decide that the difference between the ⟨handshape⟩ and ⟨handshape⟩ handshape is not contrastive and therefore notate both handshapes with the same symbol.

19. Even though an excellent iconic system, Bell's Visual Speech was proposed and worked out in great detail, linguists have chosen to use the non-iconic IPA. Why did the IPA succeed when many systems with newly invented symbols, whether iconic or systematic, did not gain general acceptance? There are probably several reasons. First, many people described languages (either as a hobby or more professionally) before such specialized notation systems had been designed, or they were unaware of the existence of such systems. As many of those used the Roman alphabet, a tradition of transcription based on this alphabet simply emerged. (There are similar examples of phonetic uses of other scripts in India, China or Arabic countries.) Second, newly invented symbols must be learned and memorized, which is a stumbling block for everyone. Connected to this is the fact that those who do take the trouble of learning the new system will see their work ignored by the majority of potential readers who do not take the trouble to learn it. Third, newly invented systems pose problems to typewriters, printers and proofreaders. That the Roman alphabet and not some other alphabet became the basis for the IPA is, of course, the result of Eurocentrism. Fourth, and probably most importantly, the idea that iconicity or systematicity is a *crucial* (or even desirable) feature of a notation system is probably an illusion. As mentioned, iconicity may be a natural drive in the design of a

notation system. However, once such a system is mastered, each symbol will eventually start functioning as an arbitrary sign for a specific speech sound. This will lead to iconicity, if present initially, "wearing off," even though when people design new notation systems they find it irresistible to come up with iconic symbols.

20. The lack of iconic order does make the HamNoSys representation harder to read, but this may not be a serious drawback, since anyone trained in the system will be able to read it with adequate speed.

21. For a comprehensive overview of sign notation systems, we refer to Miller 2001.

22. There are many written speech systems that do not have a clear one-to-one relationship between the written form and the spoken form. But all sign writing systems do, although they vary to one degree or another in what is omitted. It is possible that this is a result of the relative youthfulness of all written sign systems, and that over time, historical "garbage" may accumulate. Intuitively, this seems unlikely, especially with SignWriting, and it also seems that the reasons for this are connected not with its age, but with its iconic and featural nature. While writing systems for speech can lag behind phonological change, we find it difficult to imagine a situation where, for example, a SignWriting symbol which represented the hand at the forehead was accepted as a good symbol for a sign made on the cheek (although there should be no difficulty in accepting that something is written in citation form without regard to a specific performance). This question must be left for future investigation, but we mention it as a possible significant difference between written speech and sign.

23. We propose a closed vocabulary of *English* words simply because at the present time, English is the de facto language of science, and therefore a database using English will have the largest number of scientists who will not require translation before use. Because it is a closed set of words, translation into various other languages should be relatively straightforward.

24. SignTyp can also be seen as an attribute-value structure in which a value can itself be an attribute (Scobbie 1997).

9 Verb agreement in sign language morphology

1. "Verb agreement" has been noted in, for example, American Sign Language (Padden 1983), Argentinian Sign Language (Massone & Curiel 2004), Australian Sign Language (Johnston & Schembri 2007), Brazilian Sign Language (Quadros 1999), British Sign Language (Sutton-Spence & Woll 1999), Catalan Sign Language (Quer & Frigola 2006), German Sign Language (Rathmann 2000), Greek Sign Language (Sapountzaki 2005), Indo-Pakistani Sign Language (Zeshan 2000), Israeli Sign Language (Meir 1998b), Japanese Sign Language (Fischer 1996), Korean Sign Language (Hong 2008), Sign Language of the Netherlands (Bos 1994) and Taiwanese Sign Language (Smith 1990), among others.

2. As suggested in recent literature, e.g., Pfau and Glueck 1999, Zwitserlood 2003 and Mathur and Rathmann 2007, these constructions may involve agreement between a classifier predicate and a noun phrase in its class feature, such as *person*, *animal* or *vehicle*. Owing to space limitation, this type of agreement is not discussed in detail here.

10 Functional markers in sign languages

For the LIS research, we thank our informants Giuseppe Amorini, Giammarco Eletto, Anna Folchi, Graziella Anselmo, Emiliano Mereghetti, Mirko Pasquotto and Mirko Santoro. For the ASL research, we are grateful to Robert Lee, Michael Schlang, Dana Schlang, Lana Cook, Ben Bahan, Norma Tourangeau, Ken Mikos, Tyler Richard, Joan Nash and

Paul Hagstrom. None of these people bears responsibility for any errors. Thanks also to Stan Sclaroff and Vassilis Athitsos for assistance with video data capture. This research was supported in part by funding from the National Science Foundation (#IIS-0329009, #CNS-0427988, #IIS-0705749).

1. See, for example, Bybee, Perkins and Pagliuca (1994).
2. A "perfective" form describes a complete event. "Completives," according to Dahl and Velupillai (2008), "are used of completed events but only if some additional nuance of meaning is intended, for instance if emphasis is put on the result being complete or affecting the object totally." For the notion of complete event, see section 2 of this chapter.
3. Similarities between sign languages and creoles were first noted in Fischer 1978.
4. This informal characterization of perfectivity is widely adopted in descriptive studies of aspect. For example, according to Dahl and Velupillai (2008), "To be interpreted as a perfective, ... a form should be the default way of referring to a completed event in the language in question." According to Jakobson (1957), "perfective [is] ... concerned with the absolute completion of the [narrated event]."
5. See, for example, Heim 1997 for a way of representing the present perfect along these lines.
6. Some of our informants also produced sentences like (i), in which FATTO is possibly analyzed as taking MANGIARE ('eat') as a complement:

   (i)   GIANNI   DOLCE   FATTO   MANGIARE
           Gianni   cake   done   eat
           'Gianni finished eating the cake.'

7. Determiners may also occur before the noun.
8. Depending on the context, a sentence like (9) may also describe past or future events. For a discussion of how temporal information may be conveyed in LIS, see Zucchi 2009.
9. If this hypothesis is correct, the example sentences with FATTO would be best translated by the English simple past rather than, as we do in the text, by the English perfect.
10. See Chomsky and Lasnik 1993 and Chomsky 1995.
11. See Bahan (1996) and Padden (1988).
12. Similar aspectual markers have developed from the adverb meaning 'already' or an adjective meaning 'ready' in German Sign Language (DGS) and in the Sign Language of the Netherlands (NGT) as well (Pfau & Steinbach 2006).
13. Recognized for its perfective meaning by Aarons *et al.* (1992), ASL FINISH, on the usage in question, is analyzed by Neidle and MacLaughlin (2002) as a perfect marker occurring structurally in an Aspect projection under the scope of Tense. Here it is proposed to mark both perfect and perfective.
14. See Duffy 2007 for a different interpretation of some of the data presented by Rathmann (2005).
15. See www.bu.edu/asllrp/SignStream, and www.bu.edu/asllrp/cslgr/.
16. For discussion of apparent exceptions, see Duffy 2007.
17. Perfective aspect, however, is not ungrammatical with negation in Russian, as shown by the following example from Comrie 1976:

   (i)   On dolgo ugovarival (Impf.) menja, no ne ugovoril (Pfv.)
          'He was trying to persuade me for a long time, but he didn't persuade me.'

18. Despite what the gloss suggests, NON-ANCORA is not phonologically derived by incorporating negation with ANCORA.

19. Here, we leave open the issue of how the inference that John won't do his homework is generated for (57), whether it simply follows from the grammatical meaning of (57) or from the interaction of the semantics of (57) with additional pragmatic principles.

20. Similarly, ASL sentence (62) may be used as the negative counterpart of the sentence with FINISH in (18).

21. Thus, for example, the Norwegian negative NP *ingen bøker* ('no book') cannot appear in postverbal object position, as in (ii), while it can appear preverbally, as in (iii). If the object remains postverbal, the discontinuous strategy must be used as in (iv), with the postverbal NP *noen bøker* ('any books') licensed by preverbal negation, *ikke* ('not'):

(i) | Jon | har | kjøpt | en | bok |
|---|---|---|---|---|
| Jon | has | bought | a | book |

'Jon has bought a book.'

(ii) | * Jon | har | kjøpt | ingen | bøker |
|---|---|---|---|---|
| Jon | has | bought | no | books |

'Jon has bought no books.'

(iii) | Jon | har | ingen | bøker | kjøpt |
|---|---|---|---|---|
| Jon | has | no | books | bought |

'Jon has bought no books.'

(iv) | Jon | har | ikke | kjøpt | noen | bøker |
|---|---|---|---|---|---|
| Jon | has | not | bought | any | books |

'Jon has not bought any books.'

22. Christensen's theory develops an idea originally proposed for English *nobody* by Klima (1964), according to which *nobody* is derived from conflation of *not* and *anybody* under syntactic adjacency.

23. Since LIS lacks articles, the indefiniteness of the NP CASA in (68) is not marked overtly, but is inferred from the context.

24. See Geraci (2006) for this observation and for discussion of N-words in LIS.

25. The question why in some cases the discontinuous strategy is chosen, as in (68), and in other cases negative NPs are used, as in (81)–(82), is one for which we do not have an answer at the moment. What is crucial for our point, however, is that in LIS the canonical position of negative NPs is postverbal, and so is the position of negation.

26. Geraci assumes that negation is also located in SpecNegP to account for the fact that negative NPs and negation cannot co-occur. Notice that, on this account, this fact may be explained also under the assumption that negation heads NegP, since the negative NP arises from conflating negation with the existential NP, and thus we should not expect them to co-occur.

27. The sign FATTO, as it appears from Figure 10.1, starts with open hands and palms facing the chest of the signer, then the hands move downwards and the palms end up facing the ground. In the sign for NON, the index finger moves repeatedly to the right and to the left with the palm facing the addressee. In the sign for NON-ANCORA, the palms face the addressee, the thumb and the index finger form a ring while the other fingers are extended, and the hands alternatively move close and far. In the sign for NIENTE, hands and palms are configured in the same way as for NON-ANCORA, but they move apart once and with a wider movement.

28. According to this proposal, LF structures carry information only about the structural components of meaning (quantifier scope, etc.), and not about the lexical meaning of individual nouns and verbs. See Marantz (1994) on how semantic interpretation is determined in a DM approach.

11 Clause structure

1. See Rathman and Mathur's chapter (this volume) for a more extended discussion of verb agreement in sign language. Padden's (1990) terminology uses "agreeing" to refer to verbs displaying person inflection while "spatial" verbs display location information. For our analysis, agreeing verbs are understood as agreeing with person and/or with location features. The distribution of these verbs in the phrase structure seems to be the same, but we recognize the lexical/semantic difference between these two kinds of agreement.

2. Many of our examples are grammatical with the same word order in ASL and LSB. We will generally alternate between using ASL examples and using LSB examples, indicating that the other language allows the same word order by noting (also ASL/LSB). Where only one language shows a particular pattern, we will indicate this.

3. See Wood 1999 for discussion of the placement and interpretation of NEVER in ASL.

4. Whether such an ordering effect is seen in ASL remains to be tested. See Wilcox and Wilcox (1995) and Shaffer (2000) for a discussion of modality in ASL.

5. Note that we follow Liddell's original notation (as we do throughout the chapter). Some researchers have claimed that the nonmanual marking of negation does not extend over the subject, as in Liddell's example (e.g., Neidle *et al.* 2000). Some consultants have told us that the subject can be marked with the negative nonmanual, particularly with a prosodic break between the subject and verb phrase.

6. See Sandler and Lillo-Martin (2006) for comparison of these constructions and Germanic object shift.

7. Brentari (1998) presents an analysis of this phenomenon in terms of the phonological heaviness of the verb.

8. In ASL (and in LSB as well), the sign for READ can be analyzed as containing a classifier, at least historically.

9. Just how high the position is, and whether it is a special projection or can be collapsed with inflectional projections, is a matter for further research.

10. The nonmanual for emphatic focus will be somewhat different depending on the type of utterance (e.g., declarative, question, negative). The manual signs are also emphasized, being produced with greater muscle tension. We use the notation E-foc as a cover term. The nonmanual marking is also different between LSB (where it extends beyond the manual sign) and ASL (where it does not).

11. For more details on this structure and evidence supporting it, see Lillo-Martin and Quadros 2008.

12. Bahan (1996) and Bahan *et al.* (2000) argue against Lillo-Martin's analysis of the existence of two kinds of null arguments in ASL. They claim that the existence of null arguments with plain verbs is licensed by non-manual marking. However, Thompson, Emmoray and Kluender (2006) show that nonmanual marking generally does not accompany null arguments with plain verbs. Thus, we follow the analysis of Lillo-Martin (1986) and Quadros (1995).

13. It is also possible to find negation preceding a *plain verb* when the subject is topicalized. This case will not be considered in the present work. This negation is probably related to modality, since its meaning is related to "shouldn't." If this is the case, the position occupied by the negation in this case can be the same position occupied by the sign "CAN'T."

12 Factors that form classifier signs

I would like to thank Diane Brentari, Adam Schembri and an anonymous reviewer for comments on earlier versions of this chapter. Any remaining errors and shortcomings are mine.

1. The data and the method of collection are described in section 5. The photos of signs in this chapter were made as close to the ones in the tapes as possible with a native Danish signer, Eva Abildgaard, as the model.

2. Since the term "classifier" has become established in the sign linguistics literature, I shall use it in this chapter. There is no widely used term for the entirety of the linguistic unit seen in Figure 12.1, whether it belongs to the word class of verbs or should rather be described by its syntactic function as a predicate, and whether it is one or more "verbs." In this chapter, I shall talk about "classifier signs."

3. As will appear from section 2.3, Liddell's (2003a) analysis of signs with classifiers as (partially) lexicalized verbs should not be confused with descriptions where a lexical verb MEET is distinguished from productively formed signs. Johnson and Liddell (1984) presented contrasting analyses of what they described as a monomorphemic, lexical verb MEET and a multimorphemic sign denoting 'One person, upright at location A and facing location B, moves toward another person, upright at location B, facing location A, and upon contact, stops moving' (Johnson & Liddell 1984:182). In the 1984 paper, Johnson and Liddell analyzed the last sign within Supalla's framework of multimorphemic signs, but in later work, Liddell (2003a) criticizes this type of analysis (see section 2.1).

4. As pointed out, data in the NSF project, from which the data in my analysis stem, disconfirm some of Liddell's claims of constraints on combinations of classifiers and movements in ASL (see also Benedicto & Brentari 2004). The discrepancy points to a general problem in sign linguistics and a special problem in relation to classifier signs. All sign languages are used in a context with few native signers and many non-native signers (see the chapters on transmission of sign languages in this volume). This sociolinguistic fact can be expected to influence the acceptability judgments made by native signers who are confronted with many ways of signing in their daily lives. Specifically, classifier signs, which – as will appear and as is pointed out by both Cogill-Koez (2000a) and Liddell (2003a) – can be adapted for specific descriptive purposes, are difficult to judge. By way of comparison: Google has about 3,750,000 hits for *seniority* and 13,000 hits for *juniority*, i.e., *seniority* is firmly established in the English language (and found in the online versions of *Encyclopædia Britannica* and *Merriam-Webster Dictionary & Thesaurus*); *juniority* has a marginal status (and is found in neither dictionary) but does indeed occur.

5. I would like to thank Diane Brentari and her collaborators for letting me use the data.

6. Mayer's picture book has been used in several studies of motion descriptions in sign languages (e.g., Taub & Galvan 2001, Engberg-Pedersen 2003).

7. This may be somewhat surprising because of the classifier's name. The V-handshape with the fingers clearly bent in its citation form is, however, a classifier for animals in many sign languages. The orientation of the hand denotes the orientation of an animal in the same way as the orientation of the biped classifier. Iconically, the animal classifier can thus be seen as a one-handed, stylized depiction of a creature with legs. In signed discourse, the two classifiers may look very similar, especially in cases where there is a possibility of the weak hand's form assimilating to the strong hand's form, and the strong hand is used for the biped classifier as in some of the descriptions of the boy's fall onto the deer.

8. ASL signer A's description in Figure 12.10 may be seen as an exception. It is, however, not clear whether the upward movement of the signer's left hand has significance in itself ('the deer rose'), or whether it assimilates to the movement of the right hand and prepares for the final downward movement ('come to rest').

13 Handshape constrasts in sign language phonology

This work was supported in part by National Science Foundation (NSF) grants to Brentari (BCS 0112391 and BCS0547554) and by a Purdue Research Foundation Grant to Eccarius.

1. A few key works that contributed to our understanding of handshape from various methodological points of view are Stokoe, Casterline and Croneberg 1965, Battison 1978; Mandel 1981; Liddell and Johnson 1989; Sandler 1989, 1996b; Brentari 1990, 1998, 2005; van der Hulst 1993, 1995; Ann 1993; Channon 2002a; van der Kooij 2002; and from an experimental point of view, Lane, Boyes Braem and Bellugi 1976; Emmorey and Corina 1990, and Carreiras *et al.* (2008).

2. [hu] is still disallowed in the periphery, an issue that will be taken up in section 6.

3. We consider the handshape to have two groups of selected fingers: the index and thumb as "primary selected fingers" and the remaining three fingers as the "secondary selected fingers." See Eccarius 2002 for more information about this distinction.

4. The handshape has two possible selected finger groups. Here, we refer to the form with the three extended fingers selected.

5. These signs are believed not to be derived from character signs (Tang, personal communication).

6. In ASL '6' and '9' look like and respectively, but '6' is analyzed as having the pinkie + thumb selected, since they move in the number '16' (i.e., the three extended fingers are not selected), and '9' is analyzed as having the index and thumb selected for the same reason (the index finger moves in '19'). The status of numbers themselves in the organization of the lexicon has not yet been determined and is a topic for future research.

7. Further research is needed to determine whether or not these observations hold true on a greater scale and in more naturalistic settings.

8. It is interesting to note here, however, that the character sign INTRODUCE 介紹, which could potentially use to represent the top two strokes of the written form, uses a handshape instead.

9. As mentioned before, the lack of attested forms in the foreign component of HKSL may be more related to the general rarity of character signs.

10. Despite this proliferation of joint configurations, no [stacked] handshapes were observed for this classifier type.

11. The difference between use of the index finger and the middle finger with the thumb to represent thin, disc-shaped objects (e.g., 'plate') may result from a stylistic difference.

12. For an example, see the "Thumb-3 Finger" grasp in Cutkosky's (1989) taxonomy of grasp types used in manufacturing tasks, which uses the index, middle and ring fingers.

13. Only the first two criteria are helpful for sign languages because long-distance effects have not been observed in these languages, and many-to-one association is observed almost everywhere throughout the system and so would not reveal anything new. ("Many-to-one" association occurs, for example, when one handshape has more than one place of articulation – e.g., ASL compounds – or when one location has more than one handshape – e.g., in disyllabic signs [such as DESTROY, BACKGROUND in ASL]. These many-to-one relationships exist for all combinations of parameters.)

14. In particular, Underspecification Theory (Archangeli 1988a, 1988b, Steriade 1995) has discussed this issue at length.

15. Despite this shift in some foreign forms, there are also many initialized forms that remain in the foreign component in a stable manner. In fact, it has been observed that some initialized 3FHSs in ASL are quite old and show no indication of changing, as is evidenced in the sign WATER (Supalla 2004).

16. This alternation can also be seen in four-finger forms such as SALAD.

17. In SCLs, only one meaningful joint alteration – from extended to bent – is allowed in some forms (e.g., to to indicate a crashed car; first mentioned in Supalla 1982). However, this change is unusual in many respects, and therefore warrants further study. For example, it seems to be a sequential morpheme rather than a simultaneous one

(cf. Aronoff, Meir & Sandler 2005), and it is less iconic than prominent contrasts in other classifier types (e.g., a signer cannot bend the thumb instead of the fingers to indicate different crashed locations on the vehicle).

18. Even distinctive contrasts do not hold absolutely everywhere. For example, the voicing contrast in English is true for obstruents (stops and fricatives), but suspended in onset clusters and syllable codas.

19. Underspecification Theory (Archangeli 1988a,1988b; Steriade 1995 and references contained therein) is insufficient to explain the possible distribution types in (3) because all parts of the lexicon are treated alike in this theory.

20. Unselected fingers are located above the joints and SF nodes in the representation (and not shown in Figure 13.4), but since these phenomena are rare, it is worth mentioning.

21. Movements or locations may be neutralized to some extent, but they will not be neutralized to as great a degree as in spoken languages (see Johnson & Liddell 1984 for movement changes, and see van der Hulst and van der Kooij 2006 for changes in location).

22. The anatomy of the hand definitely affects the frequency of certain types of handshapes over others, as Ann (1993, 2006) and Greftegreff (1993) have shown. Allophonic flexion of the knuckles (Crasborn 2001) and the closing of the fist and extension of the wrist (Mandel 1979, Brentari 1998) are two further examples.

14 Syllable structure in sign language phonology

1. Typologically, despite of the fact that most descriptions of the spoken syllable use the structure CVC as an example, the most common syllable type in spoken language is CV (Maddieson 2005).

2. Specific solutions have been devised for these problems in English (Fudge 1969) and Spanish (Harris 1983).

3. The term "movement" has been used in different senses by different researchers (for two overviews, see Brentari 1998 and Crasborn 2001). In this section, unless otherwise directly indicated, the term movement is used in the general sense referring to the dynamic properties of a sign stream.

4. In photographs from Malm (1998), simple straight arrow(s) indicate(s) the path or trajectory of the movement (see MUSTA 'black' in Figure 14.1; see also Figures 14.3 and 14.7). Two arrows indicate repetition (see TIETÄÄ 'to know' in Figure 14.1). The design above the hands in the sign VÄHETÄ 'to decrease' (Figure 14.1) indicates wiggling; a dashed line indicates that the movement is produced in a slowed manner. Double or triple direction lines indicate that the handshape either closes or opens (see VÄHETÄ and KULTTUURI 'culture' in Figure 14.1; see also Figures 14.7 and 14.8).

5. In general, it is possible to analyze lexical signs that have a repeated movement either as true disyllabic forms or as forms that are derived from monosyllables by reduplication. Regarding the FinSL sign TIETÄÄ 'to know' (see Figure 14.1), we do not find the (formal, semantic or etymological) evidence to support the reduplication analysis. In other words, we consider TIETÄÄ to be similar to the disyllabic Finnish word *koko* 'size.'

6. Brentari's (1998) hierarchy of joints is slightly simplified for there are actually two joints that can be manipulated at the "elbow" – one producing movement as in the ASL sign THANK-YOU and another producing forearm rotation as in the ASL sign TREE. For more see Mirus, Rathmann and Meier 2001.

7. Brentari's (1998) Prosodic model includes a built-in option to deal also with nonmanual movements.

8. Jantunen's (2005) study is conducted in a slightly modified framework of Brentari's (1998) Prosodic model. In this framework, head and upper body movements are separated, if necessary, in the IF-branch under the nonmanual-node.

9. The other type of mouth movements, i.e., *mouthings*, Jantunen (2005, 2006) considers to be spoken language-induced code-mixing with no phonological relevance. The analysis follows that of Hohenberger and Happ (2001).

10. In Figure 14.2, as well as in all the other photographs from Malm (1998), the small straight line in front of the arrow head indicates a clear stop (see also Figure 14.7).

11. Obviously, the principle of ease of perception conflicts here with the principle of ease of articulation.

12. Jantunen (2005) gives the status of nonmanual articulator to the *mouth, head* and *torso* on the grounds that they are the only nonmanual articulators found in Malm (1998; *Suomaloisen viittomakielen perussanakirja* [Basic Dictionary of FinSL]) which are independently responsible for the production of a lexical movement (cf. KYLLÄ 'yes,' ON-KUULLUT 'has/have heard' and MUKAVA 'nice,' respectively).

13. Other studies have shown that, particularly in the earliest stages, hearing non-signing children produce manual babbles very similar to those produced by deaf children, suggesting that in the beginning, motoric development might be playing more of a part than phonology (e.g., Meier & Willerman 1995).

14. It should be noted that although core lexemes may include two syllables, there is a strong tendency in signed language lexemes in general to be monosyllabic (e.g., Wilbur 1990, Jantunen 2007).

15. Both Perlmutter (1992) and Sandler (1993) take the trisegmental PMP/LML-type syllable to be the prototypical syllable in signed language. This breaks down their analog between signed and spoken syllables since in spoken languages it is the two-segmental CV-type syllable which must be treated as prototypical (e.g., Maddieson 2005).

16. In the earlier version of the Prosodic model (Brentari & Goldsmith 1993), dominant and non-dominant hands were treated as being functionally analogous to spoken syllable-internal unit onset and coda, respectively. In the current version of the model (Brentari 1998), this analogy is dropped since, for example, the data from disyllabic compounds suggests that the non-dominant hand is a word-level appendix-like unit.

17. According to Brentari (1998), simple syllables, i.e., syllables with only one weight unit, seem to be the most frequent syllables also in ASL. In a study of signs described in the *Dictionary of American Sign Language on Linguistic Principles* (*DASL*; Stokoe, Casterline & Croneberg 1965), she found that 82 percent of the signs had simple movement. Conversely, 18 percent of *DASL* signs were characterizable as containing a complex movement.

18. The circle in Figure 14.8 (see EI-TUNNE 'does not know him/her') indicates the pivot point of the movement that changes the orientation of the hand.

15 Grammaticalization in sign languages

The research reported in this chapter stems from work conducted on American Sign Language (ASL) modal forms (Wilcox & Wilcox 1995), subsequently extended to other signed languages. We wish to thank the American, Catalan and Italian signers who participated in different studies we draw upon for the present work. The collection and part of the analyses of the data on Italian Sign Language (LIS) were made possible by funding provided by the Italian National Research Council (CNR), Short-Term Mobility Program "Cross-linguistic typological studies of signed languages: A pilot comparative study of American and Italian Sign Languages" (1999) and "The expression of modality in signed languages: A comparative exploration of American and Italian Sign Languages" (2001). We thank several friends and colleagues for the many helpful comments and suggestions they generously provided at different stages of our research: Maria Luisa Franchi, Silvia Del Vecchio and

Virginia Volterra. A special thought of gratitude to Tommaso Russo Cardona who is no longer with us, but whose rich and passioned scientific rigor will always remain inside us as a source of inspiration.

1. Throughout the text, the signs under discussion are represented via English glosses in capital letters that roughly correspond to the translations in Italian words given for these signs by LIS signers and/or in LIS dictionaries (e.g., Radutzky 1992, Romeo 1991). Because some of the signs can be translated with the same English words, we use letters suffixed in parentheses to distinguish them by some of their formational properties. (H), (SS), (O), (F) indicate one or two-handed signs whose initial handshapes, following Stokoe, Casterline and Croneberg's (1965) notation for ASL handshapes, can be described as, respectively: H-, S-, O-, and F-handshapes; 'fff,' and 'pa-pa' indicate mouth gestures that obligatorily accompany two of the signs we discuss. In agreement with analyses of these mouth gestures conducted by Franchi (1987/2004) and Ajello, Mazzoni and Nikolai (2001), 'fff' denotes a prolonged emission of air, 'pa-pa' a constrained puff of air. Note also that in actual discourse the signs in Figures 15.3, 15.5, 15.7 and 15.8 are almost always accompanied by a side to side negative head shake.

2. Aldrete later came to suspect that it was "one of the basic gestures used by speakers (both elite orators and stage actors) while they were speaking in order to accentuate the rhythm of their words. As such, it would not really have a specific meaning other than that the person making it was speaking at that moment, and the motion of the arm could be used to emphasize the rhythm of their words" (Aldrete, personal communication, December 15, 2007).

3. Note that this implies that modal verbs are conceptually dependent on their main verbs. This A/D relationship is likely to be a fruitful area of further exploration.

4. Although we do not address the historical development of modals other than IMPOSSIBLE (H) in this chapter, we should point out that modal forms often derive historically from content words expressing ability or power. *Can* originally referred to the subject's knowledge or mental ability to do something; *may* derives from a meaning of strength or physical ability. The LIS modal POSSIBLE(SS) clearly has its origin in a gesture indicating physical strength, as does the comparable ASL form CAN (Wilcox 2002). Finally, of course, the Italian modal *potere* has its origin in the Latin meaning 'potent'.

16 The semantics–phonology interface

This research is partially funded by the National Institutes of Health DC05241 and the National Science Foundation Linguistics Program 0345314 and 0414953.

1. The examples in (3) are taken from Bohnemeyer *et al.* (2007).

2. The original source of the term "macro-event" is Talmy (1991, 2000).

3. If an event occurs iteratively or habitually, this does not affect the path of any single occurrence.

4. In his paper "Semantic phonology," Stokoe (1991) suggested that a sign should be treated as a "marriage of a noun and a verb" and as an "agent–verb" construction, with no separation of phonology and semantics. Thompson, Emmorey and Golan (2005) provide counter-evidence for this proposal. The model proposed here does not pursue this particular analogy but recognizes form–meaning mappings of varying degrees of transparency.

5. Path movement *between* repetitions also reflects Extent, that is, elapsed time between such events (Wilbur 2005). Even when spatial predicates are reduplicated, the path movement between each occurrence of the event is still time between events.

6. Alternately, a semi-circle.

7. This is further evidence that EndState is not at the point in space but merely indicates it – it is the argument reference that is referred to by the point in space.

17 Nonmanuals: their grammatical and prosodic roles

We are indebted to Santiago Frigola and Sibaji Panda for help with LSC and IPSL illustra-tions. Moreover, we are grateful to Diane Brentari and an anonymous reviewer for insightful comments on an earlier version of this chapter. Part of this research has been possible thanks to the project grant HUM2006–08164 awarded to Josep Quer by the Spanish Ministry of Education and Science.

1. Pfau (2002) and Pfau and Quer (2002) also include DGS in the comparison. Interestingly, DGS (which – just like LSC – has the order S-V-O-Neg) exhibits yet another pattern. In contrast to ASL and LSC, headshake on the negative particle only is ungrammatical in DGS, while, as in LSC, headshake on only the predicate is possible in the absence of NOT.

2. Another specialized construction that fulfills a pragmatic function, namely focusing, is the *wh*-cleft construction, as analyzed by Wilbur (1994b). In example (i), the constituent LEE in the main clause is the focus while the subordinate *wh*-clause is the presupposition (Wilbur 1994b:653). Among other things, Wilbur stresses the fact that the nonmanual accompanying the *wh*-clause is not the one found in ASL *wh*-questions (see section 2.3.2).

        re   hn

(i)   CHAIR PAINT WHO, LEE
        'The one who painted the chair was Lee.'

3. At least in ASL, DGS and ISL, temporal adverbial clauses ("when" clauses) also appear in sentence-initial position and are marked by raised eyebrows. Owing to the similarity in nonmanual marking, a sentence may sometimes be ambiguous between an adverbial and a conditional reading, as, for example, in (i) from Coulter (1979:26).

    re

(i)   RAIN, NOT GO PICNIC
        'If it rains, we won't go on the picnic.'
        'When it rains, we don't go on picnics.'

4. Note that the two studies offer different accounts for LIS relative clauses. According to Cecchetto, Geraci and Zucchi (2006), LIS has correlatives and PE is correlative marker. In contrast, Branchini and Donati (2009) argue that LIS relatives are internally headed and that PE is a determiner-like element.

5. Thompson, Emmorey and Kluender (2006) also investigate eye gaze patterns accompany-ing spatial verbs such as PUT-DOWN and MOVE. In spatial verbs, the movement is not determined by subject and object but rather by locatives, as, for example, in 'I move the book from the shelf to the table.' Bahan (1996) claims that in spatial verbs, too, eye gaze targets the object location. That is, eye gaze should follow the movement of the hand which manipulates the object (the book). Thompson *et al.*, however, find that eye gaze in spatial verbs systematically targets the goal location (the table).

6. See Brentari and Crossley 2002 for discussion of comparable ASL examples and Boyes Braem 2001c on the use of mouthings and mouth gestures as prosodic markers in early and late learners of Swiss German Sign Language.

18 Sign languages in West Africa

1. Some ASL-based sign languages figure twice, once as separate sign languages, and once under ASL as well.

2. Where relevant, the convention to write Deaf with a capital to indicate cultural Deafness, rather than hearing impairment has been maintained. However, in many cases too little

information is available to make the distinction. In other cases, the distinction seems to be of relatively little relevance to the people involved.

3. "a certain number of linguistic codes/performances and gestures that are important to them" (translation is mine).

4. IDCS, n.d. Sign Language development in Guinea Bissau on www.idcs.info/learning_from_dperience/sign_language.html#visited on 10/09/2007.

19 Sign languages in the Arab world

Special thanks to Manal Hamzeh, Najah Taffal and the Palestine Red Crescent Society for their permission to reprint images.This research was supported by a National Institute of Health grant DC6473 "Emergence of Grammar in a New Sign Language."

1. LIU is the abbreviated form of the Arabic–English phonetic translation, *Lughat al-Ishara al-Urduniyah*.

2. The twenty-two countries are Algeria, Bahrain, Comoros, Djibouti, Egypt, Iraq, Jordan, Kuwait, Lebanon, Libya, Mauritania, Morocco, Oman, Palestine, Qatar, Saudi Arabia, Somalia, Sudan, Syria, Tunisia, United Arab Emirates and Yemen (League of Arab States, n.d.).

3. ABSL is used in the Al-Sayyid community in the Negev Desert in Israel.

4. Dictionaries used for this study are: Hamzeh 1993 for LIU, Palestine Red Crescent Society 2000 for PSL, Kuwaiti Sign Language Dictionary 1995 for KuSL, Suwayd 1992 for LSL, Tennant and Gluszak Brown 1998 for ASL.

5. The LIU sign for KORAN shows an arrow pointing upward on the left, below the chin. The PSL sign for KORAN shows an arrow moving toward the forehead.

6. The LIU sign for ELEPHANT has a D-handshape. The LSL sign for ELEPHANT has a flattened O-handshape.

7. The LIU signs for HOUSE and UNIVERSITY show arrows, each pointing both upward and downward.

20 Variation in American Sign Language

Portions of this chapter are adapted from Lucas, Bayley and Valli (2001), Lucas and Bayley (2005) and Lucas (2007). We are grateful to M. J. Bienvenu and Paul Seltzer for the illustrations in this chapter.

1. Upper-case D is used to denote communities and language users who are culturally deaf, that is, who share values, beliefs and behaviors about deafness. Lower-case d is used to denote audiological deafness, that is, the physiological condition of not being able to hear. Individuals who are deaf may not necessarily be Deaf.

2. See www.asd-1817.org/history/history-deafed.html.

3. Reviewers suggested that we draw a distinction between language particular "constraints" and language-external "factors." We have, however, retained the terminology commonly used in variationist sociolinguistics because these terms have specific technical meanings. A factor group refers to a linguistic feature (e.g., the location of the segment following the target variable) or a social feature (e.g., the signer's social class) that is hypothesized to correlate with greater or lesser use of a particular variant of the target variable. Factors within factor groups are linguistic (e.g., high or low location of the following sign) or social (e.g., working or middle class). We may say that a particular factor constrains the use of a variant, that is, it is a constraint, regardless of whether it is linguistic or social.

4. The data for Maryland in Lucas *et al.* (2001) include only White signers. Because we also wished to compare the results for African American and White signers, we excluded those tokens from the larger study.

21 Sociolinguistic variation in BANZSL

Sections of this chapter are adapted from T. Johnston and A. Schembri, Australian Sign Language. An Introduction to Sign Language Linguistics (Cambridge: Cambridge University Press, 2007).

22 Variation in East Asian sign language structures

We are grateful to all of the Deaf people in Asia who have enlightened us about their languages, especially Chengxiang Shen, Yan Zhang, Junhui Yang, Tetuo Itiyosi, Harumi Kimura, Yutaka Osugi and the many students at Tsukuba University of Technology with whom we have had the pleasure of working. Jean Ann provided information about phonology and character signs in Taiwan Sign Language. We were enlightened on TSL morphology and syntax by Hsin-Hsien Lee, Shou-fen Su and Yijun Chen. Soya Mori provided valuable information about Japanese demographics; and Sung-Eun Hong and Kang-Suk Byun provided information about Korean Sign Language. Thanks to Gladys Tang for permission to use some of her data, and to Midori Matsufuji for all of her logistical support. Some of Fischer's work was supported by a grant from the Japan Foundation. The editor and external reviewer provided many helpful comments and suggestions. All remaining errors are our own.

1. Perhaps a word is in order about the names and abbreviations of these languages. In the case of Western sign languages, the tradition has become the use of the term for the sign language in the surrounding spoken language, e.g., the sign language of Germany, Deutsche Gebärdensprache, is abbreviated as DGS. We have decided to follow the English names and abbreviations for the sign languages on which we are focusing for two reasons: first, these names and abbreviations have been in use for some time among linguists including ourselves; and second, none of the countries where these sign languages are used uses a Roman alphabet for its writing system. Thus, any alphabetic abbreviation would already be a distortion of the spoken language name for the sign language.
2. As in Western sign languages, there is a distinction between the natural sign languages of China, Taiwan, Japan and Korea and signed Chinese, Japanese and Korean, which follow the grammatical order of the spoken language and may lack features of the natural sign languages such as verb agreement, classifiers and aspect marking. For example, in signed Japanese, there is a question sign KA that corresponds to the Japanese question particle *ka*, but in JSL, questions are formed with particular non-manual markers and KA is not used.
3. See www.dpa.org.sg/services/hear/signlang.htm.
4. See www8.cao.go.jp/shougai/whitepaper/h18hakusho/zenbun.pdf/pdf/02_01_01.pdf.
5. See www.webtelevi.com/sokuho/kokunaiseiji/070809kokunaiseiji.htm.
6. Okamoto (1997) shows that the Osaka deaf school had more deaf teachers than any other, and for a longer time.
7. See Brentari and Eccarius (this volume) for differences in handshape inventories between Western sign languages and HKSL, one member of the Chinese family.
8. TI (O with pinkie extended) and TU (O with pinkie and ring finger extended) are used with added motion for 'Y100' and 'Y1000' in the Osaka dialect of JSL (Tetuo Itiyosi, personal communication, January 2008).
9. See http://en.wikipedia.org/wiki/Korean_manual_alphabet.
10. As mentioned above, written Korean no longer uses Chinese characters; however, KSL still has character signs for some place names in KSL (Kang-Suk Byun, personal communication, February 2008).

11. See Ann (1998) for more examples of each of these in TSL. Ann was the first person to our knowledge to discuss character signs in a widely available English publication. Our present analysis, based on our own observations of JSL and CSL in addition to TSL, is consistent with Ann's findings.

12. Three different sign languages have three different ways of depicting 品; JSL does a one-handed serial depiction using F-handshapes; CSL depicts one of the squares with one F hand and holds it steady while the other hand shows the other two squares; in TSL, two F hands are placed on either side of the mouth, which represents the top square (口 means 'mouth')! Ann (1998) discusses the use of the mouth for the depiction of 中 in TSL.

13. In JSL, the depictions of 中 middle', 日 'sun, day', 小 ('small') and 田 ('rice paddy') are generally used only in name signs; other signs not based on Chinese characters are used for talking about middles and rice paddies. Similarly, some character signs in CSL are used only in common name signs. TSL, perhaps because it lacks a fingerspelling alternative, appears to use more character signs for denotative meaning than JSL or CSL. It is also interesting to note that although both JSL and CSL depict 田, they do it with different fingers, following the phonology of the sign language in question: JSL uses a W-handshape while CSL uses the F-handshape, mirroring the number systems, where the F-handshape is used for the number 3 in CSL but the W-handshape is used in JSL.

14. Japan has forty-seven prefectures, and each has a name sign, as do almost all large cities; all competent signers know these signs. In the United States, by contrast, most signs for place names are very local, and many are based on fingerspelled abbreviations, e.g., TJ for Tijuana in the San Diego area, and FP for Fairport in the Rochester area.

15. For further information, see Sohn 1999.

16. This sign is highly unusual in that the two arguments participating in agreement are both objects. The JSL sign for 'introduce' is a plain verb and must use an auxiliary to show agreement. See Fischer 1996.

17. This is not grammatical gender, but real-world gender, and is generally reserved for humans or personified humans.

18. One domain in JSL where compounds are frequent is name signs. For anyone named Kimura, their default name sign will be KI ('tree') ˄MURA ('village'), matching the meanings of the components of their name. Alongside these signs many people from Deaf families also have unique nickname signs usually based on personal characteristics.

19. Smith (1990) claimed to have found three auxiliaries; further research by Tai and Su (2006) suggests that in fact there is only one, and it is essentially the same as that found in JSL.

20. See Pfau and Quer (this volume) for a survey of common uses of nonmanuals in sign languages, and Tang *et al.* (this volume) for more specific differences among HKSL, ASL and Swiss German Sign language (DSGS).

21. Quinto-Pozos (personal communication, April 2004) notes that LSM, the sign language of Mexico, also does not seem to require nonmanual marking of topic.

22. Van Gijn (2004) has similar examples in NGT (Sign Language of the Netherlands). For example:

neg
INGE INDEX$_a$ $\overline{\text{WANT}}$ ROLAND$_b$ $_b$VISIT$_c$ MARIJKE INDEX$_c$
'Inge doesn't want Roland to visit Marijke.'

23. This section is based on Osugi and Fischer 1998. See also Morgan (2006).

23 Crosslinguistic variation in prosodic cues

This work was supported by National Science Foundation (NSF) grants BCS 0112391 and BCS 0547554, awarded to Diane Brentari.

1. This prosodic hierarchy can be further analyzed into Foot → Syllable → Mora in models of prosodic analysis. Also, in the original hierarchy of Nespor and Vogel (1986), there is an intermediate level Clitic Group which is a level above the P-Word; however, we will not discuss this level in our analysis.
2. Here we provide a simplified version of the Strict Layer Hypothesis, which can in fact be decomposed into four "prosodic domination" constraints, namely LAYERNESS, HEADEDNESS, EXHAUSTIVITY and NONRECURSIVITY (Selkirk 1995).
3. Lengthening plays a role in our analyses in Studies 2 and 3. H2-spread is optional, and the non-dominant hand behaves differently when it plays a morphological role, as it does in classifier constructions (Nespor & Sandler 1999, Brentari & Crossley 2002), so it will not be a factor in our analyses.
4. Although reduplication has been reported to be a prosodic cue for P-Phrases in ISL and Langue des signes québécoise (LSQ; Miller 1996), it also occurs at I-Phrase boundaries (Brentari & Crossley 2002).
5. The pictures used in this work were a subset of those developed by Zwitserlood (2003) in her study on classifier constructions in Sign Language of the Netherlands.
6. See notational conventions in the Appendix.
7. By "native" we mean that the signers had Deaf signing parents, as well as being immersed in the Deaf communities of their respective countries.
8. Available at www.lat-mpi.eu/tools/elan.
9. The longest episodes were the same for all participants.
10. Pauses are the spaces between signs. Here they included the period of time from the beginning of the disintegration of the final handshape to the moment when the handshape of the next sign was assumed.
11. For each sign language, we divided the total numbers of signs by the total number of blinks produced in the three episodes.
12. We are calling this effect cultural, since deaf signers have limited access to the speech signal.
13. We suspected that dynamic movie clips like Tweety and Sylvester cartoon might induce the production of some discourse-driven constructions or nonmanuals in different sign languages that might have confounded our analysis.
14. We will see later on that two types of lengthening are operating in HKSL: a stronger form for I-Phrases and a weaker form for P-Phrases.
15. In our corpus, only path + trill combinations occurred phrase-internally. The other two types of complex movements – "path + path" or "path + local" – were all phrase-final (either P-Phrase or I-Phrase).
16. Sign duration was calculated from the beginning of the well-formed handshape to the beginning of the disintegration of the handshape at the end of a sign.
17. These passages are transcribed so that the reader can focus on comparing the forms across languages, so only rough glosses, the I-Phrase boundaries and prosodic cues used are provided.
18. This corpus differed from that in Sze's study, which was conversational data and which contained a larger variety of sentence types. The corpus in the current study contains more classifier constructions.
19. The percentages of having a blink to mark I-Phrases (R) boundaries in HKSL are higher than those reported in Sze's study, perhaps due to the nature of the task (i.e., conversational vs. picture description).

20. The percentages were derived by adding the two columns of figures in Table 23.8 " + Length, + blink" and " + Length, –blink."
21. " + Length" is based on the duration of the P-Word at the I-Phrase(R) boundary, including duration of movement, syllable repetitions and hold time.
22. Signer 1 in (9) and Signer 2 in (10) used different lexical forms for ROCKET. Signer 2's was a complex two-handed form as her base form.
23. The term "agent" means "handling classifier" in these structures. They have been shown to be agentive in HKSL and ASL (Tang & Yang 2007, Benedicto & Brentari 2004).
24. Other potential cues observed were eye gaze and return of head position to neutral, but these cues were even less consistent than blinks, and their status remains uncertain.

24 Deixis in an emerging sign language

We are grateful to our Nicaraguan participants for their enthusiastic involvement, and thank the authors of Chapter 25 and the editor for their helpful comments on an earlier version. This research was funded by National Institutes of Health (NIH)/NIDCD grant 2R56-DC005407 to Ann Senghas, NIH/NIDCD grant R01 DC00491 to Susan Goldin-Meadow; and National Science Foundation grant BCS 0547554 to Diane Brentari.

1. This cartoon was selected because it has been used extensively in crosslinguistic research on gesture. A full description of the cartoon can be found in McNeill 1992.
2. Diessel 1999 proposes a similar grammaticalization cline of demonstratives in spoken languages, in which an exophoric demonstrative must always pass through a stage of anaphoric use before acquiring a grammatical function.
3. We posit a contrast between *linguistic* and *grammatical* elements. Linguistic elements show language-like behavior, and are part of the language, but do not necessarily play a role in the grammar. The noun *dog* is a linguistic element but not a grammatical one; an agreement morpheme is both linguistic and grammatical; the gestured 'thumbs-up' is neither linguistic nor grammatical.
4. Another form of deixis that has been observed in Nicaragua among hearing and deaf people is the lip point (Kegl 2002). However, this form was not attested in the present dataset.
5. All data were coded by the first author; a subset of the data was coded by the second author to ensure reliability of the coding categories. Intercoder reliability for IX:chest was 1.00; ANOTHER, .97; and locative vs. nominal reference, .95.
6. Pyers and Senghas 2007 provide more detail on these constructions, which they gloss as *IX:self*.
7. We present the ordering analyses based on raw numbers in order to preserve frequency information; the same analyses conducted on the proportion data (that is, taking into account the total number of signs produced by each participant) reveals a similar pattern of results.
8. Of these fifty-one combinations, forty-three were with nouns or verbs and are shown in Figure 24.6; two appeared in sandwiches, and the remaining six were with adjectives or other elements.
9. This appears to be a "switch reference" device. Rather than indicating the previous referent (the way an anaphor does), it indicates a new referent, different from the previous referent. For example, in a language with a switch reference marker, a sentence like *The cat climbed the pole, and **he[anaphor]** fell* would mean that the cat fell, while *The cat climbed the pole, and **he[switch]** fell* would mean that someone other than the cat fell.
10. It has been suggested that even spoken language demonstratives may not have developed from a lexical source (Diessel 1999).

25 The grammar of space in two new sign languages

Our work is supported by grants from the National Institute on Deafness and other Communication Disorders (R01 DC 6473) and the Israel Science Foundation (#553/04). Thanks to Sara Lanseman for her help in obtaining the ISL data, and to Adi Lifshitz for her help in coding and organizing the ISL data.

1. We thank Yoav Moriah for this seminal thought.
2. Indeed, Fischer and Gough (1978) refer to the two types of verbs as "directional verbs."
3. In our other publications about ABSL, we have used estimates of the number of deaf people based on the work of other researchers. We are now working with members of the village to create a map of all deaf people in the community, to help us arrive at a more precise figure.
4. As far as we know, only one of the first generation deaf signers had deaf children. However, the deaf children from that family did not participate in the study reported here.
5. For a description of the history of the Deaf community in Israel and the development of ISL, see Meir and Sandler 2007.
6. The oldest subject is ninety-one years old and the first member of the Association of the Deaf in Israel.
7. The overall theory developed in Aronoff, Meir, and Sandler 2005 is still valid: that sign languages typically develop "simultaneous" morphology motivated by visuo-spatial cognition early in their histories, while affixal morphology that arises through grammaticalization is language-particular and takes much longer to develop. What the present study teaches us is that even the sign-language-typical and motivated morphology develops gradually.
8. *Webster's Third International Dictionary, Unabridged.* Merriam-Webster 2002. Available at http://unabridged.merriam-webster.com.
9. This pattern of setting up both referents in space, but then moving the verb straight out from the body, along the Z-axis, is quite common among hearing people who are asked to describe events without using speech (Coppola & Newport 2005).

REFERENCES

Aarons, D. (1994). *Aspects of the Syntax of American Sign Language.* PhD dissertation, Boston University.

Aarons, D., Bahan, B., Kegl, J. & Neidle, C. (1992). Clausal structure and a tier for grammatical marking in American Sign Language. *Nordic Journal of Linguistics*, **15**, 103–142.

(1995). Lexical tense markers in American Sign Language. In K. Emmorey & J. S. Reilly (eds.), *Language, Gesture and Space* (pp. 225–253). Hillsdale, NJ: Lawrence Erlbaum Associates.

Abdel-Fattah, M. (2005). Arabic Sign Language: A perspective. *Journal of Deaf Studies and Deaf Education*, **10**, 212–221.

Abercrombie, D. (1967). *Elements of General Phonetics.* Edinburgh: Edinburgh University Press.

Aboh, E. O., Pfau, R. & Zeshan, U. (2005). When a wh-word is not a wh-word: The case of Indian Sign Language. In T. Bhattacharya (ed.), *The Yearbook of South Asian Languages and Linguistics 2005* (pp. 11–43). Berlin: Mouton de Gruyter.

Adamiec, T. (2003). Głuchoniemi i ich świadectwa zycia od starozytności do końca XVIII wieku – przeglad problematyki. In M. Świdziński & T. Gałkowski (eds.), *Studia nad Kompetencja Jezykowa i Komunikacyjna Niesłyszacych.* Warsaw: Uniwersytet Warszawski.

Adams, M. (2003). *Historia de la Educación de los Sordos en México y Lenguaje por Señas Mexicano.* Spring Valley, CA: Fundación de Sordos Hispanos de San Diego.

Aitchison, J. (1991). *Language Change: Progress or Decay?* Cambridge: Cambridge Unversity Press.

Ajavon, P. A. (2003). *The Incorporation of Nigerian Signs in Deaf Education in Nigeria: A Pilot Study.* Frankfurt am Main. Brussels: Peter Lang.

Ajello, R., Mazzoni, L. & Nicolai, F. (2001). Linguistic gestures: Mouthing in Italian Sign Language (LIS). In P. Boyes Braem & R. Sutton-Spence (eds.), *The Hands Are the Head of the Mouth: The Mouth as an Articulator in Sign Languages* (pp. 231–246). Hamburg: Signum.

Akach, A. O. (1993). Squibbles barriers. *Sign Post*, **6**(1), 2–4.

Aldersson, R. & McEntee-Atalinanis L. J. (2007). A lexical comparison of Icelandic and Danish Sign Language. *Birkbeck Studies in Applied Linguistics*, **2**, 41–67.

Aldrete, G. S. (1999). *Gestures and Acclamations in Ancient Rome (Ancient Society and History).* Baltimore, MD/London: Johns Hopkins University Press.

Alibašić Ciciliani, T. & Wilbur, R. B. (2006). Pronominal system in Croatian Sign Language. *Sign Language and Linguistics*, **9**, 95–132.

Alisedo, G. & Skliar, C. (1993). The influence of Italian oralism in Argentina. In R. Fischer & H. Lane (eds.), *Looking Back: A Reader on the History of Deaf Communities and their Sign Languages* (pp. 307–332). Hamburg: Signum.

Allen, G. D., Wilbur, R. B. & Schick, B. S. (1991). Aspects of rhythm in ASL. *Sign Language Studies*, **72**, 297–320.

Allott, R. (2000). *Brain, Lexicon, Syntax*. Rutgers, NJ: Language Origins Society.

American School for the Deaf (1818). *Second Report of the Directors of the Connecticut Asylum for the Education and Instruction of Deaf and Dumb Persons. 5*. Hartford: American School for the Deaf.

Anderson, J. M. (1971). *The Grammar of Case: Towards a Localist Theory*. London: Cambridge University Press.

Ann, J. (1993). A linguistic investigation of the relationship between physiology and handshape. PhD dissertation. University of Arizona, Tucson.

   (1998). Contact between a sign language and a written language: Character signs in Taiwan Sign Langauge. In C. Lucas (ed.), *Pinky Extension and Eye Gaze: Language Use in Deaf Communities* (pp. 59–99). Washington, DC: Gallaudet University Press.

   (2006). *Frequency of Occurrence and Ease of Articulation of Sign Language Handshapes: The Taiwanese example*. Washington, DC: Gallaudet University Press.

Aramburo, A. (1989). Sociolinguistic aspects of the Black Deaf community. In C. Lucas (ed.), *The Sociolinguistics of the Deaf Community* (pp. 103–119). San Diego, CA: Academic Press.

Archangeli, D. (1988a). Aspects of underspecification theory. *Phonology*, **5**, 183–208.

   (1988b). *Underspecification in Yawelmani Phonology and Morphology*. New York: Garland Press.

Arends, J., Muysken, P. & Smith, N. (1995). *Pidgins and Creoles: An Introduction*. Amsterdam: John Benjamins Associates.

Ariko, C. (2006). Deaf demand special news. *The New Vision*, March 28th Edition.

Aronoff, M., Meir, I. & Sandler, W. (2005). The paradox of sign language morphology. *Language*, **81**(2), 301–344.

Aronoff, M., Meir, I., Padden, C. & Sandler, W. (2003). Classifier constructions and morphology in two sign languages. In K. Emmorey (ed.), *Perspectives on Classifier Constructions in Sign Languages* (pp. 53–86). Mahwah, NJ: Lawrence Erlbaum Associates.

   (2004). Morphological universals and the sign language type. In G. Booj & J. van Marle (eds.), *Yearbook of Morphology 2004* (pp. 19–39). Dordrecht/Boston, MA: Kluwer Academic Publishers.

   (2008). The roots of linguistic organization in a new language. In *Interaction Studies: A Special issue on Holophrasis vs. Compositionality in the Emergence of Protolanguage*, **9**(1), 131–150.

Arrotéia, J. (2003). Papel do marcador 'aceno de cabeça' em sentenças não-conônicas. Paper presented at III Seminário Internacional Abralin, UFRJ (Universidade Federal do Rio de Janeiro), Rio de Janeiro.

Askins, D. & Perlmutter, D. (1995). Allomorphy explained through phonological representation: Person and number inflection of American Sign Language. Paper presented at the Annual Meeting of the German Linguistic Society, Gottingen.

Atkinson, J., Campbell, R., Marshall, J., Thacker, A. & Woll, B. (2004). Understanding "not": Neuropsychological dissociations between hand and head markers of negation in BSL. *Neuropsychologia*, **42**, 214–229.

Avery, P. & Idsardi, W. (2001). Laryngeal dimensions, completion and enhancement. In T. A. Hall (ed.), *Distinctive Feature Theory* (pp. 41–70). Berlin: Mouton de Gruyter.

Babiński, G. (1998). *Metodologiczne problemy badań etnicznych.* Kraków: Zakład Wydawniczy "NOMOS."

Bahan, B. (1996). Non-manual realization of agreement in American Sign Language. PhD dissertation, Boston University.

Bahan, B., Kegl, J., Lee, R., MacLaughlin, D. & Neidle, C. (2000). The licensing of null arguments in American Sign Language. *Linguistic Inquiry,* **31,** 1–27.

Bailey, C.-J. N. (1970). Lectal groupings in matrices generated with waves along the temporal parameter. *Working Papers in Linguistics,* 2, 214.

   (1971). Variation and language theory. Unpublished manuscript, Arlington, VA: Center for Applied Linguistics.

Bailey, C. S. & Dolby, K. (2002). *The Canadian Dictionary of ASL.* Edmonton, Canada: University of Alberta Press.

Baker, A. E. (2000). Official recognition of sign language in the Netherlands. *Deaf Worlds,* **16**(2), 34–38.

Baker, A. E. & van der Hulst, H. (1996). Sign linguistics: Phonetics, phonology and morpho-syntax. *Lingua,* **98,** 1–3.

Baker, A. E. & Woll, B. (eds.) (2009). *Sign Language Acquisition.* Amsterdam: John Benjamins.

Baker, C. & Cokely, D. (1980). *American Sign Language: A Teacher's Resource Text on Grammar and Culture.* Silver Spring, MD: T. J. Publishers.

Baker, C. & Padden, C. (1978). Focusing on the non-manual components of American Sign Language. In P. Siple (ed.), *Understanding Language Through Sign Language Research* (pp. 27–57). New York: Academic Press.

Baker-Shenk, C. (1983). A micro-analysis of the non-manual components of questions in American Sign Language. PhD dissertation, University of California, Berkeley.

Baker-Shenk, A. E., van den Bogaerde, B. & Woll, B. (2005). Methods and procedures in sign language acquisition studies. *Sign Language and Linguistics,* **8**(1/2), 7–59.

Barakat, R. (1973). Arabic gestures. *Journal of Popular Culture,* **6,** 749–791.

Barasch, M. (1987). *Giotto and the Language of Gesture.* Cambridge, MA: Cambridge University Press.

Barnplantorna, Riksförbundet för Barn med Cochleaimplantat och Barn med Hörapparat. (n.d.). Cochleaimplantat: en fantastisk möjlighet för döva att få höra. Available at www.barnplantora.se.

Basu, D. (2005). Verb compounds in Bangla: An event based analysis. Master's thesis, Purdue University, West Lafayette, IN.

Bates, E., Benigni, L. Bretherton, I., Camioni, L. & Volterra, V. (1979). *The Emergence of Symbols: Cognition and Communication in Infancy.* New York: Academic Press.

Battison, R. (1974). Phonological deletion in American Sign Language. *Sign Language Studies,* **5,** 1–19.

   (1978). *Lexical Borrowing in American Sign Language.* Silver Spring, MD: Linstok Press. Repr. 2003, Burtonsville, MD: Sign Media, Inc..

Battison, R., Markowicz, H. & Woodward J. (1975). A good rule of thumb: Variable phonology in American Sign Language. In R. W. Fasold & R. W. Shuy (eds.), *Analyzing Variation in Language* (pp. 291–302). Washington, DC: Georgetown University Press.

Bayley, R. (2002). The quantitative paradigm. In J. K. Chambers, P. Trudgill & N. Schilling-Estes (eds.), *The Handbook of Language Variation and Change* (pp. 117–141). Oxford: Blackwell.

Bayley, R., & Lucas C. (in press). Phonological variation in Louisiana ASL: An exploratory study. In M. Picone & C. Davies (eds.), *Language Variety in the South: Historical and Contemporary Perspectives.* Tuscaloosa, AL: University of Alabama Press.

Bayley, R. & Pease-Alvarez, L. (1997). Null pronoun variation in Mexican-descent children's narrative discourse. *Language Variation and Change*, **9**, 349–371.

Baynton, C. D. (1996). *Forbidden Signs: American Culture and the Campaign Against Sign Language*. Chicago, IL: University of Chicago Press.

Bébian, Roch-Ambroise A. (1825). *Mimographie ou essai d'écriture mimique, propre à régulariser le langage des sourds-muets*. Paris: Colas.

Beecken, A., Keller, J., Prillwitz, S. & Zienert, H. (1999). *Grundkurs Deutsche Gebärdensprache. Lehrbuch Stufe 1*. Hamburg: Signum.

Behares, L. E. & Massone, M. I. (1996). The sociolinguistics of Uruguayan and Argentinian deaf communities as a language-conflict situation. *Journal of the Sociology of Language*, **117**, 99–113.

Bell, A. M. (1867). *Visible Speech: The Science of Universal Alphabetics or Self-Interpreting Physiological Letters, for the Writing of All Languages in One Alphabet*. London/New York: Simpkin, Marshall & Co.

  (1881). *Sounds and Their Relations: A Complete Manual of Universal Alphabetics, Illustrated by Means of Visible Speech*. Salem, MA: J. P. Burbank.

Bellugi, U. & Klima, E. (1982). From gesture to sign: Deixis in a visuo-gestural language. In R. J. Jarvella & W. Klein (eds.), *Speech, Place, and Action: Studies in Deixis and Related Topics* (pp. 279–313). Chichester, NY: Wiley.

Benalcázar, O. (1994). Principles, changes, and current guidelines in the education of the Deaf. In C. J. Erting, R. C. Johnson, D. L. Smith & B. D. Snider (eds.), *The Deaf Way: Perspectives from the International Conferences on Deaf Culture* (pp. 127–128). Washington, DC: Gallaudet Unversity Press.

Benedicto, E. & Brentari, D. (2004). Where did all the arguments go?: Argument-changing properties of classifiers in ASL. *Natural Language and Linguistic Theory*, **22**(4), 743–810.

Berenz, N. (1998). The case for Brazilian Sign Language: A deaf community finds its voice. In D. A. Kibbee (ed.), *Language Legislation and Linguistic Rights* (pp. 269–287). Amsterdam/Philidelphia, PA: John Benjamins Associates.

  (2002). Insights into person deixis. *Sign Language and Linguistics*, **5**(2), 203–227.

  (2003). Sudros venceremos: The rise of the Brazilian Deaf Community. In L. Monaghan, C. Schmaling, K. Nakamura & G. Turner (eds.), *Many Ways to Be Deaf* (pp. 173–193). Washington, DC: Gallaudet University Press.

Bergman, B. (1979). *Signed Swedish [translated from Tecnad svenska (1977)]*. Stockholm: Liber Distribution.

  (1983). Studies in Swedish Sign Language. Doctoral dissertation, Stockholm University.

Bergman, B. & Wallin, L. (1994). The study of sign language in society. In C. Erting, R. C. Johnson, D. Smith & B. Snider (eds.), *The Deaf Way: Perspectives from the International Conference on Deaf Culture* (pp. 309–330). Washington, DC: Gallaudet University Press.

Bezzina, F. (n.d.). *Niftiehmu bis-sinjali: Gabra mil-Lingwi tas-Sinjali Maltin*. Malta: Gozo Association for the Deaf.

Bickford, A. (1991). Lexical variation in Mexican Sign Language. *Sign Language Studies*, **72**, 241–276.

Biesold, H. (1999). *Crying Hands: Eugenics and Deaf People in Nazi Germany*. Washington, DC: Gallaudet University Press.

Birch-Rasmussen, S. (1989). *Lærebog i Mundhåndsystem*. København: Døves Center for Total Kommunikation (KC).

Biritwum, R. B., Devres, J. P., Ofosu-Amaah, S., Marfo, C. & Essah, E. R. (2001). Prevalence of children with disabilities in central region. Ghana. *West African Journal of Medicine*, **20**(3), 249–255.

Black, P. & Kruskal, J. (1997). Comparative lexicostatistics: A brief history and bibliography of key words. Available at www.ntu.edu.au/education/langs/ielex/BIBLIOG.html.

Blench, R. & Nyst, V. (2003). An unreported African sign language in Northeast Nigeria. *OGMIOS Newsletter*, Vol. **2**.10, 22.

Blench, R. & Warren, A. (2005). An unreported African sign language for the deaf among the Bura in Northeast Nigeria. Available at http://homepage.ntlworld.com/roger_blench/Language%20data.htm.

Blevins, J. (1995). The syllable in phonological theory. In J. A. Goldsmith (ed.), *The Handbook of Phonological Theory* (pp. 206–244). Oxford: Blackwell.

Bloomfield, L. (1933). *Language*. New York: Henry Holt and Co.

Bobaljik, J. (1995). Morphosyntax: The Syntax of Verbal Inflection. PhD dissertation, MIT, Cambridge, MA.

Boeters, G. (1926). Lex Zwickau. *Zeitschrift für Volksaufartung und Erbkunde*, **1**, 148–150.

Bohnemeyer, J. (2003). The unique vector constraint. In E. van der Zee, & J. Slack (eds.), *Representing Direction in Language and Space* (pp. 86–110). Oxford: Oxford University Press.

Bohnemeyer, J., Enfield, N., Essegbey, J., Ibarretxe-Atunaño, I., Kita, S., Lüpke, F. & Ameka, F. (2007). Principles of event segmentation in language: The case of motion events. *Language*, **83**(3), 495–532.

Bolinger, D. (1986). *Intonation and Its Parts*. Stanford, CA: Stanford University Press.

Bonvillian, R. J. & Folven, J. D. (1991). The transition from non-referential to referential language in children acquiring ASL development. *Psychology*, **25**(5), 806–816.

(1993). Sign language acquisition: Developmental aspects. In M. Marschark & D. M. Clark (eds.), *Psychological Perspective on Deafness* (pp. 229–265). Hillsdale, NJ: Lawrence Erlbaum Associates.

Bonvillian, R. J., Orlansky, M. D., Novack, L. L., Folven, R. J. & Wilcox, P. H. (1985). Language cognition and chirological development: The first steps in language acquisition. In W. Stokoe & V. Volterra (eds.), *Sign Language Research '83: Proceedings of the III International Symposium on Sign Language Research* (pp. 10–23). Silver Spring, MD: Linstok Press.

Bos, H. F. (1990). Person and location marking in SLN: Some implications of a spatially expressed syntactic system. In S. Prillwitz & T. Vollhaber (eds.), *Current Trends in European Sign Language Research: Proceedings of the 3rd European Congress on Sign Language Research* (pp. 231–246). Hamburg: Signum. (International Studies on Sign Language and Communication of the Deaf; vol. 9)

(1993). Agreement and pro drop in sign language of the Netherlands. In K. Hengeveld & F. Drijkoningen (eds.), *Linguistics in the Netherlands* (pp. 37–48). Amsterdam/Philadelphia, PA: John Benjamins Associates. (AVT Publications; vol. **10**)

(1994). An auxilary verb in Sign Language of the Netherlands. In I. Ahlgren, B. Bergman & M. Brennan (eds.), *Perspectives on Sign Language Structure: Papers Presented from the Fifth International Symposium on Sign Language Research (SLR)*, Vol. I (pp. 37–53). Durham: International Sign Linguistic Association.

(1995). Pronoun copy in Sign Language of the Netherlands. In H. F. Bos & G. M. Schermer (eds.), *Sign Language Research 1994: Proceedings of the Fourth European Congress on Sign Language Research, Munich* (pp. 121–148). Hamburg: Signum. (International Studies on Sign Language and Communication of the Deaf; vol. **29**)

Bošković, Z. & Lasnik, H. (2007). *Minimalist Syntax: The Essential Readings*. Oxford: Blackwell.

Bouchard, D. (1996). Sign language & language universals: The status of order & position in grammar. *Sign Language Studies*, **91**, 99–139.

Bouchard, D. & Dubuisson, C. (1995). Grammar, order & position of wh-signs in Quebec Sign Language. *Sign Language Studies*, **87**, 99–139.

Bourgerie, D. S. (1990). A quantitative study of sociolinguistic variation in Cantonese (China). PhD dissertation, Ohio State University, Columbus.

Boyes Braem, P. (1990a). Acquisition of the handshape in American Sign Language: A preliminary analysis. In V. Volterra & C. Erting (eds.), *From Gesture to Language in Hearing and Deaf Children* (pp. 107–127). New York: Springer.

(1990b). *Einführung in die Gebärdensprache und ihre Erforschung*. Hamburg: Signum.

(1996). *Eine Untersuchung über den Einfluß des Erwerbsalters auf die in der deutschsprachigen Schweiz verwendeten Formen von Gebärdensprache*. Informationsheft Nr. 27. Zurich: Verein zur Unterstützung der Gebärdensprache der Gehörlosen.

(1999). Rhythmic temporal patterns in the signing of early and late learners of German Swiss Sign Language. *Language and Speech*, **42**(2/3), 177–208.

(2001a). A multimedia bilingual database for the lexicon of Swiss German Sign Language. *Sign Language and Linguistics*, **4**(1/2), 133–143.

(2001b). Functions of the mouthing component in the signing of deaf early and late learners of Swiss German Sign Language. In D. Brentari (ed.), *Foreign Vocabulary in Sign Language* (pp. 1–47). Mahwah, NJ: Lawrence Erlbaum Associates.

(2001c). Functions of the mouthings in the signing of Deaf early and late learners of Swiss German Sign Language (DSGS). In P. Boyes Braem & R. Sutton-Spence (eds.), *The Hands Are the Head of the Mouth: The Mouth as Articulator in Sign Language* (pp. 99–131). Hamburg: Signum.

(2003–2005). *Linguistic Descriptions of DSGS, as Printable Texts in the Four CD-ROMS*. Zurich: Schweizerischer Gehörlosenbund-DS.

Boyes Braem, P. & Sutton-Spence, R. (2001). *The Hands Are the Head of the Mouth: The Mouth as Articulator in Sign Languages*. Hamburg: Signum.

Boyes Braem, P., Pizzuto, E. & Volterra, V. (2002). The interpretation of signs by (hearing and deaf) members of different cultures. In R. Schulmeister & H. Reinitzer (eds.), *Progress in Sign Language Research: In Honor of Siegmund Prillwitz* (pp. 187–219). Hamburg: Signum. (International Studies on Sign Language and Communication of the Deaf; vol. **40**)

Boyes Braem, P., Fournier, M. L., Rickli, F., Corazza, S., Franchi, M. L. & Volterra, V. (1990). A comparision of techniques for expressing semantic roles and locative relations in two different sign languages. In W. H. Edmondson & F. Karlsson (eds.), *Papers from the Fourth International Symposium on Sign Language Research (SLR 1987)* (pp. 114–120). Hamburg: Signum.

Boyes Braem, P., Caramore, B., Herman, R. & Shores-Hermann, P. (2000). Romance and reality: Sociolinguistic similarities and differences between Swiss German Sign Language and Rhaeto-Romansh. In L. Monaghan (ed.), *Many Ways to BE Deaf: International Variation in Language, Identity and Ideology* (pp. 89–113). Hamburg: Signum.

Branchini, C. & Donati, C. (2009). Relatively different: Italian Sign Language relative clauses in a typological perspective. In A. Liptàk (ed.), *Correlatives Cross-Linguistically* (pp. 157–191). Amsterdam: Benjamins.

Braze, F. D. (2004). Aspectual inflection, verb raising, and object fronting in American Sign Language. *Lingua*, **114**, 29–58.

Brennan, M. (1990). Word Formation in British Sign Language. PhD dissertation, University of Stockholm.

(1992). The visual world of BSL: An Introduction. In D. Brien (ed.), *Dictionary of British Sign Language/English* (pp. 1–133). London: Faber & Faber.

624   *References*

624   *References*

(2005). Conjoining word and image in British Sign Language (BSL): An exploration of metaphorical signs in BSL. *Sign Language Studies*, **5**, 360–382.

Brennan, M. & Turner, G. (1994). *Word-Order Issues in Sign Language*. Durham: International Sign Linguistics Association.

Brentari, D. (1990). Theoretical foundations in American Sign Language phonology. PhD dissertation, University of Chicago.

(1998). *A Prosodic Model of Sign Language Phonology*. Cambridge, MA: MIT Press.

(2002). Modality differences in sign language phonology and morphophonemics. In R. Meier, D. Quinto & K. Cormier (eds.), *Modality in Language and Linguistic Theory* (pp. 35–64). Cambridge: Cambridge University Press.

(2005) The use of morphological templates to specify handshapes in sign languages. *Linguistische Berichte*, **13**, 145–177.

(in press). Sign language phonology. In J. Goldsmith, A. Yu & J. Riggles (eds.), *Handbook of Phonological Theory*. 2nd edn. Oxford/New York: Blackwell.

Brentari, D. & Crossley, L. (2002). Prosody on the hands and face: Evidence from American Sign Language. *Sign Language and Linguistics*, **5**(2), 105–130.

Brentari, D. & Goldsmith, J. (1993). Secondary licensing and the non-dominant hand in ASL phonology. In G. Coulter (ed.), *Current Issues in ASL Phonology* (pp. 19–41). New York: Academic Press.

Brentari, D. & Padden, C. A. (2001). Native and foreign vocabulary in American Sign Language: A lexicon with multiple origins. In D. Brentari (ed.), *Foreign Vocabulary in Sign Languages* (pp. 87–119). Mahwah, NJ: Lawrence Erlbaum Associates.

Brentari, D., González, C., Seidl, A. & Wilbur, R. (in press). Sensitivity to visual prosodic cues in signers and nonsigners. *Language and Speech*.

Brentari, D., van der Hulst, E., van der Kooij & Sandler, W. (1996). [One] Over [All]; [All] Over [One]: A dependency phonology analysis of handshape in sign languages. Unpublished manuscript, Purdue University, University of Connecticut and the University of Haifa.

Brenzinger, M., Heine, B. & Sommer, G. (1991). Language death in Africa. In R. H. Robins & E. M. Uhlenbeck (eds.), *Endangered Languages* (pp. 19–45). Oxford/New York: Berg.

Brien, D. (1992). *Dictionary of British Sign Language/English*. London: Faber & Faber.

Briggs, C. L. & Guede, N. (1964). *No More For Ever: A Saharan Jewish Town*. Cambridge, MA: Peabody Museum.

Brito, L. F. (1984). Similarities and differences in two Brazilian Sign Languages. *Sign Language Studies*, **42**, 45–56.

Brouland, J. (1855). *Language Mimique: Spécimen d'un Dictionnaire des Signes*. Washington, DC: Gallaudet Archives.

Bruce, V. & Green, P. (1990). Visual perception. In *Physiology, Psychology, and Ecology*. 2nd edn. London/Hillsdale, NJ: Lawrence Erlbaum Associates.

Brugman, H., Crasborn, O. & Russel, A. (2004). Collaborative annotation of sign language data with peer-to-peer technology. Paper presented at the Fourth International Conference on Language Resources and Evaluation (LREC 2004), Lisbon.

Buhler, D. (2007). Friendships in Costa Rica: Mobility International USA. Available at www.miusa.org/ncde/stories/buhler.

Bühler, K. (1990). *Theory of Language: The Representational Function of Language*. Amsterdam: John Benjamins Associates.

Bulwer, J. (1644). *Chirologia: Or the Natural Language of the Hand*. London: R. Whitaker.

Bulwer, J. (1648). *Philocophus: Or the Deafe and Dumbe Man's Friend*. London: Humphrey Moseley.

Butler, J. (2003). A Minimalist treatment of modality. *Lingua*, **113**, 967–996.

Bybee, J. (2003). Cognitive processes in grammaticalization. In M. Tomasello (ed.), *The New Psychology of Language: Cognitive and Functional Approaches to Language Structure* (pp. 145–168). Mahwah, NJ: Lawrence Erlbaum Associates.

Bybee, J., Perkins, R. & Pagliuca, W. (1994). *The Evolution of Grammar: Tense, Aspect, and Modality in the Languages of the World.* Chicago, IL: University of Chicago Press.

Byun, K.-S. (2004). Gender marking in Korean Sign Language. Paper presented at the Mini-Conference on Sign Language Research, Nijmegen.

Callaway, A. (1998). Deaf children in China. *China Review*, Spring, 28–32.

Campos de Abreu, A. (1994). The Deaf social life in Brazil. In C. J. Erting, R. C. Johnson, D. L. Smith & B. D. Snider (eds.), *The Deaf Way: Perspectives from the International Conference on Deaf Culture* (pp. 114–116). Washington, DC: Gallaudet University Press.

Caramore, B. (1988). *Die Gebärdensprache in der Schweizerischen Gehörlosenpädagogik des 19. Jahrhunderts.* Zurich, Hamburg: Verlag Hörgeschädigte Kinder.

  (1990). Sign language in the education of the deaf in 19th century Switzerland. In S. Prillwitz & T. Vollhaber (eds.), *Current Trends in European Sign Language Research: Proceedings of the Third European Congress on Sign Language Research. Hamburg July 26–29, 1989* (pp. 23–34). Hamburg: Signum.

Carew, R. (1602). *Survey of Cornwall.* London: John Jaggard.

Carreiras, M., Gutierrez-Sigut, E., Baquero, S. & Corina, D. (2008). Lexical processing in Spanish Sign Language (LSE). *Journal of Memory and Language*, **58**, 100–122.

Carroll, C. & Mather, S. (1997). *Movers & Shakers: Deaf People Who Changed the World.* San Diego, CA: Dawn Sign Press.

Carty, B. (2000). John Carmichael: Australian Deaf pioneer. In A. Schembri, J. Napier, R. Beattie & G. R. Leigh (eds.), *Proceedings of the Australasian Deaf Studies Research Symposium, Renwick College, Sydney, Australia* (pp. 9–20). Sydney: North Rocks Press.

Carty, B. (2004). Managing their own affairs: The Australian deaf community during the 1920s and 1930s. PhD dissertation, Griffith University, Brisbane.

Caselli, M. C., Maragna, S. & Volterra, V. (2006). *Linguaggio e sordità: Gesti, segni e parole nello sviluppo e nell'educazione.* Bologna: Il Mulino.

Casey, S. (2003). "Agreement" in gestures and signed languages: The use of directionality to indicate referents involved in actions. PhD dissertation, University of California, San Diego, CA.

Castberg, P. A. (1809). *Om Tegn- eller Gebærde-Sproget med Hensyn paa dets Brug af Døvstumme og dets Anvendelighed ved deres Undervisning.* Kiøbenhavn: Andreas Seidelin.

Cecchetto, C., Geraci, C. & Zucchi, S. (2006). Strategies of relativization in Italian Sign Language. *Natural Language and Linguistic Theory*, **24**, 945–975.

Channon, R. (2002a). Signs are single segments: phonological representations and temporal sequencing in ASL and other sign languages. PhD dissertation, University of Maryland, College Park.

Channon, R. (2002b). Beads on a string? Representations of repetition in spoken and signed languages. In R. Meier, D. Quinto & K. Cormier (eds.), *Modality and Structure in Signed and Spoken Languages* (pp. 65–87). Cambridge: Cambridge University Press.

Cheikh, E. B. (2007). Un apprentissage du langage des signes.. *Le Soleil*, August 7.

Chen Pichler, Deborah. (2001). Word order variability and acquisition in American Sign Language. PhD dissertation, University of Connecticut, Storrs.

Chomsky, N. (1957). *Syntactic Structures.* The Hague: Mouton de Gruyter.

Chomsky, N. (1965). *Aspects of the Theory of Syntax.* Cambridge, MA: MIT Press.

Chomsky, N. (1977). On wh-movement. In P. Culicover, T. Wasow & A. Akmajian (eds.), *Formal Syntax* (pp. 71–132). New York: Academic Press.

Chomsky, N. (1995). *The Minimalist Program*. Cambridge, MA: MIT Press.
Chomsky, N. & Halle, M. (1968). *The Sound Pattern of English*. New York: Harper and Row.
Chomsky, N. & Lasnik, H. (1993). The theory of principles and parameters. In J. Jacobs, A. Von Stechow, W. Sternefeld, & T. Venneman (eds.), *Syntax: An International Handbook of Contemporary Research*, Vol. I (pp. 506–569). Berlin: Mouton de Gruyter. Repr. with minor revisions in Chomsky (1995).
Christensen, K. K. (1986). Norwegian *ingen*: A case of post-syntactic lexicalization. In Ö. Dahl & A. Holmberg (eds.), *Scandinavian Syntax* (pp. 21–35). Stockholm: Institute of Linguistics, Stockholm University.
Cinque, G. (1999). *Adverbs and Functional Heads*. Oxford: Oxford University Press.
Clark, H. (1973). Space, time, semantics, and the child. In T. E. Moore (ed.), *Cognitive Development and the Acquisition of Language* (pp. 27–63). New York: Academic Press.
Clements, G. N. (2001). Representational economy in constraint-based phonology. In T. A. Hall (ed.), *Distinctive Feature Theory* (pp. 71–146). Berlin: Mouton de Gruyter.
Coates, J. Sutton-Spence, R. (2001). Turn taking patterns in deaf conversation. *Journal of Sociolinguistics*, **2**, 2–34.
Coerts, J. (1990). The analysis of interrogatives and negation in SLN. In S. Prillwitz & T. Vollhaber (eds.), *Proceedings of the Third European Congress on Sign Language Research. Hamburg* (pp. 265–277). Hamburg: Signum. (International Studies on Sign Language and Communication of the Deaf; vol. **9**)
  (1992). Non-manual grammatical markers: An analysis of interrrogatives, negation and topicalizations in Sign Language of the Netherlands. PhD dissertation, University of Amsterdam.
  (1994). Constituent order in Sign Language of the Netherlands and the functions of orientations. In I. Ahlgren, B. Bergman & M. Brennan (eds.), *Perspectives on Sign Language Structure: Papers from the Fifth International Symposium of Sign Language Research*, Vol. I (pp. 69–88). Durham: International Sign Linguistic Association.
  (2000). Early sign combinations in the acquisition of Sign Language of the Netherlands: Evidence for language-specific features. In C. D. Chamberlain, J. P. Morford & R. I. Mayberry (eds.), *Language Acquisition by Eye* (pp. 91–109). Mahwah, NJ: Lawrence Erlbaum Associates.
Cogill-Koez, D. (2000a). A model of signed language "classifier predicates" as templated visual representation. *Sign Language and Linguistics*, **3**, 209–236.
  (2000b). Signed language classifier predicates: Linguistic structures or schematic visual representation? *Sign Language and Linguistics*, **3**, 153–207.
Collins, S. (2004). Adverbial morphemes in tactile American Sign Language. PhD Dissertation, The Union Institute, Cincinnati, OH.
Collins, S. & Petronio, K. (1998). What happens in Tactile ASL? In C. Lucas (ed.), *Pinky Extension and Eye Gaze: Language Use in Deaf Communities* (pp. 18–37). Washington, DC: Gallaudet University Press. (Sociolinguistics in Deaf Communities, vol. **4**)
Collins-Ahlgren, M. (1989). Aspects of New Zealand Sign Language. Doctoral Dissertation, Victoria University of Wellington.
Comité Prociegos y Sordos de Guatemala. (2006). Guatemala División de Educación. Available at www.prociegosysordos.org.gt/index.php?id = 3.
Comrie, B. (1976). *Aspect*. Cambridge: Cambridge University Press.
Coppola, M. (2002). The emergence of the grammatical category of Subject in home sign: Evidence from family-based gesture systems in Nicaragua. PhD dissertation: University of Rochester, NY.

Coppola, M. (2007). Gestures to signs: The origins of words in Nicaraguan Sign Language. Paper presented at the Workshop Current Issues in Sign Language Research, University of Köln, Köln.

Coppola, M. & Newport, E. L. (2005). Grammatical subjects in home sign: Abstract linguistic structure in adult primary gesture systems without linguistic input. *Proceedings of the National Academy of Science*, **102**(52), 19249–19253.

Coppola, M. & So, W. C. (2005). Abstract and object-anchored deixis: pointing and spatial layout in adult homesign systems in Nicaragua. In M. R. Clark-Cotton, A. Brugos & S. Ha (eds.), *BUCLD 29: Proceedings of the Twenty-Ninth Annual Boston University Conference on Language Development* (pp. 144–155). Somerville, MA: Cascadilla Press.

(2006). The seeds of spatial grammar: Spatial modulation and coreference in homesigning and hearing adults. In D. T. M. Bamman & C. Zaller (eds.), *BUCLD 30: Proceedings of the Thirtieth Annual Boston University Conference on Language Development* (pp. 119–130). Somerville, MA: Cascadilla Press.

Corazza, S. (1993). The history of sign language in Italian education of the deaf. In R. Fischer & H. Lane (eds.), *Looking Back: A Reader on the History of Deaf Communities and Their Sign Languages* (pp. 219–229). Hamburg: Signum.

(1997). La sezione ENS di Trieste. In A. Z Zuccalà (ed.), *Cultura del gesto e cultura della parola: Viaggio antropologico nel mondo dei sordi* (pp. 107–112). Milan: Meltemi.

Corbett, G. (2006). *Agreement*. Cambridge: Cambridge University Press.

Corina, D. P. (1993). To branch or not to branch: Underspecification in American Sign Language handshape contours. In G. R. Coulter (ed.), *Current Issues in ASL Phonology* (pp. 63–95). New York: Academic Press.

Corina, D. P. & Sandler, W. (1990). Reassessing the role of sonority in syllable structure: Evidence from a visual-gestural language. In M. Ziolkowski, M. Noske & K. Deaton (eds.), *Proceedings for the Annual Meeting of the Chicago Linguistic Society, 26*; Vol. II: *The Parasession on the Syllable in Phonetics and Phonology* (pp. 33–43). Chicago, IL: Chicago Linguistic Society.

(1993). On the nature of phonological structure in sign language. *Phonology*, **10**, 165–201.

Corina, D. P., Bellugi, U. & Reilly, J. (1999). Neuropsychological studies of linguistic and affective facial expressions in deaf signers. *Language and Speech*, **42**(2/3), 307–331.

Cormier, K. (1998). Grammatical and anaphoric agreement in American Sign Language. Master's thesis, University of Texas, Austin.

(2002). Grammaticization of indexic signs: How American Sign Language expresses numerosity. PhD dissertation, University of Texas, Austin.

Coulter, G. R. (1979). American Sign Language typology. PhD dissertation, University of California, San Diego.

(1993). *Current Issues in American Sign Language Phonology*. San Diego, CA: Academic Press.

Council of Arab Ministers of Social Affairs (2004). *Background paper on the international convention for the protection and promotion of the rights and dignity of persons with disabilities*. Available at www.un.org/esa/socdev/enable/rights/contrib-arab1.htm.

Crain, R. C. (1996). Representing a sign as a single segment in American Sign Language. Paper presented at the Proceedings of the Eastern States Conference on Linguistics, 13 (ESCOL), University of New Brunswick, St. John.

Crasborn, O. (2001). *Phonetic Implementation of Phonological Categories in Sign Language of the Netherlands*. Utrecht: LOT (Netherlands Graduate School of Linguistics).

(2006). A linguistic analysis of the use of the two hands in sign language poetry. In J. van de Weijer & B. Los (eds.), *Linguistics in the Netherlands 2006* (pp. 65–77). Amsterdam: John Benjamins Associates.

Crasborn, O. & de Wit, M. (2005). Ethical implications of language standardization for sign language interpreters. In J. Mole (ed.), *International Perspectives on Interpreting: Selected Proceedings from the Supporting Deaf People Online Conferences 2001–2005* (pp. 41–150). Bassinton: Direct Learn Services.

Crasborn, O. & van der Kooij, E. (2003). Base joint configuration in Sign Language of the Netherlands: Phonetic variation and phonological specification. In J. van de Weijer (ed.), *The Phonological Spectrum*. Vol. I: *Segmental Structure* (pp. 257–287). Amsterdam/ Philadelphia, PA: John Benjamins Associates.

Crasborn, O., van der Hulst, H., & van der Kooij, E. (2001). SignPhon: A phonological database for sign language. *Sign Language and Linguistics*, **4**(1/2), 215–228.

Crasborn, O., Sloetjes, H., Auer, E. & Wittenburg, P. (2006). Combining video and numeric data in the analysis of sign language with the ELAN annotation software. In E. Vettori (ed.), *Proceedings of the Second Workshop on the Representation and Processing of Sign Languages: Lexicographic Matters and Didactic Scenarios* (pp. 82–87). Paris: European Language Resources Association (ELRA).

Crasborn, O., van der Kooj, E., Waters, D., Woll, B. & Mesch, J. (2008). Frequency distribution and spreading behavior of different types of mouth actions in three sign languages. *Sign Language and Linguistics*, **11**(1): 45–67.

Crowley, T. (1992). *An Introduction to Historical Linguistics*. Oxford: Oxford University Press.

Crystal, D. (1987). *Child Language, Learning and Linguistics: An Overview for the Teaching and Therapeutic Professions*. London: Edward Arnold.

(1995). *The Cambridge Encyclopedia of the English Language*. Cambridge: Cambridge University Press.

Croneberg, C. (1965a). Appendix C: The linguistic community. In W. Stokoe, D. Casterline & C. Croneberg, *The Dictionary of American Sign Language on Linguistic Principles* (pp. 297–311). Silver Spring, MD: Linstok Press. Repr. 1976.

(1965b). Appendix D: Sign Language dialects. In W. Stokoe, D. Casterline & C. Croneberg, *The Dictionary of American Sign Language on Linguistic Principles* (pp. 313–319). Silver Spring, MD: Linstok Press. Repr. 1976.

Cutkosky, M. R. (1989). On grasp choice, grasp models, and the design of hands for manufacturing tasks. *IEEE Transactions on Robotics and Automation*, **5**(3), 269–279.

Cuxac, C. (2000). *La Langue des Signes Française: Les voies de l'iconicité*. Paris: éditions Ophrys.

Czajkowska-Kisil, M. (2005). Dwujęzyczność w nauczaniu głuchych. *Nauczyciel w Świecie Ciszy*, **7**, 3–9.

Dachkovsky, S. (2008). Facial expression as intonation in Israeli Sign Language: The case of neutral and counterfactual conditionals. In J. Quer (ed.), *Signs of the Time: Selected Papers from TISLR, 2004* (pp. 61–82). Hamburg: Signum.

Dahl, Ö. & Velupillai, V. (2008). Perfective/Imperfective aspect. In M. Haspelmath, M. S. Dryer, D. Gil & B. Comrie (eds.), *The World Atlas of Language Structures*, Ch. 65. Munich: Max Planck Digital Library. Available at http://wals.info/feature/65.

Dänzer, P., Hemmi, P. & de Marco, E. (1997). *Dance of Hands: The Renaissance of the Sign Language of the Deaf in Europe*. Zürich: Etoile Productions.

Deaf Society of New South Wales. (1989). *Operation Knock Knock: A Profile of the Deaf Community of New South Wales*. Parramatta, NSW: Deaf Society of New South Wales.

De Jorio, A. (1832/2000). *La mimica degli antichi investigata nel gestire Napoletano, Napoli: Fibreno 1832*. Repr. Sala Bolognese: Arnaldo Forni, 1979. [Trans. *Gesture in Naples and Gesture in Classical Antiquity*, by Adam Kendon. Bloomington, IN: Indiana University Press, 2000]

DeGraff, M. (1999). *Language Creation and Language Change*. Cambridge, MA: MIT Press.

DeMatteo, A. (1977). Visual imagery and visual analogues in American Sign Language. In L. Friedman (ed.), *On the Other Hand* (pp. 109–136). New York: Academic Press.

DeSantis, S. (1977). Elbow to Hand Shift in French and American Sign Languages. Paper presented at the Conference on New Ways of Analyzing Variation, Georgetown University, Washington, DC.

Det Danske Bibelselskab (2004). *Bibelske og liturgiske tekster på dansk tegnsprog*. DVD. København, Denmark: Det Danske Bibelselskab.

Deuchar, M. (1981). Variation in British Sign Language. In B. Woll, J. G. Kyle & M. Deuchar (eds.), *Perspectives on British Sign Language and Deafness* (pp. 109–119). London: Croom Helm.

(1983). Is BSL an SVO language? In J. Kyle & B. Woll (eds.), *Language in Sign* (pp. 69–76). London: Croom Helm.

(1984). *British Sign Language*. London: Routledge.

Deverson, T. (1991). New Zealand lexis: The Maori dimension. *English Today*, **26**, 18–25.

Di Renzo, A. (2006). Le produzioni narrative in LIS di bambini e ragazzi sordi. Thesis, Università degli studi di Roma "La Sapienza," Roma.

Diccionario Español-Lengua de Señas Mexicana (DIELSEME). (Dirección de Educación Especial en el Distrito Federal. 2004). México DF: SEP/Subsecretaría de Servicios Educativos para el Distrito Federal.

Diessel, H. (1999). *Demonstratives: Form, Function & Grammaticalization: Typology Studies in Language*. Amsterdam: John Benjamins Associates.

Dively, V. (2001). Sign without hands: Nonhanded signs in American Sign Language. In V. Dively, M. Metzger, S. Taub & A. M. Baer (eds.), *Sign Languages: Discoveries from International Research* (pp. 62–73). Washington, DC: Gallaudet University Press.

División de Educación. Benemérito comité Pro Ciegosy Sordos de Guatemala (2006). Available at www.prociegosysordos.org.gt/educacion.htm.

Dresher, B. E. (2003). Contrasts and asymmetries in inventories. In A. M. DiScuillo (ed.), *Asymmetry in Grammar,* Vol. III*: Morphology, Phonology, Acquisition* (pp. 239–257). Amsterdam: John Benjamins Associates.

Duffy, Q. (2007). *The ASL Perfect Formed by Preverbal FINISH*. American Sign Language Linguistic Research Project No. 14, Boston University.

Dugdale, P. O. (2000). Being Deaf in New Zealand: A case study of the Wellington Deaf community. PhD dissertation: Victoria University of Wellington.

Duncan, S. (2002). Gesture, verb aspect, and the nature of iconic imagery in natural discourse. *Gesture*, **2**(2), 183–206.

Eccarius, P. (2002). Finding common ground: A comparison of handshape across multiple sign languages. Master's thesis, Purdue University, West Lafayette, IN.

Eccarius, P. (2008). A constraint-based account of handshape contrast in sign languages. PhD dissertation, Purdue University, West Lafayette, IN.

Eccarius, P. & Brentari, D. (2007). Symmetry and dominance: A cross-linguistic study of signs and classifier construction. *Lingua*, **117**, 1169–1201.

Edinburgh & East of Scotland Society for the Deaf. (1985). *Seeing the Signs in Scotland*. Edinburgh: Edinburgh & East of Scotland, Society for the Deaf.

Eckman, P., Friesen, W. V. & Hager, J. C. (2002). *The Facial Action Coding System*. Salt Lake City, UT: Research Nexus eBook.

Elton, F. & Squelch, L. (2008). *British Sign Language: London and South East Regional Signs*. London: Lexisigns.

Emmerik, W., Meyer, G., Hiddinga, A. & Pot, L. (1993). *Poëzie in gebarentaal*. Amsterdam: Nijghand van Ditma.

Emmerik, W., Meyer, G., Hiddinga, A. & Pot, L. (2005). *Bewogen: Filmgedichten in Gebarentaal.* The Netherlands: Stichting Geelprodukt.

Emmorey, K. (1991). Repetition priming with aspect and agreement morphology in American Sign Language. *Journal of Psycholinguistics Research*, **20**, 365–388.

(1999a). Do signers gesture? In L. S. Messing & R. Campbell (eds.), *Gesture, Speech and Sign* (pp. 133–159). Oxford: Oxford University Press.

(1999b). The confluence of space and language in signed languages. In P. Bloom, M. A. Peterson, L. Nodel & M. F. Garrett (eds.), *Language and Space* (pp. 171–209). Cambridge, MA: MIT Press.

(2002). *Language, Cognition and the Brain: Insights from Sign Language Research.* Mahwah, NJ: Lawrence Erlbaum Associates.

(2003). *Perspectives on Classifier Constructions in Sign Languages.* Mahwah, NJ: Lawrence Erlbaum Associates.

Emmorey, K. & Corina, D. (1990). Lexical recognition in sign language: Effects of phonetic structure and morphology. *Perceptual and Motor Skills*, **71**, 1227–1252.

Emmorey, K. & Herzig, M. (2003). Categorical vs. gradient properties in classifer constructions in ASL. In K. Emmorey (ed.), *Perspectives on Classifier Constructions in Sign Languages* (pp. 221–246). Mahwah, NJ: Lawrence Erlbaum Associates.

Engberg-Pedersen, E. (1993). *Space in Danish Sign Language: The Semantics and Morphosyntax of the Use of Space in a Visual Language.* Hamburg: Signum.

(1994). Some simultaneous constructions in Danish Sign Language. In M. Brennan & G. H. Turner (eds.), *Word-order Issues in Sign Language* (pp. 73–87). Durham: International Sign Linguistics Association.

(1996). Iconicity and arbitrariness. In E. Engberg-Pedersen, M. Fortescue, P. Harder, L. Heltoft & L. Falster Jakobsen (eds.), *Content, Expression and Structure: Studies in Danish Functional Grammar* (pp. 453–468). Amsterdam: John Benjamins Associates.

(2003). How composite is a fall? Adults' and childrens' descriptions of different types of falls in Danish Sign Language. In K. Emmorey (ed.), *Perspectives on Classifier Constructions in Sign Languages* (pp. 311–332). Mahwah, NJ: Lawrence Erlbaum Associates.

(2007). Internal structure: Backgrounding in classifier constructions. Paper presented at the Economic and Social Research Council (ESRC) Workshop on Sign vs. Gesture, Rome.

Engberg-Pedersen, E. & Pedersen, A. (1983). Proforms in Danish Sign Language: Their use in figurative signing. In W. Stokoe & V. Volterra (eds.), *Proceedings of the III International Symposium on Sign Language Research, Rome 1983* (pp. 202–209). Silver Spring, MD: Linstok Press & Roma: Istituto di Psicologia CNR.

Falk, Y. (2006). *Subjects and Universal Grammar.* Cambridge/New York: Cambridge University Press.

Faurot, K., Dellinger, D., Eatough, A. & Parkhurst, S. (1999). The identity of Mexican sign as a language. Unpublished manuscript. Summer Institute of Linguistics.

Feige, H.-U. (2006). *Denn taube Personen folgen ihren thierischen Trieben …* Leipzig: Gutenberg Verlag.

Feige, H.-U., Muhs, J., Vogel, H., Winkler, J. & Wolff, S. (2001). Leipziger Gespräche II "Wir machen Geschichte!" Deaf History im neuen Jahrtausend. *Das Zeichen*, **15**(56), 316–322.

Felipe, T. (1989). *A estrutura frasal na LSCB.* IV Encontro Nacional da ANPOLL: Recife.

Ferreira-Brito, L. (1995). *Por Uma Gramática das Línguas de Sinais.* Rio de Janeiro: Tempo Brasileiro.

Fillmore, C. (1968). The case for case. In E. Bach & R. Harms (eds.), *Universals in Linguistic Theory* (pp. 1–90). New York: Holt, Rinehart & Winston.

Fischer, J. L. (1958). Social influences on the choice of a linguistic variant. *Word*, **14**, 47–56.

Fischer, R. & Vollhaber, T. (1996). *Collage: Works on International Deaf History*. Hamburg: Signum.

Fischer, R., Wempe, K., Lamprecht, S. & Seeberger, I. (1995). John E. Pacher (1842–1898) – ein "Taubstummer" aus Hamburg. (Teil I und II). *Das Zeichen*, **9**(32)/9(33), 122–133/412–421.

Fischer, S. (1974). Sign language and linguistic universals. In T. Rohrer, & N. Ruwet (eds.), *Actes de Colloque Franco-Allemand de Grammaire Transformationelle* (pp. 187–204). Tübingen: Niemeyer.

(1975). Influences on word order change in American Sign Language. In C. N. Li (ed.), *Word Order and Word Order Change* (pp. 1–25). Austin, TX: University of Texas Press.

(1978). Sign language and creoles. In P. Siple (ed.), *Understanding Language Through Sign Language Research: Perspectives in Neurolinguistics and Psycholinguistics* (pp. 309–331). New York/San Francisco, CA/London: Academic Press.

(1996). The role of agreement and auxiliaries in sign languages. *Lingua*, **98**, 103–120.

(2006). Questions and negation in American Sign Language. In U. Zeshan (ed.), *Interrogative and Negative Constructions in Sign Language*: (pp. 165–197). Nijmegen: Ishara Press. (Sign Language Typology Series No. 1).

Fischer, S. (in preparation). Verb agreement in the Japanese sign language family. University of California, San Diego.

Fischer, S. & Gough, B. (1978). Verbs in American Sign Language. *Sign Language Studies*, **7**(18), 17–48.

(1999). Some Unfinished Thoughts on FINISH. *Sign Language and Linguistics*, **2**, 67–77.

Fischer, S. & Osugi, Y. (1998). Feature movement in Wh-questions: Evidence from sign languages. Paper presented at the Sixth Theoretical Issues in Sign Language Research Conference (TISLR 6), Washington, DC.

(2000). Thumbs up vs. giving the finger: Indexical classifiers in in NS and ASL. Paper presented at the Seventh Conference on Theoretical Issues in Sign Language Research (TISLR 7), Amsterdam,.

Fishman, J. A. (1991). *Reversing Language Shift: Theoretical and Empirical Foundations of Assistance to Threatened Languages*. Clevedon, UK: Multilingual Matters.

Fitzgerald, S. (1999). *Open Minds, Open Hearts: Stories of the Australian Catholic Deaf Community*. Lidcombe, NSW: CCOD.

Fletcher, T., Dejud, C., Klingler, C. & Lopez Mariscal, I. (2003). The changing paradigm of special education in Mexico: Voices from the field. *Bilingual Research Journal*, **27**(3), 409–430.

Flood, C. M. (2002). *How do deaf and hard of hearing students experience learning how to write using signwriting, a way to read and write signs*? PhD dissertation, University of New Mexico. Available from University Microfilms, Ann Arbor, MI.

Flores-Ferrán, N. (2007). A bend in the road: Subject personal pronoun expression in Spanish after thirty years of sociolinguistic research. *Language and Linguistics Compass*, **1**, 624–652.

Flynn, J. W. (1984). *No Longer By Gaslight*. Melbourne: Adult Deaf Society of Victoria.

Fodor, J. (1970). Three reasons for not deriving "kill" from "cause to die." *Linguistic Inquiry*, **1**, 429–438.

Folchi, A. & Mereghetti, E. (1995). Tre educatori sordi italiani. In G. P. Li Destri & V. Volterra (eds.), *Passato e presente: Uno sguardo sull'educazione dei sordi in Italia* (pp. 61–75). Napoli: Gnocchi.

Fónagy, I. (1983). Preconceptual thinking in language (An essay in paleontology). In E. D. Grolier, A. Lock, C. R. Peters & J. Wind (eds.), *Glossogenetics: The Origin and Evolution of Language* (pp. 329–353). London: Harwood Academic.

Forman, W. (2003). The ABCs of New Zealand Sign Language: Aerial spelling. *Journal of Deaf Studies and Deaf Education*, **8**(1), 92–96.

Fortgens, C. & Knoors, H. (1994). Distinguishing between Sign Language of the Netherlands and Sign-Supported Dutch. In B. Van den Bogaerde, H. Knoors, & M. Verrips (eds.), *Language Acquisition with Non-Native Input* (pp. 93–117). Amsterdam: University of Amsterdam. (Amsterdam Series in Child Language Development, 2)

Fortgens, C. (2003). Taalkeuze van dove kinderen [Language choice of deaf children]. PhD dissertation, University of Amsterdam. Gouda: Koninklijke Auris groep.

Foster, A. (1975). The social aspect of deafness: School years. Paper presented at the Seventh World Congress of the Deaf, Washington, DC.

Foucault, M. (2001). Les mailles du pouvoir. In D. Defert & F. Ewald (eds.), *Dits et écrits II, 1976–1988* (pp. 1001–1020). Paris: Gallimard.

Franchi, M. L. (1987/2004). Componenti non manuali. In V. Volterra (ed.), *La Lingua Italiana dei Segni: La Comunicazione visivo, Gestuale dei Sordi*. 2nd edn (pp. 159–177). Bologna: Il Mulino.

Frege, G. (1879). *Begriffsschrift: Eine der Arithmetischen nachgebildete Formelsprach des reinen Denkens*. Halle: Verlag von Louis Nebert.

Fridman-Mintz, B. (2005). Tense and aspect inflections in Mexican Sign Language verbs. PhD dissertation, Georgetown University, Washington, DC.

Friedman, L. A. (1976). The manifestation of subject, object and topic in ASL. In C. N. Li (ed.), *Subject and Topic* (pp. 127–148). New York: Academic Press.

   (1977). *On the Other Hand: New Perspectives on American Sign Language*. New York: Academic Press.

Frishberg, N. (1975). Arbitrariness and iconicity: Historical change in American Sign Language. *Language*, **51**, 696–719.

   (1987). Ghanaian Sign Language. In J. van Cleve (ed.), *Gallaudet Encyclopedia of Deaf People and Deafness*, Vol. III, (pp. 778–779). New York: McGraw-Hill.

Frishberg, N. & Gough, B. (2000). Morphology in American Sign Language. *Sign Language and Linguistics*, **3**(1), 103–131.

Fromkin, V. & Rodman, R. (1998). *An Introduction of Language*. 6th edn. Orlando, FL: Harcourt Brace College.

Fu, Y. & Mei, C. (1986). *Longren Shouyu Gailun*. Shanghai: Xuelin.

Fuchs, B. (2004). *Phonetische Aspekte einer Didaktik der Finnischen Gebärdensprache als Fremdsprache*. Jyväskylä, Finland. (Studies in Humanities, Vol. 21)

Fudge, E. (1969). Syllables. *Journal of Linguistics*, **5**, 253–287.

Fusellier-Souza, I. (2006). Emergence and development of signed languages: From a semiogenetic point of view. *Sign Language Studies*, **7**(1), 30–56.

Gałkowski, T., Kunicka-Kaiser, I. & Smoleńska, J. (1976). *Psychologia Dziecka Głuchego*. Warsaw: PIPS.

Gambian Association of the Deaf and Hard of Hearing (2002). *Gambian Sign Language*. Available at www.gadhoh.com/history.htm.

García, N. (1994). The art and culture of the Deaf. In C. J. Erting, R. C. Johnson, D. L. Smith & B. D. Snider (eds.), *The Deaf Way: Perspectives from the International Conference on Deaf Culture* (pp. 128–130). Washington, DC: Gallaudet University Press.

Gascón Ricao, A. & Storch de Gracia y Asensio, J. G. (2004). *Historia de la Educación de los Sordos en España y su Influencia en Europa y América*. Madrid: Editorial Universitaria Ramón Areces.

Gasser, M. (2004). The origins of arbitrariness in language. In K. Forbus, D. Gentner & T. Reiger (eds.), *Proceedings of the Cognitive Science Society Conference* (pp. 434–439). Hillsdale, NJ: Lawrence Erlbaum Associates.

Gasser, M., Sethuraman, N. & Hockema, S. (2005). Iconicity in expressives: An empirical investigation. In S. Rice & J. Newman (eds.), *Experimental and Empirical Methods in Cognitive Functional Research* (pp. 1–18). Stanford, CA: Center for the Study of Language and Information (CSLI) Publications.

Gebhard, M. (2007). *Hören lernen – hörbehindert bleiben: Die Geschichte der Gehörlosen- und Schwerhörigenorganisationen in den letzten 200 Jahren.* Baden: hier + jetzt, Verlag für Kultur und Geschichte.

Geraci, C. (2006). Negation in LIS (Italian Sign Language). In L. Bateman & C. Ussery (eds.), *Proceedings of the Thirty-Fifth Annual Meeting of the North East Linguistic Society* (pp. 217–230). Amherst, MA: GLSA (Graduate Linguistic Student Association), University of Massachusetts.

Gerner de Garcia B. (1995). Communication and language use of Spanish-speaking families with Deaf children. In C. Lucas (ed.), *Sociolinguistics in Deaf Communities* (pp. 221–252). Washington, DC: Gallaudet University Press.

Ghanaian Sign Language. (~2001) *Ghanaian National Association of the Deaf.* Accra: Accra Catholic Press.

Gillian, R. & Easterbrook, S. (1997). Educating children who are deaf or hard of hearing: Residential life, ASL & Deaf culture. Available at www.ericdigests.org/1998–2/life.htm.

Giuranna, R. & Giuranna, G. (2000). Poesia in LIS: Iconicità e arbitrarietà, concreto e astratto. In C. Bagnara, G. Chiappini & M. P. Conte (eds.), *Viaggio Nella Città Invisibile* (pp. 341–348). Del Cerro: Pisa.

(2003). *Sette poesie in lingua dei segni italiana (LIS).* CD-Rom. Pisa: Gdizioni del Cerro.

Givón, T. (1984). *Syntax: A Functional-Typological Introduction,* Vol. I. Amsterdam: John Benjamins Associates.

Givón, T. (1991). Isomophism in the grammatical code: Cognitive and biological considerations. *Studies in Language*, **15**, 85–114.

Goeke, A. (2006). Variation in American Sign Language: Articulator deletion in two-handed signs. Unpublished Master's thesis.

Goldin-Meadow, S. (1982). The resilience of recursion: A study of a communication system developed without a conventional language model. In E. Wanner & L. R. Gleitman (eds.), *Language Acquisition: The State of the Art* (pp. 51–77). Cambridge/New York: Cambridge University Press.

(2003a). *Hearing Gesture: How Our Hands Help Us Think.* Cambridge, MA: Harvard University Press.

(2003b). *The Resilience of Language: What Gesture Creation in Deaf Children Can Tell Us About How All Children Learn Language.* New York: Psychology Press.

(2008). Gesture, speech, and language. Paper presented at the Annual Meeting of the Linguistic Society of America, Chicago, IL.

Goldin-Meadow, S. & Mylander, C. (1984). *Gestural Communication in Deaf Children: The Effects and Noneffects of Parental Input on Early Language Development.* Monographs of the Society for Research in Child Development, vol. 49. Boston, MA: Blackwell.

Goldsmith, J. (1976). Autosegmental phonology. PhD dissertation, MIT, Cambridge, MA. [Published New York: Garland Press, 1979].

(1995). Introduction: Phonotactics, alternations, contrasts; Representations, rules, levels. In J. Goldsmith (ed.), *Handbook of Phonological Theory* (pp. 1–23). Oxford/Cambridge, MA: Blackwell.

Gombrich, E. H. (1966). Ritualized gesture and expression in art. *Philosophical Transactions of the Royal Society of London.* Series B, **251**, 393–401.

Gong, Q. (2005a). Shouyu wenti jianghua. In Y. Shen, A. Wu, & C. Chu (eds.), *Shuangyu Longjiaoyu de Lilun yu Shijian* (pp. 39–60). Beijing: Huaxia.

(2005b). Zhongguo longren yuyan ji yuyan jiaoyu wenti. In Y. Shen, A. Wu & C. Chu (eds.), *Shuangyu Longjiaoyu de Lilun yu Shijian* (pp. 61–90). Beijing: Huaxia.

Gordon, R. (2005). *Ethnologue: Languages of the World*, Summer Institute of Linguistics. Available at www.ethnologue.com/.

Gras Ferrer, V. (2006). La comunidad sorda como comunidad lingüística: Panorama sociolingüístico de la/s lengua/s de signos en España. PhD dissertation, Universitat de Barcelona.

Green, F. (1783). *Vox oculis subjecta*. London: Benjamin White Publishers.

Green, L. (2004). Research on African American English since 1998. *Journal of English Linguistics*, **32**, 210–229.

Greenberg, J. (1957). *Essays in Linguistics*. Chicago, IL: Chicago University Press.
(1966). *Universals of Language*. Cambridge, MA: MIT Press.

Greftegreff, I. (1993). A few notes on anatomy and distinctive features in NTS handshapes. *University of Trondheim, Working Papers in Linguistics*, **17**, 48–68. Dragvoll, Norway.

Grenoble, L. A. & Whaley, L. J. (2008). *Saving Languages: An Introduction to Language Revitalization*. Cambridge: Cambridge University Press.

Grimshaw, J. (1990). *Argument Structure*. Cambridge, MA: MIT Press.

Groce, N. E. (1985). *Everyone Here Spoke Sign Language: Hereditary Deafness on Martha's Vineyard*. Cambridge, MA: Harvard University Press.

Grose, D. 2008. The geometry of events: Evidence from English and ASL. PhD dissertation, Purdue University, West Lafayette, IN.

Grose, D., Wilbur, R. B. & Schalber, K. (2007). Events and telicity in classifier predicates: A reanalysis of body part classifier predicates in ASL. *Lingua*, **17**, 1258–1284.

Grosjean, F. (1998). Living with two languages and two cultures. In I. Parasnis (ed.), *Cultural and Language Diversity and the Deaf Experience* (pp. 20–37). Cambridge: Cambridge University Press.

Grzegorzewska, M. 1964. *Pedagogika specjalna*. Warszawa: PIPS.Warsaw: PIPS

Guerra Currie, A.-M. (1999). A Mexican Sign Language lexicon: Internal and cross-linguistic similarities and variations. PhD dissertation, University of Texas, Austin.

Guerra Currie, A.-M. P., Meier, R. P. & Walters, K. (2002). A crosslinguistic examination of the lexicons of four signed languages. In R. P. Meier, K. A. Cormier & D. Quinto-Pozos (eds.), *Modality and Structure in Signed and Spoken Languages* (pp. 224–236). Cambridge: Cambridge University Press.

Guggenheim, L. (1993). Ethnic variation in ASL: The signing of African Americans and how it is influenced by conversational topic. In E. Winston (ed.), *Communication Forum* (pp. 51–76). Washington, DC: Gallaudet University Department of Linguistics and Interpreting.

Günther, K.-B. (2004). Der Hamburger Bilinguale Schulversuch – Ergebnisse, Perspektiven und offene Fragen. *Hörgeschädigte Kinder*, **41**(2), 78–91.

Guy, G. R. (1980). Variation in the group and in the individual: The case of final stop deletion. In W. Labov (ed.), *Locating Language in Time and Space* (pp. 1–36). New York: Academic Press.

Hagège, C. (1993). *The Language Builder: An Essay on the Human Signature in Linguistic Morphogenesis*. Amsterdam: John Benjamins Associates.

Hagman, R. (1977). *Nama Hottentot Grammar*. Language Science Monographs, No. 15. Bloomington, IN: Indiana University Publications.

Haiman, J. (1978). Conditionals are topics. *Language*, **54**, 564–589.
(1983). Iconic and economic motivation. *Language*, **59**, 781–819.
(1985). *Iconicity in Syntax*. Amsterdam: John Benjamins Associates.
(1994). *Ritualization and the Development of Language*. Amsterdam: John Benjamins Associates.

(1998). *Talk is Cheap: Sarcasm, Alienation, and the Evolution of Language*. Oxford: Oxford University Press.
Hairston, E. & Smith, L. (1983). *Black and Deaf in America: Are We That Different?* Silver Spring, MD: T. J. Publishers.
Hale, K. & Keyser, S. J. (1993). On argument structure and the lexical expression of syntactic relations. In K. Hale & S. J. Keyser (eds.), *The View from Building 20: Essays in Honor of Sylvain Bromberger* (pp. 53–109). Cambridge, MA: MIT Press.
Hale, K. & Keyser, S. J. (2001). *Prolegomenon to a Theory of Argument Structure*. Cambridge, MA: MIT Press.
Hallahan, D. (1998). International perspectives on special education reform. *European Journal of Special Needs Education*, **13**, 123–127.
Halle, M. & Marantz, A. (1993). Distributed morphology and the pieces of inflection. In K. Hale & S. J. Keyser (eds.), *The View from Building 20* (pp. 111–176). Cambridge, MA: MIT Press.
(1994). Some key features of distributed morphology. In A. Carnie & H. Harley (eds.), *MIT Working Papers in Linguistics 21: Papers on Phonology and Morphology* (pp. 275–288). Cambridge, MA: MIT Press.
Hamano, S. (1998). *The Sound Symbolic System in Japanese*. Stanford, CA: Center for the Study of Language and Information (CSLI) Publications.
Hamzah, M. & Taffal, N. (1993). *Lughah al-ishara al-Urduniyah al-Arabiyah*. Amman, Jordan: Specialized Audiology Center.
Hänel, B. (2005). The acquisition of agreement in DGS: Early steps into a spatially expressed syntax. In H. Leuninger & D. Happ (eds.), *Linguistische Berichte (Gebardensprachen: Struktur, Erwerb, Berwendung)*, Special Issue **13** (pp. 201–232).
Harder, R. (2003). Meervoud in de NGT. Manuscript, Nederlands Gebarencentrum.
Harder, R. & Schermer, G. M. (1986). A first analysis of handshapes in the Sign Language of the Netherlands. In B. T. Tervoort (ed.), *Proceedings of the Second European Congress on Sign Language Research, Amsterdam July 14–18, 1985* (pp. 47–51). Amsterdam: University of Amsterdam.
Harris, J. (1983). *Syllable Structure and Stress in Spanish*. Cambridge, MA: MIT Press.
Harris, Z. (1951). *Methods in Structural Linguistics*. Chicago, IL: University of Chicago Press.
Hawayek, A. & Cappelli, G. (2004). Identificación y recuperación del sujeto nulo: evidencia de una lengua signada (LSM). In I. Barreras Aguilar, & M. Castro Llaamas (eds.), *Memorias del VII Encuentro Internacional de Lingüística en el Noroeste* (pp. 411–430). Hermosillo: Universidad de Sonora.
Hazen, K. (2007). The study of variation in historical perspective. In R. Bayley & C. Lucas (eds.), *Sociolinguistic Variation: Theories, Methods, and Applications* (pp. 70–89). Cambridge: Cambridge University Press.
Heim, I. (1997). Tense in compositional semantics: introduction. Hand-out for the MIT seminar on Tense, Aspect and Events.
Heine, B., Claudi, U. & Hünnemeyer, F. (1991a). *From Cognition to Grammar: Evidence from African Languages*, Vol. I. Amsterdam: John Benjamins Associates.
(1991b). *Grammaticalization: A Conceptual Framework*. Chicago, IL: University of Chicago Press.
Hendriks, B. (2004). *An Introduction to the Grammar of Jordanian Sign Language*. Salt, Jordan: Al-Balqa University.
Hendzel, J. K. (1986). *Słownik Polskiego Jezyka Miganego*. Olsztyn: Wydawnictwo "Pojezierze."
Hepp, I. & Nager, F. (1926). *Die Taubstummheit im Kanton Zürich*. Zürich: [No publisher listed].
Herbst, J. M. (1987). South African Sign Language. In J. van Cleve (ed.), *Gallaudet Encyclopedia of Deaf People and Deafness* (pp. 106–108). New York: McGraw-Hill.

Higgins, D. D. (1923). *How to Talk to the Deaf.* St. Louis, MO: Catholic Church at 1118 N. Grand Blvd.

Hintermair, M. (2007). *Psychosoziales Wohlbefinden hörgeschädigter Menschen.* Hamburg: Signum.

Hirn, D. F. (1910). *De dövstummas åtbördsspråk i Finland – Kuuromykkäin viittomakieli Suomessa, I.* Helsingfors: Finlands Dövstumförbunds Förlag.

History of Deaf Education in America. (American School for the Deaf, n.d.).

Hockett, C. F. (1954). Two models of grammatical description. *Word,* **10**, 210–231.

  (1960). The origin of speech. *Scientific American,* **203**, 89–96.

  (1966). The problem of universals in language. In J. Greenberg (ed.), *Universals of Language* (pp. 1–29). Cambridge, MA: MIT Press.

Hoffman, B. (1979). *Rewalidacja niestyszacych: Podstawy Poste powania pedagogicznego.* Warsaw: PWN.

Hoffmeister, R. J. (1978). The development of demonstrative pronouns, locatives, and personal pronouns in the acquisition of ASL by deaf children of deaf parents. PhD dissertation, University of Minnesota, Minneapolis.

Hohenberger, A. & Happ, D. (2001). The linguistic primacy of signs and mouth gestures over mouthings: Evidence from language production in German Sign Language (DGS). In P. Boyes Braem & R. Sutton-Spence (eds.), *The Hands Are the Head of the Mouth: The Mouth as Articulator in Sign Languages* (pp. 153–190). Hamburg: Signum.

Hoiting, N. & Slobin, D. I. (2001). Typological and modality constraints on borrowing: Examples from the Sign Language of the Netherlands. In D. Brentari (ed.), *Foreign Vocabulary in Sign Languages: A Cross-Linguistic Investigation of Word Formation* (pp. 121–137). Mahwah, NJ: Lawrence Erlbaum Associates.

Hoiting, N. & Slobin, D. I. (2002). Transcription as a tool for understanding: The Berkeley Transcription System for sign language research (BTS). In G. Morgan & B. Woll (eds.), *Directions in Sign Language Acquisition* (pp. 55–75). Amsterdam: John Benjamins Associates. (Trends in Language Acquisition Research; vol. 2)

Holdsworth, W. & Aldridge, W. (1766). Natural short-hand, wherein the nature of speech and the manner of pronunciation are briefly explained. London: Self-published.

Hollak, J. & Jagodziński, T. (1879). *Słownik Mimiczny dla Głuchoniemych i Osób z Nimi Styczność Majacych.* Warsaw: Nasza Ksiegarnia.

Holm, A., Gudman, S., Rasmussen, J. W. & Vestberg Rasmussen, P. (1983). *Døveundervisning i Danmark 1807–1982: Med et Tillæg om Voksne Døve.* København: Døveforsorgens Historiske Selskab.

Holy Land Institute for the Deaf. (2004). *Holy Land Institute for the Deaf – Salt, Jordan [Brochure].* Salt, Jordan.

Honduran Deaf Projects. (n.d). Logos International Ministry Association. Pamphlet.

Hong, S. (2006). Agreement verbs in Korean Sign Language (KSL). Paper presented at the Ninth conference on Theoretical Issues in Sign Language Research (TISLR 9), Florianópolis, Brazil.

Hong, S. (2008). Eine empirische Untersuchung zu Kongruenzverben in der Koreanischen Gebärdensprache. PhD dissertation, Universität Hamburg.

Hoopes, R. (1998). A preliminary examination of pinky extension: Suggestions regarding its occurrence, constraints, and function. In C. Lucas (ed.), *Pinky Extension and Eye Gaze: Language Use in Deaf Communities* (pp. 3–17). Washington, DC: Gallaudet University Press.

Hopper, P. J. (1991). On some principles of grammaticalization. In E. C. Traugott & B. Heine (ed.), *Approaches to Grammaticalization,* Vol. I (pp. 17–36). Amsterdam/Philadelphia: John Benjamins Associates.

Hopper, P. J. & Traugott, E. C. (1993). *Grammaticalization*. Cambridge/ New York: Cambridge University Press.

Houston, A. (1991). A grammatical continuum for (ING). In P. Trudgill & J. K. Chambers (eds.), *Dialects of English: Studies in Grammatical Variation* (pp. 241–257). London: Longman.

Hoyer, K. (2004). The sociolinguistic situation of Finland-Swedish deaf people and their language, Finland-Swedish Sign Language. In M. Van Herreweghe & M. Vermeerbergen (eds.), *To the Lexicon and Beyond: Sociolinguistics in European Deaf Communities* (pp. 3–23). Washington, DC: Gallaudet University Press.

(2005). Vi kallade dem Borgåtecken: Det Finlandssvenska Teckenspråket i Går och i Dag. In J. Östman (ed.), *FinSSL: Finlandssvenskt Teckenspråk* (pp. 21–77). Helsingfors, Finland: Institutionen för nordiska språk och nordisk litteratur, Helsingfors universitet.

Hoyer, K., Londen, M. & Östman, J. (2006). *Teckenspråk: Sociala och Historiska Perspektiv. Nordica*. Helsingfors, Finland: Institutionen för nordiska språk och nordisk litteratur, Helsingfors universitet.

Huang, C.-T. J. (2003). The distribution of negative NPs and some typological correlates. In Y. A. Li & A. Simpson (eds.), *Functional Structure(s), Form and Interpretation* (pp. 262–280). New York/Milton Park, UK: Routledge (Taylor and Francis).

Hyman, L. (1985). *A Theory of Phonological Weight*. Dordrecht: Foris.

Iatridou, S., Anagnostopoulou, E. & Izvorski, R. (2001). Observations about the form and meaning of the perfect. In M. Kenstowicz (ed.), *Ken Hale: A Life in Language* (pp. 189–238). Cambridge, MA: MIT Press.

Itô, J. & Mester, A. (1995a). Japanese Phonology. In J. Goldsmith (ed.), *Handbook of Phonological Theory* (pp. 817–838). Oxford/New York: Blackwell.

Itô, J. & Mester, A. (1995b). The core-periphery structure of the lexicon and constraints on reranking. In J. Beckman, L. Walsh Dickey & S Urbanczyk (eds.), *University of Massachusetts Occasional Papers 18: Papers in Optimality Theory* (pp. 181–209). Amherst, MA: GLSA (Graduate Linguistic Students Association), University of Massachusetts.

Iverson, J. M. & Goldin-Meadow, S. (1998). *The Nature and Functions of Gesture in Children's Communication*. San Francisco: Jossey-Bass Publishers.

Iyute, D. & Nkwangu, R. (2007). Uganda's second international Deaf awareness week to be commemorated in September 2007. *Uganda National Associaton of the Deaf Newsletter, July 18th Edition*.

Jackendoff, R. (1990). *Semantic Structures*. Cambridge, MA: MIT Press.

(2002). *Foundations of Language: Brain, Meaning, Grammar, Evolution*. Oxford: Oxford University.

(2007). A parallel architecture perspective on language processing. *Brain Research*, 1146, 2–22.

(2008). Your theory of language evolution depends on your theory of language. Paper presented at the Annual Meeting of the Linguistic Society of America, Chicago, IL.

Jackson, P. W. (2001). *A Pictorial History of Deaf Britain*. Winsford, UK: Deafprint.

Jacobucci, G. (1997). Strategie di normalizzazione. Il bambino sordo nella scuola dell'obbligo. In A. Zuccalà (ed.) *Cultura del gesto e cultura della parola. Viaggio antropologico nel mondo dei sordi* (pp. 90–106). Meltemi: Milano.

Jakobson, R. (1941). *Kindersprache, aphasie, and allgemeine lautgesetze*. Repr. 1968 as *Child Language, Aphasia and Phonological Universals*. The Hague: Mouton de Gruyter.

Jakobson, R. (1971 [1957]). Shifters, verbal categories, and the Russian verb. In *Roman Jakobson: selected Writings*. Vol. II: *Word and Language* (pp. 130–147). The Hague: Mouton de Gruyter.

Jakobson, R. (1971). Quest for the essence of language. In *Roman Jakobson: Selected Writings*. Vol. II: *Word and Language* (pp. 345–359). The Hague: Mouton de Gruyter.

Jakobson, R., Fant, G. & Halle, M. (1951). *Preliminaries of Speech Analysis.* Cambridge, MA: MIT Press. Repr. 1961.

Janis, W. (1995). A crosslinguistic perspective on ASL verb agreement. In K. Emmorey & J. Reilly (eds.), *Language, Gesture, and Space* (pp. 195–223). Hillsdale, NJ: Lawrence Erlbaum Associates.

Jansma, S., Knoors, H. & Baker, A. (1997). Sign language assessment: A Dutch project, in Deafness and education. *Special Focus Edition: Sign Language in the Education of Deaf Children,* **21**(3), 39–46.

Jantunen, T. (2003). Viittomien historiallinen muutos ja deikonisaatio suomalaisessa viittomakielessä. [Historical Change and Deiconisation in Finnish Sign Language Signs; with English abstract] *Puhe ja kieli,* **23**, 43–60.

(2005). Mistä on pienet tavut tehty? Analyysi suomalaisen viittomakielen tavusta prosodisen mallin viitekehyksessä. Licentiate thesis, University of Jyväskylä, Finland.

(2006). The complexity of lexical movements in FinSL. In M. Suominen, A. Arppe, A. Airola, O. Heinamaki, M. Miestamo, U. Määttä, J. Niemi, K. K. Pitkänen & K. Sinnemäki (eds.), *A Man of Measure: Festschrift in Honour of Fred Karlsson on His 60th Birthday* (pp. 335–344). Turku: The Linguistic Association of Finland. (Special Supplement to SKY Journal of Linguistics; vol. **19**, 2006)

(2007). Tavu suomalaisessa viittomakielessä. [The Syllable in Finnish Sign Language; with English abstract] *Puhe ja kieli,* **27**, 109–126.

Janzen, T. (1999). The grammaticalization of topics in American Sign Language. *Studies in Language,* **23**(2), 271–306.

Janzen, T. & Shaffer, B. (2002). Gesture as the substrate in the process of ASL grammaticalization. In R. Meier, K. Cormier & D. Quinto-Pozos (eds.), *Modality and Structure in Signed and Spoken Languages* (pp. 199–223). Cambridge: Cambridge University Press.

Jewish Deaf Association. (2003). *Sign Language in Judaism.* London: Jewish Deaf Association.

Jia, L. & Bayley, R. (2002). Null pronoun variation in Mandarin Chinese. *University of Pennsylvania Working Papers in Linguistics,* **8**(3), 103–116.

Jirou, G. (2000). *Analyse descriptive du parler gestuel de Mbour (Sénégal).* Mémoire de maîtrise de Sciences du Langage, Université Paris VIII.

Johnson, R. E. (1990). Distinctive features for handshapes in American Sign Language. Paper presented at the Fourth Conference on Theoretical Issues in Sign Language Research (TISLR 4), Boston, MA.

(1991). Sign language, culture & community in a traditional Yucatec Maya village. *Sign Language Studies,* **20**(73), 461–474.

Johnson, R. E. & Liddell, S. (1984). Structural diversity in the American Sign Language lexicon. In D. Testen, V. Mishra & J. Drogo (eds.), *Papers from the Twentieth Regional Meeting of the Chicago Linguistic Society (CLS* 20) (pp. 173–186). Chicago, IL: Chicago Linguistic Society.

Johnston, T. (1989). Auslan: The sign language of the Australian deaf community. Doctoral Dissertation, University of Sydney.

(1998). *Signs of Australia: A New Dictionary of Auslan.* Sydney: North Rocks Press.

(2001). Nouns and verbs in Australian Sign Language: An open and shut case? *Journal of Deaf Studies and Deaf Education,* **6**, 235–257.

(2003). BSL, Auslan and NZSL: Three signed languages or one? In A. Baker, B. van den Bogaerde & O. Crasborn (eds.), *Cross-Linguistic Perspectives in Sign Language Research: Selected Papers from Theoretical Issues in Sign Language Research (TISLR), 2000* (pp. 47–69). Hamburg: Signum.

(2004). W(h)ither the deaf community? Population, genetics, and the future of Australian Sign Language. *American Annals of the Deaf*, **148**(5), 358–375.

Johnston, T. & Schembri, A. (2006). Issues in the creation of a digital archive of a signed language. In L. Barwick & N. Thieberger (eds.), *Sustainable Data from Digital Fieldwork: Proceedings of the Conference Held at the University of Sydney, Australia* (pp. 7–16). Sydney: Sydney University Press.

(2007). *Australian Sign Language: An Introduction to Sign Language Linguistics.* Cambridge: Cambridge University Press.

Julien, M. (1991). Gebärdensprach-Theater in den Niederlanden: Eine kurze Geschichte des Handtheaters. *Das Zeichen*, **5**(16), 143–152.

Julliann Montañez, C. (2003). Génesis de la Comunidad Silente en México. La Escuela Nacional de Sordomudos (1867–1896). PhD dissertation for Licenciatura in History, Universidad Nacional Autónoma de México, Mexico City.

Jusczyk, P. W. (1997). *The Discovery of Spoken Language*. Cambridge, MA: MIT Press.

Kafando, A. (1990). *Les Mains qui parlent*. Introduction à la Communication manuelle au Burkina-Faso.

Kamei, N. (2006). The birth of Langue des Signes Franco-Africaine: Creole ASL in West and Central French-speaking Africa. Online conference paper of Languages and Education in Africa Conference (LEA 2006). Oslo: University of Oslo. Available at www.pfi.uio.no/konferanse/LEA 2006/.

Kamp, H. & Reyle, U. (1993). *From Discourse to Logic*. Dordrecht: Kluwer Academic Publishers.

Kato, M. A. & Raposo, E. (1994). European and Brazilian Portuguese word order: questions, focus and topic constructions. In C. Parodi, A. C. Quicoli, M. Saltarelli & L. Zubizarreta (eds.), *Aspects of Romance Linguistics: Selected Papers from the Linguistic Symposium on Romance Languages XXIV* (pp. 267–278). Washington, DC: Georgetown University Press.

Kayne, R. S. (1996). *Lectures of Grammatical Theory*. Technical report, University of Girona, Girona Summer Institute in Linguistics.

(1998). Overt vs. covert movement. *Syntax*, **1**, 128–191.

Keep, J. R. (1857). The mode of learning the sign language. In *Convention of American Instructors of the Deaf, Proceedings* (pp. 133–153). Bedford, TX: American Instructors of the Deaf.

Kegl, J. (1985). Causative marking and the construal of agency in American Sign Language. In W. H. Eilfort, P. D. Kroeber & K. L. Peterson (eds.), *Proceedings from the Twenty-First Regional Meeting of the Chicago Linguistic Society (CLS 21)* (pp. 120–137). Chicago, IL: Chicago Linguistic Society.

(2002). Language emergence in a language-ready brain: Acquisition. In G. Morgan & B. Woll (eds.), *Directions in Sign Language Acquisition* (pp. 207–254). Amsterdam: John Benjamins Associates.

Kegl, J. & Iwata, G. (1989). Lenguaje de Signos Nicaragüense: A pidgin sheds light on the "creole?" ASL. In R. Carlson, S. DeLancey, S. Gilden, D. Payne & A. Saxena (eds.), *Fourth Annual Meeting of the Pacific Linguistics Conference* (pp. 266–294). Eugene, OR: University of Oregon, Department of Linguistics.

Kegl, J., Neidle, C., MacLaughlin, D., Hoza, J. & Bahan, B. (1996). The case for grammar, order and position in ASL: A reply to Bouchard and Dubuisson. *Sign Language Studies*, **90**, 1–23.

Kegl, J. A., Senghas, A. & Coppola, M. (1999). Creation through contact: Sign language emergence and sign language change in Nicaragua. In M. DeGraff (ed.), *Language Creation and Language Change: Creolization, Diachrony & Development* (pp. 179–237). Cambridge, MA: MIT Press.

Kelman, C. & Branco, A. (2004). Deaf children in regular classrooms: A sociocultural approach to a Brazilian experience. *American Annals of the Deaf*, **149**(3), 274–280.

Kendon, A. (2003). Pointing by Hand in "Neapolitan." In S. Kita (ed.), *Pointing: Where Language, Culture, and Cognition Meet* (pp. 243–268). Mahwah, NJ: Lawrence Erlbaum Associates.

(2004). *Gesture: Visible Action as Utterance*. Cambridge: Cambridge University Press.

Kennedy, G., Arnold, R., Dugdale, P., Fahey, S. & Moskovitz, D. (1997). *A Dictionary of New Zealand Sign Language*. Auckland: Auckland University Press with Bridget William Books.

Kenstowicz, M. (1994). *Phonology in Generative Grammar*. Cambridge, MA: Blackwell.

Kim, J.-S. (1997). *Syntactic Focus Movement and Ellipsis: A Minimalist Approach*. Storrs, CT: University of Connecticut.

Kimura, H. & Ichida, Y. (1995). *Hazimete no Syuwa*. Tokoyo: Nihonbungeisha.

Kirejczyk, K. 1967. *Ewolucja systemów kształcenia dzieci głuchych*. Warsaw: Nasza ksiegarnia.

Kisch, S. (2000). "Deaf discourse": The social construction of deafness in a Bedouin community. Master's thesis, University of Tel Aviv.

Kisch, S. (2004). Negotiating (genetic) deafness in a Bedouin community. In J. van Cleve (ed.), *Genetics, Disability and Deafness* (pp. 148–173). Washington, DC: Gallaudet University Press.

Kita, S. (2003). Pointing: A foundational building block of human communication. In S. Kita (ed.), *Pointing: Where Language, Culture, and Cognition Meet* (pp. 1–9). Mahwah, NJ: Lawrence Erlbaum Associates.

Kita, S. & Özyürek, A. (2003). What does cross-linguistic variation in semantic coordination of speech and gesture reveal?: Evidence for an interface representation of spatial thinking and speaking. *Journal of Memory and Language*, **48**, 16–32.

Kiyaga, N. B. & Moores, D. F. (2003). Deafness in Sub-Saharan Africa. *American Annals of the Deaf*, **148**(1), 18–24.

Klee, E. (1985). *Euthanasie im NS-Staat: die "Vernichtung lebensunwerten Lebens."* Frankfurt/Main: Fischer.

Klima, E. S. (1964). Negation in English. In J. Fodor & J. Katz (eds.), *The Structure of Language* (pp. 246–323). Englewood Cliffs, NJ: Prentice-Hall.

Klima, E. S. & Bellugi, U. (1979). *The Signs of Language*. Cambridge, MA: Harvard University Press.

Knoors, H. (1992). Exploratie van de gebarenruimte. PhD dissertation, University of Amsterdam. Delft: Eburon.

(1994). Increasing morphological complexity as a strategy: The SLN of nonnative signing children. In B. van den Bogaerde, H. Knoors & M. Verrips (eds.), *Language Acquisition with Non-Native Input* (pp. 51–69). Amsterdam: University of Amsterdam. (Amsterdam Series in Child Language Development; 2)

(1999). The education of deaf children in the Netherlands. In H. W. Brelje (ed.), *Global Perspectives on the Education of the Deaf* (pp. 249–260). Hillsboro, OR: Butte.

Kobosko, J. (1999). Wybrać czy nie? – Rozmowa o jezyku migowym. In J. Kobosko (ed.), *Moje dziecko nie słyszy. Materiały dla rodziców dzieci z wada słuchu, 5* (pp. 147–155). Warsaw: Stowarzyszenie Przyjaciół Osób Niesłyszacych i Niedosłyszacych "Człowiek - Człowiekowi."

Kobosko, J., Szuchnik, J. & Wojda, P. (2004). Kwestionariusz "JA-INNI" jako narzedzie słuzace do opisu tozsamości własnej młodziezy głuchej. *Audiofonologia*, **26**, 119–133.

Korbus, C. (2006). On the situation of the Deaf, of sign language interpreters and of interpreters' education in Uganda. Diploma thesis, Zwickau, University of Applied Sciences.

Kourbetis, V. (1999). Elliniki Noimatiki Glossa: Mithi ke Pragmatikotita. In V. Kourbetis (ed.), *Noima stin Ekpedefsi. I Elliniki Noimatiki Glossa ke I didaskalia tis sta scholia Kofon* (pp. 53–92). Athens: Ministry of Education and Religious Affairs, Pedagogical Institute.

(2005). Education of the deaf in Greece: from oralism to bilingualism and special education in Greece: State of the art and curriculum development. Unpublished manuscript presented at Zunich University, Switzerland, November 2005.

Kourbetis, V. & Kostas, G. (2006). Deaf empowerment in Greece. In H. Goodstein (ed.), *The Deaf Way II Reader: Perspectives from the Second International Conference on Deaf Culture* (pp. 42–47). Washington, DC: Gallaudet University Press.

Krakowiak, K. (1995). *Fonogesty jako narzedzie formowania jezyka dzieci z uszkodzonym słuchem*. Lublin: Wyd. UMCS.

(1998). *W Sprawie Kształcenia Jezyka Dzieci i Młodziezy z Uszkodzonym Słuchem*. Lublin: Wyd. UMCS.

(2003). *Kim Jest Moje Niesłyszace Dziecko? Rozwazania o Ukrytych Załozeniach Antropologicznych Współczesnych Koncepcji Surdopedagogiki i Audiofonologii*. Lublin: GAUDIUM.

(2004). Nowe podstawy wychowania jezykowego dzieci z głebokimi prelingwalnymi uszkodzeniami słuchu. *Audiofonologia*, **25**, 1–9.

(2006). Pedagogiczna typologia uszkodzeń słuchu. In K. Krakowiak & A. Dziurda-Multan (eds.), *Nie Głos, Ale Słowo: Przekraczanie Barier w Wychowaniu Osób z Uszkodzeniami Słuchu* (pp. 255–288). Lublin: Wydawnictwo KUL.

Krakowiak, K., Muzyka, E. & Wojda, P. (2002). Oczekiwania rozmówców niesłyszacych i słyszacych wobec siebie jako przesłanki do programów pracy logopedycznej. *Logopedia*, **30**, 67–85.

Kruth, L. (1996). *En Tyst Värld – Full av Liv*. Örebro: SIH Läromedel.

Kuwaiti Sign Language Dictionary. (1995). Available at www.mym.4mg.com/.

Kweller, D. (2005). Políticas educativas: La educación del niño sordo. Algunas reflexiones. La *Revista Iberoamericana de Educación*. Available at www.rieoei.org/opinion04.htm.

Kyle, J. & Allsop, L. (1982). *Deaf People and the Community*. Bristol, UK: Centre for Deaf Studies, School for Education, University of Bristol.

Kyle, J. & Woll, B. (1985). *Sign Language: The Study of Deaf People and Their Language*. Cambridge: Cambridge University Press.

(1993). *Language in Sign: The Development of Deaf Children's Communication in Sign Language*. Bristol, UK: University of Bristol.

Labov, W. (1963). The social motivation for sound change. *Word*, **19**, 273–309.

(1966). *The Social Stratification of English in New York City*. Washington, DC: Center for Applied Linguistics.

(1969). Contraction, deletion, and inherent variability of the English copula. *Language*, **45**, 715–762.

(1990). The intersection of sex and social class in the course of language change. *Language Variation and Change*, **2**, 205–254.

Labov, W., Cohen, P., Robins, C. & Lewis, J. (1968). *A Study of the Non-Standard English of Negro and Puerto Rican Speakers in New York City*. Philadelphia, PA: US Regional Survey.

Ladd, P. (2003). *Understanding Deaf Culture: In Search of Deafhood*. Clevedon, UK/Buffalo, NY: Multilingual Matters.

Ladefoged, P. (1975). *A Course in Phonetics*. New York: Hartcourt, Brace, Jovanovich.

Ladis, A. (1992). Review: Moshe Barasch, "Giotto and the Language of Gesture," (Cambridge Studies in the History of Art). *The Art Bulletin*, **74**(71), 159–161.

Lakoff, G. (1965). *On the Nature of Syntactic Irregularity*. In Mathematical Linguistic and
    Automatic Translation, NSF-16 (National Science Foundation, Technical Report 16).
    Cambridge, MA: Harvard Computation Laboratory.
Lambropoulou, V. (1994a). The history of deaf education in Greece. In C. Erting,
    R. Johnson, D. Smith & B. Snider (eds.), *The Deaf Way: Perspectives from the
    International Conference on Deaf Culture* (pp. 239–249). Washington, DC: Gallaudet
    University Press.
    (1994b). The vocational distribution of deaf people in Greece. In C. Erting, R. Johnson,
    D. Smith & B. Snider (eds.), *The Deaf Way: Perspectives from the International
    Conference on Deaf Culture* (pp. 791–793). Washington, DC: Gallaudet University Press.
    (1999). The education of the deaf in Greece. In H. W. Brelje (ed.), *Global Perspectives on the
    Education of the Deaf* (pp. 157–174). Hillsboro, OR: Butte.
Lane, H. (1984). *When the Mind Hears*. New York: Random House.
Lane, H., Boyes Braem, P. & Bellugi, U. (1976). Preliminaries to distinctive feature analysis of
    handshapes in American Sign Language. *Cognitive Psychology*, **8**, 263–289.
Lane, H., Hoffmeister, R. & Bahan, B. (1996). *A Journey into the Deaf World*. San Diego, CA:
    Dawn Sign Press.
Lanesman, S. & Meir, I. (2007). The sign language of Algerian immigrants in Israel. Paper
    presented at the workshop entitled, Cross-linguistic Research and International
    Cooperation in Sign Language Linguistics, Nijmegen, The Netherlands.
Langacker, R. W. (1987). *Foundations of Cognitive Grammar*. Vol. I: *Theoretical
    Prerequisites*. Stanford, CA: Stanford University Press.
    (1991). *Foundations of Cognitive Grammar*. Vol. II: *Descriptive Application*. Stanford, CA:
    Stanford University Press.
Lasnik, H. (1995). Verbal morphology: Syntactic structures meet the minimalist program. In
    H. Campos & P. Kempchinsky (eds.), *Evolution and Revolution in Linguistic Theory:
    Essays in Honor of Carlos Otero* (pp. 251–275). Washington, DC: Georgetown
    University Press.
Lazanas, V. (1984). *The Problems of the Deaf*. Athens: St. A. Tsepepas.
League of Arab States. (2006). Member States. Available at www.arableagueonline.org/las/
    arabic/categoryList.jsp?level_id = 61.
Lee, D. M. (1982). Are there really signs of diglossia? Re-examining the situation. *Sign
    Language Studies*, **35**, 127–152.
Lee, R. (2004). *A Beginner's Introduction to Deaf History*. Feltham, UK: British Deaf History
    Society.
Lehmann, C. (1988). On the function of agreement. In M. Barlow & C. Ferguson (eds.),
    Agreement in Natural Language: Approaches, Theories, Descriptions (pp. 55–65).
    Stanford, CA: Center for the Study of Language and Information (CSLI) Publications.
Lewis, J. (1998). Ebonics in American Sign Language: Stylistic variation in African American
    signers. In C. Carroll (ed.), *Deaf Studies V: Toward Unity and Diversity* (pp. 229–240),
    Washington, DC: Gallaudet University, College for Continuing Education.
Lewis, J., Palmer, C. & Williams, L. (1995). Existence of and attitudes toward Black
    variations of sign language. In L. Byers, J. Chaiken & M. Mueller (eds.), *Communication
    Forum 1995* (pp. 17–48). Washington, DC: Gallaudet University Department of ASL,
    Linguistics, and Interpretation.
Liddell, S. (1977). An investigation into the syntactic structure of American Sign Language.
    PhD dissertation, University of California, San Diego.
    (1980). *American Sign Language Syntax*. The Hague: Mouton de Gruyter.
    (1984). Unrealized inceptive aspect in ASL: Feature insertion in syllabic frames. In
    J. Drogo, V. Mishra & D. Testen (eds.), *Proceedings from the Twentieth Regional Meeting*

of the Chicago Linguistic Society (CLS 20) (pp. 257–270). Chicago, IL: Chicago Linguistic Society.

(1986). Head thrust in ASL conditional sentences. *Sign Language Studies*, **52**, 243–262.

(1995). Real, surrogate, and token space: Grammatical consequences in ASL. In K. Emmorey & J. Reilly (eds.), *Language, Gesture and Space* (pp. 19–42). Hillsdale, NJ: Lawrence Erlbaum Associates.

(1996). Spatial representation in discourse: Comparing spoken and signed language. *Lingua*, **98**, 145–167.

(2000). Indicating verbs and pronouns: Pointing away from agreement. In K. Emmorey & H. Lane (eds.), *The Signs of Language Revisited: An Anthology to Honor Ursula Bellugi and Edward Klima* (pp. 303–320). Mahwah, NJ: Lawrence Erlbaum Associates.

(2003a). Sources of meaning in ASL classifier predicates. In K. Emmorey (ed.), *Perspectives on Classifier Construction in Sign Languages* (pp. 199–220). Mahwah, NJ: Lawrence Erlbaum Associates.

(2003b). *Grammar, Gesture, and Meaning in American Sign Language*. Cambridge: Cambridge University Press.

Liddell, S. & Johnson, R. E. (1986). American Sign Language compound formation processes, lexicalization and phonological remnants. *Natural Language and Linguistic Theory*, **4**, 445–513.

(1989). American Sign Language: The phonological base. *Sign Language Studies*, **64**, 197–277.

Liddell, S. & Metzger, M. (1998). Gesture in sign language discourse. *Journal of Pragmatics*, **30**(6), 657–697.

Lillo-Martin, D. (1986). Two kinds of null arguments in American Sign Language. *Natural Language and Linguistic Theory*, **4**, 415–444.

(1991). *Universal Grammar and American Sign Language: Setting the Null Argument Parameters*. Dordrecht: Kluwer Academic Publishers.

(2002). Where are all the modality effects? In R. Meier, K. Cormier & D. Quinto-Pozos (eds.), *Modality and Structure in Signed and Spoken Languages* (pp. 241–262). Cambridge: Cambridge University Press.

Lillo-Martin, D. & Fischer, S. (1992). Overt and covert Wh-questions in ASL. Paper presented at the Fifth International Symposium on Sign Language Research, Salamanca, Spain.

Lillo-Martin, D. & Quadros, R. M. (2008). Focus constructions in American Sign Language and Língua de Sinais Brasileira. In J. Quer (ed.), *Signs of the Time: Selected Papers from TISLR 2004* (pp. 166–176). Hamburg: Signum.

Lillo-Martin, D., Quadros, R. M. & Mathur, G. (1998). Acquisition of verb agreement in American Sign Language and Brazilian Sign Language: A cross-linguistic study. Paper presented at the Sixth Conference on Theoretical Issues in Sign Language Research (TISLR 6), Washington, DC.

Lipka, L. (1994). Lexicalization and institutionalization. In R. E. Asher (ed.), *The Encyclopedia of Language and Linguistics* (pp. 2164–2167). Oxford: Pergamon Press Ltd.

List, G. (1993). Deaf history: A suppressed part of general history. In J. van Cleve. (ed.), *Deaf History Unveiled. Interpretations from the New Scholarship* (pp. 113–126). Washington, DC: Gallaudet University Press.

Lockwood, E. M. (2002). Uruguayan Deaf Education and its Effects on the Deaf Community (Fulbright Uruguay Annual). Available at www.sordos.com.uy/foros/la_educacion_del_sordo_uruguaya.htm.

Los sordos no tienen acceso a la secundaria ni a la universidad. *Voces en Silencio*, 2006.

Lucas, C. (1995). Sociolinguistic variation in ASL: The case of DEAF. In C. Lucas (ed.), *Sociolinguistics in Deaf Communities* (pp. 3–25). Washington, DC: Gallaudet University Press.

(2007). Variation and modality. In R. Bayley & C. Lucas (eds.), *Sociolinguistic Variation: Theories, Methods, and Applications* (pp. 145–161). Cambridge: Cambridge University Press.

Lucas, C. & Bayley, R. (2005). Variation in ASL: The role of grammatical function. *Sign Language Studies*, **6**, 38–75.

Lucas, C. & Valli, C. (1992). *Language Contact in the American Deaf Community*. San Diego, CA: Academic Press.

Lucas, C., Bayley, R. & Valli, C. (2001). *Sociolinguistic Variation in American Sign Language: Sociolinguistics in Deaf Communities*, Vol. VII. Washington, DC: Gallaudet University Press.

Lucas, C., Bayley, R., Reed, R. & Wulf, A. (2001). Lexical variation in African American and white signing. *American Speech*, **76**(4), 339–360.

Lucas, C., Goeke, A., Briesacher, R. & Bayley, R. (2007). Variation in ASL: 2 Hands or 1? Paper presented at the Conference on New Ways of Analyzing Variation 36, University of Pennsylvania.

Lule, D. (2001). Regional variation in USL. Baccalaureate thesis, University of Bristol.

Maddieson, I. (2005). Syllable structure. In M. S. Dryer, D. Gil & B. Comrie (eds.), *The World Atlas of Language Structures* (pp. 54–57). Oxford: Oxford University Press.

Mallery, G. (1893). *Picture Writing of the American Indians: Tenth Annual Report of the Bureau of American Ethnology*. Washington, DC: Smithsonian.

Mally, G. (1993a). The long road to self-confidence of the deaf in Germany. In R. Fischer & H. Lane (eds.), *Looking Back: A Reader on the History of Deaf Communities and Their Sign Languages* (pp. 177–198). Hamburg: Signum.

(1993b). *Redewendungen der Deutschen Gebärdensprache: Münchner Dialekt*. Hamburg: Signum.

Malm, A. (1998). *Suomalaisen viittomakielen perussanakirja 2003*. Helsinki: Kuurojen Liitto ry. [Available at http://suvi.viittomat.net/.]

Mandel, M. (1977). Iconic devices in American Sign Language. In L. Friedman (ed.), *On the Other Hand: New Perspectives on American Sign Language* (pp. 57–107). New York: Academic Press.

(1979). Natural constraints in sign language phonology: Data from anatomy. *Sign Language Studies*, **24**, 215–229.

(1981). Phonotactics and morphophonology in American Sign Language. PhD dissertation. University of California, Berkeley.

Manteau, E. & Thivilliers-Goyard, B. (2002). A propos de la situation des enfants sourds dans les pays d'Afrique subharienne. *La Lettre d'Orthophonistes du Monde*.

Marantz, A. (1994). A late note on late insertion. In Y-S. Kim, K-J. Lee, B-C. Lee, H-K. Yang & J-Y. Yoon (eds.), *Explorations in Generative Grammar. A Festschrift for Dong-Whee Yang* (pp. 396–413). Seoul: Hankuk Publishing Company.

Maroney, E. (2004). Aspect in American Sign Language. PhD dissertation, University of New Mexico, Albuquerque.

Marotta, G. (1985). *Modelli e misure ritmiche: La durata vocalica in italiano*. Bologna: Zanichelli.

Marsaja, I. G. (2008). *Desa Kolok: A Deaf Village and its Sign Language in Bali, Indonesia*. Nijmegen: Ishara Press.

Martin, J. (2000). A linguistic comparison of two notation systems for signed languages: Stokoe Notation and Sutton SignWriting. Unpublished manuscript, Western Washington University.

Massone, M. & Curiel, M. (2004). Sign order in Argentine Sign Language. *Sign Language Studies*, **5**, 63–93.

Massone, M. & Famularo, R. (2000). Semiotic aspects of Argentine Sign Language: Analysis of a videotaped "Interview." In M. Metzger (ed.), *Bilingualism and Identity in Deaf Communities*, Vol. VI (pp. 204–216). Washington, DC: Gallaudet University Press.

Massone, M. & Johnson, R. E. (1991). Kinship terms in Argentine Sign Language. *Sign Language Studies*, **73**, 347–360.

Massone, M. & Menéndez, S. M. (1992). An interactional approach to the analysis of Argentine Sign Language. *Cuadernos de Estudios Lingüísticos*, **33**, 75–82.

Mathur, G. (2000). Verb agreement as alignment in signed languages. PhD dissertation, MIT, Cambridge, MA.

Mathur, G. & Rathmann, C. (2004). Cross-sign-linguistic variation in the frequency of verb agreement forms. Paper presented at the Annual Meeting of DGfS, Mainz, Germany.

(2006). Variability in verb agreement forms in four sign languages. In L. Goldstein, C. Best & D. Whalen (eds.), *Laboratory Phonology VIII: Varieties of Phonological Competence* (pp. 287–314). The Hague: Mouton de Gruyter.

(2007). The argument structure of classifier predicates in American Sign Language. In A. Rose Deal (ed.), *Proceedings of the Fourth Meeting of Semantics of Underrepresented Languages of Americas*. Amherst, MA: GLSA (Graduate Linguistic Students Association).

(forthcoming). The features of verb agreement in signed languages. In R. Pfau, M. Steinbach and B. Woll (eds.), *Handbooks of Linguistics and Communication Sciences on Sign Languages*. Berlin: Mouton de Gruyter.

Matsuoka, K. (1997). Verb raising in American Sign Language. *Lingua*, **103**, 127–149.

Matthews, P. A. (1996). *The Irish Deaf Community Volume 1: Survey Report, History of Education, Language and Culture*. Dublin: Linguistics Institute of Ireland.

Matthews, S. (1990). A cognitive approach to the typology of verbal aspect. PhD dissertation, University of Southern California, Los Angeles.

Mayberry, R. & Eichen, E. (1991). The long-lasting advantage of learning sign language in childhood: Another look at the critical period for language acquisition. *Journal of Memory and Language*, **31**, 486–512.

Maye, C., Ringli, G. & Boyes Braem, P. (1987). The use of signs in Switzerland: Projects in the Zurich and Geneva Schools. In J. Kyle (ed.), *Sign and School: Using Signs in Deaf Children's Development* (pp. 162–170). Clevedon, UK: Multilingual Matters.

Mayer, M. (1969). *Frog, Where Are You?* New York: Dial Books for Young Readers.

Mbulamwana, J. (2004a). Implement the enacted disability friendly legislations. *Uganda National Association of the Deaf Newsletter*, 12–13.

(2004b). Silent Theatre launched. *Uganda National Association of the Deaf Newsletter*, December 13th Edition.

(2004c). WBS introduce Sign Language. *Uganda Association of the Deaf Newsletter*, June 12th Edition.

(2005). Ndeezi castigates stigmatization of the Deaf. *Uganda Association of the Deaf Newsletter*, December 15th Edition.

McBurney, S. (2002). Pronominal reference in signed and spoken language: Are grammatical categories modality-dependent? In R. Meier, K. Cormier & D. Quinto-Pozos (eds.), *Modality and Structure in Signed and Spoken Languages* (pp. 329–369). Cambridge: Cambridge University Press.

McCarthy, J. & Prince, A. (1993). Constraint interaction and satisfaction.Unpublished manuscript, University of Massachusetts/Rutgers University.

McClave, E. Z. (2000). Linguistic functions of head movements in the context of speech. *Journal of Pragmatics*, **32**(7), 855.

(2001). The relationship between spontaneous gestures of the hearing and American Sign Language. *Gesture*, **1**(1), 51–72.

McDonald, B. H. (1982). Aspects of the American Sign Language predicate System. PhD dissertation, University of Buffalo, New York.

McIntire, M. (1980). *Locatives in ASL*. PhD dissertation, University of California, Los Angeles.

McKee, R. (2007). Hand to mouth: Findings on the role of mouthing in New Zealand Sign Language. Paper presented at the Australian Sign Language Interpreters Association National Conference, Macquarie University, Sydney.

McKee, D. & Kennedy, G. (2000). Lexical comparisions of signs from American, Australian, British and New Zealand Sign Languages. In K. Emmorey, & H. Lane (eds.), *The Signs of Language Revisited: An Anthology to Honor Ursula Bellugi and Edward Klima* (pp. 49–76). Mahwah, NJ: Lawrence Erlbaum Associates.

McKee, D., McKee, R. & Major, G. (2008). Variation in the NZSL number system. In R. M. de Quadros (ed.), *Sign Languages: Spinning and unraveling the past, present and future.* TISLR9 (pp. 296–313). Published online at: www.editora-arara-azul.com.br.

McKee, D., McKee, D., Smiler, K. & Pointon, K. (2008). Maori signs: The construction of indigenous Deaf identity in New Zealand Sign Language. In D. Quinto-Pozos (ed.), *Sign Languages in Contact* (pp. 31–81). Washington, DC: Gallaudet University Press.

McNeill, D. (1992). *Hand and Mind: What Gestures Reveal About Thought*. Chicago, IL: University of Chicago Press.

(2000). *Language and Gesture*. Cambridge/New York: Cambridge University Press.

(2005). *Gesture and Thought*. Chicago, IL: University of Chicago Press.

McPherson, B. & Swart, S. M. (1997). Childhood hearing loss in sub-Saharan Africa: A review and recommendations. *International Journal of Pediatric Otorhinolaryngology 1997*, **40**, 1–18.

Meier, R. P. (1982). Icons, analogues and morphemes: The acquistion of verb agreement in American Sign Language. PhD dissertation, University of California, San Diego.

(1990). Person deixis in American Sign Language. In S. Fischer & P. Siple (eds.), *Theoretical Issues in Sign Language Research*. Vol.I: *Linguistics* (pp. 175–190). Chicago, IL: University of Chicago Press.

(2002). The acquisition of verb agreement: Pointing out arguments for the linguistic status of agreement in signed languages. In G. Morgan & B. Woll (eds.), *Directions in Sign Language Acquisition* (pp. 115–141). Amsterdam: John Benjamins Associates.

Meier, R. P. & Willerman, R. (1995). Prelinguistic gesture in deaf and hearing infants. In K. Emmorey & J. Reilly (eds.), *Language, Gesture and Space* (pp. 391–409). Hillsdale, NJ: Lawrence Erlbaum Associates.

Meillet, A. (1929). Le Développement des langues. In J. Chevalier, (ed.), *Continu et discontinu* (pp. 119ff.) Paris: Blood & Gay. Repr. in A. Meillet, (1951). *Linguistique historique et linguistique générale*, Vol. II. (pp. 53–69). Paris: Klincksieck.

Meir, I. (1995). Explaining backwards verbs in Israeli Sign Language: Syntax–semantic interaction. In H. Bos & G. Schermer (eds.), *Sign Language Research* (pp. 105–120). Hamburg: Signum.

(1998a). Syntactic–semantic interaction in Israeli sign language verbs: The case of backwards verbs. *Sign Language and Linguistics*, **1**(1), 3–37.

(1998b). Thematic structure and verb agreement in Israeli Sign Language. PhD dissertation, The Hebrew University of Jerusalem.

(1999). A perfect marker in Israeli Sign Language. *Sign Language and Linguistics*, **2**, 43–62.

(2002). A cross-modality perspective on verb agreement. *Natural Language and Linguistic Theory*, **20**(2), 413–450.

Meir, I. & Sandler, W. (2008). *Language in Space: The Story of Israeli Sign Language*. New York: Lawrence Erlbaum Associates.

Meir, I., Padden, C., Aronoff, M. & Sandler, W. (2007). Body as subject. *Journal of Linguistics*, **43**, 531–563.

Meir, I., Sandler, W., Padden, C. & Aronoff, M. (in press). Emerging Sign Languages. In M. Marschark & P. Spencer (eds.), *Oxford Handbook of Deaf Studies, Language, and Education*, Vol II. Oxford: Oxford University Press.

Mesch, J. (1998). *Teckenspråk i Taktil Form: Turtagning och Frågor i Dövblindas Samtal på Teckenspråk*. Hamburg: Signum. (International Studies on Sign Language and Communication of the Deaf; vol. 38)

(2000). Tactile Swedish Sign Language: Turn taking in signed conversations of people who are Deaf and blind. In M. Metzger (ed.), *Bilingualism and Identity in Deaf Communities* (pp. 187–203). Washington, DC: Gallaudet University Press. (Sociolinguistics in Deaf Communities; vol. 6)

(2006). Påminner nationella teckenspråk om varandre? In K. Hoyer, M. Londen & J. Östman (eds.), *Teckenspråk: Sociale och Historiska Perspektiv* (pp. 71–95). Helsingfors, Finland: Institutionen för Nordiska Språk och Nordisk Litteratur, Helsingfors Universitet.

Meyerhoff, M. (2000). *Constraints on Null Nubjects in Bislama (Vanuatu): Social and Linguistic Factors*. Canberra: Pacific Linguistic Publications.

Miestamo, M. & van der Auwera, J. (2006). Negation and perfective vs. imperfective aspect. Paper presented at the Chronos 7 Conference, Antwerp.

Milewski, T. (1993). *Teoria, Typologia i Historia Jezyka*. Kraków: UNIVERSITAS.

Miller, C. (1996). Phonologie de la langue des signes québecoise: Structure simultanée et axe temporel. PhD dissertation, Université de Québec a Montréal.

(2001). Some reflections on the need for a common sign notation. *Sign Language and Linguistics*, **4**(1/2), 11–28.

Mirus, G., Rathmann, C. & Meier, R. P. (2001). Proximalization and distalization of sign movement in adult learners. In V. Dively, M. Metzger, S. Taub & A. M. Baer (eds.), *Signed Languages: Discoveries from International Research* (pp. 103–119). Washington, DC: Gallaudet University Press.

Mitchell, R. E., Young, T. A., Bachleda, B. & Karchmer, M. A. (2006). How many people use ASL in the United States? Why estimates need updating. *Sign Language Studies, Spring* **6**(3), 306–356.

Morales-López, E. (2004). *Educación bilingüe en lengua de signos y lengua(s) oral(es) en Barcelona y Madrid*. Barcelona: Asociació de Pares de Nens Sords de Catalunya (APANSCE). Available at www.apansce.org.

Morales-López, E., Agliaga-Emeterio, D., Alonso-Rodriguez, J. A., Boldú-Menasanch, R. M., Garrusta-Ribes, J. & Gras-Ferrer, V. (2002). Deaf people in bilingual speaking communities: The case of Deaf people in Barcelona. In C. Lucas (ed.), *Turn-Taking, Fingerspelling, and Contact in Signed Languages* (pp. 107–155). Washington, DC: Gallaudet University Press. (Sociolinguistics in Deaf Communities; Vol. 8)

Morford, J. P. (1993). Creating the language of thought: The development of displaced reference in child-generated language. PhD dissertation, University of Chicago.

(1996). Insights to language from the study of gesture: A review of research on the gestural communication of non-signing deaf people. *Language and Communication*, **16**(2), 165–178.

Morgan, G., Barriere, I. & Woll, B. (2006). The influence of typology and modality on the acquisition of verb agreement morphology in British Sign Language. *First Language*, **26**, 19–43.

Morgan, M. W. (2006). Interrogatives and negatives in Japanese Sign Language. In
U. Zeshan (ed.), *Interrogatives and Negative Constructions in Sign Languages* (pp. 91–127). Nijmegen: Ishara Press.

Mubangizi, M. (2006). Five of eight siblings are deaf. *The Weekly Observer*, December, 14–20.
(2007). PWD write to Museveni over neglect. *The Weekly Observer*, July, 5–11.

Mufwene, S. (2008). *Language Evolution: Contact, Competition and Change.*
London/NewYork: Continuum.

Mufwene, S., Rickford, J. R., Bailey, G. & Baugh, J. (1998). *African American English:
History, Structure, and Use.* London: Routledge.

Mugenyi, S. (2003). Deaf children still denied access to secondary school. *The New Vision*,
January 27th Edition.

Muhs, J. (1994). Eduard Fürstenberg. *Das Zeichen*, **8**(30), 422–423.

Mulrooney, K. (2002). Variation in ASL fingerspelling. In C. Lucas (ed.), *Turn-Taking,
Fingerspelling, and Contact in Signed Languages* (pp. 3–23). Washington, DC: Gallaudet
University Press.

Nadolske, M. & Rosenstock, R. (2007). Occurrence of mouthings in American Sign
Language: A preliminary study. In P. Perniss, R. Pfau & M. Steinbach (eds.), *Visible
Variation: Cross-Linguistic Studies on Sign Language Structure* (pp. 35–61). Berlin:
Mouton de Gruyter.

Nakagwa, F. (2006). Isanga appeals for the deaf. *The New Vision*, September 20th Edition.

Nakamura, K. (2006). *Deaf in Japan.* Ithaca NY: Cornell University Press.

Nampala, M. (2007). Raising six deaf dumb children single-handed. *The New Vision*, April
27th Edition.

Naro, A. J. (1981). Morphological constraints on subject deletion. In D. Sankoff &
H. Cedergren (eds.), *Variation Omnibus* (pp. 351–357). Edmonton, AB: Linguistic
Research.

Ndeezi, A. (2004). *The Disability Movement in Uganda: Progress and Challenges with
Constitutional and Legal Provisions on Disability.* Kampala: Oscar Industries Ltd.

Ndeezi, A. & Ssendagire, E. (1998). How UNAD was formed: A brief history. *Uganda
Association of the Deaf Newsletter*, December, Special edition.

Neidle, C. (2002). ASL focus and question constructions. *Linguistic Variation Yearbook*, **2**,
71–98.
(2003). SignStream-Version 2.2 CD-ROM. American Sign Language Linguistics Research
Project, Boston University. Also available at www.bu.edu/asllrp/SignStream/.
(2004). *NCSLGR Sign Stream Database Volume 1.* American Sign Language Linguistic
Research Project (Distributed on CD-ROM), Boston University.
(2007). NCSLGR SignStream Databases *Volumes 2–7.* American Sign Language Linguistic
Research Project (Distributed on CD-ROM), Boston University.

Neidle, C. & MacLaughlin, D. (1998). SignStream. A Tool for Linguistic Research on Signed
Languages. *Sign Language and Linguistics*, **1**, 111–114.
(2002). The distribution of functional projections in ASL: Evidence from overt expressions
of syntactic features. In G. Cinque (ed.), *Functional Structure in the DP and IP: The
Cartography of Syntactic Structures* (pp. 195–224). Oxford: Oxford University Press.

Neidle, C., Sclaroff, S. & Athitsos, V. (2001). SignStream. A tool for linguistic and computer
vision research on visual-gestural language data. *Behavior Research Methods,
Instruments, and Computers*, **33**, 311–320.

Neidle, C., Kegl, J., MacLaughlin, D., Bahan, B. & Lee, R. G. (2000). *The Syntax of American
Sign Language: Functional Categories and Hierarchical Structure.* Cambridge, MA: MIT
Press.

Nespor, M. & Vogel, I. (1986). *Prosodic Phonology.* Dordrecht: Foris.

Nespor, M. & Sandler, W. (1999). Prosody in Israeli Sign Language. *Language and Speech*, **42**(2/3), 143–176.

Newport, E. L. & Supalla, T. (2000). Sign language research at the millennium. In K. Emmorey & H. L. Lane (eds.), *The Signs of Language Revisited: An Anthology to Honor Ursula Bellugi and Edward Klima* (pp. 103–114). Mahwah, NJ: Lawrence Erlbaum Associates.

Niederberger, N. A. (2004). Capacités langagières en langue des signes française et en français écrit chez l'enfant sourd bilingue: quelles relations? PhD dissertation, University of Geneva.

Nippon Foundation (2007). *Gallaudet students visit the Nippon Foundation*. Tokyo: Nippon Foundation

Nkwangu, R. (2006). Uganda commemorates the International Deaf Awareness Week for the first time. *Uganda National Association of the Deaf Newsletter*, December 17th Edition.

Nunes, J. (2004). *Linearization of Chains and Sideward Movement*. Cambridge, MA: MIT Press.

Nunes, J. & Quadros, R. M. de, R. (2006). Focus duplication of wh-elements in Brazilian Sign Language. Paper presented at the Proceedings of the North Eastern Linguistic Society 35, Charleston, SC.

  (2008). Phonetically realized traces in American Sign Language and Brazilian Sign Language. In J. Quer (ed.), *Signs of the Time: Selected Papers from TISLR 2004* (pp.177–190). Hamburg: Signum.

Nurowski, E. (1983). *Surdopedagogika Polska: Zarys Historyczny*. Warsaw: PWN.

Nyst, V. (1999). Variation in Handshape in USL. Unpublished manuscript, University of Leiden.

  (2007). *A Descriptive Analysis of Adamorobe Sign Language (Ghana)*. Utrecht: LOT (Netherlands Graduate School of Linguistics).

Nyst, V. & Baker, A. E. (2003). The phonology of name signs: A comparison between the sign languages of Uganda, Mali, Adamorobe and the Netherlands. In A. Baker, B. van den Bogaerde & O. Crasborn (eds.), *Cross-Linguistic Perspective in Sign Language Research: Selected Papers from Theoretical Issues in Sign Language Research (TISLR 2000)* (pp. 71–80). Hamburg: Signum.

O'Reilly, S. (2005). *Indigenous Sign Language and Culture: The Interpreting and Access Needs of Deaf People who are Aboriginal and/or Torres Strait Islander in Far North Queensland*. Kewarra Beach, Australia: Australian Sign Language Interpreters Association.

Östman, J. (ed.) (2005). *FinSSL:Finlandssvenskt teckenspråk*. Nordica. Vol. 4. Helsingfors, Finland: Institutionen för nordiska språk och nordisk litteratur, Helsingfors unversitet.

Ohala, J. J. (1990). Alternatives to the sonority hierarchy for explaining segmental sequential constraints. In M. Ziolkowski, M. Noske & K. Deaton (eds.), *Proceedings for the Annual Meeting of the Chicago Linguistic Society, 26*. Vol. II: *The Parasession on the Syllable in Phonetics and Phonology* (pp. 319–338). Chicago, IL: Chicago Linguistic Society.

Ohala, J. J. & Kawasaki, H. (1984). Phonetics and prosodic phonology. *Phonology Yearbook*, **1**, 113–127.

Okamoto, I. (1997). *Kindai moorookyooiku no seirittu to hatten: Hurukawa Toisiroo no syoogai kara*. [The Rise and Development of Modern Blind/Deaf Education: From the Life of Toshiro Furukawa.] Tokyo: NHK (Nihon Hoosoo Kyookai).

Okombo, D. O. (1991). The place of sign language in the African language situation. Unpublished manuscript, Nairobi University.

Oliveri, F. (2000). *La Gestualità dei Siciliani*. Palermo: Krea.

Oluoch, B. P. (2006). 1,000 March for USL Policy. *Uganda National Association of the Deaf Newsletter*, December 17th Edition.

Ordbog over Dansk Tegnsprog (2008). Professions-højskolen VCC (http://www.tegnsprog.dk).

Oteng, F. S. (1997). *Deaf Adwoa Benewaa*. Kumasi: Kumasi Catholic Press.

Otheguy, R., Zentella, A. C. & Livert, D. (2007). Language and dialect contact in Spanish in New York: Towards the formation of a speech community. *Language*, **83**, 770–802.

Oviedo, A. (1996). Bilingual deaf education in Venezuela: Linguistic comments on the current situation. In C. Lucas (ed.), *Multicultural Apects of Sociolinguistics in Deaf Communities*, (Vol. II pp. 61–79). Washington, DC: Gallaudet University Press.

Padden, C. (1980). The deaf community and the culture of deaf people. In C. Baker & R. Battison (eds.), *Sign Language and Deaf Community: Essays in Honor of William C. Stokoe* (pp. 89–104). Silver Spring, MD: National Association for the Deaf.

(1983). Interaction of morphology and syntax in American Sign Language. PhD dissertation, University of California, San Diego.

(1988). *Interaction of Morphology and Syntax in American Sign Language*. New York: Garland Press.

(1990). The relation between space and grammar in ASL verb morphology. In C. Lucas (ed.), *Sign Language Research: Theoretical Isssues* (pp. 118–132). Washington, DC: Gallaudet University Press.

Padden, C. & Gunsauls, D. C. (2003). How the alphabet came to be used in sign language. *Sign Language Studies*, **4**, 10–33.

Padden, C. & Humphries, T. (1988). *Deaf in America: Voices from a Culture*. Cambridge, MA: Harvard University Press.

(2005). *Inside Deaf Culture*. Cambridge, MA: Harvard University Press.

Padden, C. & Rayman, J. (2004). The future of American Sign Language. In J. van Cleve & D. Armstrong (eds.), *The Study of Signed Languages: Essays in Honor of William C. Stokoe* (pp. 247–263). Washington, DC: Gallaudet University Press.

Palestine Red Crescent Society (2000). *Qamus lughat al-ishara al-Falasteeniyah*. Ramallah, Palestine: Matba'et Al Manar.

Paliza Farfan, A. (1994). The problem of the Peruvian deaf person. In C. J. Erting, R. C. Johnson, D. L. Smith & B. D. Snider (eds.), *The Deaf Way: Perspectives from the International Conference on Deaf Culture* (pp. 804–810). Washington, DC: Gallaudet University Press.

Panther, K.-U. & Thornburg, L. L. (2003). *Metonymy and Pragmatic Inferencing*. Amsterdam: John Benjamins Associates.

Parasnis, I. (1998). *Culture and Language Diversity and the Deaf Experience*. Cambridge: Cambridge Unversity Press.

Parkhurst, S. & Parkhurst, D. (2001). *Un estudio lingüístico: Variación de las lenguas de signos usadas en España*. Madrid: RELLS.

Parrill, F. (2001). Linguistic aspect and gestural cues to backstage cognition. Paper presented at the Seventh International Cognitive Linguistics Conference, Santa Barbara, CA.

Parsons, T. (1990). *Events in the Semantics of English: A Study in Subatomic Semantics*. Cambridge, MA: MIT Press.

Patrick, P. L. & Metzger, M. (1996). Sociolinguistic factors in sign language research. In J. Arnold, R. Blake, B. Davidson, S. Schwenter & J. Solomon (eds.), *Sociolinguistic Variation: Data, Theory and Analysis*, (pp. 229–242). Stanford, CA: Center for the study of Language and Information (CSLI) Publications.

Pedersen, B. (2004). Thought from a Dane. *Uganda National Association of the Deaf Newsletter*, December 13th Edition.

Penn, C., Ogilvy-Foreman, D., Goldin, D. & Anderson-Forbes, M. (1992). *Dictionary of Southern African Signs for Communicating with the Deaf*. Johannesburg: Human Science Research Council.

Percy-Smith, L. (2006). *Danske Børn med Cochlear Implant: Undersøgelse af Medvindsfaktorer for Børnenes Hørelse, Talesprog og Trivsel*. Virum, Denmark: Videnscenter for døvblevne, døve og hørehæmmede.

Pérez, Y. (2008). Los Marcadores en conversaciones entre Sordos en Lengua de Señas Venezolana. PhD dissertation, Universidad de los Andes.

Perlin, J. (1993). *Lingwistyczny Opis Polskiego Jezyka Migowego*. Warsaw: WSiP.

Perlin, J. & Szczepankowski, B. (1992). *Jezyk Migowy dla Pedagogów. Opis Lingwistyczny*. Warsaw: WSiP.

Perlmutter, D. (1990). On the segmental representation of transitional and bidirectional movements in ASL phonology. In S. Fischer & P. Siple (eds.), *Theoretical Issues in Sign Language Research (TISLR)*. Vol. I: *Linguistics* (pp. 67–80). Chicago, IL: University of Chicago Press.

  (1992). Sonority and syllable structure in American Sign Language. *Linguistic Inquiry*, **23**, 407–442.

  (1995). Phonological quantity and multiple association. In J. A. Goldsmith (ed.), *The Handbook of Phonological Theory* (pp. 307–317). Oxford: Blackwell.

Perniss, P. M. (2007). *Space and Iconicity in German Sign Language (DGS)*. Nijmegen: Max Planck Institute for Psycholinguistics. (Max Planck Institute (MPI) Series in Psycholinguistics; 45)

Petitto, L. A. & Marentette, P. F. (1991). Babbling in the manual mode: Evidence for the ontogeny of language. *Science*, **251**, 1493–1496.

Petronio, K. (1993). Clause structure in American Sign Language. PhD dissertation, University of Washington.

Petronio, K. & Lillo-Martin, D. (1997). Wh-Movement and the position of spec CP: Evidence from American Sign Language. *Language*, 73, 18–57.

Pfau, R. (2002). Applying morphosyntactic and phonological readjustment rules in natural language negation. In R. P. Meier, K. A. Cormier & D. G. Quinto-Pozos (eds.), *Modality and Structure in Signed and Spoken Languages* (pp. 263–295). Cambridge: Cambridge University Press.

Pfau, R. & Glück, S. (1999). The pseudo-simultaneous nature of complex verb forms in German Sign Language. Paper presented at the Western Conference on Linguistics, El Paso, TX.

Pfau, R. & Quer, J. (2002). V-to-Neg raising and negative concord in three sign languages. *Rivista di Grammatica Generativa*, 27, 73–86.

Pfau, R. & Steinbach, M. (2005). Relative clauses in German Sign Language: Extraposition and reconstruction. In L. Bateman, & C. Ussery (eds.), *Proceedings of the Thirty-Fifth Annual Meeting of the North East Linguistic Society (NELS 35)*, Vol. II (pp. 507–521). Amherst, MA: GLSA (Graduate Linguistics Student Association).

Pfau, R. & Steinbach, M. (2006). Modality-Independent and Modality-Specific Aspects of Grammaticalization in Sign Languages. *Linguistics in Potsdam*, 24, 3–98. Available at www.ling.uni-potsdam.de/lip/.

Pierrehumbert, J. (1980). The phonology and phonetics of English intonation. PhD dissertation, MIT, Cambridge, MA.

Pierrehumbert, J. & Hirschberg, J. (1990). The meaning of intonational contours in discourse. In P. Cohen, J. Morgan & M. Pollack (eds.), *Intentions in Communication* (pp. 271–311). Cambridge, MA: MIT Press.

Pietrzak, W. (1992). *Jezyk Migowy dla Pedagogów*. Warsaw: WSiP.

Pigliacampo, R. (2001). *Il genio negato: Giacomo Carbonieri psicolinguista sordomuto del XIX secolo*. Siena: Cantagalli.

Pinsonneault, D. (1999). *Lexique des Signes Utilisés par les Sourds au Mali*. Mali: Editions Donniya.

Pitman, Isaac (1837). *Stenographic Soundhand*. London: Samuel Bagster.

Pizzuto, E. (1987/2004). Aspetti morfosintattici. In V. Volterra (ed.), *La Lingua Italiana dei Segni: La Comunicazione Visivo, Gestuale dei Sordi*. 2nd edn (pp. 179–209). Bologna: Il Mulino.

Pizzuto, E. (2002). The development of Italian Sign Language (LIS) in deaf preschools. In G. Morgan & B. Woll (eds.), *Directions in Sign Language Acquisition* (pp. 77–114). Amsterdam: John Benjamins Associates.

Pizzuto, E. & Wilcox, S. (2001). *A Study of Modal Verbs, Subjectivity, and Gesture in Italian Sign Language.* Final Report, Italian National Research Council, Short Term Mobility Grant Programme, Rome.

Plann, S. (1997). *A Silent Minority: Deaf Education in Spain, 1550–1835.* Berkeley, CA: University of California Press.

Plum, O. M., Søndergaard, L., Artmann, D., Kjær Sørensen, R., Hagedorn-Olsen, O. & Pedersen, A. (1979). *Dansk-tegnordbog.* København, Denmark: Danske Døves Landsforbund.

Poggi, I. (2007). *Minds, Hands, Face and Body: A Goal and Brief View of Multimodal Communication.* Buchverlag, Berlin: Weidler.

Polich, L. (2000). The search for proto-NSL: Looking for the roots of the Nicaraguan Deaf community. In M. Metzger (ed.), *Bilingualism and Identity in Deaf Communities*, Vol. VI (pp. 255–305). Washington, DC: Gallaudet University Press.

(2005). *The Emergence of the Deaf Community in Nicaragua: "With Sign Language You Can Learn So Much."* Washington, DC: Gallaudet University Press.

Pollock, J.-Y. (1989). Verb movement, UG, and the structure of IP. *Linguistic Inquiry*, **20**, 365–424.

Prałat-Pyrzewicz, I. & Bajewska, J. (1994). *Jezyk Migowy w Szkole i Internacie.* Warsaw: WSiP.

Prawitz, J. (1913). *Manilla Dövstumskola 1812–1912.* Stockholm: Beckman.

Prillwitz, S., Leven, R., von Meyenn, A., Schmidt, W. & Zienert, H. (1985). *Skizzen zueiner Grammatik der Deutschen Gebärdensprache.* Hamburg: Forschungsstelle DGS.

Prillwitz, S., Leven, R., Zienert, H., Hanke, T. & Henning, J. (1989). *Hamburg Notation System for Sign Language: An Introductory Guide.* Hamburg: Signum.

Pustejovsky, J. (1995). *The Generative Lexicon.* Cambridge, MA: MIT Press.

(2000). Events and the semantics of opposition. In C. Tenny (ed.), *Events as Grammatical Objects* (pp. 445–482). Stanford, CA: Center for the Study of Language and Information (CSLI) Publications.

Pyers, J. E. & Emmorey K. (2007). Two-Faced: How Knowledge of a Sign Language Affects facial gesture. Paper presented at the International Society for Gesture Studies, Evanston, IL.

Pyers, J. E. & Senghas, A. (2007). Reported action in Nicaraguan and American Sign Languages: Emerging versus established systems. In P. Perniss, R. Pfau, M. Steinbach (eds.), *Visible Variation: Comparative Studies on Sign Language Structure* (pp. 279–302). Berlin: Mouton de Gruyer.

Quadros, R. M. de (1995). *As Categorias Vazias Pronominais: Uma Análise Alternativa com Base na Língua de Sinais Brasileira e Reflexos no Processo de Aquisição.* Porto Alegre, Brazil: Pontifícia Universidade do Rio Grande do Sul (PUCRS).

(1999). Phrase structure of Brazilian Sign Language. PhD dissertation, Pontifícia Universidade Católica do Rio Grande do Sul, Porto Alegre, Brazil.

(2003). Phrase structure of Brazilian Sign Language. In A. Baker, B. van den Bogaerde & O. Crasborn (eds.), *Cross-Linguistic Perspectives in Sign Language Research: Selected Papers from TISLR 2000* (pp. 141–162). Hamburg: Signum.

(2004). *O 'bi' em Bilingüismo na Educação de Surdos.* Unpublished manuscript, Universidade Federal de Santa Catarina.

Quadros, R. M. de & Lillo-Martin, D. (2007). Gesture and the acquisition of verb agreement in sign languages. In H. Caunt-Nulton, S. Kulatilake & I. Woo (eds.), *BUCLD 31:*

Proceedings of the Thirty-First Annual Boston Conference on Language Development (pp. 520–531). Somerville, MA: Cascadilla Press.

Quadros, R. M. de, Lillo-Martin, D. & Chen-Pichler, D. (2004). Clause structure in LSB and ASL. Paper presented at the Deutschen Gesellschaft für Sprachwissenschaft (DGfS), [German Linguistics Association], Mainz, Germany.

Quer, J. (2005). Context shift and indexical variables in sign language. In E. Georgala & J. Howell (eds.), *Proceeding from Semantics and Linguistic Theory 15* (pp. 152–168). Ithaca, NY: CLC Publications.

Quer, J. & Frigola, S. (2006). Cross-linguistic research and particular grammars: A case study on auxiliary predicates in Catalan Sign Language (LSC). Paper presented at the Workshop on Cross-Linguistic Sign Language Research, Max Planck Institute for Psycholinguistics, Nijmegen.

Quigley, S. P. & Paul, P. V. (1984). *Language and Deafness*. San Diego, CA: Singular Publishing Group, INC.

Quinto-Pozos, D. (2002). Contact between Mexican Sign Language and American Sign Language in two Texas border areas. PhD dissertation, University of Texas, Austin.

   (2007). *Sign Languages in Contact*. Washington, DC: Gallaudet University Press.

   (2008). Sign language contact and interference: ASL & LSM. *Language in Society*, **37**, 161–190.

Quinto-Pozos, D. (2009). Code-switching between sign languages. In B. Bullock & J. Toribio (eds.), *The Cambridge Handbook of Linguistic Code-Switching* (pp. 221–237). Cambridge: Cambridge University Press.

Raanes, E. (2006). Å gripe inntrykk og uttrykk: interaksjon og meningsdanning i døvblindes samtaler. En studie av et utvalg dialoger på taktilt norsk tegnspråk. PhD dissertation, Sor-Trondelag University College, Norway.

Radutzky, E. (1992). *Dizionario Bilingue Elementare della Lingua Italiana dei Segni*. Roma: Edizioni Kappa.

Rainò, P. (2004). *Henkilöviittomien synty ja kehitys suomalaisessa viittomakieliyhteisössä* [The birth and development of personal name signs in the Finnish Sign Language society]. Deaf Studies in Finland 2. Helsinki: Kuurojen Liitto ry (CD).

Ramchand, G. (2008). *Verb Meaning and the Lexicon: A First Phase Syntax*. Cambridge: Cambridge University.

Ramos, E. & Fletcher, T. (1998). Special education and education reform in Mexico: Providing quality education to a diverse student population. *European Journal of Special Needs Education*, **13**, 29–42.

Ramsey, C. (1997). *Deaf Children in Public Schools: Placement, Contexts, and Consequences*. Washington, DC: Gallaudet University Press.

   (2007). Survey of Lenguaje de Señas de México. Paper presented at the Center for Research on Educational Equity, Assessment, and Teaching Excellence, University of California, San Diego.

Ramsey, C. & Noriega, J. (2000). Niños milagrizados [Miracle-ized Children]: Language attitudes, deaf education and miracle cures in Mexico. In M. Metzger (ed.), *Bilingualism and Identity in Deaf Communities, Sociolinguistics in Deaf Communities*, Vol. VI (pp. 117–141). Washington, DC: Gallaudet University Press.

Ramsey, C. & Ruiz Beddla, F. (2004). Where there is no school: The Mexican Sign Language network and Language Transmission across Generations. Paper presented at the Eighth International Conference on Theoretical Issues in Sign Language Research (TISLR 8), Barcelona.

   (2006). *Seeking Sign Language in Two Contexts: With and Without a School*. Poster presented at the Ninth International Conference on Theoretical Issues in Sign Language Research (TISLR 9), Florianópolis, Brazil.

(in press). *The Deaf People who Spell: The Surviving Students of the Mexican National School for the Deaf.* Washington, DC: Gallaudet University Press.

Rathmann, C. (2000). The optionality of agreement phrase: Evidence from signed languages. Master's thesis, University of Texas, Austin.

Rathmann, C. (2005). Event Structure in American Sign Language. Doctoral Dissertation, University of Texas, Austin.

Rathmann, C. & Mathur, G. (2002). Is verb agreement different cross-modally? In R. Meier, K. Cormier & D. Quinto-Pozos (eds.), *Modality and Structure in Signed and Spoken Languages* (pp. 370–404). Cambridge: Cambridge University Press.

(2004). Verb agreement as a linguistic innovation in signed languages. Paper presented at the Eighth Conference on Theoretical Issues in Sign Language Research (TISLR 8), Barcelona.

(2005). Unexpressed features of verb agreement in signed languages. In G. Booij, E. Guevara, A. Ralli, S. Sgroi & S. Scalise (eds.), *Morphology and Linguistic Typology: Proceedings of the Fourth Mediterranean Morphology Meeting (MMM4)* (pp. 235–250). Bologna: University of Bologna. Available at http://morbo.lingue.unibo.it/mmm/.

(2008). Verb agreement as a linguistic innovation in signed languages. In J. Quer (ed.), *Signs of the Time: Selected Papers from TISLR 2004* (pp. 193–218). Hamburg: Signum.

Rathmann, C., Mathur, G. & Meier, R. P. (2003). From gesture to verb agreement. Paper presented at the Proceedings of the International Society for Gesture Studies, Austin, TX.

Reddy, M. (1979). The conduit metaphor: A case of frame conflict in our language about language. In A. Ortony (ed.), *Metaphor and Thought* (pp. 164–201). Cambridge: Cambridge University Press.

Rée, J. (1999). *I See a Voice: Language, Deafness and the Senses: A Philosophical History.* London: Harper Collins.

Regional Bureau of Education for Latin America and the Caribbean. (2007a). *Quality Education for All: A Human Rights Issue.* Santiago: United Nations Educational, Scientific and Cultural Organization (UNESCO).

(2007b). *The State of Education in Latin America and the Caribbean Guaranteeing Quality Education for All.* Santiago: United Nations Educational, Scientific and Cultural Organization (UNESCO).

Reilly, J. & Anderson, D. (2002). FACES: The acquisition of non-manual morphology in ASL. In G. Morgan & B. Woll (eds.), *Directions in Sign Language Acquisition* (pp. 159–181). Amsterdam: John Benjamins Associates.

Rhodes, R. (2000). School psychology and special education in Mexico: An introduction for practitioners. *School Psychology International,* **21**(3), 252–264.

Riberio Hutzler, C. (1994). Are deaf children "allowed" signing? In C. J. Erting, R. C. Johnson, D. L. Smith & B. D. Snider (eds.), *The Deaf Way: Perspectives from the International Conference on Deaf Culture* (pp. 811–816). Washington, DC: Gallaudet University Press.

Rissanen, T. (1998). The categories of nominals and verbals and their morphology in Finnish Sign Language. Licentiate thesis in General Linguistics, Department of Finnish and General Linguistics, University of Turku, Finland.

Romeo, O. (1991). *Dizionario dei Segni. La Lingua dei Segni in 1400 Immagini.* Bologna: Zanichelli.

Rosenstein, O. (2001). ISL as a topic prominent language. Master's thesis, University of Haifa.

Rosellini, T. L. (1998). *Adama, the Fulani Magician* [Documentary]. Santa Cruz, CA: African Family Films.

Royal Commission. (1889). *On the Education of the Blind, Deaf and Dumb.* London: Her Majesty's Stationery Office (HMSO).

Royal National Institute for the Deaf. (1981). *Sign and Say*. London: The Royal National Institute for Deaf and Hard of Hearing People (RNID).

Russo, T. (2005). A cross-cultural, cross-linguistic analysis of metaphors in two Italian Sign Language registers. *Sign Language Studies*, **5**, 333–359.

Russo, T., Giuranna, R. & Pizzuto, E. (2001). Italian Sign Language (LIS) poetry: Iconic properties and structural regularities. *Sign Language Studies*, **2**(1), 84–112.

Saito, M. (1985). Some asymmetries in Japanese and their theoretical implications. PhD dissertation, MIT, Cambridge, MA.

Salmi, E. & Laakso, M. (2005). *Maahan Lämpimään: Suomen Viittomakielisten Historia.*. Helsinki: Kuurojen Liitto ry.

Sandler, W. (1986). The spreading hand autosegment of American Sign Language. *Sign Language Studies*, **50**, 1–28.

   (1989). *Phonological Representation of the Sign: Linearity and Nonlinearity in American Sign Language*. Dordrecht: Foris.

   (1993). A sonority cycle in American Sign Language. *Phonology*, **10**, 243–279.

   (1996a). Phonological features and feature classes: The case of movements in sign language. *Lingua*, **98**, 197–220.

   (1996b). Representing handshapes. *International Review of Sign Language Linguistics*, **1**, 115–158.

   (1999a). Prosody in two natural language modalities. *Language and Speech*, **42**(2/3), 127–142.

   (1999b). The medium and the message: Prosodic interpretation of linguistic content in Israeli Sign Language. *Sign Language and Linguistics*, **2**(2), 187–215.

   (1999c). Cliticization and prosodic words in a sign language. In T. Hall & U. Kleinhenz (eds.), *Studies on the Phonological Word* (pp. 223–255). Amsterdam: John Benjamins Associates.

Sandler, W. & Lillo-Martin, D. (2006). *Sign Language and Linguistic Universals*. Cambridge/ New York: Cambridge University Press.

Sandler, W., Meir, I., Padden, C. & Aronoff, M. (2005). The emergence of grammar: Systematic structure in a new language. *Proceedings of the National Academy of Sciences*, **102**, 2656–2665.

Santillán, M. (1994). The Ecuadorian Deaf community: History of the Deaf in Ecuador and the moment of awareness. In C. J. Erting, R. C. Johnson, D. L. Smith & B. D. Snider (eds.), *The Deaf Way: Perspectives from the International Conference on Deaf Culture* (pp. 119–122). Washington, DC: Gallaudet University Press.

Sapir, E. (1925). Sound patterns in language. *Language*, **1**, 37–51.

Sapountzaki, G. (2005). Free functional elements of tense, aspect, modality and agreement as possible auxilaries in Greek Sign Language. PhD dissertation, Centre of Deaf Studies, University of Bristol.

Sasaki, D. (2003). Comparing the lexicon of sign languages in East Asia: A preliminary study focusing on the influence of Japanese Sign Language on Taiwan Sign Language. Unpublished manuscript, University of Texas, Austin.

Saussure, F. de (1916). *Cours de Linguistique Générale*. Paris: Payot. [*Course in General Linguistics*. 10th printing. Peru, IL: Open Court Publishing, 2000]

Schalber, K. (2004). Phonological visibility of event structure in Austrian Sign Language: A comparison of ASL and ÖGS. Master's thesis, Purdue University., West Lafayette, IN.

Schalber, K. (2006). Event visibility in Austrian Sign Language (ÖGS). *Sign Language & Linguistics*, **9**(1/2), 207–231.

Schalber, K., & Grose, D. (2006). The semantics, syntax and phonology of event related nonmanuals in two sign languages. Paper presented at the Ninth Conference on Theoretical Issues in Sign Language Research (TISLR 9), Florianópolis, Brazil.

Schein, J. D. (1968). *The Deaf Community: Studies in the Social Psychology of Deafness.* Washington, DC: Gallaudet University Press.

Schein, J. D. & Delk, M. T. J. (1974). *The Deaf Population of the United States.* Silver Spring, MD: The National Association of the Deaf.

Schembri, A. (2002). The representation of motion events in signed language and gesture. In R. Schulmeister & H. Reinitzer (eds.), *Progress in Sign Language Research: In Honor of Siegmund Prillwitz* (pp. 99–125). Hamburg: Signum.

(2003). Rethinking "classifiers" in signed languages. In K. Emmorey (ed.), *Perspectives on Classifier Constructions in Sign Languages* (pp. 3–34). Mahwah, NJ: Lawrence Erlbaum Associates.

Schembri, A. & Johnston, T. (2006). Sociolinguistic variation in Australian Sign Language Project: Grammatical and lexical variation. Paper presented at the Ninth International Conference on Theoretical Issues in Sign Language Research (TISLR 9), Universidade Federal de Santa Catarina, Florianópolis, Brazil.

(2007). Sociolinguistic variation in the use of fingerspelling in Australian Sign Language (Auslan): A pilot study. *Sign Language Studies*, **7**(3), 319–347.

Schembri, A., Jones, C. & Burnham, D. (2005). Comparing action gestures and classifier verbs of motion: Evidence from Australian Sign Language, Taiwan Sign Language, and nonsigners' gesture without speech. *Journal of Deaf Studies and Deaf Education*, **10**, 272–290.

Schembri, A., Johnston, T. & Goswell, D. (2006). NAME dropping: Location variation in Australian Sign Language. In C. Lucas (ed.), *Multilingualism and Sign Languages: From the Great Plains to Australia* (pp. 121–156). Sociolinguistics in Deaf Communities, Vol. 12. Washington, DC: Gallaudet University Press.

Schembri, A., Cormier, K., Deuchar, M., Elton, F., Sutton-Spence, R., Turner, G. & Woll, B. (2007). The British Sign Language Corpus Project. Paper presented at the UK Council on Deafness Annual Deafness Conference, London.

Schermer, G. M. (1985). Analysis of natural discourse of deaf adults in the Netherlands: Observations of Dutch Sign Language. In W. C. Stokoe & V. Volterra (eds.), *SLR '83: Proceedings of the Third International Symposium on Sign Language Research. Rome, June 22–26, 1983* (pp. 269–273). Rome/Silver Spring, MD: CNR (Consiglio Nazionale delle Ricerche)/Linstok Press.

(1990). In search of a language: Influences from spoken Dutch on Sign Language of the Netherlands. PhD dissertation, University of Amsterdam.

(2003). From variant to standard: An overview of the standardization process of the lexicon of sign language of the Netherlands over two decades. *Sign Language Studies*, **3**(4), 469–486.

(2004). Lexical variations in Sign Language of the Netherlands. In M. van Herreweghe & M. Vermeerbergen (eds.), *To the Lexicon and Beyond: Sociolinguistics in European Deaf Communities* (pp. 91–110). Washington, DC: Gallaudet University Press.

Schermer, G. M. & Harder, R. (1985). Lexical variation in Dutch Sign Language: some implications for language planning. In B. T. Tervoort (ed.), *Signs of Life: Proceedings of the Second European Congress on Sign Language Research*, (pp. 134–141). Amsterdam: University of Amsterdam.

Schermer, G. M. & Koolhof, C. (1990). The reality of time-lines: Aspects of tense in SLN. In S. Prillwitz & T. Vollhaber (eds.), *Current Trends in European Sign Language Research: Proceedings of the Third European Congress on Sign Language Research*. (pp. 295–305). Hamburg: Signum.

Schermer, G. M., Brien, D. & Brennan, M. (2001). Developing linguistic specifications for a sign language database: The development of Signbase. *Sign Language and Linguistics*, **4**(1/2), 253–274.

Schermer, G. M. Harder, R. & Bos, H. (1988). *Handen uit de Mouwen: Gebaren uit de Nederlandse Gebarentaal in kaart gebracht.* Amsterdam: NSDSK/Dovenraad.

Schermer, T. (2001). The role of mouthings in Sign Language of the Netherlands: Some implications for the production of sign language dictionaries. In P. Boyes Braem & R. Sutton-Spence (eds.), *The Hands Are the Head of the Mouth: The Mouth as Articulator in Sign Language* (pp. 273–284). Hamburg: Signum.

Schermer, T., Geuze, J., Koolhof, C., Meijer, E. & Muller, S. (2006). *Standaard Lexicon Nederlandse Gebarentaal, Deel 1 en 2 (DVD-ROM).* Bunnik: Nederlands Gebarencentrum.

Schmaling, C. (2000). *Maganar Hannu: Language of the Hands: A Descriptive Analysis of Hausa Sign Language.* Hamburg: Signum. (International Studies on Sign Language and Communication of the Deaf; vol. 35)

(2001). ASL in northern Nigeria: Will Hausa Sign Language survive? In V. Dively, A. Baer, M. Metzger & S. Taub (eds.), *Signed Languages: Discoveries from International Research* (pp. 180–193). Washington DC: Gallaudet University Press.

Schmid, M. A. (1980). Co-occurrence restrictions in negative, interrogative, and conditional clauses: A cross-linguistic study. PhD dissertation, SUNY Buffalo, New York.

Schröder, O.-I. (1993). Introduction to the history of Norwegian Sign Language. In R. Fischer & Lane, H. (eds.), *Looking Back: A Reader on the History of Deaf Communities and Their Sign Languages* (pp. 231–248). Hamburg: Signum.

Scobbie, J. (1997). *Autosegmental Representation in a Declarative Constraint-Based Framework.* New York/London: Garland Press [Original dissertation title: Attribute value phonology. Edinburgh].

Scott, D., Carmi, R., Eldebour, K., Duyk, G., Stone, E. & Sheffield, V. (1995). Nonsyndromic autosomal recessive deafness is linked to the DFNB1 locus in a large inbred Bedouin family from Israel. *American Journal of Human Genetics,* **57**, 965–968.

Sebba, M. (1997). *Contact Languages.* New York: St. Mark's Press.

Seely, D. R., Gloyd, S. S., Wright, A. D. & Norton, J. (1995). Hearing loss prevalence and risk factors among Sierra Leonean children. *Archives of Otolaryngology Head and Neck Surgery,* **121**, 8.

Seidl, A. (2001). *Minimal Indirect Reference: A Theory of the Syntax–Phonology Interface.* New York: Routledge.

(2007). Infants' use and weighting of prosodic cues in clause segmentation. *Journal of Memory and Language,* **57**, 24–48.

Selkirk, E. (1982). The syllable. In H. van der Hulst & N. Smith (eds.), *The Structure of Phonological Representation,* Vol. II (pp. 337–383). Dordrecht: Foris.

(1984). *Phonology and Syntax: The Relation Between Sound and Structure.* Cambridge, MA: MIT Press.

(1995). Sentence prosody: Intonation stress and phrasing. In J. Goldsmith (ed.), *The Handbook of Phonological Theory* (pp. 550–569). London: Blackwell.

(2005). Comments on intonational phrasing in English. In S. Frota, M. Vigario & J. Freitas (eds.), *Prosodies: Selected Papers from the Phonetics and Phonology in Iberia Conference, 2003* (pp. 11–58). Berlin: Mouton de Gruyter.

Senghas, A. (2003). Intergenerational influence and ontogenetic development in the emergence of spatial grammar in Nicaraguan Sign Language. *Cognitive Development,* **18**(4), 511–531.

Senghas, A., Kita, S. & Özyürek, A. (2004). Children creating core properties of language: Evidence from an emerging Sign Language in Nicaragua. *Science,* **305**(5691), 1779–1782.

Senghas, A., Roman, D. & Mavillapalli, S. (eds.), *Simply Unique: What the Nicaraguan Deaf Community Can Teach the World.* London/Managua: Leonard Cheshire International.

Senghas, A., Coppola, M., Newport, E. & Supalla, T. (1997). Argument structure in Nicaraguan Sign Language: The emergence of grammatical devices. In E. Hughes, M. Hughes & A. Greenhill (eds.), *BUCLD 21: Proceedings of the Twenty-First Annual Boston University Conference on Language Development* (pp. 550–561). Somerville, MA: Cascadilla Press.

Senghas, R. J. (2003). New ways to be deaf in Nicaragua: Changes in language, personhood, and community. In L. Monaghan, K. Nakamura, C. Schmaling & G. H. Turner (eds.), *Many Ways to Be Deaf: International, Linguistic, and Sociocultural Variation* (pp. 260–282). Washington, DC: Gallaudet University Press.

Serpell, R. & Mbewe, M. (1990). Dialectal flexibility in sign language in Africa. In C. Lucas (ed.), *Sign Language Research Theoretical Issues*. Washington, DC: Gallaudet University Press.

Shaffer, B. (2000). A syntactic, pragmatic analysis of the expression of necessity and possibility in American Sign Language. PhD dissertation, University of New Mexico, Albuquerque.

Shahin, H., Walsh, T., Sobe, T., Lynch, E., King, M., Avraham, K. & Kanaan, M. (2002). Genetics of congenital deafness in the Palestinian population: Multiple connexin 26 alleles with shared origins in the Middle East. *Human Genetics*, **110**, 284–289.

Shannon, C. E. & Weaver, W. (1949). *The Mathematical Theory of Communication*. Urbana, IL: University of Illinois Press.

Shepard-Kegl, J. (1985). Locative relations in American Sign Language word formation syntax and discourse. PhD dissertation, MIT, Cambridge, MA.

(2006). Deaf teachers have a critical role in effective teaching of deaf children. In A. Senghas, D. Roman & S. Mavillapalli (eds.), *Simply Unique: What the Nicaraguan Deaf Community Can Teach the World* (pp. 45–52). London, Managua: Leonard Cheshire International.

Shuman, M. K. (1980). Culture and deafness in Mayan Indian Society: An examination of illness roles. *Medical Anthropology Newsletter*, **2**(5), 9–13.

Shuy, R. W., Wolfram, W. & Riley, W. (1968). *A Study of Social Dialects in Detroit*. Washington, DC: Educational Resources Information Center.

Siple, P. (1978). Visual constraints for sign language communication. *Sign Language Studies*, **19**, 97–112.

Skarzyński, H. (2004). Nowa era w otochirurgii. *Audiofonologia*, **25**, 11–17.

Skliar, C., & Quadros, R. M. de (2004). Bilingual deaf education in the south of Brazil. *Bilingual Education and Biligualism*, **7**(5), 368–380.

Skolöverstyrelsen. (1983). *Läroplan för Specialskolan. Kompletterande Föreskrifter till LGr80*. Stockholm: Liber Utbildningsförlaget.

Slobin, D. I. (2006). Issues of linguistic typology in the study of sign language development of deaf children. In B. Schick, M. Marschark & P. E. Spencer (eds.), *Advances in the Sign Language Development of Deaf Children* (pp. 20–45). Oxford: Oxford University Press.

Slobin, D. I. & Hoiting, N. (1994). Reference to movement in spoken and signed languages: Typological considerations. In S. Gahl, A. Dolbey & C. Johnson (eds.), *Proceedings of the Twentieth Annual Meeting of the Berkeley Linguistics Society, 20* (pp. 487–505). Berkeley, CA: University of California.

Slobin, D. I., Hoiting, N., Anthony, M., Biederman, Y., Kuntze, K., Lindert, R., Pyers, J., Thumann, H. & Weinberg, A. (2001). Sign language transcription at the level of meaning components: Berkeley Transcription System (BTS). *Sign Language and Linguistics*, **4**, 63–96.

Slobin, D. I., Hoiting, N., Kuntze, M., Lindert, R., Weinberg, A., Pyers, J., Anthony, M., Biederman, Y., & Thumann, H. (2003). A cognitive/functional perspective on the acquisition of "classifiers." In K. Emmorey (ed.), *Perspectives on Classifier Constructions in Sign Languages* (pp. 271–296). Mahwah, NJ: Lawrence Erlbaum Associates.

Smith, C. R. (2007). "Almost" in ASL: Insights into event structure. Master's thesis, Purdue University, West Lafayette, IN.

Smith, E. (2003). "Deaf Ways": The literacy teaching strategies of deaf teachers in New Zealand. Master's thesis, Victoria University of Wellington.

Smith, W. (1989). The morphological characteristics of verbs in Taiwan Sign Language. Doctoral Dissertation, Indiana University, Bloomington.

(1990). Evidence for auxiliaries in Taiwan Sign Language. In S. Fischer & P. Siple (eds.), *Theoretical Issues in Sign Language Research (TISLR)*. Vol.I: *Linguistics* (pp. 211–228). Chicago, IL: University of Chicago Press.

(2005). Taiwan Sign Language: An historical overview. *Language and Linguistics*, **6**, 187–215.

Sohn, H.-M. (1999). *The Korean Language*. Cambridge: Cambridge University Press.

Sorin-Barreteau, L. (1996). Le Langage Gestuel des Mofu-Gudur au Cameroun. Doctoral Dissertation, University of Paris V-René Descartes.

Souza Campello, A. R. S. (1994). The origin of the Deaf community in Brazil. In C. J. Erting, R. C. Johnson, D. L. Smith & B. D. Snider (eds.), *The Deaf Way: Perspectives from the International Conference on Deaf Culture* (pp. 117–118). Washington, DC: Gallaudet University Press.

Statistics New Zealand. (2001). *New Zealand Disability Survey Snapshot 6: Sensory Disabilities*. Wellington: Statistics New Zealand.

Steele, S. (1978). Word order variation: A typological study. In J. Greenberg, C. Ferguson & E. Moravcsik (eds.), *Universals of Human Language*. Vol. IV: *Syntax* (pp. 585–623). Stanford, CA: Stanford University Press.

Steinbach, M. & Pfau, R. (2007). Grammaticalization of auxiliaries in sign language. In P. Perniss, R. Pfau & M. Steinbach (eds.), *Visible Variation: Cross-Linguistic Studies on Sign Language Structure* (pp. 303–339). Berlin: Mouton de Gruyter.

Steriade, D. (1995). Underspecification and markedness. In J. Goldsmith (ed.), *Handbook of Phonological Theory* (pp. 114–174). Oxford/Cambridge, MA: Blackwell.

Stevenson, R. C. (1969). *Bagirmi Grammar*. (Linguistic Monograph Series 3) Research Unit. University of Khartoum.

Stocker, K. (2002). Cochlea-Implantat, Gebärden und Frühschriftsprache. PhD dissertation, University of Zurich. Zurich: Edition Schweizerische Zentralstelle für Heilpädagogik (SZH).

Stokoe, W. (1960). *Sign Language Structure: An Outline of the Visual Communication Systems of the American Deaf*. Buffalo, NY: University of Buffalo. (Occasional Papers 8)

(1969). Sign Language diglossia. *Studies in Linguistics*, **21**, 27–41.

(1991). Semantic Phonology. *Sign Language Studies*, **71**, 107–114.

Stokoe, W., Casterline, D. & Croneberg, C. (1965). *A Dictionary of American Sign Language on Linguistic Principles*. Silver Spring, MD: Linstok Press. Repr. 1976.

Stone, C. & Woll, B. (2008). Dumb O Jemmy and others: Deaf people, interpreters and the London courts in the 18th and 19th centuries. *Sign Language Studies*, **8**(3), 226–240.

Stroombergen, M. & Schermer, G. M. (1988). *Notatiesysteem Voor Nederlandse gebaren*. [Notationsystem for Dutch Signs]. Amsterdam: NSDSK.

Suleiman, Y. (2003). *The Arabic Language and National Identity*. Edinburgh: Edinburgh University Press.

Supalla, S. (1991). Manually Coded English: The modality question in signed language development. In P. Siple & S. Fischer (eds.), *Theoretical Issues in Sign Language Research (TISLR)*. Vol. II: *Psychology* (pp. 85–110). Chicago, IL: University of Chicago Press.

Supalla, S., Cripps, J. H. & McKee, C. (2008). *Revealing Sound in the Signed Medium Through an Alphabetic System*. Poster presented at the First SignTyp Conference, Storrs, CT, June 2008.

Supalla, T. (1982). Structure and acquisition of verbs of motion and location in American Sign Language. PhD dissertation, University of California, San Diego.

  (1985). The classifier system in American Sign Language. In C. Craig (ed.), *Noun Classification and Categorization* (pp. 181–214). Philadelphia, PA: John Benjamins Associates.

  (1997). An implicational hierarchy in verb agreement in American Sign Language. Unpublished manuscript, University of Rochester, NY.

  (2003). Revisiting visual analogy in ASL classifier predicates. In K. Emmorey (ed.), *Perspectives on Classifier Constructions in Sign Languages* (pp. 249–257). Mahwah, NJ: Lawrence Erlbaum Associates.

  (2004). The validity of the Gallaudet lecture films. *Sign Language Studies*, **4**, 261–292.

Supalla, T. & Newport, E. (1978). How many seats in a chair? The derivation of nouns and verbs in ASL. In P. Siple (ed.), *Understanding Language Through Sign Language Research* (pp. 91–132). New York: Academic Press.

Sutermeister, E. (1929). *Quellenbuch zur Geschichte des Schweizerischen Taubstummenwesens*. Bern: Self-Published.

Sutton-Spence, R. & Boyes Braem, P. (2001). *Introduction*. In P. Boyes Braem & R. Sutton-Spence (eds.), *The Hands Are the Head of the Mouth. The Mouth as Articulator in Sign Languages* (pp. 1–7). Hamburg: Signum.

Sutton-Spence, R. & Woll, B. (1993). The status and functional role of fingerspelling in BSL. In M. Marschark & D. Clark (eds.), *Psychological Perspectives on Deafness* (pp. 185–207). Mahwah, NJ: Lawrence Erlbaum Associates.

  (1999). *The Linguistics of British Sign Language: An Introduction*. Cambridge: Cambridge University Press.

Sutton-Spence, R., Woll, B. & Allsop, L. (1990). Variation and recent change in fingerspelling in British Sign Language. *Language Variation and Change*, **2**, 313–330.

Suwayd, A. (1992). *Al-qamus al-ishari*. Triploi, Libya: Dar Al-Madinah Al-Kadeemah Lil-kitab.

Svorou, S. (1994). *The Grammar of Space*. Amsterdam/Philadelphia, PA: John Benjamins Associates.

Swedish Government survey on the status of Swedish Sign Language. (1955). *Det döva barnets språk- och talutveckling*. Stockholm: Swedish Government survey on the status of Swedish Sign Language, 20.

Swedish Government survey on the status of Swedish Sign Language. (2006a). *Teckenspråk och teckenspråkiga. Kunskaps- och forskningsöversikt*. Stockholm: Swedish Government survey on the status of Swedish Sign Language, 29.

Swedish Government survey on the status of Swedish Sign Language. (2006b). *Teckenspråk och teckenspråkiga. Översyn av teckenspråkets ställning*. Stockholm: Swedish Government survey on the status of Swedish Sign Language, 54.

Świdziński, M. (1998). Bardzo wstepne uwagi o opisie gramatycznym Polskiego Jezyka Migowego. Cześć I. *Audiofonologia*, **12**, 69–83.

Świdziński, M. & Czajkowska-Kisil, M. (1998). Czy głuchoniemy jest naprawde niemy? *Kosmos*, **47**, 243–250.

Swisher, V., Christie, K. & Miller, S. (1989). The reception of signs in peripheral vision by deaf persons. *Sign Language Studies*, **63**, 99–125.

Szagun, G. (2003). Spracherwerb bei Kindern mit Cochlear-Implantat im Vergleich mit normal hörenden Kindern. *DFGS forum (Deutscher Fachverband für Gehörlosen- und Schwerhörigenpädagogik)*, **11**, 71–82.

Szczepankowski, B. (1973). *Problemy Rehabilitacji Inwalidów Słuchu.* Warsaw: PZG.
   (1988). *Podstawy Jezyka Migowego.* Warsaw: WSiP.
   (1996). *Zarys historii stowarzyszeń głuchoniemych 1876–1946.* Warsaw: PZG.
   (1999). *Niesłyszacy – Głusi – Głuchoniemi. Wyrównywanie Szans.* Warsaw: WSiP. Spółka
      Akcyjna.
   (2001). O jezyku migowym, jezyku miganym i systemie jezykowo-migowym. In J. Kobosko
      (ed.) *Blizej Zycia. Materiały dla Rodziców Dzieci i Młodziezy z Wada Słuchu* (pp.
      231–237). Warsaw: Stowarzyszenie Przyjaciół Osób Niesłyszacych i Niedosłyszacych
      "Człowiek-Człowiekowi."
Sze, F. (2008). Blinks and intonational phrases in Hong Kong Sign Language. In J. Quer
   (ed.), *Signs of the Time: Selected Papers from TISLR 2004* (pp. 83–107). Hamburg:
   Signum.
Tagliamonte, S. (2007). Quantitative analysis. In R. Bayley & C. Lucas (eds.), *Sociolinguistic
   Variation: Theories, Methods, and Applications* (pp. 190–214). Cambridge: Cambridge
   University Press.
Tai, J. H.-Y. & Su, S-F. (2006). Taiwan shouyu de huying gangshi [Agreement in Taiwan Sign
   Language]. *Language and Linguistics, Monograph Series Number W-5,* 341–363.
Takkinen, R. (1995). The Finnish Sign Language as the second language of a hearing family.
   In H. Bos & T. Schermer (eds.), *Proceedings of the Fourth European Congress on Sign
   Language Research, Munich, Germany* (pp. 231–240). Hamburg: Signum.
   (2002). Käsimuotojen Salat: Viittomakielisten lasten käsimuotojen omaksuminen 2–7
      vuoden iässä. Deaf Studies in Finland. Helsinki: Kuurojen Liitto ry.
Takkinen, R., Jokinen, M. & Sandholm, T. (2000). Comparing language and interaction skills
   of deaf children living in a native and non-native language environment. In *XIII World
   Congress of the Deaf Proceedings* (pp. 342–355). Brisbane: Australian Association of the
   Deaf.
Talmy, L. 1975. Semantics and syntax of motion. In J. P. Kimball (ed.), *Syntax and Semantics,*
   (pp. 181–238). New York: Academic Press.
   (1991). Path to realization: A typology of event conflation. *Berkeley Linguistics Society,* **17,**
      (pp. 480–519). Berkeley, CA: University of California.
   (2000). *Toward a Cognitive Semantics.* Cambridge, MA: MIT Press.
Tamomo, S. (1994). *Le Langage des Signes du Sourd Africain Francophone.* Cotonou, Bénin:
   PEFISS (Programme d'éducation de formation et d'intégration social des sourds).
Tang, G. (2003). Verbs of motion and location in Hong Kong Sign Language: Conflation and
   lexicalization. In K. Emmorey (ed.), *Perspectives on Classifier Constructions in Sign
   Languages* (pp. 143–166). Mahwah, NJ: Lawrence Erlbaum Associates.
   (2006). Questions and Negations in Hong Kong Sign Language. In U. Zeshan (ed.),
      Interrogative and Negative Constructions in Sign Languages (pp. 198–224). Nijmegen:
      Ishara Press.
   (2007). *Dictionary of Hong Kong Sign Language.* Hong Kong: Chinese University of Hong
      Kong Press.
Tang, G., Lam, S., Sze, F. & Lau, P. (2006). Acquisition of verb agreement in Hong Kong
   Sign Language. Paper presented at the Ninth Conference on Theoretical Issues on Sign
   Language Research (TISLR 9), Florianópolis, Brazil.
Tang, G. & Yang, G. (2007). Events of motion and causation in Hong Kong Sign Language.
   Lingua, **117,** 1216–1257.
Taub, S. (2001). *Language from the Body: Iconicity and Metaphor in American Sign Language.*
   Cambridge: Cambridge University Press.
Taub, S. & Galvan, D. (2001). Patterns of conceptual encoding in ASL motion descriptions.
   Sign Language Studies, **1,** 175–200.

Taylor, J. R. (2006). Where do phonemes come from? A view from the bottom. *International Journal of English Studies*, **6**(2), 19–54.

Tennant, R. & Gluszak-Brown, M. (1998). *The American Sign Language Handshape Dictionary*. Washington, DC: Gallaudet University Press.

Terpstra, A. & Schermer, T. (2006). 'Wat is NmG en waarom gebruik je het?' *Van Horen Zeggen* February 2006, 1–10.

Tervoort, B. T. (1987). Dutch Sign Language. In J. van Cleve (ed.), *Gallaudet Encyclopedia of Deaf People and Deafness*, Vol. III (pp. 70–71). New York: McGraw-Hill.

Thompson, R., Emmorey, K. & Gollan, T. H. (2005). "Tip of the fingers" experiences by deaf signers: Insights into the organization of a sign-based lexicon. *Psychological Science*, **16**(11), 856–860.

Thompson, R., Emmorey, K. & Kluender, R. (2006). The relationship between eye gaze and verb agreement in American Sign Language: An eye-tracking study. *Natural Language and Linguistic Theory*, **24**, 571–604.

Thrift, E. (2003). Object drop in the L1 acquisition of Dutch. Doctoral Dissertation, University of Amsterdam. Utrecht: LOT (Netherlands Graduate School of Linguistics).

Tomaszewski, P. (2005). Rola wychowania dwujezycznego w procesie depatologizacji głuchoty. *Polskie Forum Psychologiczne*, **10**(2), 174–190.

Tomaszewski, P. & Rosik, P. (2002). Czy polski jezyk migowy jest prawdziwym jezykiem? In G. Jastrzebowska and Z. Tarnowski (eds.), *Człowiek wobec ograniczeń: Niepełnosprawność, komunikacja, terapia* (pp. 133–164). Lublin: Wyd. Fundacja ORATOR.

Torigoe, T. (1994). Resumptive X structures in Japanese Sign Language. In I. Ahlgren & B. Bergman (eds.), *Perspectives on Sign Language Structure* (pp. 187–200). Durham: International Sign Linguistics Association.

Torigoe, T. (2000). Grammaticalization of pointings and oral movements in a home sign. Paper presented at the Seventh Conference on Theoretical Issues in Sign Language Research, (TISLR 7), Amsterdam.

Tovar, L. A. (1998). Reflexiones acerca de la educación de los Sordos Colombianos para el Siglo XXI. *Lenguaje*, **26**, 24–37.

Traugott, E. C. & Heine, B. (1991). *Approaches to Grammaticalization*. Amsterdam/ Philadelphia, PA: John Benjamins Associates.

Traugott, E. & König, E. (1991). The semantics–pragmatics of grammaticalization revisited. In E. C. Traugott & E. König (eds.), *Approaches to Grammaticalization*, Vol. I (pp. 189–218). Amsterdam: John Benjamins Associates.

Travis, L. (2000). Event structure in syntax. In C. Tenny & J. Pustejovsky (eds.), *Events as Grammatical Objects* (pp. 145–185). Stanford, CA: Center for the Study of Language and Information (CSLI) Publications.

Trubetzkoy, N. (1939). *Grundzüge der phonologie [Principles of Phonology]*. Göttingen: Vandenhoeck and Ruprecht (trans. 1969, University of California Press, Berkeley).

Truckenbrodt, H. (1999). On the relation between syntactic phrases and phonological phrases. *Linguistic Inquiry*, **30**, 219–255.

Trudgill, P. (1974). *The Social Differentiation of English in Norwich*. Cambridge: Cambridge University Press.

Turner, G. H. (1995). Contact signing and language shift. In H. Bos & G. M. Schermer (eds.), *Sign Language Research 1994: Proceedings of the Fourth European Congress on Sign Language Research, Munich, Germany* (pp. 211–230). Hamburg: Signum.

Tylor, E. B. (1874). *Researches Into the Early History of Mankind*. London: Murray Publishers.

Tywonek, M. (2006). Opanowywanie jezyka migowego przez niesłyszace dzieci rodziców niesłyszacych i słyszacych. In K. Krakowiak & A. Dziurda-Multan (eds.), *Nie Głos, Ale Słowo: Przekraczanie Barier w Wychowaniu Osób z Uszkodzeniami Słuchu* (pp. 187–196). Lublin: Wydawnictwo KUL.

Uganda National Association of the Deaf (UNAD) (2004). *Information Handbook.* Kampala: UNAD.

Ugandan Government. (1995). *The Constitution of the Republic of Uganda.* Kampala: Law Development Centre.

Undervisningsministeriet (1982). *Undervisningsvejledning for folkeskolen.* Vol. II: *Specialpædagogisk bistand til elever med hørevanskeligheder.* København: Undervisningsministeriet.

(1991). *Undervisningsvejledning for folkeskolen.* Vol. V: *Tegnsprog.* København: Undervisningsministeriet.

(2007). *Dansk tegnsprog i folkeskolen: god praksis for tilrettelæggelse og gennemførelse.* København: Undervisningsministeriet.

UNESCO (United Nations Educational, Scientific, and Cultural Organization) (1994). *The Salamanca Statement and Framework for Action on Special Needs Education.* Spain: UNESCO.

UNICEF. (1985). *UNICEF Report on Prevention of Deafness: Hearing Aids.* London: UNICEF.

Valli, C. (2005). *The Gallaudet Dictionary of American Sign Language.* Washington, DC: Gallaudet University Press.

Vallverdú, R. (2000). The sign language communities. In M. Turell (ed.), *Multilingualism in Spain: Sociolinguistic and Psycholinguistic Aspects of Linguistic Minority Groups* (pp. 183–214). Clevedon, UK: Multilingual Matters.

van Cleve, J. (1987). *Gallaudet Encyclopedia of Deaf People and Deafness.* New York: McGraw-Hill.

van Cleve, J. & Crouch, B. (1993). *A Place of Their Own: Creating the Deaf Community in America.* Washington, DC: Gallaudet University.

van den Bogaerde, B. (2000). Input and Interaction in Deaf Families. Doctoral Dissertation, University of Amsterdam, Utrecht: LOT (Netherlands Graduate School of Linguistics).

van den Bogaerde, B. & Baker, A. (1996). *Verbs in the language production of one deaf and one hearing child of deaf parents.* Paper presented at the the Fifth Conference on Theoretical Issues on Sign Language Research (TISLR 5), Montreal, Canada.

(2005). Code mixing in mother–child interaction in deaf families. *Sign Language and Linguistics,* **8**(1/2), 155–178.

van den Bogaerde, B. & Mills, A. E. (1994a). Word order in language input to children: SLN or Dutch. In M. Brennan, G. H. Turner & H. Graham (eds.), *Word-order Issues in Sign Language: Working Papers Presented at a Workshop Held in Durham, 18–22 September 1991.* Durham: International Sign Language Association.

van den Bogaerde, B., Knoors, H. & Verrips, M. (1994b). *Language Acquisition with Non-Native Input.* Amsterdam: University of Amsterdam. (Amsterdam Series in Child Language Development; 2)

van der Hulst, H. (1993). Units in the analysis of signs. *Phonology,* **10**(2), 209–241.

(1995). The composition of handshapes. *University of Trondheim, Working Papers in Linguistics,* 1–18. Dragvoll, Norway.

(2000). Modularity and modality in phonology. In N. Burton-Roberts, P. Carr & G. Docherty (eds.), *Phonological Knowledge: Its Nature* (pp. 207–244). Oxford: Oxford University Press.

(2009). Brackets and grid marks or theories of primary accent and rhythm. In C. Cairns & E. Raimy (eds.), *Contemporary View on Architecture and Representations in Phonological Theory* (pp 225–245). Cambridge, MA: MIT Press.

van der Hulst, H. & van der Kooij, E. (2006). Phonetic implementation and phonetic pre-specification in sign language phonology. In L. Goldstein, D. Whalen, & C. Best (eds.), *Papers in Laboratory Phonology, 8* (pp. 265–286). Berlin/New York: Mouton de Gruyter.

van der Kooij, E. (2002). *Reducing Phonological Categories in Sign Language of the Netherlands: Phonetic Implementation and Iconic Motivation.* Utrecht: LOT (Netherlands Graduate School of Linguistics).

van der Kooij, E., Crasborn, O. & Emmerik, W. (2001). Weak drop in sign language of the Netherlands. In V. L. Dively, M. Metzger, S. Taub & A. M. Baer (eds.), *Signed Languages: Discoveries from International Research* (pp. 27–44). Washington, DC: Gallaudet University Press.

(2006). Explaining prosodic body leans in Sign Language of the Netherlands: Pragmatics required. *Journal of Pragmatics, 38,* 1598–1614.

van der Leer, B. (2006). *The Italian Mobile Dipthongs: A Test Case for Experimental Phonetics and Phonological Theory.* Utrecht: LOT (Netherlands Graduate School of Lingustics).

van Gijn, I. (2004). *The Quest for Syntactic Dependency: Sentential Complementation in Sign Language of the Netherlands.* Utrecht: LOT (The Netherlands Graduate School of Linguistics).

van Gijn, I. & Baker, A. (2003). Testing for syntactic dependency: Some results from NGT. In A. Baker, B. van den Bogaerde & O. Crasborn (eds.), *Cross-Linguistic Perspectives in Sign Language Research: Selected Papers from Theoretical Issues in Sign Language Research (TISLR 2000)* (pp. 193–208). Hamburg: Signum.

van Gils, G. (2007). Dove tolken: partner of concurrent? [Deaf interpreters: partner or competition?]. Master's thesis, Hogeschool Utrecht.

Van Herreweghe, M. & Vermeerbergen, M. (2006). Interrogatives and negatives in Flemish Sign Language. In U. Zeshan (ed.), *Interrogative and Negative Constructions in Sign Languages* (pp. 225–256). Nijmegen: Ishara Press. (Sign Language Typology Series No. 1)

van Lambalgen, M. & Hamm, F. (2005). *The Proper Treatment of Events.* Oxford: Blackwell.

Vanguardia. (2005). Matriculan a sordos en enseñanza regular. Available at www.vanguardia.co.cu/index.php?+pl=design/secciones/lectura/portada.tpl.html&newsid_obj_id=8954.

Vashishta, M., Woodward, J. C. & DeSantis, S. (1985). *An Introduction to the Bangalore Variety of Indian Sign Language.* Washington, DC: Gallaudet Research Institute.

Velásquez Garciá, C. (1994). The birth of Ecuadorian Sign Language. In C. J. Erting, R. C. Johnson, D. L. Smith & B. D. Snider (eds.), *The Deaf Way: Perspectives from the International Coference on Deaf Culture* (pp. 123–126). Washington, DC: Gallaudet University Press.

Vendler, Z. (1967). *Linguistics in Philosophy.* Ithaca, NY: Cornell University Press.

Vermeerbergen, M., Leeson, L. & Crasborn, O. (2007). *Simultaneity in Signed Languages: Form and Function.* Amsterdam: John Benjamins Associates.

Vianna Martins, R. (2006). Linguistic development and Deaf identity in rural Rio Grande do Sul, Brazil. In H. Goodstein (ed.), *Deaf Way II Reader* (pp. 336–339). Washington, DC: Gallaudet University Press.

Vogel, H. (1999). Gebärdensprache und Lautsprache in der deutschen Taubstummenpädagogik im 19. Jahrhundert. Historische Darstellung der kombinierten Methode. Master's thesis, University of Hamburg.

(2002a). Otto Friedrich Kruse (1801–1880): Gehörloser Lehrer und Publizist. Part One. *Das Zeichen, 15*(56), 198–207.

(2002b). Otto Friedrich Kruse (1801–1880): Mahner gegen die Unterdrückung der Gebärdensprache. Part Two. *Das Zeichen*, **15**(57), 370–376.

Vogt-Svendsen, M. (2001). A comparison of mouth gestures and mouthings in Norwegian Sign Language (NSL). In P. Boyes Braem & R. Sutton-Spence (eds.), *The Hands Are the Head of the Mouth: The Mouth as Articulator in Sign Language* (pp. 9–40). Hamburg: Signum.

Voice for the Deaf. (n.d.) School today. Available at www.voiceforthedeaf.org/voiceforthedeaf/Today.html.

Volterra, V. (1981). Gestures, signs, and words at two years: When does communication become language? *Sign Language Studies*, **33**, 351–361.

(1987). *La lingua italiana dei segni: La comunicazione visivo-gestuale dei sordi.* Bologna: Il Mulino.

Wallin, L. (1994). Polysynthetic signs in Swedish Sign Language. PhD dissertation, University of Stockholm.

(1996). Polysynthetic Signs in Swedish Sign Language, translated from Polysyntetiska Tecken i Svenska Teckenspråket (1994). PhD dissertation. University of Stockholm.

Wallin, L., Lule, D., Lutalo, S. & Busingye, B. (2006). *The Uganda Sign Language Dictionary.* Kampala: Sign Language Research Project, Kyambogo University.

Wallvik, B. (2006). Det finländska dövsamfundets historia: några nyckelpersoners liv och leverne. In K. Hoyer, M. Londen & J. Östman (eds.), *Teckenspråk: Sociale och Historiska Perspektiv* (pp. 145–164). Helsingfors, Finland: Institutionen för nordiska språk och nordisk litteratur, Helsingfors universitet.

Walsh, T., Rayan, A., Sa'ed, A., Shahin, H., Shepshelovich, J. *et al.* (2006). Genomic analysis of a heterogeneous Mendelian phenotype: Multiple novel alleles for inherited hearing loss in the Palestinian population. *Human Genome*, **2**, 203–211.

Washabaugh, W. (1979). Hearing and deaf signers on Providence Island. *Sign Language Studies*, **24**, 191–214.

Watson, J. (1809). *Instruction of the Deaf and Dumb.* London: Darton and Harvey.

Widell, J. (1994). Historical phases of Deaf culture in Denmark. In C. J. Erting, R. C. Johnson, D. L. Smith & B. D. Snider (eds.), *The Deaf Way: Perspectives from the International Conference on Deaf Culture* (pp. 212–219). Washington, DC: Gallaudet University Press.

Wilbur, R. B. (1990). Metaphors in American Sign Language and English. In W. H. Edmondson & F. Karlsson (eds.), *SLR '87: International Symposium on Sign Language Research. Finland* (pp. 163–170). Hamburg: Signum. (International Studies on Sign Language and Communication of the Deaf; Vol. 10)

(1993). Syllables and segments: Hold the movement and move the holds! In G. R. Coulter (ed.), *Current Issues in ASL Phonology* (pp. 135–168). New York/San Francisco, CA/ London: Academic Press. (Phonetics and Phonology, 3)

(1994a). Eyeblinks & ASL phrase structure. *Sign Language Studies*, **84**, 221–240.

(1994b). Foregrounding structures in American Sign Language. *Journal of Pragmatics*, **22**, 647–672.

(1997). A prosodic/pragmatic explanation for word order variation in ASL with typological implications. In M. Verspoor, K. D. Lee & E. Sweetser, (eds.) *Lexical and Syntactical Constructions and the Constructions of Meaning* (pp. 89–104). Amsterdam/ Philadelphia, PA: John Benjamins Associates.

(2000). Phonological and prosodic layering of nonmanuals in American Sign Language. In K. Emmorey & H. Lane (eds.), *The Signs of Language Revisited: Festschrift for Ursula Bellugi and Edward Klima* (pp. 213–244). Mahwah, NJ: Lawrence Erlbaum Associates.

(2003). Representations of telicity in ASL. *Chicago Linguistic Society*, **39**, 354–368.

(2005). A reanalysis of reduplication in American Sign Language. In B. Hurch (ed.), *Studies in Reduplication* (pp. 593–620). Berlin/New York: Mouton de Gruyter.

(2008). Complex predicates involving events, time and aspect: Is this why sign languages look so similar? In J. Quer (ed.), *Signs of the Time: Selected Papers from TISLR 2004* (pp. 219–250). Hamburg: Signum.

(2009). Productive reduplication in ASL, a fundamentally monosyllabic language. In M. Kenstowicz (ed.), *Data and Theory: Papers in Phonology in Celebration of Charles W. Kisseberth*. special issue of *Language Sciences* **31**, 325–342.

Wilbur, R. B. & Allen, G. D. (1991). Perceptual evidence against internal syllable structure in American Sign Language syllables. *Language and Speech*, **34**, 27–46.

Wilbur, R. B. & Malaia, E. (2008). *Event Visibility Hypothesis: Motion Capture Evidence for Overt Marking of Telicity in ASL*. Chicago, IL: Linguistic Society of America.

Wilbur, R. B. & Petersen, L. (1990). Why syllables? What the notion means for ASL research. In S. Fischer, & P. Siple (eds.), *Theoretical Issues in Sign Language Research (TISLR)*, Vol. I: *Linguistics* (pp. 81–108). Chicago, IL/London: University of Chicago Press.

(1997). Backwards signing in ASL syllable structure. *Language and Speech*, **40**, 63–90.

Wilbur, R. B. & Schick, B. (1987). The effects of linguistic stress on ASL signs. *Language and Speech*, **30**(4), 301–323.

Wilbur, R. B., & Patschke, C. G. (1998). Body leans and the marking of contrast in American Sign Language. *Journal of Pragmatics*, **30**, 275–303.

(1999). Syntactic correlates of brow raise in ASL. *Sign Language & Linguistics*, **2**, 3–30.

Wilcox, P. (2000). *Metaphor in American Sign Language*. Washington, DC: Gallaudet University Press.

(2004). A cognitive key: Metonymic and metaphoric mappings in ASL. *Cognitive Linguistics*, **15**(2), 197–222.

Wilcox, P. & Wilcox, S. (1995). The gestural expression of modality in American Sign Language. In J. Bybee & S. Fleischman (eds.), *Modality in Grammar and Discourse* (pp. 135–162). Amsterdam: John Benjamins Associates.

Wilcox, S. (1992). *The Phonetics of Fingerspelling*. Amsterdam/Philadelphia, PA: John Benjamins Associates.

(2002). The gesture-language interface: Evidence from signed languages. In R. Schulmeister & H. Reinitzer (eds.), *Progress in Sign Language Research: In Honor of Siegmund Prillwitz* (pp. 66–81). Hamburg: Signum.

(2004a). Gesture and language: Cross-linguistic and historical data from signed languages. *Gesture*, **4**(1), 43–73.

(2004b). Cognitive iconicity: Conceptual spaces, meaning, and gesture in signed language. *Cognitive Linguistics*, **15**(2), 119–147.

(2005). Routes from gesture to language. *Revista da ABRALIN – Associação Brasileira de Lingüística*, **4**(1/2), 11–45.

(2007). Routes from gesture to language. In E. Pizzuto, P. Pietrandrea & R. Simone (eds.), *Verbal and Signed Languages: Comparing Structures, Constructs and Methodologies* (pp. 107–131). Berlin: Mouton de Gruyter.

Wilcox, S., Rossini, P. & Pizzuto, E. (2001). The interplay of subjectivity, gesture and prosody: POSSIBLE and IMPOSSIBLE in Italian Sign Language. Paper presented at the Seminar at the Institute of Psychology, National Research Council, Rome.

Wilcox, S., Shaffer, B., Jarque, M. J., Valenti, J. M. S. I., Pizzuto, E. & Rossini, P. (2000). The emergence of grammar from word and gesture: A cross-linguistic study of modal verbs in three signed languages. Paper presented at the Seventh Conference on Theoretical Issues in Sign Language Research (TISLR 7), Amsterdam.

Winteler, G. (1995). Ich hätte gerne geheiratet: Aus dem Leben gehörloser Frauen im 20. Jahrhundert. Master's Thesis: Höhere Fachschule für Soziokulturelle Animation, Zurich.

Wojda, P. (1999). Jezyk migowy – "spojrzenie od wewnatrz." In J. K Kobosko (ed.), *Moje Dziecko Nie Słyszy: Materiały dla Rodziców Dzieci z Wada Słuchu* (pp. 166–171). Warsaw: Stowarzyszenie Przyjaciół Osób Niesłyszacych i Niedosłyszacych "Człowiek-Człowiekowi."

(2000). Rola jezyka migowego w rodzinie dziecka niesłyszacego. In D. Kornas-Biela (ed.), *Źródło Życia i Szkoła Miłości* (pp. 491–510). Lublin: Towarzystwo Naukowe KUL.

(2001). Czy mozna nauczyć sie jezyka migowego? In J. Kobosko (ed.), *Blizej Zycia: Materiały Dla Rodziców Dzieci i Młodziezy z Wada Słuchu*. Warsaw: Stowarzyszenie Przyjaciół Osób Niesłyszacych i Niedosłyszacych "Człowiek-Człowiekowi."

(2005). Nieprzyzwoite Migi' we Współczesnym Polskim Jezyku Migowym. Postgraduate thesis: Wyzsza Szkoła Pedagogiczna, Łódź.

(2006). Jezyk Migowy Jako Przejaw Kreatywności Jezykowej Osób Niesłyszacych. In K. Krakowiak & A. Dziurda-Multan (eds.), *Nie Głos, ale Słowo: Przekraczanie Barier w Wychowaniu Osób z Uszkodzeniami Słuchu* (pp. 107–124). Lublin: Wydawnictwo KUL.

Wolff, S. (2000a). Taubstumme zu glücklichen Erdnern bilden? Lehren, Lernen und Gebärdensprache am Berliner Taubstummeninstitut. Teil I: Selbstverständlich Gebärdensprache! Ernst Adolf Eschke in der Zeit von 1788 bis 1811. *Das Zeichen*, **14**(51), 20–29.

(2000b). Lehren, Lernen und Gebärdensprache am Berliner Taubstummen-Institut. Teil II: Die Willkür der Zeichen. *Das Zeichen*, **14**(52), 198–207.

(2000c). Erst bildbar? dann vorzeigbar: Karl Heinrich Wilke und seine Bilderwelt. *Das Zeichen*, **22**(78), 8–17.

(2008). Vom Taubstummenlehrer zum Gebärdensprachpädagogen: Die Rolle der Gebärdensprache: in einer 200-jährigen Professionsgeschichte. *Das Zeichen*, **22**(78), 8–17.

Wolfram, W. (1969). *A Linguistic Description of Detroit Negro Speech*. Washington DC: Center for Applied Linguistics.

Woll, B. (1981). Borrowing and change in BSL. Paper presented at the Linguistics Association of Great Britain Autumn Meeting, York.

Woll, B. (1983). The comparative study of different sign languages. In J. Kyle (ed.), *Sign and School* (pp. 12–34). Clevedon, UK: Multilingual Matters.

(1987). Historical and comparative aspects in BSL. In J. Kyle (ed.), *Sign and School* (pp. 12–34). Clevedon, UK: Multilingual Matters.

(1994). The influence of television on the deaf community in Britain. In I. Ahlgren, B. Bergman & M. Brennan (eds.), *Perspectives on Sign Language Usage: Papers Presented from the Fifth International Symposium on Sign Language Research (SLR)*, Vol. I (pp. 293–301). Durham: International Sign Linguistics Association.

(2001). The sign that dares to speak its name: Echo phonology in British Sign Language (BSL). In P. Boyes Braem & R. Sutton-Spence (eds.), *The Hands Are the Head of the Mouth: The Mouth as Articulator in Sign Languages* (pp. 87–98). Hamburg: Signum.

Woll, B., Kyle, J. G. & Deuchar, M. (1981). Borrowing and change in BSL. Paper presented at the Linguistics Association of Great Britain Autumn Meeting, New York.

Woll, B., Kyle, J. G. & Deuchar, M. (1983). Historical change in British Sign Language. Unpublished manuscript, University college London.

Woll, B., Allsop, L., & Sutton-Spence, R. (1991). *Variation and Recent Change in British Sign Language: Final Report to the Economic and Social Research Council (ESRC)*. Bristol, UK: University of Bristol.

Woll, B., Sutton-Spence, R. & Elton, F. (2001). Multilingualism: The global approach to sign languages. In C. Lucas (ed.), *The Sociolinguistics of Sign Languages* (pp. 8–32). Cambridge: Cambridge University Press.

Wood, S. K. (1999). Semantic and syntactic aspects of negation of ASL. Master's thesis, Purdue University, West Lafayette, IN.

Woodward, J. (1972). Implications for sign language study among the deaf. *Sign Language Studies*, **1**, 1–17.

(1973). Implicational lects on the Deaf diglossic continuum. PhD dissertation, Georgetown University, Washington, D.C.

(1976). Black southern signing. *Language in Society*, **5**, 211–218.

(1978). Historical bases of American Sign Language. In P. Siple (ed.), *Understanding Language Through Sign Language Research* (pp. 333–348). New York: Academic Press.

(1979). The selflessness of Providence Island Sign Language: Personal pronoun morphology. *Sign Language Studies*, **23**, 167–174.

(1985). Universal constraints on two-finger adjacency and choice. *Sign Language Studies*, **46**, 53–72.

(1987). Universal constraints across sign languages: One-finger contact handshapes. *Sign Language Studies*, **57**, 375–383.

(1991). Sign language varieties in Costa Rica. *Sign Language Studies*, **73**, 329–346.

(1993). The relationship of sign language varieties in India, Pakistan, and Nepal. *Sign Language Studies*, **78**, 15–22.

(1996). Modern Standard Thai Sign Language: Influence from ASL, and its relationship to original Thai sign varieties. *Sign Language Studies*, **92**, 227–252.

(2000). Sign languages and sign language families in Thailand and Viet Nam. In K. Emmorey & H. Lane (eds.), *The Signs of Language Revisited: An Anthology to Honor Ursula Bellugi and Edward Klima* (pp. 23–47). Mahwah, NJ: Lawrence Erlbaum Associates.

Woodward, J., Erting, C. & Oliver, S. (1976). Facing and handling variation in American Sign Language. *Sign Language Studies*, **10**, 43–52.

Woodward, J. & DeSantis, S. (1977). Two to one it happens: Dynamic phonology in two sign languages. *Sign Language Studies*, **17**, 329–346.

Worseck, T. & Meyenn, A. Von (2007). Opportunities of Deaf Associations for the empowerment of Deaf and sign language communities in industrial countries. Paper presented at the Fifteenth World Congress of WFD (World Federation of the Deaf), Madrid.

Wrigley, O. (1997). *The Politics of Deafness*. Washington DC: Gallaudet University Press.

Yang, J. (2004). The linguistic status of finger wiggling in Chinese Sign Language interrogatives. Paper presented at the Theoretical Issues in Sign Language Research 8, Barcelona, Spain.

Yang, J. & Fischer, S. (2002). Expressing negation in Chinese Sign Language. *Sign Language and Linguistics*, **5**, 167–202.

Zatini, F. (1993). *Di tutto e di tutti circa il mondo della sordità (Enciclopedia)*. Firenze: Offset System.

Zaurov, M. (2003). *Gehörlose Juden: eine doppelte kulturelle Minderheit*. Frankfurt/Main: Lang.

Zeshan, U. (2000). *Sign Language in Indo-Pakistan: A Description of a Signed Language*. Amsterdam: John Benjamins Associates.

(2004a). Hand, head, and face: Negative constructions in sign languages. *Linguistic Typology*, **8**, 1–58.

(2004b). Interrogative constructions in signed languages: Cross-linguistic perspectives. *Language*, **80**(1), 7–39.

(2006a). *Interrogative and Negative Constructions in Sign Languages.* Nijmegen: Ishara Press.

(2006b). Negative and interrogative constructions in sign languages: A case study in sign language typology. In U. Zeshan (ed.), *Interrogative and Negative Constructions in Sign Languages* (pp. 28–68). Nijmegen: Ishara Press.

Zhang, Q. (2001). Changing economy, changing markets: A sociolinguistic study of Chinese yuppies. PhD dissertation. Stanford University, CA.

Zhongguo shouyu (2003). Beijing: Huaxia.

Zimmer, J. & Patschke, C. G. (1990). A class of determiners in ASL. In C. Lucas (ed.), *Sign Language Research: Theoretical Issues* (pp. 201–222). Washington, DC: Gallaudet University Press.

Zuccalà, A. (1997). *Cultura del Gesto e Cultura Della Parola. Viaggio Antropologico nel Mondo dei Sordi.* Milano: Meltemi.

Zucchi, A. (2009). Along the time line: Tense and time adverbs in Italian Sign Language. *Natural Language Semantics,* 17, 99-139.

Zwitserlood, I. (2003). *Classifying Hand Configurations in Nederlandse Gebarentaal [Sign Language of the Netherlands].* Utrecht: LOT (Netherlands Graduate School of Linguistics).

Zwitserlood, I. & Nijhof, S. (1999). Pluralization in Sign Language of the Netherlands. In J. Don & T. Sanders (eds.), *Utrecht Institute of Linguistics OTS Yearbook 1998–1999* (pp. 58–78). Utrecht: UiL (Utrecht institute of Linguistics)/OTS (Onderzoeksinstituut voor Taal en Spraak).

INDEX